PERSIA

PERSIA

AND THE

PERSIAN QUESTION

George N. Curzon

VOLUME TWO

NEW YORK

BARNES & NOBLE, INC.

Publishers · Booksellers · Since 1873

Published by Frank Cass & Co. Ltd.,
10 Woburn Walk, London W.C.1
by arrangement with Longmans Green, & Co.

Published in the United States
in 1966
by Barnes & Noble, Inc.
105 Fifth Avenue, New York, N.Y. 10003.

First edition	1892
Second impression	1966

Printed in Great Britain

CONTENTS

OF

THE SECOND VOLUME

CHAPTER XIX

FROM TEHERAN TO ISFAHAN

CHAPTER XX

FROM ISFAHAN TO SHIRAZ

CHAPTER XXI

PERSEPOLIS, AND OTHER RUINS

CHAPTER XXII

FROM SHIRAZ TO BUSHIRE

CHAPTER XXVI

THE NAVY

CHAPTER XXVII

THE PERSIAN GULF

CHAPTER XXVIII

REVENUE, RESOURCES, AND MANUFACTURES

CHAPTER XXIX

COMMERCE AND TRADE

PART I. *History of Perso-European Trade*

Part II. *The Modern Trade of Persia*

CHAPTER XXX

BRITISH AND RUSSIAN POLICY IN PERSIA

LIST OF ILLUSTRATIONS

FULL-PAGE ILLUSTRATIONS

ILLUSTRATIONS IN TEXT

MAPS

PERSIA

AND

THE PERSIAN QUESTION

CHAPTER XIX

FROM TEHERAN TO ISFAHAN

Then pomp and pleasure dwelt within her walls,
The merchants of the East and of the West
    Met in her arched bazaars.
    All day the active poor
Showered a cool comfort o'er her thronging streets.
    Labour was busy in her looms,
    Through all her open gates
Long troops of laden camels lined the roads.

SOUTHEY, *Thalaba the Destroyer*, bk. v.

The southerly route

AFTER some weeks spent in the enjoyment of the hospitality of the British Legation, and in the interesting and often highly-charged political atmosphere of the capital, it was with no slight reluctance that I again resigned myself to the tender mercies of the *chapar-khaneh* and the Persian post-horse, and started forth on my 800 miles' ride to the Gulf. In justice, however, to a much abused institution and animal, I must observe that along the stretch of road from Teheran to Shiraz, which is the most frequented in Persia, the former is in a better state of repair, and the latter is sprightlier in his movements, than in other parts of the country. Execrable horses and an inhospitable track had been the distinguishing features of my ride from Meshed to Teheran. With a tolerable mount, with the chance of European converse and entertainment in the Telegraph stations, encountered at distances of from sixty to seventy miles along the road, and with the prospect of great cities and world-famed ruins before him, with leisure to rest in the one or to linger over the other, the southward journey soon loses the visionary horrors with which the traveller has credited it, and proves to be deficient neither in comfort nor charm. To the student of works on Persia it will present little novelty. It has been traversed by almost every visitor who has either entered or left the country on the south, and it has on many occasions been excellently and conscientiously described.[1] There remains for me the task of faithfully depicting its features as they now exist, and of doing somewhat fuller justice to the great and historic cities through which it passes than is commonly rendered by the scribe of travel.

Postal table

Along the first section of the road, namely, from Teheran to Isfahan, the following is a table of the post-houses and distances :—

Name of station	Distance in *farsakhs*	Approximate distance in miles	Name of station	Distance in *farsakhs*	Approximate distance in miles
Teheran † (3,800 ft.)	—	—	Kuhrud (7,250 ft.) .	7	26
Robat Kerim . .	7	28	Bideshk (Soh †) .	6	25
Pik	6	24	Murchakhar . . .	6	24
Kushk-i-Bahram .	4	16	Gez	6	24
Rahmetabad . . .	6	25	Isfahan † (5,300 ft.)	3	12
Kum † (3,100 ft.) .	4	14	Julfa	1	4
Pasangun . . .	4	15			
Sinsin	7	26			
Kashan (3,200 ft.) .	6	22	Total . . .	73	285

† = Telegraph stations.

Three roads lead, or have been followed in recent times, from Teheran to Kum, a distance of about 100 miles; and the history of their competition has in it something peculiarly Persian.

Roads to Kum. 1. Old caravan track

The first of these roads is the old caravan track, which was pursued by every traveller up till the last decade, and has been frequently described. It left Teheran by the Shah

[1] I may cite the following: J. P. Morier (1809), *First Journey*, cap. x.; (1811) *Second Journey*, cap. x.; Sir J. Malcolm (1810), *Sketches*, caps. xiv.–xvi.; Sir W. Ouseley (1811), *Travels*, vol. iii. cap. xv.; W. Price (1811), *Journal of British Embassy*, vol. i. pp. 19–28; Colonel J. Johnson (1817), *Journey from India*, caps. ix. x. Sir R. K. Porter (1818), *Travels*, vol. i. pp. 367–406; J. B. Fraser (1821), *Journey into Khorasan*, cap. vi.; Baron C. De Bode (1840), *Travels*, vol. i. pp. 5–42; R. B. Binning (1851), *Two Years' Travel*, vol. ii. caps. xxvii.–xxviii.; J. Ussher (1861), *Journey*, cap. xxx.; A. Vambéry (1862), *Life and Adventures*, caps. ix.–xi.; J. Bassett (1874), *Land of the Imams*, p. 145, *et seq.*; A. Arnold (1875), *Through Persia by Caravan*, vol. i. caps. xiii.–xv.; Madame Dieulafoy (1881), *La Perse*, caps. ix.–xi.; Mrs. Bishop (1890), *Journeys in Persia*, vol. i. letters x.–xii.

TEHERAN TO ISFAHAN.

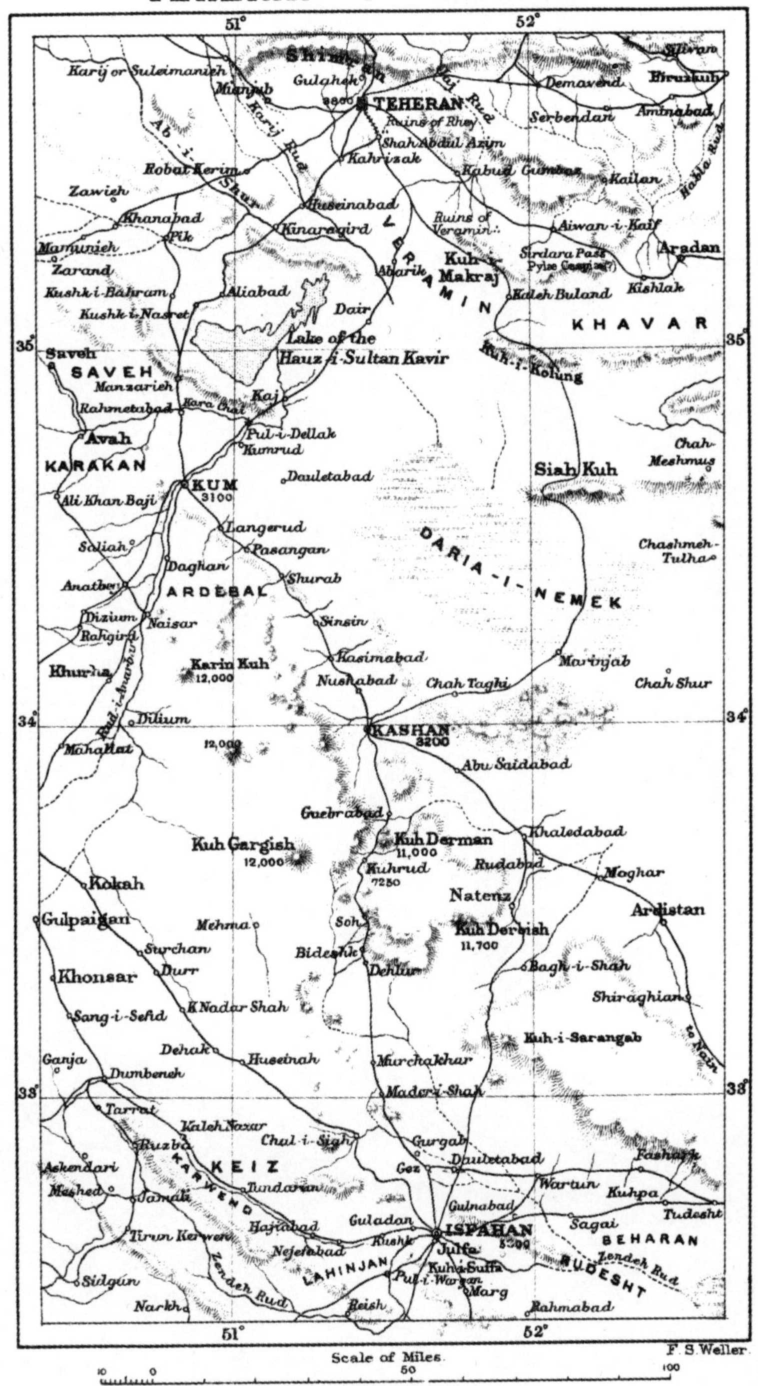

Abdul Azim gate, passed the shrine of that name, and proceeded to the village of Kinaregird (i.e. Border-town), soon after which it entered a succession of barren and gloomy defiles known as the Malek-el-Maut Dareh, or Valley of the Angel of Death,[1] so called because the superstitious fancies of the Persians infested it with jins and ghouls and fabulous shapes of monsters.[2] This pass, which in no sense differs from scores of others in Persia, and is a hundred-fold less rugged and repellent than many, has impressed the European traveller in a variety of ways; for, whilst the romantic Ker Porter saw in it only 'a dun and drowthy vale,' Sir J. Malcolm, for once forsaken by sound sense, described it as containing 'the most frightful precipices and ravines he had ever seen.' On quitting the mountainous tract, the road debouched upon the Hauz-i-Sultan, or Reservoir of the King, where was a caravanserai containing a tank that was fed by several *kanats* on the northern outskirts of the *kavir*. This *kavir*, or salt desert, was commonly regarded as the most westerly bay or extension of the Dasht-i-Kavir, or Great Salt Desert of northern Persia, and must have approached, further to the east, if it did not actually join, the Daria-i-Nemek, or Sea of Salt, which has been for the first time brought to light in the present year.[3] Popular legend avers that the sea, which is supposed to have covered the whole expanse, dried up on the birth of the Prophet; but attributes the still surviving swamps to the sweat that poured from the brow of Shamr, the murderer of the saintly Husein, who fled to this wilderness in the agony of an inexpiable remorse. After traversing the *kavir*, which was over ten miles in width, the road crossed the Kara Su, or Kara Chai river by the Pul-i-Dellak, or Barber's Bridge, a stone structure either erected or repaired by some famous barber of the past, commonly supposed to have officiated in that capacity to Shah Abbas.[4] It then proceeded to Kum.

The second road, which is followed by the wires of the Indo-

[1] Jeremiah ii. 6 has been appositely quoted: 'A land of deserts and of pits, a land of drought and of the shadow of death, a land that no man passed through, and where no man dwells.'

[2] For local legends about it, *vide* Malcolm's *Sketches*, cap. xvi., and R. B. Binning, *Two Years' Travel*, vol. ii. p. 202.

[3] *Vide* cap. xxiii.

[4] Sir R. Ker Porter is at his very best in describing this functionary, whoever he may have been, as 'the public-spirited barber and honest shaver, Poohl-Dowlak'!

European Telegraph, is the so-called carriage-road before spoken of, that was constructed by the father of the present Amin-es-Sultan in 1883–84, and was originally supplied or intended to be supplied with a service of *telegas* and *tarantasses*, for the more affluent pilgrims to the sacred shrine. For their comfort, too, a series of magnificent tile-fronted caravanserais (rented by the present Amin-es-Sultan) were erected at Aliabad, Manzarieh, and Kum, the distances being as follows: Teheran to Huseinabad (six *farsakhs*), Aliabad (eight), Manzarieh (five), Kum (six); total, twenty-five *farsakhs*, or ninety-one miles. The carriage service appears to have been a failure, or at least to have been inadequately patronised from the start; but as this section of the road has now been purchased from the Amin by the association who are responsible for the new Teheran-Burujird-Shushter wagon-road, there is a chance of its being properly organised and worked.

2. Carriage road

Now, however, occurs the interesting part of the story. Soon after the construction of the new road, the *kavir* of which I have spoken, and across which ran the old caravan track, became covered with a salt lake of considerable size; a phenomenon which excited such general interest that it was visited by the Shah, and received the honour of a description from the royal pen in the 'Iran' of May 10 and 19, 1888, which was translated by General Schindler and published with a map in the Proceedings of the R.G.S.[1] His Majesty discreetly attributed the formation of the lake to 'waters bubbling up in the *kavir* like fountains from underground;' but it must be added that other and less fortuitous explanations prevail. According to one account, a dam on the Kara Chai below the Pul-i-Dellak burst in 1883, so that the waters of the river poured through the gap into the depression of the *kavir*. But according to another and the more probable version, the dam did not collapse of its own accord, but was intentionally cut by the Amin-es-Sultan or his agents, in order to swamp the old caravan track, and force traffic and travellers on to the new road and into the new caravanserais. Anyhow, there is the lake;[2] and as it now receives the overflow of two rivers,

The new lake

[1] Vol. x. (1889), pp. 624–633.

[2] The Shah said it is 30 *farsakhs*, or 120 miles, in circumference This is a ridiculous exaggeration. That the lake, or rather a lake on the spot, is not an altogether novel phenomenon is evident from Mounsey, *Journey through the Caucasus*, p. 173. He crossed the *kavir* on March 28, 1866, and found it covered by a lake nearly a mile broad, after the melting of the snows.

the Kara Chai from Saveh, and the Rud-i-Anarbar (sometimes miscalled Ab-i-Khonsar and Ab-i-Jerbadegan) from Kum, there it is likely to remain.

But the Amin-es-Sultan, having successfully defeated the old caravan-route, had yet to deal with the postal authorities and the

3. Postal road

chapar service; and here a further disagreement between him and the Amin-ed-Dowleh, Minister of Posts, is said to have been the reason for which a third road started into existence, still more to the west, and at the time of my visit to Persia, in 1889, was taken by the *chapar* rider to Kum. This was the track that I pursued.[1] Leaving Teheran by the Hamadan Gate, it follows the main caravan-route to the west, to a little beyond the village of Robat Kerim, the single wire to Baghdad, originally erected by English engineers, and afterwards handed over to the Persian Government, taking the same direction. At about sixteen miles from Teheran I crossed the slender stream of the Karij, flowing in a deep fissure between high banks, by a single-arched bridge. Robat Kerim is a straggling village with a filthy ditch running down the main street. Thence the road to Pik is as devoid of interest as it is wholly destitute of life; although running as it does over a level expanse, it is a welcome stage to the *chapar* rider. Low ranges of hills enclose the plain on either side; and towards one of these the track wends, plunging into a series of rolling hollows and undulations about four miles before reaching Pik. Demavend and the Elburz range were always behind me, the one snow-robed, the other snow-besprinkled; and with every quarter of an hour they took on a different light, from pink to ashen grey, through all the dwindling gradations of rose and saffron, as the afternoon died down into dusk. At Pik I found a *chapar-khaneh* with two separate towers and *bala-khanehs*, one of which had the usual overplus of open windows and flapping unshut doors. From there the track cuts across the surrounding fields in an easterly direction, and enters a low pass in the surrounding hills, down the further slope of which runs a stream strongly impregnated with salt, on its way to the new lake, which flashed before me in the morning sun, its borders marked by a glittering fringe of saline scum. I may here

[1] It has since been superseded by a more direct route, starting from Teheran by the old caravan-track *viâ* Kinaregird, and joining the carriage-road; the total distance being charged as 24 *farsakhs*.

quote, as a sample of His Persian Majesty's style, the passage in which he described the surrounding scene:—

At this season (April) when most of the camels had brought forth their young, the greenness of the plains, the clearness of the air, the lake and the reflection of the sun on its waters, the vastness of the plain, the many camels and their young, the camel men and their children who were all busily tending the camels, the black tents of the Nomads, the many flocks of sheep, which were grazing in the plain, were wonderful to see.

Skirting the west shore of the lake the carriage-road from Teheran is here first encountered, driven in a bee-line across the valley (which is about sixteen miles in width), and joined by the *chapar* route on the crest of the further hill. On descending from this ridge by an easy pass on the south, we come to the magnificent new caravanserai of Manzarieh, with gorgeous tile-covered façade and emblem of the Lion and Sun sculped in stone. Further down, and just before reaching the solitary post-house of Rahmet-abad, the river Kara Chai, which flows from Saveh,[1] is crossed by a prodigious stone bridge, the most solid construction of the kind that I had so far seen. Another low ridge is climbed, another valley opens out, towards the southern end of which extends the belt of mingled brown and green that in the East signifies a large city. Above it the sun flames on the burnished cupolas and the soaring minars of Fatima's mosque. As we approach, the sacred buildings loom larger, and are presently seen to consist of two domes overlaid with gilded plates, and five lofty minarets, disposed in two pairs and a single standing in close proximity to the larger dome. Emerging from small clumps of trees, or standing in soli-

[1] Saveh is interesting as being Marco Polo's 'city of Saba, from which the three Magi set out when they went to worship Jesus Christ; and in this city they are buried, in three very large and beautiful monuments, side by side. And above them there is a square building, carefully kept. The bodies are still entire, with the hair and beard remaining' (Yule's *Marco Polo*, vol. i. p. 73). The localisation of the home of the Magi at Saveh arose, no doubt, from a purely arbitrary application of the text in the Psalms (lxxii. 10)—'The kings of Tharsis and of the isles shall give presents; the kings of Arabia and Saba shall bring gifts'—whence it was supposed that one of them came from Tarsia in Eastern Turkestan, the second from Arabia, and the third from Saveh. No trace of either the sepulchres or the legend is found in the pages of any traveller in Persia subsequent to Marco Polo, and he himself said that, when he asked the people many questions, 'no one knew anything except that there were three kings who were buried there in days of old.' (*Vide* Keith Abbott (1849), *Journal of the R. G.S.*, vol. xxv. pp. 1–8; and Madame Dieulafoy (1881), *La Perse*, caps. ix. x.)

tary prominence are to be seen the conical tiled roofs of scores of *imamzadehs* erected over the remains of famous saints and prophets, whose bones have been transported hither and laid to rest in the consecrated dust of Kum. There were formerly said to be over 400 of these structures in and around the city. Some of them are in good repair, and contain beautiful panels or lintel-bands of tiles with Kufic inscriptions from the Koran. Others are in a state of shocking ruin, the blue tiles having peeled off their cupolas, upon whose summits repose enormous storks' nests. The landscape is framed on the south by a range of hills of splintered outline and peculiar sterility, whose forbidding aspect is in harmony with the traditional and fanatical superstition of the holy city.[1]

Kum

The approach to the town lies through richly-cultivated fields; and at the very end of the road, which supplies a vista thereto, flashes the holy Fatima's dome. Immediately outside the gates flows, in the direction of the new lake, the Rud-i-Anarbar, which is crossed by a substantial bridge of nine arches. Some of the houses on the further bank have two storeys, with windows and balconies overlooking the stream—a more advanced degree of exterior embellishment than is usually attained by Persian domiciles. The remainder of the city, viewed from the outside, consists of a multitude of squat clay domes, the roof of nearly every building being shaped into half a dozen or a dozen of these protuberances. I traversed the entire length of the bazaar on my way to the *chapar-khaneh*, which, having recently been shifted, is now situated in a caravanserai opening out of the bazaar. The latter is vaulted throughout, and consists of one long alley, with a few parallel and transverse aisles. The roadway is broad, the shops large and well-furnished; and the jostle of human beings, camels, donkeys, horses, and cattle, was greater than I had yet seen in Persia. I subsequently retraced my footsteps to see as much of the mosque as is permissible to a Christian and an unbeliever. Outside its encircling wall extends a vast necropolis, adorned with thousands of stone slabs and crumbling mounds. A conjurer had selected this incongruous spot as his theatre, and was holding spell-bound a large crowd. I

[1] The name Kum is fancifully, but improbably, derived from *Kuh-i-mis*, mountain of copper, a mineral which is undoubtedly found in the adjacent hills. Its ancient name was Kumindan, or Kumidan, and it was one of seven villages which, in the eighth century A.D., were formed into a town, and called Kum.

rode up to the gateway of the big court of the mosque and, gazing in, not without attracting a large concourse of the curious, could see an immense quadrangle, with arched and tile-faced recesses all round the walls, and a tank for ablutions in the centre. Fraser, in 1821, entered the mosque in disguise, and visited the tomb-chamber. A Dr. Bicknell, who had already been to Mecca, made a similar entry in 1869, disguised as a Haji. Arnold, in 1875, having entered the outer court, remembered that discretion is the better part of valour, and beat a retreat; while any less adventurous Giaour must be content with what he can see through the open gate.

Kum is the site of the second most sacred shrine in Persia, and the Westminster Abbey of many of her kings. I have already spoken of the solicitous regard for the welfare of his devotees that led the Imam Reza to scatter his relatives while living, and their corpses when dead, throughout the country that he loved so well. At Kum are deposited the remains of his sister, Fatima-el-Masuma, i.e. the Immaculate, who, according to one account, lived and died here, having fled from Baghdad to escape the persecution of the Khalifs; according to another, sickened and died at Kum, on her way to see her brother at Tus. He, for his part, is believed by the pious Shiahs to return the compliment by paying her a visit every Friday from his shrine at Meshed. Kum[1] appears to have existed from an earlier period, although we may be absolved from accepting the legendary Persian foundation by Tahmuras or Kai Kobad. It was not, however, till it became the sepulchre of the illustrious Fatima, nor, after that, until the Shiah faith had become the national religion, that the town attained its reputation for especial sanctity. It was, of course, sacked by Timur, and has been in a state of greater or less ruin ever since. As the quaint Herbert phrased it, 'in the Sable weed she is still apparelled; for great Coom is now onely *magni nominis umbra*.' Nevertheless, under the patronage of the Sefavi sovereigns, the city revived; fine quays adorned the banks of the river; extensive bazaars and handsome caravanserais received or

History

[1] Kum has been described at greater or less length by a succession of eminent travellers, whose works I have so frequently cited that I need not recapitulate them here: Sir T. Herbert (1627), J. B. Tavernier (1632), Sir J. Chardin (*circ.* 1670), J. Struys (1671), C. Le Brun (1703), Sir J. Malcolm (1800), J. P. Morier (1809), Sir J. M. Kinneir (1810), Sir W. Ouseley (1811), Sir R. Ker Porter (1818), J. B. Fraser (1821), R. B. Binning (1851), J. Ussher (1861), Colonel Euan Smith (1870), Mrs. Bishop (1890).

CEMETERY AND MOSQUE OF KUM

dispensed a considerable trade; and the shrine was added to and adorned by the devout munificence of successive sovereigns. Chardin said that in his day the city contained '15,000 houses, as the people say;' but a measure, both to our own credulity and to the local hyperbole, is set by the earlier Herbert and the later Le Brun, who unite in crediting it with only 2,000 houses, albeit these were 'wel-built, sweet, and wel-furnished.' In 1722 it found in the Afghans an even more savage enemy than it had experienced in Timur, and was all but destroyed. A century later Fraser still described it as 'a wretched mass of ruins.' Its population was estimated as 4,000 in 1872, and as 7,000 in 1884; and when later lists have returned it as 20,000 to 30,000 persons, I imagine that the discrepancy is to be reconciled by regarding the smaller total as the permanent, and the higher as the fluctuating population, which is much swollen by pilgrims.

From the seventeenth century onwards Kum has been in high favour as the sepulchre of many of the Persian kings. Here repose the bodies of Shah Sefi I., Shah Abbas II., Shah Suleiman, and Shah Sultan Husein of the Sefavi dynasty; and here, among the Kajar monarchs, have been laid the remains of Fath Ali Shah (with two of his sons) in a separate building in the outskirts of the town, and of Mohammed Shah. Other sovereigns must also have been interred in the same spot; for the Persian records speak of the graves of 444 saints and princes, and of ten kings. Over their bodies, enshrined in magnificent sarcophagi of alabaster, of marble and ivory, of ebony, and camphor wood inlaid, which are covered with rich draperies, *mullahs* day and night read passages from the Koran. But of small account, it may be imagined, in the pilgrim's eyes, is even the royal dust, compared with that of the Lady Fatima herself.

Royal tombs

Chardin, Tavernier, Le Brun, and others have given minute descriptions or illustrations of the principal shrine; of which Herbert obscurely remarks that 'the mesquit is of Epirotique form.' It is preceded by several courts, the outermost of which is planted with trees. From the inner or principal quadrangle twelve marble steps lead up to the enclosure containing the saint's tomb. Three large doors, one of which is overlaid with silver plates, open into an octagonal chamber beneath the gilded dome.

Shrine of Fatima

In the midst of that chappel stands the tomb of Fatima, overlaid with tiles of China, painted à la Moresca, and overspread with cloth of gold that hangs down to the ground on every side. It is enclosed with a gate of massy silver, ten foot high, distant half a foot from the tomb, and at each corner crowned as it were with large apples of fine gold. Several breadths of velvet, hung about the inside of the gate, hide it from the view of the people, so that only favour or money can procure a sight of it. Over the tomb, about ten foot in height, hang several silver vessels, which they call candil, being a sort of lamp. But they never light up any fire therein, which they are not made to hold, nor any sort of Liquor, as not having any bottom. Upon the grate hang several inscriptions in Letters of gold upon thick velloms, as large as a large sheet of paper, which inscriptions contain the elegies of the saint and her family.[1]

It is when he ascends the twelve marble steps that the pilgrim removes his shoes, and leaves behind his staff or his arms. Then, as he enters, he kneels and kisses the threshold. Again he kisses the silver rails, through which he peers at the shrouded sarcophagus; he breathes the prescribed prayers; and with further genuflection and salutations, and fees to the hovering *mullahs*, he retires. He is one step nearer to heaven.

For its present splendour of golden cupola and tile-encrusted minars the shrine is indebted to the reigning family. In his early life Fath Ali Shah registered a vow that should he ever succeed to the throne, he would enrich Kum, and relieve its people of taxation. It is more than doubtful whether he ever carried out the latter pledge, though he gave the city and district as a private estate to his mother; but his promise as to the shrine was amply redeemed. He stripped off the tiles with which the dome had hitherto been covered, and replaced them with plates of gilt copper; he erected a neighbouring *madresseh* or religious college, with endowments and quarters for 100 students; he built at Kum a hospital and a *mehman-khaneh* or inn; he was said to have spent 100,000 *tomans* annually upon the shrine; when he visited it, he always came on foot; and when he died, hard by his body was by his orders laid to rest. In more recent times a second dome has been gilt; a clock was erected by one of the royal princes, who was Governor of Hamadan; and the glittering elegance of the large court into which I gazed was due, as I heard,

Restoration

[1] *Travels* of Sir J. Chardin, p. 394. Fraser, however, in 1821 (*Journey into Khorasan*, p. 139), said that the tomb was enclosed in a sandal-wood box, 12 feet by 8, and 7 to 8 feet high. The silver grating is still there.

to a restoration by the late Amin-es-Sultan. In one of the sanctuaries is an inscription to Ali, the refreshing originality of which entitles it to be quoted. It runs thus: 'Oh, inexpressible man! By thee, in truth, is Nature enriched and adorned! Had not thy perfect self been in the Creator's thought, Eve had remained for ever a virgin, and Adam a bachelor.'

Kum is indeed the possessor of a situation that might appear, at first sight, to recommend it for the capital city of Persia. It stands upon a river; it occupies a very central position; and it is the meeting-point of many important roads, from Teheran, from Kazvin, from Sultanabad and Burujird, from Yezd, and from Isfahan. It contains one of the two only inns or hotels in Persia that are worthy of the name,—a fine building standing in close proximity to the mosque. On the other hand, although there is a river, the water-supply is inadequate for a great city; and the heat in summer is excruciating. The city has been famous in past and present times chiefly for its melons and cucumbers, its armourers, its shoemakers, and its long-necked earthenware jars for cooling water. Of the last-named Chardin observed:—

The city

> This is peculiar to the white ware which is thence transported, that in the summer it cools the water wonderfully and very suddenly by reason of continual transpiration. So that they who desire to drink cool and deliciously never drink in the same pot above five or six days at most. They wash it with rose water the first time, to take away the ill smell of the Earth; and they hang it in the air full of water, wrapt up in a moist linen cloth. A fourth part of the water transpires in six hours the first time, after that, still less from day to day, till at last the pores are closed up by the thick matter contained in the water which stops in the pores. But so soon as the pores are stopped, the water stinks in the pots, and you must take new ones.

As might be expected from so holy a place, the population contains a large number of *seyids*—fanatics inured to long impunity of conduct—and is much addicted to bigotry and superstition. No Jews or Parsis live here; and English ladies, resident in the Telegraph offices, have usually found it prudent to veil in public. These superstitions are now dying fast throughout the East; but Kum is one of the places where an accidental spark might still be fanned into a disagreeable flame. Its title of Dar-el-Aman or Seat of Safety is an indication that its

Its people

shrine is a particularly favourite sanctuary for Mussulman refugees; and many is the malefactor who has escaped retribution by a flight to the inviolate asylum of its walls. Apparently, too, the good folk of Kum are without honour in their own country; for there is a Persian proverb that says: 'A dog of Kashan is better than a noble of Kum, albeit a dog is better than a man of Kashan.'

Postal road

In leaving Kum, it took me three-quarters of an hour to get quit of the maze of intricate streets and alleys of which the greater part of the city outside the bazaar is composed, and to emerge upon the open country. There a fast gallop on an excellent little horse conducted me to the post-house of Pasangun, standing, with a caravanserai, near the base of a range of hills on the south-east. Skirting this range, the track now becomes very stony, then crosses a stream, passes the big caravanserai of Shurab (salt water), which was built about eighty years ago, and winds by a long and arid pass through the range, till it debouches upon another plain, whereon the *chapar-khaneh* and caravanserai of Sinsin (erected by the Amin-ed-Dowleh, a prominent minister of Fath Ali Shah) are situated immediately at the foot of the hills. Sinsin was once a flourishing place, but was ruined by the Turkomans at the end of the last century—to such a distance did those incorrigible freebooters (of the Yomut tribe in this instance) push their marauding expeditions. Malcolm, on his way up to Teheran in 1810, himself conversed with one of the survivors of the catastrophe. Thence, over a perfectly level expanse, we press forward to Kashan, thin wreaths of smoke in the distance betraying the existence of the city at the base of what is sometimes called, for want of a general title, the Kuhrud range (from the village of which I shall speak presently), but is in reality a spur of the same mountain system that continues without a break from Kashan to Yezd, and thence to Kerman.

Kashan

Local tradition ascribes the foundation of Kashan[1] to Zobeideh, the wife of Harun-er-Rashid. But it appears certain that the town existed much earlier; for there is in a native historian a reference both to Kashan and Kum as having contributed a force of 20,000 soldiers to the army of the last Sassanian monarch; and some have seen in the name a contraction from

[1] For Kashan, in addition to the authorities quoted in the case of Kum, *vide* Olearius (1637), *Narrative of Embassy*; John Bell (1717), *Travels*; and Madame Dieulafoy (1881), *La Perse*.

Kai-ashian, or King's dwelling. From a very remote period Kashan appears to have been famous for five things: the industrial aptitudes of its inhabitants, its silk manufactures, its brass and copper utensils, its earthenware or *faïence*, and its scorpions. Geoffrey Ducket, one of the English factors who sailed to Persia in the fifth venture of the British Moscovy Company in the sixteenth century,[1] went up to Kashan in 1573 and reported it to be:—

A town that consisteth altogether of merchaundise, and the best trade of all the lande is there, beyng greatly frequented by the merchauntes of India. The towne is much to be commended for the civill and good government that is there used. An idle person is not suffered to live amongst them. The childe that is but five yeeres olde is set to some labour. Playing at dice or cardes is by the lawe present death.[2]

John Cartwright, preacher, in 1600, called it 'the very magazeen and warehouse of all the Persian cities for stuffes.'[3] Sir T. Herbert in 1627 said:—

This noble city is in comparison not less than York or Norwich, about 4,000 families being accounted in her. A more industrious and civil People or a town better governed Persia elsewhere has not. The Carravans-raw, is an unparallel'd fabrick, and precedes all other I saw in Persia.[4]

Chardin also spoke of 'the Royal Inn, built by Abbas the Great,' as 'the finest in all Persia,' and said that in his day the city had a double wall, five gates, 6,500 houses (including the suburbs), forty mosques, three colleges, and 200 sepulchres of Seyids.

Its manufactures

The silks, satins, velvets, and brocades of Kashan have long been famous throughout the East. In former times the silkworm was largely cultivated in the neighbourhood, and there was further a considerable import of raw material from Gilan. A number of beautiful silk, and silk with cotton, fabrics are still manufactured here (of which the shawls called Husein Kuli Khani, from the name of some early designer or patron, are perhaps the most artistic textile production of Persia), as well as velvets with a peculiar mottled pattern. The pierced and inlaid brass

1 For further details, *vide* a later chapter on Persian Commerce.

2 *Early Voyages in Russia and Persia* (Hakluyt Society), vol. ii. p. 428.

3 Purchas' *Pilgrims*, vol. ii. lib. ix. cap. 4.

4 *Some Yeares' Travels*, p. 222. The Royal Caravanserai has long ago fallen into ruin.

and copper wares are also remarkable; and Kashan is the great native manufactory of domestic utensils in copper. Formerly the metal was procured from Sivas in Asiatic Turkey, *viâ* Erzerum and Tabriz, but it is now imported in bars or sheets from England. The bazaars and busy part of the town are in its southern quarter, where also are the principal buildings, consisting of the Musjid-i-Meidan, which contains a superb *mihrab*, or prayer niche, in embossed and enamelled *faïence*, a tall leaning minaret, and vast caravanserais for the storage or barter of merchandise. In 1870, Colonel Euan Smith reported the city to contain twenty-four caravanserais for the sale of goods, thirty-five for the accommodation of strangers, thirty-four public baths, eighteen larger mosques, and ninety smaller shrines. He returned its population as 90,000—an altogether exorbitant estimate, although General Gasteiger Khan's calculation of 5,000 in 1881 is scarcely less inaccurate at the opposite extreme. In 1885, Schindler reckoned it as 30,000, though where these people are stowed away one is at a loss to imagine after inspecting what is outwardly one of the most dilapidated cities in Persia. A more funereal place I had not yet seen. Scarcely a

MINARET OF KASHAN

building was in repair, barely a wall intact. Both the cobbled roadway and the houses that lined it were in an equal state of decay, and it was as melancholy to see the one as it was to ride over the other.

From Kashan, the still surviving name for Persian earthenware, viz. *Kashi-kari*, was derived, and this city, in whose neighbourhood good clay was to be found, as well as colouring materials, was one of the chief centres of the industry. A larger number of the beautiful vases with iridescent lustre, or *reflet métallique*, which are the most cherished among the curios of Persia, have been found at Kashan than elsewhere, but there is no positive proof that they were manufactured here. On the other hand, most of the tiles, so plentifully and effectively employed in the decoration of mosques, were burned in Kashani ovens.[1]

Kashi

It is, perhaps, to mercantile habits, pursued without a break for centuries, that must be attributed the widespread reputation of the Kashanis for pusillanimity of character. Their fame in this respect has passed into a proverb, even in a country where courage did not appear to me to be popular; and among the many stories to which it has given birth, perhaps the best is that of the 30,000 men of Kashan and Isfahan (a sister-city as regards the same attributes), who, when Nadir Shah disbanded his army on their return from India, applied for an escort of 100 musketeers to conduct them safely to their homes. Possibly a somewhat enervating effect is produced by the great heat in summer, which Chardin ascribed to 'the high mountain on the south, the reverberation of which so furiously heats the place in the dog days that it scalds again.'

People

Touching the scorpions, the black variety of Kashan has enjoyed a prodigious fame, and was commemorated by El Istakhri as early as the tenth century. So venomous was their bite that one of the familar forms of expressing hatred was to pray that your enemy might either be stung by a Kashani scorpion or be made Governor of Gilan. John Struys, the Dutchman, declared that, in order to escape these pests, the people slept in hammocks, and took an antidote made of filings of copper tempered with vinegar and honey. But the more popular cure was the homœopathic application of the oil of the scorpion itself, which was extracted by frying the insect. Olearius, the secretary to the Holstein Embassy in 1637, was bitten by a scorpion at Kashan and derived great

Scorpions

[1] For the entire subject, *vide* Sir R. Murdoch Smith's *Handbook on Persian Art*; Benjamin's *Persia*, cap. xi.; 'Persian Ceramics,' by Professor W. A. Neumann, in *Oester. Monats.* (1884), pp. 257–63; and *Persian Ceramic Art*, by H. Wallis, 1891.

relief from this remedy.[1] There is a tradition that still survives that the creatures do not attack strangers, but this modest display of hospitality is hardly likely to induce a longer stay than is possible in so unattractive a spot.

About four miles to the south-west of Kashan, on the slopes of the mountains, is situated the palace of Fin, the springs of which have rendered it a favourite resort of royalty from early times. Shah Abbas built a residence here, but the present structure, now in a state of great decay, is the work of Fath Ali Shah, who made it one of his favourite summer retreats, though originally intended for his brother Husein Kuli Khan. Cypress avenues, water flowing in marble canals, and jets for fountains adorned its gardens; a picture of Fath Ali and his sons and hunting and battle scenes hung upon its walls. Sir J. Malcolm and his escort were accommodated here on their upward march to Teheran in 1810. In later times, a gloomier memory has attached to the palace of Fin; for here, in 1852, Mirza Taki Khan, the first great minister of the reigning Shah, and brother-in-law of the king, was put to death by the Royal order, his veins being opened in a bath. The place is now deserted.

Palace of Fin

After leaving Kashan, the track runs for a distance of about sixteen miles over a stony expanse, nearly flat, though with a slight rise, to the foot of the mountains, where it turns sharply to the right and plunges into the main range. At a little distance up the pass, in what the foolish Ker Porter described as 'a confined dell of this darkling labyrinth,' stands the large dilapidated caravanserai of Guebrabad—a ruined settlement of the Zoroastrians. Here we finally lose sight of the snowy spire of Demavend, which has accompanied us all the way from Teheran, gaining each day in pride and stature as his inferior satellites have sunk from view, and the monarch has stood forth alone with his crowned head in the heavens. The distance, as the crow flies, is a little over 150 miles.[2] Continuing up the pass, the road enters

Bund of Shah Abbas

[1] The same notion has prevailed in countries widely removed from Persia. Madame de Sévigné, in a letter dated July 8, 1672, wrote: 'Je vous prie, quoi qu'on dise, de faire faire de l'huile de scorpion, afin que nous trouvions en même temps les maux et les médecines.'

[2] Demavend has been seen at much greater distances. Morier (*First Journey*, p. 402) was told that it could be seen from the minaret of the Musjid-i-Shah at Isfahan, a distance of 230 miles; but this, for physical reasons, must be impossible. General Monteith (*Proc. R.G.S.* vol. iii. p. 18) saw it from Mount Savalan, above Ardebil, a distance of 270 miles. Similarly, P. H. Bruce (*Memoirs*, p. 282) saw Mount Ararat from Derbend on the Caspian, a distance of 240 miles.

a rocky gorge, which, of course, elicits from Porter the descriptive epithets of 'a tremendous abyss, an insurmountable pass, overwhelmingly grand, vieing with any part of the Caucasus for sublimity in form, hue, and bearing.' The rhodomontade of the worthy baronet proceeds from such inexhaustible wells that he could afford to leave the tap perpetually running. Presently we arrive at the great stone *bund* of Ali Verdi Khan, Commander-in-Chief under Shah Abbas and builder of the famous galleried bridge of Isfahan. This great structure, which completely blocks the valley from side to side, damming up the waters of a mountain stream in spring

PASS AND BUND OF KUHRUD

time, and forming thereby a lake of some depth and size, whose outflow towards the plain of Kashan is regulated by a sluice, still answers to the description of it left by Tavernier :—

At the end of the valley you meet a great wall which crosses it and joyns the two mountains together. This wall is above 100 paces long, above thirty foot thick, and fifty high. It was the work of the great Sha Abas, whose design it was to stop the waters that fall from the mountain, and to make a receptacle for water in that place to serve his occasions. At the foot of the wall there is a sluice, which being let down keeps in the water ; but is pull'd up to let out the water over all the neighbouring lands to the plains of Cachan.[1]

When I passed in the early winter the bed of the lake was dry, and such water as remained in the stream was frozen, for at this elevation, about 7,000 feet, it was very cold. Other travellers have reported the reservoir as half-full, or full, with the water spilling over the *bund* in a fine cascade. In January and February, after the deep snows have fallen, the pass, which below Kuhrud has an altitude of 7,250, and further on, at its highest point, of 8,750 feet, is sometimes impassable.

Above this point the valley widens somewhat, and, about four miles further on, encloses a succession of charming orchards thickly planted with walnut, pear, plum, and apple trees, for the fruit of which Kuhrud is famous. The sight of a little timber was a welcome relief after the long leagues of bare plain and brown mountain, and Kuhrud is to be congratulated on its snug little inheritance, which in summer-time is considered a terrestrial Paradise by the sentimental sons of Iran. Above the terraced orchards is situated the village—a typical Persian mountain hamlet of rude houses built one above the other in ascending tiers upon the side of the hill, such as I had seen daily in Khorasan, but not before in Central Persia.[2] The people of Kuhrud and Soh speak a dialect or patois of their own, containing many archaic words and idioms, and said by philologists to be closely allied to the Lur dialect, to the Dari of Yezd, and to that of Sivend near Persepolis.[3]

Kuhrud

Thence for over twenty miles the track lies amid the spurs and ramifications of the mountain range, climbing one ridge only to reveal another beyond, and wearying the tired traveller with the perpetual new vista of the same mountain maze. At length the caravanserai and imposing Telegraph station of Soh are reached, at a point where the ridge really begins to dip towards the plain of Isfahan. A *farsakh* further are the village and post-house of Bideshk. A descent among the lower undulations carries us on to the flat, where a canter can be enjoyed for miles, a thin streak of verdure in the distant hollow of the plain marking the

Road to Isfahan

[1] *Voyages*, lib. i. cap. vi.

[2] I have called the place Kuhrud (i.e. Mountain River), vulg. Kohrud, which appears to be the generally accepted name; though Kahrud (i.e. Laughing River) has been suggested, and is, perhaps, supported, by the Carou of Chardin.

[3] *Vide* A. H. Schindler, 'Beiträge zum Kurdischen Wortschatze,' in *Zeit. d. M. G.*, 1884.

SECTION OF PIGEON-TOWER

village of Murchakhar, near to which, on November 13, 1729, Nadir Shah inflicted a decisive defeat on the Afghans, who were soon expelled root and branch from the country. Here also in 1785 died Ali Murad Khan, who enjoyed a brief reign of four years in the anarchy that succeeded the death of Kerim Khan Zend. A short rise leads past the large Mader-i-Shah caravanserai, built of brick upon a foundation of blueish stone by the mother of Shah Abbas, to the crest of a low ridge that separates the plains of Murchakhar and Isfahan. Thence over the flat we speed in the direction of the Sefavi capital, already indicated by faint blue smoke-wreaths and by the converging lines of innumerable *kanats*. Behind it the panorama is closed by mountains of striking and irregular outline.[1]

As we approach the city the most conspicuous objects in the landscape are a number of large circular towers with smaller turrets projecting from their summits, sometimes sixty to seventy feet in total height, planted in the midst of enclosures and gardens, and suggesting to the untutored eye the fortalices of a feudal baronage. The real explanation is deplorably material and deficient in the slenderest element of romance. They are pigeon-towers, erected for the preservation of the dung and for the breeding of those birds, who spend the day afield and return at night to these comfortable quarters. The photograph which I present of a section of the interior will show that the towers contain an infinite number of cells [2] and a well in the middle for collecting the manure, which is spread upon the melon-beds in the surrounding fields.[3] They are opened and cleaned once a year, but I should imagine that the damage inflicted on the grain crops by the depredations of the birds would all but counterbalance the profit accruing from the distribution of their guano. In Chardin's time there were reckoned to be 3,000 of these pigeon-towers

Pigeon-towers

[1] From Kashan to Isfahan, an alternative, but more circuitous, route runs to the east *viâ* Natanz. It was followed and described by several of the seventeenth century travellers, e.g. John Struys (1672), *Travels*, cap. xxx., and C. Le Brun (1703), *Travels*, cap. xxxvii. Compare A. H. Schindler (1879), *Zeit. d. Gesell. f. Erd. z. Berlin*, vol. xiv. pp. 307–66.

[2] Dr. Wills mentions a single tower as containing 7,000 cells, and giving accommodation, therefore, to 14,000 pigeons. Since Isfahan, however, ceased to be a capital, melons do not fetch so high a price; and, accordingly, the majority of the towers have fallen into ruin.

[3] Dr. Fryer (*Travels into Persia*, 1676, letter v.) is responsible for the statement that the pigeons' dung was used 'to supply the Magazines with Salt-Petre for making gunpowder,' a use which is, I confess, novel to me.

outside Isfahan, and we read in the pages of Olearius of the king stationing himself on the summit and anticipating the Hurlingham or the Monte Carlo of the nineteenth century by shooting the birds (which represent two varieties of the genuine 'blue-rock,' and are called by the Persians *kabutar*, or 'the blue one') as they bolted from the apertures.

Above the low buildings of the city, as we draw nearer, emerge a blue dome and a single minaret. Presently the road passes between garden walls, and, through the familiar labyrinth of intricate lanes, we enter the former capital of Persia. Traversing the town, but avoiding its principal marts and thoroughfares, I came out on the far side into the Avenue of the Chehar Bagh, crossed the Zendeh Rud by the great bridge of Ali Verdi Khan, and having spent another half-hour in diving in and out of the still more intricate alleys of Julfa, arrived at the house of my host. Here I shall pause to give a detailed account of the past and present of the renowned capital of Shah Abbas.[1]

Approach to the city

Isfahan or Ispahan (the former is the commoner pronunciation, the *p* being softened into *f*, as in the case of Fars for Pars [Persis]), is probably the same name as the Aspadana of Ptolemy,[2] and may possibly be derived from the family name of the race of Feraidan, who were called Aspiyan in the Pehlevi dialect, elsewhere Athriyan. Whatever part, however, may have been played by myth in determining the nomenclature of the place, we need not admit the same element into a discussion of its actual history, which we will therefore not pursue into the nebulous period of Jamshid and his successors. Under the Achæmenian kings, a

History

[1] For descriptions of Isfahan at various periods, I recommend the following, in addition to the works already cited in a footnote upon the route from Teheran: P. della Valle (1618), *Viaggi*; Sir T. Herbert (1627), *Some Yeares' Travels*, pp. 154–69; Olearius (1637), *Narrative of Embassy*, p. 291 *et seq.*; J. B. Tavernier (1640–70), *Travels*, bk. iv. cap. v.; Sir J. Chardin (1665–77), *Coronation of Solyman* and *Voyages* (edit. Langlès), vols. vii. and viii. p. 141; A. Daulier-Deslandes (1665), *Les Beautez de la Perse*, pp. 19–53; J. Thévenot (1665–7), *Travels*, caps. iv. *et seq.*; J. Struys (1672), *Voyages*, caps. xxxi.–xxxii.; J. Fryer (1676), *Travels*; P. Sanson (1683), *Mémoire*; E. Kaempfer (1684–8), *Amœnit. Exot.*, lib. i. ii.; C. Le Brun (1703), *Travels*, caps. xxxviii.–xlviii.; Krusinski (1700–22), *History of Revolution*, p. 90 *et seq.*; J. Bell (1717), *Travels*; A. Dupré (1808), *Voyage*, caps. xliv.–v.; Ch. Texier (1840), *L'Arménie, la Perse*, &c., vols. i. and ii.; E. Flandin (1840–1), *Voyage en Perse*, vol. i. caps. xviii.–xxii., vol. ii. caps. xxx.–ii.; Sir H. Rawlinson, *Encyclopædia Britannica* (9th edit.); E. Stack (1881), *Six Months in Persia*, vol. ii. cap. ii.

[2] Lib. vi. cap. 4.

city named Gabal or Gavi seems to have existed on this site, and later to have become the Jai of the Sassanian epoch, which was captured by the conquering Omar in 641 A.D., after the battle of Nihavend.[1] In the early Mohammedan period, about 931 A.D., the city, already known as Isfahan, passed into the hands of the Dilemi or Buyah dynasty, who ruled as petty princes in Fars and Irak, at which time it consisted of two quarters, known as Yehudieh, or Jews' Town, and Shehristan, or Medinah, i.e. the city proper, which were finally united within a single wall by Husein, the Rukn-ed-Dowleh, father of the even more famous Asad-ed-Dowleh, of that line. About this time Isfahan was visited by El Istakhri, who reported it as a very flourishing place, renowned for its silks and fine linen.[2] Early in the eleventh century it was taken by Mahmud of Ghuzni, and next fell under the control of the Seljuks, having been besieged and captured by Togrul Beg. Nasiri Khosru, who was there in 1052 A.D., soon after the siege, found that the city had quite recovered, and occupied a walled space three and a half *farsakhs* in circumference. Benjamin of Tudela, a few years later, corroborates these dimensions, calls Isfahan 'capital of the kingdom of Persia,' and says that it contained 15,000 Jews.[3] Jenghiz Khan pillaged it; but was outdone in this instance by Timur, who, in revenge for an attack made by the citizens upon the garrison which he had quartered in the city, ordered a general massacre, the fruits of which, in the shape of 70,000 heads, were piled up in pyramids of skulls. At about the same time that Henry VII. was ascending the throne of England, 'Spahaun' was visited by the Venetians, Barbaro and Contarini, who found there installed the court of Uzun Hasan, or Long Hasan, of the White Sheep Dynasty. Thus we are brought down to the period when, always having been a capital city, though of a restricted dominion, Isfahan was promoted to the metropolitan rank of the entire Persian empire by the renowned Shah Abbas.

This great monarch would ill have sustained his own conception of royalty had he not provided for himself, and adorned with all the magnificence that an enlightened taste could suggest, a new seat of residence and power. Some chroniclers have attributed to

[1] Arab authors represent a force of 20,000 men as having been contributed to the Persian army from Spahan.

[2] *Oriental Geography*, p. 169.

[3] *Itinerary*, p. 128. It has, of course, been said in consequence that these were the descendants of Jews deported by Nebuchadnezzar.

him inferior or subsidiary motives: the unhealthiness of Kazvin, the distance of Sultanieh, the omens of astrology. Behind the superficial vainglory which he so dearly loved, lurked, however, an idea of true statesmanship. Of the new empire which he had won, and which stretched from Georgia to Aghanistan, Isfahan was the natural geographical centre. The instincts of a prudent centralisation commanded him to fix his capital at a spot where he would be within equal distance of all corners of his huge dominion, and where, in reasonable proximity to the Persian Gulf, he could at once overawe the maritime provinces, control the foreign trade, and enter into easy diplomatic relations with the potentates of Europe. This decision arrived at, he sketched the outlines of a colossal plan. A new city, approached by superb bridges and stately avenues, furnished with public buildings, as beautiful as they were large, and embellished by terraced gardens, and palaces, and pavilions, sprang into existence. The embassies of mighty sovereigns flocked to the new capital from the uttermost parts of Europe, and were received with all the splendour of a court immensely rich and versed in a fanciful and fastidious etiquette. The factors of great trading corporations occupied a position little short of the accredited representatives of royalty; and a life of gorgeous ceremonial, mingled with holiday festivity, rendered Isfahan the most famous and romantic of the cities of the East. It is fortunate that the cosmopolitan tastes of this great monarch—the contemporary of Elizabeth in England, of Henri IV. in France, of Gustavus Adolphus in Sweden, and of Akbar in India—and his successors, should have tempted so many intelligent foreigners to the Persian court; for it is to their presence and, in some cases, prolonged residence in the city throughout the seventeenth century, that we owe a minute knowledge of the life and habits, the pomp and parade, the virtues and the vices of the Sefavi kings. Pietro della Valle, Herbert, Olearius, Tavernier, Chardin, Sanson, Daulier-Deslandes, Kaempfer, and Le Brun successively shed the light of an acute and instructed scrutiny upon the scene, and have added to the respective literatures of Italy, Great Britain, Germany, France, and Holland.

Abbas the Great

In the middle of the seventeenth century we have the estimate of Chardin that within ten leagues of Isfahan were 1,500 villages; that the city itself was 24 miles round; that inside the walls, which were pierced by 12 gates, were 162 mosques, 48 *madressehs*, 1802 caravanserais, 273 baths, and twelve cemeteries; and that the various computations of the total of inhabitants varied between 600,000 and 1,100,000.[1] The figures of Olearius, viz. 18,000 houses and 500,000 people. do not fall greatly below the lesser total. No wonder that the Oriental hyperbole should have vented itself in the vainglorious boast that 'Isfahan nisf i Jehan,' i.e. 'Isfahan is half the world.' Kaempfer and Struys credited it, the suburbs included, with an even ampler circuit, which they fixed at sixteen *farsakhs*, or forty-eight miles. In the time of Abbas II. the king possessed, in addition to his own numerous residences, 137 royal palaces (probably in many cases only private mansions) in different parts of the city, acquired either by inheritance, purchase, or seizure, and devoted to the entertainment of foreign envoys and strangers of consideration. When the former were received in public audience in the Chehel Situn, or Forty Pillars, all business was suspended for the day; a magnificent but tedious ceremonial preceded and delayed the approach of the ambassador to the footstool of royalty; gorgeous banquets, culminating in general intoxication, followed; while in the Great Square the populace were regaled with the exhibitions of wrestlers, fencers, jugglers, and acrobats, with polo-matches and puppet-shows; and with combats of animals, bulls, rams, buffaloes, wolves, and, on great occasions, lions and panthers. When night fell fantastic fireworks illumined and prolonged the festive scene. In one part of the city stood a great tower sixty feet high, and twenty feet thick, called the Kelleh Minar, composed of the horns and skulls of wild animals slain by one of the earlier monarchs in the chase.[2] The favour and the prestige in which foreigners were held, and the latitude allowed by the liberal-minded Abbas and his successors to the Christian religion, were exemplified by the establishments and

The Sefavi capital

[1] In illustration of the immense size of Isfahan, Chardin tells the story of a slave who fled from his master to another part of the city, opened a shop there, and remained undiscovered for years. He did not himself, however, think the population greater than that of London.

[2] Commonly attributed to Shah Ismail or Shah Tahmasp, but doubtless of later origin. Olearius says there were the heads of two thousand stags and gazelles that were all killed at one hunting by Shah Tahmasp. Chardin mentions the popular belief that the architect's head was placed on the apex by the royal sportsman, because he had said that the skull of some peculiar great beast was wanted for the summit. Engravings of the tower occur in the works of Chardin and Sanson. Herbert and Tavernier both declared that a great many of the skulls were human.

churches of the principal monastic fraternities of Europe in the city. The Augustines, Carmelites, and Capuchins were allowed separate quarters belonging to the Crown in Isfahan ; [1] the Jesuits and Dominicans had convents in Julfa. Of the various factories, that of the representative of the British East India Company, from 1617 to the Afghan invasion in 1722, was situated in the Bazaar near the Great Meidan. It is perhaps only fair to quote, as a set-off to the doubtless exaggerated descriptions of some of the afore-mentioned travellers when relating the wonders of Isfahan, the cooler and more cynical verdict of the French jeweller Tavernier, who was not to be deluded by surface show or factitious pomp, but who mercilessly stripped the tinsel from the gilt gingerbread. This is what he said :—

> Ispahan in general, unless it be the Meydan, and some few arch'd streets, where the merchants live, is more like a great village than a city ; the Houses standing at a distance one from the other with every one a garden, but ill look'd after, not having anything in it perchance but only one pitiful tree . . . . As for the King's Palace, I cannot make any handsome description of it in regard there is nothing of beauty either in the Building or in the Gardens. Excepting only four rooms which they call Divans, I saw nothing but pitiful low galleries and so narrrow that hardly two men could pass abrest in 'em.

As for the Christian Missions and monks, he entertained a very poor opinion of their propaganda, for he wrote :—

> The number of the Religious Teachers is far greater than the number of hearers, for in all Ispahan and Julfa, take the Franks that come out of Europe, or born in Persia, as well men as women, there are not 600 persons that profess the Catholic Religion.

He further declared that the city was ill laid-out, the walls broken by great gaps, the streets narrow, unequal, and dark, encumbered with heaps of ordure and the carcasses of dead animals, and buried in summer dust or winter mire. We are justified, indeed, in believing that the pomp of Isfahan was limited to outer show, and to the appurtenances of royalty ; and that, one grade only below

[1] Of these the Augustines were the first European monks who ever lived in Isfahan. Their first representative was Antonio di Govea, who in 1598 was sent by the Archbishop of Goa as ambassador for Spain and Portugal. The Carmelites under Père Simon arrived as envoys from Pope Clement VIII. to Shah Abbas in 1608. The Capuchins (Père Pacifique de Provins and Père Gabriel) were sent out by Richelieu with letters from Louis XIV. in 1628. *Vide* the published works of A. di Govea, P. Pacif. de Provins, and P. Gabriel de Chinon.

these, were encountered the slovenliness and the filth of the unregenerate East. Such as it was, however—a strange but truly Oriental mixture of splendour and squalor, of dignity and decay—the city continued with little alteration till the first quarter of the eighteenth century, when, the virtues of the reigning dynasty having been sapped by an inherited course of debauchery and intoxication, the capital and its monarch both fell a disgraceful prey to the Afghans in 1722. The horrors of the siege—when the Zendeh Rud was choked with corpses, when mothers devoured their children in the extremity of famine, and when the inhuman conqueror, after massacring all the princes and nobles on whom he could lay hands, surrendered the city for fifteen days to an indiscriminate carnage—have been powerfully described by the Polish Jesuit Krusinski, who was himself a resident in the capital at the time.[1] From this shock, and from the brutal savagery of the Afghans, who overturned, and sacked, and defiled out of all recognition, palaces, and avenues, and gardens, and whatever of beauty or grandeur met the eye, Isfahan has never recovered. It was patronised by Nadir Shah, but was less esteemed by him than Meshed. Kerim Khan Zend shifted the seat of Government to Shiraz. Agha Mohammed Khan Kajar shifted it again to Teheran, when he dismantled the fortifications of Isfahan. Fath Ali Shah sometimes visited the city, and ultimately died there in 1834. It has only once, in 1851, been favoured by the presence of the reigning monarch. Under the depressing influence of all these circumstances, Isfahan has fallen from its high estate, and now in perpetual sackcloth and ashes—no inapt metaphor to apply to the present appearance of the town—bewails an irrecoverable past.

Plan of the city

The method which I shall adopt of describing the city will be to give an indication of its general features, and then, step by step, to visit its most renowned or interesting localities, depicting at each stage the contrast between a past of grandeur and a present of sorrowfulness and decay. The only plan of Isfahan that I know appears among the plates of M. Coste's splendid work, entitled 'Monuments Modernes de la Perse.' Roughly speaking, Isfahan lies to the north of the Zendeh Rud, Julfa to the south. In about the centre of the former is situated the great block of buildings, gardens, and pavilions constituting

[1] *History of the Revolutions of Persia*, taken from the Memoirs of Father Krusinski, by Père Ducerceau. Translated into English. 1729.

the Palace enclosure, and abutting on the western side upon the Great Meidan, a parallelogram, whose length is from north to south and width from east to west. South-east of the Meidan is the Ark or Citadel. From the western flank of the palace enclosure runs the Chehar Bagh, or principal avenue to the great bridge of Ali Verdi Khan, conducting to Julfa. Further to the east, a similar avenue leads down to the second storeyed bridge, known as Pul-i-Khaju. Older bridges exist at some little distance both to the east and west of these two structures, while between them a fifth conducts to the palace of Haft Dest.

Meidan-i-Shah

The centre of Isfahan is the Meidan-i-Shah, or Royal Square, which is undoubtedly one of the most imposing piazzas in the world. It was laid out and surrounded with buildings by Shah Abbas; the king's palace, the principal mosque, and the Great Bazaar opened on to it; and it was both the scene of the principal royal pageants, and the nucleus of city life. This Meidan is 560 yards in length by 174 in width.[1] It is surrounded by a long low range of brick buildings, divided into two storeys of recessed arches, one above the other. Originally the lower of these were shops, opening on to the Meidan, and communicating at the back with the big Bazaar, while the upper storey consisted of chambers with balconies, that were thronged on festival occasions. They have since been used as barracks, and now present a blank and deserted appearance. A row of trees was planted all round in front of these arcades, and in front of the trees was a stone-edged canal filled with water. In 1809 Morier reported that there was not a single tree in the Meidan and that the canal was empty. A scanty row of *chenars* and poplars has

[1] Nowhere have I been so bewildered at the confusing and contradictory accounts of previous travellers as in their descriptions of the sights of Isfahan. They differ irreconcilably in their orientation of buildings, in their figures of dimensions, in the number of avenues, pillars, bridges, arches, &c. To correct or even to notice these countless inaccuracies would be a futile task. But as an illustration of them I may here give the dimensions in yards or paces of the Meidan-i-Shah as recorded by the principal historians of Isfahan, from which it will be seen how absurd is the divergence between two independent visions. Della Valle 690–230, Olearius 700–250, Tavernier 700–250, Chardin 440–160, Sanson 600–300, D. Deslandes 600–400, Kaempfer 660–212, Struys 700–250, Le Brun 710–210, Olivier 700–230, Johnson 500–200, Porter 860–230, Binning 800–200, Ussher 880–250, Pollington 600–200, Stack 300–180, Wills 440–220, Rawlinson 660–230. Here there is a maximum divergence of 580 yards in length, and 240 yards in width, or a cumulative error of over 125 per cent.

ROYAL SQUARE AT ISFAHAN

since been planted; but the canal was dry when I saw it, a substitute being provided by occasional fountains of drinking-water. In the centre of the Meidan, in the Sefavi days, stood a mast or maypole, twenty-five feet high, on which was placed, on great occasions, a cup of gold, but on ordinary occasions an apple or melon, to be shot at by archers passing at full gallop below.[1] Its place was afterwards taken by a more sinister object, viz., the *kapuk*, or execution pole, with notches on the side, by which the culprit was hanged up by the heels, and subsequently dashed to the ground, or else had his throat cut. This, too, has disappeared. Two great basins of water with porphyry coping adorned the two ends of the piazza, both of which survive, and are kept full. In front of the Ali Kapi, or Palace Gate, over 100 cannon, the spoils of Ormuz, were planted behind a wooden balustrade. These also have vanished. The only other permanent objects in the Meidan were two marble columns, which served as the goal posts in the game of Pall Mall or Polo, called *chugan*, which was very popular with the old Persian nobility, but has also died a natural death.[2] In the daytime the Meidan was all but filled with booths or tents balanced on poles, under which the petty hucksters displayed their wares upon the ground;[3] but on great occasions all these were cleared away, and in the evenings were ordinarily replaced by the shows of mummers, jugglers, and acrobats, by groups of story-tellers, wrestlers and dervishes, by cock-fights and ram-fights, and by the tents of prostitutes. All these are gone, with the exception of a few stalls at the northern extremity.

Here there still stands in a bay or recess a majestic portico, flanked by arched galleries, and opening into the Kaiserieh or main Bazaar. This lofty and ornamental structure, in the main arch of which is a painting of Shah Ismail or Abbas in combat, is the Nakkara-Khaneh or Drum-Tower of

Nakkara-Khaneh.

[1] Angiolello saw Shah Ismail bring down seven out of ten shots at Tabriz, *circ.* 1510; and Tavernier saw Shah Sefi I., who was a great athlete, strike three cups in five courses at Isfahan.

[2] It was played by numbers varying from five to twenty a side. P. della Valle described a game that he saw at Kazvin in 1618. Abdul Malek of the Samanid dynasty was killed by a fall from his horse while playing *chugan*. Sefi I. and Abbas II. were both excellent performers. Ouseley has an erudite note on the game (*Travels*, vol. i. app. 6), but is very wide of the mark when he traces to it the Cricket of England and the Golf of Scotland.

[3] Tavernier's illustration of the Meidan represents it as covered with these booths.

Isfahan; for here, in the flanking galleries, is dispensed the appalling music at sundown which indicates the residence of royalty, and of which I have already spoken at Teheran.[1] In the lower galleries, looking out into the square, the people used to smoke and drink their morning coffee; and here the paternally-minded Shah Abbas deputed *mullahs* to entertain them with serious discourse. Above the main arch, in a space still visible, but filled with modern tile-work, was fixed a great clock (Tavernier alone calls it a sun-dial) which, according to Olearius, was made by an Englishman named Festy for Shah Abbas; but, the maker having been killed by a Persian, it remained out of order ever afterwards. Above the clock was a big bronze bell, which contained an inscription round the edge: 'Sancta Maria, ora pro nobis mulieribus,' and had, in fact, been wrested from a Portuguese nunnery at Ormuz. It was never sounded, and nearly a hundred years ago was taken down and melted for cannon. The clock survived till the beginning of this century, and was seen by Olivier in 1796; but in 1808 it was removed by Haji Mohammed Husein, Amin-ed-Dowleh, and Beglerbeg of Isfahan under Fath Ali Shah, on the pretext of repairing the fresco in the archway.

Mosque of Lutfullah.

On the eastern side of the square stood, and still stands, the Mosque of Sheikh Lutfullah, frequently called the Mosque of the Grand Pontiff, i.e. the Sadr or Chief Priest (Chardin wrote it Cèdre) of Isfahan. In modern times it seems to have been less frequented than was once the case; but its dome is still covered by the ancient enamelled tiles, with a flowing, almost Florentine, pattern. A little beyond, or to the south of this, formerly existed a tower, which the French writers called Pavilion des Horloges, or des Machines, and which was built for the amusement of Shah Abbas II. by some of his European artificers. It contained a mechanical clock with marionnettes and figures of animals that moved. Not a trace of it now remains.

[1] Chardin says it sounded at sunset and midnight; Sanson at noon, sunset, and two hours after midnight; and on fête days almost all the day and night. A passage in the *Ghazaliat* of Sadi seems to suggest a morning performance also: 'Till you hear in early morning from the Friday mosque, or from the door of the Atabeg's palace, the noise of the big drum.' Le Brun names the instruments employed, and they have changed but little: 'tambours, trumpets, tymbals, clavecins, haûtbois, drums, flutes, harps, cymbals.' Thévenot says the trumpets were over 8 feet long. The custom is referred by Persian MSS. to as far back as the time of Alexander.

MUSJID-I-SHAH, ISFAHAN

In the centre of the southern or narrow end of the Meidan stands the Musjid-i-Shah or Royal Mosque of Isfahan. Erected on the site of a melon-garden in 1612–13 by Shah Abbas, and originally intended as the Musjid-i-Jama or Friday Mosque, it cost over 175,000*l.*, and was from the beginning one of the noblest fabrics in the city. Shah Sefi I. covered its doors with silver plates. Inside were preserved the blood-stained shirt of the martyred Husein, and a Koran written by the Imam Reza. It has been many times restored, notably by Nadir Shah, after the Afghan usurpation, and again by Ali Murad Khan. A lofty archway framed in a recess, embellished with interior honey-comb groining in enamelled faïence, surrounded by tile inscriptions from the Koran, and flanked by two minarets with spiral bands of similar ornamentation, leads from the Meidan through a porch, containing a great vase or font of porphyry, into the inner court. Here the peculiar construction of the Mosque, already visible from the exterior, is fully apparent. The axis of the Meidan being almost due north and south, the architect required to incline the axis of the mosque considerably to the south-west, in order that the *mihrab* or prayer-niche might be turned in the direction of Mecca. This purpose was effected by architectural means that are at once grandiose and simple. The inner court, marble-paved and containing a great tank for ablutions in the centre, is surrounded by a two-storeyed arcade, undecorated save by bands of Kufic inscription in tile-work, white letters upon a blue ground. The arches are kept for the accommodation of priests and attendants. On either side rises a lofty tile-faced *aiwan*, a mighty arch in which opens access to a space covered by a low dome. The only Europeans of whom I know as having penetrated beyond this quadrangle into the mosque itself, were J. S. Buckingham in 1816, and E. Flandin in 1840.[1] Opposite the entrance a third *aiwan*, flanked by minarets, conducts into the mosque proper, which is surmounted by the principal cupola, whose exterior, covered with exquisite tiles containing patterns in dark blue and green arabesque on an azure ground, is one of the principal land-

Musjid-i-Shah.

[1] Admirable plans, elevations, and restorations of the entire building have been published by Ch. Texier, *L'Arménie, la Perse*, &c., vol. i. pls. 70–72; and P. Coste, *Monuments Modernes de la Perse*. Mme. Dieulafoy borrows from these works without acknowledgment; but was herself admitted on to the roofs of the buildings looking down into the great court.

marks in the city. On either side of the shrine are further courts, with basins and porticoes, to which the public are admitted on Fridays. The decorative treatment of this beautiful building, though falling, like all other works of art in Persia, into decay, yet remains a superb sample of the style of the Sefavi kings. The four minarets have never been used by the *muezzin*, the kings being afraid that from their summits too much might be seen of the secrets of the royal seraglio adjoining. Their place for the call to prayer is taken by an ugly and stunted cage on the summit of one of the *aiwans*.

GATE OF ALI KAPI AND TALAR

We now pass to the western side of the Meidan, the principal structure in which, near the southern end, is a lofty building in the form of a great archway overlooking the square, and itself crowned in the fore part by an immense open throne-room or verandah supported by wooden columns, while the hinder part is elevated to a height of three storeys higher. This is the *talar* of the royal palace, and the porch below is the celebrated Ali Kapi or Sacred Gate. The name of the latter has been variously explained by different writers, some writing it as Allah Kapi, or the Gate of God, so called because of its extreme sanctity; others as Ali

Gate of Ali Kapi.

Kapi, the Gate of Ali, there being a tradition that Shah Abbas carried it off in its entirety from the sepulchre of Ali at Nejef (Meshed Ali) near the Euphrates, where he replaced the original by a jewelled substitute. The true meaning would appear, however, to be Ali (i.e. Aali) Kapi or the Sublime Porte. Its sanctity has now fallen into comparative abeyance, although any one sitting under the chain at the back, which is covered with rags as offerings, has *bast* and cannot be touched; but in the Sefavi days it was great and unquestioned. No one might walk over the threshold; the king never crossed it on horseback; all recipients of the king's favour went and kissed the gate; and it was held an inviolable asylum, from which none but the sovereign could drag a fugitive, and he by starvation only. Tavernier gave still further particulars:—

> Tis the custom of all Ambassadors to salute the Gate of Ali by reason of a white marble stone made like an asses back, and which serves for a step; being, as they report, brought anciently out of Arabia, where Ali liv'd. That day that the new King receives his Ensignia of Royalty, he goes to stride over that Stone, and if by negligence he should chance to touch it, there are four guards at the gate that would make a show of thrusting him back again.

From Thévenot it appears that this sacred stone was not situated in the gateway, but at the end of an alley leading from the Ali Kapi.

In the *talar* or open portal above, supported by twelve wooden columns and containing a marble basin in the centre, the king gave audience to the ambassadors at No Ruz; and there he sat to witness the horse races and polo, the wild beast fights and public entertainments below. The building, when I visited it, was unoccupied; and presented a very forlorn and deserted appearance.

This portal is the most advanced portion of the Royal Palace, the various courts and gardens and pavilions of which occupy an

The Palace

immense space, estimated by Chardin as four and a half miles in circuit, along the entire western side of the Meidan, terminating on the far side in the avenue of the Chehar Bagh. In this palace still lives the Zil-es-Sultan as Governor of Isfahan; but some of its courts abutting on the square are surrendered to public officials, and, in the absence of the prince, were crowded by the applicants for ministerial or magisterial favour. A ground plan of the entire block would alone reveal or explain its intricate and bewildering partitions. As is common in Persian buildings, all the beauty was showered upon a few special courts or halls, and there can never have been any general effect, either of art or magnificence. Tavernier, indeed, in a passage already quoted, spoke very contemptuously of its features. A few structures, however, always deserved, and still deserve, admiring attention.

Of these the most famous is the Chehel Situn or Hall of Forty Pillars, which was the principal *talar* or verandahed throne-room in the palace, where the king gave audience to ambassadors, and received his ministers in Levée. About the origin of the name there has been some dispute. As the loggia is supported by twenty columns only, the number of forty has been obtained by some too ingenious spirits by counting their reflections in the basin of water that stretches in front. I myself imagined that there might once have been a similar porch, with twenty more columns, on the back or further side of the central hall; and I have been informed that restorations, carried out in the past year (1891) have revealed traces of such an original addition. At the same time I can find, neither in the letterpress nor in the engravings of the old travellers, any hint of such a structure; and I have very little doubt, therefore, that the designation is merely a numerical title, intended to express size and magnificence. For this purpose the number *chehel* or forty is in common use in Persia. Persepolis is called Chehel Minar, or the Forty Towers; and other familiar appellations are Chehel Chashmeh (Forty Springs), Chehel Dokhteran (Forty Maidens), and Chehel Chiragh (Forty Lamps, commonly applied to a European chandelier).[1] The hall is situated at the end of a large garden, down the centre of which extends a tank which, when I saw it, was empty. A row of wires, stretched round it on tall blue and green poles, was a relic of a recent illumination. The gateways opening on to this garden are adorned with the heads of ibex, mountain-sheep, and similar trophies of the chase. The Chehel Situn was originally built by Shah Abbas; but, according to Krusinski, who was resident in Persia at the time, the greater part of the old fabric was destroyed by fire in the reign of Shah Sultan Husein, 100 years later; the latter monarch, who was childishly superstitious, declining to

Chehel Situn

[1] To the same class, in all probability, belonged the Hekatompylæ, or Hundred Gates of the Greeks. We may also compare the Forty Thieves of Aladdin.

CHEHEL SITUN

interfere with the flames, whose ravages he regarded as a dispensation of the divine will. However, when they had fulfilled their mission, he set about rebuilding the edifice; a fact which, though it has passed unnoticed by every writer with scarcely an exception, doubtless accounts for the occasional differences between the present fabric and that described by Chardin, Tavernier, etc., in the days before Shah Sultan Husein.

The building consists of four stages or compartments. Of these the outermost is the pillared verandah. Its roof, which is flat and immensely solid, some of the rafters being composed of the boles of entire *chenars* or planes, seven feet round, and unhewn, is supported upon twenty wooden columns, in four rows of three each, and two rows of four each.[1] The outer row of these were originally covered with small facets of looking-glass, set diamond-wise in perpendicular bands; the inner rows with glass set in spirals. All these facings had, at the time of my visit, been recently removed, a vulgar restoration having apparently been attempted, with the result of irreparable damage to the artistic beauty of the fabric. The interior columns rest on groups of stone lions, each facing outwards, and the four central pillars stood formerly at the angles of a marble basin, into which the lions that look that way spouted water from their mouths. But the basin had been filled in, and the lions, too, had succumbed to a recent daub of paint. The walls of this beautiful loggia, whose effulgence drew from the rhapsodical Ker Porter the following tribute:—

Verandah

> The exhaustless profusion of its splendid materials reflected not merely their own golden or crystal lights on each other, but all the variegated colours of the garden; so that the whole surface seemed formed of polished silver and mother of pearl, set with precious stones,

were formerly covered at the bottom with a wainscoting of white marble, painted and gilt, and above with the beautiful *aineh-kari*, or mirror-work, set in facets and panels, for which the Persian artificers were justly renowned. The bulk of this superb decoration, which still remains in the throne-room behind to point the bitter contrast, had, on the walls of the loggia, been ruthlessly obliterated

[1] Nevertheless Morier, Binning, and Dieulafoy, as also Chardin, give the number as eighteen, not reckoning, I imagine, the two columns that support the architrave of the throne-room. The dimensions of the various compartments are: Verandah, 44 yards by 22; Talar, 19 yards by 16; Shahnishin, 23 feet by 19; Picture-gallery, 80 feet by 40.

by the brush of the painter, who had left in its place a pale pink wash. Had I caught the pagan, I would gladly have suffocated him in a barrel of his own paint.

Immediately behind the verandah is the *talar*, or throne-room; and from this, but on a rather higher level, opens a deeply recessed compartment or dais, or Shahnishin, whereon stood the royal throne. The decorations of this chamber, when I saw it, were still intact; and the prismatic flash of the mirror panels and facets on the walls, the painting in gold, blue, red and green on the coffered ceiling, and the honeycomb vaulting of the recess, produced a sumptuous effect. Out of the throne-room small compartments open on either side, that were intended for the king's ministers.

Throne-room

Finally, behind the throne-room, and communicating with it by three doors, is a great hall, extending the entire length of the building (Lumsden gives its dimensions as seventy-five feet by forty-five feet), crowned by three low cupolas, and adorned over almost the entire surface of its walls by six immense oil-paintings, three on either side. Pietro della Valle, speaking of the paintings in the palace at Isfahan in the reign of Shah Abbas, made the remark that they were so badly drawn that he was very apprehensive of losing the European artist whom he had brought out to take private pictures for himself, if the king should become aware of his merit. Notwithstanding this criticism, which is so far just that the ignorance of perspective, the ill proportion, and the angular stiffness apparent in all Persian portraiture might well have shocked a seventeenth-century European, whose vision had been trained in the school of the Italian Renaissance, these pictures of the Chehel Situn are both admirable as works of art and invaluable as historical documents. They transport us straight to the court of the lordly Abbas and his predecessors or successors on the throne. We see the king engaged in combat, or at some royal festivity, enjoying the pleasures of the bowl. The big moustaches and smooth chins, and abundant turbans, represent a fashion of coiffure that has long expired. The arms and accoutrements of the warriors, the instruments of the musicians, the very gestures of the dancing-girls, open to us the locked doors of the past; and we seem to share in the feasts and fights, in the pomp and dalliance of the Sefavi kings. Whether these pictures are the originals that were painted by order of those sovereigns, or whether

Picture gallery

the originals were burned in the conflagration under Shah Sultan Husein, and repeated by command of that monarch, is not related. But from their correspondence with the description of Chardin I entertain very little doubt that four of them at least are the identical pictures described by him *circ.* 1670; that of Nadir Shah is, of course, a later addition.

I have found in the explanation of these pictures the same hopeless jumble of mistakes in previous writers that is the inevitable consequence of scant historical knowledge combined with perfunctory observation. On the wall facing the entrance are three of the six panels. One of these represents Shah Ismail engaged in combat with the Janissaries of Sultan Soliman. The redoubtable Shah is slicing the Agha of the Janissaries in twain, a red streak marking the downward passage of the royal blade. Adjoining is the picture of Shah Tahmasp entertaining the refugee Indian prince, Humaiun, at a banquet in 1543.[1] The two kings are kneeling upon a dais; around are disposed the singers and orchestra, the bodyguard and royal falconers with the birds perched on their wrists; while in the foreground two dancing-girls are performing with gestures none too prudish. The figures are not far short of life-size. The third picture on the western wall depicts a scene of even more advanced conviviality, the central figures of which are Abbas the Great and Abdul Mohammed, Khan of the Uzbegs.[2] There is the same background of royal attendants; but the carouse has evidently made considerable progress; for the king is holding out his cup for more wine, while an inebriated guest is lying in a state of extreme intoxication on the floor, with a flask pressed to his lips. This picture is said to contain a likeness of Ali Verdi Khan, the celebrated generalissimo of Shah Abbas, and the especial patron of the Sherleys. On the near wall are three corresponding panels. In one of these Shah Ismail at the head of his cavalry is engaged in conflict with the Uzbeg Tartars. In the second Shah Abbas II. is entertaining Khalif Sultan, ambassador from the Great Mogul, with the usual accompaniment of musicians and dancing-girls, the latter performing with

Description

[1] Texier, who alone gives engraved reproductions of three of the pictures, makes a ludicrous mistake about this one in particular. In his letterpress, he describes the Persian monarch as Shah Abbas, who did not ascend the throne till nearly fifty years later, and, in his title to the plate, as Fath Ali Shah, who did not reign till the present century.

[2] Lady Sheil calls him the Turkish ambassador.

tambourines and castanets. The last picture represents the battle between Nadir Shah and Sultan Mahmud (mounted on a white elephant), that decided the fate of Delhi. The colours and the gilding on these pictures retain an extraordinary vividness. A portrait of the reigning Shah has been added on the archway of the roof between two of the ancient panels. The lower portion of this great hall, as well as the walls of the side rooms, have been painted an ugly green. There are four fire-places, two on each of the longer sides. In the past year (1891) the picture-gallery has been turned into a species of conservatory, being filled with flowering plants. Smaller cabinets originally opened out at either end, and were adorned with portraits of European ladies and gentlemen of the days of Shah Abbas. All round the Chehel Situn were, and I dare say still are, hung great curtains of needle-work and brocade, which were let down against the sun. Mounsey in 1866, and Madame Dieulafoy in 1881, found the loggia employed as a workshop for the tent-makers of the Prince-Governor. This particular form of desecration has been abandoned; and quite recently (1891) I hear of the Zil-es-Sultan as sitting in daily audience in one of the cabinets to receive the addresses or complaints of his astonished subjects.

Courts and pavilions

Among the other pavilions or courts in the palace enclosure, which I have not the space more minutely to describe, may be mentioned the Sar Puchideh (of which Coste publishes an engraving), a hall of which the octagonal pillars, encrusted with glass, rest upon the shoulders of female figures in marble, themselves holding lions' heads which spout water into a basin; the Imaret-i-Ashraf, or pavilion built by the Afghan usurper; the Imaret-i-Nau, built for Fath Ali Shah by the Amin-ed-Dowleh, and containing many pictures of the king and his family;[1] and the Talar-i-Tavileh, or Hall of the Stables, a part of the palace now used for official business.

Hasht Behesht

On the extreme western side of the royal precincts, opening on to the Chehar Bagh, are a garden and building that merit a less curt notice. These are the Hasht Behesht, or Eight Paradises, a title which some writers have erroneously ascribed to the eight gardens bordering on either side upon the Chehar Bagh. The name, which appears, like the Chehel Situn, to be a numerical expression indicating size and splendour, was

[1] It is well described by Morier, *First Journey*, p. 167.

given to the place by Shah Suleiman when, in about 1670, he built this palace in a garden previously called Bagh-i-Bulbul, or Garden of the Nightingale. The chief building is a pavilion standing in the centre of a large enclosure. At its prime this must have been a remarkable structure, for it was thus described in 1677 by the rhetorical Dr. Fryer:—

It is a sweet Place, doubtless, were it cloathed with its glory ; but as it is, it is a Rich Piece ; the Summer House in the middle is saluted by two Channels, in which are Ships and Boats to represent a Naval scene of War ; Swans and Pelicans find here their diversion ; the Summer House is built entirely of polished Marble, the Arch of the Cupilo is Inlaid with Massy Gold, upon the Walls are depainted the famous Actions of their Heroes ; the Tank in the middle is all of Silver, the Posts are stuck with Looking glasses, reflecting the Posture of the Body, and the Figures of the whole Fabrick ; an Hemispherical Turret presses on Four Pillars which are the main supporters.[1]

Even Chardin, enthusiastic but seldom sentimental, was inspired to an unwonted outburst by the charms of the Hasht Behesht.

When one walks in this place expressly made for the delights of love, and when one passes through all these cabinets and niches, one's heart is melted to such an extent that, to speak candidly, one always leaves with a very ill grace. The climate without doubt contributes much towards exciting this amorous disposition ; but assuredly these places, although in some respects little more than cardboard castles, are nevertheless more smiling and agreeable than our most sumptuous palaces.[2]

Later on this pavilion fell into decay, but it was rebuilt or restored by Fath Ali Shah, who in the main hall, covered by a dome and surrounded by galleries with small chambers in the angles, caused to be executed frescoes and oil-paintings of himself seated in state with his court, and mounted on horseback spearing a lion. Other contemporary pictures adorn the neighbouring walls, including one of Istarji, or Strachey, the English Adonis. This heptagonal pavilion, which is now neglected and falling to decay, is sometimes placed by the Governor at the disposal of strangers of consideration or officials of foreign governments. It stands in a garden laid out in parterres, planted with fruit-trees, and with avenues bordered with cypresses and *chenars*. Like all Persian gardens, this is no

[1] *Travels in Persia*, p. 214.

[2] *Voyages* (ed. Langlès), vol. viii. p. 43.

doubt very lovely in spring-time and summer, but at any other season of the year it has an unkempt and bedraggled appearance. Tavernier very truly remarked of the royal gardens of Isfahan, even at the zenith of their splendour, that

> You must not imagine that these gardens are so curiously set out nor so well kept as ours in Europe. For they have no such lovely borders, nor such close walks of honeysuckles and jasmin as are to be seen in the Gardens of Europe. They suffer the grass to grow in many places; contented only with a good many great Fruit Trees, tufted atop, and planted in a line, which is all the grace of the Gardens of Persia.

Chehar Bagh

From the palace I now pass to the Great Avenue, already mentioned, that conducts from the centre of the city for a distance of 1,350 yards to the Bridge of Ali Verdi Khan. Its name, the Chehar Bagh, or Four Gardens, is not derived from the gardens that open out of it, but recalls the fact that the site was originally occupied by four vineyards which Shah Abbas rented at 9,000 *francs* a year and converted into a splendid approach to his capital. Of all the sights of Isfahan, this in its present state is the most pathetic in the utter and pitiless decay of its beauty. Let me indicate what it was and what it is. At the upper extremity, a two-storeyed pavilion, connected by a corridor with the Seraglio of the palace, so as to enable the ladies of the harem to gaze unobserved upon the merry scene below, looked out upon the centre of the avenue. Water, conducted in stone channels, ran down the centre, falling in miniature cascades from terrace to terrace, and was occasionally collected in great square or octagonal basins, where cross roads cut the avenue. On either side of the central channel was a row of *chenars* and a paved pathway for pedestrians. Then occurred a succession of open parterres, usually planted or sown. Next on either side was a second row of *chenars*, between which and the flanking walls was a raised causeway for horsemen. The total breadth is now 52 yards. At intervals corresponding with the successive terraces and basins, arched doorways with recessed open chambers overhead conducted through these walls into the various royal or noble gardens that stretched on either side, and were known as the Gardens of the Throne, Nightingale, Vines, Mulberries, Dervishes, &c. Some of these pavilions were places of public resort and were used as coffee-houses, where, when the business of the day was over, the good burghers of

Isfahan assembled to sip that beverage and to inhale their *kalians*, the while, as Fryer puts it,

> Night drawing on, all the Pride of Spahaun was met in the Chaurbaug, and the Grandees were Airing themselves, prancing about with their numerous Trains, striving to outvie each other in Pomp and Generosity.

At the bottom, quays lined the banks of the river, and were bordered with the mansions of the nobility.

Such was the Chehar Bagh in the plenitude of its fame. But now what a tragical contrast! The channels are empty, their stone borders crumbled and shattered, the terraces are broken down, the parterres are unsightly bare patches, the trees, all lopped and pollarded, have been chipped and hollowed out[1] or cut down for fuel by the soldiery of the Zil, the side pavilions are abandoned and tumbling to pieces, and the gardens are wildernesses. Two centuries of decay could never make the Champs Elysées in Paris, the Unter der Linden in Berlin, or Rotten Row in London, look one half as miserable as does the ruined avenue of Shah Abbas. It is in itself an epitome of modern Iran.

Madresseh-i-Shah Husein

Towards the upper end of the Chehar Bagh on the eastern side, is a once splendid covered bazaar, through which one can turn aside to enter the Meidan. It is now empty and forlorn; but a short time ago was turned into stables for his *gholams*, by the Zil-es-Sultan.[2] On the same side is the entrance to the Hasht Behesht. A little further down stands a building that is still one of the spectacles of Isfahan. This is the Madresseh-i-Shah Husein, called also Madresseh-i-Mader-i-Shah, which was built, according to Krusinski, about the year 1710, by that monarch as 'a monastery for the Dervishes.' The Polish Jesuit further says that the chief gate was of solid silver; but he probably alludes to the chased silver plates with which the wooden doors are adorned. Beneath a deeply recessed archway, vaulted with honeycomb decoration, we pass into a dome-covered portico or vestibule, on either side of which petty hucksters sell fruit on

[1] Fraser (*A Winter's Journey*, vol. ii. p. 70) mentions a native superstition that when the *chenar* attains three hundred years, it perishes of self-combustion, and appears to have been taken in by it. I prefer the Isfahan rationalisation.

[2] In the early part of the century, a riot having broken out in this bazaar, the governor planted a cannon at its entrance, and fired straight down the central avenue into the crowd, killing or maiming everyone there—a slight contrast to the methods of Trafalgar Square.

stalls, and thence into the main court of the *madresseh*, which contains long basins filled with water, and is planted with flower-beds and overshadowed by trees. On the right-hand side opens the mosque or prayer-chamber, flanked by two minarets and crowned by a dome. In the centre of the remaining sides are similar arched chambers. Two storeys of arched cells for the students extend all round, and the corners are cut off by recessed arches. But it is in the surface decoration of the walls that this noble building still arrests and compels admiration. A wainscoting of the marble of Yezd runs round the base; and above this the archways and recesses, the lintels and façades, are covered with magnificent tiles and panels of enamelled arabesque. It was one of the stateliest ruins that I saw in Persia. I was informed that though there are 160 chambers or cells, there were only 50 pupils, and that the *vakf* or endowment had seriously dwindled, being for the most part appropriated by the Government.

Before I pass from Isfahan to the southern bank of the river and to Julfa, I may mention a few other buildings of interest. Of these the most considerable is the Musjid-i-Jama, or Friday mosque, said to have been originally raised by Abbas Khalif Al Mansur, in 755 A.D. The successive restorations of Malek Shah the Seljuk, of Shah Tahmasp, and of Abbas II., have deprived it of genuine artistic value, and it fell into the second rank after the erection of the Musjid-i-Shah by Abbas the Great. But it still retains titular pre-eminence as the Town Mosque, though its minarets and quadrangle are in a state of decay. There is also another and older *meidan*, entrance to which is gained through the bazaars.

Musjid-i-Jama

The bazaars of Isfahan are very fine, stretching for a great distance on the north and east sides of the Meidan-i-Shah. Several of them are unoccupied or but partially occupied; but those where business still centres are, next to Kerim Khan Zend's bazaar at Shiraz, the finest in Asia. All the life of the city throbs in the daytime in their packed and clamorous alleys; here is visible an ever-changing kaleidoscope of the unchanged Orient; and the crush of men and beasts renders locomotion slow and bewildering. From the main avenues open out immense courts or caravanserais, piled high with bales of merchandise; and here the clank of weighing-machines, the jostle of camels and mules, and the noise of human barter, are incessant.

Bazaars

MADRESSEH-I-SHAH HUSEIN

The European merchants have their quarters in these caravanserais or in buildings opening out of the main bazaar; and many was the business colloquy, attended with coffee and pipes, and protracted by interminable haggling, at which I assisted as an amused spectator.

In spite of its physical decay Isfahan is still the second largest trading emporium in Persia, yielding supremacy only to Tabriz.

Trade

The English eye is gratified by the sight of English trade marks or figures on nine out of every ten bales of merchandise that pass on camel, donkey, or mule; and inquiry elicits the satisfactory fact that Manchester is still the universal clothier of Isfahan; and that though this city marks the northern limit of undisputed British commercial predominance, yet that ascendency is both firmly secured and shows signs of increase rather than of diminution. From the fact that the principal European houses of business in Isfahan bear foreign names—I allude to the firms of Ziegler and Hotz—it has been erroneously inferred that British enterprise has supinely allowed the trade of the city to pass into other hands. No more incorrect induction could be made. Both these firms, as well as the Persian Gulf Trading Company, who have a representative in Isfahan, trade almost exclusively in English goods; and the considerable profits accruing from their transactions find their way in the last resort as wages into the pockets of Lancashire artisans. It is a further evidence of the importance of British mercantile interests in Isfahan that Lord Salisbury has recently taken the wise step of appointing a British Consul to that place, his choice having fallen upon Mr. J. R. Preece, for many years one of the leading officers of the Indo-European Telegraph, than whom no better selection could possibly have been made.

The imports into Isfahan, the vast majority of which come from Bushire, may be classified as follows in the approximate order

Imports and exports

of their bulk:—Manufactured cotton goods, almost wholly from Manchester and Glasgow; copper sheets from London, tin and zinc from India and Java, woollen stuffs and cloths from Austria and Germany, loaf sugar from Marseilles and Hamburg, raw sugar from Java and Mauritius, *viâ* Bombay; tea from India, China, and Java; candles from England, Holland, and in a less degree Russia; crockery from England, glass from Austria, oil and a few prints from Russia. By far the most valuable portion of this import is either English or Indian, and it will argue great imbecility if this advantage is ever lost. Of the exports, whose value and bulk are both greatly inferior to the imports, the principal are:—Opium, a great deal of which is grown in the Isfahan district, and about 4,500 cases of which, with an average value of 70*l.* to 90*l.* per case, are annually exported from the city, in the proportion of three-fourths to China and one-fourth to London; tobacco, the average annual yield of which from the same district is 60,000 bags, of from 100lb. to 110lb. each, with a value of 45,000*l*, of which 30,000 bags are exported *viâ* Bushire to Egypt and Syria, 20,000 *viâ* Tabriz to Constantinople, and 10,000 to Baghdad; carpets, manufactured in the provinces of Ferahan, Kurdistan, Khorasan, and Fars, and exported to the annual value of 100,000*l.* from the whole of Persia to England, America, and France; cotton, of which about 50,000 *shahmans* (one *shahman* = 12⅘ lb.), with an approximate value of 25,000*l.*, are exported *viâ* Bushire, mainly to Bombay; almonds, sent to India, Russia, and London; and rice for consumption within the country itself. A good deal of trade is done by native merchants; but the bulk of mercantile transactions passes through the hands of what may indisputably be described as English firms, whose activity here is in pleasing contrast with the apathy that has been displayed in other parts of Central Asia. Further observations upon trade I reserve for a subsequent chapter upon the Commerce of Persia.

Manufactures

Formerly Isfahan was famous for its armour; and a certain amount is now manufactured in imitation of the old. A good deal of the local industry appears indeed to be devoted to the reproduction of articles or styles that once won a world-wide renown. Of these, perhaps the most noticeable are the chiselled brass ware, in bowls, vases, trays, lamps, and ornaments (far superior, in my judgment, to the analogous products of Benares or Lucknow), the *kalemdans* or painted pen-cases, the mirror cases, and book-backs similarly painted and varnished; and the pottery and tiles, directly copying old patterns, which may be seen stacked in the curio-shops of Constantinople, or, for the matter of that, of London. Also celebrated are the *kalemkars* or printed calicoes of Isfahan, in which elegant native designs are stamped by hand-dies on cotton fabrics imported from England, and the *kadaks*, a sort of nankeen, much used in dress.

At different times since the Afghan invasion, and the great fall of Isfahan, exaggerated and conflicting accounts have been given of its population. In 1784–5, Ferrières-Sauvebœuf actually named 300,000 as the total. In 1810, Malcolm reduced this to 200,000; but in the previous year Morier had doubled it to 400,000; although the value of his own figures, as well as their correspondence with contemporary calculations, are betrayed by the figures which he gave only two years later, in 1811, when, at the very same time that he returned a census of 60,000, Ouseley, a member of the same party, mentioned 200,000. Any Persian will probably give the last-named total at the present day; but it is reduced by competent authorities to a maximum of not more than 70,000 to 80,000, although the city and its trade have recently experienced an undoubted revival. Amid their own countrymen the Isfahanis enjoy an unenviable reputation alike for cowardice and morals. They are inordinately vain of their city and of themselves, and in a country where lying is a fine art, are said to be incomparable artists. Their niggardliness and closeness in business matters are illustrated by a story told by Malcolm,[1] which has been crystallised into the saying that 'The merchant of Isfahan will put his cheese into a bottle, and rub his bread on the outside to give it a flavour.' Cowardly though the people are alleged to be, they have also acquired a reputation for petty disorder; and the *lutis* of Isfahan are justly regarded as the biggest blackguards in Persia.

Population and character

Isfahan is also one of those places where a spirit of religious intolerance prevails or can easily be excited, its victims being as a rule the Jews, who are here treated with great contumely; the Babis, whose numbers are vastly on the increase, and against whom sallies are frequently stimulated by the *mullahs*; and in a less degree the Armenians and other Christian communities, who require to conduct themselves with circumspection. The arrogance of the clerical order has been very much augmented since the fall from high estate of the Zil-es-Sultan, as described in a previous chapter. When at the zenith of his power he maintained a style at Isfahan, and ruled with an autocratic independence that kept these unruly gentry in order; but, in his present contracted state of authority, he courts support or popularity wherever he can get it, and fawns upon those whom he once despised. A

Court

[1] *Sketches of Persia*, cap. xiii. Compare also Morier's *Adventures of Haji Baba*, passim.

greater contrast cannot be imagined than between Isfahan a few years ago, and the same seat of government now. Then it was the capital of a prince who affected the monarch, and resounded with the pomp and circumstance of military rule ; now it is the residence of a provincial governor, whose power is precarious, and who is all but destitute of armed men. Such is no uninteresting example of the operation in Persia of the irresponsible authority of the sovereign.

I have elsewhere mentioned that at the height of his power the Zil controlled an army of nearly 21,000 men. He took immense interest in the equipment and proficiency of these troops, whom he clad in a variety of foreign uniforms, and whom he constantly paraded for the edification of foreign visitors. One Kerim Khan, known as the Mir-i-Panj, commanded the Zil's cavalry in those days and still follows the fortunes of his master; but only 400 to 500 horsemen are now available, although in the barracks and stores, which were well built and maintained, are equipments and arms for 1,000 cavalry, and rifles and ammunition it is said, for 10,000 men. The policy of the Zil, in treacherously slaying the Ilkhani of the Bakhtiari tribes, has permanently alienated from him those potent auxiliaries, upon whom a wise and ambitious governor of the central provinces would have relied for help.

Army

South of Isfahan, and separating it from a number of former suburbs, of which the sole survival is the Armenian colony of Julfa, flows the Zendeh or Zaiendeh Rud. In a later chapter I shall trace this river to its springs in the Kuh-i-rang among the Bakhtiari mountains. Rapid and rushing in its upper courses, it spreads over a wider bed as it enters the plain of Lahinjan, to the south-west of Isfahan. There its waters are largely drawn off for purposes of irrigation, and by the time the river has reached the storeyed bridges of the capital, though swollen in spring time to a powerful torrent, at other seasons it fills but a contracted channel or lies in detached pools. Below Isfahan it fertilises the districts of Berahan and Rudesht, in which its flow is regulated by the *bunds* or dykes of Ali Kuli Khan and Mervan. Later on its surplus waters are lost in the Gavkhaneh marsh.

The Zendeh Rud

At Isfahan the Zendeh Rud is crossed by five bridges of differing style and antiquity. Highest up the stream and most ancient of these is the Pul-i-Marnun,[1] which was built by Shah Tahmasp,

[1] Kaempfer named it Maranbuun, and explained it as meaning 'viper-hunter'

who reigned 1523–75 A.D., to conduct to the Mohammedan suburb of Marnun to the west of Julfa. The bridge is built of brick, and is pierced by arches of every size and shape resting upon piers of roughly hewn stones. The city having so greatly contracted its borders, this bridge is now little used. The Armenians call it the Sarfaraz bridge, and ascribe its erection to one of their own countrymen.

Bridge of Marnun

Next in order on the east comes the famous Bridge of Ali Verdi Khan, the general of Shah Abbas, which is also known as the Bridge of Julfa, and the Pul-i-Chehar Bagh, from the fact that it conducts from the base of that avenue to the southern bank of the river. This beautiful structure, whose main features and proportions the march of decay has been powerless to destroy, is alone worth a visit to Isfahan to see; albeit, *a priori*, one would hardly expect to have to travel to Persia to see what may, in all probability, be termed the stateliest bridge in the world. Approached by a paved ramp or causeway from the avenue, the bridge is entered at the north end under a gateway. Its entire length is 388 yards, the breadth of the paved roadway is thirty feet.[1] Upon either side a narrow pathway, or covered arcade, two and a half feet in width, is pierced, along the entire length of the bridge, in the outer wall, communicating with the main roadway by frequent arches. and opening by similar arches, over ninety in number, on to the river view. In a few places, this gallery expands into larger chambers, which were originally adorned by not too proper paintings, of the time of Abbas II. Access can also be gained by staircases in the round towers at the corners of the bridge to an upper platform, upon which are now planted the telegraphic poles supporting the wires to Julfa, but which was formerly used as a promenade in the warm weather. Similar staircases, cut in the basements of the towers and also at regular intervals in the main piers, conduct from the road level to a lower storey, where, but little elevated

Bridge of Ali Verdi Khan

(*Amœn. Exot.*, p. 166); Chardin, Marenon. Krusinski called it the Bridge of Abbasabad, the name, as we learn from Chardin, of the finest suburb of old Isfahan, containing 2,000 houses, 12 mosques, 19 baths, 24 caravanserais, and 5 *madressehs*, peopled by a colony which Shah Abbas had transplanted from Tabriz.

[1] Again the measurements of our authorities differ irreconcilably—Chardin, 360–13 yards; Tavernier, 350–23 yards; Bembo, 250–20; Kaempfer, 490–12; Le Brun, 540–17. All these writers referred to the entire breadth, including the side galleries.

above the bed of the river, a vaulted passage runs along the entire length of the bridge, through arches pierced in the central piers, crossing the channel of the river by huge stepping stones planted in its bed. Colonel Johnson gives the dimensions of these transverse arches as ten feet span and nine feet high ; and of the main arches, thirty-three in number, which they bisect, as twenty feet span, and fifteen feet high, separated by piers eleven feet thick. There is thus a triple promenade in this remarkable bridge—the vaulted passage below, the roadway and lateral galleries above, and the open footpath at the top of all. I should add that the upper part

BRIDGE OF ALI VERDI KHAN

of the bridge is of brick, the piers and towers of stone. When I saw it in December, but little water was flowing through the arches ; and the banks of the river, and the shingle in its bed, were completely covered with native cotton stuffs and chintzes, which men and women were perpetually rinsing and bleaching in the shallow pools, and laying out to dry.

Formerly this bridge opened immediately upon another avenue, which was practically a continuation of the Chehar Bagh on the

Hazar Jerib

south bank of the river, the united length of the three sections being given by Kaempfer as : Chehar Bagh 1,620 yards, bridge 490, avenue beyond 2,200, total 4,310 yards, or nearly 2½ miles.[1] This avenue was laid out in the same style as the Chehar Bagh, being planted with rows of trees and adorned by channels filled with water, that fell from tier to tier and at regular intervals expanded into larger basins or pools. On either side also were situated the palaces and mansions of the princes or grandees; whilst at the upper end was a royal enclosure, known as the Hazar Jerib or Thousand Acres.[2] This great pleasaunce was laid out in terraces, built on stone walls one above the other, and adorned with alleys and canals. It was Crown property, but was apparently open to the public. The surrounding enclosure was utilised as a game preserve, and we read in Olearius of wild asses being hunted there by the king. Of the Hazar Jerib not a trace now remains; whilst the southern avenue is far more ruined even than the Chehar Bagh, and speaks only in choked and faltering accents of its vanished glory.

Pul-i-Jhubi

Three hundred yards below the Bridge of Julfa, and at about the same distance above the Pul-i-Khaju, the river is crossed by the Pul-i-Jhubi,[3] a plain brick bridge of fourteen uniform arches, which was constructed as an aqueduct to convey water to the Palace of Haft Dest on the southern bank. Hence the origin of the name *jui*, vulgo, *jûb*, signifying a watercourse. In the company of its splendid neighbours it excites no attention.

Haft Dest and Aineh-Khaneh

The suburb upon the southern bank at this spot was originally known as Guebristan, from being inhabited by the Zoroastrians; but the ground was cleared by Abbas II., and converted into a royal residence, which he designated Sadetabad, or Abode of Felicity, and where he kept his seraglio. The bank of the river from the Pul-i-Khaju upwards was lined with gardens, and by means of the sluice-gates at the lower bridge the king was in the habit of damming up the river, till it formed a great lake before the *talar* known as the Aineh-Khaneh, upon which he disported himself in boats with his ladies, and which at

[1] Le Brun's measurements were not broadly different—1,751 + 540 + 2,045 = 4,336 yards.

[2] The *jerib* was a land measurement, amounting to 1,000 to 1,066 Persian square yards (of 41·34 inches). The total of 1,000 was, however, a numerical title, and must not be taken to indicate the actual area.

[3] The name is spelt Pul-i-Choop by Price, Pul-i-Joole by Binning. Most writers have ignored the existence of the bridge, which has also been called the Bridge of Sadetabad, because it led from that quarter.

night was made the scene of fairy illuminations. The actual building of the *harem* was known as Haft Dest, the Seven Suites, or Compartments. Here were received and entertained Sir Harford Jones and Sir Gore Ouseley, on their respective missions in 1810 and 1811, and here also have been accommodated subsequent distinguished guests. In one of the lower chambers of the Haft Dest, surrounded by a wainscoting of Tabriz marble, and adorned with a marble cistern, Fath Ali Shah died in 1834. No attention has since been bestowed upon the place, which, when I visited it, looked as if it had been abandoned for years. Hard by the Haft

AINEH-KHANEH

Dest stands a *talar*, very similar to that of the Chehel Situn. It is called the Aineh-Khaneh, or Hall of Mirrors, from the glass facets that formerly adorned its pillars and walls, and consists of a great projecting verandah, sustained by twelve wooden columns, the inner of which repose upon the clustered bodies of marble lions. A *hauz*, or basin, occupies the centre, and a second stands in the recessed throne-room at the back, behind which open several chambers, once embellished with paintings of Shah Abbas and his Circassian ladies. The lower walls were wainscoted with marble, upon which were painted and gilded designs of flowers and birds. In the garden at the back stood the Nemekdan or Salt Cellar, a pavilion of the class described by the Persians as *Kolah Feringhi*, from their supposed resemblance to the crown and brim of a European hat, which was occupied by some of Ouseley's suite. It would appear that in the last eighty years not a step has been taken to arrest the march of decay in these once elegant and beautiful structures. The Nemekdan, after tumbling almost to pieces, has been pulled down. The Aineh-Khaneh is in the last throes of dissolution, the pavement being broken, the decorations peeled off, the chambers defiled, and the whole place open to any loafer to camp in, or any vandal so-minded to destroy. Almost touching it on the eastern side is a solitary pine, sole relic of the vanished pleasure-ground. Its tufted crown waves like a funeral plume over the scene of departed grandeur.

At a slight distance below the Aineh-Khaneh, the Zendeh Rud is spanned by the second of the historic bridges of the Sefavi kings.

Pul-i-Khaju.

This is variously known as the Pul-i-Khaju, from the quarter of the city of that name; the Pul-i-Baba Rukn, from a famous dervish named Rukn-ed-Din, who was interred in an adjacent cemetery; the Bridge of the Guebres (Krusinski), because it led to the suburb of Guebristan, and was built by Abbas II., in order that the Guebres might not pass across the main bridge to Julfa; and the Bridge of Hasanabad, because it led to the Bazaar of that name in Isfahan, which was restored by the Governor of Isfahan under Fath Ali Shah, who also replanted an avenue, like the Chehar Bagh, from the bridge to the city. The Pul-i-Khaju is shorter than the bridge of Ali Verdi Khan, being only 154 yards in length, owing to a contraction in the bed of the river, which here flows over a ledge of rock. The structure consists, in fact, of a bridge superimposed upon a dam. The latter is built of solid blocks of stone and is pierced by narrow channels, the flow in which can be regulated by sluices. This great platform is broken on its outer edge, the stones being arranged in the form of steps descending to the river-level. Upon the platform or dam repose the twenty-four main arches of the bridge, which is of brick, and the chief external features of which are four projecting two-storeyed hexagonal pavilions, one at each corner, and two larger pavilions of similar shape in the centre, a third storey being erected upon the roof of the more westerly of the two. As in the case of the Julfa bridge, the basement is pierced by a vaulted passage, running the entire length of the bridge through the piers on the top of the dam, and crossing the successive channels by stepping-stones six feet deep. The main roadway of the bridge, twenty-four feet broad, is also flanked by a covered gallery on either side, leading to the hexagonal pavilions, and opening by a succession of arches on to the outer air. Finally, there is a terrace-walk at the top, which was originally protected by a double parapet and screens. The pavilions were once adorned with rich paintings and gilding, and with panels containing inscriptions. The decoration is now more jejune and vulgar; and the spandrels of the arches are mostly filled in with modern tiles. In olden days this bridge was a favourite resort in the evening, where the young gallants of Isfáhan marched up and down, or sat and smoked in the embayed archways overlooking the stream. Now it is well-nigh deserted save in spring time, when the snows melt in the mountains, and in a few hours the Zendeh Rud is converted from a petty stream into a foaming torrent. Then the good folk of Isfahan crowd the galleries and arcades of the bridge, and shout with delight as the water first rushes through the narrow sluices, then mounts to the level of the causeway and spills in a noisy cascade down each successive stairway or weir, and finally pours through the main arches, still splitting into a series of cataracts, as it leaps the broken edges of the dam. This is one of the annual holidays of Isfahan. Upon either side of the Pul-i-Khaju are planted avenues, as in the case of the approaches to the larger bridge; but they have fared no better at the hands of Time.

Bridge of Shehristan

Lowest of the bridges of Isfahan, and at the distance of some miles from the modern city, the Pul-i-Shehristan conducts to a village of that name which contains a very tall minaret, but is otherwise in ruins; although it was originally one of the two quarters of the earliest city and was the residence of the nobles. The superstructure of the bridge is of brick, and is apparently of later date than the foundations and piers, which are of stone.

Julfa

South of the Zendeh Rud, and a little to the west of the Pul-i-Chehar Bagh, extends the once populous and still interesting suburb of Julfa; interesting because it is inhabited by a Christian colony nearly three hundred years old, because it is the abode of all such Europeans as reside for business or other purposes in Isfahan, and because it is the theatre of a missionary effort directed by our own countrymen. After crossing the big bridge we turn to the right, and are presently involved in a wilderness of intricate alleys, many of them closed at the end by wooden

PUL-I-KHAJU

doors—the relic of a less secure age—or entered by tunnel-like arches. Narrow ditches fringed with a single row of pollarded willows or poplars run down the sides of the streets, which are little more than pathways, and are plentifully perforated with open sewers. The principal street or boulevard of Julfa contains a double row of trees. But in winter there is no beauty in the place (though I see that in spring Mrs. Bishop returns a very different verdict); everything is meagre and narrow; the exteriors of the houses are blank walls of mud, pierced by a single door. Life in Julfa struck me as cribbed, cabined, and confined to an intolerable degree; and it was a relief to escape from its squalid precincts even to the spacious ruin of Isfahan. There is a marked contrast of appearance in the people of Julfa with the inhabitants of an ordinary Persian town; for the customary blue *chadar* or veil of the Mussulman female is replaced by the spotless white sheet, covering a red gown, of the Armenian woman, whose black eyes and eyebrows flash above a white cotton cloth that conceals the mouth and chin and presses upon the lower part of the nose. Around their waists are visible broad girdles adorned with silver plates. There must be a good deal of market gardening in Julfa, for piles of vegetables are exposed for sale in the streets; and fruit is cheap and excellent.

History

It is well known that both the name [1] and the first inhabitants of Julfa were borrowed from the town of the same title on the River Araxes, in Azerbaijan. From there, in 1604, Shah Abbas, pursuing his favourite policy of forcible colonisation, transported several thousand families of Armenians to his new capital, where he conceded them the sparse consolation of a revival of their patrimonial name. His design has been attributed by some to a wish to despoil the Turkish army of its chief mart for provisions; but it is more credibly referred to the monarch's confidence in the thrift and commercial aptitudes of the Christians, and to his desire to give his subjects at Isfahan the benefit at once of their industry and example. Chardin speaks of an Old and a New Julfa as the colonies respectively of Abbas the Great and

[1] Some Persian writers, however, call it Julahieh, a name which signifies 'weavers' quarter,' and which often appears in Government documents, instead of Julfa. They further assert that this was the original and earlier name, before the Armenian immigration. History, however, lends no corroboration to this hypothesis.

Abbas II.; but I infer that the latter connoted new streets and buildings rather than a second immigration, of which I have found no corroborative record. Encouraged by its royal founder, who gave the new arrivals many privileges, exempting them from servitude, granting them the free exercise of their religion, and a *kalantar* or mayor of their own nationality, and lending them money without interest, Julfa soon became a thriving and populous place. By the time of Herbert's visit (1627), the number had swollen to 10,000 souls. In Chardin's day Julfa contained 3,400 houses and 30,000 persons (Fryer at the same time says 6,000 families), more than a dozen churches or chapels,[1] a monastery, a nunnery, 'where were about thirty poor widows or girls, ugly and ill-shapen,' and 100 to 120 priests. The Jesuits possessed an establishment there (the ruins of their church can still be seen), having arrived in 1645 under Père Rigourdi with letters from the Pope and the King of France. For a time the prosperity of the colony was free from cloud or blemish, although the taxation levied from it gradually increased in proportion to the dwindling sympathies or the growing cupidity of the later Sefavi kings. Shah Suleiman was the first who systematically overtaxed and persecuted the Armenians. Under Shah Sultan Husein, who prided himself upon an unbending orthodoxy, the outlook became blacker still, a law being promulgated that if a Persian killed an Armenian he need only pay one load of corn to the family of the deceased. In and after the Afghan invasion, the Julfans suffered terribly; but the storm did not finally culminate till the reign of Nadir Shah, who alleging, most unjustifiably, that they had helped the Afghans in the siege of Isfahan, visited them with savage penalties and exactions, interdicted their worship, and placed them under a ban of permanent social ostracism. Immediately upon the news of his death in 1747, the miserable Armenians flocked away in hundreds, if not thousands, to Georgia, to India, and to Baghdad; and the population shrank to limits upon which it has never since been able to make any appreciable advance. Olivier in 1796 reported 800 families, Morier and Ouseley 300 to 400 in 1811, Martyn 500 in 1812, Ker Porter 300 in 1818, Lumsden 500 in

[1] The foundations of the principal churches were as follows: St. Joseph, or the Cathedral, in 1605; St. Stephen in 1691; St. John in 1695. St. George is not now used for worship, but is a great place of pilgrimage, owing to its possession of some miracle-working stones, prayer in front of which is fraught with great benefit to the sick.

1820, Ussher 3,000 souls in 1861, Goldsmid 500 families in 1874. The total population of Julfa was given to me as 2,500, of whom eighty per cent. are Armenians.[1]

Armenian community

There are practically four distinct ingredients in the population of Julfa; (1) the Armenians proper, constituting the bulk of the community; (2) the United or Catholic Armenians, a small schism; (3) the Church of England Mission; and (4) the European mercantile and Telegraph element. A few words about each of these. The Armenians proper are under the spiritual jurisdiction of an Arachnurt or Archbishop, who is invariably a monk from Echmiadzin. He resides in a building, formerly a convent, adjoining the Egglesia Wang (Big Church) or Cathedral. Attached to this establishment is also a nunnery, whose annals have not been free from flagrant scandal, and which shelters a number of old spinsters who visit the sick, teach, and knit socks. The younger and more active part of the male population is annually drafted to India, Java, and other places in the East, where, in situations of business and profit, they speedily lose all desire to return to their unprepossessing homes. The consequence is, that only the residuum is left behind; and while some of these are engaged in business as carpenters, market gardeners, etc., a good many have embarked on a trade which secures them neither popularity nor consideration, viz., the manufacture of liquor, quite as much for surreptitious Persian, as well as for avowed home consumption. Dr. Wills, who lived in Julfa many years, presents a very unfavourable portrait of the Julfa Armenian. So common is drunkenness, that his Armenian cook would say to him on a Sunday night: 'Dinner finished, sir; if you no orders, I go get drunk with my priest;' while of the average specimen he drew the following picture:—

The Hamadan Armenian is hardworking and respectable, if occasionally a drunkard, looked on by his Persian fellow-subjects as a friend and a good citizen. The Isfahani looks upon the Julfa Armenian as a race apart, and merely the panderer to his vices and the maker of intoxicating liquors; and the hangdog Armenian with his sham Turk or European dress, and the bottle of arrack in his pocket, scowls staggering along in secure insolence, confident in the moral

[1] For the Armenians of Julfa, *vide* a report by Eugène Boré in his *Correspondance et Mémoires*, vol. ii. pp. 374–92; and for modern Julfa, *vide* C. J. Wills, *In the Land, &c.*, caps. xii. and xiv.; and Mrs. Bishop, *Journeys in Persia*, vol. i. letters xii. xiii.

protection given him by the presence of the English whom he robs; respecting neither his priest, whom he has been taught to despise; nor the missionary whom he dislikes at heart (though he has educated his children gratuitously) and whom his priest openly reviles.

It is, I fear, too true that the Armenian of Julfa cannot be credited with the virtues or gifts that have made his race successful, if also unpopular, elsewhere in the East. He has suffered from a too long expatriation among the tents of Kedar.

The main church or cathedral was built under the auspices of Shah Abbas by his imported colonists. Having lately been repaired and decorated with new tiles it presents a smart appearance. In the courtyard outside stands a big detached belfry. Four stone pillars support a brick gallery with a railing, to which there is no access from below. Above this rises the bell-tower and bell, which is pulled by a rope communicating with the church opposite. In the corner of the courtyard are a number of graves, of Protestant Christians as well as of Armenians. Upon a passage immediately outside the church, open a number of small cells. Entering the main building we find that its shape is a parallelogram, consisting of two squares, with a semicircular apse at the end. The first square is the nave, the second is the choir beneath a dome. A wainscoting of ornamental tiles runs round the base, and above this the walls are covered with strange old paintings of rich and sombre hue. Chardin tells us that they were the gift of a wealthy Armenian merchant, named Avadich, who, having travelled in Italy and acquired a taste for art, persuaded his co-religionists to allow of the execution of these paintings, greatly to the scandal of the Mohammedans, who were shocked at the delineation of the human form. The pictures depict Old Testament scenes, and the sufferings of saints and martyrs, whilst over the door is a great and gruesome tableau of the Day of Judgment. Above is the heavenly host, but all the skill of the artist has been lavished on the tortures of the damned, who are being ushered into perdition by huge devils and symbolical monsters. Higher up in the walls are windows filled with stained glass; while the apse is painted with miniatures of saints and cherubim, and with a figure of Christ. It should be added that the liturgy in this and the other churches is conducted in the ancient Armenian tongue, which is gibberish to ninety-nine out of every hundred Armenians who repeat it.

Cathedral

Outside Julfa, on the desolate stony plain that stretches to the

ARMENIAN CATHEDRAL AT JULFA

foot of Kuh-i-Suffa, is the cemetery, where three centuries of Christians have been laid to rest. Here are not merely the tombstones of hundreds of departed Armenians—great blocks or slabs of stone, chiselled and sculptured—but also of many Europeans, English, French, Dutch, and Russian, who, during the same period, have lived and died at Isfahan or Julfa, in the employment of the various factories or in other pursuits. Among them is the well-known gravestone bearing the inscription *Cy git Rodolfe*, and covering the remains of Ralph or Rodolph Stadler, a Swiss watchmaker, who enjoyed great favour at the Court of Sefi I., but was ultimately put to death by that monarch in 1637, upon his refusal to turn Mohammedan.[1] The Armenians converted him into a saint and raised a tomb over his remains.

Cemetery

The small community of United or Catholic Armenians, now numbering some sixty families, is the representative at Julfa of a schism two hundred years old, a Jesuit missionary at Erzerum having converted an Armenian bishop and a large number of his flock in the year 1688. The schism spread in spite of the vigorous persecution of the Armenian hierarchy; and later a young Armenian priest named Mechitar founded an order of Armenian monks on the little island of St. Lazarus near the Lido. In Julfa the church of this small community was built in the year 1705; but the present movement is the fruit of a revival, that was effected early in the present century by Catholic Armenians from India, and sustained by an energetic priest named Bertoni. It is now under the jurisdiction of a Jesuit Monsignor, and of a well-known monk, Père Pascal Arakélian, who is one of the most popular and agreeable figures in Julfan society. Relations with the Armenian Church have commonly been strained and frequently hostile; but an outward harmony appears now to have been established.

United Armenians

The real jealousy, it is useless to deny, is between the Armenians of both persuasions, and the Mission, sent out and supported by the Church of England Missionary Society, which has selected Julfa as the scene of an active propaganda and a large annual outlay. This mission is under the control of the well-known and greatly

[1] Different versions are given of the circumstances that led to his death by Olearius and Tavernier, the former alleging that Stadler had first killed a Persian whom he caught breaking into his house, the latter that the burglarious Persian had violated the watchmaker's harem.

respected Dr. Bruce, of whom it may be said that he is as good a type as can anywhere be seen of the nineteenth-century Crusader. In an earlier age the red cross would have been upon his shoulder, and he would have been hewing infidels in conflict for the Holy Sepulchre, instead of translating the Bible, and teaching in schools at Julfa. Going out to Persia for the first time in 1869, he has been engaged ever since in a revision of the translation of the New and Old Testaments into Persian, and in a translation of the Book of Common Prayer into the Armenian dialect of Julfa. The establishment over which he presides is large and commodious, comprising a fine church with accommodation for 300, and a congregation in 1889 of 184 native baptised Christians and 90 communicants; a boys' school, which in the same year was attended by 177 pupils, from the ages of six to sixteen; a girls' school with an attendance of 164; a staff of two or three European clergy, and of thirty lay teachers, native and Europeans, and a dispensary for Mohammedans and Christians alike. I shall, I hope, be doing no injustice to Dr. Bruce's self-sacrificing and unflagging labours, if I say that his converts are drawn exclusively from the Christian and not from the Moslem fold. Mohammedans have been baptised; but as I have elsewhere said they have relapsed, and I have never myself encountered a full-grown converted Mussulman. It would, perhaps, savour of disrespect to an institution excellently managed, if I added that here, as in many other parts of the East, the results do not, in my opinion, justify the expenditure both of labour and of money. The mission is not over popular with the Zil-es-Sultan, and is naturally much disliked by the Armenian hierarchy, who look upon its agents as poachers on their own preserves. To an English traveller it is in the highest degree agreeable to alight, in a strange land, upon a small colony of his own countrymen, which is also a centre of hospitable culture and of learning.

Church of England Mission

Finally, there is resident at Julfa a small European lay community numbering about a dozen and composed of the officials of the Indo-European Telegraph Department, and of the representatives of the British or foreign mercantile houses already named, who are engaged in trade in Isfahan. Nothing can exceed the friendliness and warmth of welcome that are extended by this little community to strangers. I see no reason myself, beyond that of old custom, why they should continue to reside in Julfa

European colony

rather than in the city, where are their places of business, and whither they have to walk or ride a distance of three miles every morning. Rents are much higher in Julfa, and the atmosphere is, as I have said, cramped and narrow. In former times the large Christian population of Julfa conferred a sort of protection upon European Christians compelled to live in or near the capital. But the obligation is now entirely reversed. There is no doubt that foreigners might reside in Isfahan with perfect impunity, and it is the Armenians of Julfa who benefit by the existing arrangement, which gives them a security that they would not otherwise enjoy. In considering the small estimation in which Christians generally are held by the uneducated masses in Persia, it must further be remembered that the Armenians are the only Christian population known to them; and that if a traveller protests his faith and finds the declaration received either with indifference or with contempt, it is in nine cases out of ten because he is at once associated with the none too desirable attainments of his fellow-Christians of Julfa.

In conclusion, let me devote a paragraph to the few sights of interest in the immediate neighbourhood of Isfahan. Of these the best known are the Minari Jumban, or Shaking Minarets, of Kalehdan, or Guladan, a village about six miles to the west of Isfahan. Here there is the tomb of a Sheikh Abdullah, though what particular Abdullah no one appears to know. His sarcophagus, a big rectangular chest, stands in an open, vaulted recess, and upon either side of the façade above the arch rise the two minarets to an additional height of about twenty feet, the entire structure being of brick. A small spiral staircase in the interior of either minaret leads to the summit, which is pierced with open arches.[1] An individual usually ascends the right-hand tower, where, by pressing against the walls and swaying to and fro, he imparts an oscillation to the minaret, which, passing along the intervening platform about thirty feet in length, is communicated to the other tower; so that both of them visibly sway in company with the operator, describing a deviation of several inches from the perpendicular. Writers have exhausted their ingenuity in the attempt to explain this phenomenon, which is, of course, attributed by the Persians to the wonderful properties of the defunct Sheikh.

Shaking minarets

[1] Tavernier included in his *Travels* an engraving of the Shaking Minarets, which shook in his day; although why he should represent a figure as swarming up the exterior of the minaret, in contempt of the stairway, I cannot explain.

One traveller is convinced that the towers are connected by a chain concealed beneath the platform; another says that from the ground to the summit they are detached from and, so to speak, enclosed in the main building, which experiences and transmits the oscillation easily excited in the separate towers. Mme. Dieulafoy says that each tower has for its vertical axis a wooden framework fixed in the staircase, and can thus, when agitated, describe slight oscillations round its own axis. More probably the elasticity of the bricks and mortar employed have something to do with it, the vibration easily excited in one tower being then communicated along the

THE SHAKING MINARETS

tympanum of the main arch to the other. Dr. Wills calls them 'a terrible fraud,' though for what reason I do not understand. There is no fraud, and still less is there any miracle. The only folly is that of the visitor who is in the smallest degree excited by so commonplace, even if uncommon, a manifestation.

At a slight distance from the Shrine of Abdullah rises an isolated rocky hill, the summit of which is crowned by some ruined buildings of mud-brick. This is called the Atesh Gah, from a tradition that a fire-altar was here erected by Ardeshir (Artaxerxes) Longimanus. The tradition may be true, but the present ruins are not old. Immediately to the south of Julfa the red rocky ramparts of the Kuh-i-Suffa (from an Arabic

Sites and ruins

word signifying a house on a high place or terrace) frame the landscape with their gaunt and ragged outlines. In a recess or terrace on their northern front, less than half-way up and overlooking the capital, a pavilion or summer-house was built by Shah Suleiman, and called Takht-i-Suleïman, upon the site of a former hermitage. Only the ruins of the villa now remain, but the climb is repaid by the fine view. A neighbouring rocky height supports some ruins, also of modern date, but bearing the name of Kaleh or Takht-i-Rustam, from a tradition that the national hero built a fortress on this site. At the foot of the Kuh-i-Suffa was situated the famous palace of Ferahabad (Abode of Joy), to which its royal architect and master, Shah Sultan Husein, was so devotedly attached that when the Afghans invaded Persia, he was quite ready to sacrifice his capital if only the barbarians would leave him his palace. The latter was distinguished less for its buildings than for its wonderful terraces, and lakes, and gardens, which were the admiration of observers. The Afghans, it is needless to say, spared neither the scruples nor the person of the accommodating monarch. Ferahabad, having been hastily evacuated by him, was occupied by them and was burned to the ground when, a few years later, they were expelled from Isfahan. Its site is now a wilderness of ruins. But little more imposing are the remains of the celebrated castle of Tabarrak, which was the deposit of the Royal Treasure under the Sefavi kings, and whose fortifications were described in such glowing terms by Chardin, Kaempfer, and others. Already, in 1704, Le Brun found them shattered and tottering, and the surviving walls are now little more than heaps of clay.

Truly, as he turns his back on Isfahan after completing the local itinerary, which I have here marked out for him, may the traveller observe, in the words of Shelley—

> Look on my works, ye mighty, and despair!
> Nothing beside remains. Round the decay
> Of that colossal wreck, boundless and bare
> The lone and level sands stretch far away.

Supplementary Routes.

Kashan to Isfahan (*viâ* Natanz), A. H. Schindler (1879), *Zeit. d. Gesell. f. Erd. z. Berlin*, 1881, pp. 307–66.

Kum to Gulpaigan or Khonsar, E. Stack (1881), *Six Months in Persia*, vol. ii. cap. v.; Col. M. S. Bell (1884), *Blackwood's Magazine*, June 1889.

Isfahan to Gulpaigan, E. Stack (1881), *ibid.*; Col. Bell (1884), *ibid.*

Isfahan to Kangavar, E. Flandin (1840), *Voyage en Perse*, vol. i. cap. xxviii.; E. Floyer (1877), *Unexplored Beluchistan*, caps. xvi.–xviii.

CHAPTER XX

FROM ISFAHAN TO SHIRAZ

Out of the ivory palaces whereby they have made thee glad.—*Psalm* xlv. 9.

ALTHOUGH the European traveller will have made Julfa his head-quarters during his residence at Isfahan, his post-horses will upon arrival have been obliged to return upon their tracks for a distance of over three miles—paid for as one *farsakh*—to the *chapar-khaneh* in Isfahan, and from there they will have to be ordered beforehand to come out again to Julfa when he is ready to start upon his forward way. The table of stations and distances upon the road to Shiraz is as follows:[1]—

Postal road

Name of Station	Distance in *farsakhs*	Approximate distance in miles	Name of Station	Distance in *farsakhs*	Approximate distance in miles
Isfahan†(5,300 ft.)	—	—	Khan-i-Khoreh .	7	24
Marg . . .	4	13	Dehbid † (7,500 ft.)	5	18
Mayar . . .	6	19	Murghab (6,200 ft.)	7	29
Kumisheh † . .	5	21	Kawamabad (Sivend †) . .	6	24
Maksud Beggi .	4	17	Puzeh . . .	6	21
Yezdikhast (6,500 ft.) . . .	6	25	Zerghun . .	5	19
Shulgistan . .	6	24	Shiraz † (4,750 ft.)	5	21
Abadeh † . .	5	22			
Surmek . .	4	15	Total . .	81	312

† = Telegraph stations.

Quitting the squalid and dusty precincts of Julfa and leaving the Armenian cemetery, with its shattered gravestones, on the right, the track mounts the slopes of the Kuh-i-Suffa, until we reach a point where, as the road dips into a hollow, we inevitably turn round in the saddle to take a parting look at Isfahan. There, outspread over

[1] In addition to the authorities already quoted for the journey from Teheran to Isfahan, and most, if not all, of whom have also described the march from Isfahan to Shiraz, I may cite for the latter the following works: J. B. Tavernier (1665), *Travels*, lib. v. cap. xx.; J. Struys (1672), *Voyages*, cap. xxxiii.–iv.; Sir J. Chardin (1674), *Voyages* (edit. Langlès), vol. viii. pp. 195–314; C. Le Brun (1704–5), *Travels*, cap. l.–lv.; A. Dupré (1808), *Voyage en Perse*, vol. i. caps. xxv.–xxviii.; J. S. Buckingham (1816), *Travels*, vol. i. cap. xii. to end; Lieutenant T. Lumsden (1820), *Journey from India*, pp. 72–116.

ISFAHAN TO SHIRAZ.

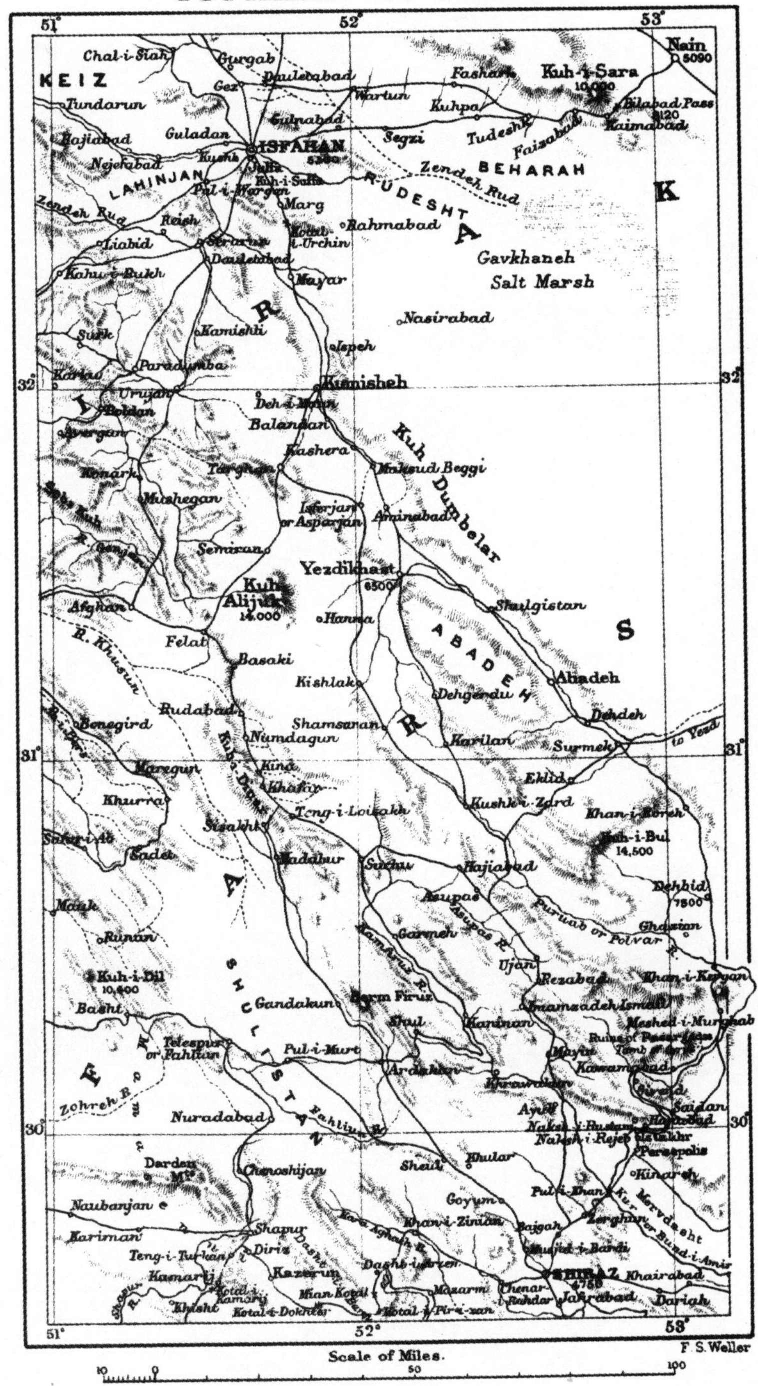

Scale of Miles.

10 0 50 100

the wide plain, are the cupolas and minars, the pigeon-towers and terraced bridges, the long avenues and straggling suburbs of the fallen capital. From this distance the pitiless handiwork of decay is blurred and imperceptible, and a certain majesty seems still to hover over the wreck of departed grandeur. I know of no city in the world that has ever struck me with a greater pathos, or whose figure is wrapped in so melancholy a garb of woe. The road descends to the post-station of Marg in a small desolate valley, in which, with the exception of a ruined caravanserai, it is the solitary building. After leaving Marg, the track climbs a steep acclivity, known as the Kotal-i-Urchin, or Pass of the Stairway, from the fact that steps have in places been hewn in the rock. This pass, however, although to the timid vision of Sir R. Ker Porter it seemed 'literally a ladder hewn in the mountain for the surer footing of the horses and beasts of burthen, who, as we viewed them indistinctly from below, appeared hanging from the rock in the air,' is in no sense remarkable, and is child's play compared with the famous *kotals* of the Shiraz-Bushire route that will be encountered later on. Having crossed the ridge, I cantered gaily along the level plain to Mayar, passing on the way a band of six Russians, who had excited great interest in Julfa by their mysterious movements and by the unexplained character of their mission in these parts. No one knew whether they were traders or Government agents. I entered into conversation with them; their leader told me that they were private travellers, journeying for their own amusement to Bushire, a statement which was belied by their obscure appearance, and was subsequently invalidated by the discovery that they were engaged on sort of roving expedition to Abyssinia, for which place they ultimately embarked from Bombay. The character and quality of the men whom Russia employs on these semi-political undertakings, disguised under a mask of colonisation, are among the puzzles of the East.

Mayar

Mayar was once a flourishing and agreeable place, and, in Tavernier's day, 'consisted of above 1,000 houses.' Its walls and towers are now in ruins, and almost the sole relic of the good days gone by is the caravanserai, originally built by the mother of Shah Abbas and afterwards restored by Shah Suleiman. This structure, which is built of brick upon a massive stone foundation, is now in a state of dilapidation, but in the early years of the century it was described by travellers as the finest erection of the kind in Persia. I do not know that Mayar or its surroundings possess any other interest, however faint, although the hills which surround its valley awoke in the bosom of the susceptible Porter a paroxysm of the most profound emotion:—

I might have thought myself again amongst the most savage tracks of the Caucasus, climbing the scarred ridges of a shattered, rocky world. The whole seems as if the Titans had really been at war, and this the scene of their tearing up the hills and pitching them against each other, to fall, at any hazard, in the pell-mell heaps in which they stand.

If the transports of the worthy Baronet have never served any other purpose, at least I have often been grateful to them for the relief they have imparted to monotonous sections of my journey.

Kumisheh

The road follows the valley, which is barren and without interest, to Kumisheh. A confused vision of big pigeon-towers; of a tattered graveyard, to which a crowd was hurrying a newly-deceased corpse, with the strange mixture of irreverence and mourning that characterises a Mussulman funeral; of a tumble-down city with crumbled walls and mouldering towers; and of a large blue dome surrounded by old *chenars*, and gleaming fitfully through an opaque whirlwind of dust—still remains in my memory as I think of Kumisheh. This place, which is the Komsu of Della Valle and the Comicha of Chardin, was over three miles in circuit in the latter's time, though even then it had fallen greatly from the epoch of its prime under the earlier Sefavi sovereigns. Its present desolation is over a century and a half in age, having been inflicted by the Afghans in their northward march against Isfahan in 1722, a visitation from which the place has never recovered. The blue dome covers the last resting-place of Shah Reza, who is described by Chardin as a grandson of the Imam Reza, but appears more probably to have been his brother and a son of the Imam Musa el Kazim (the Forbearing). In the early part of the century the Persian Shiahs were much less fanatical about the entry of Christians into their mosques and sanctuaries than they now are; and we have records of visits by former travellers to shrines which are now only accessible at a certain risk. Buckingham, who, however, spoke the language and posed as a pilgrim to the Moslem shrines, entered the Mosque of Kumisheh in 1816,[1] and described its interior. The inner court, around which are cells for dervishes and pilgrims, contains two tanks, in one of which

[1] *Travels*, vol. i. pp. 430–2.

have always been kept a number of sacred fish. Two centuries ago the sanctity of these creatures was indicated, as Chardin and Dr. Fryer acquaint us, by 'their Noses and Finns being hung with Gold Rings; besides these here were Ducks devoted to as foppish a Maintenance.' The declining fervour or the more practical temper of modern times may be variously held accountable for the disappearance of these evidences of distinction, but the fish still remain. The tomb of the saint reposes behind a brass trellis or grating beneath the blue-tiled dome.

Battle-field of 1835

On the further side of Kumisheh extends a level plain, fringed by mountains on the left or eastern side, which was the scene of a battle fought in 1835 between the army of Mohammed Shah, commanded by Sir H. Lindsay-Bethune, and the combined forces of two of his uncles, the Firman Firma (previously Governor-General of Fars) and his brother, Hasan Ali Mirza (the Shuja-es-Sultaneh), who, upon the death of old Fath Ali Shah, combined to dispute the succession of their nephew to the throne. The royal forces consisted only of two regiments of regular infantry, some cavalry, and twenty guns—less than 4,000 men in all. The pretenders had a much larger army, but were deficient in artillery, in which Lindsay (or Linji, as the Persians called him) had a decided advantage. A mist separated the two forces, who are said to have been unaware of each other's propinquity until the Armenian wife of Colonel Shee, serving in the Shah's army, heard a shot fired in the opposite camp. Bethune then took the enemy by surprise, and aided by his guns, which battered down the walls of a deserted village in which they had stationed themselves, soon put them to flight. Marching rapidly upon Shiraz, he there took prisoner the two claimants and sent them captive to Teheran. The rebellion was thus crushed at the outset.

Maksud Beggi

Several villages are passed in the hollow of the plain on the right hand, and eventually the hamlet of Kishara is reached lying in a depression at a little distance off the road. Here is a village and the *chapar-khaneh*, but the stage takes its name from the walled village of Maksud Beggi (a little further on and nearer the eastern valley-wall), which itself, according to Chardin, was named from 'the late Lord Steward of Persia,' to whom it owed its elevation. On the next stage to Yezdikhast, a distance of twenty-five miles, I only passed one place on the way. This was Aminabad, the Abode of Trust or Safety, originally erected as a fortified redoubt against the Bakhtiari freebooters by Daud Khan, brother of Imam Kuli Khan, the celebrated Governor-General of Fars under Shah Abbas. For two cen'uries the locality continued to attract the hostile notice of those formidable tribesmen, and in about 1815 the whole place was rebuilt for the protection of wayfarers, the walled enclosure including a mud fort, a caravanserai, a mosque, and baths. The members of the early British Embassies to Persia and travellers in the first half of the present century were always instructed to keep a very sharp look-out in the belt of country stretching southwards from this neighbourhood to Dehbid; and in their pages Bakhtiari is a designation almost interchangeable with the name of robber. The nomads are now kept in better order, and Aminabad is no longer a necessary haven of security. Nevertheless, there are but few signs of life or habitation on this part of the southward track, so effectually have the risks and exactions arising from contiguity to the main road driven away a sedentary population. Neither on the road from Isfahan to the Gulf did I observe many signs of through traffic. Caravans of mules and camels are passed, but there is no general stream of wayfarers nor any migration of families similar to those so frequently encountered on the Meshed-Teheran road. If the present extent of traffic between the capital and the cities of Isfahan and Shiraz is of at all a fixed or normal description there would be some difficulty in filling a single railway train *per diem* between those centres. On the plains hereabouts grows the wild plant from which the gum ammoniac, or *ushak*, is derived, and which is more or less common in the hilly country from Kerman to Kermanshah.

Fars

A little beyond Aminabad, the administrative frontier between Irak-Ajemi and Fars is crossed; and we enter upon the province which, both in name, in history, and in population, has the best right to be regarded as Persia Proper, and as the central hearthstone of Iran. Fars, or Farsistan, is the same word as the Greek Persis; and, originally the title of a section only of the empire of Iran, has begotten the name which Europeans have, from remote times, applied to the whole. In this province were the capitals of the Achæmenian kings, Pasargadæ, Persepolis, Istakhr; here the Sassanian monarchs, whilst they favoured a more western capital, frequently resided, and have left, in close proximity to the palaces and tombs of their predecessors, the sculptured records of their own majestic rule;

and here, in the cradle of the native race, a succession of ambitious soldiers of fortune, springing, as a rule, from a humble stock, found it possible in the early disorganisation and ultimate atrophy of the unwieldy empire of the Khalifs, to carve, with their own swords, the scarcely-disguised reality of an independent kingdom. The first of these was Yakub bin Leith, of Seistan, founder of the Sufari or Coppersmith dynasty, in the latter part of the ninth century, whose earliest conquests were Herat, Kerman, and Fars. In the reign of his brother and successor, the Khalifs recovered their sway, but only to cede it a few years later to the Dilemi, or Al-i-Buyah family, whose founder was a fisherman, and who, nominally as viceroys of the Khalif, ruled with great authority and splendour at Shiraz. Next came the Seljuk invasion. A Turkish general was appointed Governor of Fars, and managed affairs so skilfully as to transmit that office to his son, who again passed it on in like fashion, seven viceroys, whose rule extended from 1066 to 1149 A.D., being thus derived from the same family. Sunkur ibn Modud, a chieftain of the Turkoman tribe of Salghuris, who had been moved by the Seljuks from Khorasan to Fars, threw off the Seljuk yoke and proclaimed his own independence in 1149 A.D. It was during the reign of Abubekr, one of his successors, that Sadi, the poet, lived for thirty years at Shiraz, composed his 'Gulistan' and 'Bostan.' and died. At this time Fars was an extensive and powerful kingdom, seeing that it comprised Kerman, Isfahan, the coast-line and islands of the Gulf, and even the opposite or Arab shore. When Jenghiz Khan appeared upon the scene, Abubekr was wise enough to proffer his allegiance to the Mongol, who responded by confirming him in his office, a patronage that was ratified a little later by the marriage of a Salghur princess with the son of Hulaku Khan. Here, however, the independent line of Atabegs terminated; and Fars remained a Mongol province until a fresh principality was created by one Mubariz-ed-Din Mohammed, whose title, El Muzaffer, the Victorious, was transferred to the dynasty of which he was the founder. It was during the reign of the fifth prince of this family that Timur first came to Shiraz (which prudently submitted to his arms), and there enjoyed that friendly interview with the poet Hafiz, that reflected equal credit upon the wit of the bard and the clemency of the sovereign. This was in 1387. A few years later, however, Shah Mansur, taking advantage of the Great Tartar's absence, ventured upon rebellion. Timur knew no mercy. The Persian army was routed, Mansur was slain, and all the princes of his house were put to death. After the break-up of the empire of the conqueror, Fars fell successively into the hands of the Turkoman Black Sheep and White Sheep Dynasties; from whom it passed with the rest of Persia under the sway of Shah Ismail, the founder of the Sefavi royal line; since which time it has remained an appanage of the Persian crown. Few territories have ever succeeded in retaining for so long a period, namely six centuries, the almost continuous reality of an *imperium in imperio*; an achievement largely due to the mountainous barriers by which it is on all sides defended.

Yezdikhast

In every book upon Persia that I had studied, I had read of Yezdikhast (explained by the old writers as a Pehlevi word, signifying 'God willed it') as a village perched upon a remarkable rock in the centre of a deep valley. Great, therefore, was my surprise, as I drew near the end of my stage, to see what looked like a low line of houses, just emerging above the level of the plain. This, I thought, could never be Yezdikhast; and I must have alighted once more upon the elastic *farsakh* of Khorasan. It was not till I was within 200 yards of the place that I realised my mistake, or that the exact nature of the phenomenon became visible. Yezdikhast is, truly enough, built on the top of a remarkable rock, and this rock does stand in the middle of a deep valley; but the latter, so far from being a valley in the ordinary application of the term, is a deep gash or trench cut down to a depth of over 100 feet, without the slightest warning, in the middle of the plain, the edge being as clearly defined as Shakspeare's Cliff at Dover. One is almost on the brink of the gully before one is aware of its existence. At the bottom flows a swift and dirty stream towards the east; and upon the far side the plain resumes its normal level at the top of the fissure, as though nothing had occurred to break its even expanse. Fraser said the trench was 200 yards in width, Binning half mile. The former is much nearer the mark, but is somewhat below it. This extraordinary trench has exactly the appearance of the dried-up bed of a great river; and there is a tradition, probably founded on fact, that it was once so filled, and was navigable by boats. Fraser said that a road to Yezd lies for three days in the hollow; while Chardin declared that the latter extended for twenty leagues, seven to the east, and thirteen to the west of Yezdikhast. But I

YEZDIKHAST

am not aware that any traveller has either traced or surveyed its course; and I would recommend to some future explorer a march across the desert, by this track, to Yezd.

Right in the middle of this strange ditch, which was the old boundary between Fars and Irak, is a long, narrow hump of rock, from 300 to 400 yards in length, severed from the ravine walls on either side, and standing absolutely isolated in the gully bottom. Upon the summit of this rock have been built tiers of cottages, not unlike the man-roost of Lasgird, which I have described in my ride from Meshed to Teheran, to a height of perhaps 120 to 150 feet from the valley bottom; and it was the topmost storey of these edifices, peering above the level of the plain, that had looked, on my approach, like a Persian village of the familiar squat elevation. I own I should never myself have detected any analogy in the rock of Yezdikhast to the hanging gardens of Babylon; but the matter presented itself in a different light two centuries ago to the vision of the excellent Dr. Fryer, who wrote:—

Exterior

> Here, at Esduchos, was truly verified what might be Fabulously delivered of Semiramis's Pendulous Gardens and Summer Houses, there being Tenements made over this Moat out of the ancient Fortifications, barring the Persian Incroachments on their Confines, whose Mouldring Sands have left the jetting Rocks the bare supporters of these hanging Buildings.

Entrance to the village is gained at one spot only, on the south-west (Binning erroneously says north-east) side, by a bridge of wooden rafters thrown across the ravine and leading to a single low doorway pierced in the rock. When this drawbridge is removed or destroyed the place is quite inaccessible, and its inhabitants can laugh at marauding Bakhtiari or soldiers demanding a billet, or tax-collectors unduly extortionate. I entered on foot and made my way down the main street, which is more like a tunnel than a road, inasmuch as the greater part of it is under-ground or has been so completely built over as to form a veritable subterranean alley. Small vaulted passages diverge from this, and flights of steps lead up to the higher cottages, which have rude projecting balconies with wooden palings on the exterior. From any one of these a fall would mean certain death. I entered with-out hindrance a decrepit mosque, which is said to be the *imamzadeh* of Seyid Ali, son of the Imam Musa, who is reported to have

Interior

endowed the world with an offspring numbered at 1,000—a performance that must have greatly stirred the envy of Fath Ali Shah, the philoprogenitive Kajar. The rock, with its strange superstructure, narrows towards the eastern end, where, from below, it looks like the bow of some gigantic ship. This was the spot from which Zeki Khan, the inhuman half-brother of Kerim Khan Zend, who had assumed the real sovereignty on the Vekil's death, while marching northwards in 1779 against his nephew Ali Murad Khan, ordered the leading inhabitants of Yezdikhast, one after the other, to be hurled down, because the villagers declined to satisfy his merciless cupidity. Eighteen had already perished. For his nineteenth victim the monster selected a *seyid*, whose wife and daughter he commanded at the same time to be delivered to the soldiery. This sacrilege proved too much for the tolerance even of his own attendants. That night they cut the ropes of his tent, which collapsed upon him. The villagers rushed in and satisfied a legitimate vengeance by stabbing the brute to death.[1]

At the base of the cliffs are a number of caves hewn in the rocks, which are used as sheep-folds and stables. The *chapar-khaneh* is in the bottom of the ravine on the near side of the stream below the town. On the far side is a caravanserai, originally of the Sefavi age, but restored in the early years of the present century by a governor of Fars. Climbing the reverse side of the gully, I turned my back on Yezdikhast with the reflection that it was one of the most curious places I had ever seen, and continued my ride towards Shulgistan.

Alternative route

In summer an alternative route, lying more to the west and shorter by twenty-five miles than the postal road, is frequently taken from Yezdikhast to Shiraz. It runs *viâ* Dehgerdu, Asupas, Ujan (where Bahram Gur, the sporting Sassanian monarch, lost his life in a quicksand while pursuing the wild ass, from which he was named), and Mayin.[2] But it is not to be

[1] The story is first related by Ensign Franklin, who was at Yezdikhast only seven years after the tragedy had occurred (*Observations made on a Tour*, &c., pp. 316–22). Sir R. K. Porter, in 1818, and other travellers at about the same time, conversed at Yezdikhast with an old man, the sole survivor of the catastrophe, who, though cruelly maimed by the fall, had not been killed by it, but had managed to crawl away and save his life.

[2] This route was taken and is described by both Tavernier and Thévenot in the seventeenth century, and in more recent times by J. S. Buckingham (1816), *Travels*, vol. i. pp. 450–75; Colonel Johnson (1817), *Journey from India*, cap. vii.; Sir

recommended to the stranger, seeing that (unless a deviation be made) it misses both Pasargadæ and Persepolis.

Nothing of interest marked my ride over a desolate, gravelly plain, bounded by high hills on the right, to Shulgistan. There are a ruined caravanserai of Shah Abbas, and a dirty *imamzadeh* with a green-tiled cupola, covering the remains of Mohammed, a son of the Imam Zein-el-Abidin. A similar stage conducts to Abadeh, a large walled village, surrounded by numerous gardens, well-watered, and planted with trees. Having galloped on in front of the post-boy, I tried to find my own way to the Telegraph-office by following the wires, but got involved in the stuffy alleys and amid the blank mud-walls of the town. At the time of my visit Abadeh was temporarily celebrated for two young panthers, which had been brought up as pets by the officer of the Telegraph Department stationed there, and which roamed about his house and garden at their own sweet will; although having reached a period of adolescence they were rapidly becoming rather ugly customers. The place has a more abiding fame for the beautifully-carved *kashuks*, or sherbet-spoons, and boxes, which are made from *gulabi*, or pear-wood, and *shimshad*, or boxwood, in the neighbouring villages. The former, though wrought by simple peasants, are veritable works of art; the bowls of the spoons being hollowed out from a single piece of wood till they are almost as thin as paper, and quite transparent; while the handles are models of fragile and delicate filagree-work. The carvings for the box covers and sides are worked on thin slips, which are then glued on to a rustic box.

Abadeh

Continuous villages and evidences of cultivation border on the road, which continues in a south-east direction, from Abadeh to the next post-station of Surmek, whence a well-known caravan route diverges *viâ* Abarguh to Yezd. For several miles after leaving Surmek, we proceed along the flat, and then commence a steady rise till the sixteenth mile, where a deviation from the track, along the line of the telegraph poles more to the left, may be recommended to the traveller as saving him from a needless détour. The ascent continues by easy inclines to Khan-i-Khoreh, which is merely a post-house and a caravanserai

Dehbid

R. K. Porter (1818), *Travels*, vol. ii. pp. 1–26; J. B. Fraser (1821), *Journey into Khorasan*, cap. vi.; and A. H. Mounsey (1866), *Journey through the Caucasus*, pp. 255–64.

in a bleak desert. Already, since leaving Surmek, we have risen 500 feet; but a further climb of 700 is necessary before we arrive at our next halting-place, which is the highest point on the route between Isfahan and Shiraz. Very desolate and unattractive is this belt of country; nor is Dehbid (lit. Village of the Willow), the place of which I speak, situated in its least unattractive portion. In the middle of a bleak upland plain, surrounded by a network of small watercourses, are seen the post-house, telegraph-station, and one or two huts that constitute the sum total of Dehbid. There is no village, and there are no willows. An artificial mound of earth is attributed by MacGregor to the era of the Fire Worshippers in Persia, and in the first half of the present century was called by the natives Gumbaz-i-Bahur, and explained by them as the site of one of the eight shooting-boxes of Bahram Gur. Dehbid is 7,500 feet above the sea, and though healthy enough from its bracing atmosphere, is considered one of the coldest inhabited places in Persia. A few days before my arrival the thermometer had registered twenty degrees of frost; but a change in the weather had fortunately occurred; and I found travelling very pleasant. The rolling hills and upland plains round Dehbid are the haunts of the Kashkais and other nomad tribes of Fars, who pass to and fro, at regular seasons of the year, driving their flocks to the highlands in the spring, grazing as they go, exchanging milk for bread, and thieving wherever they get the chance. I shall have something more to say about them at the close of this chapter.

Murghab

On leaving Dehbid the track continues to wind over the hills, until, at about the fourteenth mile, it crosses a stream by a very high-backed bridge of five arches, built by a recent Governor of Fars. Close to this is the large ruined caravanserai of Khaneh Kurgan, originally built by Kerim Khan Vekil. The stream is the upper part of the Polvar River, which from this point is almost continually with us, watering successively the plains of Murghab, Hajiabad, and Mervdasht or Persepolis, until it flows into the Kur or Bund-Amir, at the Pul-i-Khan. Following the valley down for a short distance the track then turns abruptly to the right, and climbs a big range of hills by a steep and very stony path. A succession of desolate valleys and ridges follow, until the source of a stream is reached that presently irrigates the villages of Kadarabad and Murghab. Gushing out in great abundance from the hillside it races down the slope, for all the world just like an English trout-stream. At the bottom of the descent, the village of Murghab is seen, clustered against the hillside in an open valley. The distance from Dehbid is reckoned as seven *farsakhs*, but is probably a little more, or about twenty-nine miles. It took me exactly four hours to accomplish, cantering whenever there was fifty yards of possible ground. At Murghab the stream was peopled by a number of wild fowl. I saw several wild duck, a number of snipe, which were quite tame, and a great many plovers. Riding down the valley by the side of a creek infested with these and other water-fowl, I crossed a second small valley containing the tiny hamlet of Deh-i-Nau, and passed over a slight acclivity into a third, which contains the ruins of the famous capital of Cyrus. Here I must pause to deal with some fulness with a question that has throughout this century been a disputed point of archæology and history, and which, if it cannot be definitely solved by travellers who have been to the spot, can still less be decided *ex cathedrâ* by professors or students sitting, with their Arrian and Strabo, or with translations of the cuneiform inscriptions open before them, at home. I have endeavoured to master both sides of the controversy; and the result at which I arrive, even if it carries conviction to the mind of any reader, is advanced with no dogmatism.

Ruins of Pasargadæ. 1. Platform

The method that I propose to adopt will be first to describe the nature of the remains still surviving in the valley of the Polvar, and, secondly, to state the arguments that have been, or can be, advanced for or against their identification with the ancient Pasargadæ. The ruins fall into six separate groups, the site and relative positions of which have been much confused by writers who have not been to the spot.[1]

[1] The names of the scholars who have discussed the question without ocular knowledge will be given presently. The travellers who have visited and described the remains at Murghab are as follows: J. P. Morier (1809), *First Journey*, p. 144, (1811) *Second Journey*, p. 117; Sir W. Ouseley (1811), *Travels*, vol. ii. cap. xii. and App. xiii.; Sir R. K. Porter (1818), *Travels*, vol. i. p. 485 *et seq.*; C. J. Rich (1821), *Journey to Persepolis*, p. 240; Ch. Texier (1840), *L'Arménie*, &c., vol. ii.; Baron de Bode (1841), *Travels*, vol. i. p. 71 *et seq.*; E. Flandin and P. Coste (1841), *Perse Ancienne*, Text, pp. 156–63, vol. iv. pls. 194–203; R. B. Binning (1851), *Two Years' Travel*, vol. ii. cap. xxiii.; M. Dieulafoy (1881), *L'Art Antique de la Perse*, part i. Ker Porter and Flandin both give useful maps of the ruins. For their present condition, *vide* the photographs in Stolze's *Persepolis*, and in Dieulafoy. That a comparative idea may be formed of their state at different periods,

The first of these that are encountered by a traveller coming from the north are the remains of a great terrace or platform, built out from the summit of a hill on the left-hand side of the road, at about 300 yards distance. This is known as the Takht-i-Suleiman, or Throne of Solomon, that potentate being the Persian's synonym for any great unknown monarch of the past. The terrace consists of a parallelogram, two of the sides of which have recessed centres and projecting wings, their dimensions being as follows: left wing 72 feet long, retiring angle 54 feet, central recess 168 feet, corresponding returning angle 54 feet, right wing 48 feet, or about 290 feet in total length. The length of the main front, facing towards the north-west, is about the same. Its height is 38½ feet, and is composed of fourteen layers of stone. The whole is built of great blocks of a whitish stone resembling marble, the outer surface of which is rusticated—i.e. chiselled in low relief—at a slight distance from the edge, exactly like the great blocks that are said to have formed part of the substructure of the Temple at Jerusalem, and that are kissed by the Jews in the Friday observance at the 'Place of Wailing.' So beautifully are the stones (of which Rich measured one over fourteen feet in length[1]) adjusted, that no mortar was used between them. At most of the angles of junction deep holes have been wantonly scooped in the blocks, in order to extract the metal clamps (probably of iron and lead) by which they were originally held together. These interstices are now the homes of crowds of pigeons. Many of the blocks contain on their outer surface curious workmen's signs; and it appears probable from the evidence of the upper part of the platform and from the absence of any staircase, that it was never completed. The outer facing has peeled or been stripped off from much of the surface, and the character of the interior masonry, which is composed of the blue limestone of the mountain, can clearly be seen. It seems to be generally admitted that this platform must have been intended to support

and of the work of the various artists above mentioned, I append a table that may be useful to the student:—

Subject of Plate	Texier (1840), vol. ii.	Fl. & Coste (1841), vol. iv.	Stolze (1878), vol. ii.	Dieulafoy (1881), Part I.
Takht-i-Suleiman	—	201–2	136	3, 4
Zindan, or Tomb	85	200	135	5
General remains	—	197	131	12–14
Inscriptions	—	199	133, 134	—
Bas-reliefs	—	—	137	—
Figure of Cyrus	84	198	132	17
Tomb of Cyrus	81–3	194–6	128, 129	18–20

[1] Flandin said that some of the stones are fifteen to seventeen metres long; but no one else has observed these.

a palace or hall of audience, similar to those that were raised by the successors of Cyrus at Persepolis.

Descending towards the south on to the level of the plain, the next ruin, at a distance of over 300 yards, is that of the single wall of a four

2. Not a fire-temple

sided building that has been commonly called the Fire-temple; (Ouseley said that the local designation was Zindan-i-Suleiman or Prison of Solomon). I am not aware that there is the slightest justification for this purely arbitrary nomenclature, beyond the fact that this building appears to have been an exact facsimile of the square tower that stands in front of the royal rock-tombs at Naksh-i-Rustam (*vide* the next chapter) and the interior chamber of which, being blackened by smoke, was hastily conjectured to have been used for the rites of their worship by the Zoroastrians. There is, however, every reason to suppose that neither edifice ever was, or could have been, a fire-temple. The upper chamber in each, entered by a staircase from outside, was an apartment without aperture or outlet except the door. It was roofed over, and had no communication with the roof; nor could the latter have supported a fire-altar, seeing that it was slightly convex in shape. Moreover, the form of the Persian *atesh-gahs*, or fire-altars, still remaining or reproduced in sculptures and on coins, is entirely different. There can be little doubt that both of these towers were sepulchral in character, the means of hauling up the heavy weight of a sarcophagus having even been traced in that of Naksh-i-Rustam; and the analogy to some of the Lycian tombs discovered in Asia Minor, notably that at Telmessus, is so minute as to confirm this belief. We need not, however, rush to the conjectural extreme of M. Dieulafoy in identifying the Murghab tomb as that of Cambyses, the father of Cyrus. The aperture of the doorway that led into the inner chamber gapes in the still surviving wall,[1] and the remains of the staircase are visible below it. The entire structure is 42 ft. 3 in. high, and 23 ft. 3 in. square, and the blocks are of the same material as the Takht-i-Suleiman, held together, not by mortar, but by cramps. They are also pitted with the same incised orifices, probably designed with decorative intent, that are visible in the tower at Naksh-i-Rustam.

At about the same distance to the south, the third ruin is visible in the shape of a single tall monolith, or block of chiselled stone,

3. Inscribed pillar

eighteen feet high, one side of which is hollowed in the form of a niche (perhaps in order to receive the crude brick-work of which we may assume the walls of the building to have been composed), while high up on the exterior surface are engraved in four

[1] Early in the century parts of all four walls were standing, and as late as 1840 parts of two. The stones are carried off by the natives for housebuilding purposes.

lines a trilingual inscription, containing the words 'Adam Kurush Khshayathiya Hakhamanishiya,' in the Persian, Susian and Assyrian tongues—i.e. 'I am Cyrus, the King, the Achæmenian.' The upper extremity of this great shaft is curiously mortised in order to receive the beams of the roof that covered the hall of whose walls it formed a portion.

Another 300 yards in a southerly direction conducts us to the fourth collection of remains, which consists of a single circular limestone column, 36 feet high, and 3 ft. 4 in. diameter at the base, destitute of a capital, and standing on a small plinth of black basalt, in the centre of an oblong paved space, the outer walls of which are marked by three hollowed angle-piers, similar to that already described, each bearing on one of its surfaces the same trilingual inscription that proclaims the handiwork of Cyrus. This is one of the few unfluted columns that now remain in Persia,[1] and may with little hesitation be referred to an earlier and less developed architectural style than the fluted pillars of Istakhr and Persepolis. The enclosure further contains remains of the bases of eight columns, and the stumps or bases of former doorways, on which are visible a row of feet, that doubtless once belonged to a processional bas-relief similar to those at Persepolis. The probable character of the building has secured for it from recent writers the name of the Palace of Cyrus.

4. Column and pilasters

At about half the distance to the south-east is the platform that once supported another building or palace, the bases of some of whose columns, in two rows of six each, are still visible; while at the distance of eight yards from one of these stands a squared limestone block, 11 ft. 7 in. high, whose upper surface formerly displayed the same proud assertion of authorship,[2] while below it is sculped in low relief—now defaced and indistinct from ill usage and the lapse of time—the famous winged figure that has been variously taken for the *fravashi* or genius of Cyrus, and for Cyrus himself. The figure is in profile, more than life-size, and faces towards the right. From the head springs the strange symbolical crown that has been found on Egyptian sculptures, and which puzzled travellers have compared to three decanters in a row with balls on the top. It is formed of two rams' horns, surmounted by two *uræi*, which in turn are surmounted by the *hemhem* or crown of Harpocrates. The

5. Alleged figure of Cyrus

[1] Morier in 1809 mentioned the remains of another at Istakhr (*First Journey*, p. 142), but it has since disappeared. The columns of the *peribolos* of the tomb of Cyrus were also unfluted. So are the single column on the cliff-top at Naksh-i-Rustam, and a fragment which I shall mention at Persepolis; and so are the columns on the façades of the royal tombs at the same place.

[2] The drawings of Porter and others reproduce the inscription. The engraved part of the monolith has since been broken off and has disappeared.

body is clothed in a long closely-fitting fringed garment from the neck to the ankles. The hair and beard are crisply curled, and somewhat resemble the well-known archaic figure at Athens, called the Warrior of Marathon. Two pairs of immense wings spring from the shoulders, the one pair uplifted, the other sweeping to the ground, and the figure carries in its right hand an object which no one has been able to explain, until the fanciful vision of M. Dieulafoy detected in it a statuette surmounted with the Egyptian *pshent* or double crown, and the sacred *uræus.* The majority of writers have seen in this likeness the tutelary genius of Cyrus.[1] Others, relying upon the literal accuracy of the inscription, believe that it is the conqueror himself, adorned with attributes borrowed from the pantheon of the peoples whom he had vanquished. M. Perrot, seeing that Egypt was not subdued by the Persians until the reign of Cambyses, suggests that the pillar was not erected in the lifetime of Cyrus, but after his death and deification, either by Cambyses or by Darius. Mr. Cecil Smith reminds me, in furtherance of the same idea, of the fact that the wife of Cyrus, and mother of Cambyses, was, according to one account, an Egyptian, Nitetis (Herod. iii. 1–3), a name evidently connected with the goddess Nit, or Neith, and the daughter of Apries, who was king of that country. If there be any truth in this story, which Herodotus rejected, but which the Egyptians affirmed, we may find therein a simultaneous explanation of the Egyptian attributes accorded to Cyrus in the bas-relief, and of the invasion of Egypt by his son Cambyses.

BAS RELIEF OF CYRUS AT PASARGADÆ

The sixth ruin, situated considerably to the west, is the most interesting of all; for it is the structure that, according to the theory which I shall sustain, in all probability once held the gold coffin and the corpse of Cyrus. It consists of a small fabric built of great blocks of white limestone, with a pedimented roof, like that of a Greek temple, the whole standing upon the summit

6. Musjid-i-Mader-i-Suleiman

[1] The four-winged genius is a conception directly borrowed from the religion and art of Assyria. So are the fringed robe and the curled hair of the king. *Vide* Babelon's *Manual of Oriental Antiquities* (translated), pp. 92–3. Compare with these the winged cherubim of the Jewish Ark.

of a pedestal, which consists of seven successive steps or tiers of stone diminishing in size as they approach the summit. The total height from the level of the ground to the top of the roof—which, however, is much worn away—is at present thirty-six feet. This curious edifice, which is called by the natives Kabr or Musjid-i-Mader-i-Suleiman—i.e. the Tomb or the Mosque of the Mother of Solomon—stands in a forlorn and dilapidated enclosure, thickly strewn with the slabs of Mussulman graves. The bases or shattered drums of a number of pillars are still seen embedded in a low mud wall, or standing alone in

TOMB OF CYRUS

what was once evidently a surrounding colonnade. It appears to be uncertain whether this colonnade encompassed the tomb all round, for there are no traces of it on one of the longer sides. The back of the monument is towards the present roadway, and its doorway is upon the reverse, or northern, face. Nor, strange to say, did it stand in the centre of the enclosure, the entrances to which can still be traced. It was placed in a different axis from them ; the design being apparently to prevent the doorway and interior of the sepulchre from being visible outside. Entering the enclosure we see that the entire structure, both mausoleum and pedestal, is composed of great blocks of white, calcareous stone like marble, as smoothly cut and perfectly laid as those in the preceding fabrics, and like them held together in several places with metal cramps, which have been as ruthlessly dug out and plundered. The lowest terrace is a plinth, elevated only thirteen inches above the ground.[1] The next three courses are much deeper, and are composed of enormous blocks.[2] The three uppermost are shallower.[3] The dimensions of the plinth at the base are 47 ft. 2 in. by 43 ft. 9 in. ; those of the topmost tier are 26 ft. by 20 ft. ; and upon this stands the tomb, which is 21 ft. long by 17 ft. wide and 18 ft. 2 in. high. A bush has intruded its roots into the crannies of one of the upper terraces on the south-west side, while another has established a lodgment on the roof itself.

The tomb-chamber

Climbing the terraced steps we are confronted with the mausoleum, which is built of three courses of limestone blocks, the lowest corresponding in depth with the height of the doorway. Above the highest runs a thin projecting cornice, and upon this is superimposed the gabled roof, consisting of two tiers of immense stones, two blocks composing the lower course, and one being laid upon them for the summit. Access is gained to the interior by a low, narrow doorway, 2 ft. 3 in. in width and only 4 ft. 3 in. in height. If M. Dieulafoy is right, the entrance, which is commensurate with the thickness of the surrounding walls, was once closed by two doors opening upon each other, so that both could not be thrown back at the same time—a further device for securing the interior from the sacrilege of prying eyes. Crouching so as to enter, we find ourselves in an empty chamber, the ceiling and walls of which are blackened with smoke. The floor consists of two great slabs, polished quite smooth with age, the larger one being mutilated by great holes, perhaps hacked open with a view to the discovery of what lay below. There are similar mutilations in the walls, and at the far end a string suspended from side to side bears a number of brass, bell-shaped trinkets or offerings. On the right-hand wall is carved an Arabic inscription within an ornamented border, in the form of a *mihrab* or prayer-niche. The dimensions of the cell are : length 10 ft. 5 in., breadth 7 ft. 6 in., height 6 ft. 10 in. I have entered into these particulars with a view to the theory of identification which I shall presently sustain.

[1] In the early part of the century it was all but concealed beneath the surface, whence some travellers have only reported six terraces instead of seven. Some limestone steps are reared against the lower tiers, which Flandin says belong to one of two *atesh-gahs*, or fire-altars, whose remains are to be seen on the banks of a small tributary of the Polvar, to the north-west of the Takht-i-Suleiman (vol. iv. pl. 203).

[2] Their depths are 5 ft. 5 in., 3 ft. 5 in., and 3 ft. 5 in.

[3] Their depth is uniform, 1 ft. 10 in. each.

I have said that the Persians entitle this edifice the Tomb of the Mother of Solomon; and such appears to have been the tradition throughout the Mussulman epoch. Barbaro, the Venetian, in 1474 A.D., calls it by that name, and mentions the Arabic inscription in the interior. Mandelslo's description in 1638 might answer for its present condition; whilst his natural bewilderment as to the origin of the legend was solved for him by the Carmelite Friars of Shiraz, who explained that the Solomon in question was doubtless the fourteenth Khalif of that name, who reigned in 715 A.D. Father Angelo, a little later, corroborates Mandelslo. John Struys, in 1672, mentions that it was already a place of pilgrimage for 'many devout women, who pushed the tomb with their head three times, and as often stooped to kiss it, then muttered out a short prayer, and so departed.' Le Brun in 1706 found it difficult to understand why Bathsheba should be there interred; there being no record in Holy Writ of Solomon having left the Holy Land. The superstition as to an exclusively female place of worship has survived till the present century, when Morier, in 1809, was not allowed to enter. Later travellers have either disregarded the natives' protests, or have entered, as I did, without let or hindrance.

Persian tradition

Morier, in 1809, has received the universal credit of being the first to opine that this was the Tomb of Cyrus, which was found despoiled by Alexander, as narrated by Arrian, Strabo, and other classical writers. And yet, strange to say, on referring to his pages I find that he only made the suggestion in order to reject it.[1] Ouseley, who was there in the same year, adopted a similar attitude. Ker Porter was, I believe, the first Englishman to adopt the identification; but I fancy that its original author was Professor Grotefend.[2] The acceptance or rejection of this theory depends upon a collation of the passages relating to the actual Tomb of Cyrus in classical writers with the allusions to Pasargadæ in the Bisitun inscription, and with the local indications which I have described on the plain of Murghab. For this purpose the first essential is a correct reproduction of what the Greek and Latin historians actually did say; and here

First identification with Tomb of Cyrus

[1] These are his words (*First Journey*, p. 148): 'If the position of the place had corresponded with the site of Pasargadæ as well as the form of this structure accords with the description of the tomb of Cyrus near that city, I should have been tempted to assign to the present building so illustrious an origin.' On the occasion of his second visit in 1811 he says nothing whatever about the identity, but merely that 'the whole of the remains at Moorghaub attest the site of some considerable city, and furnish a subject the investigation of which will be well worthy the labours of an antiquary' (*Second Journey*, p. 119).

[2] *Hallische Allgem. Litt. Zeitung*, No. 140, June 1820; and App. III. to vol. ii. of Heeren's *Historical Researches*.

I must record my surprise that I have not discovered a faithful translation of them in a single work, even in those of great scholars; and that in some cases hypotheses have actually been sustained or rejected upon a palpable mistranslation of the original texts.

The Classical writers

The authorities upon whom we have chiefly to rely are Arrian, Strabo, Pliny, Quintus Curtius, Plutarch. The two first of these, of whom Arrian wrote a work in Greek on the Expedition of Alexander at the end of the first century A.D., while the date of Strabo was about A.D. 20, base their account upon the testimony of Aristobulus, a companion of Alexander in his Eastern Campaign, who became its historian in his old age, but of whose work only fragments remain; and of Onesicritus, a less trustworthy authority, but also a companion of Alexander and a probable eye-witness. Quintus Curtius wrote a life of Alexander about 50 A.D.; but his work is uncritical and sacrificed to rhetorical effect. The date of Pliny, as is well known, is about 70 A.D., of Plutarch about 100 A.D. With this preface I will proceed to quote the words of the several writers.

Arrian's reference to the Tomb of Cyrus and the visit of Alexander thereto in 324 A.D. is as follows:[1]—

Alexander himself with his lightest infantry and with his cavalry-guard and some of his bowmen, marched (from Carmania) towards Pasargadæ in Persis. And he was grieved at the insult inflicted upon the tomb of Cyrus, the son of Cambyses, seeing that he found the tomb of Cyrus broken open and despoiled, as Aristobulus tells us. For the latter says that there was in Persis, in the royal paradise, the tomb of that Cyrus. About it had been planted a grove of all kinds of trees, and it was watered with streams, and deep grass had grown up in the meadow. The tomb itself in its lower parts had been wrought of squared stone in the form of a square; and above was a house (οἴκημα) upon it, of stone, roofed, having a door that led within, so narrow that hardly could one man, and he of no great stature, enter even with much difficulty. In the house was placed a golden coffin, where the body of Cyrus was buried, and a couch beside the coffin; and the feet of the couch were of hammer-beaten gold, and it had a coverlet of Babylonian tapestries, and thick carpets (or cloaks) of purple were strewn beneath it; and there were also upon it a tunic and other garments of Babylonian workmanship. He says further that Median trousers and purple-dyed vestments were placed there (and some of these were of purple, and some of other colours), and collar-chains, and swords, and earrings of gold inlaid with stones, and a table was placed there. And in the middle of the couch was placed the coffin, which held the body of Cyrus. And there was within the enclosure, hard by the ascent that led to the tomb, a small house that had been made for the Magi, who guarded the tomb of Cyrus, from the time of Cambyses the son of Cyrus to now, father handing down the guardianship to son. To these a sheep was given every day from the king, and fixed measures of flour and wine, and a horse every month for sacrifice to Cyrus. And the tomb was inscribed with Persian characters; and they said in Persian as follows: 'O man, I am Cyrus the son of Cambyses, who founded the

---

[1] *De Exped. Alex.*, vi. 29.

Empire of Persia, and was King of Asia. Grudge me not therefore this monument.'

Alexander (for it had been an object of great care to him, when he should take Persia, to come to the tomb of Cyrus) found all the other things carried away save only the coffin and the couch. Nay, they had outraged the very body of Cyrus, having carried off the lid of the coffin, and had cast forth the corpse; and the coffin itself they had tried to make light of burden for themselves, and in this wise light to carry, cutting part of it in pieces, and battering part of it in. But when this work of theirs did not fare well, then they had left the coffin and gone. And Aristobulus says that he himself was appointed by Alexander to adorn anew the tomb of Cyrus, and to put back such parts of the body as still remained in the coffin, and to put the lid upon it, and to repair such parts of the coffin as had been injured; and to tie fillets upon the couch, and to restore all the other things that had been placed there for adornment, both in number and likeness to those of old time; and to do away with the door by building it up with stone and plastering it over with mortar, and to stamp upon the mortar the royal signet. And Alexander seized the Magi who were guardians of the tomb, and tortured them, so that they should confess the doers of the deed. But they, albeit tortured, confessed nothing, neither against themselves nor any other, nor were convicted in any other way of being privy to the deed. And upon this they were let go by Alexander.[1]

[1] In connection with the Egyptian attributes of the bas-relief of Cyrus, and with the suggestion concerning Nitetis that has already been made, and in explanation of the above passage, which appears to indicate a form of sepulture strictly Egyptian in character—in fact, no less than the mummification of Cyrus' corpse—Mr. Cecil Smith sends me the following interesting note: 'In contrast with the usual mode of interment practised by the Achæmenian kings, whose bodies were laid in sarcophagi of stone, the πύελος of Cyrus was evidently of some light material, for it stood upon a κλίνη, and was easily breakable, for the plunderers had *cut* and battered it to make it portable. It was valuable (otherwise they would not have wished to carry it off)—"golden," according to Strabo (though not of gold, as it would have been too heavy for the κλίνη). Presumably the "gold" was principally on the lid, because they carried that off, leaving the lower part of the coffin behind. Further, the actual body was still in a condition to be broken up, τὸ σῶμα being the expression employed, whereas one would expect τὰ ὄστεα. These facts are intelligible, if we suppose that the body had been mummified. In accordance with the usual practice, the mummy would be enclosed in a cedarwood case following the outline of the mummy, with lid richly decorated and gilt. The natural Greek word for this would be πύελος, as opposed to σορὸς, a sarcophagus. Such a lid would be worth carrying off. This would account, too, for the breaking-up of the "body," in the search for ornaments, &c., among the mummy-cloths. The mummy in its case would have stood (as usual in the Egyptian rite) upon a couch, with feet in the form of lions' claws (σφυρήλατον, the term employed by Arrian, is the natural word for the usual Egyptian method of decorating wooden furniture with sheets of *repoussé* metal, nailed on); and in front of this couch (analogous to the banqueting couch) would have stood the table of offerings (the τράπεζα of Arrian). It is in keeping with this idea that the monument should have taken the general form of a pyramid, the natural shape for the tomb of an Egyptian sovereign. Finally, the "gold inlaid with stones," mentioned both by Arrian and Strabo, may

Strabo,[1] utilising the same materials, differs in unimportant details, but generally corroborates Arrian :—

Then he (Alexander) came to Pasargadæ; and this was the ancient abode of the kings. And there he saw the tomb of Cyrus in a paradise, a tower of no great size, concealed beneath the thicket of trees, in its lower parts massive, but in its upper parts having a roof and a shrine, with a very narrow entrance. By this Aristobulus says that he entered. And he saw there a golden couch and a table with drinking-cups, and a golden coffin, and much raiment, and ornaments inlaid with stones. At his first visit he saw these things; but afterwards they had been despoiled, and the other things had been carried away, and the couch had been shattered, and the coffin, while they had shifted the corpse. From which it was clear that it was the work of plunderers, and not of the satrap, since they had left behind the things that it was not possible to carry away with ease. And these things had happened, although a guard of Magi had been set about the tomb, who received every day a sheep for food, and every month a horse. Now the absence of the army of Alexander in Bactria and the Indies was the occasion of many other renovations being made, of which renovations this was one. So said Aristobulus; and the inscription he related from memory as follows: 'O man, I am Cyrus, who founded the Empire of the Persians, and was King of Asia. Grudge me not therefore this monument.' Onesicritus further said the tower was ten storeys high; and in the uppermost storey was placed Cyrus; and the inscription was in Greek, engraved in Persian characters: 'Here I lie, Cyrus, King of Kings'; and there was another in Persian of the same sense.

Pliny merely said :[2]—

On the east (of Persepolis) the Magi hold the fortress of Passagarda, in which is the tomb of Cyrus.

Plutarch, in his Life of Alexander, wrote as follows :—

Then finding the tomb of Cyrus broken open, he slew the man that had done the wrong, though the offender was a Pellæan, and not of the least distinguished, by name Polymachus. And having read the inscription he ordered it to be engraved again below in Greek characters; and it ran thus: 'O man, whosoever thou art, and from whencesoever thou comest (for that thou wilt come I know), I am Cyrus, who founded the Empire of the Persians. Grudge me not, therefore, this little earth that covers my body.' These things caused Alexander to be sore moved, when he called to mind the uncertainty and the vicissitudes of things.

Finally, Quintus Curtius,[3] obviously untrustworthy, gave the following version :—

For it happened that Alexander ordered the tomb of Cyrus to be opened, wherein had been buried his body, to which he wished to offer obsequies. He

---

probably be referred to the specially Egyptian jewellery of gold inlaid with enamel, which would not, naturally, have been found at so early a date except in Egypt.' To his Egyptian queen, Nitetis, therefore, the treatment of the corpse of Cyrus according to the custom of her country may conceivably have been due; by her orders, even, it may, in common with the winged bas-relief, have been executed. How entirely the structure at Murghab harmonises with the dispositions required by such a mode of sepulture is manifest.

[1] *Geog.* lib. xv. 1061. [2] *Hist. Nat.* vi. 29. [3] *Hist. Alex.* x. 1.

believed that it was filled with gold and silver, since the Persians had spread that report abroad; but beyond the rotten shield of Cyrus, and two Scythian bows, and a sword, he found nothing. However, he placed a crown of gold upon the coffin, and covered it with the cloak which he himself was wont to wear, wondering that a king of such great name, and endowed with such riches, should have been buried in no more costly fashion than if he had been one of the populace.

Points of resemblance

Now without attempting to form a connected narrative from the above excerpts—the salient features of which are, however, unmistakable —let us see what points there are in them, in which the tomb that I have described at Murghab either corresponds with, or differs from, the original Tomb of Cyrus. I will first note the points of resemblance or identity: (1) The Tomb of Cyrus stood in an enclosure (περίβολος), within which was also a small building for the accommodation of the guardians. The tomb at Murghab, as I have shown, was surrounded on three sides by a covered colonnade, that may well have contained such a building. (2) The Tomb of Cyrus was not large, and consisted of two parts, an upper and a lower; the lower massive and resting upon a squared stone base, the upper resembling a house (οἴκημα) roofed over, and containing the coffin. To this there was an ἀνάβασις or ascent. Here the correspondence is minute and exact, the dimensions of the base, which I have previously given as 47 ft. by 43 ft. 9 ins., being little short of a square, although the Greek words employed (τετράπεδον and τετράγωνος) imply a quadrangular shape rather than one necessarily square. (3) The Tomb of Cyrus had a conspicuously small and narrow entrance, a further point of absolute correspondence. (4) Finally, Onesicritus, who probably saw it (and I am surprised that this statement, which appears to me of considerable importance, has been so little noticed), says that the Tomb of Cyrus was in ten storeys or tiers. Now, however untrustworthy Onesicritus may have been, this is the kind of statement that he could hardly have invented for no purpose. The discrepancy between his figure of ten, and the seven terraces (or eight, including the sepulchre) of the tomb at Murghab is so slight as to count for nothing compared with the startling resemblance of the two fabrics in this essential detail of external structure.[1]

[1] The pyramidal, or terraced, form of structure has, as I have said, been regarded by some critics as a reminder of Egypt; whilst most writers have seen in the gabled tomb a legacy from the Greek art of Ionia. It should not, however, be forgotten that the elevation of buildings on seven terraces was a familiar feature of Chaldæo-Assyrian architecture—the number seven having a planetary reference – and there is in Herodotus (lib. i. 181) a description of the seven-staged Temple of Bel at Babylon, which suggests a curious parallel: 'Upon the last tower stands a spacious shrine, in which is a large couch with rich coverings, and by it a golden table.' Furthermore, a pedimented structure, so far from being necessarily of Greek origin, already exists on a bas-relief in the Khorsabad palace of Sargon (Botta, pl. 141).

On the other hand, the opponents of the theory of identification advance the following arguments, to which I will append such replies as appear to be both reasonable and adequate. (1) The Tomb of Cyrus was surrounded by gardens and streams and grass, and was overshadowed with the foliage of trees, whereas there is now no sign at Murghab of any of these. I really cannot think that this argument is of the slightest value, looking to the prodigious change in the face of a country that is effected in a single century, let alone 2,200 years. Upon this hypothesis, scarcely a single site in Persia could now be identified with its forerunner in ancient days. There is abundance of water in the valley of Murghab, for the river runs at no distance; and the little sepulchre and its surrounding colonnade may well have stood in a copse of trees. Moreover, the modest height of the existing building, over which a sylvan canopy might easily have been formed, itself indirectly corroborates the assertion of Strabo. (2) M. Dieulafoy says that a Greek would never have compared the edifice at Murghab to a square tower. Here I have to complain of the mistranslation or misrepresentation of the originals, of which no critic has been so fragrantly and frequently guilty as M. Dieulafoy. The answer is very simple. None of the Greeks did so compare it. Strabo called it a tower (πύργος)—a term frequently applied in later Greek to isolated buildings—but never said that it was square. Arrian added that it rested upon a squared base, which I have shown to be true.[1] (3) M. Dieulafoy argues that the tomb chamber at Murghab is too small to have contained the objects before enumerated, to which he gratuitously adds, without the slightest excuse, 'une auge dorée propre à se laver ou à se baigner.'[2] This is largely a matter of opinion. I gather myself from the passages before cited that the contents of the mausoleum of Cyrus were a decorated couch upon which the coffin was laid, and a table covered with cups, ornaments, and arms. For these there appears to me to have been ample room. (4) M. Dieulafoy, perpetrating a still further enormity, says that in the tomb at Murghab there is no trace of an inner staircase leading down to the chamber of the guards. Neither, I reply, was there in the Tomb of Cyrus. The staircase is an unpardonable figment of M. Dieulafoy's own imagination.[3] (5) There

Points of difference

[1] His words are: ἀυτὸν δὲ τὸν τάφον τὰ μὲν κάτω λίθου τετραπέδου ἐς τετράγωνον σχῆμα πεποιῆσθαι.

[2] This is a second mistranslation. M. Dieulafoy translates πύελος in its primary meaning of a bathing-tub, ignoring that Arrian is applying it, in its secondary meaning of a coffin, to the receptacle that held the body of Cyrus. This is clear enough from Arrian's own words: ἡ πύελος ἡ τὸ σῶμα τοῦ Κύρου ἔχουσα.

[3] To make this point clear, let me cite the words both of M. Dieulafoy and of Arrian. The former says (*L'Art Antique de la Perse*, p. 26): 'On communiquait

is no trace on the walls at Murghab of the Persian or Greek epitaphs of Cyrus. These, however, may very conceivably have been inscribed on tablets affixed to the wall, or in some position since destroyed.[1] So much for the arguments *pro* and *con.* suggested by the descriptions of the original and the appearance of the actual tomb—an ordeal from which it cannot, I think, be doubted that the theory which I have defended emerges with superior laurels. I should add that, of the two most formidable opponents of this hypothesis, Professor Oppert, attaching a not wholly improper or irrational weight to tradition, which, as I have shown, ascribes the tomb at Murghab to a woman, believes it to have been that of Cassandane, the wife of Cyrus,[2] while M. Dieulafoy prefers Mandane, his mother.[3] There is, of course, not a tittle of positive evidence in support of either ; and why M. Dieulafoy, admitting that this is the Pasargadæ of Cyrus, and locating here the tomb both of his father and of his mother, should at the same time place the conqueror's own tomb in some other place, locality unknown, it passes my wits to determine.

Even so, however, the matter is far from having been determined ; for there arises the question whether the ancient Pasargadæ, the royal

au moyen d'un escalier intérieur avec la chambre où se tenaient les prêtres préposés à la garde du monument.' What Arrian wrote was εἶναι δε ἐντὸς τοῦ περιβόλου πρὸς τῇ ἀναβάσει τῇ ἐπὶ τὸν τάφον φερούσῃ οἴκημα σμικρὸν τοῖς Μάγοις πεποιημένον, words which I have already literally rendered in my translation. Would it be believed that, on the threshold of these achievements, M. Dieulafoy thus addresses his readers : 'J'engage les personnes qui voudraient consulter Strabon ou Arrien à avoir recours au texte grec, les mots techniques étant généralement mal interprétés' !

[1] Stolze says that above the door of the tomb at Murghab the actual holes by which such a tablet may have been affixed are still visible (*Persepolis, Bemerkungen*).

[2] Oppert, indeed, goes further, and finds in the gabled roof an irrefragable argument in favour of a feminine connection : 'Incontestablement ce tombeau est celui d'une femme, ainsi que le prouve son toit à bât d'âne. Ce caractère distinctif des sépulcres féminins se retrouve déjà dans les caveaux taillés dans le roc à Persépolis ; il remonte donc à une haute antiquité. Ce n'est que par l'oubli de toutes les possibilités archéologiques et géographiques qu'on a identifié le tombeau de Mourghab avec le tombeau de Cyrus' (*Le Peuple et la Langue des Mèdes*, p 110; cf. *Records of the Past*, vol. vii. p. 89). This is very tall talk ; but the remark about the tombs at Persepolis, upon which the reasoning rests, is pure conjecture.

[3] If a lady is to be selected, why not Nitetis, the alleged Egyptian queen of Cyrus, before mentioned? There is more to be said in favour of an Egyptian than of a Persian female occupant of the sepulchre. Indeed, if such enormous weight is to be attached to the traditional association of the Gabr with a woman, we may conceive that the mummy of Nitetis may have been deposited there along with that of Cyrus. But this, I think, is treating tradition too seriously.

city of the Achæmenians, in which it is beyond doubt that the tomb of Cyrus was situated,[1] can be identified with the ruins which I have described in the valley of the Polvar. Again let me state the *pros* and *cons*.[2] (1) Anaximenes tells us that the city of Pasargadæ was built by Cyrus on the site of his famous victory over Astyages the Mede, and Strabo that this city contained both his palace and his tomb.[3] Now we happen to have an account of this battle in the fragments of Nicolaus of Damascus, a contemporary and friend of Herod the Great, who composed a Universal History in 144 books, of which some excerpts have been preserved by Photius, Patriarch of Constantinople.[4] His narrative, which is here very circumstantial, can scarcely leave a doubt that it was in the valley of the Polvar, commanding the sole entrance from the north into Fars (Astyages was marching from Media and Ecbatana), that the decisive conflict was waged, Cyrus and the Persians having naturally selected the most advantageous field of combat. Moreover, Nicolaus connects the name Pasargadæ with this site, describing it as *τὸ ὑψηλότατον ὄρος*, the very lofty mountain, overlooking the plain, to which Cyrus sent the women and children for safety during the battle. Finally, we have already seen on this very plain the remains of buildings inscribed with the name and titles of Cyrus, and one or more of which are certainly palaces of the Achæmenian type; whilst in another edifice I have shown what certainly bears an extraordinary likeness to the authentic descriptions of his tomb. (2) Strabo says of the river at Pasargadæ: 'There is the river Kuros flowing through Persis which is called Koile, round Pasargadæ, of which the king changed the name, calling it Kuros, instead of Agradates.'[5] Now this is not strictly correct; for the river at Murghab is the Polvar (or Medus of the ancients, also mentioned by Strabo); while the Kuros or Kur is another name for the Araxes, or

Identity of Pasargadæ

[1] This Pasargadæ was associated with many religious observances of the Achæmenian monarchs. Here they were consecrated by the Magi, and invested with the robe of Cyrus. Here they partook of the sacred banquet (Plutarch's *Artaxerxes*), and made many offerings. Cyrus, the younger, performed the pilgrimage to Pasargadæ no less than seven times (Xenophon, *Cyrop.* viii.). Darius, son of Hystaspes, made the same journey (Ctesias, *Pers.*, cap. xix.).

[2] The chief advocates of the identification have been Rennell, Burnouf, Heeren, Grotefend, Tychsen, Fergusson, C. Ritter, Spiegel, Kiepert, Rawlinson, Menke, Justi. Its chief opponents are Hoeck, *Veteris Persiæ et Mediæ Monumenta*, p. 58; P. Lassen, *Encycl. d'Ersch et Grüber*, *sub tit.* Pasargada; J. Oppert, the works above quoted and *Journal de la Société Asiatique*, vol. xix. 1872; Prof. A. H. Sayce, *Encycl. Britannica*, 9th edit. *sub tit.* Cyrus; M. Dieulafoy, *L'Art Antique de la Perse*, part i.

[3] *Geog.* xv. 1061.

[4] *Fragmenta*, edit. Muller, vol. iii. p. 101. The passages are collected and abstracted in a footnote by M. Dieulafoy.

[5] *Geog.* xv. 1061.

Bund-Amir, after the Polvar has joined it in the plain of Mervdasht in front of Persepolis. I think, however, it will be seen that this mistake is in itself corroborative of our theory, inasmuch as Strabo has merely transferred to an upper branch of the river the name which the whole of it bears lower down ; a mistake which is also found in later writers, who have compounded the Kur-ab with the Pur-ab, which is the old Persian name for the Polvar. Moreover, Strabo's classification of the rivers of Central and Southern Persia in geographical sequence, as the Choaspes, Coprates, Pasitigris, Kuros, Araxes and Medus, makes it clear that the Kuros is to be sought in this neighbourhood, and not, as the hostile school would have us believe, in the south-east, near Darabjird. (3) There is, in the descriptions of both Strabo and Arrian, every indication that Persepolis and Pasargadæ were situated at no great distance from each other. Arrian relates that Alexander (in 331 B.C.), marching from Susa and the Pasitigris (Karun) through the territory of the Uxii, fought and won a great battle, and then advanced in hot haste to Pasargadæ, where he seized the treasure of Cyrus, continuing from thence to Persepolis. This exactly tallies with the situations of Murghab and Persepolis. Strabo says of Alexander that, after burning the palace at Persepolis, εἶτ' ἐς Πασαργάδας ἧκε, 'then he came to Pasargadæ.' Again Arrian, describing his return march from India, in 324 B.C., depicts him as leaving Hephæstion and the bulk of his army to march along the coast from Carmania, while he himself, with a detachment of light-armed troops, 'came to the borders of Persis and so to Pasargadæ,' and thence to Persepolis, the two names being bracketed in the same sentence (ὡς δὲ ἐς Πασαργάδας τε καὶ ἐς Περσεπόλιν ἀφίκετο), an almost certain index of proximity.

It being clear, therefore, to my mind that in the valley of the Polvar was fought the battle that made Cyrus the master of Persia, and it being certain that in that valley he built a royal city and palace, and called it Pasargadæ, where he was ultimately buried, and that name having also been shown to be already connected with the locality, and the remains of a palace indubitably erected by Cyrus, because inscribed with his own name, having also been shown to exist there, as well as a tomb answering to his sepulchre, I am brought to the conclusion that the ruins of Murghab are the very Pasargadæ which Cyrus built, and that the Tomb of the Mother of Solomon is the very sepulchre where his body lay.

What, however, are the counter-propositions that have influenced the vote of the learned authorities before mentioned? They are of a two-fold source, being derived partly from discrepancies in the classical writers, partly from the evidence of the cuneiform inscription at Bisitun.

Let me state both. (1) Pliny says that Pasargadæ was east of Persepolis (Inde ad orientem Magi obtinent Passagardas castellum), whereas Murghab is north-east. This, I think, is hyper-criticism. (2) The same writer, describing the naval cruise of Nearchus along the shore of the Persian Gulf, speaks of the 'river Sitiogagus, by which Pasargadæ is reached by boat on the seventh day.'[1] This of course can in no wise be reconciled with the Kur or the Polvar. It is the Sitakus of Arrian (*Indica*, cap. 93), and the modern Kara Aghach, one branch of which rises south of Darabjird, where, as I shall presently show, it is probable that there was either another Pasargadæ, or a city of very similar name. (3) Ptolemy (who, however, did not write till the second century A.D.) in giving the latitudes and longitudes of Persepolis and Pasargadæ, represents the latter as a good deal to the south-east, and not to the north-east, of the former. One answer to this might be that Ptolemy in his Persian tables made many egregious mistakes, although, as I shall show, I think it quite possible that in this case he was referring to another city of a similar name, further to the south-east.[2] (4) It is argued that Alexander, in marching into Fars from Carmania (Kerman), would probably have adopted the ordinary caravan track from the south, in which case he would have reached Persepolis before Murghab, instead of in the inverse order. But the very fact that he only took a small detachment of his lightest troops on this expedition seems to imply that he went by a less ordinary and, possibly, by a desert route. (5) Finally, we come to the argument from the cuneiform inscription of Bisitun, which is of more weighty calibre. There we read of Pisiyauwada or Pisyachada, a name bearing a strong verbal resemblance to Pasargadæ. The first pseudo-Smerdis, Gomates, we are told, rose here. Hither the second pseudo-Smerdis, Veisdates, fled after a defeat at Rakha. 'From that place (i.e. Pisyachada) with an army he came back, arraying battle before Artabardes. The mountains named Parga, there they fought.' There, too, the pretender was taken prisoner and put to death. In another paragraph it is mentioned that he had sent his troops to Arachotia—i.e. Western Afghanistan. Upon these details Professor Oppert grounds a minute scheme of identification, Rakha, according to him, being the Pasarracha of Ptolemy, on the site of the modern Fasa or Pasa; Parga being the modern Forg, and Pisyachada, or Pasargadæ, being the modern Darabjird, or rather a ruined enclosure known as the Kaleh-i-Darab, four miles south-west of that town.[3] Here, he says, was the royal city of Cyrus and the

Hostile arguments

[1] *Hist. Nat.* vi. 25.

[2] *Geog.* vi. 4. In the best manuscript moreover, the name is written, not Pasargadæ, but *Pasarracha*.

[3] I may point out (accepting Sir H. Rawlinson's translation of the inscription as correct) that Professor Oppert has strained the text in what appears to be an

Achæmenians, here Cyrus was buried, and here must be sought his tomb.[1]

Now the negative arguments against Darabjird being the site of the city and tomb of Cyrus are, I think, overpowering. The plain round Darabjird cannot well have been the site of the battle between him and Astyages. There is no ὑψηλότατον ὄρος here at all. Neither is there any river Kuros. Nor does the place correspond with the indications of the Greek or Latin writers whom I have quoted, with the exception of the latest in date, Ptolemy. Moreover, it is at such a distance from Persepolis (190 miles) as to render it highly improbable that the two names would have been constantly

Darabjird

unwarrantable manner in order to suit his assumptions. He says (*Journ. Asiat.*, vol. xix. 1872) that 'starting from Pisyachada Veisdates fought a second battle at Parraga (Forg), whence his beaten troops fell back upon Arachotia in the extreme east.' The inscription says nothing of the kind. On the contrary, it says that he *came back* to Parga, whereas had Parga been Forg, he would have required to go on. Nor is the expedition to Arachotia in the inscription justifiably represented as a retreat of beaten troops from Forg. The context shows that it was an independent military venture.

[1] Oppert derives the name Pisyachada from *fiseh*, springs, and *kheveh*, valley—i.e. the valley of springs. But this is purely conjectural. The old explanation of Pasargadæ, or Parsagardæ (as it was written by Q. Curtius), was given by Stephen of Byzantium, quoting Anaximenes, as the encampment of the Persians. (Compare Las-gird, Buru-jird, etc.) Oppert, having thus identified Pasargadæ with Darabjird, has also to dispose of the remains of the city built by Cyrus in the valley of the Polvar. This he does by identifying the latter with Marrhasium, cited by Ptolemy (*Geog.* viii. 21, 14) as one of the four principal cities of Persia, the geographical positions of the two places corresponding very fairly. Dr. Andreas solves the difficulty by supposing that the Cyrus of Murghab is Cyrus, brother of Xerxes, and Viceroy of Egypt, who was called Achæmenides by Ctesias, and whose body was brought after death to Persia to be buried there. To which the answer is that this Cyrus could never have been described in the inscriptions as Khshayathiya, or king, an objection which applies equally to the suggestion of the younger Cyrus. Sayce is hardly to be congratulated upon his statement of the case (*Encycl. Britannica*): 'The tomb at Murghab cannot be that of Cyrus, as is often supposed. Murghab, like Persepolis, is on the Araxes, while Pasargadæ where Cyrus was buried, was on the Cyrus (Kur). The cuneiform inscription at Murghab points to a period subsequent to the accession of Darius, as does also the Egyptian head-dress of the figure below it.' Now, as regards the above, neither Murghab nor Persepolis are on the Araxes or Kur. If the former had been, the case would be settled at once against Professor Sayce. Both are on the Medus or Polvar, although lower down the river *is* called the Kur, after joining the Kamfiruz. Nor is the cuneiform character of Murghab of late date; for Oppert himself is constrained to admit that 'the character of the sculptures at Murghab is more ancient than that of any other Persian antiquities;' whilst the Egyptian character of the head-dress of Cyrus may be explained by the theory, previously suggested, that the figure was sculped after his death and deification either by Nitetis or by one of his successors.

bracketed as they were. Furthermore, we know from the inscriptions on Babylonian cylinders that Cyrus was originally king of Anzan; and if Anzan, as appears probable, was identical with the west part of modern Persia, perhaps with Susiana, it is unlikely that he would be found fighting Astyages and founding a royal city in the distant east. Above all, there is not at or near Darabjird the smallest vestige of palace or tomb of Cyrus, not a single cuneiform inscription, nor, indeed, any remains that can conceivably be regarded as Achæmenian, with the possible exception of a species of rampart in the middle of which rises a rugged rock, identified by tradition with the citadel of Darab or Darius,[1] generally supposed to be the Darius Nothus of the Greeks, who reigned 423 B.C. It is difficult to believe, in a country where some relics, at least, have been found of nearly all the great contemporary cities, that Pasargadæ, had it been here, could have been so completely blotted out from the face of the earth.

Conclusion

I am disposed myself to think that the name Pasargadæ, which, as we know from Herodotus, was that of the royal tribe of Persia, may have been given to more than one site, and may thus very naturally have confused the Greek and Latin writers, who were compiling their works about countries which they had never themselves seen from the testimony of earlier writers, whose accounts they could not invariably reconcile, and who thus led them astray. We have already seen that the title of Pasargadæ was applied to a lofty mountain in one locality (which I have identified with the valley of the Polvar); whilst in another passage of Ptolemy we find a second place of the same name in Kerman. I even think it likely, for reasons that will be stated in the next chapter, that Pasargadæ may have been the Persian title of Persepolis itself. It is possible, therefore, that there may also have been a Pasargadæ or Pasarracha in south-east Fars, at or near Darabjird or Fasa, to which the few allusions in the classical writers which postulate such a situation may have referred. But that

[1] Ouseley, who visited it in 1811, called it Kaleh-i-Dehayeh (probably a misunderstanding of Darayeh), *Travels*, vol. ii. p. 177. Keith Abbot in 1850 described it as a mud rampart, thirty to forty feet high, surrounding an isolated rock at a distance of 800 yards (*Journal of the R. G. S.*, vol. xxvii. p. 189). Flandin and Coste visited it in 1841, and have included a ground plan and illustration in their beautiful collection of plates, vol. i. plate 31. J. R. Preece, the latest visitor, in 1884, said that the remains consisted of walls of clay, twenty feet high, with a ditch forty feet broad, surrounding two small rocky hills, the higher of which is 100 feet. He added: 'After searching the whole place and most carefully examining the rocks all about, not the slightest trace of a stonemason's handiwork could be found, and the rocks show no sign of ever having been touched. The place did not give the idea of any great antiquity. It doubtless belongs to the Sassanian period, and not to the Achæmenian, as we surmised and hoped.' (*Supplementary Proceedings of R. G. S.*, vol. i. part iii.)

the Pasargadæ of Cyrus, in life and in death, was the city whose fragmentary ruins I have described in the valley of the Polvar, I am inclined strongly to believe; and therefore it is that in face of the recent attacks that have been made upon it by men of science, I have ventured to refurbish the armoury of its defence.[1]

Approach to Persepolis

Soon after leaving the Musjid-i-Mader-i-Suleiman, the walls of which gleam like a white patch on the sombre landscape, we bid farewell to the plain of Murghab, and enter a lofty range of mountains by a fine gorge, along the base of which rushes the river Polvar. When the water is low, the bed of the stream, or its banks, provide a roadway; for seasons when the channel is full, a path, called Sangbur, has been hewn many centuries ago, for a distance of over fifty yards in the side of the lofty limestone cliff.[2] Twice this dark ravine expands into open valleys, and twice again contracts into narrow defiles, admitting little beyond the track and the noisy river. So we continue for several miles, until, at the far end of one of the valley-windings, we espy the miserable post-house and imposing caravanserai of Kawamabad. This place takes its name from its founder, the Haji Kawam, who was minister at Shiraz fifty years ago. Turning to the left, and pursuing the same ravine, I came, after thirty-five minutes' sharp riding to the village and Telegraph-station of Sivend. The village, which is said to be inhabited by Lurs, is built in ascending tiers on the mountain side, while the valley bottom is thickly planted with vines. From here the track continues in a south-easterly direction, skirting the river, and arrives at the Lur village of Saidan, to which point there is also a shorter track from Murghab than that followed by the postal and telegraph route, running over the hills *viâ* Kamin. An abrupt turn to the right, or west, then brings us into a valley, bordered on either side by mountains and cut up by watercourses and irrigation channels, which, in the darkness, the sun

[1] Since writing the above lengthy—but not, I hope, gratuitous—argument, I have seen the new volume of MM. Perrot and Chipiez' magnificent work, entitled *Histoire de l'Art dans l'Antiquité*, tome v., *Perse* (1890); and I am delighted to find that, limiting his own discussion to the identity of the tomb, without embarking upon the larger question of Pasargadæ, M. Perrot has arrived by arguments very similar to my own at precisely the same conclusion; although he has hardly realised the full measure of M. Dieulafoy's peccadilloes, and has based his identification upon structural, rather than topographical, resemblances.

[2] *Vide* Stolze, vol. ii. pl. 127.

having set, made riding anything but easy and pleasant, and caused my Persian servant to describe two complete somersaults over the head of his tired and stumbling steed. As we ride down this valley, we are approaching scenes of historic greatness, and on the morrow there lies before us the exciting prospect of a first day amid the ruined palaces and indestructible tombs of Persia's greatest sovereigns. At the end of the cliff wall that borders the valley on the right, or north, are hewn in the face of the rock the sepulchres of Darius and his fellow kings, and the pompous bas-reliefs of Shapur. At the base of the hills on the left lie the vanishing ruins of Istakhr, the capital of Darius. Round the corner of these same hills, but fronting in a westerly direction the wide plain of Mervdasht, into which the valley we have been descending here opens, is built out from the mountain side the great platform that sustains the columns of Persepolis and the shattered halls of Darius and of Xerxes. These three sites of ancient fame will be described and examined in the succeeding chapter, which I shall specially devote to a subject that appertains to archæology rather than to travel. Here I shall proceed with the narrative of my journey. The *chapar-khaneh*, which the visitor makes his head-quarters while he inspects the monuments of the Achæmenids, is that of Puzeh, situated at the western extremity of the valley of the Polvar, which flows in a deep gully just below and almost on the site of the ancient Istakhr. Here he is within easy distance of all the ruins; and if the blackened walls, the smoky fire-place, the mud flooring, and the crazy, hingeless door of the *bala-khaneh* of the post-house at Puzeh do not constitute an appetising domicile, at least the wayfarer can reflect, with a positive gush of delight, that this is the last *chapar-khaneh* in which he will be called upon to spend the night in Persia.

The plain of Mervdasht, over which the monarchs of the Medes and Persians looked out as they sat in state in their marble halls, is a flat expanse, about fifteen miles in width from north to south, while its south-easterly extension is said to stretch for forty miles. *Kanats* and irrigation ditches, dug from the river, intersect it in every direction, and have always rendered it a fertile spot; though the decline of modern Persia could not be more pertinently illustrated than by the fact that, whereas in Le Brun's day, not two centuries ago, it contained over eight

The Bund-Amir

hundred villages, this total has now dwindled to fifty; while so inadequate is the control of the water-supply, that the plain often lies half under water, and is converted into stagnant pools and swamps. As I left Persepolis, after completing my study of its ruins, I was obliged to strike back in a north-westerly direction, in order to escape this network of watery trenches. Passing the village of Kushk, I then kept straight forward in a south-westerly line, towards the Pul-i-Khan, a very lofty bridge, with two main arches of irregular size and shape, which crosses the river Kur (the Araxes of the ancients) a little below its confluence with the Polvar.[1] The conjoint stream formed a deep, wide pool below the bridge, and there was more water in it than in any river that I had yet seen in Persia. From the fact that eight miles further down, this river is crossed by a great dam, upon which stands a bridge of thirteen arches, 120 yards in length, the work of an enlightened ruler of the Al-i-Buyah or Dilemi dynasty, known as the Asad-ed-Dowleh, in about 970 A.D., its lower course has received the name of the Bund-Amir[2] (*lit.* dyke of the Amir), or Bendemeer of Moore, whose rhapsodical description of its charms I shall allow myself, almost alone among modern writers on Persia, the luxury of not quoting.

From here the road continues towards the mountains that fringe the plain of Mervdasht on the south-west side, and, entering a deep bay in these, proceeds for a distance of some miles over an expanse that is occupied, in the rainy season, by a marsh, across which the track is carried for over

Approach to Shiraz

[1] Higher up the Kur, whose main source is the Chashmeh-i-Durdaneh, is known successively as the Asupas and Ḳamfiruz. Eight *farsakhs* above the Pul-i-Khan it is dammed by the Bund-i-Nasiri, so called from the reigning Shah, who in 1890 repaired a structure, originally erected by the Achæmenian kings, and frequently restored since. The Polvar, whose course I have followed, and which flows in above the Pul-i-Khan, is the Medus of the ancients, and the Faruab or Puruab of Persian geographers. After the confluence the river is called the Kur. Two *farsakhs* lower down is the celebrated dam of Asad-ed-Dowleh, from which the river derives its title in these lower reaches of Bund-Amir. Five more dams obstruct its course and divert its waters, before the remainder finally falls into the great salt lake of Bakhtegan (called by the natives Bichegan), or Niriz. *Vide* 'Notes on the Kur River' by A. H. Schindler in *Proceedings of the R. G. S.*, vol. xiii. p. 287 (1891).

[2] The dam was visited and described by J. P. Morier (1811), *Second Journey*, p. 73; Sir W. Ouseley (1811), *Travels*, vol. ii. p. 180–5; C. J. Rich (1821), *Journey to Persepolis*, p. 261.

TENG-I-ALLAHU AKBAR, SHIRAZ

a mile upon a narrow and irregular causeway. Turning a sharp corner to the left, we presently arrive at the village of Zerghun, famous for its muleteers, built at the base of a rocky chain. From a distance of about three miles from Zerghun, to the very outskirts of Shiraz—for this is the last stage that separates us from the capital of Fars—the post-road is one of the stoniest and most disagreeable in Persia. Its course lies over a succession of mountain ridges, in whose valleys and undulations, and over whose peaks and crests, it is conducted in a line that in many places resembles a torrent-bed rather than a made road. The ground is completely covered with loose stones and boulders, from the size of an orange to the dimensions of a football; and riding over these, particularly at any pace, is one of the most painful of human experiences. Rather more than half-way in a naked mountain-plain, at a spot called Bajgah, or Place of the Tolls, from the fact that there was formerly a station here of *rahdars*, or toll-gatherers upon the *kafilahs* or caravans, is a large, forlorn-looking caravanserai (mentioned by Thévenot in 1666) with a tank of water in front. It is after crossing the subsequent ridge of the Kuh-i-Bamu that we notice, by the roadside, a tiny channel filled with running water that accompanies us for some distance on our march. Lest none should guess it, let me say that this slender rivulet is no less a stream than the Ruknabad, which, rising in the hills twelve miles away, races gaily down to Shiraz, and was celebrated by the patriotic Hafiz in terms that would lead one to expect some less insignificant channel.

Teng-i-Allahu Akbar

It was with no slight relief that, two and three-quarter hours after leaving Zerghun, and while descending the ultimate ridge of this seemingly interminable chain, I caught sight, in the opening of a mountain pass, of a great cluster of solemn cypresses, and, below, the shimmer of mingled smoke and mist that floated above the roofs of a large town, lying in the hollow of a considerable plain. This was Shiraz, which, in the words of its own singer, Sadi, 'turns aside the heart of the traveller from his native land;' Shiraz, the home of poets, and rose-bowers, and nightingales, the haunt of jollity, and the Elysian fields of love, praised in a hundred odes as the fairest gem of Iran. So overwhelmed with astonishment at the beauty of the panorama is the wayfarer expected to be, that even the pass takes its name of Teng-i-Allahu Akbar, the Pass of God is Most Great, from the expression that is supposed to leap to his lips as he gazes upon the entrancing spectacle. I confess that my own gratitude to Providence bore far less relation to the view, in which I saw nothing very wonderful, than to the relief which I experienced at having reached the end of this section of my journey. In the Sefavi days, an aqueduct brought water into Shiraz down this pass, but is now in complete ruin. In the rock on the right-hand side of the road is sculped here a bas-relief of Fath Ali Shah, smoking a *kalian* with two of his sons; and hard by is another of Rustam transfixing a lion which holds a man in its claws. The end of this pass was formerly fortified and completely filled by an arched gateway, stretching from mountain to mountain. This gateway fell into ruin, but was rebuilt by Zeki Khan, who was Vizier of Shiraz in 1820, in the style and manner apparent in the accompanying photograph. In the upper storey, above the arch, is a chamber, containing, upon a desk surrounded by a wooden rail, a ponderous and monumental Koran. This colossal manuscript, which is said to weigh seventeen *mans*, or eight stone, and of which it is popularly believed that if one leaf were withdrawn, it would equal in weight the entire volume, is variously reported to have been written by the younger Ali or Imam Zein-el-Abidin (Ornament of the Pious), the son of Husein, or by Sultan Ibrahim, the son of Shah Rukh, and grandson of Timur. One may be reconciled to either legend, according as one prefers a sacred or a secular authorship.

View of the city

In the Sefavean days a species of Chehar Bagh, or broad avenue, planted with cypresses, adorned with marble basins of water in the middle, and lined with rows of walled gardens, entered by arched pavilions, led from the mountain gate to a bridge over the stream that flows outside the city walls. Almost all traces of this approach have disappeared, and the intervening stretch of road is bare and desolate. The stream was all but dry at the time of my visit, though, when the snows melt, it sometimes contains a good deal of water. The panorama of the modern town contains nothing of distinction except three blue domes appearing above a crumbling wall and numerous enclosures thickly planted with cypresses, which seem, in their sable stoles, to mourn like funeral mutes over a vanished past. A low wall of mud, flanked with semicircular towers—both of them in a state of ruin—describes a circumference of between three and four miles, although in the security of modern times the suburbs

PANORAMA OF SHIRAZ

have encroached upon and obscured the outlines of the earlier city. The valley in which Shiraz lies is about ten miles in width by thirty in length, and is completely surrounded by mountains, whose snows in winter heighten the funereal contrast of the cypress-spires. The population, which stood at 50,000 under Kerim Khan Vekil, 120 years ago, has not greatly fluctuated during the present century, but has usually been reckoned at 20,000 to 30,000; figures which indicate the stationary condition of the modern city.[1]

History

I find in most histories that Shiraz (variously derived from *shir* = milk, or *shir* = lion, an allusion in the one case to the richness of its pastures, in the other to the prowess of its people) was founded in 694 A.D., i.e. subsequent to the Arab conquest, by Mohammed, son of Yusuf Zekfi. I cannot, however, accept this as a correct version of the earliest foundation, for I regard it as more than probable that there was a city here both of the Achæmenian and Sassanian kings. To a very early and ante-Mussulman origin must be ascribed the castle on the northern mountain and the great well, of which I shall speak presently. Again, there are, within a slight distance of the modern city—which, like all Persian towns, has shifted its site somewhat at different times—remains both of Achæmenian and Sassanian sculptures, which invariably herald the neighbourhood of a royal residence or capital. The former are of the same character and age as the Persepolitan edifices, and are thought by some to have been bodily removed from the Takht-i-Jamshid, while others have been inclined to see in them a later reproduction; the latter are inferior editions of the great bas-reliefs elsewhere encountered and described.[2] I am supported in my belief by the ingenious Herbert,

[1] For accounts of Shiraz in addition to (1) the works mentioned for the route Teheran to Isfahan; (2) the works mentioned upon Isfahan; (3) the works mentioned for the route Isfahan to Shiraz, nearly all of which include descriptions of the latter city, *vide* C. Niebuhr (1765), *Voyage en Arabie*, vol. ii. pp. 91–7, 135–144; W. Franklin (1786-7), *Observations on a Tour*, pp. 51–108; J. Scott Waring (1802), *Tour to Sheeraz*, caps. vi. to x.; C. J. Rich (1821), *Journey to Persepolis*, p. 224 *et seq.*; (Sir) C. MacGregor (1875), *Journey through Khorasan*, vol. i. cap. ii.; C. J. Wills (circ. 1880), *In the Land, etc.*, p. 218 *et seq.*

[2] The earlier remains consist of three portals of stone, with human figures chiselled in relief on the inner side of the jambs, situated on a hill about four miles south-east of Shiraz. They were formerly called Mader-i-Suleiman, and were described by Niebuhr, Ouseley (*Travels*, vol. ii. pp. 41–6), Ker Porter (*Travels*, vol. i. p. 706), and Flandin, *Voyage en Perse*, vol. i., pl. 55. Binning in 1851 found that they were known as Takht-i-Abu Nasir, Schindler in 1878 Takht-i-Bukhtun-

although I cannot say that the evidences of antiquity which he cites would stand the test of the modern scientific school.

> Here art magick was first hatched ; here Nimrod for some time lived ; here Cyrus, the most excellent of Heathen Princes, was born ; and here (all but his head, which was sent to Pisigard) intombed. Here the Great Macedonian glutted his avarice and Bacchism. Here the first Sibylla sung our Saviour's incarnation. Hence the Magi are thought to have set out towards Bethlehem, and here a series of 200 Kings have swayed their scepters.

However, no other record that I am aware of, beyond those before mentioned, exists of this ancient Shiraz. The later city was much improved and beautified by the Dilemi rulers, of whom the Samsam-ed-Dowleh, son of the famous Asad-ed-Dowleh, was the first to surround it with a wall, twelve miles in circuit, while the channel of Ruknabad had already been excavated and named by the Rukn-ed-Dowleh, father of the latter prince. The various dynasties of Atabegs, whom I have previously described, and who governed Fars, with Shiraz as their capital, still further adorned the city. Towers were added to the wall by Sherif-ed-Din Mahmud Shah. Ibn Batutah, in about 1330, said that its most celebrated mosque was that of Ahmed ibn Musa, a brother of Imam Reza, in which also was the tomb of Abu Abdullah, who wandered about Ceylon with a sanctity so well established that it was recognised even by the elephants. The mercy of Jenghiz Khan, and the vengeance of Timur have already been recorded. Nevertheless, the city continued to grow in size and importance—as a memory of which, in later days, the vainglorious saying arose, 'When Shiraz was Shiraz, Cairo was one of its suburbs'—until the Venetian Josafa Barbaro, in 1474, represented it as twenty miles in circumference, including the outskirts, while his countryman, Angiolello, said that it contained 200,000 inhabitants, and was larger and more

Nasr. Mme. Dieulafoy in 1881 reported that the stones had been upset by a recent governor digging underneath them for the treasure which Persians invariably connect with inscriptions that they cannot read. *Vide* also Stolze, vol ii. pl. 96, and Perrot and Chipiez, *Histoire de l'Art*, vol. v. p. 754. The Sassanian sculptures are situated a little further on, nearer the Maharlu lake, and consist of three tablets, sculped in the rock above a pool. They were described by Chardin, Thévenot, Kaempfer, Mandelslo, Le Brun, etc., under the title Kadamgah, but are called by Binning Naksh-i-Burmedillek, i.e. Barm-i-dilek from the name of the pool. *Vide* Flandin, *ibid.* pl. 56, and Stolze, *ibid.* pl. 145.

beautiful than the capital of the Mamelukes. With the disappearance of local dynasties, and the centralisation of Persia, that followed upon the accession of the Sefavi line, Shiraz lost much of its importance; although the rule of Imam Kuli Khan, the celebrated Governor of Fars under Shah Abbas, invested it with almost the distinction of a capital; while the subject rivalled his sovereign at Isfahan in the beautification of his seat of government. The old walls, seven miles round, were still standing in 1627, when Herbert passed through the city; but these had disappeared in the time of Tavernier and Chardin; and the march of decay, assisted by a severe inundation in 1668, had made such wholesale inroads that both writers described Shiraz as little better than a ruin. So the town remained for nearly a century, the ferocity of the Afghans and the anarchy that attended the fall of Nadir, accentuating its decline; until, in the hands of a second powerful and liberal-minded viceroy, it enjoyed a bright spell of rejuvenescence. This was Kerim Khan Zend, who, ruling at Shiraz as Vekil or Regent, on behalf of a Sefavi puppet, from 1751 to 1779, was practically sovereign of all Persia. He rebuilt the walls of stone, with bastions, twenty-eight feet high and ten feet thick, dug a deep fosse outside, and adorned the interior with a citadel and palace, and with beautiful mosques, *madressehs*, caravanserais, and bazaars. Indeed, whatever of stateliness or elegance remains in modern Shiraz, may almost as certainly be attributed to Kerim Khan, as in other Persian cities it must be to Shah Abbas; and the two are among the few monarchs of Iran who have deserved well of their country. After the death of Kerim Khan, there was a brief revival of the halcyon days under the ill-fated Lutf Ali Khan, at which time (1789) Sir Harford Jones, British Resident at Baghdad, was the guest and friend of that unfortunate prince at Shiraz. The triumph of the Kajars and their eunuch chieftain, Agha Mohammed Khan, involved a sure retribution upon the capital of the Zends. Its stone walls were levelled to the ground and replaced by the present mean erections of mud; the ditch was filled up; and Shiraz was degraded from the rank and appearance of a capital to that of a provincial town. Its government, however, remained an appanage of royalty, and has usually been held by a member of the reigning family. Fath Ali Shah was Governor-General of Fars during his uncle's lifetime. When Shah himself, he deputed more than one of his sons to the post, one of these,

Husein Ali Mirza, the Firman Firma, utilising the position to embark upon an independent rebellion when the old king died in 1834. The speedy discomfiture of this pretender I have already related. He died, soon after, in Teheran; but three of his sons fled to England, where, for political reasons, they were much fêted, Mr. Baillie Fraser, the Persian traveller, acting as their cicerone,[1] and were ultimately pensioned. In the present reign the office has been filled by various of the Shah's relatives, the most conspicuous of whom was one of his uncles, Ferhad Mirza, who, twenty years ago, earned a widespread reputation for bad government but pitiless severity, and whose son now fills the post with moderation and popularity. Fars was one of the many governments united in the person of the Zil-es-Sultan ten years ago, and was nominally administered by his son, the Jelal-ed-Dowleh, then a mere boy, the leading-strings being committed to the wealthy but extortionate noble known as the Sahib Diwan, who has lately been nominated to Meshed. In his long reign the Shah has never once visited Shiraz.

The Ark

The interior features of the city are not to be compared for size or splendour with those of the more northern capitals. The Ark or citadel is a fortified enclosure eighty yards square, surrounded by lofty mud walls, with towers at the four corners adorned with bricks arranged in patterns. Its interior is occupied by the courtyards and pavilions of the governor's residence, which struck me as in no sense remarkable. When, upon his courteous initiative, I paid a visit to the Motemed-ed-Dowleh, the present Governor, I passed through two large garden-courts, one of which contained a marble dado of warriors sculped in relief and painted, a relic of the palace of Kerim Khan. The Governor, who is a first cousin of the Shah, is a man of about fifty years of age, tall, urbane, of polished manner and address, speaking French and familiar with European habits and politics, having, as he told me, visited Europe four times, and having accompanied the Shah in 1873. He also possessed a French-speaking secretary. In conversation he showed a thorough acquaintance with the strategical situation in Persia, and very rightly ridiculed a Bushire-Shiraz railway as preposterous. As I have said, he enjoys a good reputation, and is much liked by the English residents at Shiraz. The

[1] He wrote the record of their visit, *Narrative of the Persian Princes in London* (2 vols. 1838).

interests of the latter are officially represented in the city by the Nawab Haider Ali Khan, a member of a distinguished family once prominent in the Deccan, but for many years resident in Persia.

One face of the palace fronts the principal Meidan, which is a desolate expanse containing a number of guns.[1] On its northern side is a large building, now occupied by the Indo-European and Persian Telegraph establishments, but formerly the *diwan-khaneh*, or audience-chamber, of the palace of Kerim Khan. An arched gateway opens from the square on to a fine garden, containing a *hauz* or tank, at whose upper end, on a platform, the face of which is adorned with sculptured bas-reliefs in marble, is the large recessed chamber, now filled with official bureaux and counters, that once held the twisted marble columns and the Takht-i-Marmor, or Marble Throne, previously described as standing in the *talar* or throne-room at Teheran, whither they were removed a hundred years ago by Agha Mohammed.

Old Palace

From the Meidan, access is gained to the Bazaar-i-Vekil, or Regent's Bazaar, an enduring monument of the public-spirited rule of Kerim Khan. This bazaar, which is the finest in Persia, consists of a covered avenue, built of yellow burnt bricks, and arched at the top, about five hundred yards in total length. It is crossed by a shorter transept, 120 yards long, a rotunda or circular domed place marking the point of intersection, where are a cistern and a platform above it, at which the merchants meet for talk or consultation. From the bazaar, gateways lead into extensive caravanserais, the most spacious of which appeared to be that occupied by the Persian Custom-house. In the Bazaar-i-Vekil were all the din and jabber, the crush and jostle, of an Eastern mart, which is the focus of city life in the daytime, and is apt to give to a stranger an exaggerated impression of the volume of business. In the increased activity, however, of the southern trade-routes in Persia in recent years, Shiraz, both as a consuming and as an export market, has borne its share. An immense trade in all European goods has sprung up with Bombay, most of the Persian merchants having agents in that city. The chief imports are cotton fabrics from Manchester; woollen tissues from Austria and Germany; loaf sugar from Marseilles (Russian loaf sugar stopping short at

Bazaar and trade

[1] There were reported to me to be only 1,800 infantry and 300 artillery in the province.

Isfahan); raw sugar from Java and Mauritius; French, German and Austrian cutlery and crockery; copper sheets from England and Holland; tea from India, Java, Ceylon, and China, and candles from Amsterdam. I found the Shirazis very apprehensive of the opening of the new trade route by the Karun, which, without interfering with their local traffic, would, if it superseded the Teheran-Bushire line as the main commercial avenue into Persia from the south, destroy their transit trade altogether. I had myself quite sufficient confidence in the temperate pace at which progress advances in Iran to assure them that there was no immediate ground for alarm. So obstinate is custom in the East, that to kill a caravan track that has been followed for a century is no slight undertaking. I found the chief exports to consist of opium, 10,000 to 15,000 cases of which were said to be despatched yearly from the neighbourhoods of Shiraz and Yezd; cotton, pressed in Bushire and sold in Bombay; dried fruits, especially almonds and apricots; and the famous *tumbaku*, or tobacco of Shiraz, of which the local crops appeared to be, for the most part, locally consumed, the bulk of the export to Syria and Turkey coming from other districts. The wine, for which Shiraz is famous, is also in such extensive local demand as to leave no residue for exportation.

Vintage of Shiraz

Of the vintage of Shiraz I shall have something to say in a later chapter upon the resources and products of Persia. I may here mention that there are two varieties, a red and a white wine, which are stored in jars and sold in glass bottles of curious shape, locally manufactured. I thought that some old Shiraz wine which I tasted was by far the best that I had drunk in Persia, an opinion which has apparently been shared by others before me, seeing that, two centuries ago, John Struys plaintively remarked that it was 'held in such esteem that it was as dear as Canary Sack in the Low Countreys,' whilst Dr. Fryer, who may be supposed to have given a more scientific verdict, observed :—

> The Wines of the Growth of this Country are esteemed the most Stomachical and Generous in all Persia, and fittest for common drinking, when allayed a little with Water, otherwise too heady for the Brain and heavy for the Stomach, their Passage being retarded for want of that proper Vehicle. It is incredible to see what quantities they drink at a merry meeting, and how unconcerned the next day they appear, and

brisk about their Business, and will quaff you thus a whole week together.[1]

Worthy doctor! His genial testamur would have raised a tempest about his ears, and have provoked a fortnight's controversy in the 'Times,' had it been proffered in another country nearer home at the latter end of the nineteenth century.

Among the other manufactures of Shiraz which came under my notice, and for which the place is famous, are the enamelled bowls and stems of *kalians* or water-pipes, *repoussé* silver work, of which very elegant frames and salt-cellars with Oriental designs are fabricated for European customers; *khatem bandi*, a species of mosaic work in wood, brass, silver, ivory, and stained bone, small fragments of which are fixed in a bed of glue, and then planed smooth, the strips being fitted together as the sides and lids of very pretty boxes; seals, engraved on cornelians and other stones; and jewellery. Of the natural products I may mention the moss-roses and the *bulbul* or nightingale, which appears to be almost the precise counterpart of the English bird.

Other manufactures

Shiraz, like most Persian cities, has its epithet of personal glorification, which is in this case Dar-el-Ilm, or Abode of Science, a pretension for which I should have thought that its notoriously convivial habits would have admittedly disqualified it. Nevertheless, for a city of its present size, it is well supplied with religious edifices, although these, alike by their size and decay, tell the story of a deposed capital rather than of a devout population.[2] The oldest mosque is the Musjid-i-Jama, built in 875 A.D. by Amru bin Leith, brother and successor of the famous Yakub of that name. But little remains of the original structure, the whole being in a shocking state of ruin from earthquakes and the ravages of time; but in the centre of the main court is a small, square, stone building, reported to be a copy of the Kaaba at Mecca, with circular towers at the corners, presenting in blue Kufic inscriptions round their summits the date 1450 A.D. This curious edifice is known as the Khoda-Khaneh, or House of

Mosques and colleges

[1] *Travels in Persia*, p. 245. Compare Chardin, *Voyages* (edit. Langlès), vol. viii. pp. 436–7; Kaempfer, *Amœn. Exot.*, pp. 376–381, and Franklin, *Observations on Tour*, vol. iii. p. 17.

[2] The only good account that I know of the buildings of Shiraz at the present day is contained in Mme. Dieulafoy's book, accompanied by admirable illustrations. *La Perse*, cap. xxiv.

God. In the walls of the main fabric is also inserted a block of porphyry which is looked upon as a sacred stone. Another old building, in spite of its name, viz. the Musjid-i-No, or New Mosque, an immensely large edifice, is in rather a better state of preservation, having luckily escaped the worst earthquakes. This mosque, which consists of a flat-roofed cloister round a court, is said to have been originally the palace of the Atabegs; but to have been converted to the worship of God by one of those princes named Ali bu Said in 1226 A.D., the *mullahs*, whom he had consulted upon the illness of his son, having instructed him to devote to the service of Allah his most valued possession. The only fabrics, however, in anything approaching repair are those erected by Kerim Khan, the most beautiful of which is the Musjid-i-Vekil near the Meidan, left unfinished by the Regent at his death and never yet completed. A *madresseh* also survives and is still frequently designated by his name; while another, styled the Madresseh-i-Baba Khan, in the vegetable market, is deserted and in ruins, although retaining traces of magnificence. The decorative treatment of Kerim Khan's buildings is less conventional and more secular in type than that of the earlier Mohammedan mosques, bunches of roses and flowers and bright colours being largely employed in the eighteenth century *faïence*, which depended more upon the splendour of polychrome than upon hieratic correctness. The largest of the domes of Shiraz, which are all of a somewhat elongated pattern, that has been irreverently compared to the head of a big asparagus, is that of Shah Chiragh, at no great distance from the Ark. It contains the tomb of one of the sons of Imam Musa, behind a silver grating. Other notable tombs are those of Seyid Mir Ahmed, in a good state of preservation, and of Seyid Allah-ed-Din Husein, another son of Imam Musa, which was described by Buckingham in 1816 as the then finest building in Shiraz. The tomb of Shah Mirza Hamza, outside the walls on the north, which was restored by Kerim Khan, has almost fallen to pieces, and its once conspicuous cupola has collapsed.

People and life

The life and beauty of Shiraz were always, however, extra-mural in character and location, and were centred in the umbrageous gardens and beside the poets' graves that have won for it such a place in the realm of song. The superb climate of the southern capital admitted of an almost wholly out-of-door existence; while the vivacious temperament of its people disposed them to jollity and to a life of light-hearted nonchalance and gay carousal. The people of Fars pride themselves upon the purity of their origin, the correctness of their tongue, and the excellence of their wit. No doubt we encounter here a less mixed Iranian type than elsewhere, as is evident from the darker complexions and clear-cut features, the brown hair and blue or grey eyes of the northern provinces being rarely met with in the south. 'In all my life,' said the amiable Herbert, who gleefully welcomed the opportunity of bursting into doggerel, 'I never saw people more jocund and less quarrelsome:—

They revel all the night, and drink the round
Till wine and sleep their giddy brains confound.'

Others have been more sceptical about the second attribute; the excitability of the Shirazi being a property that renders him sensitive and irritable, and sometimes prone to outbursts of intolerance. The Babi movement started here, and has always claimed a large number of disciples.

The character of Persian gardens, for its number and quality of which Shiraz has always been renowned, is, as I have explained in other chapters, very different from the European pattern.

Gardens

From the outside, a square or oblong enclosure is visible, enclosed by a high mud wall, over the top of which appears a dense bouquet of trees. The interior is thickly planted with these, or, as Herbert phrased it, 'with lofty pyramidal cypresses, broad spreading chenawrs, tough elm, straight ash, knotty pines, fragrant masticks, kingly oaks, sweet myrtles, useful maples.' They are planted down the sides of long alleys, admitting of no view but a vista, the surrounding plots being a jungle of bushes and shrubs. Water courses along in channels or is conducted into tanks. Sometimes these gardens rise in terraces to a pavilion at the summit, whose reflection in the pool below is regarded as a triumph of landscape gardening. There are no neat walks, or shaped flower-beds, or stretches of sward. All is tangled and untrimmed. Such beauty as arises from shade and the purling of water is all that the Persian requires. Here he comes with a party, or his family, or his friends; they establish themselves under the trees, and, with smoking, and tea-drinking, and singing, wile away the idle hour. Of such a character are the gardens of Shiraz.

The most northerly of these, at a distance of about one and a half mile from the city, is that known as the Bagh-i-Takht, i.e. Garden of the Throne, or Takht-i-Kajar, i.e. Throne of the Kajars. A palace was first built on this site by one of the Salghur Atabegs, named Karajeh, and was called from him Takht-i-Karajieh. Seven hundred years later Agha Mohammed Khan Kajar commenced the rebuilding of a palace on the same site, whose name, by a slight verbal transposition, became Takht-i-Kajarieh. The building was completed by Fath Ali, when Governor of Fars, and was occupied for three months by the Mission of Sir Gore Ouseley, in 1811, when on their way to the Persian capital. It stood, as the name indicates, upon the hillside, the conformation of the latter being utilised to construct seven terraces, one above the other, faced with tiles, with a long *hauz* or tank, called the *dariacheh*, or little sea, at the bottom, and a two-storeyed edifice at the summit. The whole is now in a state of utter ruin. The wall is broken down, the alleys, planted with orange trees, are unkempt and deserted, the pavilion is falling to pieces. In common with many other of the gardens of Shiraz, this is Crown property; but the notorious parsimony of the Shah forbids him from issuing funds adequate for their maintenance; and accordingly decay makes unimpeded progress.

Bagh-i-Takht

I also visited the Bagh-i-No, or New Garden, on the right of the Isfahan road, leading down into Shiraz. It was new about seventy years ago, when it was constructed, with the usual features of walks, canals, and cascades, by Husein Ali Mirza, son of Fath Ali Shah. In one of its *imarets*, or pavilions, was a portrait of the latter monarch, seated in state, and receiving the British Mission of Sir John Malcolm. The walled enclosure is still filled with cypress and fruit-trees; but I found the summer palace at the top in a state of complete ruin, the wood-work crumbling away and the painting and stucco peeling off the walls. Water remained in a large circular tank, but was covered with an unsightly scum.

Bagh-i-No

On the other side of the Isfahan road, and a little above the Hafizieh, is the Jehan Nemah,[1] or Displayer of the World, which was known as the Bagh-i-Vekil in the time of Kerim Khan, but changed its name under Fath Ali, who, when Governor of Fars,

[1] Dr. Wills has explained it as Bagh-i-Jan-i-ma, i.e. Garden of our Souls, but this is wrong.

built a summer-house here. It occupies a walled enclosure, about 200 yards square, but contains little beyond cypresses and ruin. In the early part of the century its central pavilion, or Kolah Feringhi, was in good repair, and was assigned to English travellers of distinction, of whom C. J. Rich, British Resident at Baghdad and the explorer of Kurdistan, died there of cholera, on October 5, 1821, and was buried in the garden.

Jehan Nemah

Higher up, on the same side of the road, is the Dilgusha or Heart's Ease, which was laid out by Haji Ibrahim, when *Kalantar*, over a hundred years ago, and is irrigated by a stream that flows down from the Sadieh, a little above. In 1811 Morier reported it as in a state of ruin; but when I visited it in 1889 it was in better repair than any other garden in the outskirts of Shiraz, having passed into the hands of the Sahib Diwan. Its alleys and trees and tank were in good condition, and a large party of closely-veiled Persian ladies, waddling along like bales of blue cotton set up on end, had been spending an agreeable afternoon under its shade.

Dilgusha

But, after all, the chief suburban glory of Shiraz is neither its cypresses, nor its tanks, nor its gardens, but its two poets' graves. The literature of a country never produced two more differently constituted exponents than Sadi and Hafiz, nor two whose opposite temperaments and philosophy appealed more closely to the moralising and the lighter-hearted instincts of their countrymen. Perhaps it is the predominance of the latter ingredient in the composition, at least, of the inhabitants of Fars, that has accounted for Hafiz' greater popularity. Sheikh Maslah-ed-Din, surnamed Sadi, was the elder by a century. Born at Shiraz in 1193 A.D. (some say in 1184), he lived to little short of one hundred years, although his enthusiastic countrymen have sometimes credited him with a considerable excess above the century. He was one of the greatest travellers of the Middle Ages. There were few countries between the Mediterranean and Hindustan that he did not explore in the guise of a dervish, being taken prisoner by the Crusaders in Palestine, making the pilgrimage to Mecca fourteen times, and assuming the religion of Vishnu in India in order to extend his knowledge. Well might he say of himself —and I cannot imagine a better traveller's motto—'I have wandered through many regions of the world, and everywhere have I mingled with the people. In each corner I have gathered

Sadi and Hafiz

something of good. From every sheaf I have gleaned an ear.' Returning from his peregrinations, the poet resided for the last thirty years of his life at his native city, devoting himself to literary production, of which his 'Gulistan,' or Rose Garden, and his 'Bostan,' or Fruit Garden, are the most famous. Sadi had not been long dead when Hafiz was born; this being the poetical sobriquet worn by Mohammed Shems-ed-Din, also of Shiraz. Of his life we know little, but his mingled vein of gaiety and mysticism, expressed in a hundred odes and sonnets, in praise of wine, women, music, and love, with a higher strain of allegory sometimes lurking behind, have endeared him to his emotional countrymen, while they alternately remind us of the odes of Horace and the Song of Solomon. It is disputed by erudite Persians whether the efforts of Hafiz' more abandoned Muse are to be literally or figuratively interpreted. For my own part, I would not inflict upon the genial memory of the poet the affront of misconstruction that has twisted the beautiful epithalamium of Solomon into an incomprehensible rhapsody about the Church. Hafiz died and was buried at Shiraz in A.D. 1388.

Tomb of Sadi

The Sadieh, or enclosure that holds the tomb of Sadi, is at the distance of about one mile from the town in a north-easterly direction, and lies just under the mountains. A garden precedes a building, containing some small rooms in the centre, and an arched *diwan* on either side, in one of which, with plain, whitewashed, unpretentious walls, behind a tall brass lattice or screen, reposes the sarcophagus of the poet.[1] This is an oblong chest of stone, open at the top, and covered with Arabic inscriptions. A friendly green-turbaned *seyid* did the honours of the place. A hundred years ago, when Franklin saw it, this tomb, which is the original fabric, was covered with a very ancient wooden case, painted black and inscribed with an ode of Sadi. In 1811, also, Ouseley saw a lid lying near; but I did not observe any such addition. In Tavernier's time (1665) the tomb 'had been very fair; but it runs to ruine.' Kerim Khan restored the building, without altering the sarcophagus; but at the beginning of the present century it had again fallen into such decay that Scott Waring in 1802 and Sir John Malcolm in 1810 offered to repair it at their own expense. It has since been subjected to some sort

[1] Illustrations of it are given by Ouseley, vol. ii. plate xxv., and Mme. Dieulafoy, p. 429.

of restoration, but even now has a forlorn and friendless look. Hard by is a descent by a long flight of steps to a subterranean well, containing fish that are or were regarded as sacred to Sadi, the water proceeding from a *kanat* that subsequently irrigates the garden of Dilgusha.

Above the Sadieh is a place in the mountain known as Gahwareh-i-Div or Demon's Cradle, from a fissure or channel, leading to an arched passage, cut in the rock. A little to the east on the summit of a peak are the few surviving remains of a castle commonly called Kaleh-i-Bander (Ouseley says it is properly Fahender) supposed to have been a Sassanian

Castle and wells

TOMB OF SADI

structure. Here, too, are two wells, whose shafts are hewn to an immense depth in the solid limestone of the mountains. The largest, which is commonly called Chah Ali Bunder, is of unknown or uncertain depth. Chardin said he rehearsed a *paternoster* before a stone reached the bottom. Le Brun reported 420 feet and Stack 500 feet, but Morier's servant claimed to have measured a depth of 350 yards, while Dr. Wills let down 600 yards of string and never reached the bottom. I merely mention these conflicting estimates as illustrations of the ambiguity that is found in travellers' descriptions of almost every site or object in Persia. The seventeenth century writers said that in former days women convicted of adultery were pitched down this well; but Dr. Wills speaks of this summary mode of execution as a recent practice.

Whatever be the history or origin of these remarkable shafts, for which of course the natives have a miraculous explanation, they undoubtedly appertain to a time long anterior to Mussulman days, when the hill in which they are sunk was occupied by a considerable fortress and used as a place of strength. The third well, which is called Chah-i-Murtaza Ali, is situated in a grotto hewn out of the rock, and is visited by pilgrims who regard its waters as sacred.

TOMB OF HAFIZ

Tomb of Hafiz

Nearer the city, and on the outskirts of its northern suburbs, the tomb of Hafiz stands in a cemetery crowded with Moslem graves. The enclosure, known as the Hafizieh, consists of an upper and a lower part, i.e. the graveyard and a garden, separated by a summer-house. The cemetery is of comparatively modern growth; for ancient authors describe the poet's tomb as surrounded by trees, the last survivor of which, a cypress, said to have been planted by himself at the head of his grave, was cut down about 1814 A.D. The copy of the poet's works that was once chained to the tomb was carried off by Ashraf the Afghan. Nadir Shah, having come here and been opportunely presented with an encouraging *fal* or fortune from the manuscript kept by the *mullahs*,[1] embellished and repaired the tomb. But the original

[1] This practice, an Oriental counterpart of the *Sortes Virgilianæ* (rendered

marble slab on which was said to have been sculped a cypress, was taken away by Kerim Khan, who built it into the tank in the Jehan Nemah, and replaced it by the present sarcophagus. This is made of yellow Yezd marble, and has two odes from the Diwan, or collection of the poet's works, beautifully chiselled in relief in a number of elegant panels upon its lid.[1] Of that which is sculped on the centre panels I have made a translation in elegiacs, a metre that seems to me to do least offence to the structure and spirit of the original :—

Tell the glad tidings abroad that my soul may arise in communion,
    I, with celestial wings, rise from the snares of the world.
Didst thou but call me to come and wait as a slave on thy bidding,
    Yet should I rise in esteem over the lords of the world.
Lord, may the cloud of Thy mercy descend in raindrops upon me,
    Now ere my body arise, scattered as dust on the wind.
Sit on my tomb, ye friends, with mirth of minstrel and flagon,
    So shall I rise from the grave dancing, aglow with desire.
Though I be old, one night do thou lie in my loving embraces,
    Then from thy side in the morn fresh in my youth shall I rise.
Image of deeds that are lovely, on high shine forth, that as Hafiz
    I from the grave may arise, soar above life and the world.

A frail iron railing now surrounds the tomb, which is visited by bands of admiring pilgrims, on devotional or festive aim intent; but I confess I think that in any other country in the world a greater distinction would encompass the last resting-place of a national hero and the object of adoration to millions. It is interesting to contrast the grave of the Persian poet with that of his European contemporary, Dante, whose sepulchre is not less an object of pilgrimage at Ravenna.

Adjoining the Hafizieh are two other enclosures, which are also consecrated by much-respected graves. Of these, one is the Chehel Tan, or Forty Bodies, so called from forty dervishes who were there interred, and were, I suppose, very eminent personages in their day. The other is the Haft Tan, or Seven Bodies, built by Kerim Khan over the remains of seven

Dervishes' graves

so famous by the stories of Charles I. and Lord Falkland), and which consisted in drawing an omen by opening at random the pages of the poet, was in existence even during the lifetime of Hafiz. It has been described by most writers, best by Binning, vol. i. pp. 222–5.

[1] There is an excellent engraving of this in W. Price's *Narrative of Embassy to Persia* (1811).

other holy persons, as well, it is said, as of Sultan Shuja, one of the old princes of Fars. The pavilion at the upper end of this garden contains, or contained (for I did not see its interior), a number of paintings of Bible scenes (e.g. Abraham and Isaac, Moses tending Jethro's flocks, etc.), as well as two illustrations of Sadi and Hafiz. These pictures are of no antiquity, nor is there any reason to suppose that they are likenesses. Sadi is depicted as an old man with a white beard, an axe over his shoulder, and a dervish's begging-bowl in his right hand. Hafiz is a much younger man, with an immense pair of black moustaches and a huge club.[1]

Such is a fairly complete summary of the buildings and charms, or shall I not rather say the ruins and mourning, of modern Shiraz. It is, perhaps, difficult for a foreigner to place himself in the precise mental or emotional environment that would enable him to comprehend the extraordinary effect which these have long exercised, and continue to exercise, over the imagination of Persians. I can believe that in spring-time, when the plain is a sea of verdure, and the brooks dispense a welcome coolness as they run beneath the trees, and a brilliant sun shines from the undimmed sky, the gardens of Shiraz may constitute an agreeable retreat. But it is impossible to avoid the conclusion that, in the eyes of the Shirazi, every local goose is a swan, and that there neither is nor has been in the site and surroundings of the city anything to excite such extravagance of laudation. The place is very liable to earthquakes, by one of which in 1855 half the houses are said to have been destroyed, and 10,000 persons to have perished. Some writers, notably Kinneir and Rich (the latter little thinking that he was going to die there), have extolled the climate of Shiraz as among the finest in the world; but this opinion does not appear to be altogether shared by modern European residents. The atmosphere is dry, and certainly far more equable than in the north; but intermittent fever is very rife, and is attributed by some to miasma arising from the abundance of stagnant water.

Local patriotism

About seven miles in a south-easterly direction from the city is a swamp, called Karabagh, from the mountains by which it is overhung on the south. Here, in the reed-beds and on the marsh, I

[1] Copies of these pictures are given by Ouseley, vol. ii. plate lv., and Colonel Johnson, *Journey from India*, p. 59.

enjoyed a good day's snipe-shooting, there being a great number of birds. This marsh lies at the upper end of a valley, the lower extremity of which is filled by the salt-lake of Maharlu, some twenty miles in length, into which flows the stream that irrigates the plain of Shiraz. Along its southern shore runs the caravan-track to Sarvistan, Fasa, and Darab.[1] Further to the north-east is the second largest lake in Persia, known as the Daria-i-Niriz, or Bakhtegan, which possesses a very indented and fantastic outline, being almost divided into two lakes by a big projecting promontory or island. Though the chief confluent of this lake is the Bund-Amir, or Kur river, which I have previously traced from Persepolis, its waters, which are frequented by flamingoes and wild fowl, are extremely salt, and, in dry seasons, the desiccated bed is found to be covered with a thick saline incrustation.[2] It is doubtful, indeed, whether we ought to describe this expanse of water as a lake, seeing that it is, in reality, only an area under more or less permanent inundation. There is no depth of water, Captain Wells having walked in for a quarter of a mile without getting above his knees. It would appear from the negative evidence of history that the lake cannot be of very ancient origin; seeing that it is never mentioned by the ancient writers, and that El Istakhri, in the tenth century, is the first to allude to

Salt lakes

[1] This route has been described by Dupré, Ouseley, Flandin, Keith Abbott, Stolze, Dieulafoy, and Preece, whose works will be cited in the Table of Routes at the end of this chapter. At ten miles from Sarvistan are the ruins of a great building, whose central hall is covered by a dome, and which shows traces of spacious side-galleries and courts. This is commonly supposed to have been a Sassanian palace, but is credited by some with an Achæmenian origin. (*Vide* Flandin and Coste, vol. i. pls. 28–9, Canon G. Rawlinson's *Seventh Great Oriental Monarchy*, cap. xxvii., and M. Dieulafoy, *L'Art Antique de la Perse*, pt. iv. pls. 1–8). At Fasa there are no remains of antiquity, with the exception of a big mound, apparently artificial, styled Tell-i-Zohak (Flandin and Coste, pl. 30). At Darab, or Darabjird, in addition to the ruined rampart or Kaleh-i-Darab before mentioned, there is a great Sassanian bas-relief, like those of Naksh-i-Rustam and Shapur, representing the monarch on horseback above a prostrate figure, conferring the crown of Valerian upon the obscure Cyriadis (*ibid.* pl. 31). There is also a vast underground hall hewn in the mountain, and divided into aisles by solid pillars. This is now known as the Caravanserai Dub, but is supposed to have been originally a rock-temple. It contains neither sculptures nor inscription. (*Ibid.* pls. 31–3.)

[2] *Vide* Sir W. Ouseley (1811), *Travels*, vol. ii. cap. viii.; Keith Abbott (1850), *Journal of the R.G.S.*, vol. xxvii.; and Capt. H. L. Wells (1881), *Ibid. Proceedings*, (new series), vol. v. pp. 138–144.

it. In all probability the river overflow to which it owes its existence was consumed, in earlier times, in irrigation.

In an earlier part of this chapter, while speaking of Dehbid, I alluded to the nomad tribes of the province of Fars. It will be my duty in a later chapter, dealing with the south-west provinces, where the Iliats, or migratory tribes of Persia are chiefly concentrated, to write at length of their features and organisation. Here, however, I must devote a few paragraphs to those of their number who belong, almost exclusively, to Fars and its administrative subdivision of Laristan. These fall under two heads: Turkish Lurs and Arabs, the principal tribe of the former being the Kashkai. I have called them Turks because that is their origin, the tradition being that they are the descendants of a race transplanted to Persia, by the Mongol Hulaku Khan, from Kashgar; and I have called them Lurs because they are considered to belong to the Lur family, and in manners and customs differ very little from the Bakhtiaris and Kuhgelus. The Kashkais cover, in their biennial migrations, an immense tract of country; for, whilst in winter they are to be found in their *kishlaks*, or winter quarters, in the *garmsir*, or warm region of the coast fringe, known as Dashtistan (the Land of Plains), and in Laristan, as the spring advances they move northwards, leaving a few men behind to reap the scattered fields which they have sown in the southern region, and to bury the grain in pits against the ensuing winter, marching themselves, for the most part at nights, and driving their immense flocks of sheep and goats before them. So they come to their *yeilaks*, or summer-haunts in the highlands, through which the postal route runs from Isfahan to Shiraz. In the late autumn, as the cold begins to increase, they again strike their black goats'-hair tents, and are off to the south and the sun.[1]

Nomads of Fars. Kashkais

These tribes, like those which I shall afterwards describe, are under chieftains drawn from one of their own ruling families. There are two governing offices, those of Ilkhani and Ilbegi, which may be respectively rendered as First and Second in Command. The former is also *ex officio* Governor of Firuzabad, the centre of the tribe, and of Ferashband. The

Organisation

[1] The best authorities on the Kashkais are Keith Abbott (*Journal of the R. G. S.*, vol. xxvii.); De Bode, *Travels*, vol. i. p. 256; E. Stack, *Six Months in Persia*, vol. i. caps. v., vi.; and F. C. Andreas. The name is erroneously derived by Stack from the Turkish *kachmak*, to flee.

present incumbent, Sultan Mohammed Khan, has been obliged to content himself with these distinctions, the titular rank of Ilkhani being all that is left to him of tribal power. This is a part of the policy pursued by the Government of the Shah, which, in order more effectually to control the nomad element, keeps a hold upon their chieftains, often summoning them as hostages to the provincial capitals, or to Teheran. In the meantime, the headship of the tribe is vested in the Ilbegi, a cousin of the Ilkhani, named Darab Khan, who pays in to the provincial governor the revenue, in the shape of a poll-tax upon their flocks and herds, which he collects from his followers.

The Kashkais were once a numerous and powerful aggregation; but their ranks were greatly thinned by the famine of 1871–2; yearly more and more abandon nomadic and take to settled existence; and other causes of decline were thus stated to me in a communication derived from the tribe:—

Present decline

All the Kashkai tribes are now under the Ilbegi Darab Khan. Twenty years ago there were over 60,000 families of these tribes, all under their late chief and leader Mohammed Kuli Khan, the father of Sultan Mohammed Khan, the present Ilkhani. At that time they were able to bring into the field 120,000 (?) horse, but after the death of the above chief, the tribal affairs fell into the hands of smaller Khans, which resulted in internal dissension. Owing to this, about 5,000 families went over to the Bakhtiaris, and an equal number to the Iliat Khamsah, and about 4,000 families dispersed themselves to different villages. This reduced the total to about 25,000 families, which is their present number.

I may say that I do not accept even the reduced total, the latest information which I possess rendering it doubtful whether the tribe now numbers more than 10,000 to 12,000 tents. The Kashkais were formerly great breeders of horses, and having richer pastures than their neighbours more to the west, possessed a finer stock of cattle and sheep. But this superiority is also being forfeited, while their constant propinquity to the seat of government renders them liable to a heavier taxation.

I append a table both of the Kashkai and Arab Iliats of Fars, as their clans have been returned by different authorities during recent years.[1] The Arab tribes known under the collective title

[1] I have seen yet other and longer tables, but they contain a great many names of Mamasenni and Bakhtiari tribes, who occupy in their migrations parts of eastern Fars.

Arab Iliats

of Khamsah, are far less numerous than the Turks, and are said not to number more than 3,000 tents. They are scattered over the same region, and claim descent from the Beni Sharban tribe of Arabia. They bear a much worse reputation than the Kashkais, robbers as the latter are apt to be. There is a certain well-judged immunity about nomad larceny: seeing that to-night they steal, and to-morrow their place knows them no more.

Nomads of Fars and Laristan

Kashkai Tribes (Turks)

1875	1890
Kashkuli	1. *Nomad:*
Darashuli	Kashkuli
Shish Beluki	Darashuli
Farsi Madan	Shish Beluki
Safi Khani	Farsi Madan
Igdar	Safakhani
Ali Kuli Khani	Ikdir
Gallazan	Alakuini
Kuruni	Gallazan
Karachai	Haji Masih Khan
Dadagai	Arkapan
Rahimi	Bulli
Kur-i-Shuli	Kizili
Urd-i-Shiri	Khawanin
Jafir Begi	Naukarbab
Imam Kuli Khani	2. *Stationary:*
Darab Khani	Cheharpinjah
Amala-i-Ilkhani	Pablisi
Bahadur Khani	Zangiun
Kubad Khani	Alabeglu

Khamsah Tribes (Arabs)

Col. Ross, 1875	Self, 1889	1890
	Arab	
Baseri	Bajri	Basiri
Napar	Nofar	Nafar
Baharlu	Baharlu	Baharlu
Arayalu	Apatlu	Ainalu
Abulwardi		Shaiwani
Amalah Shahi		Safari
Mamasenni[1]		Jabbarah

[1] Turks.

Routes in Fars and Laristan [1]

Shiraz to Fasa and Darab.—A. Dupré (1808), *Voyage en Perse*, vol. i. cap. xxviii.; Sir W. Ouseley (1811), *Travels*, vol. ii. cap. viii.; E. Flandin (1841), *Voyage*, vol. ii. caps. xlvii.–viii.; Keith Abbott (1850), *Journal of the R. G. S.*, vol. xxvii. p. 149; F. Stolze (1875), *Zeit. d. Gesell. f. Erd. zu Berlin*, 1877; Mme. Dieulafoy (1881), *La Perse*, caps. xxv–vi.; J. R. Preece (1884), *Supplem. Procs. of the R. G. S.*, vol. i. part iii.

Shiraz to Bunder Abbas (Gombrun).—(1), *viâ* Darab and Forg: A. Dupré (1808), *ibid.* vol. i. caps. xxix., xxx.; J. R. Preece (1884), *ibid.*; (2), *viâ* Jahrum and Lar: Sir T. Herbert (1627), *Some Yeares' Travel*, pp. 116–127; J. A. Mandelslo (1638), *Travels*, pp. 7, 8; J. B. Tavernier (1666), *Travels*, book v. cap. xxii.; J. Struys (1672), *Voyages*, caps. xxxiv.–v.; Sir J. Chardin (1673), *Voyages* (edit. Langlès), vol. viii. pp. 459–506; Dr. J. Fryer (1676), *Travels*, letter v.; C. Le Brun (1705), *Travels*, cap. lviii.; A. Dupré (1808), *ibid.*, vol. ii. cap. xl.

Shiraz to Firuzabad and Bushire.—J. Scott Waring (1802), *Tour to Sheeraz*, cap. xxvi.; Aucher Eloy (1837), *Relations de Voyages*, pp. 511–536; F. Stolze (1875), *ibid.*; E. Stack (1881), *Six Months in Persia*, vol. i. cap. iv.; Mme. Dieulafoy (1881), *ibid.*, caps. xxvi.–viii.

Firuzabad to Lar.—E. Stack (1881), *ibid.*, vol. i. cap. vi.

[1] In this table *ibid.* signifies the work by the same writer before mentioned.

CHAPTER XXI

PERSEPOLIS, AND OTHER RUINS

Among the ruined temples there,
Stupendous columns and wild images
Of more than man, where marble demons watch
The Zodiac's brazen mystery, and dead men
Hang their mute thoughts on the mute walls around,
He lingered, poring on memorials
Of the world's youth, through the long burning day
Gazed on these speechless shapes, nor when the morn
Filled the mysterious halls with floating shades
Suspended he that task, but ever gazed
And gazed, till meaning on his vacant mind
Flashed like strong inspiration, and he saw
The thrilling secrets of the birth of time.

SHELLEY, *Alastor*, 116-28.

Groups of Achæmenian and Sassanian ruins

I SHALL devote this chapter to a critical examination of the several ruins and monuments of antiquity that are encountered within the space of a few miles in the valleys of the Polvar and of Mervdasht, through which the traveller rides at a distance of forty miles to the north of Shiraz. Here, within easy reach and almost within sight of each other, is grouped in all probability the most considerable collection of important remains, belonging to widely different historical periods, that so circumscribed an area can anywhere display. They belong to two epochs, the Achæmenian and the Sassanian, and they represent three forms of antiquarian art: the structure of palaces, the excavation of rock-tombs, and the chiselling in high relief of sculptures on stone. The Achæmenian remains may be divided into four groups: (1) the ruins of the royal city at Istakhr (to which must be appended an account of its successor in Sassanian and Mohammedan days, with the few surviving relics of mediæval handiwork); (2) the royal sepulchres, the fire altars, and other remains at Naksh-i-Rustam; (3) fragments on the plain of Mervdasht; and (4) the great platform of Persepolis, with its series of ruined halls and palaces, and its rock-sepulchres behind. The Sassanian remains also fall into four groups, which will be dealt with in the order of their occurrence to a traveller coming from the north · (1) the Pehlevi inscriptions in the cave of Hajiabad; (2) the series of bas-reliefs representing the investiture, combats, and triumph of the sovereigns of this dynasty, which are carved in the cliff-face below the tombs of the Achæmenian kings, and which have given to the place the name of Naksh-i-Rustam, or Pictures of Rustam, from the prevalent Persian belief that the national hero is the individual therein depicted; (3) similar rock-carvings on the other or southern side of the valley of the Polvar, to which has been given, for a similarly foolish reason, the name of Naksh-i-Rejeb, though who Rejeb was I am unable to explain; (4) Pehlevi inscriptions on the platform of Persepolis. Though the Sassanian sculptures are later in date by at least six to seven hundred years, and in some cases by more, than the Achæmenian trophies, I shall yet deal with them first; both because they are first encountered, and because I desire to clear the ground for that which is the main object of this chapter, viz. a discussion of the architecture and ruins of Persepolis.

Sassanian remains: 1. Hajiabad Inscription

In the previous chapter I mentioned that after leaving Sivend the wayfarer whose face is turned southward enters a broad cliff-confined valley, through whose level bottom the Polvar has scoured for itself a deep bed in the soft soil. About half-way down this valley is the village of Hajiabad, the cliff-wall to the north of which, about one mile distant, is pierced by several natural caverns of considerable depth and dimensions. In the entrance to one of these, which is commonly named from Sheikh Ali, no doubt some venerable recluse who selected this spot for his retreat, but which is also known as Teng-i-Shah Sarvan, five square tablets or panels have been smoothed in the rock at a height of six to seven feet from the ground for the purpose of receiving inscriptions. Two only are so filled; and they contain the celebrated bilingual epigraph of Shapur I., which I have previously mentioned in vol. i., and upon his interpretation of which Mr. Thomas has based the theory, for which there is no external confirmation, of the conversion to Christianity of that king. Morier appears to have been the first to visit the cave;[1] Ker Porter the first to copy the inscription,[2] of which illustrations were afterwards given by Flandin and Coste,[3] and more recently by Stolze,[4] and of which plaster casts were brought to England in 1835 by Sir E. Stannus, British Resident at Bushire. That the decipherment of the Pehlevi character has reached no scientific stage of development, is manifest from the different readings that have been given of the Hajiabad lines; and sooner than pin my faith either to the philo-Christian theory of Mr. Thomas,[5] or to the bowshot theory

[1] *Second Journey*, p. 80. [2] *Travels*, vol. i. p. 513.
[3] *Perse Ancienne*, vol. ii. pl. 164; vol. iv. pl. 193.
[4] *Persepolis*, vol. ii. pl. 126. [5] *Early Sassanian Inscriptions*, pp. 73–101.

of Dr. M. Haug,[1] although I believe that the latter has secured the verdict of most scholars, I prefer the security of unshamed ignorance.

It was from the ragged *chapar-khaneh* of Puzeh, as stated in the last chapter, that I set forth to visit the combined Achæmenian and Sassanian remains at the western extremity of the cliff wall, known as Husein Kuh, that bounds the valley of the Polvar on the north, some three miles from Hajiabad, and sinks immediately beyond the sculptures into the broad plain of Mervdasht. From the post-house they cannot be more than one mile and a quarter distant in a straight line; and, standing on the roof of the stables, I could easily trace the three colossal cruciform cuttings in the rock face that marked the site of three out of the four royal tombs, a small black spot in the centre of each transverse limb indicating the violated portal. Yet, though the distance is insignificant, so cut up is the valley with gullies and water-courses that I was obliged to make a détour of at least one mile further, and to approach the cliff from the eastern side. At other seasons of the year the traveller is sometimes conducted by a similar détour to the west. The entire extent of cliff occupied by the tombs and bas-reliefs is less than two hundred yards in length; and the latter were executed by order of the Sassanian sovereigns, on panels of the rock, purposely smoothed, below the sepulchres of their illustrious predecessors, either on a level with the soil, which is here very much in excess of its original height, or a little above it.[2] Broadly speaking, the sculptures fall into two classes, those of the early Sassanian period, of Ardeshir and of Shapur I., in the middle of the third century A.D., and those of the middle Sassanian period, about the time of Varahran IV. and V. at the end of the fourth century and later. For the art of the later Sassanians, at the beginning of the seventh century, we must refer to the grottoes of Bisitun. It is only in the present century that the true historical reference of the bas-reliefs of Naksh-i-Rustam has been definitely ascertained, although Persians can still be found in abundance who decline to recognise in the crowned and bearded equestrian giant of the portraits any other than their beloved Rustam—an error which was even shared by the learned Niebuhr little more than one hundred years ago. Small wonder, then, that in the fifteenth century Barbaro the Venetian, all unconscious of the absurdity of his hypothesis, should

2. Sculptures of Naksh-i-Rustam

[1] *Essays on the Sacred Language of the Parsees.*

[2] The best accounts of Naksh-i-Rustam in modern times are those of J. P. Morier (1809), *First Journey*, pp. 125–8; Sir W. Ouseley (1811), *Travels*, vol. ii. p. 293 *et seq.*; Sir R. Ker Porter (1818), *Travels*, vol. ii. pp. 530–61; and the works, containing plates, which are cited later on. More recent writers, such as Ussher and Mounsey, have mainly copied their predecessors.

have solemnly accepted the principal figure as 'seemyng to be the ymage of a boysterouse man, who they saie was Sampson;' or that Sir T. Herbert in 1627, with a superior historical knowledge, should yet have seen in him 'a brave chevalier such time as Artaxerxes (Queen Hester's Husband) wore the diadem.' Till within the last fifty years there were writers who divided the principal figures into two groups, describing some as Sassanian kings, the others as monarchs of the Arsacid or Parthian dynasty who were their predecessors.

First tablet: Varahran and Queen

The bas-reliefs of Naksh-i-Rustam are seven in number; although it would appear from the evidence of the rock that additional panels must have been contemplated. For instance, after passing the first royal tomb, and before coming to the completed panels, there is a large incised space on the cliff-face, obviously designed for a further bas-relief. It now contains only a later Mohammedan inscription and three small holes, presumably scooped out for votive offerings or tapers. Facing west, or in the same direction as the above tomb, the first Sassanian tablet is encountered. It is on the level of the ground, which has accumulated as high as the knees of the principal figures. These are four in number, with a fifth of diminutive stature. The length of the entire panel is nineteen feet, and its height, as at present exposed, is eleven feet.[1] The central figure facing to the right is a Sassanian monarch with the symbolical globular crown, and immense streamers floating in the air behind. His hair stands out in bushy curls on either side of a handsome countenance, and his beard is tied in a knot below the chin. He is clad in the close-fitting jersey-like garment common to the Sassanian style, terminating in *shulwars*, or loose flapping trousers upon the legs. His left hand rests on the hilt of his sword; with his outstretched right hand he holds the circlet or emblem of royalty, the other half of which is grasped by a figure of scarcely inferior dimensions that confronts him from the right-hand side of the sculpture. This, too, is a royal personage, masses of curled hair projecting above the top of a mural or turreted crown. The beardless face, the long corkscrew curls hanging upon the shoulders, the apparent formation of the body in front, and the contour of the hips, have suggested to all writers, I think without exception, that this is a female figure, and the consort of one of the Sassanian kings. Porter went so far as to say that 'Beauty is sufficiently seen in the Juno port of the Queen, who seems as capable of asserting the rights of sovereignty as the really manly form of the king by her side.' The romantic but scholarly baronet accordingly identified the royal couple as Varahran V. (or

[1] Texier, vol. ii. pl. 133 (very fanciful); Flandin and Coste, vol. iv. pl. 186; Stolze, vol. ii. pl. 122; Dieulafoy, pt. v. pl. 16.

Bahram Gur, the great hunter) and his spouse, for no other apparent reason, however, than that the story of their separation and reunion is one of the most popular of Persian legends.[1] Between the images of the king and queen (if, indeed, the latter be a woman, which, in spite of *a priori* improbability, it seems somewhat difficult to doubt) is a small and terribly defaced figure, apparently that of a boy.[2] This fact has led Dieulafoy to conjecture that the royal trio are Varahran II., his wife (who, according to Darmesteter was daughter of the leading Jew of Babylon), and their son, whose united figures appear on the coins of the reign. On the other hand, it is doubtful whether the public portraiture of the female form would have been admissible as early as the end of the third century A.D. I prefer therefore to leave the indentification uncertain. Behind the king are two warriors or attendants, the foremost of whom has a thick beard and braided hair, and wears a tall helmet (Binning calls it 'a high-peaked hat') terminating, after a fashion not unfamiliar in Sassanian likenesses, in the head of an animal, generally supposed in this case to be a horse. His right hand and forefinger are uplifted in the conventional attitude of respect. Where this sculpture has escaped mutilation, it is well executed, and after the lapse of 1300 to 1500 years retains an astonishing sharpness and vigour.

Second and third tablets: Equestrian combat

The next two tablets, as well as the fifth in sequence, belong, in common with a similar bas-relief at Firuzabad (which will be mentioned in the next chapter), to a different class of monumental sculptures. They illustrate neither the pomp of regal investiture nor the triumph over a captive foe, but the equestrian prowess of warring kings. Accordingly, the stiff and somewhat ponderous forms and pose of the ceremonial panels are here replaced by a freedom of movement and a vivacity of conception which reflect infinite credit on the artist who designed them, and entitle the sculpture of the middle Sassanian period to no mean place in the history of art. The particular form of crown or helmet worn by the king in one of these bas-reliefs has suggested their connection with the name of Varahran IV. (A.D. 388–399), and whether he be the actual monarch depicted or not, it is probably to that period that all the equestrian panels should be attributed. The first two, that now claim our notice, are carved one above the other in the rock at Naksh-i-Rustam, below the second Achæmenian tomb, which is that of Darius, son of Hystaspes. It was not till fifty years

[1] Fired by a similar enthusiasm, Mounsey (*Journey*, p. 209) describes the royal circlet as 'a wreath held in token of the bond of love which united them'!

[2] Ker Porter (*Travels*, vol. i. p. 531) did not, apparently, discern this figure himself, but mentions having seen it in an old drawing at Shiraz. It is, however, clearly visible both to the naked eye and in photographs.

ago that the lower of the two panels was laid bare by Messrs. Flandin and Coste, having previously been concealed behind the accumulations of soil. It is even now buried up to the flanks of the horses.[1] Two mounted figures are depicted therein, charging each other at full gallop with lances in rest. The cavalier on the left hand is presumably the king ; he on the right wears a helmet with a knob or some sort of projection on the top. The upper panel represents a similar combat, but at a more advanced stage.[2] Here the horse of the figure on the right is thrown upon its haunches, and its rider is driven back in his saddle, while his lance is tilted up in the air by the impetuous onset of the charging king. The latter wears a peculiar helmet, consisting of two wings on either side of the Sassanian globe (the headdress of Varahran IV.), carries a great quiver at his belt, and wears a sort of tuft on either shoulder, a similar ornament decorating the head of his charger.[3] Behind him stands an attendant or standard-bearer, carrying a peculiar standard, consisting of a ring at the end of a staff and of a cross bar below it, from which depend tassels. The king's horse further tramples under foot a prostrate figure. Both on the bodies of the cavaliers in these bas-reliefs, and on their steeds, are traces of coats of mail ; and the combined panels are invaluable as documents concerning the military equipment of the period. The lower of the two, owing to its long concealment, is by far the better preserved, the upper tablet having been shockingly defaced. The latter is 24 feet long, by 12 feet high.

Fourth tablet: Shapur and Valerian

Between the second and third royal sepulchres occurs the fourth bas-relief, which is the first (hitherto mentioned) of the series at Naksh-i-Rustam, Shapur, and Darabjird devoted to the commemoration of the crowning exploit of the Perso-Roman campaigns of Shapur I., viz. the capture of the aged Roman Emperor Valerian at Edessa in 260 A.D. The humiliation of a Latin Cæsar, whether followed or not by the indignities described and perhaps invented by later historians,[4] was a

[1] Flandin and Coste, vol. iv. pl. 184 ; Stolze, vol. ii. pl. 121.

[2] *Vide*, in addition to the above, Texier, vol. ii. pl. 132.

[3] Ker Porter, who identifies the two figures with Varahran V. and a Tartar khan whom he killed in combat near Rhey, fancifully thinks that this ornament was a bladder filled with stones, in order to make a noise.

[4] Contemporary writers speak only of the emperor having been kept in captivity till his death at an advanced old age. But in the next century Lactantius, followed by other historians, set on foot the story that he was compelled to act as a footstool to Shapur when the latter mounted on horseback, that he was constantly exposed, fettered, to the multitude, and that after his death his skin was stuffed, and hung up in a frequented temple. The sculptures do not corroborate these indignities, which may have owed their origin, as Gibbon suggests, to the malice of the defeated nationality, although there was little in Persian character

FOURTH BAS-RELIEF AT NAKSH-I-RUSTAM. SHAPUR AND VALERIAN

sufficiently notable achievement to appeal to the contemporary imagination, and may be held to have justified the boastful reiteration of its accomplishment by the conqueror in the neighbourhood of his various capitals. This panel is 35½ feet long and 16 feet high, its level at the bottom being about 4 feet above the soil.[1] The central figure, of more than human stature, is Shapur, seated on horseback and receiving the homage of the two Romans, the captive Cæsar and Cyriadis or Miriades, the obscure fugitive of Antioch, who was elevated by the scorn of the conqueror to the imperial purple. The Sassanian king presents the handsome features so familiar from sculptures and coins, with thick outstanding clusters of curls, and wears the mural crown surmounted by the globe. His well-trained beard is tied in a knot below his chin; a necklet of large stones or ornaments hangs around his throat; and behind him in the air, as also from his sword hilt and plaited charger's tail, float the dynastic fillets or frilled ribands. His lower limbs are clad in the flowing *shulwars* of the period. While his left hand grasps his sword hilt, his right is outstretched to meet the uplifted hands of the standing Cyriadis, to whom he appears to be giving the *cydaris* or royal circlet. The Syrian wears the Roman dress, as also does the kneeling Cæsar, whose hands are outstretched in mute supplication, and whose face wears an expression of piteous appeal. Valerian also has a chaplet round his head; and both captives have shackles or fetters round their ankles. At the crupper of the king's horse is suspended by a chain the big ornament, seemingly a tassel, that is so frequent a feature in the Sassanian bas-reliefs.[2] In the background appears the upper part of the figure of an attendant, with uplifted forefinger of reverence, wearing a tall cap and closely braided hair. Where the lower part should have been, the rock has been smoothed to receive a long, but as yet undeciphered and lamentably defaced, inscription in the Pehlevi character.[3] No doubt it relates, though I am not clear that Dieulafoy has a right to state it as a fact, to the victory of Edessa. As regards the execution of the entire panel, its artistic merit appears to vary in different parts, and to betray the handiwork of more than one

or habits at the time to render them intrinsically improbable. *Vide* Canon G. Rawlinson's *Seventh Great Oriental Monarchy*, pp. 86–8.

[1] Texier, vol. ii. pl. 129; Flandin and Coste, vol. iv. pl. 185; Stolze, vol. ii. pl. 119; Dieulafoy, pt. v. pl. 15, pp. 115-16. Compare E. Thomas, *Early Sassanian Inscriptions*, pp. 62–9.

[2] The ingenuity of rival commentators has perfomed astonishing feats with this object. Thévenot thought it was a flask, Chardin a bullet used as a sling at the end of a chain, Ouseley a vessel for incense, and Texier a lasso. Binning calls it 'a large mass like a cabbage.'

[3] *Vide* Niebuhr, *Voyage en Arabie*, vol. ii. pl. 34; Flandin and Coste, vol. iv. pl. 181 (*ter*); Stolze, vol. ii. pl. 120.

craftsman. Shapur and Valerian are both admirably pourtrayed ; and the king's horse also is finely rendered, though it is open to the charge that can be directed against most of the horses in Sassanian sculptures, viz. that it resembles a sturdy Flemish dray-horse much more than a royal charger. I now regret very much that I did not reproduce for this work the photograph which I myself took of this bas-relief, because, though smaller, it appears to me to be infinitely better than the accompanying engraving, which I procured from the French publisher of Madame Dieulafoy's book.

FIFTH BAS-RELIEF : EQUESTRIAN COMBAT

Below the fourth of the Achæmenian tombs is the remaining panel of equestrian combat already alluded to. It is on the level of the ground, and is 20 feet long by 11½ feet high.[1] Again there are two cavaliers engaged ; again he on the right hand is worsted, his horse being thrown back on its haunches, he himself all but dislodged from his seat by his adversary's lance, which pierces him in the throat, and his own spear, snapped in twain, projecting aimlessly in the air. This warrior wears a helmet

Fifth tablet: Equestrian combat

[1] Texier, vol. ii. pl. 131 ; Flandin and Coste, vol. iv. pl. 183 ; Stolze, vol. ii. pl. 118.

surmounted by a sort of crest or knob.[1] His victorious antagonist, who advances at full gallop from the left-hand of the panel, has lost his features by mutilation, but wears a three-pointed diadem surmounted by a crest or knob. On his shoulders and on the head of his horse are tufts or ornaments similar to those before noticed. A gigantic quiver hangs at his side. Both the king and his steed appear in parts to be clad with coats of mail; behind the quarters of the latter the two customary tassels fly in the air, and beneath its belly hangs a row of metal discs or medallions. Behind the king appears his ensign, also on horseback, carrying in this case a new variety of standard. It consists of a staff, terminating in a cross-bar, crowned by three projections,[2] and with two tufts or tassels depending below. There is no prostrate figure in this bas-relief. The spirit and reality of the combat are well sustained, although it is curious that in this case, inverting the ordinary error of proportion, the horsemen are too small for their steeds.

Proceeding westward, we come to another smoothed surface on the rock, evidently prepared for a bas-relief which it has never received.

Sixth tablet: Varahran II. and courtiers

Near the end of the bluff, and beneath the solitary pillar that rises from its summit, the sixth panel is then reached.[3] Its dimensions are 17 feet by 8 feet, and it differs entirely, both in subject and treatment, from any other of the Sassanian sculptures. Chiselled on a convex, or projecting, surface of rock, it follows the contour of the cliff. Nine figures stand in a row, of whom five on the left-hand side and three on the right, facing respectively towards the central figure, have their entire stature below the chest concealed behind a species of barrier or pew. Those on the right wear lofty caps or tiaras, are bearded and curled, and have the raised right hand and forefinger. Of those on the left, two wear the pointed head-dress previously noticed as terminating in the head of an animal, variously interpreted by writers as a lion, horse, or dog. One is bare-headed, but has thick curls. The two outermost are sculped round a retreating angle of the rock. In the centre, in a gap or division between the side-pews,[4] stands the king, fronting the spectator, although his head is turned in profile over the right shoulder. He wears the winged crown of Varahran II. (which also appears on one of the

[1] Morier called it a Grecian helmet, and twisted it out of all verisimilitude in his drawing.

[2] Ker Porter foolishly sees in these a planetary reference.

[3] Texier, vol. ii. pl. 134. (This is a very incorrect plate, inasmuch as the contour of the sculpture is made concave, instead of convex.) Ker Porter committed a different error by cutting off the king at the knees. Flandin and Coste, vol. iv. pl. 188; Stolze, vol. ii. pl. 117.

[4] I am by no means clear that this apparent barricade is not merely the prepared, but unsculped, surface of the rock, the lower part of the figures having never been completed.

sculptures at Shapur), his hair is puffed and curled, and his hands rest in front upon the pommel of his sword. His figure is visible to half-way between the knees and feet, the latter being hidden from below by a projecting surface of rock, of curving outline, which has somewhat the appearance of a rostrum, but which, being smoothed in the form of an empty tablet, may, it occurs to me, have been originally designed to receive a subsidiary sculpture. The whole is at the height of several feet above the ground. Acting upon the hint of the helmet, Canon Rawlinson suggests as the subject of this bas-relief an incident in the life of Varahran II., who, having commenced to rule tyrannically, was taken to task by his principal nobles, instigated by the chief of the Magi, and in reply to their expostulations, promised amendment and reform. I doubt, however, whether a monarch would voluntarily select such an incident in his career for eternal commemoration. Had a Royal Academy existed in England in the days of King John, would he have commissioned the President to paint a great picture of Runnymede and Magna Carta?

Adjoining this panel is what Flandin describes as the *ébauche* of a figure on the rock, but of which, as I did not notice it myself, I will quote the words of other writers who did. Morier says: 'There is besides another curious figure at full length, behind the rock, close to the sculpture, but still making part of the same piece.'[1] Porter writes: 'At one end, entirely distinct from the group, is the outline of an extraordinary figure notched in the marble, not unlike the first idle drawings of a schoolboy.'[2]

Seventh tablet: Ormuzd and Ardeshir

Separated only by two or three feet of rock from the bas-relief last described, is the seventh and concluding one of the series.[3] It is, also, in all probability, the earliest in date, representing, as it does, a scene which is again pourtrayed on the opposite side of the valley in the rock-recess of Naksh-i-Rejeb, as well as in the neighbourhood of Firuzabad, namely, the investiture of Ardeshir Babekan, or Artaxerxes, son of Babek or Papak, founder of the Sassanian line, with the imperial *cydaris* by the god Ormuzd. The two main figures face each other on horseback, their steeds, which, with an excess of disproportion, are here little bigger than stout cobs or ponies, touching their foreheads in the centre of the panel, whose total length is over 22 feet. The figure on the right hand of the spectator, as an inscription on the shoulder of his horse reveals, is that of the god. Upon his head is the mural crown, with curled hair piled above it, and subsequently falling upon the shoulders. His beard is

[1] *First Journey*, p. 127.
[2] *Travels*, vol. i. p. 559.
[3] Texier, vol. ii. pl. 130; Flandin and Coste, vol. iv. pl. 182; Stolze, vol. ii. pl. 115; Dieulafoy, pt. v. pl. 14, pp. 113–14.

square-cut, not tasselled. In his left hand he holds a sceptre, which in the Sassanian sculptures appears to be an emblem of divinity. With his outstretched right he grasps one-half of the *cydaris*, or circlet with pendent ribands, the other side of which is held by the king. Both figures wear long, flowing trousers, and at each horse's hind-quarters hangs the usual big tuft or tassel. Ardeshir wears a globe-crowned helmet, of which the balloon-like, inflated globe is commonly supposed to typify fire, while the close-fitting helmet with cheek-plates and back-plate supplies an interesting contribution to the history of ancient

SEVENTH BAS-RELIEF: ORMUZD AND ARDESHIR

armour. His left hand is uplifted, and, apparently, held to his mouth. He wears a rounded beard, and hair which hangs uncurled upon his shoulders. Around his horse's chest is a band adorned with circular medallions, the corresponding ornaments upon the horse of Ormuzd being lions' heads in metal. Behind the king stands a single figure holding a fly-flap, not unlike the attendants who are so conspicuous in the processional bas-reliefs of the Achæmenian kings. A prostrate figure lies on the ground, beneath either horse's hoofs, that beneath the charger of the king wearing a helmet or head-piece with a mark on the right side and streamers behind, and being commonly supposed to represent Artabanus, the last Parthian king. On the other hand, the figure whom the god tramples underfoot appears to have snakes wreathed round his head, a symbolism which has been variously explained. Ker Porter identifies him, somewhat vaguely, with the 'gorgon-headed demon of the Arsacidian idolatry.' Thomas talks, not less obscurely, about the 'snake-crested helmet of the Mede.' Rawlinson decides for Ahriman, the embodiment of evil; Perrot, for Zohak or Azi-Dahaka, another incarnation of the evil principle.[1] Inscriptions, bilingual, but triliteral—*i.e.* in two forms of the Pehlevi character, and in Greek—are cut upon the shoulders of both horses. That upon the charger of the king, which was first deciphered by De Sacy,[2] runs as follows:—

This is the image of the Ormuzd-worshipper, the god Artakshatr (Ardeshir), King of kings Arian, of the race of the Gods, son of the God, Papak, the King.

The Greek inscription on the horse of Ormuzd says:—

This is the image of the god Zeus.

This is the sum-total of the Sassanian sculptures of Naksh-i-Rustam. We will now cross the valley again to its southern side, where, soon after turning the angle of the mountains that face the plain of Mervdasht, and setting our faces towards Persepolis, at about two miles distance from the palace-platform we come across a small natural recess[3] in the base of the cliff, the sides and back wall of which have been artificially smoothed in order to receive the work of the chisel. So snugly hidden is this rock-nook, and so littered are its approaches with loosely-piled boulders, that four travellers out of five would probably pass it unobserved. Its sides converge towards the back wall of the natural rock; and all three surfaces are adorned with bas-reliefs of the earliest Sassanian period, representing incidents similar to those which have already been described. They have suffered, however, from more deliberate and savage mutilation than their fellows on the other side of the valley, this being due, perhaps, to their greater proximity to Persepolis, whither, we are told by Chardin that the Prime Minister of Shah Sefi I. sent sixty men with orders to deface the sculptures, so as to discourage the

3. Sculptures of Naksh-i-Rejeb

[1] *Vide* Professor J. Darmesteter, *Introduction au Vendidad*, p. lxv.

[2] Stolze, vol. ii. pl. 116; E. Thomas, *Early Sassanian Inscriptions*, p. 29.

[3] Ouseley says it was artificially hewn, but I do not agree with him. For a plan, *vide* Flandin and Coste, vol. iv. pl. 189: and for authorities, *vide* J. P. Morier (1809), *First Journey*, pp. 137–9; Sir W. Ouseley (1811), *Travels*, vol. ii. pp. 291–3; Sir R. K. Porter, *Travels*, vol. i. pp. 571–5; J. Ussher (1861), *Journey*, p. 546, *et seq.*; K. D. Kiach (1878), *Ancient Persian Sculptures*; as well as the works containing engravings or photographs which will be referred to.

visits of Europeans. If the bas-reliefs of Naksh-i-Rejeb had escaped the earlier violence of the Arab invaders, to this barbarous ruffian may perhaps be attributed their cruel fate. Nevertheless, they still present one portrait-group of unsurpassed excellence, and have been preferred, by some writers, to the tablets of Naksh-i-Rustam, and by others have been ranked as equal with those of Shapur.

On the right-hand wall of the recess, the first tablet repeats the familiar scene of the investiture of Ardeshir by the god Ormuzd.[1] Its dimensions are 21 feet in length, and 9½ feet in height. The two horsemen meet in the centre of the panel; and Ormuzd, wearing, as before, the mural crown, extends the *cydaris* to the king. Here, however, are no prostrate figures beneath the horses' hoofs. The costumes and draperies have been almost obliterated by wanton outrage, and the head of Ardeshir has well-nigh disappeared.

First tablet: Ormuzd and Ardeshir

The middle panel depicts a similar scene, in which, however, the principal actors are on foot, and other accessories are introduced.[2] It is 18 feet long, and 10 feet high. The central figures, of colossal size, are again Ormuzd and Ardeshir, who stand confronting each other, holding the circlet in their right hands. The deity wears the mural crown, and carries a bâton or sceptre in his left hand. The king, on the left, is crowned with the inflated globe. Between the two, but nearly destroyed, appear two diminutive figures, seemingly those of children, whom conjecture has identified with two sons of Shapur, born before he ascended the throne. Behind the king are two attendants, one holding a fly-flap, the other being a bearded bodyguard, all but effaced. Behind Ormuzd, but in a separate panel, which may perhaps have an independent connection, are two other figures, with their backs turned upon him and their hands lifted to their faces. The beardless contour of these has led to the belief that they are women, and one commentator has gone so far as to recognise in one of the pair the daughter of Artabanus and mother of Shapur, and in the other the wife of Ardeshir's vizier. I am far from ready to accept the hypothesis that any of the earlier Sassanian sculptures contain the likenesses of women, and am more disposed to attribute a smooth face and braided hair to the palace eunuchs. To the left of the main tablet, on a fragment of the rock, is the bust of a figure, pointing with his finger to a Pehlevi inscription at

Second tablet: Ormuzd and Ardeshir

[1] Texier, vol. ii. pl. 140; Flandin and Coste, vol. iv. pl. 192 *bis*; Stolze, vol. ii. pl. 100.

[2] Texier, vol. ii. pl. 141; Flandin and Coste, vol. iv. pl. 192; Stolze, vol. ii. pl. 101; Dieulafoy, pt. v. pl. 17. The two latter photographs are obscure and unsatisfactory. But so, it may be said, is the original.

a considerable height from the ground.[1] Flandin and Coste speak of this supplemental tablet as a discovery on their part, apparently unconscious that it had been described both by Morier and Ouseley thirty years before.

By far the best-preserved of the trio, although the faces in it have been hacked to pieces, is the concluding panel, on the left-hand side of the recess.[2] Its dimensions are also greater, being 23 feet in length by 14½ feet in breadth. Shapur I. rides upon the scene, followed by nine of his principal bodyguard, whose pose and stature are accommodated to the configuration of the rock. The perspective is extremely faulty, and there are the errors of disproportion so universal in the Sassanian sculptures ; yet for a certain solemn dignity, and also as a likeness of contemporary dress and arms, this panel has a peculiar value. The king wears the globular crown, the curled hair, the tunic fastened with a clasp on the left breast, the clinging jersey, and the streaming *shulwars*, with which we are now so familiar. The charger is lifelike, and its trappings are carefully executed. His followers, with one exception, wear high round-topped caps or tiaras, upon which are symbols, supposed to be indicative of rank. Three are on foot, and stand leaning upon their long, straight swords ; the rest are mounted. The identity of the main figure is left in no doubt by an inscription, in Pehlevi and Greek, first deciphered by De Sacy, upon the chest of the king's horse,[3] there being another inscription close by, on the smooth rock. It runs as follows :—

Third tablet: Shapur and bodyguard

> This is the image of the Ormuzd-worshipper, the god, Shapur, King of kings Arian and non-Arian, of the race of the gods, son of the Ormuzd-worshipper, the God, Artakshatr (Ardeshir), King of kings Arian, of the race of the gods, the offspring of the god, Papak, the king.

Before taking final leave of the Sassanian sculptures of Naksh-i-Rustam and Naksh-i-Rejeb, let us endeavour to sum up our impressions upon the phase of art which they represent. Its defects of proportion, design, and treatment are on the surface, and are very apparent. There are a clumsiness and a ponderous solidity about the forms and movements, except in the panels of equestrian combat, that produce a sense of fatigue ; and a want of that higher imagination that at once idealises and impresses. Yet, for all that, we may observe in the work of the Sassanian artists a decided originality of conception, and a consciousness of the dignity of art.

Criticism

[1] Texier, vol. ii. pl. 142 ; Flandin and Coste, vol. iv. pl. 190 ; Stolze, vol. ii. pl. 104 ; Thomas, *Early Sassanian Inscriptions*, pp. 30–1.

[2] Texier, vol. ii. pl. 139 ; Flandin and Coste, vol. iv. pl. 191 ; Stolze, vol. ii. pl. 102 (very unsuccessful) ; Dieulafoy, pt. v. pl. 17.

[3] Stolze, vol. ii. pl. 103 ; Thomas, *Early Sassanian Inscriptions*.

Their style is in no sense borrowed from the Achæmenian models that stared them in the face. On the contrary, it is the offspring of its own age, and while it is unmistakably affected, and in its later periods may even have been actually assisted, by those Roman influences with which Persia, under its Parthian rulers, had come into such close contact, it yet remains a Persian, not a Roman, art, as its handling of Roman figures and costumes sufficiently betrays. There is a certain simplicity, and even nobility, in its presentment of the monarch, who is everywhere the centre of the piece ; and in the modelling of flesh and form, particularly of the horses' bodies, as well as in the treatment of armour, equipments, and dress, there is a notable advance upon any previous Persian sculpture. To me this appears the more remarkable because it arose in such swift succession to a period when there is little or no evidence that art existed at all. With the overthrow of the Arsacidæ, and the restitution of the national religion, there must have been a genuine re-awakening of the national spirit. This is expressed in the vigorous bas-reliefs of the first Sassanian kings, as well as in the palaces and public works which they constructed. Then followed a decline of art, until the second revival, in or about the time of Varahran IV. A further reaction was succeeded by one final effort of recovery, probably under Byzantine influence, in the days of the splendid Chosroes II. or Parviz. Into the effects of Sassanian art and sculpture upon other countries and later times, a subject which has been somewhat conjecturally treated by certain writers, I must here forbear from entering. Let me, however, recommend, in addition to M. Dieulafoy's somewhat fanciful work, a paper by Mr. A. Phené Spiers, published in the 'Proceedings' of the Institute of British Architects, 1892.

Sassanian inscriptions at Persepolis

There remain only to be noticed two Pehlevi inscriptions, one of eleven, the other of twelve lines, which occur on the south portal of the Palace of Darius on the platform at Persepolis.[1] They relate to the reigns of Shapur II. and Shapur III., and were first copied and brought to England by Ouseley in 1811.[2] Their existence must have been overlooked by those who have written that there is no trace on the Achæmenian platform either of Seleucid, Parthian, or Sassanian rule.

From the Sassanian monuments in the valley of the Polvar I now retrace my footsteps, and reascend the stream of time to discuss the far more complex and absorbing topic of the relics that exist in the same neighbourhood, belonging to the greatest epoch of Persian history, and revealing to us in stupendous, albeit ruined, guise the indestructible

[1] E. Thomas (*Early Sassanian Inscriptions*) erroneously says, in 'an inner chamber of the Hall of Columns.'

[2] *Travels*, vol. ii. p. 238, pl. 42. For a photograph, *vide* Stolze, vol. i. pl. 49.

handiwork of the Achæmenian sovereigns—of Darius, of Xerxes, and of Artaxerxes. Already a prelude to this discussion has been offered in the passages relating to the city and sepulchre of Cyrus at Pasargadæ; and from the older ruins and the earlier monarch we pass, by a natural sequence, to the later capital of his more remarkable successor.

Achæmenian remains

The subject may not inaptly be introduced by a few general remarks on the history and character of the four groups of remains that lie before us, all appertaining to the same period, and exemplifying in greater or less degree the same design. The ruins of Istakhr, the rock-tombs above Naksh-i-Rustam, the scattered fragments on the plain, and the pillar-strewn platform of Persepolis, are now recognised beyond possibility of doubt as the work of the successors of Cyrus, the abodes in life and after death of the celebrated Kings of Kings. And yet this knowledge is of no great antiquity in the modern world. The earliest mention of the Persepolitan ruins, of which I am aware by a European writer, is that of Friar Odoricus, who in about 1325 A.D. journeyed from Iest (Yezd) to Huz (Khuzistan) and on the way encountered

Ancient travellers

> a certain city named Comerum, which formerly was a great city, and in the olden time did great scathe to the Romans. The compass of its walls is a good fifty miles; and there be therein palaces yet standing entire, but without inhabitants.[1]

The worthy friar had evidently no idea of the real identity of Comerum. Even less, if possible, 150 years later, had the travelled Venetian, Josafa Barbaro, who, having recognised Samson in Rustam, naturally saw in Persepolis, which he called Camara, a work of Hebrew origin, and in the Bund-Amir a structure of Solomon. In the seventeenth century, Mandelslo was better informed:—

> The religious men of Schiras told me that the learned were clearly of opinion that the ancient Persepolis had stood thereabouts (i.e. at Chehel Minar), and that these were the ruines of Cyrus' Palace.[2]

Well would it have been if the friars of Shiraz had had a wider audience. Otherwise we should hardly have seen, as we have during the last two centuries only, the ruins of Persepolis variously interpreted as the work of Lamech and the tomb of Noah, as due to volcanic eruption and to the worship of idols; or have heard their date promiscuously bandied about over a space of 3000 years.[3]

[1] *Cathay and the Way thither* (Hakluyt Society).

[2] *Travels* (trans. by J. Davies), p. 4.

[3] In the present century, M. Bailly, author of *Histoire de l'Astronomie Ancienne*, wrote: 'I think I have demonstrated that the Persian Empire and the foundation of Persepolis mounted to 3209 B.C.' M. d'Hancarville was of the same opinion.

It is amusing enough, in the light of ascertained knowledge, to look back upon the conjectural labours of others who have toiled in darkness. That, however, should not diminish our gratitude to those who, like Chardin, Kaempfer and Le Brun, at the end of the seventeenth and beginning of the eighteenth centuries first essayed on a considerable scale the work of transcription and illustration of the Achæmenian monuments;[1] to Niebuhr, whose scholarly industry dignified the middle of the latter century; or to those who, like Rich, Ouseley, and Ker Porter, early in the nineteenth, brought back to Europe more careful drawings and reproductions than had hitherto been procurable, to assist the labours of the students, whose keen intellects were already trembling on the brink of a momentous discovery. This was no less than the decipherment of the cuneiform alphabet. There is no need here to repeat the tale, which is as romantic as it is remarkable. It is sufficient to recall the facts that first in Germany Professor Grotefend, seconded at Paris by M. Burnouf, and at Bonn by Professor Lassen; and, independently of these, Major, now Sir Henry, Rawlinson, in Persia itself, step by step, by patient analysis and happy intuition, were creating out of the symbols that had puzzled generations of inquirers, first an alphabet, and then out of this alphabet a language. Successively the riddles of the great rock of Bisitun, the chiselled epigraphs of Persepolis, and the inscriptions of Naksh-i-Rustam, were flashed upon the world, and beyond possibility of doubt men could now read the handwriting and know of a surety that they were contemplating the handiwork of Darius. In the light of these astonishing discoveries, theory was compelled to shift its ground, and, unable to question the origin, turned with avidity to the discussion of the purport of these more than ever interesting ruins. With this exercise it still shows no sign of becoming exhausted.

The cuneiform alphabet

Simultaneously with these discoveries, the enlightened liberality of the French Government was responsible for presenting to scholars and students the means of prosecuting or verifying their labours by the publication of the splendid engravings successively of Texier, and of Flandin and Coste. Though, viewed alongside of photographic representations, their work, and particularly that of Texier, is seen to be sometimes quite fanciful, and frequently incorrect, yet too much praise cannot be bestowed upon the painstaking industry with which these artists toiled in a country where those only who have travelled in it can estimate the ceaseless obstacles

Improved illustrations

[1] Several of the seventeenth-century travellers who contemplated book-making on a large scale took artists with them to Persia to make the requisite drawings. Pietro della Valle and Kaempfer both did so. Herbert got his illustrations drawn subsequently at home, with portentous results in the case of Persepolis. So did Struys.

and discouragements ; nor can the impetus be exaggerated which their labours gave to the study of Persian art and architecture. In later times, the science of photography has come to the aid of the student ; and although in the blinding glare and corresponding shadows of the Eastern atmosphere, unequal results have so far only been attained, we have, nevertheless, much to be grateful for in the plates of Stolze,[1] and of Dieulafoy.[2]

The real name

And yet, for all our modern amplitude and certainty of knowledge, to this day we have no idea what was the ancient Persian name that was used by Darius and his successors for the city and the palaces that were reared by them in the valleys of the Medus and Araxes. Istakhr and Persepolis are the titles by which they are known to us—the former applied to the city of the populace, the latter to the palace-platform of the sovereign. But the name Istakhr does not so much as occur in a single Greek writer, and is believed to be of Pehlevi origin ; while the name Persepolis, which has been consecrated in the usage of the world, is never heard of before the time of Alexander, 200 years after its edifices had begun to be raised, and then only starts into existence from the doubtful parentage of a pun.[3] These are problems upon which the cuneiform inscriptions have, so far, thrown no light, and which it appears doubtful whether the ingenuity of a future generation will be able to solve.

The several fabrics of the different Achæmenian sovereigns will come under notice in the order of their occurrence. Persepolis, though with the Macedonian invasion it leaped into a European fame, had not

[1] *Persepolis*, 2 vols., 1882. [2] *L'Art antique de la Perse*, five parts.

[3] Persepolis, if it signifies the 'city of the Persians,' should rather have been Persopolis. But the form Persepolis was, in all probability, preferred because of the play on the Greek word πέρσις (cf. the Ἰλίου πέρσις), signifying 'destruction,' and of the veiled allusion to the exploit of Alexander, from one of whose historians—probably Clitarchus—the name originated. At the same time it must have been an approximate translation of the original Persian name. What was the latter? History is silent on the point. Ctesias, Plutarch, Xenophon, and other writers frequently speak of it as Πέρσαι, but it is disputed whether this refers merely to the city or to the country. Personally, I incline to think that the name Pasargadæ, or Parsagardæ, which, as I have before shown, was the name both of the royal tribe and of the city of Cyrus, and which is explained as having signified the 'city or encampment of the Persians,' or, if not the compound word, then 'Parsa' by itself, may have been employed by Darius to denote his later capital, a little lower down the course of the same river; and that the Greeks, hearing it interpreted as above, may have adopted the punning translation, Persepolis. In the cuneiform inscription on the Propylæa of Xerxes occur the words, *ana Parsa*, which Rawlinson translates 'besides or in this Persepolis,' Oppert 'dans cette Perse,' Spiegel 'in Persien,' and Wiesbach 'in diesem Persien.' I accept Rawlinson's theory that the reference is not to the country, but to the city and platform itself. Vide *Journal of the R. A. S.*, vol. x. p. 331.

previously been much heard of outside of Persia. It was in his winter quarters at Susa, or in his summer palace at Ecbatana, that foreign ambassadors or refugees usually found the Great King. To Persepolis, which boasted a middle temperature, he appears only to have come at springtime, to receive the first-fruit offerings of his people, the reports of his officers, and the tribute of his subjects. The great platform, with its palaces and halls, was a place of ceremonial resort rather than of habitual occupation; but its proximity to the Pasargadæ of Cyrus, and its own associations, rendered it a site of peculiar importance. There its kings sat in state; there they worshipped at the fire-altars of the Magian faith; there, according to Persian tradition, Darius laid up the Avesta, written in gold and silver letters upon 12,000 tanned ox-hides; and there six of the Achæmenian monarchs were laid to rest. But while the platform was devoted to the pomp and the residence of the sovereign, around it, and far over the adjoining plain, must have stretched the city of the shopkeepers, the middle and lower classes, and the artisans; and in the ruins on the Polvar, generally denoted Istakhr, that will presently be described, are to be traced the probable relics of its shrunken greatness. With the invasion of Alexander and the conflagration of one or more of the palaces by his command—an event which will be noticed later on—Persepolis drops suddenly into the background: its name all but vanishes from existence; and when, after the blank interval of Seleucid domination (during the overthrow of which it retained sufficient importance to be plundered by Antiochus Epiphanes in 164 B.C.[1]) it reappears under the Parthian dynasty, the city, which in 200 A.D. was the seat of a local governor, has changed its title, and is known as Istakhr.[2] Here, amid the general decline of the national faith, the Zoroastrian fire-altars burned unceasingly; and here stood the temple of the goddess Anahidh,[3] one

History of Istakhr and Persepolis

[1] 2 Maccab. ix. 1, 2.

[2] Persian legend ascribes its foundation to Istakhr, son of the legendary Kaiomars. But Istakhr, or Stakhr, is said to be a Pehlevi word signifying pond or reservoir, wherein an allusion is sought to the famous tanks that were constructed on one of the three curious pointed hills that rise from the centre of the Mervdasht plain by the Asad-ed-Dowleh, a ruler of the Al-i-Buyah dynasty in the tenth century A.D. But the name is found in existence centuries before the tanks were made, and unless we are to assume that the reservoirs existed long before the Asad-ed-Dowleh's days, and were merely enlarged or reconstructed by him, I should prefer to leave the derivation unsolved, and to assume that any earlier name may afterwards have been adapted to a local interpretation. The best historical account of Istakhr is that of Ouseley (*Travels*, vol. ii. pp. 304-411).

[3] Anahita, Anahidh, or Tanata, the Anaitis of the Greeks, the ruins of a temple to whom at Kangavar I have already noticed in vol. i. p. 51, was a goddess who from the end of the fifth century B.C. played a part in the official religion

of whose priests, named Sassan, the father of Babek or Papak, was the grandfather of that Artaxerxes or Ardeshir who in 226 A.D. overthrew the Parthian yoke, and founded the dynasty that still bears his grandsire's name. In the revival of religion and of national spirit that followed, Istakhr became again the ceremonial capital of the empire; and although Ardeshir moved his own residence to Gur or Jur, and his successors theirs to Ctesiphon, and Seleucia, and Shapur, and Dastagird, yet at Istakhr remained the treasury and fire-altar of the royal house, and here the heads of conquered kings were hung up. Its population is said to have been seriously diminished by Shapur II., who transported twelve thousands families (doubtless an exaggeration) to Nisibis. When the Arabs invaded Persia in 639 A.D., Istakhr was one of the places that at first successfully resisted the assaults of Omar. Five years later it yielded, but its population having again risen in revolt in 648 and slain the Arab governor, it was forcibly reduced. In the same century its citadel, on the summit of one of the curious isolated rocks that have been mentioned, was built by the Khalif Moaviyah. In the tenth century it is alluded to by three Arab geographers: by Masudi, who saw there a book containing the portraits and history of all the Sassanian kings; by one of its own natives, Abu Ishak el-Istakhri, who described it as 'a city of middle size, with a strong citadel, about a mile in extent'; and by Mukadessi, who specially mentioned its mosque. At the close of the same century it is said to have been destroyed in consequence of frequent rebellions under the Samsam-ed-Dowleh, of the Al-i-Buyah dynasty; but it must have experienced a complete revival, if any credence is to be attached to the testimony of Hamdallah, who in the fourteenth century returned its dimensions as fourteen *farsakhs* by ten, the platform of Persepolis included, embracing, no doubt, in this generous estimate the whole of the more or less peopled plain from the Achæmenian city on the Polvar, to the mediæval citadel of Istakhr on the pointed hill. The latter was made a state-prison by the Atabegs of Fars, and was so used as late as 1576 A.D.[1] In 1621 it was found by P. della Valle in ruins. Of other remains than those of the platform and tombs of Persepolis, and the sepulchres of Naksh-i-Rustam, the seventeenth and eighteenth-century travellers do not say much, and it has been reserved for the explorers of more modern times to bring to light such relics as still exist of the city, whatever its name may have been, that must have sheltered the vast population ever buzzing round the courts of

of Persia somewhat similar to the Phœnician Astarte, the Babylonian Mylitta, the Arabian Alitta, and the Hellenic Aphrodite. According to Plutarch, statues to her were put up in all the great cities of the empire. She is supposed to have been of Armenian or Cappadocian origin. The popular translation of her name into Artemis, or Diana, appears to me to be incorrect.

[1] Sheref Nameh.

Darius and Xerxes, and that, under a succession of dynasties, was the theoretical metropolis of Iran.

The surviving ruins, to which travellers have given the name of Istakhr, fall into two groups—those on the banks of the Polvar, a little before it emerges into the plain of Mervdasht between Persepolis and Naksh-i-Rustam, and those of the hill-fortress or acropolis before alluded to. The former occupy a space of rising ground, round which the river flows in a loop, a slight distance to the east of the *chapar-khaneh* of Puzeh. Travellers have sought to recognise in the remains a palace, a temple, and a fort; but it appears to me to be doubtful how far this particularisation can be sustained.[1] What is certain is, that the ruins, such as they are, are those of an Achæmenian city contemporary with the neighbouring structures of Persepolis, and posterior to the edifices of Pasargadæ. Material, style, and treatment are closely analogous to the building upon the palace-platform, although the disposition at Istakhr is different, and even obscure. Close to the mountain, on the southern side, are the remains of a great gateway, built of blocks of limestone, which was doubtless the main eastern entrance to the city. It consists of two passages in the centre for animals and caravans, and of two side-alleys for foot-passengers, the stone piers that separate them being still *in situ*. A little to the north of this are the remains of what is thought to have been a palace, consisting of the bases and fragments of the shafts of eight pillars, of several door-cases and niches, and of a detached, dark-grey fluted column, 25 feet high, and nearly 2 feet in diameter, with a double bull-headed capital, similar to those that remain at Persepolis and have been found at Susa. The survival of this column provides a clue to, and is itself explained by, an interesting passage already alluded to in Mukadessi, where that writer says:—

1. Ruins of Istakhr

> The principal mosque of Istakhr is situated beside the bazaars. It is built in the manner of the most beautiful mosques of Syria; it has round columns. Upon the top of each column is a cow. It is said formerly to have been a fire-temple. The bazaars surround it on three sides.

This was the condition in which the place was seen in the tenth century; and it can leave no doubt in our minds that the Achæmenian structure had been converted by the Moslems into a mosque.[2] Ker

[1] The writers who have described or illustrated this (i.e. the Achæmenian Istakhr) are: J. P. Morier (1809), *First Journey*, p. 141; Sir R. K. Porter (1818), *Travels*, vol. i. p. 573; C. J. Rich (1821), *Journey to Persepolis*; Texier, vol. ii. pls. 137, 138; Flandin and Coste, vol. ii. pls. 58–61, and text; R. B. Binning (1851), *Two Years' Travel*, vol. ii.; Stolze, vol. ii. pls. 123–5.

[2] A fantastic description, and a still more ludicrous illustration, of this mosque is given, in 1672, by John Struys, the Dutchman, who, in all probability, never saw it at all. He calls it the Royal Sepulchre, and says that the bones of Noah, Shem, Ham, and Japhet were preserved there (*Voyages*, p. 332).

Porter and other modern travellers mention the local name as being the Harem of Jamshid. On the northern side, near the river, the remains are encompassed by the ruins of a wall of irregular outline, with the trace of semicircular bastions on one side, and of a ditch once filled from the Polvar. This wall is probably of much later date than the original city, and may have been added in Mohammedan times. Such are the sole surviving relics of what was no doubt the populous and mercantile quarter of the city of Darius. Excavations in the mounds and piles of débris might produce more satisfactory results.

To a person standing on the platform of Persepolis, and looking over the plain of Mervdasht, the most conspicuous objects in the landscape are three insulated rocky bluffs, rising abruptly at a distance of from seven to eight miles to the north-west. Their lower parts consist of steep slopes, above which a precipitous scarp shoots into the air, terminating in a sharp and jagged summit. These hills are known as Seh Gumbedan, or the Three Domes; and their names have been returned by Hamdallah in the fourteenth century as Istakhr, Shekesteh, and Sangwan; and in the present century by Fraser as Istakhr, Shekusteh, and Shemgan; by Binning as Istakhr, Shahrek, and Kumfiruz; and by Stack as Ghila and Ghilan. Nöldeke, who is our latest reference, says that the middlemost, which contained the mediæval citadel of Istakhr and the tanks, has now lost its old name, and is called Mian Kaleh, or Middle Fort. It has been ascended and described by Morier, De Bode, and Flandin, the last-named of whom called it Kaleb-i-Sarb, or Fort of the Cypress. He gives a plan of the three tanks or reservoirs before alluded to as dating from the tenth century.[1] Advantage was taken in their construction of natural hollows or rifts in the mountain; and they accordingly remind us of the celebrated Tanks of Aden. Upon the same rock are remains of a gateway, and of the walls and towers of the ancient castle; similar ruins being visible upon the adjacent rock of Shahrek.[2] Its summit is 1,200 feet above the plain. I imagine that the entire space between the mediæval and Achæmenian Istakhr must, at one time or another, have been more or less peopled by outskirts or suburbs, all bearing the same name. A city of the populace, which, as a rule in the East, consists of no more than mud and wattled huts, is very easily wiped out of existence.

Seh Gumbedan

I now return to the cliff-wall of the Husein Kuh, and to the sculptured section of it, nearly 200 yards in length, that presents, above the chiselled tablets of the Sassanian kings, the magnificent rock-

[1] Flandin and Coste, vol. ii. pl. 62.

[2] Fergusson is, therefore, wrong when he says (p. 91): 'No trace of buildings, I believe, exists upon them.'

sepulchres of their greater predecessors. These are four in number, and with the exception of the second from the east, which is the tomb of Darius son of Hystaspes, their general features, both structural and decorative, are so identical that one description will suffice for them all.[1] The Husein Kuh, which at its highest point has attained an elevation of 800 feet above the plain, sinks towards its western extremity to a height of from 200 to 100 feet, and finally even less; and in its sheer front to one half or two-thirds of the total height, and facing the valley were hewn by the masons of the Great King the hollow rock-vaults that were to contain the royal corpses. Outwardly, these present the appearance of a gigantic cross, of somewhat stunted dimensions, which is cut to a greater or less depth, according to the slope of the cliff, in the rock. Each limb of the cross is the same in height, viz. 24 feet, or a total height of 72 feet; but whereas the upper and lower segments are $35\frac{1}{2}$ feet in breadth, the central or transverse segment is $59\frac{1}{2}$ feet from end to end. The bottom of the lowermost cutting is as a rule from 25 to 35 feet above the surface of the ground, and is all but inaccessible to the climber, who requires to be hauled up thither, and still more to the portal in the transverse limb, by the aid of a rope. It is by these means, as I shall show, that the royal corpses were originally drawn up; and that the numerous travellers who in this century have examined the interiors of the tombs have been enabled to compass their object.

2. Tombs of the Kings at Naksh-i-Rustam

Externally, the tombs present the following features. The lowest segment of the cross is a bare cutting, 5 to 6 feet deep at the base, vertical at the back, and absolutely unadorned. Next comes the main or transverse limb, which contains the entrance to the sepulchre. This takes the shape of a reproduction in rock-carving of the façade of an Achæmenian palace. Four semi-detached bull-headed columns rise from a platform, formed by the deeply recessed incision into the cliff, and support a massive entablature, adorned with an elegant moulding or cornice. Between the two central columns is the doorway, framed in a case, the decorative treatment of the upper or projecting part of which is an unmistakable loan from Egypt. The door is divided outwardly into four compartments, the three uppermost of which were never pierced, but are of the solid rock. The lowest compartment, about four feet in height, was pierced for the entrance, but was originally closed by a stone block hung upon a pivot. This has in every instance now disappeared, and the aperture, which has in some cases suffered violent mutilation, yawns blackly in the façade.

External features

[1] For illustrations, *vide* Texier, vol. ii. pl. 135; Flandin and Coste, vol. iv. pls. 169–73; Stolze, vol. ii. pls. 106, 107, 112.

It is, however, upon the upper limb of the cross that the skill of the sculptor was mainly lavished, and that the solemn character of the entire monument is expressed. The entablature already spoken of sustains a curious platform or throne, consisting of two stages, each of which is upheld by fourteen figures (i.e. twenty-eight in the two superimposed rows), with both arms uplifted to sustain the weight above their heads.[1] These figures wear different garbs and represent differing nationalities. The sides or corner posts of the terrace, which is doubtless a copy of the platform that supported the royal throne, are curiously moulded and carved, and terminate in griffins' or bulls' heads at the top. Upon its summit appear two objects. On the left hand side is a small dais or platform of three receding steps, upon which stands the king, seven feet in stature, clad in the royal robe and tiara, holding in his left hand a bow, which rests upon the ground, while his right hand is uplifted with a gesture of oath or adoration towards an object that floats in the air overhead. This we now know from the inscriptions to be the image of the god Ahuramazda or Ormuzd; a symbolism that is directly borrowed from the representation of the god Assur in Assyrian sculptures. The deity is depicted as a small figure, with the upper part of a man, and with hair and headdress similar to those of the king, but with the lower part of his body terminating in plumes. A disc encircles his waist, long streamers float behind him, and he is upborne in space by outspread horizontal wings. He faces the king and lifts one hand in attitude of benediction; in the other he holds a ring.[2] Behind the god is sculped in relief the second object upon the platform, viz. a fire-altar, upon which the undying flame is depicted in the form of a cone of fire. In the right-hand corner above, the disc of the sun hangs in the sky. It should be added that on either side of the terraced platform, and in the returning angles of the rock, are chiselled a triple vertical row of figures, singly, or in pairs, which, according as they are armed or unarmed, represent the bodyguards or the attendants of the sovereign.

The interior arrangement differs slightly in each case, as will

[1] The fanciful use to which this platform has been put in argument by Fergusson will be noted later.

[2] Very quaint sounds the description of these sculptures given by Barbaro, the Venetian, four hundred years ago: 'There is one ymage, like unto that that we resemble to God the Father, in a cercle, who in either hande holdeth a globe, under whom arr other little ymages, and before hym the image of a man leanyng on an arche, which they saie was the fygure of Salomon. Under them arr many other ymages, which seeme to susteyne those that be above. Amongest whom there is one that seemeth to have a Popes myter on his hedde, holding up his hande open as though he ment to blesse all that arr under him, liek as they looking towardes hym seeme also to gape for his blisseng' (*Travels to Tana and Persia*, Hakluyt Society).

presently be pointed out, according to the design of the author, or the number of dead whom the sepulchre was expected to accommodate.

Interior arrangement

The structural disposition is, however, in all essentials the same. Crouching to pass through the low doorway, the visitor, who has probably been hauled up by his guides or by the neighbouring villagers to the level of the portico, enters first a sort of vestibule, usually flat-roofed, but in some cases arched, and hewn out of the solid rock. Behind this and opening from it is a series of recesses, containing deep excavations, originally covered with stone lids, for the reception of the royal dead. The maximum number of these sarcophagi, in any one of the Achæmenian tombs, is nine. The cavities have in every case been rifled many hundred years ago, and the curiosity of the explorer can expect no spoil. The interiors are black and begrimed, and redolent, like the Egyptian rock-tombs, with the odour and fluttering of bats.

The peculiarities of each royal sepulchre, where they exist, may be separately noticed. The first or easternmost has a different orientation

First tomb

from any of its fellows at Naksh-i-Rustam. Situated in a deep natural bay of the rock, it faces, not south, but west, and did not accordingly, when I saw it, admit of photographic delineation. The angle of the cliff is here so extremely abrupt, that not even the nimble-footed natives can clamber up in order to haul the traveller up after them, and I can find no record of the interior having been so visited by Europeans. It could only be attained by means of ladders or a scaffolding. The inaccessibility of this tomb, and its protection from the blinding glare of the midday sun, have enabled its sculptures to retain a greater crispness of outline than is the case with any of the others; and one might well believe that the artificer's chisel had only yesterday been laid down.

Next in order comes the most interesting of all the sepulchres, inasmuch as the unravelled mystery of the cuneiform alphabet reveals

Tomb of Darius

to us that it hid the body of the greatest of Persian kings, Darius son of Hystaspes.[1] This we learn from the crowded lines of arrow-headed inscriptions in the three tongues—Persian, Susian, and Assyrian—that fill the space between the central columns of the portico, and part of the upper surface of rock behind the king.[2] The 'writing on the wall' has suffered a good deal in the lapse of time, particularly so the Persian text. Yet from it we ascertain without doubt that it is Darius who speaks. To Ormuzd he gives honour; his own

[1] For the tomb, *vide* Texier, vol. ii. pl. 128; Flandin and Coste, vol. iv. pls. 174–8; Stolze, vol. ii. pl. 108. For the inscription, *vide* Stolze, vol. ii. pls. 109–11.

[2] There are traces of this inscription having been picked out in blue, one of the few certain relics of colour on the stone sculptures of the Achæmenians.

titles and genealogy he sets forth; the provinces of his mighty empire, and the people who paid him tribute, he unrolls.[1] Doubtless therefore the figures, of differing garb and type, who sustain the royal platform, represent the widestrewn nationalities that acknowledged him king, and King of kings. Nay, this has recently been proved; for in 1885, MM. Babin and Houssay, two of the collaborateurs of M. Dieulafoy, having ascended by means of a scaffolding, found the names of the various satrapies actually engraved beneath the feet of some of the supporters. The interior of the tomb of Darius has been visited by several travellers in this century;[2] but Ker Porter, I think, was the first who identified it as the sepulchre of the son of Hystaspes. Inside,

TOMB OF DARIUS

the disposition of the funeral chamber differs from that of any other; for there are recesses and cavities for as many as nine corpses, three of which however, opposite the entrance, clearly appertain to the original plan, while a lateral extension to the left to admit of six more coffins must have been subsequently hollowed out.[3] A pathetic interest

[1] For translations of this inscription, *vide* Sir H. Rawlinson, *Journal of the R.A.S.*, vol. x. pp. 289–312; Oppert, *Le Peuple et la Langue des Mèdes*, pp. 201–14; and Weisbach, *Die Achämenidinschriften*, pp. 79–81.

[2] The earlier explorers, such as P. della Valle, Chardin, Le Brun, and Fryer, seem with one accord to have yielded to their fears, and to have shirked the experiment.

[3] Stack, however, was needlessly oblivious of the funeral requirements of royal families when he said: 'Opening back are three recesses, each of which was the resting-place of three kings.' How did he make up his tale of monarchs?

attaches to this gloomy rock-vault, apart from the personality of the illustrious dead for whom it was hewn, in the historical fact that for seven years after his demise it provided a cell for the favourite eunuch of Darius, who could not be persuaded to forsake his master's remains. Perhaps even more interesting is the recollection of the tragedy that accompanied its execution, and that pictures itself before our eyes as we stand below. For here it was that the father and mother of the king, having expressed a wish to see the progress of the work, and forty of the Magi having been ordered by Darius to wind them up by means of ropes, the clumsy priests, frightened it is said by the sudden appearance of some serpents, let go, and the unhappy

THIRD AND FOURTH ROYAL TOMBS

couple were dashed to the ground and killed. The forty culprits, for all their sanctity, paid the penalty with their lives.[1]

The sculptured work of the third tomb is remarkable for its good preservation. Nothing at Persepolis exceeds the fresh distinctness of the bull-headed capitals of the portico columns, or the corner-posts of the terraced throne. On the other hand, the façade of the fourth tomb is more blurred and spoiled than that of any other. The capitals are quite defaced; so is the cornice above the doorway; and so are the supporters of the platform. This tomb has been more frequently explored than its fellows, because of its greater accessibility from below; Captain Sutherland, Sir W. Ouseley,

Third and fourth tombs

[1] Ctesias, *Persica*, § 19.

Colonel D'Arcy, Sir Robert Ker Porter, Baron de Bode, Flandin, and Mounsey, being among the European visitors who have ascended to it in this century. It has three arched recesses at the back, each containing a cavity, the stone slabs that formerly covered which have either been displaced or broken. None of the sepulchres, with the exception of that of Darius, which is doubtless the oldest, have any inscriptions, or present any clue to their identification. No very great stretch of fancy, however, is required to believe that they were in all probability constructed by his three successors, Xerxes, Artaxerxes I., and Darius II. When they were rifled it is impossible to tell.

Egyptian prototype

Of all the Achæmenian sculptures, these on the royal tombs alone have a purely religious character. At Persepolis, the king walks into the palace or audience-hall, or sits in state to receive the homage of his subjects; at Bisitun he triumphs over the rebels against his throne. In both cases he makes acknowledgment to the divine power. But here he is depicted as engaged in the sacrificial act, a monarch, but a Mazdean, the lord of mankind, but the servant of the deity. There is something, alike in the selection of the sepulchral site, in the mode of interment, and in the external decoration of the tomb, that is in keeping with the stately pretensions of the Achæmenian monarchy, and that at the distance of 2,500 years sounds in our ears no faint echo of the majesty of the Great King. Among the royal sepulchres that I have seen in many parts of the world, few of the fabrics reared by man, and none of those in which nature is made to play the principal part, are more impressive than these. A comparison naturally suggests itself with the royal rock-tombs of Egyptian Thebes; the more so as in my opinion the idea of the sepulchral excavations of Naksh-i-Rustam and Persepolis must have been directly borrowed from the valley of the Nile. The body of Cyrus was laid, as we have seen, in a raised mausoleum; where and how Cambyses was interred we do not positively know;[1] but Darius, profiting by the experience of the Egyptian campaign of his predecessors, and inspired with recollections, if not actually equipped with workmen, from the Nile, was content with no meaner resting-place than one which, while providing for the inviolability of his remains by the perils of access, should yet display to the world the imperishable record of his grandeur. Herein lies at once the analogy and the difference. The rulers of both empires are interred with vast toil and expense in the hollowed heart of the mountain, where their bodies should be free from touch or pollution. But whereas the Egyptian theology prescribes the uttermost concealment of the mummy, and

[1] Ctesias says his body was taken back ἐς Πέρσας, an ambiguous phrase upon which I have previously commented.

consequently ordains an architectural elaboration which is confined to the interior of the sepulchre, and was intended never again to meet the human eye, the Zoroastrian canon blazons forth to all men the personality and the splendour of the illustrious departed. If a direct Egyptian prototype is to be sought, it will be found rather in the rock-tombs that overlook the Nile from the cliffs of Beni Hasan, than in the tunnelled vaults of the Valley of the Tombs of the Kings.

But, at this point, the question may naturally arise, How came it that monarchs, professing the faith of Zoroaster, should have sanctioned and adopted a mode of sepulture so little in keeping with the well-known veto imposed by that creed upon the inhumation of the dead? To this interesting question let me attempt to give an answer. In the first place we must bear in mind that the Avesta,[1] as we know it, dates from no more remote period than the reign of the first Sassanian monarch, Ardeshir Babekan (A.D. 226–40); and that the strict application of the canon against sepulture either by cremation or interment,[2] as a desecration of the primal and semi-divine elements of nature, was only then systematically enforced. In the time of Darius the Avestan doctrines had not gained the absolute sway that they did in later days; and were probably confined, as regards strict observance, to the sacerdotal caste of the Magi. In any case the monarch who had himself overthrown the political conspiracy of that priesthood, felt himself bound by no such rigid inhibition. Cremation, as Herodotus tells us,[3] was forbidden as an insult to the divinity; and the Persians were horrified when Cambyses burned the body of the Egyptian Amasis. Exposure to birds of prey upon *dakhmas* or platforms was common; but the skeleton so denuded was, in the case of the ordinary people, coated with wax so as to prevent defilement, and was then interred.[4] What this form of burial was to his subjects, the rock-sepulchre became to the sovereign; and hence it is that we find this seeming violation of the creed of Ormuzd perpetrated under the very shadow and effigy of his name.

The Zoroastrian canon

Opposite the third and fourth royal tombs of Nahsh-i-Rustam, the ground rises in the form of a slight and mainly artificial elevation; and

[1] Zend-Avesta, the popular title started a century ago by Anquetil Duperron, is, strictly speaking, a misnomer. Avesta—i.e. Law or Revelation (like the cognate word *Veda*, from the root *vid*, to know)—is the name of the original scriptures of the creed of Zoroaster. Zend (from the root *zan*, to know) signifies Interpretation, or Commentary, and is the comparatively late body of religious exposition, written in Pehlevi, and dating from the Sassanian epoch.

[2] A corpse-burner might be killed by any passer-by. Burial of the dead was an inexpiable crime. Even Seioces, the minister of Kobad, was put to death for this offence (Procopius, *De Bell. Pers.* i. 11).

[3] Lib. iii. c. 16.

[4] *Ibid.* lib. i. c. 140.

on the summit of the hillock thus reared, and facing the fourth or westernmost sepulchre, rises a square building of peculiar shape and disputed object, to which European tradition has, for no better reasons than that the Zoroastrians were what is termed fire-worshippers, and that the interior of this structure is blackened with smoke, assigned throughout this century the designation of a fire-temple.[1] By the natives it appears to have been called at different times Kurnai-Khaneh or Nakkara-Khaneh, i.e. Drum House, and Kaabah-i-Zerdusht, or Sanctuary of Zoroaster, the former

So-called Fire-temple

TOMB (MISCALLED FIRE-TEMPLE) AT NAKSH-I-RUSTAM

one of those stupid blunders of nomenclature to which the Persian peasant is addicted, the latter a repetition of the before-quoted tradition. The building consists of a square tower, $23\frac{1}{2}$ feet in each direction, built of solid blocks of white limestone, that might almost be mistaken for marble, to a height of $35\frac{1}{2}$ feet from the real base, which is concealed below the encircling mound, but which was partially laid bare by the excavations, some fifteen years ago, of the late Motemed-ed-Dowleh, when Governor-General of Fars. Three of its sides are blank,

[1] Flandin and Coste, vol. iv. pl. 179; Stolze, vol. ii. pl. 113; Dieulafoy, pt. i. pls. 6, 8.

but are relieved by recessed window-cases or niches, into which are inserted black basaltic slabs, six in number, the lowest pair oblong, the middle pair square, the uppermost pair square but of smaller dimensions, immediately below a denticulated cornice which runs round the summit. The surface is further pitted with a number of peculiar but uniform incisions 1 foot 4 in. long, $5\frac{1}{2}$ in. broad, and $1\frac{1}{2}$ in. deep.[1] Both of these forms of ornamentation were probably introduced with a decorative object. The fourth side, facing the royal sepulchre in the cliff, is that by which access was and is gained into the interior. It contains a doorway, six feet in height, by five in width, which was originally at a height of sixteen feet, but is now only two-thirds of that distance above the ground, and to which access was formerly gained by a flight of steps. This conducts into the interior, which consists of a single chamber, twelve feet square (the walls are consequently nearly six feet thick) and eighteen feet high. The floor consists of several slabs of stone, and the flat ceiling of two huge blocks. Externally, however, the surface of the roof is slightly convex, and is composed of four slabs, one of which was partly displaced by an earthquake earlier in the century. Below the chamber the substructure of the tower is solid; some of the surface stones having at one time been torn away presumably in order to expose what lay behind. The doorway was evidently once closed by a stone block hung upon pivots, the grooves for which are still visible; while M. Dieulafoy made the discovery that in the floor was an arrangement or slide, by which, with the aid of rollers, a heavy weight could be dragged into the interior. These are the main visible features of the edifice. That it is not unique has been shown in the preceding chapter, where I have described the remains of the so-called Zindan at Pasargadæ, which was an almost identical structure. A third and similar tower, of lower elevation and inferior dimensions, also exists near Naubandajan, at the foot of the Kuh Pir-i-Mard, eleven miles to the south-east of Fasa.[2]

[1] Ker Porter (*Travels,* vol. i. p. 563), by an extraordinary inversion, describes these as 'small blocks of marble arranged at certain distances and projecting a short way from the external face,' and so depicts them in his illustration—an error which Fergusson repeats in calling them 'projecting facets.' Their meaning has been much discussed. Flandin suggests that they may have been intended to hold plates containing the names of the deceased (presuming the edifice to have been a chamber of embalmment). But their number is destructive of this hypothesis. Others have supposed a planetary reference. With these theorists it would be futile to argue. Dieulafoy conjectures that they were masons' signs. This, again, is impossible, seeing that there are sometimes two in the same block. Perrot thinks that they may have contained *plaques* of coloured *faïence* or marble. No chips or fragments, however, of such decorative additions have ever been discovered. I incline, therefore, to the opinion that they were purely ornamental, and were designed to relieve the dead level of the outer surface.

[2] Stolze, vol. ii. pl. 147.

I pass next to the discussion of its purport. That it was not a fire-temple I consider certain, from its utter lack of resemblance to any Persian fire-altar that exists, either in ruins or figured upon coins. What could have been the object of keeping the sacred flame in a prison-like cell, hermetically concealed from the outer air? Neither could a fire-altar have stood upon the roof, seeing that it is not flat. Flandin and Coste thought that the chamber might have been used for embalming and preparing the royal corpse, prior to its deposit in the rock-tomb opposite. But, although I have elsewhere shown reasons for believing that the body of Cyrus may have been mummified, there is no passage in any author, or in the Avesta itself, that favours the existence of such a practice as a general rule; and why, even if it were so, there should have been assigned to the embalmers a small unlighted cell, so little convenient for their task, it is impossible to say. Canon Rawlinson has suggested that it may have been the Royal Treasury,[1] an hypothesis for which there is equally scant support; since no reason is forthcoming why the treasure should have been stored here, in immediate proximity to the royal tombs, rather than in the city, where, according to Diodorus, it was actually kept; and since, although Pasargadæ may have had its treasure-house also, there is no conceivable reason for the existence of such a building at Naubandajan. Dieulafoy, approximating to the only possible conclusion, viz. that it was a mausoleum, suggests that the king's body may have been temporarily deposited therein, to await the process of dissolution before being committed to its final resting-place in the opposite cliff. But, again, there is no authority for the existence of such a practice; nor could the precepts of the Avesta concerning exposure have thus been carried out; nor does the chamber in the least degree resemble any *dakhma* ever encountered or described. On the contrary, Dieulafoy's own discovery, if correct (I unfortunately had not heard of it and therefore failed to verify it on the spot), suggests a more permanent form of sepulture and the introduction of a heavy weight or probable sarcophagus into the interior, although no present trace exists of such an object. I arrive, therefore, at the conclusion, which the analogy, previously mentioned, of the Lycian tombs corroborates, that this fabric, along with those at Pasargadæ and Naubandajan, was a royal or princely sepulchre,[2] the last survival probably

What was it?

[1] *Fifth Great Oriental Monarchy*, vol. iii. p. 350.

[2] I think it scarcely necessary to discuss the suggestion—which has, nevertheless, found advocates—that this mausoleum or its counterpart at Pasargadæ corresponds with the Tomb of Cyrus, as described by Arrian and Strabo. It resembles the latter in no particular except in being a πυργὸς, and square. It has no colonnade. Its solitary chamber does not answer to the description of an οἴκημα. Above all, the doorway is neither small nor narrow, but is comfortably large.

of an older fashion of interment which may have disappeared after the first rock-tomb had been hewn by order of Darius. M. Perrot, with whose reasoning I am fortunate in finding myself in harmony, carries the argument a step further, and infers that, if the Zindan at Pasargadæ was, as suggested by Dieulafoy, the mausoleum of Cambyses, the father of Cyrus, so its counterpart at Naksh-i-Rustam may have been that of Hystaspes, the father of Darius.

Before finally leaving the Husein Kuh, there remain to be noticed a few other relics, two among them far from unimportant, that occur at the western extremity of the ridge. Upon a bluff of the cliff stands a solitary shaft, hewn out of the solid rock, without either base or capital, five and a half feet high, and one and a half feet in diameter. It does not appear to have belonged to any building, but may have fulfilled some memorial or votive object. Hard by, on the top of the rock, there are some squared and levelled spaces ascended by low steps, which are conjectured to have served as *dakhmas* or platforms of exposure for the dead. Sixty yards round the corner of the cliff, where it turns in a northerly direction, two unmistakable fire-altars, of unequal dimensions, are encountered, situated side by side upon, or rather hewn out of, a projecting mass of rock, thirteen feet above the plain.[1] They are respectively five and a half and five feet high, and four and a half feet square at the base, and taper inwards towards the summit to a square of three and two-thirds feet. Their sides are shaped in the form of filled-in arches, with an engaged column at each corner. A sort of parapet runs round the top, which is excavated into a hollow for the fuel, one foot in width and eight inches deep. This form of altar does not exactly correspond with, but is, nevertheless, not materially different from, those with which we have been made familiar by rock-carvings and coins; and it is not unlikely that this interesting pair are the oldest Mazdean relic in Persia. A little further on, Morier speaks of a number of holes or windows, of various sizes, but of the same pattern, with inscriptions over them, hewn in a recess of the mountain.[2] I did not see them myself; but Ker Porter, who did, found no trace of the alleged inscriptions.

Fire-altars

We have now completed our examination of the monuments on the north side of the Mervdasht plain, and may wend our way towards the great palace-platform, which is our present goal, and its everlasting glory, noticing *en route* a few scattered relics that still exist outside the area of Persepolis itself. These are three in number. On the plain to the north of the platform, about half way between it and Naksh-i-Rustam, and nearly opposite Naksh-

3. Ruins on the plain

[1] Flandin and Coste, vol. iv. pl. 180; Stolze, vol. ii. pl. 114.

[2] *First Journey*, p. 128.

i-Rejeb, is a terrace of white limestone, composed of massive blocks, ten feet in length by four feet in depth, in two stages or tiers, the lower of which projects nearly two feet beyond the higher.[1] The upper surface is thirty-seven feet square, and rises to an elevation of seven feet above the plain. It is variously designated by the natives Takht-i-Rustam, Rustam's Throne, and Takht-i-Taous or Throne of the Peacock, a title which appears to have no specific or intelligible meaning, but is promiscuously applied to many remains of antiquity in Persia. It has been conjectured that this platform may have formed the base of a fire-altar; but the hypothesis lacks any corroboration. Half a mile from the platform to the north, and not far from the rocks, is, or was, a stone doorway, consisting of side-jambs and a lintel, with the figures of priests in long robes, chiselled in high relief upon the former, similar to the Persepolitan portals, and to the remains at Takht-i-Abu Nasr near Shiraz.[2] The third relic has for many years ceased to exist, though its site is visible. But it was so frequently mentioned by the older travellers, from Kaempfer and Le Brun downwards, that its disappearance merits passing notice. This was a solitary column, that rose among the bases of others, in the plain opposite the south-west angle of Persepolis, and formed part of some vanished structure. It was thrown down about the year 1803 by wandering Iliats, for the sake of the iron cramps, by which its drums were held together.[3]

4. Persepolis

Our survey has now brought us to the palace-platform, which, with its ruins, has for over two centuries been accepted as the Persepolis that Alexander captured and burned, and in the last quarter of that period has been proved, by the inscriptions that survive upon its buildings, to have been the veritable structure of the earlier Achæmenian kings.[4] The historical questions, whether here

[1] J. P. Morier, *First Journey*, p. 137; C. J. Rich, *Journey to Persepolis*, p. 258; R. B. Binning, *Two Years' Travel*, vol. ii. p. 40; Flandin and Coste, vol. ii. pl. 63; Stolze, vol. ii. pl. 15.

[2] Sir R. K. Porter, vol. i. p. 680; R. B. Binning, vol. ii. p. 27.

[3] Ouseley, *Travels*, vol. ii. p. 236; Flandin and Coste, vol. iii. pl. 168.

[4] The writers who have described or discussed Persepolis have been so many as only to admit of bare enumeration here. I will divide them into two classes: (1) the travellers who have visited the ruins; (2) the scholars and students who have debated the problems arising out of the sculptures and inscriptions. In neither of these cases shall I encumber this footnote by naming the titles of the works alluded to, the bulk of them having already been frequently mentioned in these pages. I shall, however, add a small third class, with titles included, of those writers who, either by the recency or the quality of their labours, deserve to be considered as the principal extant authorities. I. Friar Odoricus (circ. 1325), Josafa Barbaro (1474), Antonio di Govea (1598), Don G. de Silva y Figueroa (1619), P. della Valle (1621), Sir T. Herbert (1627), J. A. de Mandelslo (1638), J. P. Tavernier (circ. 1650), J. de Thévenot (circ. 1665), H. de Jager (circ. 1665), A. Daulier-Deslandes (1665), Sir J. Chardin (circ. 1670), Père Angelo (circ. 1670), J. Struys (1672), J. Fryer (1676), E. von Kaempfer (1694), C. Le Brun (1704),

was indeed the palace to which the Macedonian set fire, whether this was the citadel and fortress of Persepolis, which have been so minutely described by certain ancient writers, whether the buildings upon its surface were ever completed, and by what means came about their mutilation and decline—I will postpone until a description of the existing ruins has furnished us with the data whereupon to construct a reply. Similarly, the artistic problems which the remains suggest, and, in part only, avail to solve—such, for instance, as the source from which the idea of the palace-platform and its halls was derived, the origin, nature, purpose, and quality of the sculptures with which they are adorned, and the character and object of the various edifices—will be more appropriately taken in hand when we are familiar with the grounds of a possible induction. I may, however, state at once that Fergusson's theory that the palaces of Persepolis were buildings adapted to the double purpose of secular government and religious adoration will meet with no support here.[1] Indeed, I know of no source from which it is capable of receiving support at all. There is

C. Niebuhr (1765), Cte. de Ferrières-Sauvebœuf (1785), W. Franklin (1787), J. Scott Waring (1802), J. P. Morier (1809–11), Sir W. Ouseley (1811), W. Price (1811), J. S. Buckingham (1816), Sir R. K. Porter (1820), C. J. Rich (1821), Sir H. Rawlinson (circ. 1840), Ch. Texier (1840), Baron C. de Bode (1840), E. Flandin and P. Coste (1841), R. B. Binning (1851), J. Ussher (1861), A. Vambéry (1862), F. Stolze and F. C. Andreas (1877), H. D. Kiach (1878), E. Stack (1881), M. and J. Dieulafoy (1881). II. Hyde, La Crose, Leibnitz, D'Hancarville, Cuper, Caylus, Heeren, Jones, Klenker, Mannert, De Murr, Maurice, Witte, Grotefend, Hagemann, Tychsen, Hoeck, De Sacy, Langlès, De Saulcy, Norris, Rennell, Burnouf, Wall, Lassen, Westergaard, Holtzmann, Benfey, Fergusson, Ritter, Spiegel, Hitzig, Bézold, Kiepert, Hincks, Menke, Kossowicz, Oppert, Vaux, Mordtmann, Lenormant, Sayce, Ménant, Perrot and Chipiez, Nöldeke. III. Of the above I select, as the most necessary to the student: Sir H. Rawlinson, *Journal of the R.A.S.*, vols. x. xi. xiv.; J. Fergusson, *The Palaces of Nineveh and Persepolis restored*; C. Texier, *L'Arménie*, &c.; Flandin and Coste, *Perse Ancienne*; E. Ménant, *Les Achéménides et les Inscriptions de la Perse*; J. Oppert, *Le Peuple et la Langue des Mèdes* and *Les Inscriptions Achéménides*; F. Spiegel, *Die Altpersischen Keilinschriften*: F. Stolze, *Verhandl. d. Gesellsch. f. Erdk. z. Berlin*, 1883; F. Stolze and Th. Nöldeke, *Persepolis*; Th. Nöldeke, 'Persepolis,' in *Encycl. Britan.* (9th edit.); M. Dieulafoy, *L'Art antique de la Perse*; Perrot and Chipiez, *Histoire de l'Art dans l'antiquité*, vol. v.; F. H. Weisbach, *Die Achämenidinschriften Zweiter Art*.

[1] Fergusson himself saw clearly that they were not temples in the strict sense of the term. Herodotus (i. 131) said truly that the Persians had no temples, and when, on the rock of Bisitun, Darius speaks of having restored the temples which the usurper Gomates had destroyed, he is, probably, either alluding to the fire-altars of the Zoroastrian faith, or to the temples of subject nationalities and religions which the catholic and statesmanlike sympathies of the Achæmenian sovereigns induced them habitually to patronise. A temple, as understood in Assyria, Egypt, Judæa, or Greece—viz. a sanctuary of the god—was a conception necessarily alien to a belief wherein the deity was regarded as expressed in the elemental forms of nature. Fergusson's theory of religious adoration is based only on a far-fetched induction from the sculptures on the royal tombs.

not on the platform a single trace of fire-altar, fire-temple, or adjunct of worship, and I am at a loss to understand upon what grounds, other than that of a false analogy, such an hypothesis can ever have started into existence. I shall treat the platform as that which it has clearly been demonstrated to be, viz. a collection of royal audience-halls and palaces, devoted to the ceremonial aspects of the Great King's existence.[1]

[1] For the help of the student, I append a tabulated catalogue of the illustrations of Persepolis, upon which he must in a large measure depend. Those by Texier, and Flandin and Coste, are copper-plate engravings; those by Stolze, and Dieulafoy, are photographs:—

Name of Building	Texier, 1840	Flandin & Coste, 1841	Stolze, 1878	Dieulafoy, 1881–5
General view . .	Vol. ii. 91–2	Vol. ii. 66, 71	Vol. ii. 97–9	Vol. ii. 4-11
Plan . . .	„ 93–4	„ 64, 65, 67	„ 148–50	„ 2
Platform . .	—	„ 68	—	—
Inscription on ditto . .	„ 143–4	„ 71–2	„ 95	„ 3
Great Staircase .	—	—	„ 94	—
Porch of Xerxes .				
First colossi .	„ 102$^{1\,2}$, 108	„ 73, 78–80	„ 87	—
Second colossi .	„ 109	„ 77, 81, 82	„ 88	„ 12
Inscriptions .	—	„ 83–6	„ 89–92	—
Columns . .	—	„ 74–6	—	„ 21
Restoration .	—	„ 87	(cf. Perrot and Ch	ipiez, vol. v. p. 404)
Hall of Xerxes				
General view .	—	„ 89	„ 74, 75	—
Plan . . .	—	„ 90	„ —	—
Staircase and sculptures .	—	„ 91, 95–110	Vol. ii. 77–86	—
Columns . .	„ 104–7	„ 92–4, iii. 168	„ 93	Vol. ii. 20, 21
Inscriptions .	—	„ 111	„ 76	—
Sculptures .	„ 116	—	—	—
Restoration .	„ 103	„ 112	(cf. Perrot and Chi	piez, p. 548, 676, 724)
Palace of Darius				
General view .	„ 95, 117	Vol. iii. 114–7	Vol. i. 29	—
Plan . . .	—	„ 113	—	Vol. ii. 13
Staircases . .	—	„ 119–20	„ 40, 41, 66	„ 15
Inscriptions .	„ 97	„ 125–8	„ 42–9	—
Sculptures .	„ 98, 102	„ 122–4	„ 30–9	„ 16–7, iii. 17
Restoration .	—	„ 121, 122	(cf. P. and Ch. p. 644)	Vol. iii .
Palace of Artaxerxes				
Plan . . .	—	„ 128	—	—
Inscriptions .	—	„ 129	Vol. i. 26–8, 65	—
Sculptures .	—	„ 130	—	—
Palace of Xerxes				
General view .	„ 96	„ 132–4	„ 8, 16	—
Plan . .	—	„ 131	—	—
Staircases . .	—	„ 136, 137	„ 17–20	—
Inscriptions .	—	„ 138–41	„ 21–5	—
Sculptures .	„ 99	„ 135	„ 9–15	„ 18
S.E. Edifice				
General view .	—	„ 142, 143	„ 1	—
Sculptures .	—	—	„ 2–7	—
Central Edifice				
General view	—	„ 144, 145	„ 50	—
Sculptures .	—	„ 146, 147	„ 51–2	—
Hall of 100 *Columns*				
General view .	„ 100	„ 148$^{1\,2}$, 150–1	„ 53, 54	„ 1–3
Plan . . .	—	„ 149	—	Vol. ii. 14
Columns . .		—	„ 67–9	—
Sculptures .	„ 101, 110–4	„ 152–8	„ 56–64	Vol. iii. 19
Bulls of portico	—		„ 55	—
Porch . .	—	„ 160, 161	„ 67–9	—
Restoration .	—	„ 158, 159	(cf. P. and Ch. p. 192, 788)	„ 8
Tombs				
N. tomb . .	„ 123–6	„ 164–6	Vol. i. 70	„ 4
Middle tomb .	—	„ 163, 164^{2}	„ 71, 72	—
S. tomb . .	—	„ 162	„ 73	—

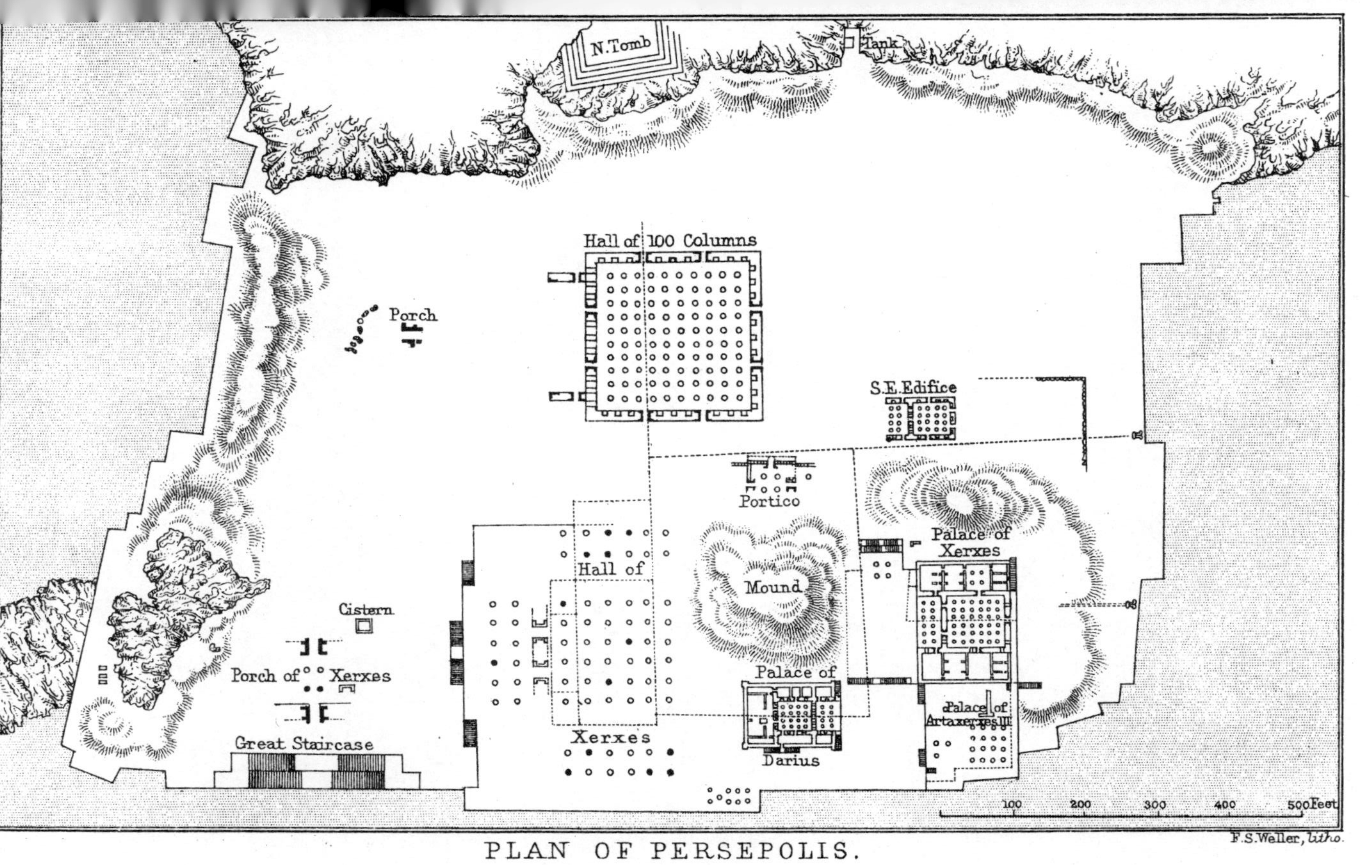

PLAN OF PERSEPOLIS.

Setting forth from Puzeh for Persepolis, I turned the corner of the cliff, passed the sculptured recess of Naksh-i-Rejeb, already described, and, keeping my face to the south, and the rock, which behind Persepolis is called Kuh-i-Rahmet or Mountain of Mercy (formerly known as Shah Kuh) on the left hand, came in sight, in about twenty minutes, of the great platform, standing boldly out from the mountain-base, and supporting on its surface the ruined piers and pillars that illustrations had rendered so familiar to my gaze. This is the northern approach to the platform ; and here an outcrop of rock juts up at the north-west corner almost to the level of its summit, so that one can reach the latter without recourse to the great stairs. The latter are at a distance of seventy yards beyond the north-west angle, and are built in a recess of the main face of the platform, which fronts the breadth of the Mervdasht plain with a westerly outlook. Remembering the famous boast that the staircase was of so gentle a slope that horsemen might ride up and down, I rounded the angle of the platform, rode up the ruined steps, and dismounted on the summit immediately before the bull-flanked Propylæa of Xerxes.

Approach

The substructure of Persepolis consists of a great platform, or three sides of a parallelogram built out from the mountain-base, whose lower slopes have been pared down and levelled to suit the architectural purpose, and have then been built up and faced with gigantic blocks of stone, constituting a perpendicular wall that rises to a height varying from twenty to nearly fifty feet above the plain. Its axis, strictly speaking, is inclined from north-west to south-east ; but for simplicity's sake I shall speak of it as north by south. Its main length is, in this direction, 1,523 feet ; its breadth from east to west is 920 feet. The original rock is in many places visible on the surface, and its inequalities in the main account both for the capriciousness of outline, and for the different terraces or levels upon which the various structures were raised. One staircase, indeed, on the platform is hewn out of the mother-rock, and a cistern is similarly hollowed in it. Great irregularity, but withal well-conceived structural relief, is lent to the external appearance of the platform by the numerous bays and angles into which, least on the main front, but chiefly on the north side, the wall is broken. Of great blocks of stone, sometimes laid horizontally, but more commonly of polygonal shape, is this composed. They are beautifully fitted and adjusted, without mortar or cement, although originally held together on their upper surface by iron cramps soldered into double dovetails with lead. Some of these great stones have been measured as much as fifty feet in length by six to ten feet in width. Originally a cornice and parapet ran round the edge of the platform, and lent it a decorative appearance from the

The platform

plain. These have now entirely disappeared. On the southern wall are engraved four cuneiform inscriptions (two in Persian, one in Susian, and one in Assyrian) which declare that it was the work of Darius, who in the manner already familiar to us from the epitaph on his sepulchre, invokes Ormuzd, enumerates his tributaries and subjects, and places his palace under the protection of the deity.[1] The surface of the platform, though littered with débris, and, in some parts, piled high with mounds of rubbish and sand, is yet clearly divisible into four levels, which are the result of natural configuration quite as much as of a deliberate architectural design. The lowest and smallest of these is a narrow platform on the south, 180 feet in breadth, and about twenty feet in height above the plain. It appears never to have borne any buildings. The second level is that upon which stand the Propylæa of Xerxes, and, further behind, the Hall of a Hundred Columns, and whose height is thirty-five to forty feet above the plain. Next comes the level, about ten feet higher, that supports the Hall of Xerxes; and finally, at an additional height of ten feet, is the terrace upon which were constructed the palaces of Darius and of Xerxes.

All these edifices, the platform itself, and the outer wall, were built of the same material. Its fine texture, its superb and manifold tints, and the high polish of which it admits, have induced most writers to describe it as marble, while many have denominated it in different parts, according to its colour, syenite, basalt, and porphyry. Le Brun, two centuries ago, and Niebuhr in the last century, were quite correct in pointing out this error. The material of which every square foot of hewn or chiselled surface at Persepolis is composed—and indeed (I believe) every relic, without exception, of the Achæmenian period in Persia—is the calcareous limestone of its native mountains. In this were hewn the royal rock-tombs; upon this was sculped the lordly proclamation of Bisitun; of this was built the Tomb of Cyrus. Short of marble, to which in grain and in surface-tone it approximates, a finer material cannot anywhere be found, while the variety of colours which it presents in its natural state, or is capable of assuming under the influence of exposure, is surprising. Sometimes it has been blanched almost snow-white, or of an amber richness, elsewhere it is brown and sombre, frequently grey, and occasionally, when polished, a rich blue-black. Nor can there be the slightest doubt as to the spot from which the material of Persepolis came. In the rock of the Kuh-i-Rahmet, in more than one place both to the north and the south of the platform, are visible the quarries from which the stonemasons hewed the stone. Big blocks

Material

[1] Rawlinson, *Journal of the R.A.S.*, vol. x. pp. 289 *et seq.*; Spiegel, *Die Altpers. Keilins.* pp. 47–51; Ménant, *Les Achéménides*, pp. 80–1.

PANORAMA OF PERSEPOLIS FROM THE EAST

are still lying there, either ready for removal, or not yet wholly separated from the mother-rock. Chipped fragments may be encountered all along the slope. The proximity of this great natural source of supply must have been one of the main reasons for the selection of the site of Persepolis, and accounts for the astonishing wealth of sculpture. Scarcely any transport was needed, and the workman could both hew and elaborate his raw material on the spot.

For about 150 years the platform has been called by the Persians Takht-i-Jamshid, or Throne of Jamshid. Its earlier name, which can

Panorama

be traced as far back as the fourteenth century, and also still survives, was Chehel Minar, i.e. Forty Minarets or Spires, an allusion to the big columns of the Hall of Xerxes, which originally numbered many more, but have steadily dwindled for centuries. Forty, as has been before remarked, is a round number in Persia; and it is accordingly fanciful to ascribe the origin of the title to a period when the columns may have amounted to exactly that total. Other and cognate Persian titles sometimes applied, have been Chehel and Hazar (Thousand) Situn. Herbert, in 1627, said that the platform reminded him of Windsor Castle from Eton. I confess that I cannot imagine any two objects more dissimilar: nor do I know of any site or structure in the world, with the single exception of the platform at Baalbec, in Syria, with which Persepolis can at all fairly be compared. The analogy of *acropoleis*, or rock-citadels, is not a fair one, inasmuch as they were commonly situated, at Athens and Pergamos, just as now at Salzburg and Königstein, on the summit of natural elevations; while the platform of Persepolis is artificially built up from the plain, whereon, owing to the stretch of surrounding flat, and the background of the Kuh-i-Rahmet, it can never have occupied a really commanding position. Indeed, I incline to think that the spectacular grandeur of Persepolis, no less than its present panoramic importance, have been uniformly exaggerated by travellers. From a distance, as we approach it, across the wide plain of Mervdasht, it appears for long to be quite insignificant: and must, even when covered with its intact palaces and halls, have always been dwarfed by its surroundings. It is only as we ride up to the great front-wall, and still more as we wander among its megalithic ruins, that the full impression of its grandeur forces itself upon the mind. Few visitors, in all probability, are not disappointed with the first *coup d'œil*. But every hour passed in scrutiny is a degree of admiration gained; until reconstructing in fancy, from the dismembered skeleton before us, the original Persepolis, glittering and pompous, as it emerged from the hands of Darius and Xerxes, we can well believe that no more sumptuous framework of regal magnificence was ever wrought by man.

It is in keeping with the bizarre outline, and with what the Greeks termed the general ἀσυμμετρία of the structural dispositions of the platform, that the main stairway, indeed the only visible access,[1] to its summit, should have been placed, not in the middle, but in close proximity to the north-west angle. The front wall of the platform is purposely recessed; and in the bay so formed, two flights are first seen, diverging to right and left, and each containing fifty-eight steps. At the top of each of these flights is a landing; and the ramps then turn towards each other and converge, this second or upper flight containing forty-eight steps each (i.e. a grand total of 212),[2] and terminating in a central landing seventy feet long, on a level with the top of the platform, which is here thirty-four feet above the plain. The steps are, as I have previously indicated, very shallow, being less than four inches deep. They are twenty-two and a half feet wide, and fifteen inches broad. Several steps, in one instance (noted by Ouseley) as many as sixteen or seventeen, are hewn out of a single block of limestone. Considering the 2,400 years of climate and conflict which they have braved, they are on the whole wonderfully well preserved; and the entire staircase formed a fitting, but not, I think, a more than fitting approach to the palaces of the Achæmenians. I certainly cannot concur in the frantic transports of most visitors, who have joined in eulogising this as the finest flight of steps in the world. The Propylæa at Athens, though representing, of course, a very different conception, constituted to my mind a far nobler approach; whilst, in the same architectural class, the great stairways that led up to the palace-terraces of Sargon and Sennacherib at Nineveh must have been considerably more imposing. It is noteworthy that neither on the walls of the stairways nor on the intervening surface of the terrace-wall, are there here either sculptures or inscriptions. The actual date of the staircase it is impossible to establish, but from the fact that it leads direct to the Portal of Xerxes, a reason might be found for associating it with the name of that monarch. On the other hand, we are then left without a direct approach from the plain to the earlier edifices of Darius.[3]

Main staircase

Immediately opposite, and at a distance of forty-five feet from the

[1] A road for wheeled vehicles, however, has been traced which ascended the platform on the south.

[2] I have given the figures of Flandin and Coste. Morier said the first flights had 54 steps; Porter and Binning, 55; Dieulafoy, 63. Perhaps more have been uncovered at the base. All agree in 48 steps for the upper flights.

[3] From the facts that the Palace of Darius stands towards the south end of the platform and faces towards the south, and that an inscription of that monarch is engraved on the extreme outside south wall, Fergusson (p. 98) infers that the original entrance was on that side, and that the northern portion of the platform was added by Xerxes. This has a certain air of likelihood; but where, then, is, or was, the staircase of Darius?

MAIN STAIRCASE

head of the staircase, stand the imposing remains of what we know, from the cuneiform inscriptions upon it, to have been the Porch of Xerxes. This was a structure consisting of three parts: a huge bull-flanked portal, facing the plain, an interior hall or court whose roof was sustained by four great columns, and a further bull-flanked portal facing in the opposite direction or towards the mountains. From its character and dimensions, not less than from the terms of the inscription, we can be certain that this structure filled no other purpose than that of a ceremonial approach or doorway to the great hall, which the same monarch built a little farther on, although its orientation is at right angles to the latter. The first objects that greet us in this portal are an unmistakable reminder of the Assyrian forerunners of Achæmenian art, and might almost have been borrowed from the halls of Nimrud or Khorsabad. They are two great figures of bulls, whose fore feet, sturdily planted on pedestals five feet above the ground, and the fronts of whose bodies face the spectator, being sculped in bold projection from the piers of the gateway. On the inner walls of the passage the hinder parts of their bodies and flanks project similarly from the surface, but in lower relief, while their hind legs, in contrast with the solid repose of their fore members, stride proudly forwards.[1] Earlier travellers used to declare that these great quadrupeds were monoliths; but it is obvious from a cursory inspection that they are built up of four courses of stone. Their dimensions are seventeen and three-quarter feet in height and nineteen feet in length, the total height of the piers whose lower parts they adorn being thirty-five and a half feet, length twenty-one feet, thickness six feet, and the breadth of the corridor between being twelve feet. The head of the monster on the right hand of the spectator has completely disappeared; the neck of that on the left survives, but the whole fore part of its head has been hacked off beyond all possibility of recognition. Round its neck hangs a collar of roses. On the chests and between the fore legs of both beasts, as also on their shoulders, ribs, and flanks, are masses of hair in tightly frizzed and rounded curls.[2] Although the ingenuity of the early travellers was severely strained in the effort to reconstruct the absent features of these colossi, and to explain the rival pair in the eastern gateway,[3]

Porch of Xerxes

[1] This is a point of difference from the Assyrian monsters, which invariably have five legs, a fifth being introduced behind the fore legs, so that, when viewed in profile, all four legs may be visible, and the verisimilitude of movement may be sustained.

[2] Some of the older writers curiously mistook these for bosses of armour.

[3] P. della Valle thought they were compounded of horse, man, and griffin; Herbert, of elephant, rhinoceros, Pegasus, and griffin; Mandelslo, of horse and lion; D. Deslandes, of elephant; Chardin, of horse, lion, rhinoceros, and elephant;

there cannot be a doubt, from the shape and anatomy of their bodies, that they were intended for bulls; and any hesitation on this score was finally removed by the discovery of the débris of one of the bull-heads by Flandin and Coste. The muscles are finely indicated on the bodies of the beasts, and their pose and mien typify the proud challenge of arrogance and strength.

Above the bulls, high up, on the inner walls of the gateway, are chiselled on either side, in parallel tablets, the inscriptions in three tongues, which reveal the handiwork of Xerxes. This is what the king says:—

Inscription of Xerxes

A great God is Ormuzd, who hath created the earth, who hath created the heavens, who hath created man, who hath given to mankind the good spirit (life), who hath made Xerxes King, the sole King of many Kings, the sole Lord of many Lords. I am Xerxes, the Great King, the King of Kings, the King of the many-tongued countries, the King of this great universe, the son of Darius, the King, the Achæmenian. Xerxes, the Great King, saith: By the grace of Ormuzd I have made this portal, whereon are depicted all the countries.[1] Many other noble monuments there are in this Parsa,[2] which I have wrought, and which my father hath wrought. That which hath been wrought is good. All of it we have wrought by the grace of Ormuzd. Xerxes the King saith, May Ormuzd protect me and my empire. Both that which I have wrought, and that which my father hath wrought, may Ormuzd protect them.[3]

From this proud memorial it is, I believe, with affected disgust that most travellers turn to the records of many generations of European visitors, who have either cut or painted their names on the lower surfaces of this gateway, in some cases even on the bodies of the bulls. I confess that I do not share this spurious emotion. A structure so hopelessly ruined is not rendered the less impressive—on the contrary, to my thinking, it becomes the more interesting—by reason of the records graven upon it, in many cases with their own hands, by famous voyagers of the past, with whose names and studies the intelligent visitor to Persepolis is likely to be almost as familiar as he

Epigraphs of travel

Kaempfer, of camelopard; Le Brun, of sphinx, horse, lion, and ape; Franklin, of lion, griffin, and elephant. Herbert's illustration represents them as most parlous-looking monsters, principally elephant. From Niebuhr downwards it became fashionable to call them sphinxes. Even Morier thought the first pair had the heads of horses.

[1] The word is Visadahyaus (derived from *visa*, for *vispa* = all, and *dahyaus*, or country). Rawlinson variously renders it 'gate of entrance' and 'public portal.' Oppert translates it as above. Spiegel has 'diesen Thorweg der alle Völker zeigt. Dieulafoy supposes it to be a proper name, and renders 'ce portique nommé Viçadhahyu.'

[2] *Vide* a previous footnote, p. 132.

[3] *Vide* Rawlinson, *Journ. R. A. S.* vol. x. pp. 329–34; Spiegel, pp. 58–9; Oppert, pp. 223–4; Dieulafoy, pt. ii. p. 19; Weisbach, pp. 82–3. The translation which I have given is a collation from several of these sources.

is with the titles of Xerxes, and whose forms seem in fancy once more to people the scene which they have revealed and illumined by their writings to thousands of their fellow-countrymen, who may never have had the chance of setting foot on Persian soil themselves. It was with no irritation therefore, but with keen interest, that I read here in large characters the name of 'Cap. John Malcolm,[1] Envoy Extraordinary, Pleni-Potentiary,' A.D. 1800, coupled with those of Captain William Campbell, Captain J. Colebrooke, and G. Briggs;[2] and, just below, those of Sir Harford Jones,[3] Bart. K.C. 1809, James Morier,[4] H. Willock,[5] T. Sheridan, J. Sutherland; and, again, Captain John Macdonald,[6] 1808, 1810, and 1826. On the right hand wall I also noticed the names of Stanley,[7] 'New York Herald,' 1870; of Gobineau;[8] of C. Texier,[9] R. Labourdonnaye, and Ph. Laguiche, 1840; of C. J. Rich,[10] A. Taylor, E. Sturmy, and I. Tod, 1821; of Malcolm's second Mission in 1810, including among other names those of H. Ellis,[11] Lieutenant Monteith,[12] Lieutenant Lindsay,[13] and Lieutenant Pottinger;[14] of S. Manesty, British Envoy in 1804, with his retinue. The earliest recorded date that I noticed was 1704.[15] To the intervening period belong Carsten Niebuhr,[16] 1765, and W. Franklin, 1787.

Beyond the entrance gateway and the first pair of colossi, there still stand two out of four lofty fluted columns, with the composite or triple Persepolitan capital, that is also found in the Hall of Xerxes, in the Hall of a Hundred Columns, and in the hall of Artaxerxes Mnemon at Susa. These four pillars, the survivors of which are forty-six and three-quarters feet high, originally supported the roof of a central hall or court, eighty-two feet square. The left hand column is composed of three blocks; but its flutings, which are thirty-nine in number, do not exactly correspond, the drums having evidently been shifted from their position by earthquake. The second right-hand

Central hall

[1] Sir John Malcolm, the historian of Persia and Governor of Bombay.
[2] The translator of Ferishta.
[3] Afterwards Sir Harford Jones Brydges.
[4] The writer so frequently mentioned, also author of *Haji Baba*, and *chargé d'affaires* at Teheran.
[5] Afterwards Sir H. Willock, *chargé d'affaires* at Teheran.
[6] Afterwards Sir J. Macdonald Kinneir, minister at Teheran and author of *Geographical Memoir of Persia*.
[7] H. M. Stanley, the African explorer, who came to Persia as a newspaper correspondent.
[8] Comte J. de Gobineau, French minister at Teheran and author of *Trois Ans en Asie*.
[9] The author, so frequently cited, of *Description de l'Arménie*, &c.
[10] British Resident at Baghdad, and traveller in Kurdistan, who died at Shiraz in 1821.
[11] Afterwards Sir H. Ellis, British envoy to Persia.
[12] Afterwards General Sir W. Monteith.
[13] Afterwards Sir H. Lindsay-Bethune.
[14] The explorer of Beluchistan, afterwards Sir H. Pottinger.
[15] Morier says that he saw here Mandelslo's name (1638) and Le Brun's (1704). I did not myself notice them.
[16] The Arabian traveller, frequently quoted.

column has fallen, and parts of its segments lie embedded in the soil. The capital and small pieces of the shaft of the corresponding left-hand column are similarly buried. In Chardin's time all four were standing. Stolze thinks that the topmost capitals of these pillars were shaped in the form of a horse; but I see no reason for supposing that they terminated in anything else than the familiar bull-headed capital of the composite Achæmenian column, like their counterparts in other contemporary fabrics.

Second gateway

This hall leads to a second or corresponding gateway on the eastern face, where, similarly projecting from the side and fronts of two massive stone piers, another pair of colossal monsters look towards the mountain. Their character and physiognomy, however, differ from their pendants on the western face, and indicate a closer adherence to the Assyrian prototype. The bodies and the legs are again those of bulls, massive, masculine, majestic; but above their backs rise lofty wings, sweeping upwards into the air (instead of being laid back, as in the case of the Assyrian colossi), with the plumes exquisitely carved in high and seemingly imperishable relief. A second and more striking difference is that these colossi are or were human-faced. The pickaxe of the destroyer has mutilated their features out of all masculine appearance; but the great ringleted beards still depend intact upon the stalwart chests; earrings hang from their ears; bunches of hair frame heavily the vanished faces; and the heads are crowned by lofty tiaras, terminating at the summit in a fringe or coronet of feathers, while circular bands, curling upwards in the shape of horns, adorn the front. The bewilderment and obfuscation which appear in equal degree to have been excited in ancient travellers by these remarkable monsters are well illustrated in the description of the excellent Dr. Fryer, two centuries ago:—

> Being entred the Pomærium of Cambyses Hall, at the Hall Gates we encountred two horrid Shapes both for Grandeur and Unwontedness, being all in Armour of Coat of Mail, striking a Terror on those about to intrude; their Countenances were of the fiercest Lions, and might pass for such had not huge Wings made them flying Gryffons, and their Bulk and Hinder Parts exceeded the largest Elephants.[1]

Why the bull-headed colossi should have been turned towards the plain, or the main front of the platform, and the winged and man-headed bulls, which are infinitely more imposing, towards the mountain, is a problem which, so far as I know, no one has discussed, and which no one is likely to solve. Similar panels of cuneiform inscription

[1] *Travels*, p. 251. The moderns have not been much wiser. M. Anquetil Duperron interpreted these monsters as symbolical representations of Noah; M. de Sacy as emblems of the mythical Kaiomurs. Of course, the truth is simply that the artist had been in Babylon or in Assyria.

COLOSSI OF THE PORCH OF XERXES

decorate the inner face of the eastern, as of the previous, gateway. As to the object of this great twofold gateway, with its interior hall, I do not conceive that there can be much dispute. Fergusson supposes it to have been a gate or seat of judgment, like those mentioned in the Old Testament, but I know of no ground for believing that the Persian monarchs so far derogated from the exalted idea of monarchy expressed upon all their sculptures, as to render themselves thus easily accessible to their subjects. Consequently, I regard the porch merely as a monumental entry to the palaces and audience-halls beyond, not unlike the pylons of Luxor and Karnak.

Cistern

To the left or north of the Porch of Xerxes, the natural rock crops up to the level of the platform, and here are the foundations of some perished structure, with the bases of pillars, and with a single drum of an unfluted column, which I do not remember to have seen noticed as such in any previous work.[1] On the other or south side of the further gateway is a tank or cistern, composed, according to Buckingham, of large stones, hollowed, according to Binning, out of a single mass of stone, but, as my notes say, hewn out of the rock itself. It is surrounded by a coping or parapet, about three feet above the surface, and is at present filled with soil to a depth of four feet from the top. Its dimensions are eighteen feet by fifteen feet; and it is supposed to have been fed by one of the subterranean aqueducts beneath the surface of the platform, to which I shall draw attention later on, and to have irrigated or embellished a garden which may have stretched between the Porch and the Audience-hall of Xerxes.

Hall of Xerxes. Staircase

We now approach the latter edifice, which must undoubtedly have been the chief glory of the original Persepolis, whose columns gave it in mediæval times its title of Chehel Minar, and whose remains are still the noblest survival of the reign of the son of Darius. At a distance of fifty-four yards from the Porch of Xerxes in a southerly direction, and at right angles both to it and to the longitudinal axis of the platform, we encounter a superb stairway, the finest of those sculptured adornments—the Achæmenian counterpart to the pylons of Egypt, the tympana and metopes and frieze of the Hellenic temple, the graven walls of the great sanctuaries of Buddha, and the western façade of the Gothic minster—that distinguish Persepolis from all other ruins, and lift the architecture of the age of Darius and his successors into an order of separate individuality and grandeur. For a total length of seventy-two yards extends the sculptured front of the elevated platform that sustains the audience-hall; and its original height was eleven and a half feet above the

[1] I have already, on p. 74, disproved Perrot's assertion that the column at Pasargadæ is the sole unfluted column in Persia.

lower level upon which stand the Propylæa. Access is gained to its summit by four flights of steps, two of which, projecting from the platform, converge towards a landing in its centre ; the remaining two ascend the platform from either extremity, north and south. Each flight contains thirty-one steps, which are fifteen and a half feet long, fourteen inches broad, and four inches deep. When we recognise, as we shall, that the building to which they conducted was the audience-hall of the Great King, the object of these four stairways to admit of the free coming and going of the vast crowds that thronged thither to do him homage, is at once apparent ; and we may admire both the ingenuity and the practical wisdom of the architect.

The front wall of the projecting central landing that is formed by the converging slope of the middle stairways, contains sculptures of a size and character that both dominate and set a tone to the remainder. In the centre is an oblong panel, designed to receive an epigraph which has never been inscribed—one among many indications that even the older buildings on the platform were never finished, and that the Achæmenian kings, like their more modern successors, were either too vain or too indolent to complete the designs of their predecessors. On the right side three armed guards, with spears and shields, on the left side four similar spearmen with quivers, face towards the empty panel. In the triangular space behind each of these groups, that is formed by the base angle of the flights of steps, is sculped on the wall a rearing bull, with a lion whose claws and teeth are fixed into its hinder flank. This is a subject so frequently reproduced in similar compartments on the stairways of Persepolis, as to deserve a passing note of examination. Some high authorities have discovered therein a subtle allegorical meaning. Layard, for instance, thinks that the victory of the lion over the bull typifies the triumph of the sun, or principle of heat, over water, or the element of moisture. But, though there is some ground for identifying the bull with the latter principle, I do not know that there is any for the connection required by the above hypothesis between the lion and the sun. A particular reference has been detected by some to the phase through which the sun passes at No Ruz. Others, again, have conjectured that the combat symbolised is that between Ormuzd and Ahriman, or the principles of good and evil, the lion representing the pernicious and destructive power—the answer to which, of course, is that on palaces adorned with the sculptured praises of Ormuzd, the victory of his adversary is hardly likely to have been pourtrayed. More probably the combat is merely a symbolical representation of the conflict, so frequently depicted in other forms on the neighbouring walls, between the king and various horrid monsters that dispute his royal power. The

Sculptures

NORTHERN STAIRCASE AND PLATFORM OF HALL OF XERXES

lion is the emblem of triumphant majesty ; the bull typifies powerful but vanquished force.

We now pass to the main wall of the terrace, whose processional bas-reliefs supply us with a clue to the ceremonies that were enacted upon its summit. In three long lines or bands they stretch away to right and left, towards the terminal staircases; although the full height of the platform has been reduced, and the integrity of the uppermost row of figures has been sadly impaired, by a mutilation that has sawn them right in twain, leaving only the lower halves of the bodies depicted. At either end the angle formed by the steps is filled with an identical lion and bull ; the group at the eastern extremity, owing to its having been buried for many centuries beneath the soil, retaining a wonderful and brilliant freshness of outline. Next to these triangular panels, at either end, come tablets for inscriptions. My notes record that that on the eastern side has been obliterated ;[1] but the western compartment contains a cuneiform inscription, combining a dedication to Ormuzd with the name of 'Xerxes, the Great King, the King of kings, the son of Darius, the king, the Achæmenian.'[2] From this panel the triple row of figures, already spoken of, each a little over three feet in height, march towards the centre ; while a corresponding procession advances from the left or opposite wing. These two sets of groups very clearly represent different classes of individuals. Those upon the left with lances and arms, and musical instruments, accompanied by chariots and horses, are manifestly the courtiers and guards of the Great King. Those upon the right, on the other hand, subdivided into smaller groups by sculptured likenesses of cypress-trees, typify, by their differing physiognomy and costumes, the various nationalities from which they were drawn ; and by the objects which they escort or convey, viz., oxen, rams, asses, camels, fruits, vases, jewels, ornaments, and offerings in general—the homage or tribute of subject peoples. There can be very little doubt, therefore, that we have here depicted the ceremonial observance that took place annually in the palace above, at such time as the Great King came to Persepolis at the vernal equinox, or No Ruz, to receive the reports of his officers, and the tribute of his subjects ; just as were chiselled upon the frieze of the Parthenon at Athens the less serious splendours of the Panathenaic procession.

Processions at No Ruz

And now having mounted to the upper level of the platform, we approach the most notable external objects among the ruins, where

The columns

[1] M. Perrot (p. 696) says that it never contained an inscription ; but this, I think, is wrong.

[2] *Vide* Rawlinson, Spiegel, Oppert, and Weisbach in the localities before cited.

Those black granite pillars, once high-reared
By Jamshid in Persepolis to bear
His house, now, 'mid their broken flights of steps,
Lie prone, enormous, down the mountain-side.

And yet that they do not all so lie the photographs will show, and we can still, amid a chaos of wilful destruction, most thankfully perceive The columns that still survive, albeit in a sadly mutilated condition, along with the yet visible bases of others that have long ago fallen or disappeared, reveal to us the plan of the building. It consisted of a central hall supported by six rows of six columns each, with advanced porticoes on three of its sides, north, east, and west, containing two rows of six columns each, or a grand total of seventy-two columns. Of these thirteen are still standing.[1] No plan that I have hitherto seen (that which accompanies this chapter has been drawn under my own instructions) places these in their right positions. To a visitor approaching from the north or principal staircase they are : (1) In the north portico, the third from the right in the outer row ; (2) in the central hall, the outermost on the left in the first row, the second from the right in the third row, and the third from the left in the fourth row ; (3) in the east portico, the third and fourth from the north in the outer row, and the second and third in the inner row ; (4) in the west portico the first, fifth, and sixth from the north in the outer row, and the third and sixth in the inner row. In many other cases the bases are still standing, with fragments of the shattered drums lying hard by. The interior surfaces of the latter, where they were originally joined to each other, are as smooth and level as on the day when they were planed, and the holes are visible in them that contained the dowels, by which they were held together. The second and third in the outer row of the west portico struck me at first as being those that must have fallen most recently (and that made up the total to fifteen at the beginning of the century), since the broken fragments of their shafts are still lying where they fell ; but a reference to the pages of Ker Porter shows me that this was a false inference, since the two additional survivors in his day belonged to the central group, and not to either of the porticoes. It is

[1] The sure, though gradual, process of decay is illustrated by the ever-dwindling number of columns that has been recorded by travellers at different times during the last three centuries, and which I have gathered from my reading. Figueroa (1619) reported 20, Della Valle (1621) 25, Herbert (1627) 19, Mandelslo (1638) 19, Tavernier (1665 ; but it appears doubtful whether he actually visited the spot himself) 12, Daulier-Deslandes (1665) 19, Chardin (circ. 1670) 20 [19 only in his illustration], Fryer (1677) 18, Kaempfer (1694) 17, Le Brun (1704) 19 [i.e. including the two in Propylæa], Niebuhr (1765) 17, Franklin (1787) 15, Morier (1809) 16, Ouseley (1811) 15, Porter (1818) 15, Rich (1821) 15, De Bode (1841) 13, Binning (1851) 13, Ussher (1861) 13, Mounsey (1866) 13, Stack (1881) 12. It will be seen that several of these writers have made mistakes.

evident from the capitals still *in situ* in a more or less mutilated condition, and from the remains of others that lie below, that the two Achæmenian orders were both represented in this fabric. In the front portico and in the central hall, the columns were surmounted by the composite or triple capital, terminating in two demi-bulls, whose hollowed necks supported the architrave, in the same manner as in the Porch of Xerxes. The shafts of these pillars are formed of three blocks. In the two lateral porticoes the simpler type of capital, consisting only of bulls' heads, superimposed upon a shaft of four blocks, prevails; although even here this nomenclature is not strictly accurate, seeing that in the east portico the animals' heads depicted seem to have been unicorns and not bulls. All the seventy-two columns, without exceptions, were fluted, and all were of the same height.[1] Those in the central hall rested upon a simple squared plinth; those in the porticoes had a more ornate circular base, resembling that of the columns in the Propylæa, which has sometimes been compared to an inverted lotus-flower, but is more correctly described as a bell-shaped block, adorned with long leaves, the points of which are turned downwards.

The outer porticoes are 140½ feet long, by 28 feet broad. A distance of 71 feet separates them from the central hall; but between the north portico and the latter are four massive substructures, the meaning of which is not clear.[2] We then enter the great hall itself, through and around which were traced by Flandin and Coste the relics of subterranean aqueducts. The exterior dimensions of this hall, which was, doubtless, the chief glory of Persepolis, are 140 feet in each direction, or not far short of a square of 50 yards.[3] It

Dimensions

[1] Fergusson (p. 163), observing the greater apparent height of the columns of the porticoes than of those of the central hall, and inferring (erroneously, I think) that the latter did not have the bull-capitals, invents a particular kind of capital for them, so as to redress the inequality. He gives the dimensions of the portico-columns as 67⅓ feet high to the top of the bulls' heads, 64 feet to the hollow of their necks; shaft, 54 feet 10 inches high, 5⅓ feet in diameter at base, 4½ feet at the top; base, 5½ feet high; capitals, 7 feet high, 12 feet 2 inches broad; and of the hall-columns: shaft, 41¾ feet high; triple capital, 16½ feet high. Ker Porter gives the number of flutings as 52 (Ouseley, 40). Flandin and Coste give the height as 63 feet 10 inches, and distance from axis to axis, 29 feet.

[2] Coste, in his restoration, suggested, and Perrot has accepted the suggestion, that these may have supported colossal figures of bulls. Fergusson and others have regarded them as the bases of doorways.

[3] Fergusson (pp. 170–1) says that it contained 40,000 square feet, or, with the walls (which are his own creation), 55,700. Adding to these, porticoes, 42,500 square feet, and guard-rooms (again imaginary) 6,800, he arrives at a total of 105,000 square feet. He then gives the dimensions of the famous buildings of ancient and modern times: Great Hall at Karnak, 58,300 square feet inside, 88,800 + halls and porticoes; Temple of Olympian Zeus at Athens, 59,000; at Agrigentum, 56,000; Cologne Cathedral, 81,500; Milan Cathedral, 107,800; and

may not inaptly be compared with the pillared hall of Karnak on the Nile; and it must, in my judgment, have been a more artistic structure, since, in spite of the cumbrous disproportion of its capitals, and its lack of the varied sculptures that adorn the surface of the Egyptian pillars, its superficial area was less crowded, and its interlacing vistas were consequently less obstructed than in the temple of the Thothmes.

Problem of walls

There remain two important questions that are suggested by the Hall of Xerxes, and that have hitherto been solved in accordance with the preconceived theories of writers, rather than from data collected on the spot. The first is that of the walls, the second is that of the roof. Was the central hall surrounded by walls; and was it connected by walls with the porticoes, so as to form one great quadrilateral? Fergusson thus conceives it. Round the hall, and framing the porticoes at either end, he places in his restoration a wall of crude brick eighteen feet thick with windows and niches similar in shape to those which we shall presently observe in the Palace of Darius. The angles at either end of the north portico he fills with imaginary guard-rooms, similarly constructed. Now it is true, so far as I know, that there is no other instance, in Persia or elsewhere (but amid what a paucity of cognate remains), of porticoes standing in entire independence of the central fabric to which structurally they belong. To this extent may we regard with suspicion the restorations of Coste and Chipiez. It is also true that the majority of the remaining buildings on the platform appear to have had walls. But the very fact that the indestructible remnants of these walls there survive; that, though mud and brick have wasted to nothing, yet the stone portals, and window cases, and niches, in every case remain *in situ*; whilst in the Hall of Xerxes there is not the faintest vestige of window, niche, or door—is to my mind an unanswerable argument against the construction at any time of a similar enclosure with stone fittings here. It is inconceivable that, if such had existed, it could have wholly disappeared. Fergusson meets this difficulty by supposing a wall of mud bricks only, faced with enamelled tiles. Not the least trace of either has however been discovered; and there seems no reason why stone should have been employed in all the other walls, and not in this. Furthermore, walls of such a character and dimensions would have deprived the building of the particular individuality which it appears to have claimed, and would have interfered with its main

concludes by saying: 'Taken all in all, Milan Cathedral is, perhaps, the building that resembles it most, both in style and the general character of the effect it must have produced on the spectator.' This is the kind of appreciation that could only have been written by a critic who had never seen the place he was describing, and was a slave to his own theories of reconstruction. As profitably might we compare Westminster Abbey with the Taj at Agra.

architectural purpose. No one now seems to deny—the sculptures indeed may be said to have proved it—that this was the Great Hall of Audience, the Imperial Talar or Throne Room, of the King of kings. Here, upon a throne and under a canopy, similar to those which we shall presently observe depicted upon the graven doorways of the other palaces, he sat in state to see and to be seen of his people. Up the stairways, and through the porticoes, and between the pillared aisles they thronged to do him homage. Broad space and light, free range of vision and movement, were required. Majesty was not called upon to conceal its radiance, but rather to shine before all men. Nor is there any difficulty in supplying the substitute for walls and doors, that may have been needed to check or to facilitate ingress and egress, and to regulate the light. There is great continuity in the East. The clue to a distant antiquity sometimes stares us in the face at our threshold; and in the *talars* or throne rooms of the modern Persian kings, from Shah Abbas downwards, as I have described them at Teheran and Isfahan, we have samples of royal audience halls, where the monarch displays himself to the assembled multitudes, and where the interior of the apartment is veiled or shaded by the dexterous use of embroidered tapestries and curtains. Nay more, if so modern an illustration be regarded with suspicion, have we not, in a contemporary document of the highest authenticity, a record of the precise system of decoration to which I allude? At Shushan or Susa, where was the winter-palace of the same princes, whose more solid erections we are here examining, 'in the court of the garden of the king's palace were white, green, and blue hangings, fastened with cords of fine linen and purple to silver rings and pillars of marble.'[1] Without, therefore, accepting in full measure the restorations of either of the French artists before mentioned, and without peremptorily denying that walls of some kind may have united the central hall with its lateral colonnades, I feel that a closer approximation to the truth is probably to be found in their hypotheses than in those of the English authority; and that whatever this great fabric may have looked like when Xerxes held therein his glittering *durbars*, it assuredly did not resemble in the least degree the hypothetical reconstruction of Fergusson.

A similar process of reasoning, starting from the premise of what actually is or was, rather than what might or ought to have been, should, I think, be applied, both here and in the remaining Persepolitan palaces, to the question of roofs There cannot be a doubt, from the hollowed centre of the bicephalous capitals in this case, no less than from the incised mortise-joints in the angle-piers of some of the other structures, that they were made to receive an

Roof

[1] Esther i. 5, 6.

architrave or roof-beam. These can hardly have been of stone, for the reasons that the pillars are neither stout enough nor close enough to have supported the weight, that not a fragment of any such ceiling has ever been found, and that the idea is foreign to the cognate architectural styles. On the other hand we have, in the statements of the Greek historians, notably of Quintus Curtius,[1] the best possible grounds for believing that the ceilings of the Persepolitan palaces were of cedar; a fact which has been corroborated by the discovery of traces of that material upon the platform itself. That the roofs so constructed were covered over and protected from the elements by a layer of rammed clay, appears highly probable from the analogy of Persian buildings for many centuries past, and would seem to have been required by the exigencies of the climate. In the absence, however, of any direct evidence I prefer neither to theorise nor to dogmatise upon this point. For similar reasons I would reject the audacious theory with regard to the roofs of the Achæmenian palaces that was started by Fergusson. Proceeding upon the solitary analogy of the rock-sculptures above the royal tombs at Naksh-i-Rustam and behind Persepolis, where, upon a roof resembling the elevation and façade of the neighbouring palaces, the king is depicted, for devotional purposes, standing upon a twofold stage or throne, he imagined that this scene was a precise reproduction of the principal secular edifices on the platform; and even went so far as to declare that 'it admits of no doubt that there were stages on the roof of the palaces as on the tombs.' It is sufficient to say that beyond the fanciful analogy alluded to there is not a single argument worthy of the name in favour of such a contention.[2] It is as though some future critic were to reason from Nelson's Column in Trafalgar Square to any other Corinthian column of the Georgian age that might be found at a later date in a mutilated or stunted condition.

Passing through the Hall of Xerxes from north to south, and pursuing the order that will naturally be followed by most visitors' footsteps, we next come, at a slight distance to the south, to another and much smaller, but also a more perfect building, to which the inscriptions upon it have been responsible for giving the title of the Palace of Darius. This structure consists of a central hall,

Palace of Darius

[1] *Hist. Alex. V.*, vii. 5. 'Multa cedro ædificata erat regia; quæ celeriter, igne concepto, late fudit incendium.' Lebanon and Taurus, the great cedar-growing nurseries of the ancient world, were connected by well-trodden caravan routes with Persia.

[2] *Vide*, however, Fergusson's own statement of the case, pp. 126–31, 167–70, 190. Had such a second storey existed, means must have existed of ascending to it. But though every other staircase on the platform is wholly or in part preserved, there is not the remotest trace of any such ascent to a higher floor.

COMBAT OF KING AND GRIFFIN—PALACE OF DARIUS

supported by sixteen columns in four rows of four each, with a portico of eight columns, in two corresponding rows on the south front, and with traces of what apparently were chambers on the longer sides and at the back. This is the only building on the platform that faces towards the south; and there two flights of steps, one at either end of the terrace on which it stands, furnished the principal means of access. In later times a third staircase was added, and another entrance effected on the west side, overlooking the brink of the main platform and the plain of Mervdasht. To a visitor approaching, as we are doing, from the north this will be the natural mode of entry; and I will therefore take the building, so to speak, in the rear, and describe it therefrom, step by step.

Side-entrance

The entire edifice stands upon a stylobate or platform, nearly ten feet higher than that of the Durbar-Hall of Xerxes. Its dimensions are 132½ feet long by 96 feet broad.[1] Ascending the small double stairway on the west front, we observe a partly buried inscription on the wall of the platform; while on the front wall of the stairway, flanked by the familiar lion and bull in either spandrel, is a tablet containing a splendidly preserved inscription, telling us that this staircase was the work of Artaxerxes III. or Ochus (B.C. 361–338),[2] 150 years posterior to the edifice itself. At the top of the steps we pass through a doorway, the side-walls of which have shifted on their bases (probably owing to earthquake) and are inclined towards each other. Continuing through a small antechamber or porch, a second doorway introduces us into the central hall. On either jamb of this doorway (which, like its predecessor, appears to have been a structural alteration of Artaxerxes) is sculped one of those symbolical combats between a king and a monster (at different times a bull, a unicorn, a griffin, or a strange compound of opposite attributes) which we shall so frequently notice in the remaining buildings. In all these bas-reliefs the king with girt loins, but in an absolutely unconcerned fashion, and with frigid uniformity of attitude, plunges a dagger into the belly of the monster, which rears on its hind legs before him, but which he sedately grasps by the horn projecting from its head.

Central hall

Owing to the introduction of this (probably later) entrance, there is an unusual lack of uniformity in the structural disposition of the central hall. Its dimensions, which are a square of fifty feet, are clearly marked by the existence *in situ* of a number of immense blocks of chiselled stone, bearing a high polish,[3] and

[1] I take these figures from Fergusson. Porter says 170 feet by 95, and another writer 180 by 96. [2] Rawlinson, *J.R.A.S.*, vol. x. p. 342; Spiegel, pp. 68–71.

[3] It must have been in this building that Don Silva y Figueroa's mastiff, from seeing itself reflected in the mirror-like polish of the walls, became so furious that it had to be chained up when it entered.

coloured almost black with exposure, which stand detached from each other all round the line which we may assume to have been occupied by the walls of the building, in which they constituted the principal feature. Some of them—the largest and loftiest—are doorways, with projecting fluted cornice; the smaller are either pierced as windows to admit light, or are hollowed into the form of niches or *takhches*, which to this day remain the favourite Persian form of mural decoration, besides supplying a receptacle for ornaments or furniture. On the north side of the hall are two doorways and three niches; on the west side, two doorways and two niches; on the east side, one doorway and three niches; on the south side, or original front, one doorway and

PALACE OF DARIUS

four windows. In this doorway is sculped another familiar Achæmenian group, viz. the king passing out of the palace with the royal parasol held by two attendants above his head.[1] On the floor are traces of the substructures of what were once sixteen columns that supported the roof, but of the plinths, shafts, or capitals of which no relics have been found.[2] Outside the wall with the windows, eight similar columns adorned a portico, the east and west walls of which contain each a doorway and a niche, besides a gigantic monolith or

[1] Binning says that the king's head-dress is perforated with numerous small holes, as though for nails to fasten plates of gold or some other substance upon it. I do not think that any other writer has noticed this.

[2] Hence the inference, in which some have indulged, that, like the columns of the Achæmenian palace at Ecbatana, they were made of wood.

angle-pier, twenty-two feet high (immediately at the summit of the two main flights of steps), the incised grooves in the summit of one of which betray to this day the manner in which the beams of the roof rested upon them. On the outer side of the portico, as also on either side of the central hall, and again behind the latter—i.e. on the north, are the somewhat obscure traces of what appear to have been apartments of greater or less dimensions.

The Palace of Darius is unusually rich in inscriptions. First may be mentioned those which are responsible for its name. They run in narrow lines round the borders of the window-frames and niches, or are chiselled in triple tablets above the bas-reliefs on the inner sides of the doors. The great angle-pier in the south-west corner has also been a favourite field for the sculptor. Here is a cuneiform inscription which tells us that Darius did not finish this palace, but that it was completed by his son Xerxes. Here, also, is a Kufic inscription, and a Persian *ghazel*, or ode, that was inscribed by Sultan Ibrahim, the son of Shah Rukh, and grandson of Timur. Hard by, as if to mark a more emphatic anti-climax, a patriotic citizen of Shiraz, thirty years ago, cut two long inscriptions in honour of Nasr-ed-Din Shah. It is on the south doorway of the same building that were engraved the Pehlevi inscriptions of Shapur II. and III., which I have previously noticed. Nor have the moderns been behindhand in their meaner but withal not meaningless epigraphs. There are several names dating from about the year 1760. On the main north doorway is a long list of the English company that passed with Colonel J. Macdonald (Sir J. M. Kinneir) in 1820; and on one of the western niches I observed, from his signature, that my friend Professor Vambéry had also succumbed to the temptation of the surroundings.

Inscriptions

As I have said, the main entrance to the Palace of Darius was on the south; and here the excavations of Flandin and Coste, fifty years ago, laid bare the sculptures and inscriptions which had been only imperfectly seen and described by the earlier travellers. As in the Great Hall of Xerxes, so here, the front of the stylobate or platform was richly carved. Two processions of armed warriors, with gigantic lances and with quivers on their backs, march towards a central panel, which, like two others at the outer extremities, contain a cuneiform repetition of the joint authorship of Darius and Xerxes. At either end a flight of steps ascends the platform, the lion and bull appearing on the outer triangle formed by the slope, while on the inner wall a row of admirably carved figures mounts the staircase along with the visitor.

South staircase

Like its predecessor, this structure suggests two questions, the solution of one of which relates to itself alone; while the other concerns equally all the edifices upon the platform. Firstly, then, what was the character and object of this building? It is too small to have been a public hall of audience. On the other hand, the surrounding chambers and apartments appear to suggest the attributes of a residence. Those only who entertain the outworn fallacy that Persepolis was a collection of sanctuaries or palace-temples, will agree with Fergusson that they may have been 'devoted to priestly mysteries, perhaps chapels.' There is no ground whatsoever for such a belief. On the other hand, if, as is now generally supposed, this was the private residence of the king, on the occasion of his annual visits to Persepolis (and we can well understand the advantages of a southern outlook in the doubtful warmth of an early Persian spring-tide), I nevertheless cannot credit, from what I have seen or read of Eastern modes of life, that anything like sufficient accommodation can have existed here both for the monarch, for his necessary guards and attendants, and for the royal harem.[1] I should feel disposed therefore to think that it must have been the official residence of the sovereign, where he transacted his private business, ate his meals, or enjoyed repose; but that the manifold equipage and accompaniment of the seraglio—the wives, concubines, female slaves, nurses, children and eunuchs—must have been accommodated in some other and neighbouring building.[2]

Character of building

The second and wider question is that of the nature and material of the walls, that must unquestionably have united the still surviving doorways, niches, and windows, not in this palace only, but in the other edifices on the platform that present similar features. I say unquestionably, not merely on *a priori* grounds, but because on the inner sides and surfaces of the stone monoliths just mentioned are unmistakable traces of their original juncture with walls

Question of walls

[1] Texier, in his plates and text, boldly so describes it.

[2] That the 'house of the women' and the 'king's house' were separate in the time of the Achæmenian kings is evident from Esther ii. 13 and v. 1. We are reminded very forcibly by the arrangement of the building on the Persepolitan platform of another Scriptural analogy—viz. the House of the Forest of Lebanon, which was built as a palace, or succession of palaces, by another great Asiatic monarch 500 years before. '(He built it) upon four rows of cedar pillars, with cedar beams upon the pillars. And it was covered with cedar above upon the beams, that lay on forty-five pillars, fifteen in a row. And there were windows in three rows, and light was against light in three ranks. And all the doors and posts were square with the windows. And he made a porch of pillars, and the porch was before them, and the other pillars and the thick beam were before them. Then he made a porch for the throne, where he might judge, even the porch of judgment; and it was covered with cedar from one side of the floor to the other. And his house where he dwelt had another court within the porch, which was of the like work. Solomon made, also, an house for Pharaoh's daughter, whom he had taken to wife, like unto this porch' (1 Kings vii. 1–8).

of another material. Though polished to a glassy smoothness on their outer surfaces, they are always here left rough, in order to facilitate the adhesion of a lighter substance. As to the nature of this, I have never myself, since having travelled somewhat widely in the East, been able to share the doubts that have found favour with so many other writers. That the walls were neither of stone, nor, as Canon Rawlinson thinks, of small stones, or rubble, is evident from the absence of even the slightest trace of any such material, either in blocks, chips, or fragments. That they were not of kiln-burnt bricks is, I think, also clear, because clay that has passed through the fire is among the most imperishable of substances; and here again only the most infinitesimal traces of such bricks have ever been discovered on the platform. But that they were of sundried bricks or crude mud is, I venture to think, absolutely certain, both from analogy, ancient and modern, the palaces of Nineveh, Babylon, and Susa having all alike been so constructed, and mud-bricks being to this day the staple of every Persian house, from the palace of the sovereign to the meanest hovel of the peasant; and because in this manner, and in this only, can we account for the total disappearance of the Persepolitan walls, which, as soon as decay had set its finger upon the place, and the platform had ceased to be occupied, would in a few score of years, much more in hundreds and thousands, have been swept away by rains and storms, or washed down into the heaps of mud that still encumber the surface. Fergusson, though he is driven to some such conclusion himself, describes it as a 'bathos in art.' When we remember the extraordinary ingenuity and skill displayed by the Eastern peoples from the time of Sennacherib to that of the present Shah, in decorating the surfaces of mud-walls either with plaster, painted and decorated,[1] or with glazed and enamelled tiles, I do

[1] In the palaces of Babylon, we learn from Ezekiel (xxiii. 14) that there were 'men pourtrayed upon the walls, the images of the Chaldæans pourtrayed with vermilion, girded with girdles upon their loins, exceeding in dyed attire upon their heads, all of them princes to look to, after the manner of the Babylonians of Chaldæa.' The suggestion of colour on the plastered surface of the walls leads me to mention the allegation of some authorities that gilding and colouring were largely employed at Persepolis, even upon the sculptured stone. Several of the seventeenth-century travellers made or repeated this assertion. Herbert (p. 152) said: 'In some other places the gold also that was laid upon the Freez and Cornish, as, also, upon the trim of vests, was also in as perfect lustre as if it had been but newly done.' Chardin (ix. 187) recorded traces of gilding in the cuneiform inscriptions. Daulier-Deslandes (p. 61) said: 'Il paroist encore à plusieurs de ces caractères qu'ils ont été dorez.' Cf. Kaempfer, p. 338. On the other hand, no subsequent visitor has made or endorsed the discovery, with the single exception of Texier, in 1840, who declared (vol. ii. pp. 188–90) that he found traces of gilded diapering on some of the robes of the king, and that the original background of the bas-reliefs was blue. He accordingly makes a plentiful use both of gilding and colour (as do Flandin and Coste) in his restorations. I searched very

not think that we shall endorse this phrase. At Persepolis the former, rather than the latter type of surface decoration would appear to have been mainly employed; but very few fragments of tiles having ever been picked up on the platform, and those in the main of doubtful antiquity. At Susa the reverse was the case; but at Susa too the main body of the interior walls appears to have been of stucco, coloured red, and adorned with tapestries and hangings. Later excavations at Persepolis in the big heaps of débris between the palaces may perhaps bring to light additional evidence, but I doubt whether, broadly speaking, they will invalidate the above conclusion.[1]

Palace of Artaxerxes III.

Before leaving this part of the platform, I may observe that on its outer edge, to the north-west of the Palace of Darius, are traces of a building, first noted by Niebuhr, and marked by Flandin and Coste. Though too indeterminate in form and size to justify reconstruction, it has been assumed by some writers to be the 'House of the Women.' Continuing in a direct line south from the Palace of Darius, we arrive at the ruins of a building occupying the extreme south-west corner of the upper platform, where the latter rises with a sheer edge above the lower or southern unoccupied level. Access is gained to this ruin by a mutilated double stairway on the north face,[2] upon the front of which are a row of processional figures, and two cuneiform inscriptions, similar to those that we have seen on the western stairway of the Palace of Darius. They proclaim the handiwork of Artaxerxes III. or Ochus; but whether they signify that

carefully, but nowhere found any trace either of gilding or colouring myself. How, then, are we to reconcile these conflicting records? I confess I think that the seventeenth-century travellers either greatly exaggerated or copied, each in turn, from the earliest who had originated the statement; for I do not see why gilding which had retained 'a perfect lustre' for 2,100 years should suddenly disappear *in toto* after the lapse of 2,200. Some of these writers may have been mistaken by the sun shining on the siliceous varnish with which the ancient Persians appear to have overlaid their sculptures. On the other hand, it is far from improbable that colour may have been employed, to some extent, even on the stone. I have elsewhere mentioned that traces of blue paint have been found on the cuneiform epitaph on Darius's tomb, and it may equally have been applied at Persepolis. The analogy of Assyrian art is in favour both of colour and gilding. Perrot points out that none of the horns or ears of the bull-capitals have been found on the platform, though the holes are there in which they were fixed. He therefore suggests that they may have been of gilt bronze.

[1] Since writing the above, I have received the satisfactory assurance from Mr. Cecil Smith that in one of the buildings on the platform he actually picked up some fragments of stucco painted red, which are now in the British Museum.

[2] Ker Porter, in his plan, places a double staircase in the north-west corner; but this is a mistake. Flandin and Coste, also, fail to do justice to the north stairways, but add a small flight of steps (which I overlooked) at right angles to the platform near the west extremity.

the building was originally raised, or was only restored, or added to, by him, it is impossible to say. From the fact that this building faced the Palace of Darius, and that, as I have pointed out, the accommodation of the latter would appear to have been inadequate for a large household, it has been called by some the House of the Women. There is nothing, however, positively to justify such a designation, and the remains consist only of a number of bases of columns, represented by Ker Porter as two rows of five, preceding three rows of four; but by Flandin and Coste as an irregular number (three only are marked on their plan), preceding four rows of four. By them the ruin is described as No. 4; by others as the south-west edifice.

To the east of this building, and in continuation of the main upper platform, on which it is the most elevated of all the Persepolitan remains, are the ruins of what must originally have been the third largest structure of the entire palace-group. The inscriptions on its staircases and doorways, and on its lofty angle-piers,[1] reveal that, like the Propylæa and the Great Audience-Hall, it was the work of Xerxes, whence it has not unnaturally been conjectured to represent the palace of that monarch. Its structural arrangements, indeed, bear a marked resemblance to those of the palace of his father, with the exception that the fabric faced towards the north, and that each component part was on a considerably larger scale. In front was a platform, to which access was gained by a quadruple flight of steps, which appears in my photograph on the east,[2] and by a double flight on the western side. They are sadly ruined. Mounting the stairs, we find the remains of the main or entrance-portico of the palace, in the shape of the bases of two rows of columns of six each. This opened by doorways into a central pillared hall, the roof of which was sustained by thirty-six columns, in six rows of six each, covering a square surface of eighty-seven and a half feet each way. Their circular bases alone survive. Down the centre of this hall runs at a slight distance below the surface, but now exposed to view, a subterranean aqueduct, which procured for it from Texier the somewhat precipitate title of the Baths. There is no ground for connecting the building with such a purpose; nor is there the faintest trace of any of the requisite dispositions; and there can be

Palace of Xerxes

[1] The inscriptions occur in a greater variety of situations in this palace than elsewhere: (1) in panels on both the east and west staircases; (2) round the doorways; (3) in tablets above the king and parasol; (4) on the folds of the king's robe in the north and east doorways; (5) round the windows; (6) on the big angle-pier.

[2] At the summit of the east staircase are four great substructures, or blocks of stone, which Fergusson conjectures, but without sufficient reason, to have been the bases of a porch or Propylæa, similar to those before the Hall of a Hundred Columns and the Hall of Xerxes.

little doubt that the conduit is merely part of the system either of drainage or of water-supply, the traces of which exist in other parts of the platform—e.g. under the Hall of Xerxes. Whether Ker Porter is justified in connecting it directly both with the relics of a tank at the foot of the mountain on the east, and with the stone cistern already noticed near the Porch of Xerxes, I have not the means of ascertaining. As in the case of the Palace of Darius, so also here, the building is flanked by a number of smaller compartments, of which there appear to have been four on either side, those two into which access is gained from the central or pillared hall having also contained four columns each, and having, therefore, constituted subsidiary pillared courts. The doorways, windows, and niches surrounding the

EAST STAIRCASE, PALACE OF XERXES

main hall are adorned with sculptures similar in character to those in the elder palace, the sovereign with parasol and fly-flap, held by attendants, being sculped on the door-jambs; but in several of the windows are depicted what appear to be evidences of royal luxury and entertainment, in the shape of attendants leading animals, or carrying cups, dishes, and vases of perfume. On the south side two staircases lead up from its eastern and western ends on to the palace platform, in the outer front of which four niches with a cornice are disposed; while—a unique feature in this structure—from the south-west corner another flight of steps, hewn in the natural rock, at right angles to the terrace, and without either parapet or sculptures, leads up from the lower or southern to the upper platform. The general remarks which have previously been made upon the purpose of Darius' Palace will apply equally to that of his son. Here, in all probability, we have the building in which Xerxes lived, and in which he conducted business of state, and gave ceremonial banquets; reserving for his great *levées* the audience-hall with the porticoes and big columns.

Before leaving this palace, let us notice that between the terrace that precedes it on the north, and the hindermost pillars of the Great Hall of Xerxes, is a space of ground about a hundred yards in length, which is now occupied only by a mound, rising in parts to a very considerable height above the true level of the platform. It has not unreasonably been conjectured that this great pile of accumulated soil may cover the relics of some other and yet unknown fabric, and Ker Porter sanguinely located here the banqueting hall where Alexander feasted, and which 'fell a sacrifice to the drunken revelry of the Macedonian.' Thirteen years ago, Messrs. Stolze and Andreas drove a trench through part of this great mound, and found no more remunerative spoil than masons' rubbish and chips. Yet I cannot but hope that a more thorough investigation might produce ampler results, even though the *trouvaille* were limited to the discovery, not of an unsuspected palace, but of what would be nearly as important, viz. authentic traces of tiles, bricks, or whatever method of mural decoration was employed by the Achæmenian architects on the platform. Personally, I shall not feel any sense of contentment that the limits of possible discovery have been reached until, like the Acropolis at Athens, the surface of the rock or true level of the platform has everywhere been laid bare. Then only will archæology have had its final say.

Great mound

On the lower or principal platform, at a distance of 180 yards behind or to the east of the Palace of Xerxes, are the remains of a further building, which has a stunted appearance, owing to the fact that it is buried in the soil up to half the height of its niches and doorways. These, which are composed of a stone the blackness of which resembles the material of the Palace of Darius, enclose a space eighty-nine feet in length by sixty-one in breadth, preceded by a portico fifty and a half feet by thirty and a half feet. The former appears to have contained sixteen columns, in four rows of four each; the latter eight columns, in two rows of four each. There are no traces of lateral chambers; and the entire building appears to have been either a reproduction or a prototype on a small scale of the great Hall of a Hundred Columns, which we shall presently notice. That it was a royal palace or hall is evident from the sculptured images of the king, with the fly-chaser in the south door, and the parasol in the north, and of the king fighting with the symbolical monster on its hind legs in the east and west; but no

South-east edifice

inscription remains to enable us to identify the monarch. Fergusson, indeed, assumes that this is the earliest structure on the platform, because it has 'a monolithic character of solidity and a massiveness of proportion greater than that possessed by any other edifice;' and he conjectures that it may have been the work of Cyrus or Cambyses. But it must be remembered, both that Fergusson never saw Persepolis himself, and also that there is not anywhere the slightest trace of any edifice or fabric on the platform prior to Darius. Indeed, it seems to me certain that Cyrus and Cambyses were both in their graves before the first stone of Persepolis was laid.

Central Edifice

Returning towards the north, we arrive, immediately behind the big mound that flanks the Palace of Darius on the east, at a building which, in the absence of any distinguishing mark or inscription, has generally been called the Central Edifice. It is of peculiar plan, and has afforded a welcome scope to the theorists. It consists of three great doorways, on the inner surface or jambs of which are chiselled the monarch, seated or standing under the royal umbrella, with the image of the god Ormuzd floating in a winged halo overhead. In the east doorway we meet with the first specimen that we have hitherto encountered of a type that is very familiar on the next ensuing building, viz. the king seated on a triple-staged throne, supported by three rows of nine figures each, with uplifted arms—a variation of the scene already depicted on the tombs at Naksh-i-Rustam. In the centre, between the north and south doorways, are the bases of four columns. What may have been the object of this small but remarkable structure it is impossible to say. Ker Porter, anxious to do a good turn to the Holy Place school of thought, supposed it to be the private oratory of the king, and the four plinths to be the bases of a fire-altar. For this suggestion there is no support. Fergusson thinks it was a second Propylæa, in front of the Palace of Xerxes. It does not, however, resemble any of the other remains of porches; and does not either confront or lead to any other building, least of all the Palace of Xerxes. I prefer therefore to classify it with the other Persepolitan halls or palaces, and not to spin cobwebs in hypothetical identification.

Hall of 100 Columns

Finally we come to the last—and if we speak of a hall itself, without adjuncts—the largest of the Persepolitan structures. This is the building which, ever since its ground plan was ascertained in the middle of the century, and with even greater precision since the excavations of 1877–8, has been known as the Hall of a Hundred Columns. It is situated on a lower level (identical with that of the Porch of Xerxes) than the edifices recently described, and is nearest of all the ruins to the mountain, from whose base it is removed but a short distance. It consists of a single great hall, the

NORTH DOORWAY—HALL OF HUNDRED COLUMNS

interior dimensions of which are a square of 225 feet, and whose roof was sustained by 100 columns, in ten rows of ten each, preceded on the north by a portico, of sixteen columns, in two rows of eight each ; or a grand total of 116 columns in the entire building. On either side of the portico, whose dimensions are 180 feet by fifty-one, were gigantic figures of bulls, facing northwards, which Ker Porter took to have been statues, and not bas-reliefs, but which there is no reason to suppose were different from the surviving remains of similar colossi, i.e. projections in bold relief from the front and sides of stone piers, as in the Porch of Xerxes. From this portico two doorways, of superior height and width to the remainder, conduct into the interior or Hall of a Hundred Columns. The latter is surrounded by forty-four stone doorways, windows,[1] or niches similar to those already observed in the palaces of Darius and Xerxes—once united to each other by a wall of sun-dried bricks, over ten feet thick, long ago completely perished. The interior, which was excavated by the workmen of Ferhad Mirza, the then Ihtisham-ed-Dowleh, and Governor-General of Fars, under the superintendence of Dr. Andreas in 1878, presents a wilderness of pillar bases,[2] with fragments of cornices, capitals, and drums, piled in inextricable ruin. Enough remains to show that the columns were of the composite or triple-headed Achæmenian order, with lotus-shaped bases and demi-bull capitals. Not a single pillar survives ; but reconstructing them from the dimensions of the plinth on the same scale as in the Hall of Xerxes, we ascertain that they were thirty-seven feet high, and twenty feet apart from axis to axis.

The bas-reliefs on the doorways of this hall are on an even more grandiose scale than the majority of those hitherto inspected. In the east and west entrances the combat between the king and a nondescript monster is again shown forth. On the south doorways he is seated on a throne, which is supported on a threefold terrace, upheld by the arms of subject nationalities, who are disposed in parallel rows of five. An exquisite canopy with tasselled fringe is outstretched over his head, and still higher the winged and protecting Ormuzd hovers in the sky. This scene we have already witnessed.

Sculptures

[1] My own notes record 9 windows on the north wall only, divided into groups of 3 by the two entrance doors. Flandin and Coste give 3 windows only, and 6 niches ; Ker Porter and Texier, 7 windows and 2 niches. The ground plans of all these travellers seem to require a maximum of 7 windows only, because of the portico-walls outside. But I hardly think I can have been mistaken, and I find that I have the support of Niebuhr.

[2] Mr. Cecil Smith informs me that on the upper surface of several of these bases he observed masons' marks, similar to those previously mentioned on the palace-platform at Pasargadæ, some of which appear to be characters from the Greek alphabet—a curious testimony to the theory of Greek collaboration.

On the north doorways, however, an even more majestic conception is pourtrayed. There the monarch sits in state on a high-backed chair or throne, with his feet upon a footstool. At his back are guards, and an attendant with the lifted fly-wisp. On the ground in front of him stand two censers, behind which two other figures, possibly ambassadors or ministers, advance to render account or to make obeisance to the

SOUTH DOORWAY, HALL OF A HUNDRED COLUMNS

sovereign. Below are five superimposed rows of warriors, with spears, bows, quivers, and bucklers, fifty in all, their differing dress and head-gear typifying the composite enlistment of the Great King's host. In the panels of royal state he himself is everywhere displayed with the royal tiara upon his head, with bushy curled hair, and with long frizzed beard, clad in the flowing purple of empire. In the scenes of combat his loins are girt, and he solemnly grapples with and transfixes the foe.

This great hall, which next to that of Karnak in Egypt was the largest in the ancient world, was doubtless, as its sculptures indicate, the throne-room or audience-hall of the Great King. Less striking, though more spacious than the Hall of Xerxes, inasmuch as it was lower in elevation, and in all probability worse lighted,[1] it must have served an analogous purpose. Here, in the manner depicted upon the doorways, one of the Achæmenian sovereigns must have sat in state to receive the homage or the tribute of his people. With which of the dynasty are we to connect it? Sir H. Rawlinson has been induced by the superior preservation of the sculptures to refer it to the latest reasonable period, viz., to the reign of Artaxerxes III. From the same premise I should draw quite the opposite conclusion. Looking to the facts, that under the reign of Darius the national art appears to have touched its apogee of splendour, that there is no other hall on the platform which we are justified in identifying with a throne-room such as he must undoubtedly have used, and that both the ground plan and structure represent the simplest and least complicated form of Persepolitan hall, I should be inclined to argue that this was the building where the son of Hystaspes sat in royal state; and that it was with the familiar ambition of the Oriental to create some novel type, at once emulating and transcending his predecessor, that Xerxes departed from the model of his father, and raised the Great Hall with the porticoes on another part of the terrace. Moreover, when the Hall of a Hundred Columns was built, the decorative massing of sculpture on the fronts of stairways had seemingly not been developed, and the scenes of royal pageantry which Xerxes depicted on the stylobate of his stately platform are here concentrated and disposed vertically on the jambs of the entrance doorways. A further difference may be noted in the absence of any groove or socket in the doorways, as in the palaces of Darius and Xerxes, to contain the pivots on which the folding doors were hung. This lends an additional support to the theory that we have here an audience-chamber merely; since the doorways can only have been closed or concealed by hangings, like those described in the book of Esther.

Design

At a distance of 190 feet to the north of the portico are the remains of what is generally admitted to have been a bull-flanked

[1] The only apparent means by which light can have been admitted to the interior was by the nine windows in the northern wall, the bays on the other side being all filled and constituting niches. The limited and feeble radiance that must have spread therefrom down the long, pillared aisles necessitates, in my opinion, the theory of windows or open spaces left to admit light in the sides of the timbered roof.

porch, or Propylæa, leading thereto. In the earlier part of the century these ruins were in a more recognisable shape than now ; and north again of them stood an enormous isolated column. My notes and photographs record only a few dilapidated blocks of stone, retaining however the unmistakable disposition of a gateway and on one side the form of what was once a bull. Flandin inferred from the apparently unfinished workmanship of some of these fragments, that the porch to which they belonged was never completed, and may have been a later addition to the original design. Such a condition, however, if true, need not necessarily postulate a later origin in the East, where, as I have frequently remarked, to leave the edifices of a predecessor either incomplete or a prey to ruin, is no uncommon manifestation of the ὕβρις of royalty.

Propylæa

A far more interesting question, however, than the date or the object of this building, is raised by its remains. Whereas none of the earlier travellers found in any of the edifices on the platform the least traces of destruction by fire, and were therefore puzzled how to reconcile with the visible ruins the story, attested by a consensus of ancient historians,[1] of the conflagration of one or more of the Persepolitan palaces by Alexander, more recent discoveries have acquainted us with the fact that the Hall of a Hundred Columns contains precisely the evidence of which we stand in need.[2] On the soil above the pavement was found, in the excavations of thirteen years ago, a thick layer of ashes, proved by microscopic analysis to be carbonised cedar, of which not a vestige has been brought to light in any other of the palaces.[3] It is probable, therefore, that these are the remains of the cedar roof, which crumbled into ashes just where it fell, carrying down with it the columns and supports that had previously sustained its splendour. It is not the least among the fascinations of the site that we can—without positive certainty it

Was it burned by Alexander?

[1] Diodorus Siculus, lib. xvii.; Strabo, lib. xv.; Q. Curtius, lib. v. c. 7; Plutarch's *Vita Alexandri*; Clitarchus in *Athenæus*, lib. xiii.; Arrian, lib. iii. c. 18. Q. Curtius is responsible for the statement that the palace set on fire was largely composed of cedar.

[2] It was with an unconscious prescience, therefore, that Ouseley wrote (*Travels*, vol. ii. p. 281) : 'From the very durable nature of charcoal, we might, perhaps, reasonably hope to discover fragments of carbonised cedar.'

[3] Texier and Stolze, however, have both opined that the stones in the Palace of Xerxes show traces of having been sundered by violent heat. Madame Dieulafoy (*La Perse*, p. 407) says: 'Seated in the doorway of the Hall of Xerxes, I reread Plutarch's account of the burning of Persepolis by Alexander, and was compelled, in presence of these calcined stones, these columns reddened by the flames, these débris of carbonised timbers, to accept the version of the Greek historian.' This I believe to be fancy. No one else, so far as I know, has observed any of these things in the Hall of Xerxes.

is true, but at least with more than moderate probability—feel ourselves contemplating, at a distance of 2,200 years, the speaking wreck of what was either, if the Greek historians are to be believed, the drunken freak of the conqueror, or, more probably, the act of a merciless but deliberate premeditation.

I have now completed my account of the still surviving ruins upon the platform of Persepolis. Before I leave it, there are one or two subsidiary features that require to be mentioned. Of these the most interesting, if also not the least obscure, is the existence of a large number of what were described by the ancient travellers as underground passages, but are more probably channels for the passage of water. The entrance to these in former times must have been far more exposed than at present; the aqueduct beneath the Palace of Xerxes being the only one that now openly attracts the eye. The most complete exploration of these underground passages that is recorded was made by Chardin over 200 years ago. He represented them as extending in every direction at a depth of five feet below the surface, but principally in the eastern corner, where he entered and walked, for thirty-five minutes, a distance of a quarter of a league, till he was compelled to retire by the terror of his attendants. Their sides, he said, were like polished glass. Morier in 1809 repeated the experiment:—

Subterranean passages

> The great aqueduct is to be discovered among a confused heap of stones in the rear of the front row of buildings, and almost adjacent to a ruined staircase. We descended into its bed, which in some cases is cut 10 feet into the rock. This bed leads east and west: to the east its descent is rapid about 25 paces; it then narrows, so that we could only crawl through it; and again it enlarges, so that a man of common height may stand upright in it.[1]

The position and direction of several of these channels, but probably of only a small proportion of their real number, is given in the plans of Flandin and Coste.[2] In parts they are hewn in the live rock; elsewhere they are paved and walled with stone. The passages quoted show that they vary in height from low drains to ample channels. A layer of mud on the floor reveals the purpose for which they were originally intended. This appears to have been two-fold; either as aqueducts to convey drinking water or water for the gardens from cisterns in the mountain,[3] or as drain-pipes to carry off rain-water

[1] *First Journey*, p. 131. On his second visit, in 1811 (*Second Journey*, p. 77), Morier took candles and lights; but was stopped by the narrowness of the passage after crawling for some time on his stomach. Ouseley (vol. ii. p. 273) recorded the same result.

[2] Vol. ii. pls. 67, 90.

[3] One such cistern, already mentioned, has been noticed by most travellers just at the foot of the mountain behind the platform, between the first and second royal tombs.

from the roofs of the palaces, and surplus water in general from the platform. A more extended examination of these passages might not be fraught with valuable consequences, but is nevertheless desirable.

I have before mentioned that, in digging into the big mound behind the palace of Darius, Messrs. Stolze and Andreas found little beyond remains of masons' unfinished work, indicating that the structures on the platform never reached completion, but were suspended either by caprice or war, or, more likely, by the fall of the monarchy itself. Similar evidences exist on other parts of the platform. Tablets gape blankly for the inscriptions that were never engraved upon them; there are staircases on which the sculptures were only in part executed. Fragments of stone may be seen on which the chisel had only wrought half of its work. Stolze even hazards the conjecture that all the columns of the Hall of Xerxes may not have been set up, because of the almost complete disappearance of the expected wealth of ruin. To the caprice of Oriental sovereigns, as I have more than once argued, quite as much as to political vicissitudes, I should be disposed to attribute this phenomenon.

Unfinished work

The contents of the platform do not, however, exhaust the interest of Persepolis. Just as Darius and three of his successors selected the cliff now known as Naksh-i-Rustam for their rock-hewn and inaccessible sepulchres, so did three other sovereigns of the same line, but doubtless later in date, make similar choice of the Kuh-i-Rahmet, in immediate proximity to the palaces where they had reigned and feasted. One of these royal mausoleums stares from the rock immediately behind the Hall of a Hundred Columns, but has an outlook inclined rather more to south than west; the second is in a recess of the mountain a little to the south-east of the platform; the third, which was never completed, is on the outer edge of the sloping rock, nearly three-quarters of a mile to the south. The mountain background here being neither so lofty nor so precipitous as at Naksh-i-Rustam, there are necessary differences between the two groups. At Persepolis the sepulchre is not hewn high up in the vertical cliff, impenetrable save by ropes or machines. On the contrary, it is now easy of access from below, although, in the case of the north tomb, an attempt was made to render approach from the platform more difficult by means of a wall built up of big polygonal stones in five tiers or terraces from the lower level. The dimensions of the Persepolitan tombs also differ slightly from their predecessors, being (as calculated from the visible parts of the cruciform cutting in the mountain): height, seventy-nine feet, breadth of the upper limb, thirty-three feet, breadth of the transverse limb, containing the tomb-chamber, fifty-four and a half feet. A third and instructive difference, pointing to a later and more ornate period of art, is perceptible in the sculptured

Royal tombs

surface of the façade. The doorways are surrounded with three rows of exquisitely carved rosettes on the lintel and jambs ; and the roof or architrave which supports the twin-staged throne has carved on its front a spirited frieze of lions.[1] The four tombs of Naksh-i-Rustam having been hypothetically assigned to Darius I. (B.C. 521–485), Xerxes (485–465), Artaxerxes I. or Longimanus (465–424), and Darius II. or Nothus (424–405), we shall not be far wrong in allotting those at Persepolis to the later sovereigns of the Achæmenian dynasty, viz. Artaxerxes II or Mnemon (405–361), Artaxerxes III. or Ochus

NORTH TOMB BEHIND PERSEPOLIS

(361–338), and the unfinished tomb either to Arses (338–336) or to Darius III. or Codomannus (336–330).

North tomb

In the early part of the century the entry to the first or northernmost tomb was choked with sand and clay. The labours of the English artillerymen, who formed part of the escort of Sir Gore Ouseley, cleared these away in 1811, and the accumulations were, by the labours of Ferhad Mirza in 1878, still further reduced ; until now the front is exposed down to the base of the doorway

[1] Mistaken by several writers for dogs.

conducting into the tomb.[1] Of this the lower part has been forcibly broken away,[2] and we can now enter without difficulty. Passing into a chamber or vestibule with arched vault, hewn out of the live rock, we encounter at a distance of nine feet from the door a wall, four feet high, also in the solid rock, constituting the front of the first of two cavities or sarcophagi, excavated one behind the other in a recess. A partition, one foot in width, separates the pair; and the furthest extends to within three feet of the end of the cutting.[3] They are four feet in depth, nine and one-third feet long, and four feet broad, and their broken lids, which formerly were arched at the top, lie across the openings.[4]

Middle tomb

At a distance of three hundred yards to the south is the second rock tomb. It differs only from its predecessor in containing three arched niches or recesses at the back of the main vestibule, each containing a rifled cavity or sarcophagus.[5]

South tomb

The most southerly tomb, at some distance from the others, was first noticed by Niebuhr in 1765. Its lower part is hewn out of the rock in the familiar fashion, but its upper portion is built up with large rectangular stones to supply the superior limb of the cross. Nor was this tomb ever finished, as the state of the sculptures sufficiently shows. The king, and Ormuzd, and the fire-altar, and the terrace, are there; but immediately below the cornice of

[1] The lower limb of the cross does not, therefore, exist in this case, being built up by the polygonal wall.

[2] Chardin declared that the door was always a sham door forming part of the natural rock, and thought that the real entry to the tomb must have been gained by a subterranean passage. There is no evidence in support of this, and analogy is against it.

[3] Flandin, both in his text and plates (vol. iii. pls. 164–6), has committed the curious error of representing only one sarcophagus in this tomb.

[4] Near this tomb Herbert, in 1627, described as being 'sculptured the Image of their grand Pagotha, a Dæmon of as uncouth and ugly a Shape as well could be imagined; and if reverenced by those wretches, sure it was not in love, but rather with a Ne noceat, base fear too often drawing dastardly spirits into vile subjection. It is of a gigantish size or magnitude, standing as upright as his deformed posture will admit, discovering a most dreadful visage twixt man and beast.' No one has ever been able to make out what this horrible and purely imaginary monster (which Herbert's London artist introduced in fine style into his drawing) can have been. I fancy that the excellent knight must have carried away an indistinct recollection of the nondescript creatures with whom the king is so often represented in combat on the doorways, and must finally have written his account at home.

[5] I am puzzled by the interior of this tomb, upon which my own notes and recollections do not enlighten me. Ouseley, Johnson, Rich, Binning, and Ussher, all of whom entered it, concur in the above description. Flandin and Coste, however (vol. iv. pls. 163–4), depict it as containing six tombs instead of three. I think they are again wrong.

the latter the work is suspended, and we may infer that the death of the monarch or the collapse of the dynasty abruptly arrested its execution. There is no sign of an entrance, and the presence of a large number of loose blocks of stone in front has led some writers to the quite gratuitous conclusion that there was projected a secret and labyrinthine avenue of approach. It is undoubtedly singular that a site should have been chosen for this tomb so very near to the level of the plain, above which, if completed, it would barely have been elevated at all. This seems to indicate a relaxation in the earlier ideas of impracticability of access.

The veritable Persepolis

I have now completed my examination of all the ruins either upon or in the immediate neighbourhood of the Persepolitan platform; and I proceed in conclusion to a discussion of such of the problems, whether of history or archæology, as have not yet been solved. I have everywhere very plainly indicated my belief that here was not merely *a* palace-platform of the Achæmenian kings—that is incontestably demonstrated by the sculptures and inscriptions—but *the* Persepolis, which was one of the wonders of the ancient world, upon which Alexander descended with the conquering might of the Macedonian phalanx, whose city he surrendered to the plunder of his triumphant soldiery, and whose palace or palaces he burned.

> The princes applaud with a furious joy,
> And the king seized a flambeau with zeal to destroy;
> Thais led the way
> To light him to his prey,
> And, like another Helen, fired another Troy.

From the early Istakhr, whose ruins we have seen at the mouth of the valley of the Polvar, to the cliff-wall and rock-tombs of Naksh-i-Rustam on the north, and to the palace-platform on the south, and far out, may be, on the fronting plain, we may presume the royal city of Darius and of Xerxes to have stretched. That city—like most Oriental cities, a compound of mud and clay—has perished off the face of the earth; and its successors have done likewise; but in the rock-sepulchres, the fortified valley gateway, and the pillared platform, we have the indestructible boundary features, between which was outspread its vast extent. On the royal platform, whether it was inside or outside the precincts of the city, the monarchs resided during their short visits to the ancient capital of the dynasty; and there were enacted the gorgeous scenes that both accounted for its erection, and are still displayed upon its ruins.

Such, even in days before the cuneiform alphabet had been deciphered, has been for long the opinion of the majority of students. It has been reserved for Stolze once again to resuscitate the exorcised spirit of doubt.[1] The character and object of the platform and its structures he does not, of course, any more than other scholars, dispute.

Stolze's doubts

But he boldly denies that this was the royal castle of Persepolis which Alexander seized, and which, whether in a drunken brawl or with a fixed purpose, he set on fire.[2] Diodorus Siculus, who wrote in the half-century immediately preceding the Christian era, and who derived most of his material for the history of Alexander from Clitarchus, is his mainstay. The Sicilian describes the citadel and palaces of Persepolis (using the names *ἄκρα* and *βασίλεια* without distinction), as surrounded by a triple wall, of which the outermost was sixteen cubits or twenty-seven feet high, crowned with battlements, the second, thirty-two cubits or fifty-four feet, and the third or innermost, sixty cubits or one hundred and two feet high. He continues :—

> The third enclosure in shape was four-sided, and the wall thereof was in height sixty cubits, made of hard stone, well suited to last for ever. Each of the sides had gates of brass, and by them palisades (the word is *σταυρούς*, lit. crosses) of brass of twenty cubits, the one set up for safety, the others to strike terror into the beholders And on the side of the citadel towards the east, at a distance of four hundred feet, is a mountain called the Royal Mountain, in which were the sepulchres of the kings. . . . In this citadel were many lodgings, both of the king and of his generals, of very costly equipment, and treasuries well contrived for the guarding of money.

He further says of the royal rock-tombs, that the coffins could only be elevated to them by means of machines.[3] From this description it is at once evident (1) that the historian is either not describing the pillared platform at all, but some other structure, or that he has hopelessly blundered ; and (2) that he is describing, not the sepulchres of Persepolis, but those at Naksh-i-Rustam. Stolze, accepting the hypothesis most favourable to Diodorus, conjectures that the citadel with triple concentric enclosure did exist ; that it was situated in the immediate neighbourhood, on the western side, of Naksh-i-Rustam, and that there were the palaces which Alexander destroyed by fire.[4] He disposes of the layer of charred cedar on the floor of the Hall of

[1] *Verhand. d. Gesell. f. Erd. z. Berlin*, 1883.

[2] The bulk of the historians, basing their narrative upon Clitarchus, favour the former theory ; and Dryden, in the famous passage above quoted, has given poetical form to the familiar story of Thais, the courtesan. Diodorus, however, suggests a more deliberate motive, viz. revenge for the burning of the temples of Athens by Xerxes. This is a far likelier hypothesis; and Nöldeke, looking to the impression produced upon an Oriental people by such a display of the power of the conqueror, regards the act as 'a well-considered measure, calculated to work on the Asiatic mind.'

[3] Diod. Sic. lib. xvii. 215.

[4] According to Diodorus, the destruction was of more than one palace—*ταχὺ πᾶς ὁ περὶ τὰ βασίλεια τόπος κατεφλέχθη*.

a Hundred Columns by supposing that it was the result of natural decomposition, and he apparently forgets the traces of conflagration, for which he has pleaded elsewhere on the ruined platform. He argues that the Naksh-i-Rustam position was a much better and more probable site for the royal residence and citadel, because of the better water-supply, and because it was out of sight of the tombs, which the Mazdean monarchs would not have consented always to keep in view. In fine, he gives the go-by to the platform altogether, and leaves it, with brilliant contumely, to account for itself.

The answer

Now, in answer to all this it may be pointed out that an ounce of fact is worth a hundredweight of theory, particularly when theory rests upon an ancient but not contemporary writer, quoting in the most perfunctory fashion from another writer, notoriously reckless. The solid and incontrovertible fact of the platform and its palaces remains; while not a trace of the great threefold structure of Diodorus and Stolze has ever been discovered. Why should all the buildings have survived in one spot, and all have perished in the other? The confusion between the two groups of royal tombs is a very natural mistake, and might easily occur; nor can any valid reasoning, in my opinion, be grounded upon this statement. What, then, are we to believe of the general description by Diodorus, or Clitarchus, whichever it really was, concerning the triple, concentric, lofty-walled enclosure? That such a description could ever have been intended to apply to the existing platform, I am quite unable to credit.[1] Two hypotheses suggest themselves. The first is

[1] Some writers have laboured the minute and possible features of identity between the two, arguing that the platform was the uppermost or innermost of the three enclosures. It is sufficient to point out that even its maximum elevation above the plain is wholly inadequate, that it must always have rested upon a wall instead of being encompassed by a wall, and that not a trace has ever been noted on the ground below of either of the two inferior enclosures, their contents, or their fortifications. Why, again, should one only have survived, and the two others have perished? Some writers have sought a feeble support in the discovery (which Texier, vol. ii. p. 161, claims for one of his party, but which was really made by Ker Porter twenty years before) of what is alleged to have been a triple line of circumvallation, consisting of mud walls and towers, on the brow of the hill behind the platform, at a little distance above the royal tombs. Such a work was a very natural and necessary scheme of protection to the platform, which might otherwise have been open either to attack or to robbery on that side; but, of course, it answers in no respect to the account of Diodorus, nor can it be proved to date from Achæmenian times. A far more reasonable hypothesis is suggested to me by Mr. Cecil Smith, who thinks that the triple wall of Diodorus may have resulted from a misunderstanding of Clitarchus' description of the three walls of the Persepolitan platform, which were of differing height and were crowned with a parapet. He also ingeniously suggests that σταυρούς, the brazen palisades above mentioned, which in themselves are an unintelligible architectural feature, may

that Diodorus may in reality have been describing another building or group of buildings at Persepolis, the citadel, in fact, as distinguished from the palaces (although he erroneously identified them), and that such an enclosure may have existed in the neighbourhood of Naksh-i-Rustam. Now, it is true that on the platform there appears to be inadequate provision for the treasure-house, the barracks of the body-guard, and the other concomitants of royal residence that we know, or must believe, to have existed at Persepolis ; and to that extent may we be prepared to believe that a citadel or fort existed in a detached situation ; though even so, there would appear to have been no reason for the erection on the plain of Mervdasht of such an imposing place-of-arms as Diodorus has described ; nor does it seem likely that palace and fort would have been placed three miles apart. But until some positive traces of the whereabouts of this citadel have been brought to light, I shall prefer myself to accept the rival hypothesis that Clitarchus or Diodorus did not know or confused what they were writing about, transferring to Persepolis the structural features which existed at Ecbatana and in other contemporaneous and neighbouring capitals, and seasoning a nucleus of fact with a magniloquent garniture of fancy.

History of destruction

We have seen when and by whom the palaces on the platform were set up. We have seen that the entire work appears to have been suspended, or, at any rate, that several of the edifices lacked completion. I have given reasons for attributing the initial destruction of one palace at least to Alexander. The only remaining historical question is at what period the sculptures and ruins were reduced to their present mutilated condition. The fall of the Persian monarchy, the neglect of the Seleucidæ and Parthians, the preference of the Sassanian sovereigns for other capitals, are all landmarks in the long history of decline. From the Arab invasion, in all probability, dated the first deliberate and wholesale mutilation, the defacement of the king's features wherever they could be reached, and the brutal employment of every available instrument of destruction. And yet I think that the moderns, too, have borne their share in the iconoclastic campaign. Centuries of Persians have carried off thousands of tons of building-material from the ruins. We have the authority of Chardin that Abbas the Great sent hither for marble [*sic*] for his palaces and mosques ; that Imam Kuli Khan, the great viceroy of Fars, did the same for his capital at Shiraz ; and that the Minister of

also have resulted from a mistaken reproduction of Clitarchus' ταύρους, a very natural allusion to the colossal bulls, who might well strike terror, where a palisade could not, and to whom the attribute brazen might easily have been shifted from the gates. On the other hand, there is no trace of gates ever having existed in the Porch of Xerxes.

Shah Sefi I., disgusted at the number of studious Europeans who visited Persepolis, and for whose entertainment he was required to provide, despatched a party of sixty men with orders to destroy every sculpture upon which they could lay hands. Nor do I feel altogether happy—for the credit of these self-same Europeans—when I read in the pages of Le Brun that he took a mason from Shiraz, and blunted all his tools, in the effort to break off and carry away desirable fragments, and that he confesses to having shattered several figures in pieces. Perhaps we may seek relief from such remorse in the fact that on the 1,200 sculptured figures, reported by that traveller to have existed in his day, only a small impression ever has been or can be produced by these petty depredations. A thousand years hence our descendants will still find ample cause both for pilgrimage and for marvel in the monuments of Persepolis.

Artistic criticism

Though this is not a treatise on art, and though I do not profess to be an art critic, I yet feel justified in making a few observations in conclusion upon the artistic features and merits of the Persepolitan ruins, having at least examined them carefully on the spot, in the comparative light that is thrown upon them by other ancient Asiatic styles of architecture which I have also inspected *in situ*—credentials that I have been astonished to find are advanced by but few of those who, from the serene solitude of their studies, have pronounced *urbi et orbi* upon the nature and origin of Achæmenian architecture. And yet our authorities do not always agree, for whilst I read in the pages of one that this art was mimetic and nothing else,[1] I am informed by another that 'in its main and best features it was, so far as we can tell, original.'[2] I shall argue that the truth lies, as it commonly does, between these extremes; but in this case very much nearer to the former than to the latter.

History a clue to art

The first and most obligatory step is to correlate this Achæmenian art with the times and circumstances in which it was produced, and to see in what respects the page of history may provide us with a clue. Essentially it was an art—so far as we can trace it—of sudden birth, of brief-lived span, and of abrupt and premature decay. It was comprised within a maximum period of about 200 years, starting into being with the union of the kingdoms of Anzan, Persia, and Media into a single empire by the Great Cyrus, and perishing beneath the assault of Alexander. Its existence, in fact, was synchronous with that of the dynasty who fostered or created it, and after expressing and immortalising their triumphs, it shared the swift

[1] Z. A. Ragozin, *Media* (Story of the Nations), p. 303: 'Persian Art was from first to last, and in its very essence, imitative, with the single exception of the Aryan principle of building, consisting in the profuse use of columns.'

[2] Canon Rawlinson, *Fifth Great Oriental Monarchy*, p. 307.

revulsion of their fall. What then was the historical environment of Persia during this period, and with what foreign peoples and styles was she brought into direct contact? The answer is simple and suggestive. The campaigns of Cyrus left the new-born dominion the heir of the glories of Nineveh and Babylon, and planted the conqueror upon those illustrious thrones. For centuries they had supported a long line of sovereigns, of exceeding magnificence and power, the stately splendour of whose courts was the talk of the ancient world, and is equally stamped upon the pages of Herodotus, on the records of Holy Writ, and on the exhumed relics of their glory. Succeeding victories threw open to the Persians the stored wealth and the highly developed arts of Asia Minor, and brought them into relations with the Hellenic colonies on the maritime fringe. Cambyses, still further widening the horizon of ambition, found and absorbed in Egypt the most ancient of civilisations, the most elaborate and systematised of arts. Finally, under Darius and Xerxes, war was waged between the invading armaments of the Great King, and those European republics, already the cradle of freedom, and soon to become the nursery of the purest and freest art that the world had seen. The East was repelled by the West; but in its retreat it carried off much plunder, and by its wealth continued to command the expanding talents of the rising nationality. Chaldæa, Assyria, Lycia, Ionia, Egypt, Greece—this was the historical sequence of conflict; and this too will be found to mark the order of artistic influence and progression.

Influence of Assyria

The nearest and the most akin of civilisations naturally exercised the most powerful control. To no one who has studied Chaldæo-Assyrian art, as unearthed from the earlier Mesopotamian *tells* or mounds, or who is familiar with the spoils of Nimrud, Khorsabad, and Kouyunjik, will the bulk of the Achæmenian forms present any novelty. Let me enumerate in the order of their occurrence on the platform at Persepolis, the indubitable legacies of the art of Sennacherib and Nebuchadnezzar. The artificially built-up terrace, or mound, stone-faced (the Assyrian platforms were usually brick-faced, but there was a stone-casing to that of the palace of Sargon), surmounted by a battlement, and ascended by great flights of steps (again in Assyria, as a rule, of brick, but sometimes also of stone), was the familiar substructure of the royal palaces on the Tigris. The winged man-faced bulls of the Propylæa are almost a facsimile of the monstrous gate-keepers of Kouyunjik and Khorsabad. There is the same pose, the same attitude, the same lofty tiara and curled hair, the same backward sweep of the feathered wings. The Persepolitan types mark, however, a later age, and a perceptible artistic refinement. There is less grotesque exaggeration in their form; the fifth leg, as before noticed, has disappeared; the muscular development of limb is kept within reasonable bounds ; the wings describe a freer upward curve ; and a notable difference in structural disposition consists in their invariably fronting the spectator, parallel to the passage of entry, instead of being placed at right angles upon the outer walls. Nor are these colossi the sole fantastic testament of Assyria. Not for the first time did the lion leap upon the hind-quarters of the bull on the Persepolitan platform. The conflict of the king with nondescript monsters had already figured for centuries on cylinders and bas-reliefs in the legendary exploits of Izdubar. Every attribute of the Persian monarch had similarly been consecrated in Assyrian symbolism or etiquette. The king upon his high-backed throne (the very seat is an Assyrian facsimile), the two-staged throne supported by caryatid subjects or soldiers, the attendants with the royal parasol and fly-flap, the processions of slaves, officers, guards, and tribute-bearers,—all of these are borrowed, and almost slavishly borrowed, conceptions. If the god Ormuzd floats in a winged disc above the sovereign of the house of Achæmenes, whom he protects, so had the god Assur done over his Ninevite counterpart. The very features and stature of the king, his colossal height, his curled hair and beard, his royal robe, are the same, whether it be Assurnasirpal or Darius who is depicted. The object of the sculpture, the *raison d'être* of the palace, is the same in either case, viz., the visible apotheosis of majesty.

Such and so commanding was the influence upon the nascent Persian style of the older and neighbouring school of art. At Susa, in immediate proximity to the Chaldæan plains, the analogy was even more direct, for there, in the absence of cliffs and quarries, brick and clay provided the only available material on a large scale ; and the stupendous mounds of Shush recall the indurated piles of Sippara and Babylon. What may have been the precise influence upon Persian art of Asia Minor and the Ionian Colonies of Greece, it is difficult to determine with accuracy ; and I prefer to confine myself to a parallelism which none will dispute, rather than to embark upon an analogical cruise which may be adventurous, but can scarcely be practical. Nevertheless in the so-called fire-temples at Pasargadæ and Naksh-i-Rustam, which I hope I have dispossessed of that spurious credit and have shown to be mausoleums for the dead, we have what can hardly be an accidental reproduction of the Lycian tombs of Telmessus, Antiphellus, Aperlæ, and Myra, and not least of the celebrated Harpy tomb at Xanthus. The rosettes round the tomb doorways at Persepolis are Greek in origin. The majority have seen in the moulded doorway and pediment of the tomb of Cyrus at Murghab, a bequest from Ionia, but this is a point upon which I am unable to feel any certainty, and in speaking of Greek influence I prefer to confine myself to the obvious impress of the Hellenic genius.

Lycia and Ionia

Nowhere is the translation of history into art and architecture more manifest, and nowhere was it ever more rapidly effected, than in the case of Egypt and Persia. Cyrus cannot have been long dead, when he is already represented with the symbolical crown of an Egyptian divinity upon his brow. There is even reason to believe, as I have argued, that his body may have been embalmed. We learn from Diodorus that Cambyses carried away with him Egyptian workmen from his Nile expedition. Very early must these artificers have been set to work; for already, in the reign of his successor, we find another and a novel form of royal sepulture coming into vogue, viz. the hewing of tombs in inaccessible places in the face of the rock. I am strongly of opinion myself that Darius derived this idea, foreign to the habits of his country, alien to the precepts of his religion, from the spectacle of the rock-tombs in the valley of the Nile. In both cases the hermetic concealment of the royal corpse, and the sculptured blazoning of his title and prowess, are the objects of the architect; although the differing religions of the two countries prescribed, in the one case secrecy, in the other publicity, for the epigraphic display. An equally obvious loan from Egypt is the fluted moulding of the elegant projecting cornices above the Persepolitan niches and windows and doors. Above all I venture to express the opinion that the Achæmenian column, though possibly based upon a Median prototype,[1] though undoubtedly adorned with Greek attributes and though crowned with an original capital, was yet Egyptian before it was either Greek, Median, or indigenous, and that it adds one more Persian debt to the artistic storehouse of the valley of the Nile.[2] I attach considerable weight to the fact that, in spite of Media and Mazanderan, the use of stone columns on a large scale, which was unknown in Assyria and Chaldæa, was equally unknown in Persia until the reign of Darius, i.e. until after the Egyptian campaign of Cambyses. From what other quarter did the architects of Persepolis

Egypt

[1] The Median columns—e.g., those in the famous palace at Ecbatana, ascribed by Herodotus to Deioces—were of wood, adorned with plates of metal. But even so they were, I believe, Chaldæan in origin, precisely the same metal-plated columns having been found in the sculptures of the Chaldæan *tells*. I observe that most writers (e.g., Rawlinson and Dieulafoy) believe that the Persians derived the original use of the pillar in palatial architecture from the wooden columns that supported the humble tenements of Mazanderan and Gilan. I see no reason for accepting this theory. Those provinces and their peoples have always existed, and still exist, in almost entire isolation from Persia proper; and I doubt if they have ever influenced in the slightest degree the Persians south of the Elburz.

[2] I cannot claim the support of Canon Rawlinson, who says: 'It is the glory of the Persians in art to have invented this style; it is certainly not from Assyria nor from Egypt.'

derive their idea of immense, and, as we may think, unduly low halls, with crowded groves of pillars, supporting a flat roof, and with branching columnar aisles stretching away in long perspective into the gloom? True, in Egypt the pillared hall preceded the sanctuary of the deity, in Persia enshrined the majesty of the king; but what the god was in the Egyptian creed, and Pharaoh as his minister, the king was by himself in the faith of Iran. In either case the hall serves architecturally the same purpose, and I conceive, therefore, the later to have been derived from the earlier model.

Critics have found some difficulty in agreeing as to the obligations, if any, under which Persia laboured to the art of Greece.[1] That intercourse between the two nations, not only on the battle-field but in the relations of peace, was frequent and common is certain. How many of the statued glories of Athens were carried off to Asia we cannot tell; but that the Attic temples were remorselessly plundered we know. After the conclusion of the war, there was a constant flow of Greek exiles and artists to the Achæmenian Court, attracted in either case by its luxury and wealth. I have spoken of Greek forms in the Persepolitan column; alluding thereby to the Ionian volutes in the composite capital, and to the strings of ovals, and *tori* or fillets, upon the base. The elasticity and freedom of the Hellenic genius may further be recognised in the movements and the draperies of the human body, as depicted in the bas-reliefs of Persepolis, which are less angular and conventional than in any earlier Asiatic style. If a more minute correspondence cannot with certainty be traced, it must be remembered, in the first place, that the genius of Greek art was plastic and of Persian art structural; and secondly that, while the earlier Achæmenian sovereigns were rearing their pillared halls and throne-rooms on the platform at Persepolis, Hellenic art was still undeveloped and impeded by archaic traditions; and that the Persian form had been finally stereotyped before, upon the sacred crag of Athens, the marble of Pentelikon leaped into life beneath the inspired chisel of Phidias.

Greece

This, then, I conceive to have been, roughly speaking, the debt of Persia to foreign peoples and styles. Nevertheless, while she borrowed much, she also added something of her own, enough, beyond all question, to lift her art from the rank of a purely imitative or servile school. The Persepolitan platform, though in its origin

Residue of originality

[1] M. Dieulafoy, for instance, somewhat obscurely says: 'La part que la Grèce a prise à l'éducation du sculpteur persan n'est sensible qu'à un œil très exercé; elle ne se trahit que dans le caractère du travail, dans l'imprévu de certaines recherches, de certaines souplesses, que l'on ne s'attendait pas à trouver en pareil lieu.' I recommend an excellent excursus on the influence of Greek upon Persian art by M. Perrot, pp. 425-54.

a foreign idea, is elevated into a class and a dignity of its own by the monumental solidity of its construction. No merely slavish copyist would have detected in the footslopes of the Kuh-i-Rahmet so magnificent an opportunity. The polygonal facing of the platform is an equally ancient contrivance ; but I doubt if anywhere it was so well executed, or displayed with such majestic effect, as on the plain of Mervdasht. It is, however, when we come to the sculptures of the staircases, with their long processional panels, their inscriptions, and their figures that ascend the steps with the ascending visitor, that we see the Persian architect at his most original and his best. For staircases, and their capacities of sculptural display, the Egyptians cared little, and the Greeks hardly at all. They had other iconostases for their delineation of the pageantry either of religious ceremonial or of royal magnificence. It was the distinction of the Persian artist to have invented and brought to its highest perfection a method which served the triple purpose of economising space, of adding to the elevation and consequent grandeur of the buildings, and of realising the sole aim and object of his employment, viz., the glorification of royalty. Similarly in the case of the rock-tombs, though the idea was Egyptian in origin, the execution owes no external debt in point of combined dignity and skill. The deeply-incised cross in the cliff, the noble façade, the repetition of the palace-frontal upon the rock, the terraced platform of the adoring king—all these are Persian, and Persian only. Native, too, in all probability, is the great demi-bull capital of the composite Græco-Egyptian column, that so successfully crowned its somewhat clumsy shape and so suitably supported the timbered rafters of the ceiling. Above all, we may congratulate the Persian artist upon his slow, but very perceptible, advance along the pathway of genuine artistic progress. Not yet had he learned to make beauty his main canon, to subordinate subject to shape, to thrill to the enchantment of movement and form. His footsteps were clearly prescribed for him : he could diverge little to the right or to the left ; the king in his majesty, and nothing but the king, was his pre-ordained theme. And yet he had left far behind the stiff and often ludicrous conventionality of the earlier styles. The bizarre, the grotesque, the disproportionate, the '*horrendum, informe, ingens,*' that form so large a feature in Egyptian and Assyrian architecture, have been relegated to a secondary place ; and although the conception of majesty and its attributes must still conform to well-established rules, the sculptor can yet find scope for some of the statelier elegances of the statuary's art.

Having thus rendered to the Persian artist his due, we are at liberty to notice his limitations, both of theme and style. No one can wander over the Persepolitan platform, from storied stairway to stairway, from sculptured doorway to graven pier, no one can contemplate the

1,200 human figures that still move in solemn reduplication upon the stone, without being struck with a sense of monotony, and fatigue. It is all the same, and the same again, and yet again. The larger structural units are identical. With but slight variations it is always the same palace, the same tomb, the same flight of steps, the same cornice and entablature, the same pillared hall, the same base, and shaft, and capital. Everywhere the monarch is the same. There is nothing to distinguish one sovereign from another; nor, though the features have been wantonly destroyed, does it appear that the face was ever intended to be a likeness. On every bas-relief he performs with proud reiteration the same royal functions; he sits, or stands, or walks, or with icy composure plunges his dagger into the belly of the rampant beast. His subjects pass in long procession to his presence. They represent different nationalities, and are clad in different garbs; but there is no variation in their steady, ceremonious tramp. The royal bodyguard hold their lances, and bows, and bucklers with the well-trained rigidity of machines; but one can scarcely conceive one of these stately automatons suddenly bringing his spear into rest, or letting an arrow whistle from the string. The same criticism applies to the choice of theme. Nowhere here, as in the Egyptian and Assyrian sculptures, do we see depicted upon the walls the vicissitudes of armed conflict, battles, camps, and sieges, Sennacherib slaughtering his foes, the pursuing car of Rameses. Still less do we observe scenes from peaceful life, whether it be the pleasures of the chase, or the incidents of domestic existence. The bas-reliefs disclose no history; they perpetuate no exploit; they are guiltless of a plot or a tale. Everything is devoted, with unashamed repetition, to a single, and that a symbolical, purpose, viz. the delineation of majesty in its most imperial guise, the pomp and panoply of him who was well styled the Great King.

Limitations

So we find and so we may leave the art of the Achæmenians and their princely palace-halls. The last expression of a strictly Asiatic genius, the heir of Chaldæa, and Assyria, and Egypt, this art at once summed up their splendour and composed their epitaph. Restricted and enfeebled by its purely artificial existence, lacking alike the stimulus of spontaneity and the inspiration of popular belief, it fell as soon as the support was withdrawn by which it had been ushered into being, and by which for two centuries it had been maintained at an almost even zenith. It was splendid while it lasted; but it had within it no organic life. To the ancient Persians it expressed the supreme visible form of human grandeur, not unworthily shown forth to mankind in the person of a Cyrus or a Darius. To us it is instinct with the solemn lesson of the ages; it takes its

Conclusion

place in the chapter of things that have ceased to be; and its mute stones find a voice, and address us with the ineffable pathos of ruin.

Note on Ruins still to be excavated in Persia

I may not unfitly append to a chapter on the chief antiquarian remains in Persia a note upon the sites, still unexplored or inadequately explored, that seem especially to invite the excavator's concern. The attention of archæologists has long been concentrated upon other countries, upon the tombs of Egypt or the mounds of Mesopotamia. And yet I think that Persia still contains, and may some day yield up, no mean increment of spoil. The sites which I commend for such future investigation are the following:—

1. Persepolis.—The principal buildings have been exposed, but no student will feel satisfied until the entire platform has been laid bare. The great mound between the Hall and the Palace of Xerxes needs careful examination by means of transverse trenches, if not bodily removal. In other parts of the platform are many yards' depth of rubbish. Not till such a painstaking scrutiny has been applied can we be certain of our data. It may solve many disputed problems touching roofs, tiles, colouring, and walls.

2. Naksh-i-Rustam.—The artificial elevation on which the so-called Fire-temple stands, opposite the cliff, needs thorough examination. All mounds in this neighbourhood should be similarly tested. Thus only can we settle the doubt raised by Diodorus and revived by Stolze, and ascertain whether there ever was a citadel of Persepolis as distinct from the palace-platform. By these means, also, we might hope to add to our very scanty knowledge of the ancient city of Persepolis, or Istakhr.

3. Susa.—Excavations should be carried down into the great mound far below the level of M. Dieulafoy's discoveries and of Achæmenian trophies. Susa, which was the capital of several dynasties before Cyrus, ought to resemble Hissarlik in its superincumbent layers of ruin; and the expenditure of a few thousand pounds —possibly of a few hundreds—might shed an incalculable light upon the dark riddles of Elam.

4. Mal Amir.—I have argued in the text that no site in Persia is more likely to repay thorough exploration and copying of inscriptions than this. Archæology has never yet had a fair field in the Bakhtiari mountains.

5. Rhey.—The mounds of Rhey, though at a distance of only six miles from the capital, have never been scientifically explored. Indeed, it is not yet known for certain whether they represent the site of Rhages or not. They are rich in minute fragments of Arabic ruin, and an ampler and earlier spoil may well lie below. The same remarks apply in a less degree to the mounds of Veramin.

6. Ecbatana.—If Hamadan be indeed the Ecbatana of the ancients, some less contemptible records of its splendour should be discovered than those which have hitherto been brought to light. A thorough examination should be made of its environs, particularly of the elevation known as the Musalla.

CHAPTER XXII

FROM SHIRAZ TO BUSHIRE

γῆν γὰρ ἐκτήμεθα ὀλίγην καὶ ταύτην τρηχέαν.

HERODOTUS, lib. ix. 122.

FROM a contemplation of the vast but ruined handiwork of man, I return to the record of my journey, and to an experience of the more stupendous freaks of nature. We are now about to descend from the central plateau of Iran, i.e. from a mean elevation of from 4,000 to 6,000 feet, to the level of the sea. In the course of this advance, we must first climb to a height of 7,400 feet, from which it may be imagined that the descent on the far side, which is accomplished within a tract of country only thirty-five miles in width, and occupied for the most part by upland plains, must be one of extraordinary steepness; while the atmospheric change through which it passes, and which is reflected in the vegetation no less than in the temperature, is not less abrupt than that from a smart winter's frost in England to a summer hotter than is ever known in our northern latitudes. This descent is only effected by a series of rocky inclines, four in number, which have aptly been compared to ladders, accessible to no baggage animals but camels, mules, and donkeys, and constituting, in their succession and severity, what may be described without hesitation as the roughest and least propitious highway of traffic in the world. That such a route should ever have been selected as a main avenue either of passage or of commerce is creditable, perhaps, not to the sense. but at least, to the resolution of the Persians. That it should be persevered in, without protest, and almost without effort for improvement, is characteristic at once of Oriental conservatism, and of a nation smitten with moral decline. Over such a tract of country, in which horses, though sometimes ridden, are commonly exchanged for the more sure-footed and little less rapid mule, it will easily be understood that no *chapar* service is, or could be, maintained. The post-horses

Descent by rock-ladders

would be knocked to pieces in a fortnight. Accordingly, we have said good-bye to the *chapar-khaneh*, the *chaparchi*, and the *chapar-shagird*, who have loomed large in our daily existence for so long; and the remaining 160 miles of our descent to the Gulf must be traversed by caravan, the traveller hiring such number of mules as are necessary for him and his baggage, and sleeping at night either, if invited, in the Telegraph stations and rest-houses, or in such surroundings, at caravanserais and elsewhere, as he can procure. The journey is usually accomplished in five or in six days, the former being regarded as fairly good time, seeing that in such a country it is cruel on the animals to expect of them much more than a *maximum* of thirty miles in the day; and that the muleteer or *charvadar*, who contracts for the party, himself accompanies it throughout on foot. For my own march I paid at the rate of five *tomans* per mule for the whole distance; this being a little above the ordinary charge, as I postulated extra speed. I preferred to ride a *yabu*, or pony, myself, having no fondness for a mule, and having accepted a challenge at Shiraz as to the number of miles over which it was possible to proceed at anything beyond a foot-pace between that city and the Gulf.

Table of route

The following is the table of stations and distances, as reckoned according to Persian and English standards of measurement:—

Name of Station	Distance in *farsakhs*	Approximate distance in miles	Name of Station	Distance in *farsakhs*	Approximate distance in miles
Shiraz * (4,750 ft.) .	—	—	Konar Takhteh * ‡ (1,800 ft.) . . .	3	12
Khan-i-Zinian ‡ (6,100 ft.) . . .	7	30	Daliki † (250 ft.) .	4	15
Dasht-i-Arzen * (6,400 ft.) . . .	3	12	Borazjun * ‡ (100 ft.)	4	15
Mian Kotal ‡ (5,500 ft.) . . .	3	11	Ahmedi ‡ or Shif .	4 or 7	15 or 25
Kazerun * (2,750 ft.)	6	21	Bushire *	6	22
Kamarij † (2,950 ft.)	5	20	Total . .	45	173[1]

* = Telegraph Station. † = Telegraph Rest-house. ‡ = Caravanserai.

[1] Total distance to Shif (whence boat to Bushire) 42 *farsakhs*, or 161 miles. The route from Shiraz to Bushire has been described by many of the travellers, whose works I have already cited as references for the journey from Shiraz to Isfahan, or from Isfahan to Teheran, viz. by C. Niebuhr (1765), W. Franklin (1787), E. Scott Waring (1802), Sir J. Malcolm (1800, 1810), J. P. Morier (1809, 1811), Sir W. Ouseley (1811), W. Price (1811), J. S. Buckingham (1816), Col. Johnson (1817), Lieutenant Lumsden (1817), Sir R. K. Porter (1818), J. B. Fraser (1821),

SHIRAZ TO BUSHIRE.

Scale of Miles.

10 0 50 100

F. S. Weller.

Leaving my kind hosts at the Bagh-i-Sheikh, on the western outskirts of Shiraz, where are the residence and club-room of the Indo-European Telegraph officials, I started at 6 A.M. on a cloudy morning upon my forward journey. The road makes for the westerly corner of the Shiraz valley, passing two small villages on the way. At the distance of eight miles we cross a slender stream by a bridge, where are a caravanserai and a guard-house, called Chenar-i-Rahdar, for the taking of tolls. Here we reach the foot hills and begin the ascent. Soon a turn in the track conceals from us the retrospect of the Shiraz plain; and, ere it is gone we turn round for a parting glance at the distant cypress spires, the scattered gardens, and the bulbous cupolas of the mosques. The road continues steadily to ascend, and after five hours of unbroken marching, conducts into an upland valley, watered by a river with wide stony bed, at present occupied by a streamlet of attenuated volume. This is the Kara Aghach (Black Tree), which in a circuitous course of at least 300 miles is known by several names, the principal of which are Kawar and Mand, and which eventually falls into the sea by a creek known as the Khor Ziarat. It is the Sitiogagus, or Sitakus of the ancients, already mentioned in my discussion of the Pasargadæ question.[1] The road follows its left bank for two miles, through a hilly country clothed with thorn bushes and a good deal of stunted scrub. At length in the distance is descried the white quadrilateral of the cavaranserai of Khan-i-Zinian,[2] built nearly thirty years ago by the Mushir-el-Mulk, a very wealthy individual, who was Vizier or Minister to the then Governor of Fars, and who signalised his administration by the repair or erection of public works along the Shiraz-Bushire route, which must have earned him the gratitude of thousands of wayfarers, even though the funds devoted to the outlay had probably been wrung from a distressed peasantry. In the old

Khan-i-Zinian

C. J. Rich (1821), R. B. Binning (1850), J. Ussher (1861), A. H. Mounsey (1866), A. Arnold (1875), (Sir) C. MacGregor (1875), E. Stack (1881). To these I may also add, for this section, J. de Thévenot (1665), *Voyages*, bk. 3, part ii.; Gen. W. Monteith (1810), *Journal of the R. G. S.*, vol. xxvii. pp. 114–8; and (Sir) O. St. John, *ibid.* vol. xxxviii. p. 411.

[1] *Vide* notes on this river by Col. E. C. Ross in the *Proceedings of the R. G. S.* (New Series), vol. v. pp. 712–7, 1883.

[2] Ouseley says that the name is Kan-i-Zinian, or Mine of *zinian*, a grain like fennel-seed in appearance, and like caraway-seed in taste, which is produced in the neighbourhood.

caravanserai here in 1860 died M. Minutoli, Prussian Minister to the Court of Teheran. It was also on the stretch of road between Shiraz and Khan-i-Zinian that in 1871 Corporal Collins, R.E., one of the original staff of the Telegraph department, while travelling with his wife and attendants, was attacked by a band of robbers and killed, though not before he had accounted for two or three of the bandits with his own hand. Three of the remainder were subsequently caught by the Governor, the redoubtable Hissam-es-Sultaneh, Ferhad Mirza, who was only too glad of an excuse for his favourite method of punishment. They were buried alive in pillars of mud, which used to be pointed out to the traveller by the side of the road, and, I dare say, are still visible, although they were not indicated to me. Crossing an affluent of the river which flows in here, by a bridge below the caravanserai, I pulled up and had lunch.

Dasht-i-Arzen

Three miles further on I crossed the main river by an imposing bridge of several arches, the causeway of which, although less than twenty years old, is already in ruins. After following up the valley for another three miles, the track commences to climb the crest of a ridge on the left, known as the Sineh Sefid, or White Breast, and for some miles is involved in steep and stony slopes, the surrounding hills being now somewhat thickly covered with thorns, and wild pear, apple, plum, and barberry trees, as well as occasional dwarf oaks. At the top of the pass a ruined tower marks the site of a former Rahdar, or combined guard and toll house. Here a new view opens to the south, on to the snug and symmetrical plain of Dasht-i-Arzen, or Plain of the Millet[1] (which abounds in these parts). In the wet season the hollow of the plain is filled with a lake, but, when I saw it, was occupied by a marsh, whose scanty pools flickered in the gleam of the declining sun. I cannot give a better illustration of the bewildering vagaries of previous travellers, than by saying that their estimates of the length of this plain, which is completely mountain-locked, and therefore incapable of elasticity, vary from sixteen miles by ten—the maximum calculation—to a minimum of five miles by two. I would diffidently venture upon the estimate of seven to eight

[1] This is the older and probably more correct form. Later writers call it Dasht-i-Arjin, or Plain of the Wild Almond.

miles by two to three. The lake is mentioned as long ago as the tenth century by El Istakhri, who said :—

> Its waters are sweet and pleasant ; they were at one time dried up, no water remained in this place. All the small fish are taken here.[1]

When I saw the valley in the winter, there was not a speck of vegetation on the plain around the marsh, and no beauty in the scrub on the hill-sides. But that the contrast between the dispositions of Nature at different seasons of the year in Persia is as wide as that between the contradictory verdicts of travellers, is evident from the description of Malcolm, who was quite ravished by the beauty of Dasht-i-Arzen.

> This small but delightful valley is encircled by mountains, down whose rugged sides a hundred rills contribute their waters to form the lake in its centre. The beauty of these streams, some of which fall in a succession of cascades from hills covered with vines ; the lake itself, in whose clear bosom is reflected the image of the mountains by which it is overhung ; the rich fields on its margin ; and the roses, hyacinths, and almost every species of flower, that grow in wild luxuriance on its borders, made us gaze with admiration on this charming scene.[2]

The village of Dasht-i-Arzen is clustered against the base of the northern hills, and immediately outside it is the compound of the Telegraph office. From my host, the occupant of this building, I heard many stories of the wild beasts with which the neighbourhood abounds. The maneless lion of Southern Persia is frequently encountered here, and it was on the far side of the valley, while ascending towards the Pir-i-zan, that Sir O. St. John was attacked, when on horseback, by a lioness, in 1867.[3] My informant told me that the last man-eater had perished thirteen years before, but that the natives, who are invincible cowards, credit every beast with similar propensities. Wild boars, hyænas, wolves, jackals, antelopes (which are coursed with greyhounds), ibex, and mountain sheep, are also found in the surrounding hills.

Wild beasts

Leaving the village next morning, I passed, at the distance of about a mile, over an abundant stream of water, which, gushing

[1] *Oriental Geography* (of the miscalled Ibn Haukal), p. 99.

[2] *Sketches of Persia*, vol. i. p. 95.

[3] Mr. A. Arnold (*Through Persia by Caravan*, 2 vols.) gratuitously transfers the adventure with the lioness to Mr. W. T. Blanford, who had never set foot in Persia at the time.—Vide *Eastern Persia*, vol. ii. p. 31.

from the base of the rock a little above, flows down through a cluster of *chenars* and willows, and wends its way to the swamp.

The lake

A small domed building here covers a *kadamgah*, or slab, that is said to bear the imprint of Ali's horse-hoofs, in connection with which an astounding miracle is, of course, related by the villagers. In the face of the rock a cave is regarded as a sacred place, and contains little tin sconces for votive tapers. Skirting the west shore of the lake, at the sixth mile we pass a ruined caravanserai. The fen was alive with wild fowl. Hundreds of geese rose from their swampy feeding-grounds, and their clamorous flight resounded for miles. I saw gazelles (the *ahu*, or so-called antelope) down in the hollow, which was white with the frost of the previous night, and a fox crossed my path. Having reached the southern extremity of the marsh, the path begins to climb the hills that confine the lake-basin. The ascent is steep and joyless; but it is as nothing compared with the descent on the other side, which is long, precipitous, and inconceivably nasty. This is the famous Kotal-i-Pir-i-zan, or Pass of the Old Woman.

Pass of the Old Woman

Some writers have wondered at the origin of the name. I feel no such surprise. On the contrary, I admire the apposite felicity of the title. For, in Persia, if one aspired, by the aid of a local metaphor, to express anything that was peculiarly uninviting, timeworn, and repulsive, a Persian old woman would be the first and most forcible simile to suggest itself. I saw many hundreds of old women during my travels in that country—they always took care to be seen (which was more than could be said of their younger, and, it is to be hoped, fairer sisters)—and I crossed the Kotal-i-Pir-i-zan, and I can honestly say that whatever derogatory or insulting remarks the most copious of vocabularies might be capable of expending upon the one, could be transferred, with equal justice, to the other. From the Lake of Dasht-i-Arzen to the top of the pass, where the descent begins, and which is 7,400 feet above the sea, is perhaps two miles; and at this point is a magnificent outlook over ridge succeeding ridge in oblique parallels, towards the Dashtistan, or Land of Plains, that is itself succeeded by the Gulf. The total descent is over 3,000 feet within a distance of four to five miles, and is down a path, which resembles an Alpine torrent-bed, minus only the torrent. No Englishman would do

PASS OF THE OLD WOMAN

otherwise than dismount and descend on foot, albeit the Persian mules are generally surefooted and reliable. The same could not be said of my little horse or *yabu*, which came down repeatedly. Rather more than half-way down the Old Woman, on a peak or platform of rock, is situated the caravanserai of Mian Kotal (or Mid-Pass), which has afforded rest and shelter to many a weary mule and cursing muleteer since travelling days began. From here can be seen outspread below a valley, five miles in length by from one to two in width, thickly sown with dwarf oaks, and known as the Dasht-i-Barm. The descent to the level occupies another two miles, and an hour is then spent in traversing the valley from end to end. I had read in previous books of the sylvan delights of this grove of oaks, and had pictured to myself a joyous ride over soft sward, under the shade, and between the gnarled boles of the noblest of trees. The oaks, it is true, are there; but sward and shade there are none. The road is a desolate track of stones, and the trees stand far too wide apart to afford any overhead canopy.[1] At the end of the valley the track turns sharply to the left, makes a slight ascent, and then, at the crest of the ridge, where a further valley and a new landscape simultaneously open, discloses a steep and hideous descent, known to fame, or infamy, as the Kotal-i-Dokhter, or Pass of the Maiden.

Pass of the Maiden

I do not know if the *dokhter* in question (the same word as the English daughter) is supposed to have been allied by the filial tie to the Old Woman whom I have already described; but from the strong family likeness between the pair, I feel justified in assuming the relationship. As I descended the Daughter, and alternately compared and contrasted her features with those of the Old Woman, I fear that I irreverently paraphrased a well-known line,

O matre læda filia lædior!

The Kotal-i-Dokhter is shorter than the Kotal-i-Pir-i-zan, but its steepest part is undeniably steeper, there being a sharp zigzag descent of 700 feet in the perpendicular, and a further drop of the same extent before the plain of Kazerun is reached Furthermore, as though the paving of nature was not bad enough, man has stepped in to make it worse. In many places the road has

[1] The acorn of this oak (called *belut*), which is very long and large, is pounded by the natives into a flour, kneaded up with barley meal, and baked into thin cakes of bread.

been buttressed up, parapetted, and artificially paved with huge boulders;[1] but whatever of soil there may once have been between these having been washed out and having disappeared, the blocks stand up like isolated reefs in the sea; and down this hideous stairway man and beast alike are compelled to scramble at imminent peril of twisted ankle, if not of broken limb. My horse jammed his foot between two stones and had a very nasty fall. The descent of the Maiden on foot took me about an hour and a half. From the summit of the *kotal* the plain of Kazerun had unrolled itself to the eye, bounded at the nearer or south-east extremity by an extensive lake, and stretching westwards to a distant range of hills. The lake is known as Daria-i-Pirishum, or Famur (from a village at its eastern end), and is the haunt of innumerable wild fowl. It terminates in a dense fringe of reeds and in swampy flats, which the sportsman eyes with enthusiasm, and which he does not quit without ample return.

At the foot of the pass the track turns sharply round a projecting angle of rock. Here in the recess of the mountain side is a favourite camping-ground of the Mamasenni or nomads, who roam over the adjacent plains. Their black goats' hair tents were pitched just under the cliff, and from the women, who were unveiled, I procured some very acceptable milk. The Mamasenni, of whom I shall have more to say in a subsequent chapter on the South-west Provinces, were formerly inveterate robbers, but were cowed into comparative innocence by the truculent severity of the afore-mentioned Prince-Governor of Fars. The nomads of this camp had, I noticed, a peculiar method of hiving honey. The hives consisted of a number of earthenware jars or cylinders, in shape like a big drain-pipe, laid side by side, and covered over with a thatch of thorns. The entrance was through

Nomads

[1] From my reading I learn that this artificial causeway was first made by the mother of Imam Kuli Khan, Viceroy of Fars under Shah Abbas, at which time Thévenot says it was called Kotal-i-Oshanek, or Pass of the wild marjoram, a name that still survives. At the end of the last century it was reconstructed by Haji Mohammed Husein, a wealthy merchant of Bushire, his motive being variously described as philanthropic, and as strictly mercenary, and having relation only to the losses previously incurred by accidents to his own caravans. About 1820 it was put in thorough repair by Kelb Ali Khan, Governor of Kazerun, and impressed Rich so greatly that he called it the Simplon of Persia! It was again repaired in 1834 by the mother of Timur Mirza, and in about 1870 by the Mushir-el-Mulk, Vizier of Fars; since which date I should imagine that not a penny has been spent upon it.

a small aperture pierced in a blue earthenware plate, with which the pipe was closed. The honey yielded is excellent.

Close by, at the back of a ruined enclosure, which was formerly the court of a rest-house built here for the accommodation of travellers, is a sculptured bas-relief on the rock, one of those degenerate imitations of the Sassanian model in which the Kajar princes have loved to indulge. The hero depicted in this case is Timur Mirza, one of the Persian Princes who came as refugees to London in 1837, after the unsuccessful rebellion of their father, Husein Ali Mirza, a son of Fath Ali Shah and Governor-General of Fars. This particular Timur was Governor of Kazerun; and on this wall of rock he had himself depicted, with a tame lion at his side, a pipe-bearer, some attendants, and a hawk. The figures are more than life size, and were originally painted and gilded. They are now almost obliterated, the dislike entertained for the Kajar dynasty in the middle of the present century having impelled the nomad tribes, and every passing wayfarer in addition, to inflict what defacement they could upon the likeness of the vain-glorious Timur. The spot is variously called Takht (Throne) or Naksh (Picture) -i-Timur.[1]

Takht-i-Timur

At the foot of the hill the track crosses the end of the marsh that borders the lake by a stone causeway called the Pul-i-Abgineh (Bridge of the Mirror), and strikes across the level plain of Kazerun, a distance to the town of that name of eight miles. In descending from Dasht-i-Arzen to Mian Kotal I had felt a very sensible difference in the temperature; and this was still further accentuated on descending to the level of Kazerun, which was 3,700 feet lower than my resting-place of the previous night. The air was warm and balmy; and presently the stately crown of date-palms, clustering in the distance, revealed a spectacle very unlike anything I had so far seen in Persia, and brought that country into immediate relation with the familiar *mise-en-scène* of the East. Kazerun, though its best days are long past, is a well-favoured spot, agreeable and healthy in climate, rich in water, and famous both for its oranges and its mules. As most of

Kazerun

[1] Would it be believed that the innocent A. Arnold speaks of this clumsy bas-relief as 'some interesting ruins of Ancient Persia, where a monarch, heavily bewigged with false hair, in the fashion of Ancient Persia, and as marvellously bearded, is seated with a lion before him, his chair of state encircled by attendants.' (*Through Persia by Caravan*, vol. ii. p. 186.) And this is how history is written!

the muleteers also hail from this village, the traveller must be on his guard against the most audacious pretexts, which are invariably devised by his *charvadar*, as the latter nears his domestic hearth, and thinks how far more agreeable would be an idle day in the bosom of his family, than a march of thirty miles over the *kotals* of the Tengistan (or country of *tengs*, defiles, as this region is appropriately termed). Kazerun is credited by patriotic Kazerunis with a very hoary antiquity; but it is doubtful whether the city existed prior to the Arab conquest. Ibn Batutah, the Moor, came here about 1330 A.D., to visit the shrine of Abu Ishak el Kazeruni; but this individual seems since those days to have lapsed into oblivion. The modern town, which consisted of an upper and a lower quarter, was ruined and dismantled of its fortifications by Jafir Khan Zend in the troubles at the end of the last century, and has never since recovered. It now contains 2,000–2,500 inhabitants. In addition to the specialities before mentioned, Kazerun has always been famous for its school of *pehlevans* or wrestlers, as also for a kind of rough shoe of cotton and hide, which MacGregor recommended for our Indian army. Outside is a shady garden, called the Bagh-i-Nazar, that formerly belonged to Arnold's 'Ancient Persian monarch,' Timur Mirza, and is sometimes placed at the disposal of strangers. I secured comfortable quarters in the Telegraph office. A good deal of opium and coarse tobacco are also cultivated in the valley, which is irrigated by *kanats*, and is well adapted for many kinds of vegetable and cereal produce.

While at Kazerun, whether in his upward or downward journey to or from the Gulf, no traveller should miss the opportunity of going to see the ruins and sculptured bas-reliefs of the ancient capital of King Shapur, which also bears his name, and the rock-tablets of which are superior both in number, size, and interest to those which I have already described at Naksh-i-Rustam. Shapur is situated at the north-western extremity of the plain of Kazerun, from which it is distant fifteen miles, one third of this distance lying along the road towards the Gulf, which can accordingly be rejoined after the deviation to Shapur, and its objects have been successfully accomplished. In coming up from the Gulf, the stranger should arrange to make the excursion from Kamarij, starting from there very early in the morning in order to have a long day at Shapur, where there is no accommodation, and to get at nightfall to Kazerun. As my own contract for mules was independent of this divergence, I was obliged to hire separate animals at Kazerun for the expedition to

Visit to the ruins of Shapur

Shapur, although I did not succeed in this without invoking the aid of the governor, who put an abrupt check upon the arrogance of the local *charvadars.*

Different travellers have been conducted to Shapur by slightly different routes over the Kazerun plain. I followed the telegraph poles along the Kamarij road for a little over five miles, and then, diverging to the right, struck across the plain in the direction of the north-westerly cliff-wall. The ground was thickly covered with a very prickly thorn bush, whose pretty green leaf is apparently a favourite dainty of the camel, large numbers of whom I saw munching the boughs, regardless of the big spines. Camps of

Ride to Shapur

NOMADS ON THE PLAIN OF KAZERUN

Mamasenni Iliats with large flocks tenant the whole of the neighbouring valleys, and I encountered many of their black tents. The men have a manly air and civil bearing, and the women take no pains to veil. Near the Shapur river their dwellings are made and thatched with reeds from the river-bed, and are of the most primitive description. A *kharbast* or fence of cut thorns takes the place of a wall, and forms an admirable enclosure for the flocks. Having crossed the plain towards its northern extremity, the track becomes involved in a wilderness of tumuli, consisting of loose stones and tumbled-down structures, filling a circuit of several miles, at the base of the mountains. These mounds rise to a height of fifty to sixty feet above the level of the surrounding plain. Right down through them hundreds of *kanat-*

shafts have been dug to the lower surface; and the accumulation of their contents, alongside of the already existing débris, makes such a litter of stones and rubbish as can scarcely be imagined. Here and there is a fragment of wall built of larger stones, so firmly welded together that it has resisted the shock of centuries. These are the ruins of the city of Shapur. I had heard and read a great deal, however, of the valley of Shapur, and of the river dancing merrily through it, and of the sculptures overhanging its banks, and began to wonder where these could be; when suddenly the northern cliff, which is here a great sloping face of bare rock, opened abruptly, and disclosed a gorge, a little over a hundred yards in width, cloven right through it from top to bottom. Down the fissure came glancing and tumbling the Shapur river, occupying a stony bed between lofty banks, fringed on either side with a dense growth of reeds, plumy grasses, and flowering trees. Already above its further bank I could discern the famous sculptures of the Sassanian monarch. The gorge, which is known as the Teng-i-Chakan, at its inner or further end widened to 400 yards, and then expanded into a valley, round which the mountains formed an amphitheatrical rampart, with a sheer rock-face in many parts of several hundred feet in height.

The Sassanian city

Though Istakhr or Persepolis was the theoretical metropolis of the Sassanid sovereigns, and long retained its ceremonial importance as the centre of the revived national religion, yet, like their Achæmenian predecessors, the monarchs of this dynasty shared the Oriental fondness for change of residence and for separate evidences of royal sumptuousness and display. Ctesiphon, the Parthian capital, was a secondary abode of the kings. In later times, under Chosroes II., we read of a splendid palace at Dastagird, also in the Chaldæan plains. Allusion is made elsewhere to the ruined palaces of Sarvistan and Firuzabad. None, however, of the Sassanian monarchs gratified, to the same extent as the first Shapur or Sapor, the taste for building on a large scale. His were the great works at Shushter, of which I shall speak later; his the city between Dizful and Shushter, whose ruins are now known as Jund-i-Shapur. To him is attributed by some the bridge of Dizful. At Naksh-i-Rustam we have seen the bas-reliefs that record his victories and his splendour; and now, on a site to which he gave his own name,[1] we have come to the royal city which he founded and adorned as the most enduring monument of his reign. Persian tradition, of course, ascribes a more remote and fabulous origin to the place, and relates that the ancient city was destroyed by Alexander, and only rebuilt, rather than founded, by

[1] Shah-pur (the classical Sapor) is a contraction of *Khshayathiya*, shah or king, and *putr*, son, *i.e.* king's son, or prince.

Shapur. It was over the gates of the Sassanian city that the skin of Mani or Manes, the founder of the Manichean heresy, was stuffed and set up on high, after he had been put to death (it is said flayed) by Varahran I., A.D. 272-5. When the Arabs overran Persia, Shapur was one of the first victims of their iconoclastic fury; the sculptures were mutilated and the city destroyed. In the tenth century El Istakhri left a very correct record of its ruined condition.

> Bishawur was built by King Shapur. It has four gates, and in the midst of it is a singular hill or eminence like a tower or dome. . . . In the territory of Shapour is a mountain, and in that mountain are the statues of all the kings and generals, and high priests, and illustrious men who have existed in Pars; and in that place are some persons who have representations of them and the stories of them written.[1]

This being so, it is curious that there is not a single record of any traveller having visited the place—although Kaempfer gives, apparently from hearsay, a short but fairly correct description of its general features, and although explorers so ardent as Tavernier and Thévenot both passed through Kazerun—until Morier in 1809. The cave containing the great statue of Shapur was not discovered till later, Kinneir saying in his 'Geographical Memoir' that 'a celebrated idol is also mentioned which its votaries used to anoint with oil; but of such an image there are no traces remaining.' Neither on his first nor his second visit was Morier fortunate enough to find the right cave, though some of the party explored an empty cavern. The discovery seems to have been reserved for Major Stone a few weeks later (in 1811), and his description was embodied in Ouseley's work. Since then a number of travellers have visited and delineated the sculptures and remains of Shapur.[2]

[1] *Oriental Geography* (of Ibn Haukal), pp. 101–129. Thévenot found the river still called Boshavir.

[2] I append a list of these: J. P. Morier (1809), *First Journey*, pp. 85–93, and *Appendix*, p. 375; (1811) *Second Journey*, pp. 49–51; Sir W. Ouseley (1811), *Travels*, vol. i. pp. 278–301; J. S. Buckingham (1816), *Travels*, vol. ii. pp. 79-97; Colonel Johnson (1817), *Journey from India*, cap. iv.; Lieutenant T. Lumsden (1817), *Journey from India*, pp. 82–9; J. B. Fraser (1821), *Journey into Khorasan*, p. 82; Captain Mignan (1830), *Travels*, p. 334; W. F. Ainsworth (1836), *Personal Narrative*, vol. ii. cap. iv.; Baron C. De Bode (1840), *Travels*, vol. i. pp. 186–8, 206–18; Ch. Texier (1840), *L'Arménie, &c.*, vol. ii. pls. 146–51, and text; E. Flandin and P. Coste (1841), *Perse Ancienne*, vol. i. pls. 45–54, and text; E. Flandin, *Voyage*, vol. i. pp. 45–54; R. B. Binning (1850), *Two Years' Travel*, vol. i. cap. xii.; Viscount Pollington (1865), *Half Round the Old World*, pp. 302–8; A. H. Mounsey (1866), *Journey*, p. 235; F. Stolze and Th. Nöldeke (1877), *Persepolis*, vol. ii.; K. D. Kiach (1878), *Ancient Persian Sculptures*. *Vide* also Silv. de Sacy, *Mém. sur div. Antiq. de la Perse*; C. Ritter, *Erdkunde von Asien*, vol. viii. p. 827; E. Thomas, *Early Sassanian Inscriptions*; F. Spiegel, *Eranische Alterthümer*, vol. iii.; and Canon G. Rawlinson, *The Seventh Great Oriental Monarchy*.

In the stony wilderness of ruin that marks the site of the ancient city, few remains are now capable of identification. Morier spoke of underground passages as believed to exist in great number, and as requiring exploration; but he could gain no information himself on the point, nor have subsequent travellers been more successful. The ruins of an enclosure, one hundred feet square, have been variously supposed to be those of a fortress or a mosque. Buckingham, in 1816, discovered two small fire altars like those of which I have spoken, near the Tomb of Cyrus; but, as he advertised their portability, it would appear that they have since been carried off. The only ruin of any moment is that of a building fifty feet square, one wall of which, composed of beautiful masonry, is still standing, though half-buried in the soil; and which presents a section of an arched window and the remains of some bull-headed capitals, no doubt an imitation of those at Persepolis, that probably once supported an architrave or roof. Behind it, Morier thought that he saw the traces of a theatre.

Existing ruins

In the very jaws of the gorge, a spur of the south-east cliff stands forward, in the shape of a solitary pinnacle-like rock, the sides of which are covered with old walls, and the summit with the remains of an old castle. There can be no doubt that this edifice, to which the Persians give the popular appellation of Kaleh-i-Dokhter, or Maiden's Fortress, is the remains of the ancient citadel, absolutely commanding as it does the mouth of the defile. It is the structure alluded to by El Istakhri in the passage already quoted.

Citadel

Turning the corner of this rock, we enter the gorge, and are immediately confronted with the sculptured bas-reliefs, which, like those at Naksh-i-Rustam, have survived the more perishable structures of brick or stone, and when all other records of man's handiwork have perished, will still transmit to future ages the proud record of Sassanian splendour. Of these, there are two on the right-hand side of the gorge, i.e. on the left bank of the river; and four on the opposite, or left-hand, side, above the right bank of the river. I will first describe the two former, which, being on the level of the spectator, and immediately alongside of the road running into the valley, are very easy of access.

Bas-reliefs

The first tablet encountered has suffered severely from time and the hands of destroyers.[1] Its upper portion has entirely perished, but in the lower part are visible the legs of two horses confronting each other, whose riders have been obliterated out of all recognition. The horse

[1] Flandin and Coste, vol. i. pl. 48. This engraving, compared with Stolze's photograph (*Persepolis*, vol. ii. pl. 142), and Dieulafoy's (*L'Art Antique de la Perse*, part v. pl. 18), as well as with my own, will be found to share the inaccuracy not uncommon in the Frenchmen's reproductions of the Sassanian sculptures.

on the right-hand side tramples under foot a prostrate figure, who lies with his face turned outwards and resting on his right hand, while his left arm is stretched along his side. In front of the horseman is a kneeling figure, dressed in the Roman tunic, with outstretched suppliant arms, and uplifted face of appeal. The features have gone, but in the pose and attitude of the suppliant's body, of which I took and here reproduce a photograph, there is a simplicity and pathos that destruction has been powerless to

First tablet: Shapur and Valerian

FIRST BAS-RELIEF AT SHAPUR: VALERIAN SUPPLIANT

destroy. There can be little doubt that the subject of this bas-relief is the familiar triumph of Shapur over the fallen Cæsar.[1] The figure on horseback before whom the suppliant kneels is the victorious king; the suppliant is Valerian; the prostrate figure typifies the vanquished Roman army.

[1] I should say here that the Shapur-Valerian series of bas-reliefs is explained by Mordtmann as referring to the victory of Shapur II., in 363 A.D., at Samàra over the Emperor Julian, who was killed in the battle, and to the ignominious peace that was wrung by the conqueror from his successor Jovian. I see nothing, however, in this incident to explain the third figure who so constantly appears in the sculptures, or to justify the imploring attitude of the suppliant.

Second tablet: Shapur, Valerian, and Cyriadis

A hundred yards further on, a second and much larger tablet comes in sight, one of the series that pourtray the investiture of the obscure Syrian of Antioch, Cyriadis, or Miriades, with the imperial purple in the presence of the captive Valerian.[1] The length of the entire panel is forty-one feet, and height twenty feet, the sculptures having been much protected by an over-hanging canopy of rock. It is divided into three portions—Shapur, on horseback, with the remaining chief actors, are in the centre, occupying a tablet 12 feet 1 inch long, by 8 feet 2 inches high; behind him—i.e. on the left-hand side of the bas-relief—are two tablets, one above the other, with five horsemen in each, following the king; facing him, three more tablets in the lower row, and two above them, each 4 feet 11 inches long, and 9 feet 10 inches high, containing warriors and other figures on foot. I will now proceed to a more minute analysis, beginning with the central tablet. Shapur is easily recognised by his turreted crown with superimposed globe, by his flowing curled locks and handsome features, and by his beard tied into a knot below the chin. From his head stream the Sassanian fillets; an immense quiver hangs at his side; upon his legs are the flowing *shulwars*, or loose Sassanian trousers. He rides a sturdy horse, disproportionate, as in all these sculptures, to the heroic size of the rider. With his right hand he holds the right hand of a figure standing by the hind-quarters of his horse, wearing a laurel wreath on his head,[2] a Roman tunic, and fetters round his ankles. As in the former bas-relief, the king's horse tramples under foot a prostrate figure, typical of the overthrown army of the Romans. Facing the king is a kneeling figure, also wearing a laurel wreath and a Roman tunic, but carrying a sword at his side. In front of the horse's head is an inscription in five lines, but not in the ordinary Persian character. Above it a winged cherub or genius floats in the air and presents an unrolled fillet, or *bandeau*, to the king.[3] The important question in this, as in all the bas-reliefs representing the same scene, is the identity of the kneeling and the standing figures. Is the suppliant Cyriadis, and the upright personage Valerian, or *vice versa*? I was at first inclined to adopt the former belief for reasons into which I need not enter. But after a careful examination of all the sculptures, I am disposed to identify the kneeling individual in each case with the deposed Emperor, and the figure whose hands are

[1] Texier, vol. ii. pl. 146; Flandin and Coste, vol. i. pl. 49; Stolze, vol. ii. pl. 143; Dieulafoy, part v. pl. 23.

[2] Morier said a helmet, but this is wrong.

[3] Morier calls this well-known Sassanian emblem 'the scroll of fame,' and the cherub's figure a Victory! Texier, quite mistaking its character, identifies it with a cornucopia, and regards this as a convincing proof that the bas-relief was executed either by Roman prisoners, or by Western artists.

SECOND BAS-RELIEF AT SHAPUR. INVESTITURE OF CYRIADIS

held by the king, with his promoted successor. Behind the kneeling figure stand two individuals, apparently Persian officers, the one with a circular, the other with a conical head-piece. The cavalry in the panels behind Shapur no doubt represent the royal bodyguard. They wear the Persian dress, and the right arm of each is uplifted, and the forefinger pointed, in the attitude familiar to many of the Sassanian sculptures, and rightly interpreted as a mark of respect. The figures in the five panels facing the king are mostly warriors, some of them carrying arms; others, objects the exact nature of which it is difficult to determine. They have been regarded by the bulk of commentators as soldiers of a vanquished army or armies;[1] by some as attendants of the royal court. The entire sculpture is chiselled in very high relief, and the depth of the recess which it occupies is from one to five feet.

Opposite bank and aqueduct

Here we will retrace our footsteps, having exhausted the bas-reliefs on the right side of the gorge; and, fording the river, at a short distance below the citadel, will take up the inspection of those on the opposite or north-west cliff. These are for the most part far more difficult of access. They are situated at heights varying from twenty to fifty feet above the river-bed; and whatever may once have been the case, there is now no roadway or pathway below them. The place of such, if it ever existed, as it must have done, is taken by an aqueduct of later and, probably, Arab origin, which has been scooped and, in places, tunnelled along the face of the natural rock—with a complete disregard for the preservation of the bas-reliefs, one of which it furrows right in twain—in order to convey the waters of a small spring in the interior of the valley to a mill which once existed lower down in the Kazerun plain. In order to examine the sculptures one is obliged to clamber along this narrow channel, which is in parts built up with walls from the river level, and to go on to one's hands and knees in order to crawl through the perforations in the rock. The reason why the channel does not in places now run along the level of the soil, but, as in the case of the bas-relief already mentioned, has scooped an indentation more than half way up its face, is that in the days when the aqueduct was made and used, the soil was banked up to the level of the groove. Messrs. Stolze and Andreas, when they came here in 1877, in order to take the photographs for their large work, removed these accumulations by digging and blasting, and laid all the sculptures entirely bare. Hence the appearance that is at first so puzzling to a stranger's eye. Of the four panels on this bank of the river, three are on the same level as the water-conduit, the fourth and furthest is some twelve feet above it.

[1] There seems to be insufficient reason for identifying them all, with Canon Rawlinson, as soldiers of the Roman army. Certainly the two figures behind Cyriadis, are not, as he supposes, Romans.

The first bas-relief, on the left-hand side of the gorge, is chiselled in a great semicircular bay or apse of the rock, more than thirty feet in length, which has been tinged a deep blue by discolouration. Hence, and on account of the great size and minute detail of the original, the photograph which I took of it will not repay reproduction.[1] The panel is divided into four parallel bands or zones, extending entirely round the apse, and crowded with figures. The two lower bands are about five and a half feet high, the two upper three feet high. In the middle of the second row from the bottom is the same king Shapur I. on horseback, enacting a scene similar to that which I have last described. Here also he holds a figure, clad in Roman costume, by the hand; here also he treads under foot a prostrate foe; the kneeling form in front of him has the same characteristics as in the former sculpture; while behind the suppliant a fifth figure holds out a royal chaplet to the king.[2] This being so, I identify the kneeling figure, as in the former case, with Valerian, the upright figure with Cyriadis, about to be invested, and the figure in the background with an attendant presenting to Shapur the wreath which he is about to bestow upon his Syrian protégé.[3] A winged genius again floats overhead, and presents an unrolled chaplet to Shapur. In the sculptured tiers behind the king are depicted his mounted and helmeted guards, fifty-seven in all, with the uplifted forefinger of reverence, fifteen in the bottom row, fourteen in each of the three upper zones. The panels on the other side, facing the monarch, are filled with a most interesting representation of prisoners, tribute-bearers, trophies of victory, and attendants. In the lowest band is a two-horsed chariot, or Roman *biga*,[4] and a standard supposed to represent a captured Roman eagle; also a number of attendants who appear to be carrying trays. The second band, parallel with the king, contains a double row of figures, of whom those in front escort the captured war-horse of

Third tablet: Investiture of Cyriadis

[1] *Vide*, however, Texier, vol. ii. pl. 147; Flandin and Coste, vol. i. pl. 53; Stolze, vol. ii. pl. 141; Dieulafoy, part v. pl. 19.

[2] Texier thinks this figure is a woman. I doubt if a woman appears in any of the earlier Sassanian sculptures.

[3] Rawlinson (p. 91), who has accepted the suppliant as Valerian in the former tablet, very strangely ignores his existence in this sculpture, including him among 'three principal tribute-bearers in front of the king'; and recognises Valerian in the prone figure. On p. 608, however, he gives a different explanation of the same bas-relief, where he calls the suppliant 'a third Roman, the representative of the defeated nation.'

[4] Canon Rawlinson (pp. 648–9) mistakes this obviously Roman chariot, part of the spoil of Valerian, for a Sassanian vehicle, although in the same paragraph he says that 'the principal change which time had brought about in Sassanian warfare was an almost entire disuse of the war-chariot,' and that 'there is no mention of their actual employment in any battle.'

FOURTH BAS-RELIEF. THE CAPTIVES

Valerian and an elephant, while, according to Texier, those behind hold up draperies in the path of the cortège. The two upper rows depict a number of attendants carrying spoil or offerings on their shoulders, and leading two lions or leopards. The figures facing the king are thirty-three in number. The bottom of the entire panel has been eaten away by the water in the channel before described.

Fourth tablet: The captives

The next tablet is that which has been defaced by the erosion of the water in the mill-stream, and the lower half of which was bared by the labours of Messrs. Stolze and Andreas.[1] It represents one of the Sassanian sovereigns on horseback, receiving the submission and offerings of captives. The monarch advances from the left hand of the sculpture, which is about twenty-one feet long, by twelve feet high. On his head he wears a winged helmet, from whose centre, between the wings, rises the symbolical globe. His hair is elaborately puffed and curled ; the dynastic fillets stream in the hair behind his head and shoulders ; his charger's tail is thickly plaited ; at its hind-quarter hangs by a chain the familiar tassel or ornament ; from the king's side depends an immense quiver. The groove of the water-conduit has cut right through the figure both of the rider and the horse, completely obliterating the nose and mouth of the latter. It defaces, in a similar manner, the figures who advance to meet the king, the first of whom is a warrior, wearing a skull cap, from which his ringlets hang in a curled bush behind, while his arms are crossed above the hilt of an enormous sword. He wears a look of resignation that is admirably pourtrayed on the stone. Behind him are three other figures, with a sort of *kefieh* or handkerchief (such as the Arabs wear) on the head, accompanying a horse. In a higher tier behind are two camels with two attendants. One camel's head is very well preserved, and an air of great dignity pervades the entire group. It is, of course, obvious that the scene represented is the victory of a Sassanid sovereign, and the submission of the conquered. From the fact that the winged helmet does not appear upon coins till the reign of Varahran II. (A.D 275–292), it has been supposed by some that the king in this portrait is that monarch ; and Canon Rawlinson suggests that the incident depicted is the submission of the Segestani, or people of Seistan, whom he fought against and subdued. On the other hand, the face is a perfect and faithful likeness of Shapur I., as elsewhere delineated ; and among the scenes in his reign, which have been suggested in explanation, are the embassy which he received, and so haughtily spurned, from Odenathus, the Arab chief of Palmyra and husband of Zenobia ; the capture of Nisibis, in his first Roman

[1] The engraving of Flandin and Coste (vol. i. pl. 51) is most unsatisfactory, and gives a very inadequate idea of the original. *Vide* Stolze, vol. ii. pl. 140, and Dieulafoy, part v. pl. 21.

campaign; or his victory over the Syrian king, Sitarun. I incline to some such hypothesis, from the resemblance of the head-dress of the captives to that of the Bedouin tribes of Mesopotamia and Syria.[1]

Fifth tablet: Ormuzd and Narses

The superior elevation of the next bas-relief has fortunately saved it from the aqueous disfigurement of the last, the channel in this case merely cutting into the hocks and pasterns of the horses at the base of the tablet. It is about sixteen to eighteen feet high.[2] Two figures on horseback meet each other, that on the left side presenting the royal circlet with streamers, which the opposing figure holds out his right hand to receive. A Pehlevi inscription in the right-hand corner, first deciphered by M. Longpérier,[3] contains these words:—

> This is the image of the Ormuzd-worshipper, the God, Narses, King of kings Arian and non-Arian, of the race of the Gods, the son of the Ormuzd-worshipper, the God, Shapur, King of kings Arian and non-Arian, of the race of the Gods, the offspring of the God, Artakshatr, King of kings.

We learn, therefore, that the figure of one of the horsemen is that of Narses, who reigned from 292 to 301 A.D., when he abdicated. He has usually been supposed to be the son or brother of Varahran II., i.e. grandson or great-grandson of Shapur I., but here he calls himself the son of the latter monarch, and the grandson of Ardeshir or Artaxerxes. It has been suggested by Thomas that this may possibly have been a figure of speech on the part of Narses, in the desire to ignore the intermediate succession of less renowned monarchs; but it appears to me that we shall do well to let Narses speak for himself, and to accept his own account of his parentage, in which there is no inherent improbability. Of the two figures, that on the right is doubtless the young king. He wears a diadem, or spiked crown, with the conventional globe rising above it. His hair is elegantly curled, and flows behind his head in ringlets;[4] his expression is mild and benign, and his short beard is tied in a knot. The left-hand figure, conferring the *cydaris*, is doubtless that of Ormuzd. He wears the mural or turreted crown, above and behind which emerge his bushy locks. The features are well preserved, and the beard and hair are those of an older man than his *vis-à-vis*. The twisted tail of his horse, the trappings of both steeds, and the veins and muscles depicted on their forelegs are in a wonderful state of preservation, and indicate no mean level of

[1] Morier is very wide afield when he calls this 'the commencement of a hunting piece.'

[2] Texier, vol. ii. pl. 148; Flandin and Coste, vol. i. pl. 52; Stolze, vol. ii. pl. 139.

[3] *Médailles des Sassanides*, 1840.

[4] It does, not, however, in the least resemble the stiff trim curls depicted by Flandin and Coste, which are wholly imaginary.

glyptic ability. The rock in which this sculpture is carved has assumed quite a bluish tint from time.

Sixth tablet: Triumph of Chosroes

The sixth and last tablet is in a much ruder and clumsier style of art, and is the least well executed of the entire series. It is in a recess so deeply shaded by a deep black tree (the *narven* or wych elm), that I found it impossible to take a photograph.[1] The tablet consists of a great oblong panel, thirty-four feet in length, divided into two rows or bands of figures, one above the other. In the middle of the upper row sits the king, directly facing the

FIFTH BAS-RELIEF: ORMUZD AND NARSES

spectator. He wears a double crown, like a quartern loaf, on his head, and his hair is puffed out in immense bushes on either side. His legs are wide apart, and his uplifted right hand grasps what Flandin describes as a standard, but what looked to me like a gigantic battle-axe, while his left hand rests on the hilt of his sword. In the left-hand upper panel are a row of his own courtiers with uplifted forefingers. In the panel below it are a number of Persian nobles (their coiffure,

[1] *Vide* Texier, vol. ii. pl. 151; Flandin and Coste, vol. i. pl. 50; and Stolze, vol. ii. pl. 138.

dress, and swords resembling the king's), following the war-horse of the monarch, which is saddled, but riderless. On the opposite or right-hand side of the tablet, the upper row shows a wounded prisoner, and another captive, with his hands tied behind his back, being led along by Persian attendants ; while in the lower row the foremost figure holds two decapitated heads in his hands, and is followed by a number of prisoners and attendants, among whom is seen a child, in suppliant attitude, probably the son of the executed leader, and a boy riding a diminutive elephant. Canon Rawlinson, reasoning from the decadent style of art, and from the fact that the only monarch on the Sassanian coins who faces the spectator, and leans both hands on a straight sword, is Chosroes Nushirwan, has no hesitation in attributing the bas-relief to the latter sovereign. He may be right, though I can see no ground whatsoever for entitling the sculpture, as he does, 'Chosroes I. receiving tribute from the Romans,' the figures of the captives neither having the features nor the dress of Romans, and every indication tending to show that the bas-relief commemorates some victory over an Eastern tribe or people, whose chief was slain.

Artistic value

Such are the sculptured tablets of Shapur. It will be seen that they share both the merits and the faults of the bas-reliefs of Naksh-i-Rustam. There is a certain lumbering heaviness of style, and a lack of spirituality or idealism. On the other hand, as contemporary likenesses, and as representations of scenes requiring a certain stateliness and rigidity of form, they are both interesting and admirable. There are not at Shapur any of those spirited equestrian combats which lend such variety and distinction to the remains at Naksh-i-Rustam and Firuzabad ; but the ceremonial tablets are the most grandiose existing record of the earlier Sassanian kings. Above all, it must be remembered that, coming directly after the Parthian or Arsacid dynasty, when art had been crushed and had disappeared, these sculptures testify to a renascence of native ability which is both creditable and surprising.

The cave and statue of Shapur

There remain to be visited and described the great cave and the image of Shapur I., the sole ancient statue (with the exception of the mutilated torso, if it still exists, at Tak-i-Bostan) that survives in the whole of Persia. Several travellers have failed to find the right cave, the Iliats of the neighbourhood being sometimes absent, and not always truthful. It is situated high up in the face of the left-hand or north-west cliff of the inner valley of Shapur, a sheer scarp of rock, 700 feet high, towering above it. The ascent is extremely long, rough, and fatiguing ; and the climber will hardly arrive at the mouth within three-quarters of an hour of leaving the valley bottom. In front of the cavern is a great perpendicular mass of rock, over which it is almost impossible to scramble without assistance. We then find ourselves in the mouth of a great black orifice in the rock, 50 feet high, and 140 feet broad. In the middle of the entrance, at a short distance inside, stands a huge pedestal, four to five feet high and ten feet in diameter, shaped from the solid mother-rock. Upon it are still standing the sandalled feet, thirty-nine inches in length, and the stumps of the legs of the fallen image. The latter, violently hurled from its site,[1] has tumbled sideways; its left arm is broken short, its right arm has been fractured at the shoulder, but the hand still rests upon the thigh, the face is terribly mutilated, and the upper part of the head and crown are buried in the soil. Nevertheless, enough remains to enable us to identify the effigy with the likeness of the first Shapur. The founder of the city and the designer of the sculptures below, it is highly likely that he would have set up his own effigy in the same place, while the claim of divinity which is invariably made for him and his successors in the inscriptions, tends to fortify the hypothesis, which tradition (as quoted by Kinneir) confirms, that the image was subsequently worshipped as that of a god. It would appear from the evidence of the vaulted roof over the spot where the statue once stood, that it was originally attached to the rock above as well as below, and was, in fact, carved out of a solid stone monolith or pillar, so as to present the semblance of the king. The height of the statue would appear to have been over twenty feet, that of the surviving portion being about fifteen feet. Flandin gives the length of the head as three feet three inches, and breadth of shoulders as eight feet two inches. Texier has published a restoration of the entire figure,[2] but I confess I prefer to his too idealistic drawing the illustrations that have appeared elsewhere of the figure in its existing condition, and which, though differing from each other in details, give a better idea of the reality.[3] The dress worn by the monarch does not vary much from that delineated in the bas-reliefs. He wears the mural crown, above and below which his hair stood out in abundant curls; his moustache and beard are trimly curled; a necklet is suspended round his throat; on the upper part of his body he wears a kind of jersey, on the lower the *shulwars*, or loose trousers; his sword, hung at his left side,

[1] By what agency has been discussed, but cannot be determined. The infiltration of water has been suggested, but is a wholly inadequate explanation. The local tradition is said to favour the theory of earthquake. I should be disposed myself—looking to the character of the statue, which was hewn out of the virgin rock, and was, therefore, part of the cavern itself, and to the mutilation which the head has suffered, to attribute the overthrow to intentional violence on the part of the Mussulman invaders in the seventh century.

[2] Vol. ii. pls. 149, 150.

[3] *Vide* Ouseley, *Travels*, vol. i. p. 292; Colonel Johnson, *Journey from India*, p. 43; Flandin and Coste, vol. i. pl. 54.

depending from a sash round his right shoulder, with a cross belt meeting it from the left; a knot of ribands is tied at his waist.

At the side of the fallen statue are places in the wall of the cavern which would appear to have been smoothed, preparatory to receiving an inscription or a bas-relief that has never been executed. If the traveller has been wise enough to provide himself with candles, he will next continue his exploration far into the bowels of the mountain. A very proper distrust of the Mamasenni guides has dissuaded a good many visitors from making this experiment. A good deal, however, remains to be seen. At fifty yards from the entrance the cave, which has steadily contracted, expands again into a large dome, 100 feet high, and 120 feet in diameter. From this two passages lead still further into the interior. One of these has at its entrance a stone cistern or tank hewn in the rock, but after running for fifty yards or so comes to an end. The other descends through pools of water into an immense hall, with huge stalactite pillars depending from the roof. The total length of this fork, to which the natives declare that there is no end, is about 400 yards. There are other galleries and ramifications which have never been properly explored.

Interior ramifications

Leaving the ruins of Shapur, after this examination, I returned in a south-western direction over the outer plain towards the exit from the Kazerun valley, and rejoined the caravan-track from Kazerun, after one and a half hour, having passed the village of Shabur, or Shabud, and left the Shapur river on the right. It is at its western corner that the road leaves the Kazerun plain, crossing a low ridge of hills, after which it traverses a piece of very broken ground, and then enters a winding gorge, known as the Teng-i-Turkan, that leads down to the plain of Kamarij. The telegraph-poles follow the crest of the hills to the right, and the track, formerly taken, followed the same line. There is also a mountain path from Kazerun direct to Kamarij, across the intervening ridge of the Kuh-i-Mahas. It is less than half the length of the other, but is very steep, and seems never to be taken by beasts of burden. It was in this neighbourhood that Captain Napier's caravan was attacked and plundered by Mamasenni robbers, in as late as 1874. At length the Teng-i-Turkan opens on to the Kamarij plain, four miles long, by two broad, at the further end of which can be distinguished the village of Kamarij, with a few date-palms waving their plumes above its miserable hovels. There is a Telegraph Rest-house here, with a *bala-khaneh*, not unlike a superior sort of *chapar-khaneh*. Here I was rejoined

Kamarij

by my original beasts which had lounged comfortably over from Kazerun.

Immediately behind the village the road rises, and climbs a stony acclivity. In about half an hour we find ourselves at the

Kotal-i-Kamarij

top of the third of the notorious natural stairways between Shiraz and the sea. It takes its name from the place just left, and is the steepest, and, in some respects, most

ROAD-GUARD ON THE KOTAL-I-KAMARIJ

perilous of the four *kotals*, there being a sheer drop of 1,200 feet in a distance of less than a mile, and the track being so narrow in parts that an up-coming cannot pass a down-going mule, without itself going over the precipice. But though so steep, it is a far less unpleasant experience than either the Old or the Young

Woman, owing to the fact that the track is worn in the bare rock, instead of being covered with loose stones, or tesselated with a broken pavement. In fact, it is neither more nor less than a staircase, the hoofs of generations of mules having worn deep indentations, at regular intervals, one above or below the other into the rock. In the steepest parts, where the road overhangs a vertical ravine, it has been artificially walled. The surrounding scenery is singularly wild and grand, the mountains being split by mighty fissures, exhibiting a stratification that is almost uniformly perpendicular, and being decked on their naked sides by streaks of many-coloured marls. It was on the worst part of this descent, known as the *kamar*, or ledge of Asad Khan, that, in 1752, the Afghan chief of that name, who, upon the death of Nadir Shah, was one of the claimants to the throne, was attacked by Kerim Khan Zend, acting upon the advice of Rustam Sultan, chief of Khisht. The followers of the latter were hidden among the crags above; the soldiery of Kerim Khan, who had already been driven out from Isfahan and Shiraz, were posted in the valley below. Between the devil and the deep sea there is small loophole for escape, as Asad Khan found to his cost, in this horrible man-trap. He himself escaped, and was subsequently pardoned, and elevated to favour by his generous conqueror. The descent of the *kotal* took me about three-quarters of an hour. Following the ravine at its foot, I then again struck the Shapur river, followed its left bank for some distance, and then turning south, across the plain of Khisht, reached the hamlet of Konar Takhteh (Plateau of *konars*), which is situated almost midway down the valley.

Plain of Khisht

I saw very little beauty in the plain of Khisht, except that arising from two extensive groves of date-palms. There was a great deal of camel-thorn and other scrub growing around; but at what opposite poles of outward complexion the seasons stand in Persia, may again be illustrated from the pages of a former traveller, who, passing this way in spring-time, left the following record :—

'Among the grain in the fields, I remarked red poppies, larkspur, daisies, wild oats, wild pinks, mallows, and some flowers of the convolvulus, and other genera which I had never seen before. This being the spring season they were all in blow, and gave an enchanting effect to the scene, which reminded me of a summer's day in England.' [1]

[1] Colonel Johnson, *Journey from India* (1817), p. 36.

The Frenchman, Petis de la Croix, was at Khisht in 1674, and found it so hot that he spent the whole day lying in the river, where he said that he was surrounded by hundreds of fish, who nosed him all over, and were so tame that he caught as many as he pleased with his hands.

For three and a half miles from Konar Takhteh, the track lies across the plain to the south, and then, mounting a slight rise, takes a downward plunge of 1,000 feet, in the Kotal-i-Mallu, or Cursed Pass.[1] The curses are, in all probability, those of the ascending, and not of the descending wayfarer; for it

Kotal-i-Mallu

THE CURSED PASS

is with the most profound relief that the latter contemplates the approaching exhaustion of the horrors of the Tengistan *kotals*; and tears of joy are far more likely to leap from his eyes than oaths from his lips. Nor is the Kotal-i-Mallu either so precipitous, so stony, or so uncomfortable as those which have preceded it; although the first part is steep, and recalls the definition that was once given of a Persian *kotal*, as the kind of mark that would be left by the impression of a gigantic corkscrew on the vertical side of a mountain. A causeway had at some time been built in zigzags up the side of this *kotal*, and was in better preservation

[1] This derivation, which would be a contraction from the Arabic *mal'un*, is popular, but doubtful.

than any work of the kind that I had seen in Persia. Its surface, however, was so slippery that it had prudently been abandoned by the caravans, which had worn a tortuous stairway in the rock alongside of it.

From a gorge far down below came the welcome roar of waters; and at a turn in the descent was visible the blue current of the so-called Daliki river, racing merrily towards the south-west. This river rises in the mountains of Fars to the south of Shiraz, runs north-west under different names, the commonest of which it derives from the village of Daliki, which it presently waters, and, having reached the Dashtistan or Plain-land, joins the Shapur river, of which I have already spoken, the two falling into the Gulf to the north of Bushire under the name of Rohillah (Rud-hillah) or Rud-i-Shapur. From the summit of the *kotal* to the banks of the river was an easy walk of one hour and twenty minutes. A light breeze ruffled the stream, which here spreads out into a wide pool, and I observed fish rising everywhere to natural flies. The road now follows, for a little over a mile, the right bank of the river, passing a ruined bridge, all but one or two arches of which have disappeared, and then crosses the stream by a fine stone bridge of six arches, terminating in a causeway on the far side. This bridge and its pavement were both in better preservation than any kindred structure that I had seen in Persia, and were the work of the Mushir-el-Mulk before mentioned. A lofty square tower guards the north entrance to the bridge; and a seedy patrol, armed with a percussion musket, was taking an airing on the parapet. Traffic over the passes is now comparatively safe, although it is not twenty years since no party could proceed without an armed guard; but a few *rahdars* or sentinels are still stationed on the road, their maintenance being a tax on the nearest village; and a few of these apologies for a *gendarmerie* I encountered. The road follows the river down a gorge for nearly two miles further, and then strikes up a lateral ravine, where an evil smell betrays the presence of sulphur in the water that oozes from the ground. In this ravine we continue for some time, until we reach the top of a steep declivity, whence a seemingly endless plain can be discerned stretching away in the direction of the sea, darkened by occasional clumps of date-palms, and terminating in sand hills that hide the waters of the Gulf. The last remaining descent, down an inclined plane formed by a peculiar pitch of the strata—a feeble parody of a *kotal*—alone remains; and we are presently on the plain, where, skirting the mountain base, we arrive in the course of a mile or two at the village of Daliki. The last stage, which is called four *farsakhs*, and is a good fifteen miles, had taken me five and a quarter hours to accomplish, for the most part on foot.

Daliki

Around the village of Daliki, which is small and wholly undistinguished, grow a number of plants, known as *ghark*, which also occur, and are called *kalablab*, between Shushter and Dizful. The shrub grows to a height of seven to ten feet, has large greyish leaves, and a flower which I did not see, but which is said to be white and purple in colour. From the fibres surrounding the seeds silk fabrics used to be made; but the material is now used for stuffing cushions. Soon after leaving the village, the road crosses a stream whose waters run an emerald green from the sulphur with which they are impregnated; while on the stagnant pools floats a bituminous scum. Sulphuretted fumes also fill the air and invade the nostrils. The Rev. H. Martyn described the place in 1810 as 'one of Nature's ulcers;' but the acerbity of the metaphor may be attributed to the fact that when the excellent missionary employed it his thermometer was standing at 126°. A little below in the plain is a bitumen pit, from which the natives have long been in the habit of collecting that substance, principally as a prescription for the sore backs of camels, and for the smearing of boat and roof timbers. It was for the working of the petroleum springs suspected to exist here that a concession was procured from the Persian Government, in 1884, by Messrs. Hotz, of Bushire. Their boring was unsuccessful; but the experiment has since been renewed by the Persian Mining Rights Corporation, whose engineers have sunk a bore to a depth of over eight hundred feet, so far without much result, but who are not likely to leave the region until its oleiferous capacities, be they great or small, have been thoroughly tested. Several other streams also flow here from the mountains; and the largest of them meanders down to the plain, and is there lost in a feverish-looking swamp. Beyond, a noble belt of date-palms supplies relief to the eye, and a living to the villagers of Daliki.

The road presently strikes southwards towards a low swell of hilly ground that still separates us from the sea-level; climbs this, alternately rises and sinks in its undulations, and finally emerges on the palm-girdled village of Borazjun (the true name is said to be Gurazdun, or Place of Boars). From a distance one might imagine this to be a place of some military importance; for several miles away can be seen the lofty walls and corner towers of an immense structure, whose outer surface is pierced with loopholes only, and presents a decidedly feudal appearance. A longer acquaintance with Persia teaches the wayfarer that it cannot possibly be a fort, because every Persian fort is in ruins, and warns him that he is gazing upon nothing more formidable than a caravanserai; although among the scores that I had seen, this was without exception both the best constructed and the best preserved. It was built in 1875–6 by the same public-spirited official whom I have before eulogised, travellers before that date having bitterly complained of the lack of any similar building. I went in and inspected the interior. It is built of solid stone, well quarried and laid, and contains, in addition to the normal recesses, rooms, and stables, opening out of the central court, a number of upstairs apartments and sleeping-places, designed for the rich and for those travelling with women in their train. The walls of these chambers had been plentifully adorned by the pencils of Persian visitors of an artistic turn; but their imagination had found no higher outlet than the reproduction of steamboats and vessels with all sails spread, the most striking maritime reminiscence, no doubt, to a people possessing an hereditary terror of the sea. From the roof of the caravanserai can be gained an extensive prospect of the plain, of the town below (reputed to contain 6,000 persons), of the site at a little distance where the Persians ignominiously evacuated their position without firing a shot, in the short Anglo-Persian campaign of 1857; and of the long line of mountains, concealing behind their grim ramparts those hideous *kotals* which it was such a profound relief to have quitted, and which I hope never to tread again. The village youths of Borazjun were busily engaged in rustic games, among which hockey and rounders (the precise equivalent to the English game) appeared to be the most popular. Considering that they played on a very rough and stony piece of ground, and with bare feet, the most eager of English schoolboys would have felt little temptation to join in the fun. I noticed at Borazjun that all the men were armed with big pistols, loosely stuck in the belt; and, upon inquiring the reason of this singularly un-Persian habit

Borazjun

heard that it is peculiar to Borazjun and a few surrounding places, the inhabitants of which revel in the open profession of robbery, and in the luxury of blood-feuds, still in a comparatively early stage of existence. The only other speciality at the time of my visit was a flight of locusts, which had recently appeared, and was doing irreparable damage to whatever of green was above ground. Not even the prospect of a good dinner cheap—for, like John the Baptist, the natives boil and eat the locusts in the manner of shrimps—could reconcile the Borazjunis to this terrible scourge.

Before bidding a final farewell to the mountain region and the *kotals*, let me here say that it would be paying a most undeserved compliment to the intelligence of the Persian muleteers to suppose that the route which I have described is the easiest or best channel of traffic between Shiraz and the Gulf. It is neither. It is a road that has been selected quite at haphazard, simply because somebody started it, and others followed suit, or because it appeared to take the shortest possible cut for the required destination. Very often it follows the steepest and least practicable of the various available lines; and the continuity with which it has now for more than a century been pursued as the main avenue of commercial entry into, and exit from, Persia on the south, is a combined monument to the apathy and resolution of the Persian character. Bad as it is from the mercantile point of view, from the strategical it is infinitely worse. No field guns in the world could be hauled up those horrible stairways, although a mule battery might negotiate them with success. Similarly they are impracticable for cavalry, except with native mounts; whilst either cavalry or infantry would frequently require to march in single file. For either commercial or military purposes it may be useful, therefore, to point out that, by a somewhat longer détour, each of the appalling *kotals* above described can be turned and avoided; the general plan to be followed being that of adhering, as closely as possible, to the channels of the rivers, instead of cutting at right angles over the intervening ridges. Thus, the descent to Daliki, the Kotal-i-Mallu, the Kotal-i-Kamarij, and the Teng-i-Turkan, can all be escaped by following up from the coast plains the left bank of the Shapur river to the point where I have traced it as flowing through the gorge with the Sassanian tablets. By still adhering to its course in the plain beyond, we turn the angle of the range that

Shirking the kotals

overhangs the Kazerun valley, and emerge into the upper end of the Dasht-i-Barm, or Valley of Oaks, thus avoiding the Kotal-i-Dokhter. Finally, the Old Woman can be escaped by striking the mountains at a point two miles east of the present road, where the range dips into the Dasht-i-Arzen.[1] There is also, of course, the more circuitous southern route, from Bushire to Shiraz by Firuzabad, but this is considerably longer, being about 210 to 220 miles.[2] It was down this latter route that the Persians brought their guns in 1857, only incontinently to abandon them as soon as they had reached the plain. The ascent would be a more difficult undertaking, and would require the preparatory labours of a large force of sappers.

Khushab

About six miles south of Borazjun is the small hamlet of Khushab, which was the scene of the night attack made by the Persians upon the British force under Sir J. Outram, on February 8, 1857—the sole exploit indulged in by

[1] *Vide* a Letter by J. J. Fahie in the *Journal of the Society of Arts*, April 1883.

[2] As I have mentioned the Bushire-Firuzabad-Shiraz line, which is taken by some travellers, I may add a reference to the sites or sights which render it notable. The route has been described by E. Scott Waring (1802), *Tour to Sheeraz*, cap. xxvi.; and Mme. Dieulafoy (1881), *La Perse*, caps xxvi–viii. For the section from Firuzabad to Shiraz, *vide* the authorities cited in the Table of Routes at the end of cap. xx. Firuzabad, or the Abode of Victory, is the name given in the tenth century by the Asad-ed-Dowleh of the Buyah dynasty to a place originally founded by the Achæmenian, and subsequently embellished by the Sassanian monarchs, and known as Jur, Khur, or Gur. Here Ardeshir Babekan built a palace and a great *atesh-gah* or fire-temple. The remains now visible at Firuzabad are four in number: (1) the Kaleh-i-Dokhter, a ruined castle upon the heights commanding the Teng-ab, a gorge to the north of the town; (2) two Sassanian bas-reliefs sculped on the walls of the same defile, the one repeating the subject of the bas-relief at Naksh-i-Rustam, viz. the investiture of Ardeshir with the imperial *cydaris* by Ormuzd, the other representing an equestrian combat; (3) the ruins of a great vaulted building, generally recognised as the palace of Ardeshir, though attributed by some to an earlier period (Stack [vol. i. pp. 91–2] very strangely mistakes it for the fire-temple); (4) a ruined tower of unhewn stone masonry, built upon a platform, and retaining traces of a winding outside ascent from terrace to terrace, like the Babylonian temples—which is commonly identified with the great *atesh-gah* or fire altar of Ardeshir, but to which Perrot (*Histoire de l'Art*, vol. v. p. 650) attributes a secular or military origin. I have already said that Firuzabad is the official residence of the nominal Ilkhani of the Kashkai tribes of Fars. For illustrations of the ruins of Firuzabad, *vide* Flandin and Coste, vol. i. pls. 34–44; and M. Dieulafoy, *L'Art Antique de la Perse*, part iv. pls. 9–20. Upon the architecture of the Sassanian palaces in general, and of Firuzabad and Sarvistan in particular, *vide* Canon S. Rawlinson's *Seventh Great Oriental Monarchy*, cap. xxvii.; Fergusson's *History of Architecture*, vol. i.; and Perrot and Chipiez' monumental work already cited.

the main Persian army in that short-lived campaign. The British troops had landed south of Bushire in December, had stormed the fort of Reshire, and had shelled and captured Bushire. Then on February 3 they advanced: 2,200 English, 2,000 Indian and Beluch troops, 420 Indian cavalry, 2 light field batteries, and 18 guns. The Persian army, under the Shuja-el-Mulk, consisting of 5,000 infantry, 800 cavalry, and 18 guns, was encamped at Borazjun. Upon the approach of Outram they bolted without firing a shot, leaving their camp, equipments, and ammunition as a prey to the British. Outram blew up their powder magazine, and, conscious that nothing was to be gained, but everything lost, by throwing himself into the *kotals*, began to march back towards Bushire—a movement which the Persians, who are learned in the casuistry of retreat, have always interpreted as a sign of discomfiture. In the night the Persian cavalry attacked the column, while the infantry were found drawn up at Khushab. The cavalry and artillery of the British very soon decided the contest, and by the early morning the Persians were in full flight, leaving 700 killed, as against 16 of the British force. The theatre of war was then transferred to the Karun, where, in a later chapter, I shall allude to the even less creditable show made by the *serbaz* of the Shah. It was probably not a very wise step to send a British force to Bushire at all, unless we meant to hold the place. As it was, the war partook of the nature of a series of demonstrations, which were rather summarily cut short by the Treaty of Paris in March.

Shif

The ordinary caravan-track from Borazjun to Bushire runs *viâ* Ahmedi (where is a caravanserai), and across the low-lying, often swampy ground, called the Mashileh, that connects the peninsula of Bushire with the mainland. The distance is a little under forty miles. For such, however, as are fortunate enough to receive the British Resident's hospitality, and the loan of his steam-launch, a shorter route is available from Borazjun to Shif, a distance of twenty-five miles; whence a short sea passage across the arm of the Gulf that severs Bushire from the coast deposits the delighted traveller at the terminus of his journey. The road to Shif is as smooth as a billiard table, crawling over which at a pace adapted to the movements of tired baggage-mules is slow work. At Khushab the inhabitants were engaged in shaking the locusts from the boughs of the tamarisk trees, and greedily picking them up and stuffing them into sacks for future use at the breakfast table. Here I left the telegraph poles, which take a more southerly line to Ahmedi, and steered a westerly course for Shif. A good many sand-grouse were visible on the way, and, after the fashion of game in general, were as annoyingly tame to the unarmed voyager on horseback as they are wild to the sportsman on foot with a gun. Though the temperature was cool and pleasant, a mirage trembled above the heated soil, and gave frequent glimpses of a sea that ever receded, and of islets that resolved themselves into tiny heaps of sand. The distorting powers of the illusion (called *sirab* by the Persians) seemed to be limited to objects near the surface, but upon that level there was no limit to its achievements; for what appeared at some distance to be the ruins of an extensive marble edifice were converted upon approach into the lank members of an old white horse browsing upon the scrub.[1] At length was visible a square building with a tower, that turned out to be the solitary glory, nay, the sole structure of Shif. It is a dilapidated caravanserai, standing within a few yards of a slimy beach, where a sluggish water laps the sand. Colonel Ross's launch was lying a quarter of a mile off; and a boat was waiting to transfer me to its welcome variety of locomotion. How glad I was to take off the saddle and saddlebags and holsters, to say good-bye to my rickety *yabu*, and to feel that I had without any accident passed through Persia from sea to sea. Shif faces a shallow bay, on the opposite side of which is the small fishing village of Sheikh Saad. Rounding this point, we came out into the open bay, and steered a line straight across for Bushire, whose wind-towers and occasional palms swelled into larger prominence above the waves. Steamers tossing in the offing, quite three miles away, revealed the nature of the anchorage at the first port in Persia. Skirting the eastern face of the town, which, though squalid enough to a new comer, deserves a high rank amongst Persian maritime cities, the launch deposited me at the Governor's Bunder. The Union Jack streaming from the top of a gigantic mast —by far the loftiest object in Bushire—proclaimed the site of the British Residency; and in ten minutes' time I was the guest and inmate of an English home.

Bushire (lit. Abu Shehr)[2] is a town without a history, or at

[1] For an excellent description of the Asiatic mirage, as encountered by Alexander in his march through Sogdiana, *vide* Quint. Curt. lib. vii. c. 5.

[2] The common derivation, i.e. Father of Cities, cannot be correct, because

least with only such a history as an existence of 150 years can supply. Originally a small fishing village, it was selected by Nadir Shah in the middle of the last century as his southern port, and as the dockyard of the navy which he aspired to create in the Gulf. A little later, after the collapse of their business at Bunder Abbas, the East India Company transferred their factory to Bushire, where they received *firmans* conferring trading privileges upon them from Kerim Khan Zend. Matters progressed very slowly at the outset, there being only one English merchant in the place when Niebuhr was there in 1765. Gradually, however, as the mercantile marine of the Gulf was developed, and caravans into the interior began to adopt the route of the *kotals*, Bushire grew in size and importance,[1] and at the beginning of the present century had about 6,000–8,000 inhabitants. Under the immense increase in recent years of traffic both by land and sea, the place has swollen to larger dimensions, and now contains a mixed population of 15,000 persons. The town is situated at the northern extremity of a peninsula, eleven miles long by four broad, which is identified with the Mesambria of Arrian, where the fleet of Nearchus cast anchor, and found plantations and gardens. This peninsula has at some period been recovered from the sea, which only a century ago used sometimes to flow across the narrow neck immediately south of the town, converting the latter into an island. Since then the land has steadily risen, and this phenomenon no longer occurs; but the water from the interior or eastern bay occasionally overflows the low-lying flats near the walls, and turns them into a swamp. The town itself has a rather better elevation, being situated upon a ledge of sandy conglomerate stone, which projects above the sea-level, and gives the place from a distance a more imposing appearance than is warranted by a closer inspection.

Bushire

The people of Bushire, as of all the coast towns in the

Shehr is singular, not plural; and because *Abu* is Arabic, while *Shehr* is Persian. General Schindler informs me that in the Karnamek of Ardeshir Babekan, the first Sassanian monarch, is a passage which says that on his retreat to the coast of the Gulf, pursued by the Parthian army, Ardeshir 'when he saw the sea praised God, and there named a place Bokht-Artakhshir, and erected a fire-temple' This may have been contracted into Bushir, on the analogy of Gavashir, Bahmeshir, Reshire.

[1] There is an interesting account of Bushire in 1775, in *Travels in Asia*, by Abraham Parsons.

Dashtistan, were formerly entirely Arabs, ruled by a sheikh of the tribe of Matarish, who had emigrated in the seventeenth century from Oman. In the middle of the last century, Sheikh Nasr (variously reported as being of this family, and of the Nejd tribe of Abu Muheiri), a very remarkable man, raised himself to a position of great authority and wealth, and retained his independence throughout the reign of Kerim Khan. He was master of Bahrein, as well as of Bushire, and much of the Dashtistan, and maintained a large fleet, with which he traded with Muscat and India, and an easily mobilised army of devoted Arabs; he imported Nejd stallions from Arabia, and greatly improved the Gulf breed of horses; and finally, upon his death, bequeathed to his son a fortune of two millions sterling. The latter, bearing the same name, received from his dying father a legacy of fidelity to the cause of the youthful Lutf Ali Khan, whom he assisted to place on the throne of Persia, although before long there was disagreement between the pair. At the beginning of the present century, Sheikh Abdur Rasul, grandson of the first, and son of the second, Nasr, was Governor of Bushire; but his sluggish and unwarlike temperament suggested to the government of Fath Ali Shah, already beginning to assert its authority over the outlying portions of the kingdom, the opportunity of interference. The sheikh was seized, by the perfidious violation of an oath upon the Koran, while the mission of Sir Harford Jones was in Bushire in 1809, and was carried off to Shiraz, where his execution was ordered. Having somehow saved his life, the sheikh, in the alternate ups and downs of Asiatic fortune, found himself again installed a few years later at Bushire, where, from 1816–30, he was continually engaged in conflict, either with a brother named Mohammed on the spot, or with the Persian Governor of Shiraz. A traveller in 1830, while Sir E. Stannus was Resident at Bushire, represented the state of affairs as so critical that guns were planted by the sheikh, and levelled at the Residency, which was barricaded with furniture and lumber, and with a breastwork of water-casks and wine-chests in the courtyard. In 1832, this troublesome chieftain, whose mischievousness had increased with his years, was murdered in the fort at Borazjun. Another brother, Sheikh Husein, and a son, Sheikh Rasul, continued the family tactics of internal dissension, varied by revolt against the sovereign power, and spent their days either

People and rulers

in a state of armed siege at Bushire, or in prison at Shiraz. So matters continued till a little after the middle of the century, when the Government finally asserted its force, and Bushire has ever since received a Persian nominee. At the time of my visit (1889–90) it was under the jurisdiction of the Saad-el-Mulk, a person of low origin, and formerly a *munshi*, or clerk, to the present Governor of Fars, who had been placed by the Amin-es-Sultan as Governor of the Gulf Ports, in charge of the coast-fringe from Bunder Dilam to Jask. The garrison of Bushire consisted of 300 to 400 *serbaz*, and 50 to 60 artillerymen, with some old and rotten guns, lying near the Governor's Bunder, miscalled the Arsenal by the Persians. In the past year (1891) the Saad-el-Mulk was displaced by his elder brother, the Nizam-es-Sultaneh, who was Governor of Arabistan when I was at Shushter.

The change effected in the rulers of Bushire has been reflected in its population. Till the last twenty years the Arab element was largely in the ascendant, although, to a great extent, Persianised both in dress and religion. As trade, however, has increased, and purely maritime occupations have declined, the Persian ingredients have gained the upper hand, and now largely predominate, although the bulk of the people are still of Arab, or mixed Arab and Persian descent. There are about a hundred Armenians in Bushire engaged in trade (fifty years ago, the missionary Dr. J. Wolff founded a school for them here, which subsequently collapsed), and a European contribution of about fifty, supplied by the staff of the Residency and Telegraph department, and by the representatives of business houses, who have much increased in recent years.

The town

The western front of Bushire, facing the open sea, is the most pretentious, for here are the British Residency—a large building with two courts, at whose doorway is always stationed an Indian guard—and the principal European residences or places of business, some of which are lofty and two-storeyed, built of stone, and with verandahs facing the sea. The horizontal lines of the natives' houses at Bushire are broken by frequent *badgirs*, or wind-towers, with narrow slits to admit the air; and on some of the roof-tops may be seen awnings, for sleeping in the summer. Considering the size of the town, the bazaars are extensive, though narrow and confined. The bulk of the streets are both narrow and filthy, and in the open spaces on the shore line may be seen encampments of low tents, and *kapars* or huts, made of date-sticks and leaves, the nauseous domiciles of the lower classes of the population. Such pretentiousness of air as the modern town can claim is largely due to the wise expenditure, by Sir L. Pelly, of part of the Mansion House Persian Famine Relief Fund in 1870–1, in the employment of local labour. On the southern side, or along the base of the triangle formed by the apex of the peninsula, the town was formerly fortified by a high wall with twelve towers and bastions and two gates, in front of which stood some old Portuguese guns, brought either from Reshire or Ormuz. The last time that this wall was repaired was in 1838, when Mohammed Shah rebuilt it, to withstand a possible attack from the English, who had occupied Kharak Island in that year. It has since fallen to pieces, and is now a model of nineteenth century Persian fortification.

Climate and water

The climate of Bushire is trying though not acutely unhealthy. In summer, however, the heat is exhausting, and the thermometer frequently registers over 100° Fahr. in the shade. The average rainfall is about twelve inches in the year. Water is scarce: and most of the neighbouring supplies are brackish. The wells most commonly in use are situated on the plain at the distance of over a mile from the town gate; but the best sources are at five and six miles distant in the direction of Reshire. At the time of my visit the price of the ordinary quality was 5–6 *puls* (¾*d.*), of the better quality 16 *puls* (2¼*d.*) per donkey-load. A large reservoir to collect rain-water was built on the sea-front some years ago by a native merchant, and was opened for the public use in April and May; but its contents were found to be infested with the *reshta* or guinea-worm, which 200 years ago was complained of by Chardin[1] and Kaempfer,[2] as tainting the water-supplies along the Gulf-coast.

The port

Though Bushire is the main port of Persia, it possesses nothing that could by the wildest exaggeration be described under present conditions as a harbour. The anchorage is in an open and unprotected roadstead at the distance of some three miles from the shore, is much exposed to gales, and in bad weather is inaccessible. Every cargo has to be embarked or disembarked in native buggalows, and the process of lading and unlading is in consequence very slow. The inner bay on the

[1] *Voyages* (edit. Langlès), vol. viii. pp. 470–4. [2] *Amœn. Exot.* pp. 525–35.

western side is intended by nature, and was formerly used, as a harbour, there being deep water close up to the town. A bar, however, has formed opposite its entrance, and boats drawing over ten feet of water cannot pass. The use of a dredger, and the expenditure of a few hundred pounds, would remedy this, without the need of any costly piers or structure; and the impotence of the Persian Government in this respect lends an additional argument to those who contend that Great Britain should not have evacuated Bushire, for the retention of which the Persians thoroughly expected us to stipulate, in 1857. Of the trade of the port I shall speak in subsequent chapters upon the Gulf, and upon Persian Commerce. I may here say that in 1889 the customs were sold by the Saad-el-Mulk for 91,000 *tomans*, or 26,000*l.* + 5,000 *tomans*, or 1,400*l.*, *pishkesh*, i.e. present to himself; the farmer also making a large profit, so that the actual amount levied upon imports and exports was greatly in excess of this sum.

Reshire

About six miles to the south of the town are the ruins of the old Portuguese fort of Reshire.[1] This was no doubt the earliest settlement on the peninsula of Mesambria; for in the mounds here have been found bricks with cuneiform characters, and other remains of a considerable antiquity.[2] The Portuguese established a trading station and built a fort here in the sixteenth century, but were turned out by the Persians after the capture of Ormuz in 1622. The fort was repaired in 1856, and occupied by Persian troops, who made a gallant but ineffectual resistance against the British, the latter losing four officers in the attack. It covers a quadrangular space, 250 yards in diameter, and the ramparts still retain a steep and lofty profile, and the remains

[1] Ouseley suggests the impossible derivation *Reis shehr*, i.e. chief or captain of cities. It might be *Ras-shehr* (cape of the city) or *Rig-shehr*. General Schindler explains it as Riv-Ardeshir.

[2] The principal of these are a number of old sculptured tombstones, probably of the Arab period (*vide* Morier's *Second Journey*, p. 45); and an immense collection of stone and earthenware vases of rude shape and fabrication, sealed up with earthenware lids or with coverings of talc, sometimes lined inside with a coating of bitumen, and containing human skulls and bones. A great number of these have been found between Bushire and Reshire, at a depth of about two feet below the surface, usually placed horizontally in a long line, one after the other. The jars are about three feet in length and one foot in diameter. They are supposed to have contained the remains of Zoroastrians, after the body had perished by exposure.—*Vide* Ouseley, vol. i. p. 217, and Colonel Johnson, *Journey from India*, pp. 19–20.

of the old ditch. Near here the Indo-European Telegraph department shifted its quarters from Bushire in 1876, to a series of fine buildings, six in number, with a club-room, garden, and lawn-tennis court. Just below, the wires run down into the sea. A little further inland is Sebzabad, the summer quarters of the British Resident, a commodious verandahed building with a pretty garden, and a mud volcano in the grounds. Hither he retires with his staff in the hot months; but it struck me that the place is situated too far from the sea to get the full benefit of whatever breeze may be generated by the Persian Gulf.

The Union Jack fluttering from the summit of the Residency flag-staff is no vain symbol of British ascendency in Bushire.

British influence

The steamers lying at the anchorage are with scarcely an exception British steamers; the goods that crowd the stalls in the bazaar are British or Indian goods; the rupee is as readily, nay more readily, accepted than the *kran*. There must be many a Persian who has contrasted the smart bodyguard of the British Resident with the slatternly escort of the native Governor. In appearance and structure the English quarter of the town is not unlike an Indian station; while the friendly sentiments of the populace were unmistakably shown by the manner in which was celebrated at Bushire the Jubilee of the British Queen. For nearly twenty years the interests of this country have been in the faithful keeping of Colonel Ross in this distant outport, not of British power, but of British influence; and he has lately handed over to his successor a position whose unwritten authority is among the many silent monuments to the British name.

CHAPTER XXIII

THE EASTERN AND SOUTH-EASTERN PROVINCES

Vadimus in campos steriles exustaque mundi,
Qua nimius Titan, et raræ in fontibus undæ,
Siccaque letiferis squalent serpentibus arva,
Durum iter.

LUCAN, *Pharsal.*, lib. ix.

IN previous chapters I have described the great province of Khorasan, occupying the entire north-eastern portion of the Shah's dominions; and also the smaller district of Seistan, which, lying on the frontier midway between Transcaspia and the Indian Ocean, is strictly speaking the most easterly portion of Iran. There remains for me to say something of what may be called the eastern-central and the south-eastern provinces, which in the one case by physical conditions, and in the other by ethnological differences, are separated from the rest of the country, and have been commonly either passed over or ignored by such travellers as prefer the beaten track, and have little taste for exploration. Nevertheless, these regions, though somewhat disconnected from the rest of Persia, are intensely Persian in their characteristics; for they contain, as a glance at the map will show, on the one hand, great commercial cities, remote from the crowded areas of population, but subsisting in the main upon export and import trade; and on the other enormous expanses of sandy or saline wilderness, responsible for ghastly voids on the map, which the intrepidity of no traveller has ever, in the face of an implacable nature, been able to fill. Of such blanks in Persian cartography there are commonly two possible explanations. Either the empty space is unexplored, or it is unexplorable. Both explanations will be found to apply to the regions which we are about to examine; although such has in recent years been the well-directed activity of British officers, sent out on surveying expeditions by the Indian Government to these parts of Persia, that my map, which embodies the results of much of their labour, will be found to contain far fewer redeemable voids

Evidence of the map

than any previously issued; while the sadly disproportionate expanse of the two mighty deserts is a visitation from which Persia will hardly free herself till the end of time.

Cities and deserts

I will deal with the cities before I come to the deserts; and from the two I will then pass to the interesting but little-known subject of Persian Beluchistan.

Yezd and Kerman

Each distinct division of the Persian territories has its populous city. In the north-west is Tabriz, in the north Teheran, in the north-east Meshed, in the centre Isfahan, in the south Shiraz. The provinces of which I speak can claim two cities of similar rank, Yezd and Kerman, the former situated 200 miles (by caravan track) south-east of Isfahan, the latter rather more than the same distance south-east of Yezd, and 380 miles from the sea at Bunder Abbas. Both are famous and populous cities: both are sustained by local industry and foreign barter; and both present much the same features of habit and appearance; although Kerman must yield to Yezd, alike in number of inhabitants, in wealth, and in general prosperity.

History of Yezd

Yezd,[1] which is the capital of a district bearing the same name, is ordinarily approached, on the north, by caravan route from Kashan *viâ* Nain, or from Isfahan; on the south by similar routes from Bunder Abbas, usually traversed by camels, either *viâ* Saidabad or *viâ* Kerman. In the Persian hyperbole the city is known as Dar-el-Ibadeh, or Seat of Worship, a not inapt designation, seeing that its people, whether Mohammedans, or Babis, or Parsis, are distinguished for great strictness and zeal, and that it contains a large number of the fanatical firebrands who call themselves *seyids*. In history it has long been known; but, from its proximity to no frontier, has played both a less troublous and a less distinguished part than other cities of less importance. It was one of the legendary halting-places of Zal and Rustam while on their march from Seistan

[1] Yezd has been visited and described by the following Europeans in the present century: A. Dupré (1808), *Voyage en Perse*, vol. ii. cap. xlii.; Dr. A. Petermann (1854), *Reisen im Orient*; N. de Khanikoff (1859), *Mémoire*, pp. 200–204 (with a map); Sir F. Goldsmid (1865), *Telegraph and Travel*, pp. 570–572; Colonel Euan-Smith (1870), *Eastern Persia*, vol. i. pp. 173–175; (Sir) C. MacGregor (1875), *Journey through Khorasan*, vol. i. pp. 71–80; E. Floyer (1877), *Unexplored Beluchistan*, cap. xiv.; A. H. Schindler (1879), *Zeit. f. Gesell. d. Erd. zu Berlin*, 1881; E. Stack (1881), *Six Months in Persia*, vol. i. p. 256; H. B. Vaughan (1888), *Proceedings of the R. G. S.* (new series), vol. xii., 1890. The first city of Yezd was also called Askizar.

to Fars. In the Achæmenian and Sassanian days I have found in various writers supposed allusions to Yezd, which a closer examination has proved to relate to Istakhr. With the Arab invasion ensued that persecution of the Zoroastrian faith which extinguished the fire altars of Media and Hyrcania, and drove its acolytes to the more secure retreat of Yezd and Kerman. Here they have ever since lingered, maltreated but undismayed; and from this centre was directed in later times that happy migration which has transformed the down-trodden Guebre of Iran into the prosperous Parsi of Bombay. For more than two centuries the Atabegs of Yezd maintained an independent rule, comparable to that of the Atabegs of Luristan in the west, until at the end of the thirteenth century they were extinguished by the Mongol Ghazan Khan. Marco Polo passed through 'the good and noble city of Yasdi' in 1272; Friar Odoricus was at Iest, as he calls it, in 1325, and the Venetian Josafa Barbaro in 1474.[1] Tavernier stayed here three days in the middle of the seventeenth century, and was much struck with the good fruits, while of the ladies of Yezd he decisively remarked that 'certainly they are the handsomest women in Persia.' He was among the first to quote the now hackneyed native proverb, that 'to live happily a man must have a wife of Yezd, must eat the bread of Yezdikhast, and drink the wine of Shiraz.' To Englishmen, however, Yezd was but little known till the present century. Christie, having left Pottinger in Beluchistan, passed through the town in 1810 on his return from Herat;[2] while a succession of writers, whose works I have already named in a footnote, have in later years co-operated to remove the prevailing ignorance.

Size and appearance

Yezd is situate, as are most Persian cities of any size, on a flat sandy plain, bounded by mountain ranges both on the north and south, the latter especially presenting a bold and rugged outline. All around the city, which evidently once covered a much larger surface, lie acres encumbered with ruin, whilst on the east the ever encroaching sands of the desert are blown right up against the walls. The new arrival finds something imposing in the great extent of buildings, in the fortified *enceinte* of the citadel rising from the interior of the town, in the numerous wind-

[1] He described it as a great silk mart, and as having a walled circumference of five miles. Marco Polo had also specified the silk manufacture.

[2] Appendix to (Sir) H. Pottinger's *Travels in Beloochistan*.

towers, and in the minars and front of the Musjid-i-Jama, or Great Mosque. The modern city covers a space about two miles in length, by one and a quarter in breadth, but is not entirely, as it once was, enclosed by walls. On the other hand, the fort in the interior, though for the most part ruined and built into or over, still retains a double wall, with a broad. deep ditch before the outer rampart; while the *ark* or citadel inside the fort, where the Governor resides, is separately walled to the height of thirty to forty feet. None of these defences, however, which are built of mud or of sun-dried brick, have any military value, and neither city nor situation has the least strength. The town is divided into two parts—the Old and the New—separated by a wall with two gates. The Old or southern town has seven quarters and three gates; the New or northern town has six quarters and five gates. Water is brought by underground channels, of which there are said to be over seventy, from the Shir Kuh, on the south and south-west; and the domed *abambars* or reservoirs, approached by steep flights of steps, are among the chief glories of Yezd. Otherwise its public buildings, although reported to comprise fifty mosques, eight *madressehs*, and sixty-five public baths, are deficient both in number and importance, the only edifice of any distinction being the Musjid-i-Jama, inside the fort, the erection of which is attributed to Amir Chakmak, an officer of Timur, and whose imposing blue-tiled façade and soaring minarets, although the main structure is a ruin, are the most imposing features in a *coup d'œil* of the city. The population, which at the beginning of the century is said to have been 100,000, but which sank to 40,000 in 1860–70, is now reported to have risen, if the suburbs be included, to something like the original figure, although 70,000 to 80,000 is a more probable estimate for the city itself. These totals include a variety of elements, there being a Jewish population now calculated at 2,000 (they are distinguished by being obliged to wear a patch in front of their coats), a fluctuating Hindu contingent, engaged in trade (in 1866 Sir F. Goldsmid found seventeen, in 1871 five), and a large Guebre or Parsi contribution.

The Guebres

To an English visitor the latter constitute perhaps the main attraction of Yezd. Here for hundreds of years has resided this interesting and venerable community, lending to the city and its neighbourhood, where they possess a number of villages, the service of untiring industry and respectable character, though receiving little but kicks and cuffs in return. Their numbers have been variously reported as from 3,500 to 7,000 at different periods in the century, confusion having been habitual between the urban residents and the total inhabiting the surrounding district.[1] In the city they possess schools of their own, a high priest, and a secular head, four fire-altars, which in the prudent obscurity of private houses sustain the undying flame,[2] and several Towers of Silence or places of exposure in the adjacent hills. A few of them are naturalised British subjects, having come from India. These are very proud of the connection, which they never cease to proclaim; and their leading merchant, one Ardeshir Mehreban, is a man of high repute. Nevertheless, in spite of their riches and respectability, the community is one that has always suffered, and is still exposed to, persecution. Severe disabilities are inflicted upon them in the transactions of daily or mercantile life. Some years ago a heavy poll-tax was imposed, which drove many away;[3] within the last twenty years a wealthy Parsi has been murdered in the open streets at the instigation of the *mullahs*, and his murderer has escaped scot-free; they are compelled to wear sober-coloured garments, and may not ride, or keep open shops, or possess high or handsome houses in the city. When they purchase property, a higher price is exacted from them than from Mohammedans; they are forced to conceal their means, and to restrict their commercial operations for fear of exciting hostile attack; while in the streets they are constantly liable to insult and personal affront. In recent years an association has been formed for their protection by their co-religionists in Bombay.

Yezd a commercial emporium

It was about fifty years ago that the Parsis of Yezd began that trade with India which has since reached such considerable dimensions, and has added to the always great commercial reputation of the city. They occupy a position here not unlike that of the Chinese *compradors* and agents in the Treaty Ports of Japan, the bulk of the foreign trade passing through their hands, and a good deal of the home

[1] In 1879 General Schindler found 1,240 Parsis living in the city, and 5,240 in 22 neighbouring villages. Total, 6,480. 'Die Parsen in Persien,' *Zeit. d. M. G.* 1882.

[2] This is the allusion in Moore's 'Yezd's eternal mansion of the Fire.'

[3] This *jezieh* or poll-tax, which was an occasion of much suffering, was finally repealed by the Shah in 1882, mainly at the instance of the British Government.

industry being likewise under their direction. In both these respects Yezd stands alone in Persia. No wars or rumours of wars affect a place situated so far inland, no *chapaus* or raids of marauding nomads now sweep up to its walls; a permanent garrison is dispensed with; the mercantile instincts of the people are even indicated in their preference for donkeys rather than horses as riding animals; and the well-kept houses and crowded bazaars sustain the impression of peaceful and busy opulence. Silk-weaving was formerly the chief local industry, the mulberry being cultivated in great abundance in the neighbourhood; and as many as 1,800 factories, employing some 9,000 hands, were in the middle of the present century engaged in the business. This has, however, declined, for reasons elsewhere displayed; and its place has been taken, particularly since the Anglo-Chinese wars and the opening of Hong Kong, by the cultivation of the poppy, 2,000 chests of the opium extracted from which are now said to leave Yezd annually. Among the remaining exports are cotton, wool, carpets, felts, madder roots, henna, almonds, and pistachios. The chief imports are English and Anglo-Indian goods from the south, and Russian wares from the north. Cotton fabrics, prints, copper, tin, lead, iron, drugs and spices, India and China teas are among the former, and are shipped from Bombay to Bunder Abbas; Russia sends oil, candles, sugar, furs, crockery, and also competes in piece-goods. A number of Russian Armenians are engaged in the import and export trade with Russia, and in the promotion of their country's interest, which is further advanced by a native Russian agent, who is a Persian merchant of high position. British interests have never been similarly safeguarded; although the appointment of a consular agent at Yezd would result in a certain and lucrative extension to Anglo-Indian commerce. Messrs. Hotz & Son and Ziegler & Co. have, however, recently established agencies here. A great deal of merchandise only passes through Yezd in transit to the bazaars of Meshed and Sebzewar, and even of Kashan and Teheran.

Revenue and government

In 1870 the revenue was reported as only 100,000 *tomans*; but in 1888 the government of the district was farmed for 250,000 *tomans*, and the customs for 47,000 *tomans*. Prior to the disgrace of the Zil-es-Sultan in 1888, Yezd was one of the many governments subjected to his all but sovereign sway. It was then separated from Fars, and was constituted an independent government under the Imad-ed-Dowleh, a competent ruler. In 1890 it was given back to the Zil, who placed his son in command. The city contains a post-office, with a weekly mail to Bunder Abbas and Bushire, and a telegraph-office, which is linked by single Persian wires with Kerman and Isfahan.

From Yezd I pass to Kerman, the cities being connected by two routes of about the same length, viz. 220 miles, running the one by Bafk on the northern, and the other by Kermanshahan on the southern side of the mountain range that stretches with scarcely an interruption between the two places.

History of Kerman

Kerman is the Caramania of the ancients, and occupies a site on the confines of the Great Desert, and at the confluence of four important routes from the south and east, that has always rendered it a great trading emporium for the merchants trafficking between the Persian Gulf and the Central Asian marts of Khorasan, Bokhara, and Balkh. The founder of the city is unknown; but its size and significance have been attested from remote times. Yezdijird, the last Persian king, fled hither and reigned a brief while, when the Arabs overran his country. It was successively ruled by the Beni Buyah dynasty, the Seljuk Turks, the kings of Kharezm (Khiva), and a Kara Khitaian family who retained the throne till 1300 A.D. Kerman was further a Nestorian see under the metropolitan of Fars. The town has been repeatedly sacked and destroyed by invaders from the east and west, the united savagery of Jenghiz Khan, Timur, the Afghans, and Nadir Shah, having been expended upon its hapless body. At the end of the last century it attracted a wide renown, as the scene both of the heroism of a noble character and the inhuman brutality of a despot. Here the lion-hearted Lutf Ali Khan, the last of the Zend family, held out for several months in 1794 with extreme bravery against the army of the Kajar eunuch, Agha Mohammed Khan. Treacherously betrayed, the young prince escaped himself; but the city fell a victim to the fiendish rage of the conqueror, who for three months surrendered it to the passions of his soldiery, and is said not to have been satisfied until 35,000 pairs of eyes had been handed to him upon a dish, while every fine building was razed to the ground, and 30,000 women and children were carried off into slavery. The city was rebuilt on a reduced scale by Fath Ali Shah a little to the north-west of the former site,[1] and about thirty years ago was raised to a pitch of great prosperity under the rule of the Vekil-el-Mulk, who, though a hard and avaricious governor, recovered for the place somewhat of its ancient prestige.

Modern city

The remains of old Kerman occupy a space about three miles in length outside the walls of the modern town, and are commanded by a big ruined fort, attributed to Ardeshir, and called the Kaleh-i-Dokhter, or Maiden's Fort, upon a steep limestone ridge to the east. The modern city is about three-quarters of a square mile in extent, and is surrounded by battlemented mud walls, after the usual Persian fashion, pierced by six gates, with a broad half-choked ditch. Like Yezd, it contains a fort and a citadel in the fort, where the Governor resides. Here also high dark mountains at a slight distance overhang the city, while the snow-streaked peaks of loftier ranges to the north-west are always in the landscape. The public buildings, naturally enough, are lacking in interest, the principal being the Musjid-i-Jama, founded A.D. 1349, the two-storeyed *madresseh* of Ibrahim Khan, and the Kuba-i-Sebz, or Green Cupola, a cylindrical dome-covered structure raised in A.D. 1155, containing a mutilated marble tomb in the centre, and the remains of a blue tile wainscoting. The population is said to be about 40,000.[2] In 1810 Pottinger found no Jews, Armenians, or Hindus; but there are now representatives of all three nationalities, the Hindus, some forty in number, and half-Persianised in dress and appearance, being traders from Shikarpur and Sind. They live in a caravanserai apart, and enthusiastically welcome any English traveller, whose notice invests them with a superior social distinction. There is also a considerable Parsi population, inhabiting a separate quarter, and possessing a funeral tower in the neighbouring hills. Stack quotes the prophecy of a local saint, who predicted a century ago that Isfahan will be destroyed by water, Yezd by sand, and Kerman by horsehoofs;

[1] In the present century it has been visited and described by (Sir) H. Pottinger (1810), *Travels in Beloochistan*, cap. x.; N. de Khanikoff (1859), *Mémoire*, pp. 186–198 (with a map); Sir F. Goldsmid (1866), *Telegraph and Travel*, pp. 582–590; Colonel Euan-Smith (1871), *Eastern Persia*, vol. i. pp. 183–191; (Sir) O. St. John (1872), *Eastern Persia*, vol. i. pp. 92–102; E. Floyer (1876), *Unexplored Baluchistan*, cap. xiii.; E. Stack (1881), *Six Months in Persia*, vol. i. p. 202.

[2] In 1878 a careful census was made by the then governor, which showed 39,718 Mohammedans, 1,341 Parsis, 85 Jews, and 26 Hindus, or a total of 41,170 persons.

and adds: 'Some morning the people of Kerman shall wake and see the Saidi hills, north of the city, all white with tents, and then they will know that the end has come.' I understand, but I do not admit the inference; for there are those who will make it their business to see pretty clearly that it is not from the northern hills that the horsehoofs will descend.

The bazaars of Kerman, which are lofty and well-built, and its caravanserais, which are numerous and handsome,[1] are worthy of the commercial and manufacturing reputation of the city. The imports from Great Britain, India, and China are of the same character as those already described in the case of Yezd. Of local manufactures the chief are *namads* or felts, most cunningly and beautifully wrought; carpets of excellent colour and original design, costing prices of from 10*s*. to 10*l*., according to quality, per square yard; and the famous Kerman shawls which resemble and rival those of Kashmir. Of these the best, costing from 16*l*. to 24*l*., are made of the hair or down that grows next to the skin of the goat; the next quality are woven from the wool of a small sheep, the neighbourhood of Kerman being celebrated for both breeds, and producing either by its climate, its vegetation, or its water, or by all combined, a quality and texture that cannot elsewhere be repeated. The shawls are made from patterns, not painted, but learned by heart—a tremendous strain upon the memory—and are manufactured in surroundings extremely injurious both to eyesight and health. The looms are set up in filthy dark holes, without light or ventilation, where the artificers, who are men and boys, work in a half-naked condition. In the middle ages Kerman possessed a great reputation for the manufacture of arms; but this, like that of Meshed, is a thing of the past.

Trade

In 1810 Pottinger gave the revenue of the city as 25,000 *tomans*, or 25,000*l*., and estimated that of the province as 50,000*l*. more. In 1871, when the Mekran Boundary Commissioners were there, the provincial revenue was stated as 310,000 *tomans*, or 124,000*l*. The tables supplied to me for 1888–89 return it, including Persian Beluchistan, as 290,000 *tomans*. The government is now one of the highest rank,

Revenue and Government

[1] In 1871 Colonel Euan-Smith reported 32 public baths, 28 caravanserais, 120 shawl factories, 80 cotton factories, and 6 really good carpet factories. In 1879 Gen. Schindler returned 42 mosques, 53 public baths, 5 *madressehs*, 50 schools, 4 large and 22 smaller bazaars, and 9 caravanserais.

inasmuch as it includes Persian Beluchistan, which is administered by a deputy of the Governor-General. The latter is usually a prince of the blood royal, and at the time of my visit was the Nasr-ed-Dowleh, a cousin of the Shah. His province contains as varied a population as can be found anywhere within the same limits in Persia; Iranians, Turkis, Kurds, Beluchis, and Rinds being included in the total.

The great deserts

Yezd and Kerman both stand, as has been seen, on the outskirts of a desert, and north of both, for league upon league, extends the appalling waste that has here stamped upon Persia the imprint of an eternal desolation. From the haunts of busy life and commerce I turn, therefore, to the contemplation of a Sahara as funereal and more unique than any that Tartary or Africa can display. In existing works upon Persia there will be found hesitating, and often conflicting, accounts about both the extent, the ramifications, and the limits of the main Persian desert or deserts, arising from the scant and often untrustworthy information upon which those descriptions have been based. The more reliable intelligence that has lately been procured enables us to formulate a more accurate conception. There are, practically speaking, two great deserts, covering a combined length, from north-west to south-east, of over 500 miles, but separated from each other, between the thirty-second and thirty-fourth parallels of latitude, by a belt of hilly country, along which runs one of the main caravan tracks from the centre to the north-east. Of these deserts, the more northerly, extending from 33° to 36° north latitude, and from 52° to 57° east longitude, is that generally known as the Great Salt Desert, or Dasht-i-Kavir. The second or southerly, extending from 29° to 32° north latitude, and from 57° to 60° east longitude, is that described on the maps as the Dasht-i-Lut. Both are salt, in so far as *nemeksar*, or saline swamp, is found in the depressions of each, which average about 1,000 feet above the sea; but the far greater proportion of *kavir* in the northern desert and the almost complete absence of vegetation have procured for it the unenviable monopoly of the name.

By some the name Dasht-i-Kavir has been simply translated Great Desert, *kavir* being presumed to be a local modification of the Arabic *kabir*, great.[1] Such a derivation, however, altogether

[1] Malcolm and Morier both spoke of it as the Daria-i-Kabir, or Great Sea, but they must have been mistaken.

loses sight of the saline characteristics, which are an essential connotation of the term as used in Persia. General Schindler, examining the various words from which it may be derived—(1) the Persian *gav*, a depression or hollow, (2) the Persian *gur* or *kur*, a grave, pool, hollow, or plain (whence *gurkhar*, the wild ass or ass of the plain), and (3) the Arabic *kafr*, or *kafreh* (plural *kufur*), a word still in use to express a desert in Africa and Arabia—gives the preference to the last.[1] In its Persian application it invariably signifies a salt desert or saline swamp, and is bestowed both upon the Great Salt Desert of which I am now speaking, and also upon smaller *kavirs* or patches of saline waste, which are to be found in other parts of the country,[2] and which may be regarded, in some cases as repetitions of the same phenomenon in detached localities, in others as bays or inlets of the Dasht-i-Kavir.

The Dasht-i-Kavir

The theory has sometimes prevailed that the latter owes its origin solely to the drainage of saline streams from the highlands depositing, as they evaporate, a white crust or efflorescence upon the ground, and in some cases forming pools and swamps; and there is this to be said in favour of the hypothesis, that the streams of Persia are very frequently and largely impregnated with salt. On the other hand, tradition is so unanimous that the site of the Dasht-i-Kavir and, in fact, the entire centre of Persia, were once occupied by a salt sea, and the present physical conditions accord so well with the theory, that we shall probably not err if we accept it. Legend asserts that this inland sea once extended from Kazvin to Kerman and the borders of Beluchistan. The ancient city of Rhages is said to have been upon its northern shore, Yezd to have been an island, and Kerman to have been upon its southern coast. The tower of Saveh is even identified as one of the lighthouses built to guide the mariners who navigated its waves. Sir F. Goldsmid mentions, as confirmatory evidence, that upon the other or eastern edge of the *kavir* he found a village named Yunsi, from a fixed tradition that Yunas, i.e. Jonah, was there cast up by the whale—a fiction

Its origin

[1] *Proceedings of the R.G.S.* (new series), vol. x. p. 627.

[2] The best known of these are the *kavir* south of Khaf, that to the east of Lake Niriz, and the *kavir* whose western limits used to be passed on the road between Teheran and Kum, but are now occupied by the lake which appeared there in 1883, and which is described in cap. xviii.

which could hardly have been localised upon dry land. Guides and superstitious villagers, living near the various *kavirs*, tell marvellous tales of the circumstances under which they ceased to be seas and were dried up; but these are interesting only to students of folklore, and need not be here repeated.

Different kinds of *kavir*

In different parts, the *kavir* presents a different aspect, according to the nature of the soil and the amount of salt water that refuses to be drained. Sometimes it is quite dry and soft, with a thin glazed crust on the top, which crackles beneath the horse's hoof, and with powdery soil beneath. Sometimes it presents an expanse of hard baked clay. Again it will take the form of mobile hillocks and dangerous quicksands. When the water is lying upon the surface, particularly in winter, it will in one place resemble a great lake, in another it will be a slimy swamp; while after the evaporation of the early summer suns the saline incrustation on the dried up patches will glitter in the distance like sheets of ice.[1]

Travellers in the Great Kavir

Of travellers who have crossed or skirted the Great Kavir there are few. Marco Polo has been said to have traversed a portion of it on his supposed route from Tabbas to Damghan about 1272; although it is more probable that he marched further to the east, and crossed the northern portion of the Dasht-i-Lut.[2] Dr. Buhse, a Russian, crossed a portion of it on a journey from Yezd to Damghan in 1849, and was said by Sir O. St. John to have been the sole European who had done so.[3] Sir F. Goldsmid and the Seistan Boundary Commission were near to its eastern fringe in 1872. Sir C. MacGregor, on his march from Yezd to Tabbas, *viâ* Khur, in 1875, was upon its southern border. Finally, in 1887 and 1888, two young Indian officers, Lieutenant R. E. Galindo and Lieutenant H. B. Vaughan, travelling, the former from Khur to Damghan, the latter from Anarek to Semnan, alighted at intervening points upon the true Dasht-i-

[1] *Vide* the description given by Colonel C. E. Stewart, *Proceedings of the R.G.S.* (new series), vol. iii. (1881), p. 518.

[2] Yule's *Marco Polo*, vol. i. p. 131. The Tunogan of the text, which was originally mistaken for Damghan, is correctly explained by Yule as Tun-o- (i.e. and) Kain.

[3] 'Notice sur trois plantes médicinales et sur le grand désert salé de la Perse.' par F. A. Buhse. Extrait du *Bulletin de la Société d'Histoire Naturelle de Moscou*, 1850, No. 4. *Vide* also a notice by Dr. C. Greninck in his 'Geographical Description of N. Persia,' published in the *Trans. of the Mineralogical Soc. of St. Petersburg* in 1852.

Kavir. The experiences of each were somewhat different. Lieutenant Galindo speaks of

Perfectly level ground, at first principally black mud, with isolated patches of white salt, and slimy pools of green water. Gradually the salt increases till it becomes a hard, almost unbroken, white crust, still with the green pools standing on it, and looking something like the little pools left by the sea in the hollows of a rocky coast at low water. It is no exaggeration to say that the whole of this track (about twenty-six miles) is marked out by carcasses of camels, averaging one for every 200 yards, in various stages of pickle.

Elsewhere there was little or no saline efflorescence, but

It appeared as if very liquid black mud had been suddenly arrested and hardened, while in a state of violent ebullition or effervescence. The ground is thickly pitted and honeycombed with round holes, from eight to twelve inches in diameter, and generally about the same depth, though some go down two or three feet. Between these are rounded nodules or ridges of mud, some of which are solid, but some are merely bubbles or blisters of earth, with a thin crust covering a treacherous hole. On the path a horse has to move with slow circumspection, stepping from knob to knob, or he would soon be lamed. Off the beaten track, of course, it is simply impassable.

Lieutenant Vaughan, more to the west, wrote as follows:—

As we quitted the defile, a sudden turn in the road presented to our astonished gaze what at first sight looked like a vast frozen sea, stretching away to the right as far as the eye could reach in one vast glistening expanse. A more careful examination proved it to be nothing more than salt formed into one immense sheet of dazzling brilliancy, while here and there upon its surface, pools of water, showing up in the most intense blue, were visible. Away to the north of it stood a distant range of low red hills. A peculiar haze, perhaps caused by evaporation, hangs over the whole scene, which, though softening the features of the distant hills, does not obliterate their details. This is the Great Salt Swamp, which, lying at a low level in the centre of the great desert, receives into its bed the drainage from an immense tract of territory. All the rivers flowing into it are more or less salt, and carry down to it annually a great volume of water. The fierce heat of the desert during the summer months causes a rapid evaporation, the result being that the salt constantly increases in proportion to the water, until at last the ground becomes caked with it.[1]

[1] *Proceedings of the R.G.S.* (new series), 1886, vol. viii. pp. 141–3. Lieutenant Vaughan thinks that the Dasht-i-Kavir contains two great depressions, one at the south base of the Kuh-i-Gugird, the other at the point formed by the junction of

In the past year (1891), yet another section of the Great Kavir, and itself a new phenomenon, has been for the first time brought to light by the same officer, travelling in company with Mr. C. E. Biddulph. This is no less than a great expanse of solid rock salt, the deposit for countless centuries of numerous salt streams, called by the natives Daria-i-Nemek, or Sea of Salt. It has apparently been traversed for long years by native caravans, crossing from the Meshed-Teheran road to Kashan, from which its southern border is distant less than 40 miles to the north-east; but during all this period no hint of its existence has reached European ears. The two English travellers suddenly came upon it, having climbed a crest of the Siah Kuh, a prominent ridge that rises from the heart of the desert. This is what they saw:—

At our feet lay what looked like a frozen sea, but was in reality a deposit of salt, which entirely filled the hollow in the plains towards the south, and stretched away as far as the eye could reach on either side, glittering in the sun like a sheet of glass.

Descending to the brink they marched across it till they came to the actual sheet of salt.

This at the edge was soft and sloppy like half-melted ice; but, as we proceeded, it gained in consistency till at a distance of 3 or 4 miles it resembled nothing more than very solid ice, strong enough to bear any weight.

The travellers tried to ascertain its depth; but it was so hard that with iron tent-pegs they could only detach a few chips. The natives said it was several feet thick. Crossing this astonishing expanse by moonlight, in order to escape the blinding glare of the sun, they estimated its breadth as 25 miles, and its length as even greater. This sea of solid rock-salt is probably without a rival in the world.[1]

Such, then, is the superficial aspect of the Dasht-i-Kavir. Traversed only with difficulty by routes lying higher than the general level, it may be said within the vast area of its limits absolutely to cut off northern from southern Persia, and to interpose a barrier between the two as grim and insurmountable as, at the opposite extreme of nature, do the mighty ramparts of the

the Kal Mura and Kal Lada rivers, both containing vast sheets of water in the rainy season.

[1] Vide *Proc. of the R.G.S.*, Nov. 1891, and *Asiatic Quarterly Review*, Oct. 1891.

Himalaya between British India and Tibet. Should it ever be the fate of Persia to submit to territorial and political partition, nature has, in this part at any rate, saved the contracting or conflicting parties the expense and trouble of a Boundary Commission.

The Dasht-i-Lut

From the Dasht-i-Kavir, or Great Salt Desert, I turn to the Dasht-i-Lut, or Great Sand Desert, separating Khorasan in the south-east from Kerman, and occupying a sorrowful parallelogram between the towns of Neh and Tabbas on the north, and Kerman and Yezd on the south. Not that this sand desert is without salt. On the contrary salt is perhaps its chief ingredient; but it is rarely *kavir*, i.e. it is rarely overlaid either with a saline incrustation or with a briny swamp; and it gives birth to a few miserable desert shrubs, which is a concession to respectability that no *kavir* has ever vouchsafed. The Lut, which some too ingenious critics have fancifully endeavoured to connect with the Lot of Holy Writ, but which is apparently a local synonym for a wilderness,[1] is situated at a much lower level than the Dasht-i-Kavir; for its normal elevation is less than 2,000 feet, and in places it sinks to only 500 feet above the sea level. Upon the maps it occupies a staring and eloquent blank. Few travellers have crossed it, fewer still having done so would voluntarily repeat the experiment. Marco Polo was here, but where was not the invincible Venetian? In the succeeding century Friar Odoricus thus described its charms, calling it the Sea of Sand :—

> Now that sea is a wondrous thing and right perilous. And there were none of us who desired to enter on that sea. For it is all of dry sand, without any moisture, and it shifteth, as the sea doth when in storm, now hither, now thither; and as it shifteth it maketh waves in like manner as the sea doth; so that countless people travelling thereon have been overwhelmed and drowned, and buried in those sands. For when blown about and buffeted by the winds, they are raised into hills, now in this place, now in that, according as the wind chanceth to blow.[2]

Khanikoff crossed the Dasht-i-Lut from Neh to Kerman in 1859. Goldsmid's party were on its borders in 1871. Colonel

[1] General Schindler, in a note in the *Indian Antiquary*, Dec. 1887, says that the word *lut* means naked, bare; and *dasht-i-lut*, therefore, the naked plain, i.e. desert. The word *lat* (originally piece, bit) is frequently combined with *lut* in common phraseology. Hence a man *lat we lut*, is a man who has nothing in the world, a beggar. From *lut* is derived the Persian *luti*, originally a sodomite, now a popular synonym for a buffoon or rogue.

[2] From *Cathay and the Way thither* (Hakluyt Society), No. 36–7.

Stewart made an expedition into it in 1882.[1] Lieutenant Galindo twice crossed it, once in six days, and once in five days, in 1887 and 1888, traversing a belt of 120 miles entirely without water. His description is almost identical with that of the worthy Minorite friar 550 years earlier. He could not fail to notice the extraordinary resemblance presented by the blown sand to the waves of a chopping sea. These sand billows alternate with bare expanses of black gravel, and with a phenomenon not previously described. This is a region of curious square-cut clay bluffs, believed by the natives to be the ruins of an ancient city, and called by them the Shehr-i-Lut, but consisting in reality of 'natural formations of hard clay, cut and carved by the fierce north-west wind into strange shapes, suggestive of walls and towers.' Lieutenant Galindo found everywhere beneath the sand a substratum of hard rock-salt some eight or nine inches below the surface, thus proving the saline character of the desert, and here and there patches of genuine *kavir*, the ground being mapped out in irregular polygons with dividing walls of solid salt, or studded with hard round white bubbles of the same material, like a lot of half-buried ostrich eggs, or covered with a sort of moss of delicate-looking salt spiculæ, standing up like needles an inch long, but strong as steel spikes. The worst part of this desert is its south-east corner between Neh and Bam, which is one of the most awful regions on the face of the earth.[2] Here the prevailing north-west winds have swept the sand together, and banked it up in huge mounds and hills, ever shifting and eddying. A fierce sun beats down upon the surface which is as fiery hot as incandescent metal; and almost always the *bad-i-sam* or simoom is blowing, 'so desiccated by its passage over hundreds of miles of burning desert, that if it overtakes man or animal its parched breath in a moment sucks every atom of moisture from his frame, and leaves him a withered and blackened mummy.'

This horrible desert extends as far south as Bam-Narmashir, for long the frontier district of Kerman. Its capital is Bam, 140 miles south-east of Kerman, now a big straggling village, situated on both banks of the Bam river, amid groves of date palms, and possessing only a mean bazaar. Bam,

Bam

[1] *Proceedings of the R.G.S.* (new series), vol. viii. pp. 141–3, 1886.

[2] *Vide* the excellent description of Elisée Reclus, *Universal Geography*, vol. ix. (South-west Asia), p. 94.

however, has filled its place in history; and its semi-ruined fort on an elevation outside the modern town was the *ark* or citadel of the former Bam, which even as late as the beginning of this century was the strongest fortified place in Persia. It owed its fame and strength originally to the Afghans who took it in 1719, and were not finally expelled till 1801. In 1795 it was the scene of the culminating tragedy in the brief but brilliant career of Lutf Ali Khan, who after escaping from Kerman fled here, only to be again betrayed to his ruthless enemy by a chief in whose fidelity he had trusted. His horse was hamstrung, just as he had sprung upon its back to fly; he himself fell to the ground, and was taken prisoner. The brutal eunuch put out his eyes with his own hands, and despatched him to a cruel death at Teheran. On the spot, in honour of the brave achievement, he erected a pyramid of the skulls of 600 of his rival's adherents, which was seen as late as 1810 by Sir H. Pottinger. The importance of Bam was considerable when it was a border town, exposed to the marauding fury of Afghan and Beluch; an ample tribute to whose bygone devastations is afforded by the numerous other ruined forts in the neighbourhood. Their fame and use have now perished; and with these words we may bid both to Bam and them good-bye.

Persian Beluchistan

In our southward advance we next come to the extensive and in parts still undefined province of Persian Beluchistan, which in its present shape is the creation of the last thirty years, and to a large extent owes its existence to the intervention and recognition of the British Government. We find ourselves standing accordingly on the threshold of politics, as well as engaged in the domain of topography. In no work that has yet been published is any succinct or satisfactory account supplied of Persian Beluchistan as a whole; nor have the materials been at the disposal of previous writers which could fit them for the task. Here, therefore, I feel that I am breaking new ground, the explorations and events of recent years enabling me to fill the gaps that were left by the admirable narratives of the members of the Boundary Commission in 1870. They were occupied in giving to Persian Beluchistan an official existence and a geographical meaning. We can scrutinise and describe the established fact.[1]

[1] I have compiled the following bibliography of Persian Beluchistan, omitting such works as relate only to Independent Beluchistan or Kelat:—Captain W. P. Grant (1809), *Journal of the Royal Asiatic Society*, vol. v. 1839; (Sir) H. Pottinger

Beluchistan comprises the Gedrosia, and parts of the Drangiana, of the ancients; and it is a significant illustration of the obscurity that has rarely lifted from these regions, and of the precarious political existence which till lately they enjoyed, that the words of Gibbon, written of a period 1700 years ago, were equally applicable to their condition up till the middle of the century still unexpired :—

Record of travel

> We can scarcely attribute to the Persian monarchy the sea coast of Gedrosia or Macran, which extends along the Indian Ocean from Cape Jask to Cape Gwadel. In the time of Alexander, and probably many ages afterwards, it was thinly inhabited by a savage people of ichthyophagi, who knew no arts, who acknowledged no master, and who were divided by inhospitable deserts from the rest of the world.[1]

It is an extraordinary, but nevertheless a true fact, that from the time of Alexander's march through Gedrosia, and the navigation of his admiral Nearchus along its shores, we have no record of the visit of a European to the interior of Beluchistan until 1809. In that year Sir J. Malcolm, who had just been appointed on his third mission to Persia, anxious to discover what overland routes there might exist from Persia to India, for the possible advance of French or Russian armies, deputed Captain Grant (who was afterwards murdered in Luristan) to report upon Western Beluchistan. In the following year, Pottinger and Christie volunteered for a similar mission in Eastern Beluchistan, and started forth disguised as the European servants of a Hindu horse-dealer of Bombay. Pottinger, having parted from Christie at Nushki, subsequently continued his journey through what is now Persian Beluchistan in

(1810), *Travels in Beloochistan*; Haji Abdun Nabi (1838–9), *Journal of the Asiatic Society of Bengal*, vol. xiii. 1844; Colonel E. C. Ross (1867), *Proceedings of the R.G.S.*, vol. xvi. pp. 139–219; Sir F. Goldsmid (1861–1871), *Correspondence on the Progress of Persia in Mekran and West Beluchistan* (Bombay Government), 1869; *Eastern Persia*, vol. i., Introduction; *Journal of the R.G.S.*, vol. xxxiii. p. 181, vol. xxxvii. p. 269, vol. xliii. p. 65; (Sir) O. St. John (1872), *Eastern Persia*, vol. i. pp. 18–117; Major B. Lovett (1870–1), *Proceedings of the R.G.S.*, vol. xvi. p. 219, *Journal*, vol. xlii. p. 202; Colonel Euan-Smith (1870–1), *Eastern Persia*, vol. i. pp. 143–225; E. A. Floyer (1876), *Unexplored Baluchistan*; A. W. Hughes, *The Country of Balochistan*, 1877; Major Mockler, *Journal of the Royal Asiatic Society* (new series), vol. ix. 1877, p. 121, vol. xi. 1879, p. 129; Mirza Mehdi Khan, *ibid.* vol. xi. p. 147; A. Gasteiger (1881), *Von Teheran nach Beludschistan.* The travels of Captain Jennings and Lieutenant Galindo (before quoted) have not been published.

[1] *Decline and Fall of the Roman Empire*, vol. i. cap. viii.

the disguise of a Mussulman pilgrim. To him we owe the first reliable information about the country. In 1831, Haji Abdun Nabi, an intelligent Afghan, was sent on a similar tour by Major Leach, the British Resident at Kelat. Next, in the year 1861, Sir F. Goldsmid appears upon the scene, charged with the investigations preliminary to the construction of a telegraphic wire along the Mekran coast from Kurrachi to Gwadur, extended later on to Jask; and for ten years he remains our authority, the surveys made and knowledge acquired by him during that period supplying the basis for the Boundary negotiations, and ultimate definition in 1870–1, to which I now turn.

History of Persian encroachment

In the first half of the eighteenth century, Beluchistan, i.e. the country between the Helmund and the Arabian Sea, and between Kerman and Sind, had, in common with its neighbours, fallen a prey to the resistless prestige of Nadir Shah. He constituted it a separate government or dependency, giving it the name which it has ever since borne, from the most numerically important of its tribes, and appointing Nasir Khan Brahui, Beglerbeg of all Beluchistan in 1739. As long as Nadir lived, therefore, the newly created province was undoubtedly subject to Persia. Upon his death, however, and in the general break-up that ensued, the astute satrap of Beluchistan at first paid allegiance to the Afghan sovereignty of Ahmed Shah Durani, as the most powerful neighbouring dominion; and later, upon its collapse, asserted his own independence. After his death in 1795 all pretence either of internal unity or external suzerainty vanished: the Beluchi chieftains, according to their strength, started business each on his own account; and the country was a prey to turbulent factions and tribal feuds, Persia being at that time too weak even to dream of interference. Such was the condition of affairs when Grant and Pottinger visited Beluchistan. There was no sign of Persian authority at the sea-ports; and the chiefs of Bampur, Geh, Bahu, and Serbaz were all independent. It appears to have been in the reign of Mohammed Shah (1834–1848), who, though utterly deficient in military instincts or capacity, had the most extravagant ambitions for conquest, and thought himself qualified to pose as a second Nadir Shah, that the Persian pretensions to authority in Beluchistan were first seriously revived. The chief of Bampur having made an incursion into the province of Kerman, a Persian army was sent to inflict condign punishment and to reduce the invader. This object was effected; but a second rebellion in 1849 was followed by a renewed Persian expedition, and by the capture of the capital, Bampur, which has ever since remained in Persian hands. Simultaneously the conquerors began to encroach upon Geh and Kasrkund. Later on, a very capable man, Ibrahim Khan, who had risen from a humble position entirely by his own talents, was appointed Persian Governor of Bam-Narmashir and Bampur, and steadily continuing a policy of aggression, began to weld the recovered territories into a compact dominion. Serbaz was occupied, being wrested from Asad Khan the powerful chief of Kharan, Bolidi reduced, and Kej threatened.

These conquests, however, testified to no more than the superior might of the victors, while they left a number of the bordering Beluchi states in a position of semi-dependence, which had no sanction save that dictated by fear. Sir F. Goldsmid in his first negotiations for the telegraph was naturally much puzzled and hampered by these unsettled conditions; and when in 1864 the question arose of extending the wires from Gwadur (up to which point they had been admittedly in the territories of Independent Beluchistan or of Muscat) to Jask, the evils resulting from the absence of any territorial definition became more acute, and the situations provocative of trouble more frequent. Moreover, in the interests of Kelat, a protected state of British India, at whose expense each successive Persian usurpation had been accomplished, a settlement was most desirable. Constant diplomatic friction ensued, until in 1869 a formal investigation was suggested by Lord Mayo, and in 1870 the appointment of a joint commission by Great Britain, Persia, and Kelat was agreed to at the instigation of the Shah. It was originally intended that this inquiry should follow that into the Seistan boundary, which had been simultaneously proposed and accepted; but the delays in starting the latter suggested to Sir F. Goldsmid, who had been named the British Commissioner, the advisability of saving time by proceeding with the inquiry in Mekran. Further difficulties and delays were encountered upon arrival in Teheran; and when, in January 1871, Goldsmid and his colleagues finally reached Bampur, he found himself compelled to act without instructions and upon his own discretion. Matters were further complicated by the miscarriage of plans, and by the impracticable obstinacy of Mirza Maasum Khan, the Persian

Boundary Commission, 1870

Commissioner, and of Ibrahim Khan of Bampur. Ultimately, finding any progress impossible, General Goldsmid retired to the sea coast, and acting upon the information which he had collected in 1861–64, and which had formed the basis of a report in which he recommended a frontier almost identical with that which was afterwards adopted, as well as upon the further knowledge collected by Major Lovett, who was sent out along parts of the proposed line, with instructions to make a map, he then returned to Teheran, and submitted an arbitral decision to the Shah. There was some squabbling about this, the king standing out for the inclusion of the small border district of Kohak, in Persian territory, whereas Goldsmid persisted in vindicating its independence ; but the line suggested by the latter was presently agreed to (September 1871), the question of Kohak being left over for future settlement—a Persian way of intimating that in the Shah's opinion possession was not nine-tenths only, but the whole of the law. The acceptance of General Goldsmid's award was undoubtedly a great compliment to that officer's integrity and discretion. Encouraged thereby, he set out upon the scarcely more thankful task of demarcating the Seistan frontier, as described in a previous chapter. Major St. John was, however, commissioned in 1872 to certify the frontier sketched by Lovett, which, though approximately determined, had not been actually followed or demarcated by the previous party. When this had been accomplished, the frontier, with the addition of the Kohak district, which Persia has declined to abandon, was settled as far north as Jalk, and has ever since been coloured as such upon maps. It runs from Gwetter Bay, a little to the east of that port, which was assigned to Persia, between the watershed of the Dasht and Dashtiari (or Kaju) rivers, then bends to the east, and finally follows the Mashkid or Mashkel river, flowing northwards into a desert *hamun* or swamp.

Persian nibbling

Persia at once took advantage of her newly recognised status to round off her possessions in these parts. Pishin had been annexed in 1870, and was confirmed to her by the award. As soon as St. John's back was turned, the Governor of Bampur settled the Kohak question by marching in and taking forcible possession. Isfandak, Murt, and Darida, in the same district, were seized in 1872. In the same year the Arabs of Muscat, who had held the port of Chahbar for nearly eighty years, were turned out by the Vekil-el-Mulk. Bashakerd remained virtually independent under Seif Allah Khan till 1874, but then also succumbed. More furtive aggressions have since been pursued in the north, particularly on the Mashkid river. But encroachment in these regions is more pardonable, if not more legitimate, since, as I have pointed out in my chapter on Seistan, no frontier has either been drawn or exists for the 200 miles of territory between the Kuh Malek-i-Siah, where Goldsmid's Seistan boundary terminated, and the confines of Jalk. Goldsmid was prepared to fill the hiatus; but nothing has ever been done; and sooner than trace on my map a purely hypothetical line which means nothing, I have preferred to leave the border in this region what it is, a blank.

Having thus narrated the history of the formation of a Persian province of Beluchistan, I pass to a short account of its features and people. The area of the province has been estimated at 60,000 square miles, as contrasted with the 80,000 of Kelat. In this extent of country may be encountered almost every variety both of scenery and climate. The Mekran Desert, composed of thin particles of wind-driven sand, is comparable, on a small scale, with those larger expanses which have been previously described. On the other hand, here are considerable rivers, great mountains, and in parts abundant cultivation. Rocks, rivers and trees combine in places to supply an entrancing landscape, but are succeeded by arid bluffs and naked ravines. On the coast the heat is sometimes terrific; and at Jalk in summer-time the exhausted gazelles are said to lie down on the plains, and suffer themselves to be captured by the hunter. In the mountain plateaux a cooler and most agreeable temperature is encountered; while eternal snow whitens the caps of the highest peaks. The prevailing tribe is that of the Beluchis, who give to the country its name. They claim to be Arabs by descent, of the Koreish tribe, and allege an ancestral migration at the end of the seventh century from the neighbourhood of Aleppo, whence their tradition represents them as having been expelled by the Khalif Yezid for taking the part of the martyred Husein. No record, however, exists of their journey, or of the people whom they found on their arrival; and from the evidence, both of their physiognomy and of their language, which is an Aryan or Aryanised tongue, akin to Pehlevi or old Persian, the hypothesis must be rejected

Country and people

in favour of a non-Arab genealogy.[1] Pottinger, on the other hand, attributed to them a Turkoman, i.e. Seljuk-Turkish descent. Though numerically the most important tribe in Beluchistan, they yield a moral and political ascendency to smaller, but more warlike, tribes of Kurds and Nushirwanis (themselves claiming descent from Nushirwan, the famous Sassanian king, but in reality deriving their name from a district so called, near Isfahan, whence they originally emigrated); while in parts, e.g. in Dashtiari, are a people, more obviously of Hindu lineage, whose ancestors, though they are unaware of it, came from Sind, and whose language contains many Hindu words. There is also throughout the country a considerable admixture of the African element, due to the large importation of slaves from Muscat and Zanzibar. Some of the faces present a thoroughly negro type. The ordinary Beluchi, of whom I have seen many, is not nearly so formidable a specimen of humanity as the Afghan, though like him he wears his long black hair in curls, frequently moistened with rancid butter. In parts of the country they are in a very backward and degraded condition, but little removed from primitive savagery. The majority are great thieves and liars, and are apt to round off every period with the swaggering assertion, 'I am a Beluch.' Politically they have but two feelings: an intense passion for tribal independence, with all its murderous accompaniments of blood feuds and border raids, and an outspoken dislike of the Persians, whom they call Gajars (pronounced not unlike the English word *cudgel*), the Beluch version of the name of the reigning dynasty. This hatred, to which every traveller without exception has testified, is accompanied by a corresponding respect for the British name and rule. The prestige of British power in India has spread far and wide through Beluchistan, and there is scarcely a native chieftain who has not appealed, or who is not willing, to

[1] Dr. Bellew (*Inquiry into the Ethnography of Afghanistan*, 1891) identifies the Beluchis with the Balaecha of the Chohan Rajput tribe who originally occupied the Nushki district. The tribe variously known as Kurush, Korish, Gorich, and Guraish, which is still widely extended on the Indus border, is the Royal Rajput Kerush, Keruch, or Kurech. When these tribes were converted to Islam, they changed their name to Koreish, and pretended an Arab descent in order to conceal the fact. Bellew, therefore, assigns to the Beluchis a Rajput or Indian pedigree, and explains their dialect as a Persianised Indian tongue. The Rinds, who are now spoken of as a branch of the Beluch stock, are in reality the tribe of which the Beluchis are a branch, the name being derived from the Rin or Run of Kuch, the Sanskrit *Aranya*, or 'waste.'

be taken under the protection of the British *raj*. Their religion is as uncouth and primitive as are their manners. They are nominally Mohammedans of the Sunni persuasion (whence an added contempt for the Persian Shiahs); but practically they know nothing of religion but the rival names and a few Arab formulæ, and have neither scriptures, ritual, nor mosques. A flavour of indigenous superstition is added by the worship of *pirs* or saints, whose shrines, bearing the same title, are looked upon as charms, particularly if a stone be added by the worshipper to the piled-up heap. In the Serbaz district is a sect, known as the Zikris, who have a belief of their own, and a holy book (which is little more or less than a modified Koran) alleged to have been miraculously communicated to them, much as the Mormon bible was to Joe Smith. They omit all mention of Mohammed from their prayers, but expect the ultimate reappearance of the Mahdi, who will rise out of the earth at the hill of Kuh-i-Murad (Mountain of Desire), at Turbat Kej, in Beluchistan proper, where are the headquarters of the sect, and where they perform their rites, sometimes alleged, though without apparent foundation, to be strange and incestuous. A Persian authority has calculated the population of Persian Beluchistan as 250,000; which is believed to be a fairly accurate estimate.

Villages and cultivation

The Beluch village is a cluster of squalid huts round a central keep or fort where the Khan resides. In the south, these huts are made of wattled palm leaves; in the north, where it is colder, of mud and sun-dried bricks. The chieftain's fort, which is typical of a primitive and semifeudal state of society, is a much more picturesque and ambitious structure than its Persian counterpart. In Persia, a fort is seldom more than a rectangular walled enclosure with flanking towers. In Beluchistan it has more the appearance, except for its material, of a mediæval European keep, having lower walled courts and a lofty central tower, with a watch turret above all. Fort and village are commonly placed in a valley or grove of date palms, whence the people derive their livelihood, at the same time that they diligently cultivate with wheat and barley the intervening spaces between the stems. The date palm which grows here, and of which those of Bampur in Persia, and of Panjgur in Kelati Beluchistan, enjoy the widest reputation, is, as is well known, impregnated by the pollen of the male tree, which is inserted in the flower of the female. The ears of one male tree are sufficient to fecundate about thirty females. There is also a variety of palmetto or dwarf palm, more strictly one of the aloe family, known as *pish*, which grows in rank abundance along the river beds. Its leaves are made use of for every variety of purpose by the Beluchis, particularly when soaked and beaten out into separate fibres for ropes and cordage, and are also twisted up into sandals, with which the peasants are shod. A dense growth of acacia, mimosa, and tamarisk jungle grows wherever there is water, a variety of the latter tree having a straight stem like a poplar.

Mekran

The country may be roughly divided into three sections or belts, distinguished by their different elevation and features. Of these the coast strip has always been known as Mekran.[1] The name is employed by the natives themselves of different parts of the country; but its strict application appears to be to the zone, some sixty to seventy miles in average width, which slopes upwards from the coast to the scarp of the main Beluch plateau, and varies in height from one to five hundred feet. This strip consists of a series of long parallel sand-chains, separating shallow valleys, for the most part bare and barren, until we come to the depression at the base of the border scarp, which is well-watered, and dotted with numerous villages and date groves. On the whole this belt has relatively not much to complain of in respect of water; Colonel Ross in his journey along the coast from Jask to Gwadur, a distance of 300 miles, having encountered eight considerable rivers. The water supply, however, is ill-regulated and unsteady; and during much of the year the river beds are empty, or contain only disconnected pools. Mekran might easily be made far more fertile than it is at present. There is splendid pasturage for camels, and sheep and goats are numerous; while date groves and grain crops spring into life at the very sight of water. In Mekran a different dialect is spoken

[1] Marco Polo (book iii. cap. xxx.) called it Kesmacoran, i.e. Kej-Mekran. The same double name has been applied to it by Ibn Batutah, Sidi Ali, Sherif-ed-Din, and P. della Valle. The name Mekran has been commonly, but erroneously, derived from Mahi Khoran, i.e. the fish-eaters, or *ichthyophagi*, which was the title given to the inhabitants of the Beluchi coast-fringe by Arrian. But the word is a Dravidian name, and appears as Makara in the *Brhat Sanhita* of Varaha Mihira in a list of the tribes contiguous to India on the west. It is also the Μακαρήνη of Stephen of Byzantium, and the Makuran of Tabari and Moses of Chorene. Even were it not a Dravidian name, in no old Aryan dialect could it signify fish-eaters.

from Northern Beluchistan, and is supposed to be a *patois* of Persian intermingled with Indian words, or *vice versa*.

Above Mekran and along the entire extent of Beluchistan, both Persian and Kelati, extends the elevated area, 3,000 to 4,000 feet in height, of what has been designated the Beluch plateau. North of the scarp, which constitutes the water parting, the rivers—as, for instance, the Bampur and Mashkid—flow away from the sea, and are ultimately lost in large *hamuns* or swamps, which at different periods of the year present the appearance of vast lagoons and shallow marshes.

The Beluch plateau

Merging on the north in the plateau of Persian Beluchistan is the mountain region of Serhad, in reality tne southern prolongation of the great elevated mass forming the highlands of Khorasan. This remote and inaccessible district has long baffled the zeal of European explorers, Pottinger and St. John having both tried in vain to enter it. At length in 1885 Captain R. H. Jennings, an officer deputed by the Indian Government, was the first to penetrate its mysteries, and to give to it an existence on the map. Its local name is, not inappropriately, Yaghistan, i.e. the country of the Yaghis, or outlaws of Beluchistan, Afghanistan, and Seistan. He reported it to consist of a mountain plateau, from 3,500 to 6,000 feet in height, surrounded by higher ranges, beyond which are deserts on the north-east and west, while on the south are the districts of Bampur and Dizak. It contains two of the *hamuns* or swamps which I have mentioned, and, what is more remarkable, an active volcano with three craters 12,681 feet in height. This extraordinary mountain, at a distance of 200 miles from the coast, might appear to violate the commonly accepted theory of a subtle connection between volcanoes and the sea, unless, which is probable, we suppose it to have stood upon the southern shore of the great central sea of prehistoric Iran. It is called the Kuh-i-Tuftan, and also the Kuh-i-Naushada, or mountain of sal ammoniac, that substance being obtained from its sides. To the south-east between Bampur and Bam is another snow-crowned peak, the Kuh-i-Basman, which is an extinct volcano, and rises in splendid isolation from the desert. Captain Jennings found Serhad to be inhabited by Beluchi, Kurd, and Brahui tribes, with an alleged total of 13,500 families.[1] All were Sunnis, all

Serhad

[1] This is, of course, a mistake. So, at the other extreme, is Mirza Mehdi Khan's estimate of 1,425 families.

detested the Persians, all subsisted upon rapine; and the Persian authority amounted to little more than a prudent recognition of local chieftains and an occasional armed expedition for the collection of revenue. Serhad produces an unlimited supply of sheep and goats, and grows an immense amount of tamarisk, camel-thorn, and asafœtida. Its principal place, and indeed the only place which has hitherto figured on the map, is Washt, a large village inhabited by Kurds.

A few of the remaining districts or subdivisions of the province are deserving of mention. Dizak in the east is administered by a deputy of the Governor of Bampur. It includes Kohak, the border district that was forcibly appropriated by the Persians in 1873, and Jalk, the extreme possession of Persia, as officially certified, on the north-east. Jalk, i.e. the 'Desolate,' consists of a number of villages, with a total population of 2,500 to 3,000, and of nine picturesque loop-holed forts in a big date grove filling the mouth of a ravine for a distance of about four miles. The principal, or Miri fort, was formerly destroyed by a detachment of Nadir Shah's army; but, though in a state of dilapidation, its walls are still fifty feet high, and it is impregnable against Beluchi attack. In the Jalk palm groves are a number of ancient brick-domed structures of various shapes from twenty to sixty feet in height, which are supposed to be tombs, and are locally attributed to a race of Kafirs many hundred years ago.

Dizak

The district of Serbaz, to the north of Chahbar and Gwetter[1] has been more frequently visited by Europeans, inasmuch as through it run the main routes from the sea to Bampur. It contains Kasrkund, the principal town and seat of government of Persian Mekran.

Serbaz

Between Serbaz and Bam-Narmashir, which I have spoken of earlier as the frontier province of Kerman, is the considerable district of Bampur,[2] whose chief town, bearing the same name, is the capital of the Governor of Persian Beluchistan, who is himself subordinate to the Prince Governor of Kerman. The chief feature of Bampur is a large, well-built mud

Bampur

[1] For these ports, I refer my readers to a future chapter on the Persian Gulf.

[2] *Pur* is the termination, signifying 'town' (Sanskrit *pura*), so common in Indian names of places, e.g. Cawnpore, Manipur. It, or its neighbour Pahura, is supposed to be the Ποῦρα, the capital of Gedrosia, through which Alexander marched on his way back from India in 324 B.C.

fort, crowning an elevation about 100 feet in height, three miles north of the Bampur river, whose waters, regulated by dykes, are distributed over the grain-producing lands, which are Crown property, of the surrounding villages. A garrison is kept here of fifty artillery with six guns, as well as three hundred regular infantry and fifty cavalry. There is also a permanent Beluch militia five hundred strong in the neighbourhood. The Persians have lately built a large new fort at Pahura (where also is a lofty old fort), about fourteen miles to the east of Bampur. It covers a square of 200 yards, has four towers, and can accommodate 1,000 men.

To the south-east of Bampur, and north of Jask, is the little known and almost unexplored region of Bashakerd, whose principal town is Anguhran. It is a backward and impracticable region, consisting of a labyrinth of rugged hills, intersected by huge rocky watercourses, and containing a scanty population of half-naked savages, with a marked infusion of negro blood. In the region between Jask and Bint, Persian authority is less firmly established than on the eastern border; and the petty chieftains in this neighbourhood are practically left alone so long as a moderate revenue is paid into the royal exchequer.

Bashakerd

I have described Persian Beluchistan as it now exists in the hands of its Persian masters. It cannot be contended that their rule has been a success. On the contrary, it has been attended with oppression, corruption, and consequent revolt. I have frequently depicted the Persian petty governor or official as one of the most undesirable and flagitious of the human race; and with a poor, unarmed population, such as they have encountered in Beluchistan, the members of his class have found ample scope for all their talents. Taxes have been collected twice over at the point of the bayonet; local chiefs have been arrested or removed; the people have been driven from their homes. The consequence is that agriculture has fallen into decay, the irrigation system has broken down, and the miserable peasants have flocked out of the country in hundreds to India or Muscat. Owing to the neglect and collapse of the dykes on all the smaller rivers, whereby their waters were held up and diffused in canals over the land, the channels of the main rivers have widened to an enormous extent, the water furrowing an aimless course down their sandy beds. Thus the Dasht, which in 1876 was 357 yards in width, in 1889 was 860; the Rapch or Rabj, which in 1869 was 220

Persian rule

yards across, in 1889 was 616. At Bampur, the exasperation aroused by the Persian Governor, one Abul Fath Khan, a notable specimen of his breed, was so great that, in June 1889, the people arose, and besieged him in his fort; nor was the revolt allayed till a more politic successor had appeared upon the scene, and sent the delinquent in chains to Kerman. The new Governor, Jemal-ed-Din Khan, is a strong man, and has ruled well. The discontent is now subsiding, and the poor Beluchis, having made their protest, will probably relapse into the stagnant acquiescence that is begotten by the fearful sight of breech-loaders and mountain-guns.

Britain across the border

The spectacle that may be witnessed across the border is not one that is calculated to increase their contentment with Persian rule, while it augments the respect in which they have long held the British name. There, their brethren in Independent or Kelati Beluchistan, under the ægis of British protection, are living in comparative security and quietude, in the enjoyment of a liberty which their own violence or mutiny alone can endanger. The recent journey of Sir R. Sandeman,[1] the capable administrator of British Beluchistan, in the winter of 1890–91, from Kurrachi *viâ* Bela to Panjgur, the border state adjoining the Persian Kohak, while projected in order to reopen the old *kafilah* route between Sind and Seistan, has had the further effect of confirming the Beluchi chieftains, from the Khan of Kelat downwards, in their loyalty to the British Crown. A detachment of Beluchi levies keeps the peace in Panjgur; the entire state of Beluchistan may be said to be passing as placidly under British rule as has Bokhara under that of her northern rival; and the real neighbour of Persia on the south-east is not the Khan of Kharan. or of Kej, or even of Kelat, but the British *raj* who holds the keys of empire at Calcutta.

Routes in the Eastern Provinces.[2]

I. Eastern-Central Provinces.

Kashan to Yezd.—Sergeant Gibbons (1831), *Journal of the R.G.S.*, vol. xi.; A. Petermann (1860), *Reisen im Orient*, vol. ii. pp. 210-220.

---

[1] I grieve to say that this excellent frontier officer has, just when starting upon a second tour in South Beluchistan, died at Lus Bela (Jan. 1892). An hour before hearing by telegram of his death, I received a long and enthusiastic letter from him about his frontier policy, of which I was a cordial advocate.

[2] In this table *ibid.* signifies the work by the same writer before mentioned.

Isfahan to Yezd (*viâ* Gulnabad, Nau Gumbaz, and Akda).—K. Abbott (1849), *Journal of the R.G.S.*, vol. xxv. pp. 10–20; Sir F. Goldsmid (1865), *Telegraph and Travel*, pp. 563–9; Colonel Euan-Smith (1870), *Eastern Persia*, vol. i. pp. 164–173; E. Floyer (1876), *Unexplored Beluchistan*, cap. xv.; E. Stack (1881), *Six Months in Persia*, vol. ii. cap. i.

Dehbid to Yezd (*viâ* Abarguh and Taft).—Colonel Trézel (1807); (Sir) C. MacGregor (1875), *Journey through Khorasan*, vol. i. cap. iii.

Shiraz to Yezd (*viâ* Zerghun, Seidun, Mehrabad, and Abarguh).—A. Dupré (1808), *Voyage en Perse*, vol. ii. cap. xli.

Yezdikhast to Kerman.—Sergeant Gibbons (1831), *ibid.*

Yezd to Kerman (*viâ* Kermanshahan, Anar, and Bahramabad).—K. Abbott (1849), *ibid.*, pp. 21–9; Sir F. Goldsmid (1866), *ibid.*, pp. 573–580; Colonel Euan-Smith (1870), *ibid.*, pp. 176–183; E. Floyer (1876), *ibid.*, cap. xiv.; E. Stack (1881), *ibid.*, vol. i.

Yezd to Kabul.—M. A'Court (1826), *Narrative of Journey.*

Yezd to Herat (*viâ* Khaf).—Captain Christie (1810), Appendix to Pottinger's *Travels in Beloochistan.*

Yezd to Meshed.—Captain Truilhier (1807), *Mémoire*, par M. Daussy.

Yezd to Tabbas (*viâ* Sukand, Pusht-i-Badan, Khur, and Mehrjan).—(Sir) C. MacGregor (1875), *ibid.*, vol. i. pp. 81–121; Colonel C. E. Stewart (1880), *Proceedings of the R.G.S.* (new series), vol. iii.

Yezd to Semnan (*viâ* Anarek).—Lieutenant H. B. Vaughan (1888), *Proceedings of the R.G.S.* (new series), vol. xii.

Kerman to Shiraz. 1. (*viâ* Shehr-i-Babek and Arsinjan).—(Sir) H. Pottinger (1810), *ibid.*, cap. xvii. 2. (*viâ* Saidabad and Niriz)—(Sir) O. St. John (1872), *Eastern Persia*, vol. i. pp. 92–111.

Shiraz to Bam (*viâ* Niriz, Saidabad, Ahmedi, and Rudbar).—K. Abbott (1850), *ibid.*, pp. 29–78.

Bam to Seistan.—Colonel Euan-Smith (1872), *ibid.*, pp. 241–255.

Kerman to Bampur (*viâ* Bam and Regan).—(Sir) H. Pottinger (1810), *ibid.*, caps. xii.–xv.; Sir F. Goldsmid (1866), *ibid.*, pp. 590–605; Colonel Euan-Smith (1871), *ibid.*, pp. 191–206; (Sir) O. St. John (1872), *ibid.*, pp. 79–91.

Kerman to Birjand.—J. P. Ferrier (1845), *Caravan Journeys*, p. 440.

Kerman to Neh.—N. de Khanikoff (1859), *Mémoire*, pp. 156–186.

Kerman to Bunder Abbas. 1. (*viâ* Baft and Urzu); 2. (*viâ* Rudbar and Rahbur).—A. H. Schindler (1879), *Zeit. der Gesell. für Erd. zu Berlin*, 1881, pp. 307–366.

Lingah to Yezd (*viâ* Bastak and Forg).—Lieutenant H. B. Vaughan (1888), *ibid.*

II. *Persian Beluchistan.*

Bunder Abbas to Bam.—Sir F. Goldsmid (1872), *Journal of the R.G.S.*, vol. xlvii. p. 188; Colonel Euan-Smith, *ibid.*, pp. 227–240.

Jask to Bunder Abbas.—Captain W. P. Grant (1809), *Journal of the Royal Asiatic Society*, vol. v., 1839.

Jask to Kerman (*viâ* Anguhran, Manujan, Kahnu, and Raian).—E. Floyer (1876), *ibid.*, caps. vii.–xii.

Jask to Bampur. 1. (*viâ* Geh).—Captain W. P. Grant (1809), *ibid.* 2. (*viâ* Bint and Fanoch Pass).—E. Floyer (1876), *ibid.*, pp. 4–78, and *Journal of the R.G.S.*, vol. xlvii. p. 188.

Jask to Gwadur (*viâ* Chahbar).—Colonel E. C. Ross (1867), *Proceedings of the R.G.S.*, vol. xvi. p. 139.

CHAHBAR TO GEH.—Captain W. P. Grant (1809), *ibid.*

CHAHBAR TO BAMPUR.—Sir F. Goldsmid (1866), *Telegraph and Travel*, pp. 605–616

GWETTER TO BAMPUR (*viâ* Kasrkund).—Captain W. P. Grant (1809), *ibid.*

GWADUR TO BAMPUR (*viâ* Chirak and Kasrkund).—Major B. Lovett (1871), *Eastern Persia*, vol. i. pp. 123–131.

GWADUR TO JALK (*viâ* Pishin).—(Sir) O. St. John (1872), *ibid.*, pp. 18–63.

BAMPUR TO PISHIN (*viâ* Serbaz).—Major B. Lovett (1871), *ibid.*, pp. 131–133; Colonel Euan-Smith (1871), *ibid.*, pp. 212–223.

JALK TO BAMPUR.—(Sir) O. St. John (1872), *ibid.*, pp. 64–78.

CHAPTER XXIV

THE SOUTH-WESTERN PROVINCES

Medus infestus sibi luctuosis
Dissidet armis.

HORACE, *Carm.* iii. 8.

The Persian, Assyrian, and Babylonian monarchies might be gained in a morning with faith and the flourish of a sabre.

B. DISRAELI, *Tancred.*

Nomad life

THE physical conformation of Persia, presenting as it does the extreme vicissitudes of climate, corresponding with those of altitude, from the enervating heat of the coast plains to the rigour of mountain heights rarely left by the snow; the racial features and archaic habits of many of its peoples; and the unsettled character of its government, are responsible for a phenomenon that has almost disappeared from the organisation of other states upon which civilisation has in any degree laid its crystallising finger. In countries with which the ordinary Englishman is familiar, be it as native, or colonist, or resident, population, attracted by agriculture or congested by industry, is settled, and for the most part sedentary, movement to and fro being limited to the more or less permanent migrations of families, in deference to the exigencies of comfort, of livelihood, or of space. An alternative residence, according to the season of year, is the privilege of wealth and the mark of luxury. In Persia, on the other hand, where population is sparse, where the cultivable area is relatively small, and where great spaces are occupied by bleak mountain districts, remote from the control of government, and adapted to pastoral rather than agricultural pursuits, the immemorial prescription of the East still survives; the tribes move in compact detachments according to the period of the year, carrying with them their entire household furniture and wealth, and exchanging the lowland valleys or riverain plains, which they have occupied during the winter, for the higher and cooler crests, where life is supportable in the summer heats. *Kishlak* (from *kish*, i.e.

winter), and *yeilak* (from *yil*, i.e. year), are Turkish words employed for the tribal haunts at the two periods. The Persian words *garmsir* (warm region) and *sardsir* (cold region) cover a similar application. At the division of the seasons the nomads may be encountered upon the march, their black goats'-hair tents, as easily pitched as struck, dotting the slopes, and thousands of sheep and goats heralding or encumbering the column. Even at other times in almost every province of Persia, but particularly in those which I now approach, the traveller off the beaten track will alight upon their encampments, and may study in nineteenth century duplicate the pastoral economy of the books of Genesis or Job.

A perusal of the pages of this work will have shown that the population of Persia is in no sense of a homogeneous description. Placed as her territories have been in the track of armies, they have been repeatedly overrun, and at times held in long-enduring pawn. As the human tide has ebbed and flowed, it has deposited large portions of its burden upon Persian soil; and the mere spectacle of a country, owning an Iranian majority among its people, an Arabian religion, and a Turkish ruling dynasty, is enough to indicate a history of storm. It is from the foreign elements thus imported into Persia, and there, so to speak, precipitated and left, that the nomad portion of her present population is chiefly, though not wholly, derived.

Foreign elements

Roughly speaking, the tribes of Persia[1] are susceptible of a fourfold classification—Turks (i.e. offshoots of the great Turki or Turkoman or Tartar stock, not to be confused with the Osmanli branch of the same root); Arabs, Beluchis, and a great nameless class, sometimes described as Leks, by those who defend their common Iranian origin, more commonly known by the names of their various constituent elements, the principal of which are the Kurds and Lurs, with the Feilis, Bakhtiaris, Mamasennis, etc., as sub-divisions of the latter title. In a greater or less

Tribes of Persia

[1] Of the few existing accounts of the tribes of Persia, I can only cite the following as in the least satisfactory: Sir J. Malcolm (1800–10), *History*, vol. ii. cap. xxiii.; M. Jouannin in Dupré's *Voyage en Perse* (1808); J. P. Morier (1814–15), *Journal of the R.G.S.*, vol. vii. pp. 230–42; C. Ritter (1838–40), *Die Erdkunde von Asien*, vol. vi.; Sir J. Sheil (1840–50), Note to Lady Sheil's *Glimpses of Life*; Comte J. de Rochechouart (1865), *Souvenirs*, cap. iv.; and F. Spiegel, *Eranische Alterthumskunde*, vol. i. Ritter's is the most comprehensive account, and corresponds more nearly than the others to the *status quo*.

degree all these tribes contain a settled population, which in the case of the Turks constitutes an enormously preponderant majority, in that of the Arabs and Beluchis a decided majority, in that of the Kurds and Lurs a decided minority. The settled peoples are known as *shehr-nishins* or *deh-nishins*, i.e. dwellers in cities or villages; the nomads as *sahra-nishins*, i.e. dwellers in the open country. All nomads may further be grouped under the designation *Iliat*, a Turkish word, which is the plural of *Il*, a family or clan. Of the entire population of Persia it has been assumed that one quarter, or over 2,000,000, are in the nomadic state.[1]

Turks

Among the Turkish tribes of Persia, which are most numerous in the north and north-west, the best known are the Kajars (the tribe of the Shah), the Afshars (the tribe of Nadir Shah), the Karaguzlus of Hamadan, the Shah Sevens of Ardebil[2] (supplying the Royal Bodyguard), the Turkomans of the Gurgan and Atrek valleys, and the Kashkai hordes of Fars and Laristan. Of these the last three contain the only remaining nomad elements, changing their pastures according to the season of the year. The Goklan and Yomut Turkomans have been dealt with in Vol. I. and the Kashkais in Chapter XX.

Arabs, Kurds, etc.

Of the Arab tribes, I have previously mentioned some sections, localised in the eastern districts of Khorasan. There are also many Persianised Arab tribes both in the neighbourhood of Teheran and along the coast-fringe of the Gulf. The Kurds I have already described, both on the north-east and north-west frontiers. Similarly the Beluchis, who are to be found in Seistan, Persian Beluchistan, and on the Gulf fringe, have been dealt with in Chapter XXIII. The most conspicuous illustrations, however, of both the second and the third class, above mentioned,

[1] It is impossible to arrive at any scientific estimate of the numbers of the nomad population. No census or register of births is kept; the scale of military contribution affords no clue; and an approximate calculation is only arrived at by taking the number of the families, which are roughly ascertained for revenue purposes by the chiefs. Equally difficult is it to explore their past history. The nomad tribes appear never to have developed a folk-lore, or produced a book, or harboured an historian. Such historical details as are contained in this chapter have been laboriously gleaned from a wide variety of sources, partly written, partly oral.

[2] The Shah Sevens or King-lovers were so called by Shah Abbas the Great, who, in order to break the excessive power of the seven Kizilbash, or Red-Head tribes, who had raised Ismail to the throne, constituted a new tribe of his own supporters.

occur in the provinces to which my survey of the Persian dominions has now brought me. Here are to be found at once the most interesting, the most original, and the least generally known, of the subjects of the Shah.

General characteristics

Before I proceed to their examination, let me premise that nomad life everywhere in Persia (and, indeed, wherever I have seen it, the Bedouin of Arabia and the Turkoman of the Desert presenting much the same characteristics) exhibits certain common features which are predicable of it, independently of race and politics. These are features, firstly, of organisation, and secondly, of character. Tribal and clan feeling is very strong. A patriarchal form of government, i.e. deference to elders or headmen, successively of the household or tent, of the village or camp, of the clan, and of the tribe, is universal. Obedience and loyalty are observed within these limits, but not outside them. Taxation is only successfully exacted by a Government that employs this machinery; and the intrusion of a civil revenue officer would be a perilous experiment. A military contribution is commonly exacted by the State, its selection and equipment being left to the chief. The semi-independence thus created renders the nomad tribes very sensitive of restraint and prone to rebellion, the more so as Government interference has never in Persia presented itself to them except in the guise of mean and odious interference with their cherished privileges, of ready-lipped perfidy, or of heartless extortion. Undeniable virtues of character are balanced in them by frank and unrepented vices. They are hospitable, domestic, simple-minded, innocent of the foul debaucheries of the city Persian. On the other hand, they are rough, ignorant, aud sometimes fierce, they glory in plunder,[1] and are, in many cases, adroit thieves. Little practical religion is known to them but that of blood, which vents itself in family feuds, pursued with unslaked ferocity till

[1] Many amusing stories are related of the hereditary taste for plunder of the nomad Asiatic tribes. Malcolm took one of their chiefs to India in 1801, and asked him what he thought of Calcutta. His eyes glistened, and he replied, 'What a noble place to plunder!' This reminds one of the anecdote of the Frenchman, who, when conducted to the polished granite tomb-chamber in the heart of the Great Pyramid, exclaimed, 'Quel joli emplacement pour un billard!' A similar story is related of an Uzbeg chief, who, hearing Begi Jan of Bokhara dilate upon the sweets of Paradise, asked him if there was any *chapau*, or raiding, there. 'No,' was the answer. 'Ah, then,' he said, 'Paradise won't do for me.'

whole households have sometimes been extirpated. The sympathetic and not too squeamish visitor will like them. They will cause the cross-grained or sensitive to blaspheme.

Persian policy

I have spoken of the attitude towards them of the State, and I may here summarise what will appear over and over again in these pages, in the statement that nowhere have the baser and more contemptible aspects of Persian government been so noticeable or so calamitous as here. The intestine warfare of the last century led Fath Ali Shah, who, though timid, was sufficiently astute, to see that the power of the sovereign could only be effectively maintained in Persia by one of two means—unquestioned military superiority on the part of the monarch, which it required a Nadir, or, in a less degree, an Agha Mohammed, to effect—or a policy of dissension among the tribes themselves. He sedulously devoted himself to the latter object, and has been followed therein by his successors. The very feuds of which I have spoken, and by which members even of the same tribe are distracted, have been made the instruments of State policy. One tribe has been pitted against another tribe, one chief against another chief; and thus the animosities of individuals or communities have served the purpose while relieving the purse of the sovereign. At the same time that the tribes have been incited to mutual destruction, their leaders have been torn from their homes and, while nominally detained as hostages, have been subjected to the corrupt and demoralising influences of the capital. Their tenure of office and their restoration to their people have been dependent upon their willingness to serve as tools of the policy and conduits to the exchequer of a corrupt administration. The only chieftains with any shadow of real power now left in Persia are the Khan of Kuchan, the Amir of Kain, and the Vali of Pusht-i-Kuh. Simultaneously, the armament of the tribes has been discouraged; the poverty of the chieftains has brought with it a decline of the horse-breeding establishments for which they were once famous; and where the Iliats of Persia formerly constituted her armed strength on the battlefield, they are now disabled, disloyal, and broken. *Divide et impera* may be a good enough motto for the *imperator*, but it is a fatal one as applied to his victims; and the Kajar kings will have the mischievous distinction in history of having sapped and decimated the manhood of their country.

In the sixteenth chapter of this work I brought my survey of the north-western and western provinces of Persia down to the parallels of Kermanshah and Hamadan, through which towns runs the main caravan track from Baghdad to Teheran. There I left the Kurds of the Turco-Persian borderland in occupation at once of the surrounding territory and of my pages. A little to the south of Kermanshah they adjoin and are merged in the cognate, or, at least, not alien, tribes of Lurs, who give their name to the obscure and mountainous province of Luristan. This territorial title has a two-fold signification, according as it is applied to the entire country inhabited by the tribes collectively known as Lurs, or to the Persian province so called, which is administered by a governor at Khorremabad. In the former sense, Luristan may be said to comprise the entire belt of mountainous country, stretching from the plains of the Tigris and the frontier-mountains on the west to the borders of Isfahan and Fars on the east, and from the districts of Kermanshah and Hamadan on the north to the plains of Arabistan on the south. The principal tribes inhabiting these mountain ranges are severally known as the Feili, Bakhtiari, Kuhgelu, and Mamasenni—all of which fall strictly under the generic classification of Lurs, although the title is disowned or has been abandoned by some of their number. In its restricted or administrative sense, in which I shall here use it, Luristan is the province inhabited in the main by the first of the above sub-divisions, viz. the Feili Lurs. Their country is known as Lur-i-Kuchik, or Lesser Luristan, and is roughly divided by the Ab-i-Diz, or River of Dizful, from Lur-i-Buzurg, or Greater Luristan, which, being peopled by the Bakhtiari tribes, who possess characteristics and interests apart, has come to be popularly known as Bakhtiari Land. The classification that I shall follow will, therefore, be threefold, relating successively to Lur-i-Kuchik, or the land of the Feili Lurs, to Bakhtiari Land, and to the districts of the remaining Lur tribes. This done, I shall pass to the province of Khuzistan, or Arabistan, which adjoins the administrative Luristan on the south, including some of the more southerly Lurs within its borders, and stretches to the Tigris Delta and the Persian Gulf.

Province of Luristan

Who the Lurs are and whence they came is one of the unsolved and insoluble riddles of history. A people without a history, a literature, or even a tradition, presents a phenomenon in face of which science stands abashed. Fifty years ago Rawlinson described them as an 'unknown and interesting people';

Origin of the Lurs

and although in these pages will be presented more aids to knowledge than can elsewhere be found, yet I cannot profess to lift the curtain of an inscrutable past. Are they Turks? Are they Persians? Are they Semites? All three hypotheses have been urged. They appear to belong to the same ethnical group as the Kurds, their neighbours on the north; nor does their language, which is a dialect of Persian, differ materially from the Kurdish tongue.[1] On the other hand, they themselves consider it an insult to be confounded with the Kurds, whom they call Leks; and the majority of writers have agreed in regarding them as the veritable relics of the old Aryan or Iranian stock, who preceded Arabs, Turks, and Tartars in the land. Rawlinson says that their language is descended from the old Farsi, which was coæval with, but distinct from, the Pehlevi tongue in the days of the Sassanian kings. Whilst, however, we may accept this as the most probable hypothesis, and may even be led thereby to regard with heightened interest these last survivals of an illustrious stock, we are not compelled to endorse the conjectural connection of Bakhtiari with Bactria, which has been propounded by some writers,[2] or to localise their ancestral home. It is sufficient to believe that they are Aryans by descent, and to know that they have lived for centuries in their present mountains. The word Feili means a rebel, while the word Lur is commonly applied as a synonym for a boor by the modern Persians, who detest the Lurs almost as cordially as they are detested by them.

Of the numbers of the Lurs it is scarcely possible to speak with greater confidence. In 1836 Rawlinson gave the numbers of the Feili Lurs and their dependencies as 56,000 families; in 1843 Layard returned them as 49,000 families. In the same years respectively, Rawlinson gave the totals of the Bakhtiaris and their dependencies as 28,000 families, Layard as 37,700 families. A calculation made in 1881 fixed the total of persons as follows: Feilis and dependencies 210,000; Bakhtiaris and dependencies, 170,000; Kuhgelus, etc., 41,000; grand total of Lurs, 421,000. I am disposed to think that this is an exaggerated census;

Numbers

[1] Rich, the traveller in Kurdistan, declared that the Bakhtiaris were Kurds (*Narrative*, etc., vol. i. p. 130).

[2] Some have gone so far as to base on this resemblance the assertion that the Bakhtiari are the relics of one of the Greek colonies left by Alexander in Asia, an hypothesis for which the further support is claimed of a similarity in the Greek and Bakhtiari national dances.

although the prevalence of polygamy among the tribes, and the large families reported by recent travellers, may be held to justify the opposite opinion.

The Feilis

Lur-i-Kuchik, or Lesser Luristan, embraces the region between Dizful on the south, and the confines of Kermanshah on the north, and between the Ab-i-Diz on the east, and the Turkish frontier on the west. It is subdivided into two sections called respectively Pish-Kuh, i.e. Before the Mountains, or Cismontane Luristan, and Pusht-i-Kuh, i.e. Behind the Mountains, or Transmontane Luristan, the dividing ridge being that section of the Zagros range which is locally known as the Kebir Kuh. Till the accession of the Kajar dynasty there was no political distinction between the two; but Pish-Kuh was taken away by Agha Mohammed Shah from the Vali of Luristan, who has ever since been forced to content himself with Pusht-i-Kuh. Hence it arises that the Feili nomenclature, which was formerly applied to the whole of Lur-i-Kuchik, has become restricted in popular usage to the Pusht-i-Kuh, the Feilis proper constituting the bulk of the population in the latter district.

Pish-Kuh

Pish-Kuh, which is the eastern portion of the Luristan province, has for its boundaries Kermanshah on the north, the Ab-i-Diz and the Bakhtiari country on the east and south, and the River Kerkhah on the west. It differs both in political organisation and in the character of its people from Pusht-i-Kuh. For since the partition before mentioned, it has remained under the control of a Persian Governor, instead of a native chief, the *tushmals* or petty chieftains (lit. heads of the house) being subordinate and answerable to him; whilst, owing to the proximity of large towns, such as Kermanshah, Khorremabad, and Burujird, to the accessibility of the district, and to the neighbourhood of the electric telegraph, its population has been much more exposed to the influence of Government, and has consequently become more sedentary than is the case in the mountain fastnesses further to the west. The two main tribal divisions of Pish-Kuh are the Gulek and Selewerzi; and these are subdivided respectively into the Amala and Bala Giriwa, and the Sila Sila and Dilfan tribes, which in Rawlinson's and Layard's time were, as now, the principal names. The subheadings or clans of these tribes have, however, changed very much since those days, having in some cases disappeared, and in others changed their names; so that it is useless for me to reproduce or refer to the old lists.[1] Among the branches of the Bala Giriwa, however, the Dirikwand have retained their old pre-eminence for turbulence and brigandage. They are now under one Mir Haji Khan, who is at chronic enmity with his nephew Mir Namdar Khan. Both are great robbers, and when not exercising their predatory inclinations at each other's expense, are apt to vent them upon travellers by the Dizful-Khorremabad road, of the greater part of which, on the principle, I imagine, of 'set a thief to catch a thief,' they have been placed in charge by the government.[2] For this service they are supposed to receive a subsidy from the latter; but as this is rarely, if ever, paid, an apologist for their excesses may find therein some excuse.

I have spoken of Khorremabad as the present seat of government in Luristan; a distinction which the central position of the town

Khorremabad

and its physical advantages have secured to it since the Middle Ages.[3] A solitary rock rises suddenly in the jaws of a pass, opening upon a rich plain. At its foot lies the modern town, which does not contain more than 2,000 inhabitants. Its summit is crowned by the Bala Hissar or ruined castle of the Atabegs, which stands up with gloomy outline of walls and towers like some robber stronghold of the Rhine. Here these all-but-independent rulers of a bygone age lived in lordly style, the castle being supplied with water by a deep shaft sunk in the rock to a magnificent spring below. Within the shell of the old fort Mohammed Ali Mirza, the eldest son of Fath Ali Shah, and governor of Luristan, built himself a palace, which is now also in a state of decay. The present governor lives in an edifice at the foot of the rock. The Khorremabad river, spanned by a long bridge of twenty-eight arches, flows below. On the opposite bank, at a little distance, lie the ruins of the Atabegs' city, of which a quadrangular

[1] The latest list that I have seen of the Pish-Kuh tribes is that of A. H. Schindler (1878), *Zeit. d. Gesell. f. Erd. z. Berlin*, vol. xiv. p. 82. They then numbered, according to official documents, 39,550 families.

[2] This is a favourite plan with the Persians. A few years ago there was a noted robber chief of the Hamawand tribe, named Jan Mir Khan, who was the terror of the frontier district near Kasr-i-Shirin. Unable to coerce him into good behaviour, the Persians, in 1886, made him guardian of the frontier, with a salary of 3,000 *tomans*. As he continued his depredations, he was invited to a friendly interview with an emissary from Teheran—another well-recognised Persian device—and was treacherously seized and slain.

[3] It is thought to have been the Samha of the Middle Ages. The castle was called Diz-i-Siah.

brick tower with a Naskh inscription, bearing the date 1123 A.D., is a speaking memorial. A battalion of 400 shabby Lurs, called out annually in the spring, is stationed here as a local garrison. The filth and misery of the present town have been well depicted by Mrs. Bishop.[1]

In the Pusht-i-Kuh, or country of the Feilis proper, we come to a region of superior interest, because of greater obscurity. This district consists of the mountain ranges, with their intervening valleys, that extend in arduous and almost impenetrable succession from the right bank of the Kerkhah to the Turkish frontier. It is a remote and inaccessible country; and it is not surprising, therefore, to find that the tribes are entirely nomadic in character, and that their chieftain occupies a position almost independent of the central Government, a position, indeed, that still leaves some flavour of distinction to the title which he continues to bear, of Vali of Pusht-i-Kuh. Of the Feili Lurs whom he rules, I have only received lists so misspelt and inaccurate, that I am unwilling to publish them; the more so as I am unable in any but the most fragmentary degree to reconcile them with the now obsolete lists of Rawlinson and Layard. The history, however, and the pedigree that I shall give of the ruling family have been derived from the Persian Governor of the adjoining province, and are correct.

Pusht-i-Kuh

In the old days Pish-Kuh and Pusht-i-Kuh, and a considerable surrounding territory in addition, were united under the rule of the aforementioned Atabegs of Luristan. The only detailed account of their dynasty, known as the Khurshidi dynasty,[2] is contained in the Sheref Nameh. They ruled from 1155 A.D. till the beginning of the seventeenth century; and their dominion was counted by Marco Polo as one of the eight kingdoms of Persia. At this early period the Lurs had already vindicated for themselves the unenviable reputation as thieves and bandits which their successors have diligently maintained. Mangu Khan the Mongol, when commissioning his brother Hulaku Khan to the government of Iran, gave him particular instructions to make things uncomfortable for the Kurds and Lurs, in revenge for their plundering on the high roads. Timur marched against them,

History

[1] *Journeys in Persia*, vol. ii. p. 122.

[2] My Persian authority says: 'They considered themselves the descendants of Akil, son of Abi Talib. But God knows best.'

because they could not keep their fingers from the caravans of the Mecca-bound pilgrims, and took both Khorremabad and Burujird in 1386 A.D. The last of the dynasty was the famous Shah Verdi Khan, Mir of Wirkond, who, by his position and power, excited the jealousy of Shah Abbas the Great, by whom he was seized and put to death. The title of Atabeg was suppressed; but the vacant office was conferred, with the new title of Vali of Luristan,[1] upon one Husein Khan, who had risen to some distinction in the service of the defunct ruler. My Persian informant declares that the family of the promoted Husein was Arab in origin, being descended from a chief of the Rubaia tribe, on the west side of the Tigris, who had quarrelled with his countrymen, migrated to Luristan, and there intermarried with the Feilis. However this may be, the dynasty thus promoted has retained the office ever since, and its present incumbent is, as the accompanying pedigree will show, a lineal descendant of the *protégé* of Shah Abbas.

PEDIGREE OF THE RULING FAMILY OF THE FEILI LURS (PUSHT-I-KUH).

HUSEIN KHAN (circ. 1600). Appointed Vali of Luristan by Shah Abbas in succession to Shah Verdi Khan

| descended from

HUSEIN KHAN, Vali

|

ISMAIL KHAN, Vali

|

ASAD KHAN, Vali

|

HASAN KHAN, Vali — related to KELB ALI KHAN, who murdered Captain Grant and Lieut. Fotheringham in 1810, and was himself murdered by Mohammed Ali Mirza
Died circ. 1840

|

ALI KHAN, Vali — AHMED KHAN — HAIDER ALI KHAN, Vali

(On the death of their father the three brothers divided the tribes. Ali Khan called himself Vali at first, but fled when the Shah recognised Haider Ali Khan)

| (son of Haider Ali Khan)

HUSEIN KULI KHAN, Vali. The present ruler, known as El Feili. Is an Amir-i-Toman, or major-general. Æt. 55.

|

REZA KULI KHAN. Æt. 28. A Persian *sertip*

I am not aware that a single English or even European traveller ever penetrated into the Pusht-i-Kuh before Captain

[1] At that time there were four Valis in Persia, all enjoying a semi-independent prestige and rule. They were the Valis of Gurjistan (Georgia), Ardelan (Persian Kurdistan), Luristan, and Hawizeh. Of these, the last two alone survive, and the third alone retains any semblance of freedom.

REZA KULI KHAN AND GROUP OF FEILI LURS

Grant, the explorer of Beluchistan, and Lieutenant Fotheringham, who were among the band of brave young officers sent out by Sir J. Malcolm as his pioneers in 1810. They were murdered at Khorremabad, by Kelb Ali Khan, a chief of the Vali's family, under circumstances which were related thirty years later by an alleged eye-witness to Sir H. Layard.[1] The next visitor was Major (afterwards Sir H.) Rawlinson, at that time an officer in the Persian army, who marched through the Feili country with a detachment of Persian troops in 1836.[2] A few years later he was followed by Layard;[3] and the joint record of their experiences and researches, together with the remarks of the Baron De Bode, a Russian diplomat, who travelled in the adjoining regions contemporaneously with Layard,[4] have remained ever since the sole text-book upon the subject. In their time Hasan Khan, a very old man, was Vali, and was at constant war with the Persian Government, though once ejected by whom he managed to return, and ruled as an almost independent prince till his death, soon after 1840. He was succeeded by his three sons, who disputed the title and fought with each other. The youngest of these, Haider Ali Khan, under the patronage of the Shah, ultimately prevailed, and it is his grandson, Husein Kuli Khan, who now holds the office. With an account of him, therefore, I shall bring my notice of the Feili Lurs up to date.

English travellers

Husein Kuli Khan, the present Vali of Pusht-i-Kuh, of whom, together with his son, I present a likeness, is a Persian vassal, and an Amir-i-Toman, or major-general in the Persian army. Nevertheless, his status approaches more nearly to independence than that of any other subject of the Shah, with the possible exception of the Amir of Kain. His summer quarters are at Dehbala, a secluded valley, very difficult of access, and easily defensible by a small number of men, at the foot of a lofty mountain, known as the Manisht Kuh. Here he was found in 1888 by Captain Maunsell, residing in a square stone fort, loopholed and bastioned, and clearly constructed for purposes of defence. In the interior, however, were a courtyard and chamber, fitted with some luxury, and containing European appointments. The retainers of the chief, numbering some 2,500, were camped around in tents and booths; his armed force con-

Husein Kuli Khan, Vali of Pusht-i-Kuh

[1] *Early Adventures*, vol. ii. pp. 324–5. [2] *Journal of the R.G.S.*, vol. ix.
[3] *Journal of the R.G.S.*, vol. xvi. [4] *Travels in Luristan*, vol. ii. pp. 270–97.

sisting of 700 horsemen, well mounted and armed, and of 2,000 infantry, provided with Martini-Peabody rifles, that had been looted from across the Turkish border. The Vali seldom leaves this position, or places himself in contact with the Persian authorities, and has evidently very little intention of falling to any decoy. He is a fine-looking man, with commanding presence, and a flowing beard, which has procured for him the appellation of *Rish-i-buzurg*, or Longbeard. He is also known as El Feili, The Feili, and from his cruel and murderous propensities as *Abu Kadareh*, or Father of the Sword. The latter title testifies to his character and rule, the severity of which has driven many of his people across the Turkish border, and has made him unpopular with his subjects. Though only fifty-five years of age, he is considerably broken down through drink. His son, Reza Kuli Khan, a young man of twenty-eight, is a *sertip* in the Persian service, and was for some time kept as an hostage for his father's good behaviour by the Zil-es-Sultan in Isfahan. He is a handsome young fellow, and a keen sportsman, and is reported to have a less tyrannical and more amiable disposition than his parent. If the Vali and his people move from their quarters, it is in the direction of Turkey rather than of Persia that they shift their tents. Their winter domicile is at Huseinieh, at the foot of the Pusht-i-Kuh, just within the Turkish border; it is with Baghdad *viâ* Kut-el-Amarah, on the Tigris, that the Vali trades; it is upon Turkish territory that he makes his raids, constant disputes occurring about the occupation by the Lurs of Ottoman soil;[1] and his sworn and inveterate enemies are the Beni Lam Arabs, who are Turkish subjects. He is probably the best living representative of the old style of Border chieftain, and is said to be able to call out 30,000 fighting men.

Mountains and rivers

Nowhere is the peculiar physical conformation of south-west Persia, analogous, as I have elsewhere remarked, in its features to that of north-east Khorasan, more observable than in the mountain abodes of the Feili Lurs. The ranges run in parallel files, inclined from north-west to south-east, projecting steep and craggy masses of limestone, which are frequently sawn at right angles to their own trend by the *tengs* or cañons through which the streams or rivers force their way.[2] In the narrow

[1] *Vide* vol. i. p. 569.

[2] A good description of these extraordinary defiles was given by W. K. Loftus in a paper on the 'Geology of Portions of the Turko-Persian Frontier,' in the *Quarterly Journal of the Geological Society* (1854), vol. xi. p. 247 *et seq.*

HUSEIN KULI KHAN, VALI OF PUSHT-I-KUH, AND SON

intervening valleys opening out into occasional plains, and abundantly watered, there is rich fodder for the flocks and herds of the nomad tribes. In sheep and goats their principal wealth consists; and they provide the towns of Khorremabad, Burujird, Kermanshah, and Hamadan with mutton, curds, and butter. On the hillsides is a somewhat scanty growth of dwarf-oak[1] and mountain shrubs, the former bearing gall-nuts, which are an article of commerce. The timber is but little respected by the Lurs, who cut it remorselessly for fuel, and supply the aforementioned towns with charcoal. El Feili himself has a splendid breed of mules which he exports through Turkish territory, and which are reputed to be the finest in Persia. The great river of North Luristan is the Kerkhah; just as Central Luristan has the Ab-i-Diz, and Southern Luristan the Karun. Three parent streams, rising in the neighbourhood of Hamadan and Burujird, unite in the plain of Kangavar, and, under the title of Gamasiab, flow west to near Bisitun. Here the Ab-i-Dinawar flows in from the north, and the augmented stream turns south-west and south, receiving successively the Kara Su, the Ab-i-Chenara, the Kashgan, and the Ab-i-Zal, until, after traversing the most magnificent scenery as it breaks the ramparts of the mighty Zagros range, it passes within ten miles of Dizful on the west, skirts the great mounds of Susa, and is dissipated in the Hawizeh marshes. Formerly the Kerkhah had two outlets into the Tigris, one by the El Khud bed at Amarah, the other a little below Kurnah into the Shat-el-Arab; but these appear now, as a rule, to be dry.

Character and life

Though the Vali enjoys an authority which is but little interfered with, he is responsible to Government for a fixed annual revenue, which is collected by the various tribal chiefs and heads of families upon a rough scale determined partly by the number of tents, partly by the pastoral wealth of the particular clan. His subjects have a bad reputation, in the main inherited, but sustained by the plundering habits of the Sagwands in particular, who are a sub-division of the Bajilan tribe. Fifty years ago these confirmed freebooters were *yaghi*, i.e. in rebellion; and, along with the Dirikwands before mentioned, they are still the terror of the passing caravan. Colonel Bell in 1884 marched with a

[1] The oak forests extend from Kurdistan in the north to Shiraz in the south. Between Burujird and Dizful the wooded zone is 110–120 miles in breadth, between Shushter and Isfahan somewhat more.

section of this people, whose chief, Haji Ali Khan, tried to rob him, and worthily sustained the tribal reputation.[1] Nevertheless Colonel Bell formed a favourable opinion of the Lurs as a whole, being struck with their decorum and obedience in camp, with their modest and frugal habits, and with their natural simplicity. They are a lighthearted people, much addicted to singing and chanting; and their rebellious and thieving propensities are more probably due to the life of semi-outlawry which the suicidal policy of the State has compelled them to lead, and to the licence that is born of a self-acquired freedom, than to any ineradicable taint of vice. The Feili Lurs are smaller in stature than the Bakhtiaris further south, and dress in brighter colours. Polygamy is the fashion among them, the extent of the *harem* depending upon the wealth of the lord and master. Colonel Bell's rascally host, for instance, possessed the respectable total of twenty-five wives. Their religion is of the most nebulous description. Most are Shiah Mohammedans, but they entertain very little respect either for the Prophet or the Koran, and have *pirs* or Holy men of their own, whose tombs are regarded as sacred places, and the chief of whom, Baba Buzurg, or the Great Father, is buried in their country. Traces of Judaism have been detected in their worship, and have excited those amiable theorists who ride the outworn hobby-horse of the Lost Tribes; and there are also to be found among them Ali Illahis, of which sect I have spoken in my chapter on Azerbaijan. The females, after the fashion of all the Lur tribes, are unveiled, and in youth are as well-favoured and comely as, at an age when a western woman is at her prime, they become shrivelled and decayed. Their costume is a loose shapeless dress, with little or no underclothing. They lead a hard life, tending and milking the flocks, churning the milk in suspended skins, and clarifying the butter, assisting to pitch and strike the tents, and weaving carpets and the black goats' hair tents in which they dwell. These are of all sizes and shapes, being supported by poles and partitioned by carpets or matting into separate chambers for the women, the kitchen, and the stables, a large *diwan-khaneh* or reception chamber being the first or outer compartment. In settled villages, mat or mud huts take the place of the tent. The men lead a life of robust but careless ease, sowing and reaping the crops where tillage is possible, cutting wood for charcoal, robbing and

[1] *Blackwood's Magazine*, April 1889.

fighting when the chance occurs, or smoking in contented idleness at the tent door.

From the Feili I pass to the Bakhtiari Lurs,[1] about whom I shall have much to say that is both interesting and new. Only

The Bakhtiaris

twenty-five years ago Mr. Watson, in his History of Persia, left on record that 'of their race and country very little is known,' and, with the exception of the scholarly writings of Rawlinson and Layard, discoverable only, until the latter published his absorbing work entitled 'Early Adventures,' in the Proceedings of Scientific Societies, and of Baron De Bode's book, I know of no work on Persia until the newly published and excellent volumes of Mrs. Bishop, that attempts to give an account either of their history or features. Here, therefore, I invoke the friendly concern of my readers, while I endeavour to fill what is perhaps the most notable existing gap in our knowledge of Iran.[2]

The Bakhtiari habitat is the belt of mountainous country between the district of the Feili Lurs and the alluvial plains that

Their country

slope to the Gulf. More strictly defined, it is bounded by two lines, which, following the prevailing trend of the mountain chains from north-west to south-east, may be said to extend from Burujird to the outskirts of Isfahan on the north, and from Dizful and Shushter to Ram Hormuz and the Behbehan

[1] In local phraseology Bakhtiari has recently come to be used as a territorial rather than an ethnical designation. Mussulman *seyids*, and even Armenians living in the Bakhtiari country, will call themselves Bakhtiaris, though they would angrily repudiate the title of Lur. The name Bakhtiari appears now to be chiefly applied to the inhabitants of the districts east of the Kuh-i-rang—i.e. the upper valleys of the Karun and its tributaries—while those to the west, in the direction of Arabistan, are more commonly known as Lurs.

[2] The only original sources of information of which I am aware concerning the Bakhtiaris are as follows: J. S. Stocqueler (1831), *Fifteen Months' Pilgrimage*, vol. i. p. 116 *et seq.*; Aucher Eloy (1835), *Relations de Voyages en Orient*, pp. 270–85, 329–31; (Sir) H. Rawlinson (1836), *Journal of the R.G.S.*, vol. ix.; (Sir) H. Layard (1840–1), *Ibid.*, vols. xii. and xvi.; *Early Adventures*, 2 vols.; Baron C. A. De Bode (1841), *Travels in Luristan*, 2 vols.; E. Duhousset, *Etudes sur les populations de la Perse*, 1863; A. H. Schindler (1877), *Zeit. der Gesell. für Erd. zu Berlin*, vol. xiv.; E. Stack (1881), *Six Months in Persia*, vol. ii. caps. iii. iv.; Captain H. L. Wells (1881), *Proceedings of the R.G.S* (new series), vol. v.; Colonel M. S. Bell (1884), *Blackwood's Magazine*, April, June, and July, 1889; A. Rodler (1887), *Petermann's Mittheilungen*, 1889; *Academische Anzeiger*, Vienna, No. xxi. 1888; H. F. B. Lynch (1889), *Proceedings of the R.G.S.* (new series), vol. xii.; Mrs. Bishop (1890), *Journeys in Persia*, 2 vols., Letters xiv.–xx. My own information is largely derived from personal inquiry and from unpublished sources.

district on the south. The territory comprised within these boundaries is susceptible of a twofold classification. First are the lofty mountain ranges, from 8,000 to 12,000 feet in height, with peaks of over 13,000 feet, in which are the sources of great rivers, the Ab-i-Diz on the north, the Karun and Zendeh Rud [1] and their confluents on the south-east; and their intervening valleys, from 6,000 to 8,000 feet in average elevation. This is Bakhtiari Land proper. Here, in a *mise en scène* which unites all the elements of natural grandeur,—snowy crags, rugged hills, mountain meres,[2] rushing torrents and profound ravines,—are the *yeilaks* or summer quarters of the tribes. There is but little cultivation; the people are poor; pasturage is the sole source of livelihood; and in the winter months snow lies deeply and closes the passes against the outer world. Secondly comes a series of plateaux, mountain valleys, and elevated plains from 2,000 to 6,000 feet in height, which, on the various sides, constitute a sort of glacis to the loftier ranges. These lower haunts are either inhabited all the year round, or are the winter resort of the nomads. They are richly watered, and very fertile. On the north-east, immediately adjoining Burujird, is the district of Silakhor. Next, almost from Burujird to Isfahan, extends a plateau 200 miles long by from 40 to 50 in width, which includes the district of Feraidan. Here are many Georgian and Armenian families, the former Mussulmans, the latter Christians, whose ancestors are reported to have been moved hither by Shah Abbas in 1614–15. To the south-east of this plateau, on the Isfahan side, lies the region of Chehar Mahal or Four Districts, again dotted with Armenian villages, living peaceably under Bakhtiari

[1] The meaning is Living river. I am not, however, confident that this is the real derivation. The oldest Persian writers have Zandah Rud, i.e. 'Great River.' Later on it was called Zendeh or Zindeh, i.e. Living, a nomenclature which is endorsed by Hafiz in his *Divan*: 'Although Zendeh Rud be "the water of life," yet is our Shiraz better than Isfahan.' Other writers have Zarin Rud, or Golden River, from the name of one of its parent streams. The name now in use appears to be Zaiendeh Rud or Life-giving River, which is explained in the Jehan Nemah of Haji Khalfeh as signifying the 'river that lives again,' because, if anywhere intercepted in its course, it breaks forth anew with equal vigour.

[2] In the north-west is a small lake, at the foot of the Shuturun Kuh (i.e. Camel Mountain, from its shape), which was discovered by Major Sawyer in 1890, and was named by him Lake Irene. In the south-east are the twin-lakes of Siligun (properly Sulejan), and the lake of Chaghkhor, which drain to the Kurang or Karun. The elevation of these lakes is 8,000 feet. They are formed by the melting snows of spring, and are usually dry in the summer and autumn.

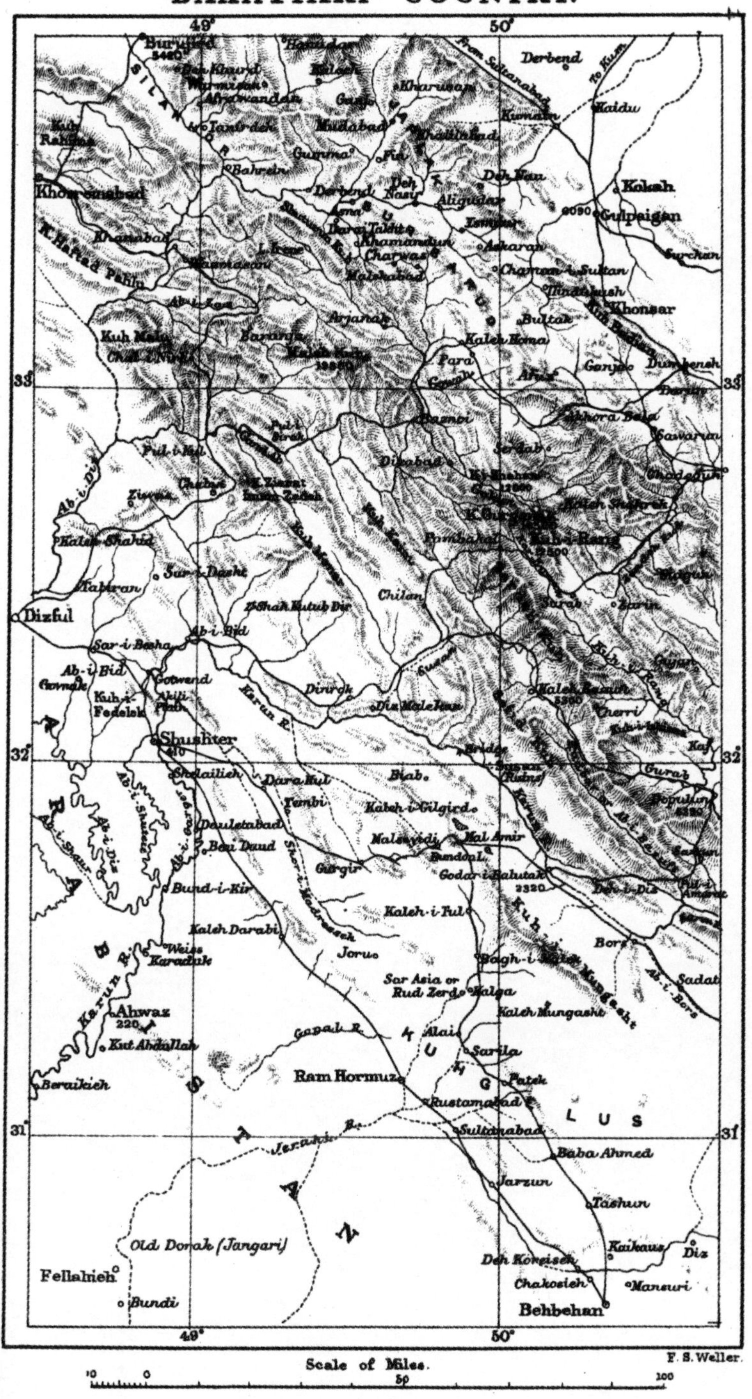
BAKHTIARI COUNTRY.
49°
50°
33°
32°
31°
Derbend
To Kum
From Sultanabad
Haidu
Kumain
Kharusan
Mudabad
Khalilabad
Gunma
Bahrein
Khorremabad
Deh Nau
Kokah
Gulpaigan
Aligudar
Ismijar
Derbend
Askaran
Surchan
Khamandun
Charwas
Chaman-i-Sultan
Khansar
R. Haftad Pahlu
Ab-i-Zaz
Kuh Malu
Arjanak
Bultak
Kaleh Homa
Kaleh Kadu
Ganjo
Dumbeneh
Pul-i-Kul
Pul-i-Bireh
Ab-i-Diz
Kaleh Shahid
Sar-i-Dasht
Mabiran
Dizful
Sar-i-Basha
Ab-i-Bid
Gotwend
Kuh-i-Fedelek
Karun R.
Shushter
Dizabad
Serdab
Kaleh Shahrek
Pambakal
Kuh-i-Rang
12500
Surab
Zarin
Chilan
Dinarek
Diz Malekan
Kaleh Rustam
Cherri
Gurab
Kaf
Biab
Dara Kul
Kaleh-i-Gilgird
Mal Amir
Deuletabad
Beni Daud
Bund-i-Kir
Gurgir
Godar-i-Balutak
2320
Kaleh-i-Tul
Kaleh Darabi
Weiss
Karaduk
Joru
Bors
Sadat
Ab-i-Bors
Bagh-i-Malek
Sar Asia or
Rud Zerd
Kalga
Kaleh Mungasht
Ahwaz
220
Kut Abdullah
Gapal R.
Alai
Sarila
Ram Hormuz
Patek
Beraikieh
Rustamabad
L U S
Sultanabad
Jerahi R.
Baba Ahmed
Jarzun
Tashun
Old Dorak (Jangari)
Kaikaus
Diz
Deh Koreiseh
Chakosieh
Mansuri
Fellahieh
Bundi
Behbehan
F. S. Weller.
Scale of Miles.
10
0
50
100

rule.[1] South of the main range are the similar elevated valleys of Mal Amir and Kaleh-i-Tul. It is a lovely country and well suited to every requirement of nomad existence. Its inhabitants can accommodate their level to the climate, choosing, according to the season of the year, any elevation from 2,000 to 12,000 feet.[2] On the hill slopes there is more timber than in any part of Persia with the exception of the Caspian provinces. Oak, ash, walnut, plane, elm, poplar, willow, ilex, beech, wild rose, briar, hawthorn, maple, wild fig, vine, hop, and almond, have all been found in the Bakhtiari hills. To the same camps or spots in the mountains come every year in the summer the same families or clans, their peculiar haunts being marked by white stones, which the tribal code forbids to move or to transgress. Before they start in the autumn they sprinkle the seed in the cultivable places; and on their return in the spring find a thirty-fold and gratuitous harvest.

Their history

What has been the history of this interesting country and people? Of the mystery of their origin I have previously spoken. From the earliest days we read of this mountain country as a wild and inaccessible region, inhabited by uncouth and formidable tribes. They set at nought the authority of the Medes and Persians; they defied Alexander,[3] and provoked Antiochus.[4] The invading Arabs found them a hard nut to crack. Between the twelfth and fourteenth centuries, however (1155 to 1424, A.D.), we find a powerful Mussulman dynasty, known as the Fasluyah, ruling the Bakhtiari country from Isfahan to Shushter under the title of Atabegs. Their stronghold was the mountain fastness of Mungasht, and their winter quarters were at Idej near Mal Amir. Ibn Batutah, the Moorish pilgrim, travelled through their dominion about 1330 A.D., and left the following testimony to its good governance:—

I then travelled (i.e. after leaving Tostar or Shushter) for three days over high mountains, and found in every stage a cell with food,

[1] Each village contains its priest and its κάτοικον, or church—a mud building unadorned outside, but more or less embellished within. The amicable juxtaposition of Armenians and Bakhtiaris in this part of Persia presents a striking contrast to the cat-and-dog existence of Nestorians and Kurds, as depicted in my chapter on the North-west Provinces.

[2] We are irresistibly reminded of Isaiah xlix. 9: 'Their pastures shall be in all high places. They shall not hunger nor thirst, neither shall the sun nor heat smite them; for he that hath mercy on them shall lead them, even by the springs of water shall he guide them.'

[3] Quintus Curtius, lib. v. cap. iii.

[4] Pliny, lib. vi. cap. xxi.

I. Haft Lang

Rawlinson, 1836	De Bode, 1841	Layard, 1844	Self, 1889	1890
Ulaki and Mal Ahmedi		Ulaki and Mal Ahmedi	Mal Ahmedi	
Bakhtiariwand	Bakhtiyarvend	Beidarwand	Bakhtiarwand	Behdarwand
Duraki	Dureki	Durkai	Duraki	Duraki
Sallaki	Zalaghi	Salak		
	Babadi		Babadi	Babadi
	Mamivend			
	Lek			
	Ashtiraki			
	Burburudi			
(Classified as Dependency)	(Dependency)	(Dependency)	Ragi or Rebgi[1]	
Dinaruni	Dinaruni	Dinaruni	Dinaruni	Dinaruni
		Sub-divisions of the above Tribes		
Bakhtiarwand		Ali Ladiwand	Allah-ed-dinwand	Alaiwand
		Beliwand	Beliwand	Belliband
		Mashmerdosi	Mahmud Shah Mor-[dosi	Mashmardusi
		Takki		
		Ushnayi		
		Gandayi		
		Makomrayi	Makum Jerri	
		Kiyurzi	Kyarsi	
		Ali Jemali		
		Leruzeni	Leller	
		Mah Sapatan		
		Akili		
		Jiveran		
		Sohrab		
		Monjezi		Munjesi
		Sheikh		
		Dinoshi		
		Gashtul		
		Bramali		
				Asmaki
				Newambli
				Iskander Khan
Duraki		Seraswand	Zurasund	Rarasfund
		Asiwand	Huseinwand	Resewand
		Bawadi		
		Ba Hamedi	Baba Ahmedi	Baba Ahmedi
		Raki		
		Mari	Mori	Maori
		Kandali	Kandali	Gandali
		Malmali		
		Berjuwi		
		Salachin		
		Sheini	Shehi	Zalaki
			Jamusi	Arab
Babadi			Ghali Anur	
			Akasha	Gosha
			Ghella	Gaila
			Ahmed Mahmedi	
			Rubathi	Reki
Dinaruni			(Classified *sub* Haft Lang)	(Classified *sub* Haft Lang)
Bawai	Bawai	Buwayi		
Urak	Urak	Aurek	Uruk	Aurak
Shaluh	Saluh	Shalu	Shahalu	Salu
	Gugirdi *or* Gulgiri	Ali Mohammedi	Ali Mahmudi	Ali Mahmudi
		Lejmi Aurek	Lah Mir Uruk	Laj Miaurak
		Serkulu	Serkulli	Sar Kulli
		Sehid		
		Goruwi	Kurui	Guhrui
		Sheikh Aliwand		
		Noruzi	Noruzi	
		Kurkhur	Kurkur	
			Tah	
			Baghiezi	Boveri

[1] Sub-divisions of Ragi or Rebgi.—Malmelli, Barjuni, Tahmasp Khani, Shemeni, Nazir Gomar, Salirchin, Serjuni Hasan Khani, Mezmullah Shaffar Khani, Mullah Haji Khosru.

II. Chehar Lang

Rawlinson, 1836	De Bode, 1841	Layard, 1844	Self, 1889	1890
Kunursi	Kumursi	Kiyunurzi	Kiyutari (?)	
Suhuni	Suhuni	Suhuni		
Mahmud Saleh	Muhammed Saleh	Mahmud Salih	Mahmud Saleh	Mahmud Saleh
Mogui	Mughui (included among Haft Lang)	Moguwi	Sakui (?)	Mogoi
Memiwand		Memiwand		
Zallaki	Zalaghi	Zalaki		Zallaghi
	Fuladvend			Fuladwand or Pulandwand
	Audilvend	Sub-divisions of Memiwand: Abdalwand		Abdulwand
	Euskhok	Busak		Bushak
		Bu Ishax Bosi Isawand Saki Basnayi Minjawi Sharafwand Zarcheguni		Sub-divisions of Fuladwand: Bosaki Isawand Hajiwand Hebedi Shillarwand Mian Kuh KhanaJemali Garawand
(Classified as Dependencies)	(Dependency)	(Dependencies)		
Janniki Garmsir	Junaki	Janniki Garmesir	Janiki Garmsir	
Janniki Sardsir		Janniki Sardesir	Janiki Sardsir	Janikis

Sub-divisions of the above Tribes

Rawlinson, 1836	De Bode, 1841	Layard, 1844	Self, 1889	1890
Kunursi				
Mohammed Jaferi			Mohammed Jaferi	
Papa Jaferi			Papa Jaferi	
Pusinah Kul			Husein-i-Sufi	
Ariwand			Ashirwand	
Arkul			Khargul	
Berun	(De Bode included Burburudi among the Haft Lang)			
Burburun			Buriwarand	
Asisafdi				
Sheikh				
Tembi			Timpi	
Karivand			Gheribwand	
Istagi			Ghaliwand	
			Sadata	
			Kahkelli	
			Samani	
Mahmud Saleh		Musawi	Mumzawi	
		Huruni	Haruni	
		Bazaras		
		Jangayi		
		Musawand		
			Arpenahi (Chehar ?)	
			Saadat-i-Shah Kut-beddin	
			Saadat-i-Buran Ali	
			Yuran	
			Dudengeh	
			Sheikh-i-Karkun	
			Shulah	
			Liwas	
			Kutali	
Mogui		Bajul		
		Bahmehshiri		
		Shirazi		
		Imari	Eimarrah	
		Duwisi	Dubisti	
		Salakchiwah	Sirlakchewah	
		Charm	Charm	
		Madevan	Makdi	
		Keimas	Kimasi	
		Shiyazi	Siasi Tufrakah	
		Albushi		
		Ghaza		
		Boroguni		
		Madiwar		
		Muri		
		Yal		
		Sowadku		

SUB-DIVISIONS OF CHEHAR LANG TRIBES—*continued.*

Rawlinson, 1836	De Bode, 1841	Layard, 1844	Self, 1889	1890
MOGUI		Gholam Ivesi Asa Khalil Husami Terdeni	Fahdar Saadat-i-Said Saadat-i-Saleh Kutah	
JANIKI GARMSIR	Makavendi Mumbeni Bulveisi Arab Gomish (Classified as Dependency) Zenghaneh	Makiyawand Mombeni Bulawasi, *i.e.* Abul Abbasi Zangenah		Makawand Mumabun Zanganah Galgiri (includ by De Bode amo the Dinaruni)

for the accommodation of travellers. I then came to the city Idhaj, which belongs to the Sultan Atabek Afrasiab. The country is called El Lur. It abounds with high mountains, and has roads cut in the rocks.[1] The extent in length is seventeen days' journey, in breadth ten. Its King sends presents to the King of Irak, and sometimes comes to see him. In every one of the stations in this country there are cells provided for the religious, enquirers, and travellers, and for every one who arrives there are bread, flesh, and sweetmeats. I travelled for ten days in this country over high mountains, with ten other religious. Having finished the districts belonging to this King, on the tenth day we entered those of Isphahan.[2]

Three centuries later we have the witness of Chardin, whose words might be taken as strictly applicable to the present day—an indication of the slow foot with which Time marches over the more remote spots of the earth's surface :—

The people that inhabit Lour-Estom (i.e. Luristan) never mind the building cities, nor have any settled abodes, but live in tents, for the most part feeding their flocks and their herds, of which they have an

[1] The allusion is no doubt to the famous paved causeway, known as the Jaddeh-i-Atabeg, or Rah-i-Sultani, which ran from Shushter, over the Bakhtiari mountains, to Isfahan (*vide* Schindler in the *Journal of the R. As. Soc.* 1880). The remains of this great work are still visible on the banks of the Karun in the elevated valley of Susan, and on the mountains above Mal Amir. It was, however, in all probability no work of the Atabegs, but may with greater likelihood be referred to Sassanian, or even to Achæmenian, days. De Bode erroneously identified it with the κλίμαξ μεγάλη, or Great Ladder road, encountered by the soldiers of Alexander (Diod. Siculus, lib. vi. cap. xix. ; Pliny, lib. vi. cap. xxxi.), and had a hankering to attribute it to the Kings of Elam, including our Old Testament friend, Chedorlaomer. The Climax Megale was more probably one of the *kotals* of Fars.

[2] *Travels* (trans. by Rev. S. Lee), cap. vii. pp. 37–8.

infinite number. They are governed by a Kaan who is set over 'em by the King of Persia, but chosen from among themselves, and for the most part all of the same race, the father succeeding the son. So that there still remains among them some shadow of Liberty; however, they pay both Tribute and Tenths. This Province furnishes Isfahan and the neighbouring parts with Cattel, which is the reason that the Governor of them is greatly respected in those parts.[1]

In the declining days of the Sefavi dynasty, Krusinski also testifies to the changelessness of things Persian when he speaks of a policy of disunion as being practised among the 'Loranis and Backtilarians,' and as having been inherited from Shah Abbas, 'who started equal factions in every city, in order to maintain the sovereignty of the crown.'[2] It is with no surprise, therefore, that we read, in the pages of Hanway, that when the Afghans appeared outside Isfahan in 1722, though Kasim Khan Bakhtiari placed 12,000 horsemen in the field, he was easily defeated by the invaders. Soon after, the Turkish Pasha of Mosul thought to take advantage of the general disorder by invading the Bakhtiari country. This he successfully accomplished; but he was not more able to hold it than any previous invader, and presently beat a retreat. Nadir Shah made the same experiment, and conquered, but did not subdue. He also tried, but without success, to transport large numbers of the tribe to Khorasan. They fought their way back again. More wisely he enlisted large numbers of the Bakhtiaris in his army, who acquitted themselves with great bravery at Herat and Kandahar. Upon his death in 1749, we are confronted with the short-lived spectacle of a Bakhtiari chieftain as the virtual occupant of the throne of Persia. Reshid Khan, one of the ruling Bakhtiari family, being at Isfahan at the time of the tyrant's assassination, seized a large treasure and fled to his native mountains, from which he soon returned with his elder brother, Ali Mardan Khan, at the head of a Lur host. Isfahan was taken; a puppet sovereign, the nephew of Shah Sultan Husein, was placed upon the throne with the title of Shah Ismail III.; Kerim Khan Zend acted as *vekil* or minister; but the real power was in the hands of his colleague in the Regency, Ali Mardan Khan, who, as commander-in-chief, controlled the army. The inevitable conflict resulted in the assassination of the aged Bakhtiari chieftain

[1] *Coronation of Solyman III.*, p. 147.
[2] *History of the Revolutions of Persia*, pp. 69, 71.

in 1751. Later in the century Agha Mohammed Khan, ambitious to fortify his rising fortunes, essayed a campaign in 1785 against these formidable mountaineers. He was not more successful than Nadir had been; and during the rest of his reign left the Bakhtiaris wisely alone. In the early years of the present century, Asad Khan, of the Haft Lang tribe, defied the Persian Government, raided up to the walls of Teheran, and when pursued took refuge in his impregnable hill-fort of the Diz near Shushter. Ultimately, however, he surrendered to Mohammed Ali Mirza, the son of Fath Ali Shah, and made his peace with the Government. At this time (1810) Morier calculated the Bakhtiaris as possessing 500,000 families, an altogether extravagant estimate. A little later, when British officers appeared in Persia to drill the native troops, a force of 3,000 Bakhtiaris was raised and placed under Major Hart, who found them orderly and tractable in their relations with him, though insubordinate and contemptuous towards Persian officers. Subsequently, Duhousset, the Frenchman, also commanded a Bakhtiari regiment. A curious story is related by Colonel Stuart and Lady Sheil of an Englishman who, in about 1830, having been captured by some Bakhtiari brigands, became domesticated and married among them, taking the name of Dervish Ali, and living as a Moslem. In process of time, having grown tired of savage life and of his Bakhtiari bride, he sold her for a jackass, which he rode to Trebizond, and embarked thence for his native country, having turned a few shillings on the speculation. Lady Sheil says that he kept a diary; if so, it is to be regretted that this has never been given to the world.

The Chehar Lang

We now come to a time when, jealous of the power of a great Bakhtiari chieftain, the Persian Government once again made a resolute attempt to assert its authority in the Lur mountains; and when, owing to the accidental presence of an Englishman, Sir H. Layard, in these regions, we have for the first time presented to us, in vivid and contemporaneous portraiture, a page of Bakhtiari history and life. The two principal subdivisions of the Bakhtiari tribes had for long been the Haft Lang (Seven Feet) and Chehar Lang (Four Feet). According to the popular account, current among the people themselves, the whole tribe originally migrated from Syria under a single chieftain, one of whose descendants left upon his death two families of seven and four sons respectively, the struggle between whom for the supremacy originated a tribal division that has lasted ever since. According to another account, the numbers of seven and four represented the respective scales of military contribution in bygone days, the Haft Lang, who were always the poorer and more nomadic section of the tribe, being taxed in the proportion of one-seventh of their property, while the Chehar Lang, who possessed villages and agricultural wealth, were assessed upon a quarter of their possessions. However this may be, a bitter enmity had from early times existed between the tribes, for which a perhaps sufficient reason was to be found in the fact that some of their pastures overlapped, and that they crossed each other while moving from their winter to their summer quarters. Between the years 1830–40, one Mohammed Taki Khan, of the Kunurzi tribe of the Chehar Lang subdivision, and a lineal descendant of Reshid, the brother of Ali Mardan Khan, before mentioned, rose by his own eminence and abilities to a commanding position among the Bakhtiari peoples. Starting as chief of his own clan, he was presently recognised as head of the Janiki (lit. Juwaniki) Garmsir, a larger tribal unit, which as a rule carried with it the supremacy of the entire Chehar Lang. At his prime his sway was likewise acknowledged by many of the Haft Lang Bakhtiaris, and by some of the Feili and Kuhgelu Lurs. This was the powerful and remarkable chieftain whom Mohammed Ali Shah, thirsting for military renown, determined to subdue; and of whose individuality and misfortunes so affecting a picture has been drawn by the pen of Layard.[1]

Mohammed Taki Khan

Mohammed Taki Khan was one of those men who exist to show that primitive surroundings and a wild existence can still develop a high ideal both of statesmanship and manhood. A brave warrior, an excellent swordsman, shot, and horseman, abstemious in his private life, affable and humane in his public relations, liberal-minded in political views, and possessed of no common abilities, 'he had a very noble air, and was the *baue idéal* of a great feudal chief.' His policy was much in advance of what might have been expected from his environment. He sternly repressed brigandage, encouraged settled as against nomadic existence, attempted colonisation on a large scale, fostered trade, and was keenly in sympathy with Layard's proposals

[1] *Vide Journal of the R.G.S.*, vol. xvi. pp. 8, 15, 47–9, and *Early Adventures*, pp. 371–5, *et passim*. Compare, also: (Sir) H. Rawlinson, *Journal of the R.G.S* vol. ix. p. 104; and Baron C. A. De Bode, *Travels in Luristan*, vol. ii. pp. 78–81.

for opening up the Bakhtiari mountains to British commerce. By his tribesmen, whom he ruled with a fair hand and from whom he collected an equitable revenue, he was respected and beloved. He wielded the power of life and death, and could command a well-armed force of 10,000 to 12,000 men, including 2,000 to 3,000 horsemen. Besides ruling his own and other kindred tribes,[1] he held Shushter, and had great influence in Dizful; he farmed Ram Hormuz from the government of Fars; he twice occupied Behbehan, and once took Hawizeh; he replaced a Ka'b Sheikh in Fellahieh. Already a Persian army, in which Rawlinson was an officer, had marched against him in 1836, but had received his submission.

KALEH-I-TUL

The Shah, however, was jealous both of his power and of his rumoured wealth. He was again declared *yaghi*, i.e. in rebellion, in 1840; and an army under Manucheher Khan, the Motemed-ed-Dowleh, who in the Government of Isfahan had acquired a reputation for merciless severity, marched into the Bakhtiari hills in 1841. The incidents of the campaign have been related by Layard, and should be read as affording an excellent illustration of Persian tactics in civil warfare. The family of the chieftain were

[1] The right of Mohammed Taki Khan to the title of Ilkhani is disputed by the Haft Lang tribe, who look upon his period of ascendency as the usurpation of a prerogative which appertains to them.

seized by an act of ill-faith; he himself took refuge with the Ka'b Sheikh Thamer, but was persuaded to surrender to the Motemed upon a guarantee of safety sworn upon the Koran. This too-familiar device of Persian government was successful. The hero was seized, cast into chains, and carried off to Teheran, where he died in imprisonment in 1851. His brothers and sons were either killed or experienced a similar fate. With the removal of Mohammed Taki Khan, the fortunes of the Chehar Lang suffered eclipse, and have never since revived. Some member of the same family has usually remained in occupation of Kaleh-i-Tul, the head-quarters of the chief; and I present a photograph of the fort and its inmates as they appeared in 1890.[1] The present head of the tribe is Chiragh Ali Khan, who married a daughter of the Haft Lang Ilkhani, Husein Kuli Khan, and is therefore brother-in-law to the present Ilbegi, Isfendiar Khan. Appended, too, is a pedigree of the Ilkhani's dynasty, which I have compiled from a number of sources.

After the fall of the Chehar Lang chieftain, the Haft Lang regained their supremacy, which has never since been disputed.

The Haft Lang

Jafir Kuli Khan, son of the Asad Khan whom I have before named, was recognised as Ilkhani by the Motemed; and if pre-eminence in crime were considered a qualification for leadership, he certainly deserved it. To attain the position, he had already slain fourteen of his relatives, including his own brother. Like his father, when engaged in hostilities with the Persian Government—a position into which he soon drifted—he withdrew to his impregnable stronghold of the Diz, where he was unsuccessfully besieged. Later he took to flight, and was succeeded by Kelb Ali Khan of the Duraki tribe, who also possessed a famous Diz, that, along with its fellow phenomenon, will presently be described. About the year 1850, however, the son of Jafir, Husein Kuli Khan, began to assert his authority over the tribes. He slew Kelb Ali Khan, and rapidly gained a predominance, which for thirty years remained uncontested, and rendered him a worthy successor to Layard's hero and patron. He was a man of com-

[1] Kaleh-i-Tul is a large stone and mud-brick fort, built upon a *tepe*, or mound about 100 feet high, in a plain 80 miles east of Shushter. The fort is a square with five towers, and is built in two tiers. In the interior it contains two courts, and would hold a powerful garrison. A village of mud huts clusters at the foot of the mound, and the black tents of the nomads are pitched around.

manding appearance and character, and ruled his followers with an iron hand. Like his prototype, he suppressed brigandage, made the caravan tracks safe, built caravanserais, constructed roads, and was willing to enter into relations with British merchants for the opening up of the route between Isfahan and Shushter.[1] Individual pre-eminence, however, has never been very safe in Persia; and least of all under a centralising administration like that of the present monarch. In June 1882, Husein Kuli Khan, who had

I. Ruling Family of the Chehar Lang (Kunurzi).

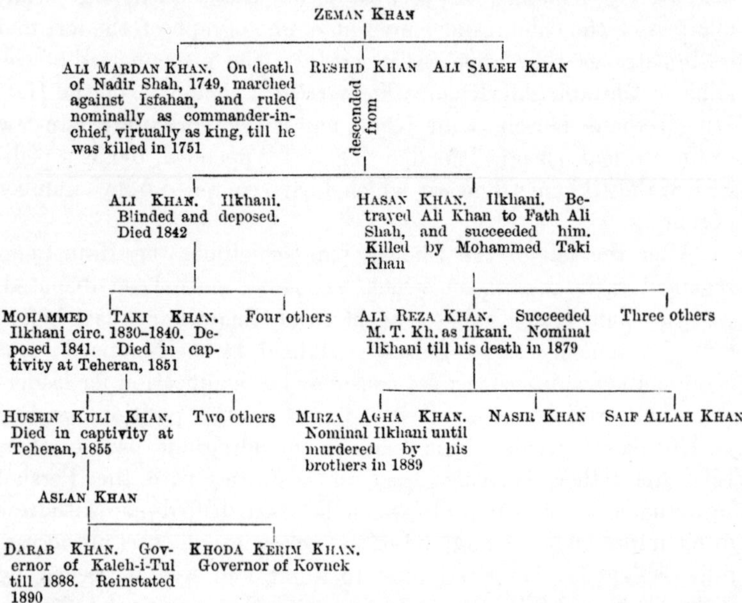

not long previously entertained the Zil-es-Sultan in regal style in his native mountains, was invited to Isfahan; and was there either strangled or poisoned by order of his princely host. The Zil-es-Sultan throws the responsibility upon the Shah. The Shah was probably aware of, even if he did not actually command, the deed. Simultaneously, Isfendiar Khan, the eldest son of the murdered man, was thrown into prison, where he remained for six years. The entire series of events was profoundly characteristic of Persian policy in its attitude towards the nomad tribes.

[1] He received, with every mark of favour, Mr. G. Mackenzie, of the firm of Gray, Paul, & Co., in 1875 and 1878; Gen. Schindler in 1877; and Captain Wells and Mr. Baring (of the Teheran Legation) in 1881.

There are three official posts associated with the leadership of the Bakhtiari tribes; and these, although never conferred upon any candidate who is not a member of the ruling family, are both salaried by, and in the gift of, the Shah—at once a fruitful source of bribery and an indication of the extent to which the Crown has succeeded in vindicating its prerogative. They are the offices of Ilkhani or Chieftain, Ilbegi or Second in Command, and Hakim, or Governor, of Chehar Mahal. The latter, although not a tribal rank *per se*, is closely bound up with tribal politics, inasmuch as the ruling family are the principal landed proprietors in the district concerned. After the assassination of Husein Kuli Khan, his next brother, Imam Kuli Khan, was appointed Ilkhani in his place, while a third brother, Reza Kuli Khan, became Ilbegi; other members of the family were kept at Teheran as hostages. With the fall of the Zil-es-Sultan, however, in February 1888, came another turn of Fortune's wheel. Isfendiar Khan, son of the late Ilkhani, was released from confinement and taken under the Shah's protection. His uncle, Imam Kuli Khan, was deposed, Reza received his place, and Isfendiar that of Ilbegi. Upon the disgraced Ilkhani refusing to evacuate his position, the successful rivals, with the aid of Persian troops, marched against him, fell upon his following at Chaghkhor, and compelled him to fly. Isfendiar emerged from the combat the bearer of the ornamental title of Samsam-es-Sultaneh, or Sword of the State. The existing arrangement was then confirmed, but only remained in operation for two years. In 1890, just after my visit, all three chiefs were ordered up to Teheran, and at No Ruz (March 21), when all offices are either renewed or change hands, the wheel described yet another and a backward revolution, inasmuch as Imam Kuli Khan was reinstated as Ilkhani, Isfendiar remaining Ilbegi, while Reza became Governor of Chehar Mahal. Such is the triangular arrangement that still prevails.

The ruling triumvirate

Though outwardly friendly, the triumvirate is secretly divided, and the present *modus vivendi* is destitute of any stability. The two uncles are separated by age, temperament, and tradition from the nephew, who carries with him the sympathies of his people. Imam Kuli Khan, the present chief, is a man of sixty-eight years of age. He is variously known as the Haji Ilkhani, from having made the pilgrimage to Mecca soon after his first accession to office, and as *El Kambakht*, or the Unfortunate,

Character and feeling

from the vicissitudes of his eventful career. With some of his subjects he is popular, being regarded as considerate and just, and he produced a favourable impression upon Colonel Bell in 1884. But his history has left its mark upon his character no less than upon his countenance, and distrust and suspicion are written on both. As Ilkhani he receives an annual salary of 1,000 *tomans* or 280*l.*, and pays a tribute to the Shah which is calculated at about two *tomans* per household. His brother, Reza, who is five years his junior, pays 5,700*l.* a year as farm-money for Chehar Mahal, and is reported to be avaricious and mean. Though he was a partisan of his nephew in 1888, the two are not now on speaking terms. His son is *sertip* of the Bakhtiari force that is maintained in their native hills. Isfendiar Khan has not passed unscathed through the ordeal of his earlier years. His father's murder and his own imprisonment have not rendered him an admirer of the powers that be, while the spectacle of others filling the place which he is entitled and qualified to occupy himself, scarcely tends to mitigate the sentiment. He is still, however, a comparatively young man, and, unless the Persian Government be contemplating any fresh wiles, is likely before long to become the *de jure* ruler of his people. The physiognomies of the three chieftains are not inadequately portrayed in the adjoining illustration. The pedigree which I have drawn up, and which has been out to Persia for confirmation, gives further particulars of the ruling family. Once annually the triumvirate meets in conference at Chaghkhor to settle the tribal affairs for the ensuing year. During the past summer (1891), I have not been surprised to hear that hostilities have again broken out. But so far they do not appear to have involved a direct rupture of the official *status quo*.

Catalogue of tribes

One result of the continued ascendency of the Haft Lang chieftains has been to bring the long-standing feud between the old tribal divisions to an end. The Chehar Lang ruling house is now united by marriage to the Ilkhani's family, and the tribal camping-grounds having ceased, to a large extent, to be distinct, there remains less ground for quarrel. As regards the sub-divisions and clans of the Bakhtiari Lurs, I have drawn up a comparative table, showing their names and numbers at different periods in the past half-century. Three previous lists have been published —by Rawlinson in 1836, by De Bode in 1841, and by Layard in 1844. In parallel columns with these I have placed a catalogue

Isfendiar Khan
Ilbegi

Imam Kuli Khan
Ilkhani

Reza Kull Khan,
Hakim of Chehar Mahal

THE BAKHTIARI KHANS

II. Ruling Family of the Haft Lang (Bakhtiarwand or Baidarwand).

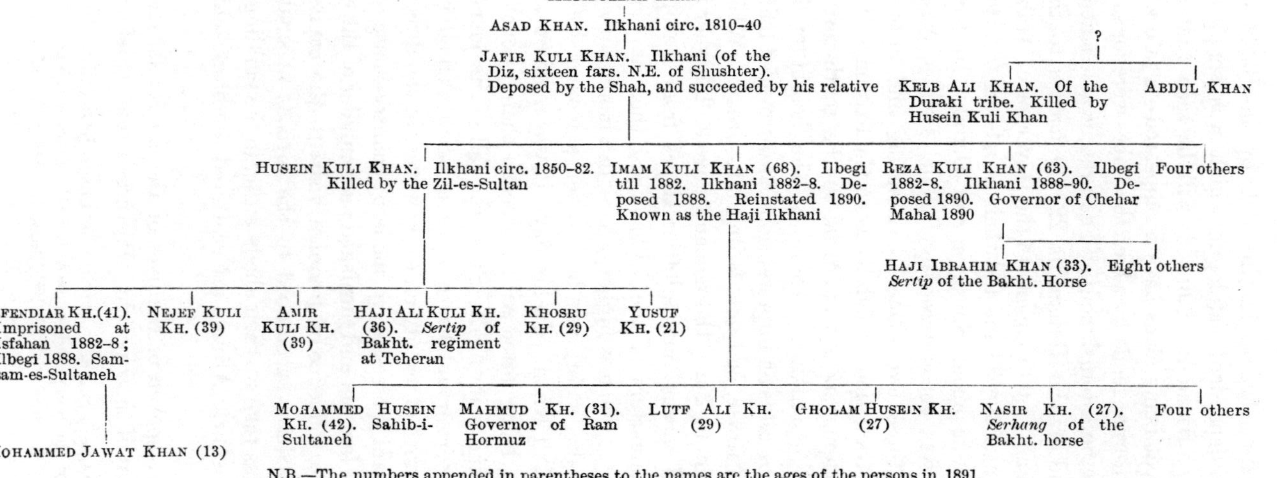

N.B.—The numbers appended in parentheses to the names are the ages of the persons in 1891.

that was furnished to me in 1889 by the Bakhtiaris themselves, and an independent catalogue which was supplied from similar sources to a friend in 1890. It will be seen that in the lapse of time a great many clans have disappeared—a fate which, considering the internal feuds by which the tribes were for so long sundered, can excite no astonishment. The present assessment of Bakhtiari Land, paid by the Ilkhani, is 22,000 *tomans* to the Governor of Isfahan, and 15,000 *tomans* to the Governor of Arabistan.

Winter and summer quarters

In winter the Khans and their people are to be found encamped in the plains about Shushter and Dizful. In 1884 the Ilkhani was encountered by Colonel Bell at Ab-i-Bid, between those two places. In spring and autumn, i.e. in the transition period between the extremes of cold and heat, their headquarters are at Ardal in the south-east portion of the Bakhtiari mountains. There, at the height of 6,000 feet, the Ilkhani possesses an unpretentious, two-storeyed building, adjoining a fortified tower, and now falling into decay. When the summer suns begin to burn, the nomads move still higher into the mountains, and encamp on the loftier slopes from Burujird to Isfahan. The headquarters of the Ilkhani are then at Chaghkhor,[1] near Ardal, but 2,000 feet higher, where, in a mountain valley containing a small lake, a fort was built, upon a mound 100 feet high, by Husein Kuli Khan. In his days it was a smart and pretentious residence, being fitted with European chairs, couches, chandeliers, mirrors, and paintings.[2] Since the fall of its founder it has itself fallen into ruin and has also been much shaken by earthquakes. At a distance of twenty miles, however, in the direction of Isfahan, the Ilkhani possesses a modern country-house at Paradumba, elegantly laid out and furnished; a reminder of the extent to which, under the influence of frequent visits to the capital, these nomad chieftains have succumbed to the inroads of civilisation. They themselves take up their abode either in the buildings or in pavilions pitched below. Around are scattered the black tents of the tribesmen.

I have spoken of the lives of the chiefs; let me say something about that of their people. Pasture is their chief occupation, sheep

[1] The name is variously derived from Chagh-Khor (Hill of Pasturage), Chaghakhor (Hill of the Sun), and Jah-i-Akhor (the Place of Horses, or Paddock).

[2] There he was visited by Stack in 1881 (*Six Months in Persia*, vol. ii. pp. 59–71), and his successor by Mrs. Bishop in 1890 (*Journeys in Persia*, vol. i p. 375).

and cows the principal source of wealth. Of the former there are estimated to be 300,000 in the Bakhtiari mountains. But little trade is conducted by the nomads except the supply of mutton to the Isfahan market and the growth of tobacco in the plains towards Shushter and Dizful. A scanty surplus of grain is sometimes exported, but the bulk disappears in home consumption. In former days the chiefs kept large studs of horses, and the Bakhtiari breed gained a repute that has not yet perished. These animals, which are of a mixed stock with a strong strain of Arab blood, are admirably adapted to the country, being nimble, sure-footed, and enduring; but their number has greatly diminished, and the tribe could no longer turn out, as in the days of Mohammed Taki Khan, a cavalry contingent of several thousand men. Mules are not now reared or kept by the Bakhtiaris, except for transport purposes, but they have a fine breed of donkeys. The bulk of the tribesmen are very poor, and in their black tents will be found neither gold nor silver, but vessels only of iron and copper. There is next to no education, except among the families of the chiefs, who sometimes keep a *munshi*. In the settled villages the parish *mullah* acts as a sort of self-constituted schoolmaster, but his attainments and curriculum are equally narrow. Outwardly and by hereditary descent the Bakhtiaris are Mohammedans, but they care little for Koran or Prophet, scoff at *mullahs* and *seyids*, and have no mosques. The shrines of *pirs*, or departed saints, are an object of attention and pilgrimage, and each stone added to the little commemorative pile signifies a vow fulfilled or a prayer uttered. Nevertheless the Bakhtiaris are not without a crude and simple faith of their own. They are believers alike in the existence and in the unity of God, and entertain elementary notions of Heaven and Hell, of a future life, and of a judgment day. Their burial places are usually located on low mounds, unfenced. A rough-hewn lion, whereon are sculped in rude imagery the sword, musket, dagger, powder-flask, and cartridge-belt of the deceased, marks the tribesman's grave.[1] Their character presents a strange combination of dignity and licence. For, on the one hand, they are modest,

Bakhtiari life and habits

[1] Fryer, in the seventeenth century (*Travels*, p. 385), was told in Persia that the emblem of a lion on a tombstone denoted one who had died in the strength of his age. Compare the tale related by Pausanias (*Bœot.* 40) of the Thebans who had perished in battle against Philip, and whose graves were marked by a lion to signify their magnanimous heroism.

though self-contained, in deportment, obedient and hospitable, loyal to family and tribal ties, and wholly free from the abominable vices of the Persians. On the other hand, they are savage when excited, particularly in the pursuit of blood feuds, which are perpetuated from generation to generation, until sometimes entire families have been extinguished, and are adroit and incurable thieves. There is not a traveller amongst them who has not spoken with suffering admiration of their dexterity in the latter respect, from Stocqueler in 1831 to Mrs. Bishop in 1890. To the denizen of cities their bearing presents a refreshing contrast to that of the urban Persian. Smooth rascality finds no place here, but in their character and mien is the free breath of their native hills.

Appearance and dress

Alike in costume and complexion, darkness is the prevailing hue of the external man. Their hair is black, with its two long uncut tufts curled behind the ear, black their bushy eyebrows and flashing eyes beneath, black the beard and moustache, black the small skull-cap upon the head, black the coat of the male, and blue-black the indigo-dyed cloak of the female. The men are robust and muscular in appearance, and have a very manly bearing. They wear loose trousers and a skirted coat. Round the waist a cartridge-belt holds the ammunition for the Martini-Peabody that is slung over the shoulder, a sword hangs under the saddle flaps, a dagger and pistol are carried in the belt. The women are tall and dark, of shapely limbs and erect carriage. They are not veiled, and but little privacy marks the economy of tented life. Polygamy appears to be almost universal, even amongst the poor. On the other hand, matrimonial infidelity is rare and domestic happiness common. The picture drawn by Layard of the family life of the Chehar Lang chieftain is one of the most touching features of his romantic tale. The women wear full Turkish trousers, or, in the *fin de siècle* vernacular, a divided skirt, a loose chemisette, and a shawl above all. Cleanliness, it is to be feared, is little known or appreciated by the nomads, and to this must be attributed the diseases, both of the skin and eye, to which they are liable. The latter ailment is exaggerated by the blinding glare of the sun from rock and sand, and by the scant protection afforded by the national head-dress.[1]

It is as a horseman that the Bakhtiari has always been famous.

[1] By far the best modern account of the habits and beliefs of the Bakhtiaris is to be found in the vivacious pages of Mrs. Bishop.

GROUP OF BAKHTIARIS ON THE UPPER KARUN

Trained from his youth to the saddle, he is a rough-rider of the finest type, able to fire while going at full gallop, and to perform feats on horseback that recall the prowess of the Western Hemisphere. He is a fine shot, with rifle or shot gun, particularly at short ranges; and it is to his insatiable desire to be always letting off at something, that the great diminution in the game that was once to be found in the Bakhtiari mountains is attributable. Fifty years ago, when Layard was there, ibex (*pasang* or rock-footed), mouflon, deer, gazelles, wolves, and bears were reported as numerous. Recent travellers have discovered little wherewith to slake the sportsman's appetite. Such men, however, it will readily be comprehended, afford the finest raw material for troops; and, as I have elsewhere hinted, it is possible that in the future the Bakhtiari highlanders may be seen in line with European comrades. At present they are ignorant of discipline, and are merely a loose collection of capable units. Nominally, the Shah claims the right to levy one horseman and two foot-soldiers upon every ten families. In practice, there are only two mobilised troops of Bakhtiari horse, each 100 strong, one of which is stationed at Teheran, really as a hostage for the good behaviour of the tribe, rather than as an addition to the fighting strength of Persia; the other in their native mountains. Both are commanded by scions of the ruling family; nor would the Shah venture to wrest from them the inherited prerogative of lead. Both these troops are equipped, mounted, and armed by the Ilkhani (they are distinguishable by a white instead of a black cap), but they are paid by the Shah in the form of a rebate on the revenue due from the chieftain. Of irregulars, in the strictest sense of the term, it is probable that the latter could put in all 8,000 to 10,000 in the field.

Military qualities

There are further natural features of the Bakhtiari country which merit specification. One of the most remarkable of these is the occurrence in the mountainous regions of natural hill-forts, known in Persia as *diz*. These strongholds, which, as a rule, consist of isolated mountain or hill-tops, artificially scarped, and difficult of access, containing pasture on the summits, and possessing natural wells or springs, have both lent themselves to and been utilised by the requirements of a semi-feudal and turbulent mode of existence. In days before artillery was invented, they supplied an impregnable retreat to the rebellious or

Hill-forts

outlawed chieftain. They are still formidable in a country which does not lend itself to the easy transport of guns. Of these natural phenomena the most remarkable are two in the neighbourhood of Shushter and Dizful. The Diz Asad Khan (so called because it was the winter residence of that chief, and subsequently of his son, Jafir Kuli Khan), is situated sixteen *farsakhs*, or two days' march, north-east of Shushter. Before belonging to the Haft Lang, it was the stronghold of the Moguwi tribe, and was known as Diz Malekan, or Fort of the Angels, from the idea that so wonderful a place could only have been rendered accessible to man by favour of the heavenly powers. Layard resided for several days upon its summit, and described it as a rock, three miles round, and ascended only by long ladders and holes in the cliff, conducting to a lower platform, where were natural springs and a collection of huts, a still higher platform being attained by an equally precipitous climb.[1] The second Diz, known as Diz Shahi, or Kaleh-i-Diz, was in Layard's time the property of Kelb Ali Khan, before mentioned, but passed, upon his death, to Husein Kuli Khan. It is situated fifteen miles north-east of Dizful, near the Ab-i-Diz, and consists of an elevated tableland, several miles in circumference, on the summit of a hill, with perpendicular sides, 150 feet sheer. A single pathway, partly hewn, partly built out, conducts to the top, where are huts, caves, springs, and good cultivated soil. Both of these hill-forts now belong to the Ilkhani of the Bakhtiari tribes. A third and analogous *diz* is that of Mungasht, which was the stronghold of the Atabegs in the Middle Ages, and held out for nine months against the Mongol Hulaku Khan. In the first half of this century it was the fastness of Mohammed Taki Khan, and is said never to have been taken. Like its fellows, it consists of a rock artificially scarped to a depth of 150 feet, with a summit half a mile round, containing perennial springs, and natural caves, capable of accommodating 1,000 men. Similar hill-forts exist more to the south in the Mamasenni country, notably that of Gul-i-Gulab, south of Behbehan,[2] and the famous Diz-i-Sefid, which will be mentioned later on. Another and different sort of *diz* is encountered in the cañon of Arjanak, in the north-west portion of the Bakhtiari mountains. There the *diz* consists of a number of shallow caves piercing the perpendicular

[1] *Journal of the R.G.S.*, vol. xvi. pp. 16, 17; *Early Adventures*, vol. ii. pp. 244–6.

[2] De Bode, *Travels*, vol. i. p. 292.

face of one of the cliff walls of the valley. The largest of these, twelve feet deep by twenty feet long, is defended by a loop-holed parapet, and is only accessible by a single steep path. It is the possession of Mihrab Khan, chief of the Isawand tribe of Bakhtiari Lurs. It is characteristic of every one of the natural fortresses here described that, though impervious to pedestrian attack, they could easily be shelled from opposite or neighbouring eminences. In modern warfare, therefore, their strategic value would dwindle.

In the extreme north-east corner of the Bakhtiari country lies the important town of Burujird (5,400 feet).[1] The district of which it is the centre and capital belongs, strictly speaking, to Irak; but inasmuch as several of the *mahals* which it contains are peopled by Bakhtiaris, and as its governor exercises jurisdiction over a large number of the latter tribe, it is more appropriately mentioned here. The commercial importance of the town, as situated at the junction of routes leading from Dizful, Kermanshah, Hamadan, Teheran, and Isfahan, has been pointed out in other chapters, and must always render it a place of importance either for trading or strategical purposes. Burujird is a thriving resort of business, with a population of 17,000, well situated in a valley watered by the upper springs of the Ab-i-Diz, and thickly studded with villages, whose orchards are renowned for their fruits. It is surrounded by a mud wall, five miles in circumference, pierced by five gates. The chief local manufacture is a species of printed calico, on which native designs are stamped by means of hand-dies cut in wood.

Burujird

On the western limits of Bakhtiari Land, and on the lower reaches of the Ab-i-Diz, is situated the less important but interesting town of Dizful. Its name (Diz-pul, i.e. Fort of the Bridge) is derived from the splendid bridge, doubtless of Sassanian structure, that here spans the stream.[2] Its lower part is of stone, and evidently of greater antiquity than the superstructure, which is of brick. It is 430 yards in length, and contains twenty-two arches of varying shape and span. Like its fellow and contemporary at Shushter, it is in a dilapidated condition, two of the arches having recently fallen in, although communication between the opposite banks is not thereby suspended as at Shushter. At a little distance upstream, a number of flour-mills

Dizful

[1] For modern Burujird, *vide* Mrs. Bishop, vol. ii. Letter xxi.

[2] *Vide* M. Dieulafoy *L'Art antique de la Perse*, part v. pp. 105–9.

built on rocks and connected by frail bridges or causeways, are turned by the current, and present a picturesque appearance. Dizful is in most respects so faithful a counterpart of Shushter (from which it is distant less than forty miles) that I shall dispense with a detailed description of its features, referring my readers to the next chapter, wherein will be related my own experiences at the sister-city. The population of Dizful, which was once inferior to that of Shushter, is said now to amount to over 16,000, or double the latter's total. Both places contain crowds of holy but fanatical impostors; life and its surroundings are much the same in each;

RIVER AND WATER-MILLS AT DIZFUL

alike in architecture the towns are similar, in general neglect of trade and tillage, and in contented evidence of universal and incorrigible decay. The chief local manufacture at Dizful is indigo, of which there are said to be 120 factories in the town. But so little has the value of the combined waterways of its own river and of the Karun, into which the Ab-i-Diz flows further down, been appraised by native merchants, that the import and export trade of the place, which might easily be doubled or trebled in volume, is at present conducted by an overland track from the Turkish landing-place of Amarah on the Tigris, merchandise being brought up the river from Busrah, and despatched by mule caravans starting twice a month for Dizful.[1] In the earlier part of this century, until replaced by Shushter, it was the seat of government of Arabistan, and a large palace was built here by Mohammed Ali Mirza.

Sabians

At Dizful, at Shushter, at Hawizeh, and at Mohammerah, are still to be found a few relics of the interesting and obscure community, known as the Sabians, frequently miscalled the Christians of St. John. In former days the sectaries of this faith were very numerous in Mesopotamia; and in the seventeenth century Petis de la Croix reported 10,000 in Busrah alone. Even in 1840 Layard found 300 to 400 families in Shushter; but in 1877 Schindler only heard of 50 families on Persian soil, and of not more than 500 families elsewhere. These are very poor, and are mostly employed either as peasants or as silversmiths. I have some engraved seals of their workmanship. The greatest uncertainty and confusion have prevailed as to the religious beliefs of this sect, who have been alternately classified as Hebrews and Christians, though widely removed from either. A still further and more serious confusion has arisen from their name, which has caused them to be mistaken for the Sabæans, who were star-worshippers and who are mentioned as such in the Old Testament, the name of the latter (which appears in the Koran as Sabiuna) being variously derived from the Arabic *Saba*, the heavenly host, or Sab, grandson of Enoch, who was a great prophet of that sect. Similarly in the time of the Khalif Mamun, A.D. 830, the people of Harran, who were polytheists and star-worshippers, appear, perhaps for the protection that it might afford them, to have assumed the name of Sabians, to which in all probability they had no right. The name of the true Sabians is believed to be derived from the Aramaic *Sabi-yun*, i.e. Baptists. They call themselves Mandai Yahiai or Followers of St. John. The latter, i.e. the Baptist, is their chief prophet, although they recognise the divinity of God, and are said to have some conception of the Trinity. They have no churches, but water plays a large part in their ritual observance, baptism, frequently renewed, being the principal ceremony, while marriage and prayer both require the use of running water. Some of them employ the sign of the Cross, which is variously explained as an act of symbolism, or as a relic of a possible conversion to Christianity

[1] This route was followed by Madame Dieulafoy in 1882 (*La Perse*, cap. xxxvii.).

in bygone days. They have five books, the principal of which is the Sidra or Book of Adam, written in a dialect of the Aramaic language, with an alphabet closely allied to the Syriac. Though the present Sidra is post-Mohammedan in date, its language and ideas alike point to an earlier origin. The Sabians are monogamous and do not practise circumcision, but have peculiar ordinances with regard to the eating of meat. Some of them also entertain a hazy belief in the gnostic idea of dualism, or a war of rival principles. But no two travellers ever received from them either a coherent or a consistent account of their faith. In appearance and dress they are not to be distinguished from the Arabs, among whom their lot is cast. They only intermarry amongst themselves; but their general poverty and obscurity are reflected in their numerical decline.[1]

I have more than once indicated that in ancient days the whole country which I have been describing was the scene of greater population and busier life, and of a truly royal rule. Evidences of bygone splendour, both of the Elamite or Susian period, that mysterious blank space in history, of the Achæmenian times, the golden age of the Medes and Persians, and of the later but still notable Sassanian epoch—in each of which Persia attained to considerable grandeur—lie scattered throughout this region from east to west. In the neighbourhood of Dizful, where the mountain ranges are succeeded by the plains of Susiana or Elam, occurs the most stately of these monuments to a vanished order, in the shape of the great mounds of Shush, or Susa.

Ruins of the past

A problem that agitated and divided the *savants* of an earlier generation,[2] and misled even so penetrative a critic as Rawlinson

[1] For a short bibliography of the Sabians, I may mention, in addition to the standard works of D'Anville, Assemann, D'Herbelot, Hyde, Ritter, De Sacy, Picart, Hottinger, Gobineau, the following: Tavernier, bk. iii. cap. viii.; Langlès on Chardin, vol. vi. pp. 136–152; Sir. W. Ouseley, *Travels*, vol. i. app. xii.; Dr. Wolff, *Travels*, vol. i. pp. 330–4; (Sir) H. Layard, *Early Adventures*, vol. ii. pp. 163–4, 171–2; De Bode, *Travels*, vol. ii. pp. 171–9; Madame Dieulafoy, *La Perse*, p. 547; and the following learned essays: Gesenius, *Mandaer o Zabier*, 1817; Chwolsohn, *Ssabier und Ssabismus*, 1856; Nöldeke, *Mundart der Mandaer*, 1862, and *Mandaische Grammatik*, 1875; *Edinburgh Review*, July 1880; Siouffi, *Etudes sur la religion des Soubbas ou Sabiens*, Paris, 1880; Babelon, *Les Mandites, leur histoire et leur doctrine*, Paris, 1882. *Vide* also A. H. Schindler, *Proc. of the R G.S.* Nov. 1891.

[2] Among those who debated the Shushan-Susa question, may be cited the names of Ouseley, Kinneir, Gosselin (ed. of Strabo), Long, Barbié du Bocage, Hoeck, D'Herbelot, D'Anville, Vincent, Mannert, Von Hammer. A hint might

—namely, the identity of the Shushan of the ancients—may now be considered as definitively settled. Shushter, Susan, and other claimants have disappeared from the lists, and the site to which I now turn has established its incontestable identity. From the dawn of history Shushan has figured in the pageants and combats of kings. Here, in the earliest recorded times, a Turanian people, ruled by a Semitic nobility,[1] lifted to a pitch of great power the independent kingdom of Elam.[2] They spoke the language, generally designated Susian, which appears in the second place in the trilingual inscriptions of the Achæmenian monarchs, but which has not yet been deciphered. Shushinak was their capital; about 2000 B.C. Chedorlaomer (Khudar Lagamar) was one of their most famous sovereigns. Elam was engaged in perpetual warfare with the neighbouring empires of Babylonia and Assyria, and suffered as much, if not more, injury than she dealt. The great invasion of Sennacherib was arrested by the winter snows of 697 B.C.; but fifty years later, in 645 B.C., Assurbanipal, the son and successor of Esarhaddon, appeared in triumph outside the walls of Shushan, broke open the Royal Treasure House, whence he carried off thirty-two statues of its kings 'of silver and gold and bronze and alabaster,' penetrated to the Holy of Holies in the Elamite temple and plundered the image of the national god, upon which to look was death, levelled the Great Tower of Shushan, and burned the city to the ground. Such was the vengeance of Assyria and the fate of the first Shushan.[3]

Shushan

well have been taken by some of these learned disputants from the Spanish Jew, Rabbi Benjamin of Tudela, who, having visited Susa in the course of his travels 700 years before, remarked: 'Among the ruins of the province of Khuzistan, the Elam of Scripture, are the remains of Shushan, the metropolis and palace of King Achashverosh, which still contains very large and handsome buildings of ancient date' (*Itinerary*, vol. i. p. 117.)

[1] This is supposed to be referred to in the representation of Elam as a son of Shem in Genesis x. 22.

[2] Elam, which is the title found in Scripture, is a Semitic version of the Accadian *numma*, or 'highlands.' It was afterwards called Susiana by the classical writers, from its capital Shushan, or Susa. Professor Sayce says that Susa or Susun signified the 'old city,' and was derived from *suse-ti*, which means 'former' in the Susian texts.

[3] The conquest of Assurbanipal is depicted on the sculptures of Nineveh discovered by Sir H. Layard and Mr. H. Rassam. For the verdict of scholars, *vide* A. H. Sayce, 'Cuneiform Inscriptions of Elam and Media,' in the *Trans. of the Soc. of Bibl. Arch.* vol. iii. 1874; and J. Oppert, *Trans. of Oriental Congress*, 1854, and *Records of the Past*, vol. vii. 1877.

Less than a century and a half later the second Shushan sprang into existence under the magnificent hand of Darius, son of Hystaspes. There, 'at Shushan, in the palace, which is in the province of Elam,'[1] Daniel saw the vision of the ram with the two horns. Thence ran the Royal Road to Sardis, by which Xerxes started forth for Greece. There the beauty of Esther the Jewess shone upon the vision of Ahasuerus (Xerxes or Artaxerxes). There were received the ambassadors and refugees from Greece, in whose eyes Susa was, far more than Persepolis or Ecbatana, the true capital of the Empire. There Æschylus laid the scene of his tragedy of the Persæ. Shushan was in fact the winter palace of the Achæmenian sovereigns. About it stretched a great city, whose walls were compared by Strabo to those of Babylon. It was bisected by the river Choaspes (Kerkhah) the water of which was borne in silver vessels to the table of the King of Kings. It was upon this splendid structure of royal pride and opulence that Alexander descended in triumph, and found there a treasure in bullion of nearly ten millions sterling. After the Macedonian epoch the city fell into ruin, but was rebuilt by Shapur II. under the title Iranshahr Shapur.[2] At the time of the Arab invasion its fortifications were dismantled; but the town continued to exist, and in the Middle Ages was, along with Ahwaz, a centre of the sugar-cultivation of Khuzistan.[3] Its pillars and stones were rifled to build the cities of the Sassanian kings; and no vestige remained of the ancient glory except the stupendous mounds, overgrown with scrub and low bushes, that reared their heads from the plain between the rivers Kerkhah and Ab-i-Diz, until, in the middle of this century, Loftus and Williams appeared upon the scene with the excavator's spade.

Loftus and Dieulafoy

The results of Loftus' explorations, which are contained in his work,[4] were at once satisfactory and meagre; satisfactory in so far as, by discovering the remains of a palace begun, according to cuneiform inscriptions that were laid bare at the same time, by Darius, son of Hystaspes, and completed by Artaxerxes, he conclusively established the identity of the *tumuli* of Shush with the classical Susa and the Scriptural Shushan; meagre, because his trenches and tunnels, which are still visible in the

[1] Daniel viii. 2. [2] Th. Nöldeke, *Gesch. d. Perser aus Tabari*, p. 58.

[3] Mukadessi, *Descriptio Imperii Moslemici*, p. 307.

[4] *Travels and Researches in Chaldæa and Susiana*, 1857.

great mound, brought so little to light, and left the larger spoil for a later worker in the same field. This was the Frenchman, M. Dieulafoy, who, having previously visited Persia in 1881–82 with his versatile wife, who became the historian of their travels,[1] and having inspected the mounds of Susa, returned in 1884, with the permission of the Shah and the assistance of the French Government, to prosecute investigations upon a large and scientific scale. The results of these labours have been given to the world in literary shape by the explorer and his wife; [2] their visible outcome is proudly displayed in a *salon* of the Musée du Louvre at Paris.

Mounds of Susa

It is at a distance of fifteen miles in a south-west direction from Dizful that the prodigious mounds of Shush, or Susa, stand up against the sky. They are situated on the left bank of the little river Shaur (originally Shapur), which rises at no great distance to the north and flows in a deep, narrow bed below the Tomb of Daniel, and between the larger rivers Ab-i-Diz (Eulæus), six and a half miles distant on the east, and the Kerkhah (Choaspes) one and a half mile distant on the west. The latter river divided the populous quarter of the ancient city from the citadel and palace. The entire circumference of the mounds is from six to seven miles. They consist of three levels: the lowest conceals the remains of the ancient city; the second, which is a rectangular platform two and a half miles round and 72 feet high, was the fortified enceinte that contained the palace; the uppermost, 120 feet in height, 1,100 yards round the base, and 850 yards round the summit, was the citadel, and is still known as Kaleh-i-Shush.

M. Dieulafoy's discoveries

M. Dieulafoy discovered that the palace of Darius had been in the main destroyed by fire, and that upon its ruins another and more splendid edifice was raised, over a century later, by Artaxerxes Mnemon (405–359 B.C.). Of this edifice there is a fancifully restored model by M. Dieulafoy in the Louvre.[3] The principal relics of the original fabric that were

[1] *La Perse, la Chaldée et la Susiane*, 1887.

[2] Mme. Dieulafoy, *A Suse; Journal de fouilles*, 1888; M. Dieulafoy, *L'Acropole de la Suse*, 1890; Perrot and Chipiez, *Histoire de l'Art*, vol. v. p. 757 *et seq.*

[3] The Hall of Darius and Artaxerxes at Susa (for it appears probable that the edifice was to a large extent a restoration of the older building) seems in shape and design to have been almost a facsimile on a larger scale of the Hall or Throne Room of Xerxes at Persepolis. There were three porticoes with twelve columns each, of the simple order of Achæmenian capital. The central hall contained thirty-six columns with the complex or triple bull-headed capital, of which M. Dieulafoy transported a magnificent specimen to the Louvre.

recovered by him were the remains, since most carefully pieced together and liberally restored, of the two superb friezes of the Archers and the Lions that decorated the façade of the later palace. They are the finest existing specimens of that art of enamelling in polychrome upon brick which was invented by the Babylonians (though unknown to Nineveh), and was adopted from them by the Achæmenian monarchs, more especially for the decoration of the palace of Susa, itself at no great distance from Babylon and situated in a region where stone was not, as at Persepolis, easily procurable, but where there was abundance of clay for bricks. The Frieze of Archers represents a procession of warriors in relief, some five feet in height. Their beard and hair are close-curled, after the Assyrian fashion; on their back they carry a big quiver and a curving bow; they wear a yellow tunic, patterned and diapered. The twisted turbans on their heads and the golden-knobbed spears which they hold in their hands identify these warriors with the Ten Thousand Immortals, as described by Herodotus, who formed the Body-guard of the Great King.[1] Their complexions, which vary from black to white, typify the opposite quarters of the globe from which they were recruited. The Frieze of the Lions, which is framed between bricks presenting elegant symmetrical designs, represents the beasts as striding forward with opened jaw and glaring eye, with swelling muscle and outstretched tail. The prevailing colours are green, pink, blue, and yellow; and a gorgeous spectacle they must have presented as they glittered under the hot sun of Susiana from the palace wall.[2] M. Dieulafoy also discovered, and there are exposed to view in the Louvre, a number of Royal seals, coins, vases, cylinders, and glass and terra-cotta implements of the same epoch. Nevertheless, what was brought to light by him is probably but little compared with the remains of a still older past that doubtless lie entombed below. The edifices of the Achæmenian monarchs, being latest in date, would naturally be encountered near the summit of the mounds. Subsequent explorers may expect to find in their lower strata the relics of a far more

[1] Lib. vii. cap. 83.

[2] The Lions' Frieze is composed of bricks in relief, 1 ft. 2 in. long by 7 in. high, and 9 in. thick. The lions are 11 ft 3 in. long, by 5 ft. 6 in. high. The Archers' Frieze is differently made, of small squares, 1 ft. 1 in. each way, and 3 in. thick, of artificial concrete, which combines the whiteness of plaster with the resistance of limestone.

remote and mysterious past, whereby we may yet be enabled to read the riddles of Susian antiquity.

A little below the great mound at Susa is the reputed Tomb of Daniel.[1] This is a somewhat mean building, surmounted by a lofty pineapple cone in plaster. In a white-washed inner chamber the sarcophagus reposes behind a modern brass railing, upon which are hung tablets inscribed with prayers from the Koran. Behind, there is a species of vault, which is shown to such pilgrims as desire the further corroboration of an actual Den of Lions. The entire building, which occupies one side of the court of a caravanserai for pilgrims, is comparatively modern and very probably covers the remains of some Mohammedan saint who has been confounded with Daniel; but from a very early period tradition has assigned the burial-place of the Jewish prophet to this spot. Rabbi Benjamin of Tudela, who reported 7,000 Jewish inhabitants of Susa in his day (1160–73 A.D.), declared that strife having arisen over the body of the saint between the different quarters of the town on opposite sides of the river, Sultan Sanjar settled the squabble by ordering the corpse to be taken out and placed in a coffin of glass, which was suspended by iron chains from the centre of the bridge. This anecdote, though supported by another pilgrim, R. Pethachia, who, however, represented the outer coffin as being made of polished copper which glittered like glass, is not generally credited, all Arab authorities being agreed in saying that the Prophet's body was interred in the bed of the stream.[2] However this may be, the Mohammedans are satisfied that they have still got the real Daniel, which is perhaps not more unlikely than Schliemann's real Agamemnon.

Tomb of Daniel

In the same neighbourhood are several Sassanian ruins: Aiwan-i-Kerkhah, a former city on the river of that name;[3] Jund-i-Shapur (the Camp of Shapur), ten miles south-east of Dizful; Teng-i-Butan (or the Gorge of Idols), north-east of Dizful, near the River Diz, where, in a small recess near the summit of a

Mal Amir

[1] *Vide* Layard, *Early Adventures*, vol. ii. pp. 295–6; De Bode, *Travels*, vol. ii. pp. 188–93; W. K. Loftus, *Travels*, cap. xxv.; Madame Dieulafoy, *La Perse*, cap. xxxix.

[2] *Vide* Sir W. Ouseley's translation of a Persian version (dated 120 A.D.) of the Tarikh, or History of Ibn Aasim el Kufi.

[3] *Vide* Mme. Dieulafoy, *La Perse*, p. 645; and M. Dieulafoy, who calls it variously Tak-Aiwan, Tak-i-Kerkhah, and Kut Gapan, *L'Art antique de la Perse*, part v. pp. 79–87, and pls. 7–9.

mountain, are twelve figures, sculped in high relief, with an inscription, upon the rock—for accounts or theories as to which I may refer my readers to the narratives of Rawlinson, Layard, and Schindler. Let me now transport them, some distance to the east, to Bakhtiari Land proper, where in the regions described a little earlier are to be found some noteworthy relics of the four periods of Susian, Achæmenian, Sassanian, and Mohammedan rule. The most conspicuous of these occur at Mal Amir,[1] a mountain plain, twelve miles long by five and a half broad, containing a small lake, in the basin of the Upper Karun, which has been described by Layard as 'the most remarkable place in the whole of the Bakhtiari mountains.'[2] The ruins here consist of five groups:—(1) The remains of an ancient city, occupying a large *tepe*, or mound, in the east part of the plain, identified with the Sassanian Idej or Izej (the Khidi of the local inscriptions and Khiteik of the Susian texts), thought by some to have been also the site of Anzan, the capital of the old Persian monarchy, and of Cyrus, before it was moved to Pasargadæ and Persepolis; (2) five tablets containing 341 small figures sculped in the rock in the ravine of Kul Fara, or Faraun, at the north end of the plain, together with a long cuneiform inscription,[3] of which Layard said that they are 'of higher antiquity than any other sculptures of the kind in Persia'; (3) a bas-relief, near the *imamzadeh* of Shah Suwar, on the east side of the plain; (4) a large number of sculptures in an extensive cavern called Shikafti Salman in a gorge on the south side of the plain, the figures representing

[1] The name signifies House, or country of the Amir; and is an obsolete Persian word (cf. *tushmal*) still used by the Lurs and Kurds.

[2] *Journal of the R.G.S.*, vol. xvi. pp. 74–80, and *Early Adventures*, vol. i. pp. 404–9, vol. ii. pp. 12–13. Compare De Bode, *Journal of the R.G.S.*, vol. xiii. pp. 100–2, and *Travels*, vol. ii. pp. 31–3 (with an illustration); A. H. Schindler, *Zeit. der Gesell. für Erd. zu Berlin*, vol. xiv.; Captain H. L. Wells, *Proc. of the R.G.S.* (new series), vol. v. 1883; H. B. Lynch, *ibid.* vol. xii. 1890.

[3] This inscription was copied by Layard, and published by him in *Cuneiform Inscriptions from Assyrian Monuments*, pls. 36–7. It has been deciphered by Professor Sayce, *Actes du 6me Congrès des Orient. à Leyde*, 1885, pp. 648, 681. He calls the third cuneiform character (which Norris interpreted as Scythian and Oppert holds to be Median) Amardian or Elamite. Cf. *Trans. of the Soc. of Bibl. Arch.*, vol. iii. p. 465. Illustrations of two of the tablets, from photographs by M. Houssay, have been published for the first time by Perrot and Chipiez, *Histoire de l'Art*, vol. v. pp. 775–6. Both represent a sacrificial scene, in which animals are or have been slaughtered in the presence of a being of superhuman size, who is doubtless a god. In the larger and more elaborate panel, the treatment and dress recall some of the Assyrian sculptures. The second is coarse and clumsy; but neither resembles, either in style or treatment, the Achæmenian sculptures.

priests and worshippers in an attitude of supplication, and being explained by an inscription of thirty-six lines in a complicated cuneiform character.[1] The above sculptures are either Susian or Achæmenian in origin, and date from the eighth or ninth centuries B.C. and later. (5) In a neighbouring gorge, called Hong, are some Sassanian sculptures, the central figure of which is a monarch with the familiar bushy mop of hair.

Susan

About twenty miles to the north-west of Mal Amir, and on the right bank of the Karun, is the small plain of Susan. The recurrence of this name, the presence here of a second, but even more insignificant, Tomb of Daniel, and the stories that were told him by the Lurs of wonderful ruins in the neighbourhood, led Rawlinson, who did not visit the locality himself, to think that here, rather than at Susa, might be the Shushan of the ancients. Layard, who visited the spot under circumstances of great difficulty and hardship,[2] reduced the patriotic hyperbole of the Lurs to its proper dimensions. Some insignificant remains of roughly-hewn stone, the probable foundations of a Sassanian building, were called by them Musjid-i-Suleiman, or the Temple of Solomon, a monarch much venerated in Lur tradition; some further heaps of old masonry were similarly designated Mal-i-Wiran, or Ruined Settlement. As the Karun enters this valley from the east, it is flanked on either side by the paved causeway, attributed to the Atabegs, which I have mentioned; and a little below are the remains of the famous bridge of Harah-zad, which here spanned the torrent, and was regarded as one of the wonders of the ancient world.[3] In mid-stream are two huge masses of brickwork, probably Sassanian, that supported the arches; on the mountain sides are visible the earlier Kaianian abutments, from which they sprang. The occurrence of these numerous relics of

[1] Also printed by Layard, *ibid.*, pls. 31–2, and deciphered by Sayce, *Actes, &c.*, pp. 653, 699. De Bode made drawings of two sculptures in an adjoining cavern, which were published by Flandin and Coste, vol. iv. pl. 228. The natives call the inscriptions Khat-i-Feringhi, or European writing, and are much disappointed when a foreigner cannot read them. Their belief, which would seem to be an unconscious corroboration of the Asiatic-Aryan theory, is that the ancient inhabitants of Persia, upon migrating to the west, buried their treasure with instructions as to the site, sculped in a language which their modern European descendants must naturally know.

[2] *Journal of the R.G.S.*, vol. xvi. pp. 61–2; *Early Adventures*, vol. i. pp. 415–28.

[3] So called from the mother of Ardeshir, the first Sassanian king. There is a long account of it in the *Athar el beldan, &c.*, of Zak. Mohammed Kazvini.

a past which has vanished from memory, and almost from knowledge, is not the least among the recompenses that await the traveller in this romantic portion of the Shah's dominions; and I at once urge and envy the scholar who, with time and means at his disposal, shall in the future visit and exhaustively examine the whole of this interesting region. I believe that he may return with a spoil that will shed a valuable light upon history, besides conferring upon himself well-merited distinction.

Further to the south, amid the mountain ranges inhabited by various tribes of the Lur family, other remains have been discovered and described.. Of these the most important are some sculptures, of which drawings were made by De Bode,[1] in a gorge called the Teng-i-Saulek, at a distance of seven *farsakhs* from Behbehan, in the territory of the Bahmei tribe of Bakhtiaris. At a Mamasenni village named Nurabad, between Behbehan and Kazerun, and on the banks of a small river, is a great Sassanian bas-relief, representing a seated monarch and his courtiers, not unlike one of the tablets at Shapur. It is called Naksh-i-Bahram, and the plain Sahra-i-Bahram.[2]

Other remains

The most remarkable natural feature of the region which I have been describing is, undoubtedly, the splendid and self-willed torrent of the Upper Karun. This river, of the lower reaches of which I shall have so much to say in the ensuing chapter, is called, in these volumes, by the name which it commonly bears, alike in Arabistan and in popular terminology. Its true orthography, however, would appear to be Kuran, from the Kuh-i-rang, or Variegated Mountain, in which it rises.[3] Though parts of the upper course of this great river have been followed or traced by the travellers to whom I have so frequently referred, and though its reputed source was visited by Stack in 1881, it was not till two years ago (1890) that its impetuous and zigzag current was tracked to its real birthplace, and pursued through the gorges and valleys of its parent mountains, by Major Sawyer, of the Indian Intelligence Department. In the very heart of Bakhtiari Land stands the lofty mountain cluster known as the Kuh-i-rang, or

The Karun river

[1] Engraved and published by Flandin and Coste, vol. iv. pls. 224–7.

[2] *Vide* Flandin and Coste, vol. iv. pl. 229; De Bode, vol. ii. p. 225; Stolze, *Persepolis*, vol. ii. pl. 146.

[3] The Portuguese writers, De Barros and Cotinho, called it Rio Carom. Other appellations in European writers of the last two centuries have been Correng, Kureng, Kuren, Keren, and Couran.

Jehan-Bin (World's View), just under 13,000 feet in height. From this great centre, which forms at the same time a water parting for the two most famous rivers of Persia, and a boundary between separate ethnological areas, spring the Karun on the south and the Zendeh Rud on the east. The former drains towards the Persian Gulf; the latter has already been encountered under the arches of the terraced bridges of Isfahan. In the peak called Haft Tanan (Seven Corpses, said to be those of the first and last party that ever reached the summit), are the real head-waters of the Karun. Fourteen miles lower down is the remarkable spring in the Zardeh Kuh,[1] which was visited by Stack[2] and by Mrs. Bishop, and which local error has christened Ser-chashmeh-i-Kurang, i.e. Head-springs of the Karun. From a hole in the bare cliff wall, communicating with a deep well at the other end of a natural cleft in the rock, the water gushes out with magnificent strength, and falls with a roar into the pool forty feet below. Hence the river rushes to its main bed, five miles distant; and from here to Shushter, a distance of seventy-five miles as the crow flies, drives a sinuous furrow for 250 miles through some of the noblest mountain scenery in the world, falling in the same interval 9,000 feet. Its normal width, even in its upper reaches, is from 50 to 100 yards, but sometimes it is compressed between sombre gorges, whose perpendicular walls, from 1,000 to 3,000 feet in sheer height, throw into perpetual shade the sea-green ribband below; whilst in one place, at the bridge of Ali Kuh, its volume is contracted within a rift only nine feet across. For the first 100 miles of its course it runs due south-east. Then, with a sharp bend, it turns south-west, and cuts a fifty miles channel through transverse ranges; then for nearly 100 miles more it flows north-west, in a direction inverse but exactly parallel to its original course; finally, it turns south, enters the plain of Akili by a gorge commanded by the ruins of two Sassanian castles, and having burst by means of another defile through the Kuh-i-Fedelek, or sandstone ridge above Shushter, debouches upon the plains of Arabistan. During this erratic progress it receives several tributaries. Of these, the most important and comparable in volume with itself is the Ab-i-Bazuft or Rudbar, which flows in from the north-west in a bed running

[1] This signifies Yellow Mountain, and is quite a modern name. The derivation, Sard Kuh—i.e. Cold Mountain—has been suggested, and is, perhaps, more probable.

[2] *Six Months in Persia*, vol. ii. pp. 91–2.

almost parallel with its own upper waters. Other noticeable confluents are a river from the east receiving the overflow of the Chaghkhor Lake, and a stream from the north, called the Ab-i-Beheshtabad (Abode of Paradise), or Darkash Warkash (from the *teng* through which it cuts its way), that drains Chehar Mahal. Near Dopulun (Two Bridges), flows in the Ab-i-Sabzu (also called Dahinur, Dinaran, and Ab-i-Gurab). From the south comes the Ab-i-Bors, hailing from the lofty Kuh-i-Dina range. From this point to Shushter its tributaries are frequent, but relatively insignificant; they include several salt or naphtha-stained streams.

I have said that the Zendeh Rud also rises in the Kuh-i-rang, although on its opposite side. Between the two rivers extends a mountain spur, through which, into the Shurab (Salt Water) valley, it was the design of the earlier Sefavi kings to divert the waters of the Karun, so as to recruit their beloved Zendeh Rud, too often a slender streamlet by the time it reached Isfahan. The place is known as Kar Kunan, or The Workers. This ambitious but sensible project, of which mention is made by Herbert,[1] Olearius,[2] Tavernier,[3] Sanson,[4] and Chardin,[5] appears to have been initiated in the sixteenth century by Shah Tahmasp, who began to excavate a tunnel, but is said to have been repelled by the noxious vapours. Abbas the Great, abandoning the tunnel scheme, for which the appliances of that age were hardly adequate, commenced a cutting, upon which, according to Herbert, he employed 40,000, and sometimes 100,000 men. He was vanquished by the snows and by the cold in winter. Abbas II. tried the simultaneous experiment of damming the river, so as to raise its level, and of mining the rock, under the direction of M. Genest, a French engineer. Both schemes were failures; and there the matter has rested till the present time. Stack visited the unfinished cutting in 1881, and reported it to be a huge cleft, sawn right across the crest of the hill, 300 yards in length, 15 in breadth, and 50 feet deep (measurements which, I believe, are not correct).[6] The quarried rocks are still symmetrically piled in heaps, and the ruins of the stone huts, built for the workmen, are

The Kar Kunan

[1] *Some Yeares' Travels*, p. 166.
[2] *Voyage*, col. 754.
[3] *Travels*, lib. iv. cap. vi.
[4] *Etat présent de la Perse*, p. 78.
[5] *Voyages* (ed. Langlès), vol. vii. pp. 279–84.
[6] *Six Months in Persia*, vol. ii. p. 84.

THE KAR KUNAN

visible. Major Sawyer estimated that less than one-twentieth of the entire work was completed. Nevertheless, the experiment was a perfectly rational one, the levels being favourable, and the obstacles not insurmountable. Modern engineering science would accomplish the purpose without difficulty by dams and tunnelling. Nor is it likely, looking to the volume of water in the Karun, and the numerous tributaries by which it is subsequently fed, that the river level would be lowered one inch thereby at Shushter. The question rather is, whether the diverted water, turned into the flat shingly bed of the Zendeh Rud, would not be scattered long before it had reached Isfahan. All such speculations, however, in a country like Persia, are in reality superfluous. The Shah is about as likely to undertake a genuinely great public work as he is to turn Protestant.

KUHGELU TRIBES (LURS).

Layard, 1844		Sheil, circ. 1850	Baring, 1882	
Chahar-banichah	Boher Ahmed	Boveir	Pusht-i-Kuh	Bah-i-Rahmet
	Nuwi	Nooee		Nowi
	Dushmanziyori	Dooshmen Zeearee		Dushmen Ziari
	Cherumi	Chooroom		Charum
Bahmehi	Ahmedi	Behmaee		Bahmei
	Mohammedi	Malahmedee		
	Kalakal			
Teibi		Tyebbee		Teibi
Bawi	Kuhmarrah	Bewee		Dehdast
		Kohmerree		
Yusofi	Shir Ali	Sheer Ali		
		Shehrooee		
Agajeri	Shahruwi	Yoosoofee	Zer-i-Kuh	Yusufi
		Aghajeree		Agha Jeri
Tekajeri	Telah Kuri	Teelehkoohee		
Geghatine	Jumah Bozurgi	Jaghatai		
		Jameh Boozoorgee		Humei
Magdeli	Afshar			Zeidan
		Thawi		Tang-i-Tekao
		Keshteel		Sirawi
		Beelehloo		Bunder Dilam

There remain to be noticed other offshoots of the Lur stock, whose camps are pitched in the same quarter of Persia. Of these

Kuhgelu Lurs

the Kuhgelu[1] occupy the country south of the Bakhtiaris, around the Kuh-i-Dina and the sources of the Jerahi River, as far as a line drawn from Ram Hormuz to Behbehan. On the west they march with the Arabs of Khuzistan, on the east

[1] *Vide* Layard, *Journal of the R.G.S.*, vol. xvi. pp. 21–5; and De Bode, *Journal of the R.G.S.*, vol. xiii. p. 75, and *Travels*, vol. i. pp. 275–89.

with the Mamasenni Lurs. I append a list of their tribal divisions as they have been recorded at different times in the past half-century by Sir H. Layard, Sir J. Sheil, and Mr. W. Baring (of the Teheran Legation). They consider themselves distinct from the Bakhtiaris, having, with few exceptions, been under separate chiefs and another government (namely, Behbehan, which is an administrative sub-division of Fars). Nevertheless they differ from the Bakhtiaris but little in dialect, and not at all in manners, customs, or religion. They had always enjoyed the worst of reputations for lawlessness and cruelty until they were severely taken in hand by Ferhad Mirza, who was Governor of Fars up till 1882, and who by his merciless visitation soon purged them of the dross of turbulence. The tribe has never raised its head since. De Bode, in whose and Layard's time they were ruled by a *seyid* of Arab origin, Mirza Koma or Kumo of Behbehan, says that their common food was bread made from pounded acorns.[1]

Mamasenni Lurs

Adjoining the Kuhgelus on the East are the tents of the Mamasenni (qy. Mohammed Huseini) Lurs,[2] occupying the country still known as Shulistan,[3] and extending as far east and south-east as Fars and the plain of Kazerun. This tribe prides itself on its origin, claiming to have come from Seistan, and to be directly descended from Rustam, whose name is still borne by one of the Mamasenni clans. Their subdivisions have been almost identically reported by different travellers in this century, and are as follows:—Rustam, Bekshi (or Bakesh), Javi, Dushman Ziari (the last-named, as has been seen, also included among the Kuhgelu Lurs, an indication of the slightness of

[1] The Arabic word for this acorn, which grows on a dwarf-oak and is of abnormal length, is *belut*, whence the title of the tree, *quercus ballota*, and whence also *bellota*, the Spanish word for acorn. Both names are possibly derived from the Greek βάλανος, and so originally from the Aryan root *gar*, *gal* (cf. the Latin *glans*). The flour derived from the crushed acorns they either eat raw in the form of paste, or baked into cakes. Compare the βαλανηφάγοι of Arcadia in Herod. i. 66.

[2] The popular etymologists, who like nothing so much as a fanciful resemblance, have connected them with the Mamakeni of Quintus Curtius (lib. vii. cap. vi.), who valiantly resisted Alexander in Bactria, near Maracanda (Samarkand). Others identify them with the Mammisei of Pliny (*Hist. Nat.* v. 19), who inhabited the tetrarchy of Mammisea in Cœle-Syria.

[3] This is the Shuolstan of Marco Polo, i.e. the country of the Shuls, who, in the twelfth century, were expelled by the Lurs from Luristan, and settled in the country between Khuzistan and Shiraz. Ibn Batutah, on his first day's march from Shiraz to Kazerun, encamped in the country of the Shuls, whom he described as 'a Persian desert tribe which includes some pious persons.'

ethnological or other difference between the two tribes). Their total number was estimated in 1884 as 19,000. They have been even more celebrated for their predatory and lawless habits than the Kuhgelu, and have always found both a rallying-place and a retreat in their celebrated hill-fortress of Kaleh or Diz-i-Sefid, the White Castle (so called from the colour of the rock), in the mountains, some fifty miles to the north-west of Shiraz. This wonderful natural stronghold—like those already described, an isolated hill summit with perpendicular sides, accessible only by a few ledges for the skilful climber, and by a single path hewn in the face of the rock, and defended by towers and a gateway—has played a conspicuous part in Persian legend and history. The great Rustam only took it by stratagem, introducing his soldiers in salt-bags placed on camels.[1] It arrested for a while the armies of Alexander. Timur captured it by the aid of Badakshan climbers. Macdonald Kinneir, who visited it in 1810, with Colonel Monteith, found it defended by huge stones poised along the brink of the precipice and ready, as in the story of Delphi, related by Herodotus, to be rolled over. Towards the latter part of Fath Ali Shah's reign the Mamasennis, under a redoubtable robber chieftain named Veli Khan Bakash, were in constant rebellion. An army of Azerbaijan troops marched against them, and besieged the Kaleh Sefid, which was at length forced to surrender. Nearly 100 of the Lur women, however, sooner than fall into the hands of the Turkish soldiery, hurled themselves with their children from the summit and perished. In 1840 the Mamasennis were still *yaghi*; and we hear of Manucheher Khan, the Motemed-ed-Dowleh, as glutting his naturally ferocious appetite by building 300 of them with mortar into a living tower. Still they continued unsubdued until Ferhad Mirza meted out to them the same drastic measure as he also dealt to the Kuhgelu; since which time they have abandoned the game of plunder and rebellion, and now content themselves with pastoral occupations and the habits of peace, the route from Shiraz to Behbehan being as safe as that from Shiraz to Bushire. In 1881 some of this tribe were encountered by Captain Wells between Kazerun and Fahliun; and he described them as 'the finest-looking men he had yet seen in Persia, with a handsome Jewish cast of countenance, very aquiline noses and long beards; the moustaches drooping and lighter coloured; the hair also light brown; the eyes often

[1] *Shah Nameh* of Firdusi.

black, but sometimes grey. They wear the tall brown felt hat of the ancient Persians, which is much more imposing than the round-headed cap of the Bakhtiari and Kuhgelu Lurs.'[1] These various tribes were once on terms of perpetual enmity and conflict; but they now collide more rarely, their leading families being united by marriage ties, and the veto of the State having become less susceptible of defiance. Of the Kashkai Lurs I have previously spoken in my chapter on the route from Isfahan to Shiraz.

From the survey of Luristan and the Lurs inhabiting the highlands, I now pass to the coast-plains and to an Arab population.

Arabistan

The administrative title of Arabistan, literally the Land of the Wanderers, is applied to a larger area than that embraced by the plains alone, many of the Bakhtiaris being under the jurisdiction of its Governor, whose official residence is at Shushter. Nevertheless the title more correctly describes the alluvial levels between the mountains and the sea, including the respective plains of Dizful, Shushter, Hawizeh, and Ram Hormuz. Its boundaries may be defined as a line from the Kerkhah River to Mohammerah on the west, the Bakhtiari hills on the north, the Shat-el-Arab and Persian Gulf on the south, and the Hindian River on the east. This province is identical with the ancient Elam, the classical Susiana, and the more modern Khuzistan. The latter designation appears now to have fallen into disuse.[2] The present administrative partition of the province is into eight districts, subordinate to the Governor-General. These are Dizful, Shushter, Hawizeh, Ahwaz, Mohammerah, Fellahieh, Deh Mullah, and Ram Hormuz, which are respectively administered by a Persian Deputy-governor or by a sheikh of one of the ruling Arab families, appointed by the Government. In olden days they were all united under the Vali of Arabistan, the Arab descendant of an illustrious family of *seyids*, who ruled at Hawizeh almost as an independent prince, and shared the proud title of Vali with only three other

[1] *Proceedings of the R.G.S.* (new series), vol. v. pp. 156–63. For other accounts of the Mamasennis and the Kaleh Sefid, *vide* Colonel Monteith, *Journal of the R.G.S.*, vol. xxvii. p. 113; (Sir) H. Layard, *ibid.*, vol. xvi. pp. 25–6; Baron De Bode, *Travels*, vol. i. pp. 229, 262–75.

[2] Khuzistan is thought to be derived from the word Uwaja, signifying aborigines, that occurs in the cuneiform inscriptions, and is, perhaps, also the origin of the Uxii of Strabo and Pliny. On the other hand, Mordtmann derives Khuzistan from a Persian word meaning sugar-cane.

Persian subjects, the rulers of Gurjistan (Georgia), Ardelan, and Luristan. The villages or camps are under their respective sheikhs, who are responsible for the revenue, paid in a lump sum to the district governor, who again passes it on to the provincial exchequer.

The Arabs

The population of this region is either pure Arab, or, more frequently, mixed Arab and Persian. The introduction of the former element commenced with the Arab conquests in 641 A.D., and has been recruited ever since by spontaneous immigration from the other side of the Tigris and the Persian Gulf, as well as by direct importation, Shah Ismail having, it is said, brought a large number of Arab colonists from the district of Nejd. Few of these Arab tribes have kept their blood undefiled. The majority have intermingled with the Persians, and the result is a strange hybrid, such as I shall afterwards describe, at Shushter and elsewhere, where the Persian dress and even the Persian religion have been in the main adopted, where sedentary has replaced nomad existence, and where the natural dignity of the Bedouin, or Wanderer, has succumbed to Persian wiles. Of the Arab peoples the most important are the Ka'b (vulg. Cha'b) Arabs, of whom there were originally seventy-two tribes. The bulk of these have died out or disappeared; but the race is still the most numerous in Arabistan. Layard in 1841 gave a tabulated list of their tribal divisions and subdivisions, many of which are not now known in the country. From a list compiled by Mr. Robertson, the late British Consul at Busrah, I take the following names as those of the Arab tribes of the province, not Ka'bs alone, who are said still to number 500 or more adult males. They are the Al-bu-Ghubaish, Asakirah, Khanafirah, Bawieh, Bait-el-Haji, Beni Rushaid, Beni Saleh, Beni Turuf, Hamudi, Humaid, Kindazli, Jurf, Kathir, Muhaisen, Naisieh, Nasara, Sharaifat, Shurafa, Suwari, Sudan, Suleiman. The number of smaller tribes is very large. On the eastern borders of the province are some other Arab tribes not included in the above list, notably the Muntefik of Hawizeh, and those dreaded robbers the Beni Lam. The bulk of these, however, particularly the Beni Lam, are in Turkish territory; and of the latter, therefore, I shall not again speak. The Arab and semi-Arab tribes of the province have been reckoned at various totals between 170,000 and 200,000, the larger sum being thus arrived at:—

Ka'b Arabs	62,000
Mixed Arabs and Persians:—	
Ram Hormuz	27,000
Shushter, Dizful, and Hawizeh . .	110,000
	199,000

The history of the Ka'b Arabs, which is typical of that of most of their neighbours, has been as follows.[1] They are said originally to have migrated from the Arabian shore of the Persian Gulf to the marshes near the junction of the Tigris and the Euphrates, where they became Turkish subjects, and acted as buffalo herdsmen; until, being propelled by drought, or expelled by another Arab tribe, they moved southwards and established a new settlement on a canal leading from the Karun, which they called Kaban or Gobban. Pushing eastwards towards the Jerahi River they presently came into collision with the tribe of Afshars, whose head-quarters were at Dorak on that river. They themselves fortified a camp at Fellahieh, twelve miles lower down, and, taking advantage of the general anarchy that followed upon the death of Nadir Shah, violently ousted the Afshars and got the whole country into their hands. About this time they were ruled by a sheikh, who owed to a powerful personality a far more than local renown. This was Sheikh Salman, or Suleiman, who for thirty years directed and aggrandised the fortunes of the tribe. In 1758, fired with a larger ambition, he commenced to build a fleet, and by 1765, when Niebuhr was in the country, had acquired ten large and seventy smaller vessels. So extensive were his depredations that Kerim Khan despatched a punitive expedition against him in that year. Malcolm says that he bought off the invader by a large indemnity, and by the promise of a regular tribute. But it is more currently believed that by cutting the dykes, which everywhere regulated the ditches, canals, and streams of a country rich in water-supply, and so converting the plains into a swamp, he reduced his adversaries to impotence.[2] His piratical

Ka'b Arabs

[1] *Vide* C. Niebuhr, *Voyage en Arabie*, vol. ii. p. 160; (Sir) H. Layard, *Journal of the R.G.S.*, vol. xvi. pp. 36–45, and *Early Adventures*, vol. ii. *passim*; (Sir) H. Rawlinson, *Journal of the R.G.S.*, vol. xxvii. p. 185; W. F. Ainsworth, *Personal Narrative of the Euphrates Expedition*, vol. ii. pp. 207–18; Baron C. A. De Bode, *Travels*, vol. ii. pp. 110–20.

[2] Colonel Monteith found the swamps still out when he passed through Dorak in 1810, and the desiccated channel of the Karun-el-Amieh, or Blind Karun, is an existing witness to the destruction of the old Ka'b dam across the Karun.

escapades now took a wider range, and he effected a seizure of some British vessels trading in the Gulf. This brought down upon him the indignation of the British Government, and a naval expedition, consisting of four vessels, was charged with the reduction of the Ka'b power in 1767. One of the flotilla blew up; an unsuccessful attack was made on the island of Kharak in May 1768; and the expedition retired with meagre laurels. With the pursuits of a corsair, however, Sheikh Salman combined the instincts of statesmanship; he was liberal-minded and far-seeing in his encouragement of agriculture, irrigation, and commerce; and he left a name worthy of remembrance. After his time the Ka'bs little by little forfeited their independence; their position, midway between Persian and Ottoman jurisdiction, exposing them to the assaults of both, and compelling them to pay tribute alternately to either power. Their own internal squabbles, moreover, are fitly illustrated in the accompanying pedigree, which I procured from Sheikh Mizal Khan, the present chief of the tribe, and which shows that out of twelve sheikhs who ruled between 1690 and 1790 A.D., no fewer than ten perished by the hand of the assassin. When Stocqueler, however, was in their country in 1831, he found Sheikh Mobadir, a lineal descendant of Salman, still 'the most powerful chieftain in south-west Persia,' possessing a revenue of 60,000 *tomans*, and an armed force of 15,000 infantry, and 6,000 to 7,000 cavalry. Fellahieh, his capital, contained a citadel one and a half mile round, and a large *meidan* with a park of artillery, mostly old Portuguese guns.[1] He was succeeded by his brother Thamer (the Samur of Stocqueler), who appears to have inherited the better, while avoiding the worse, traditions of Sheikh Salman. Though his earlier career had been stained by more than ordinary treachery and crime, yet, when his power was established, he encouraged agriculture, repaired the dams and perfected the system of irrigation, protected the caravan tracks, and opened Mohammerah (which had been built in 1812 by a sheikh of the subordinate Muhaisen tribe to resist the encroachments of Turkey) as a free port. This brought down upon him the vengeance of the Vali of Baghdad, who found that the trade of Busrah suffered severely from the competition of such a rival. Mohammerah was plundered by a Turkish force in 1837; and it was in the course of the troubles that followed that the Persians were first admitted by the Muhaisen

[1] *Fifteen Months' Pilgrimage*, vol. i. p. 72.

I. Sheikhs of the Ka'b Arabs

(belonging to the al-bu-nasir family).

1. Nasir bin Mohammed (the first known chief), murdered
2. Abdullah, murdered
3. Sarhan, murdered
4. Mir Rahmah, murdered

(1690–1722 a.d.)

5. Farajullah (1722–1734), murdered ?

Shinawa

6 Tahmaz Khanfar, murdered (1735) — 8. Salman — 9. Othman

(These two brothers ruled jointly 1737–64, when Othman died. Salman continued to rule till 1766)

7. Bander (1735–37) murdered by Salman

Son

10. Ghanim (1766–69), murdered
11. Barakat (1770–82), murdered
12. Ghadban (1782–92), murdered

Mohammed

13. Mubarek (1792–94), ousted by
14. Faris (1794–95), ousted by

Son

15. Alwan (1795–1801), ousted by
16. Barakat (1801–12)

17. Gheyth (1812–28). The first to be called Sheikh. Murdered — 18. Mobadir (1828–31) — 20. Thamer (1837–40)

19. Abdullah (1831–37)

21. Faris (1840–?)

22. Lutfullah Mohammed Khan — 23. Rahmah — 24. Mir Abdullah, Governor of Deh Mullah

(These three Sheikhs ruled conjointly)

22. Jafir Khan (1881–). Deposed 1888. Reinstated 1889. Present ruler of Fellahieh. Known as Sheikh-el-Mushaikh

II. Sheikhs of the Muhaisen Tribe.

(formerly dependent on the ka'b arabs, but now known by the same name)

Mardu

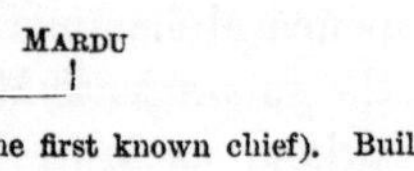

1. Haji Yusuf (the first known chief). Built Mohammerah
2. Haji Jabir Khan (?–1881). Originally acted as deputy of Sheikh Thamer at Mohammerah. Made Governor by the Persians
3. Mizal Khan (1881–). Present Sheikh of the Ka'bs, and Governor of Mohammerah — Mohammed — Khadal — Salman

III. Mullahs or Sheikhs of the Muntefik Tribe of Hawizeh.

(seyids and members of the old ruling family[1])

1. Mullah Farajullah (circ. 1840)
2. Mullah Abdullah
3. Mullah Muttalib (circ. 1883)
4. Mullah Nasrullah. Present Chief of Hawizeh

[1] For the pedigree of this family *vide* Layard, *Journal of the R.G.S.*, vol. xvi. p. 34.

Sheikh Haji Jabir Khan into that place, rewarding his complaisance with the official title of Governor. Sheikh Thamer, it may be imagined, was too prominent a figure to please the Persian Government, which, under Mohammed Shah, was beginning to show a very bellicose activity; and, having put himself out of court by harbouring the fugitive Bakhtiari chieftain, Mohammed Taki Khan, in 1840, he was proclaimed a rebel, and was compelled to fly into Turkish territory, his nephew Faris being nominated to succeed him. Sheikh Thamer was the last powerful chief of the Al-bu-Nasir or ruling family of Fellahieh, which has since then sunk into a secondary position, while the star of the Muhaisen tribe rose in its place. Sheikh Thamer's descendants are still, however, in possession both of Fellahieh and of Deh Mullah, a further Ka'b settlement more to the east.

The Muhaisen sheikhs

Haji Jabir Khan, who was a very shrewd and calculating individual, and who saw that the only practicable policy was to humour the growing power of the Persians, remained in possession of Mohammerah, with the enjoyment of a Persian title, until his death in October 1881. He was then succeeded by his younger son, Sheikh Mizal Khan, alike in the chieftainship of the tribe, and, by favour of the Shah, in the governorship of Mohammerah. The sheikh has since been yearly confirmed in this post, receiving from the Governor-General of Arabistan the annual *khelat*, or robe of honour, which in Persian public life is both the official *testamur* of reappointment, and the signal for a becoming monetary return from the presentee. Along with this, in 1889, he was granted the sonorous title of Muazz-es-Sultaneh, for which he was obliged to pay a proportionate fee.

Sheikh Mizal Khan

The sheikh resides in a fine riverside house on the Shat-el-Arab, at a spot called Feilieh, about one mile above Mohammerah, the Persian flag floating above his roof. Immediately in front of the mansion a gun is planted on the river's edge, and there attendants are ever watching to return the salute which is invariably given to their master by vessels of the British India Company in acknowledgment of a service rendered by his father several years ago to one of the company's ships, when attacked by a band of Arab robbers. No sooner has the ship's gun spoken than the answer booms from Sheikh Mizal's battery, and I doubt if he would surrender the compliment for one half of his revenues. An elder brother, named Mohammed Khan, was for some time kept as a hostage by the Persian Government, whose policy in these parts has always been to play off one member of a family against another. He has since been released, and now lives higher up on the Shat-el-Arab, in receipt of a pension of 1,200 *tomans* from the Persian Government, but is on the worst of terms with Sheikh Mizal. A younger brother resides with the latter, none of whose fifteen wives has succeeded in bearing him any children. The sheikh is a man of over fifty years of age, of fine stature and dignified appearance, and is reported to be very rich, having made a large fortune by the horse trade with Bombay.

Persian policy

For the present the relations between Sheikh Mizal and the Persian Government are ostensibly smooth and harmonious; but the Arab chief has long been apprehensive of the future. For years past he has seen the policy of Teheran directed towards the gradual suppression of all semi-dependent authority in non-Persian hands, and the centralisation of executive power. One after another the poppy-heads, to quote the old Roman fable, have been smitten off; and Arab sheikhs and Lur chieftains alike have vanished into compulsory retirement, or more frequently into the silent prisons of Teheran. For the pursuance of these tactics in south-west Persia, the opening of the Karun River to foreign trade, and the consequent necessity for new Custom-house officers and Foreign Office representatives, have supplied the Central Government with a welcome excuse; and it was with no slight alarm that Sheikh Mizal saw the first steamer of Messrs. Lynch ascend the Karun. Naturally, and by instinct a friend of the English, with whom, and particularly with the late Mr. Robertson, he has for long been upon intimate terms, he yet feels himself compelled to walk circumspectly. Accordingly, he regards everything and everybody with suspicion. He declines to go on board any vessel or steamer for fear that there may be a plot to deport him. In a creek immediately alongside of his house is moored his own paddle-steamer, the 'Karun,' ready at any moment to carry him into a safe retreat; and his deputy at Mohammerah was much distressed when I announced my intention of inspecting the new buildings at the corner, and gave private instructions that I should be deceived as to their character. More lately he has seen the wisdom of making friends with the Mammon of unrighteousness; and having invested both his interest and his wealth in the native commercial speculation for the development of the Karun trade

SHEIKH MIZAL KHAN

route, of which I shall speak in the next chapter, and which is backed by the Grand Vizier, he may succeed in retaining his twofold office. After him it is doubtful whether the Persian Government will ever again tolerate an Arab chieftain possessing any real authority.

Arab habits

The Ka'b Arabs occupy the entire extent of territory from Mohammerah and the Karun River eastwards towards the River Hindian, a distance of over one hundred miles. The natural richness of this region is enormous. It is more abundantly watered than any track of similar size in Persia, possessing the Karun, Jerahi, and Hindian rivers, and a network of canals. It is capable of producing an immense variety of cereal and other crops: wheat, barley, rice, sugar, cotton, opium, and indigo. With proper care it might become one vast grain-field, pouring much needed wealth into a depleted exchequer. As it is, tribal warfare and Government oppression have turned it into a desert over which the eye may roam unarrested for miles. Sheikh Mizal's section of the tribe dwell in the palm-groves upon the left shore of the Shat-el-Arab above and at Mohammerah, and occupy both banks of the Karun as far as Weiss. Upon the rivers they fish and trade and export their date crops; inland they camp in huts of reed, and supply their own needs by extracting an undeserved harvest from the prolific soil. Their wealth is chiefly expressed in flocks of sheep and goats, particularly the former, which supply them with their woollen blankets and tents, and with milk, curds, and clarified butter. Their breed of horses has greatly diminished; but they possess large numbers of donkeys. From long residence on Persian territories the Ka'b Arabs have lost much of their own national character. They have intermarried with the Persians, and have adopted the Shiah religion, as well as parts of the Persian dress.[1] None the less no love is lost between the two people, the Persian regarding the Arab as an interloper and a dullard, and the Arab regarding the Persian, with some justice in this region, as a plotter and a rogue.

Among the remaining Arab tribes I need only notice the Muntefik of Hawizeh, on the extreme south-eastern border of Persian territory. They appear to have migrated thither from

[1] They commonly wear the Arab *kefieh,* or silk handkerchief, on the head, kept in place by the *aghal,* or twisted camel's hair bands. But, beneath the Arab *aba* or cloak, may be seen a Persian tunic and drawers.

Turkish soil in 1812, and to have ousted that section of the Ka'b Arabs who occupied this district. Hawizeh was once an important place, with a population of 24,000 souls, at the time when it was the capital of the Vali of Arabistan. Its agricultural wealth depended upon the River Kerkhah, whose waters spread bounty over the land. In 1837, however, the main dam burst; the river dissipated itself in futile swamps, and Hawizeh shrank from a great town to a petty village. It is still governed by a sheikh of the old ruling family, claiming a sacred lineage; and according to his strength or weakness he receives the allegiance of a larger or smaller number of tribes. The majority of his people have always remained Sunnis. Surrounded by their marshes, they are fairly safe from encroachment.

The Muntefik

I have now completed my survey of the only part of the Persian dominions where anything like independence still exists among the component chiefs and tribes. That independence is fast vanishing before a power that is in command of the electric telegraph, and possesses breech-loading guns. It has already been sapped by the tribal jealousy and the petty rivalries of which the Central Government has never been slow to take advantage. Personally I shall regret its disappearance, convinced as I am that these people, Lurs and Arabs alike, have within them a manhood which alone can sustain the nation in time of need, and that firm but honourable rule and an equitable taxation were all that was needed to convert them into loyal subjects. As it is, they dislike the Persians, and detest the Government; and, when the call comes for their co-operation, 'To your tents, O Israel' is more likely to be the nomads' response.

Summary

Supplementary Routes in South-west Persia.[1]

Burujird to Hamadan.—(Sir) H. Layard (1841), *Early Adventures*, vol. i. pp. 277–88; J. P. Ferrier (1845), *ibid.*, pp. 33–4; A. H. Schindler (1877), *Zeit. der Gesell. für Erd. zu Berlin*, vol. xiv.; Mrs. Bishop (1890), *Journey in Persia*, vol. ii. Letter xxii.

Burujird to Kum.—Baron C. De Bode (1840), *Travels*, vol. ii. pp. 311–19; A. H. Schindler (1877), *ibid.*

Burujird to Isfahan (*viâ* Khonsar).—J. Otter (1737), *Voyage en Perse*; A. H. Schindler (1877), *ibid.*

Burujird to Shushter (*viâ* Khorremabad and Dizful, 250 miles).—Baron C. De Bode (1840), *ibid.*, vol. ii. pp. 162–268; A. Rivadeneyra (1874), *Viaje al*

[1] In this table *ibid.* signifies the work by the same writer before mentioned.

interior de Persia; A. H. Schindler (1877), *ibid.*; Colonel M. S. Bell (1884), *Blackwood's Magazine*, April 1889.

ZOHAB TO SHUSHTER (*viâ* Pusht-i-Kuh and Dizful).—(Sir) H. Rawlinson (1836), *Journal of the R.G.S.*, vol. ix.

DIZFUL TO SUSA (36 miles).—A. H. Schindler (1877), *ibid.*; Captain H. L. Wells (1881), *Proceedings of the R.G.S.* (new series), vol. v. pp. 183–6; Madame Dieulafoy (1882), *La Perse*, cap. xxxix.

SHUSHTER TO MOHAMMERAH (by land, 137 miles).—A. H. Schindler (1877), *ibid.*; Colonel M. S. Bell (1884), *ibid.*

SHUSHTER TO RAM HORMUZ.—A. H. Schindler (1877), *ibid.*

SHUSHTER TO ISFAHAN (*viâ* Mal Amir and Dopulun, 260 miles).—A. H. Schindler (1877), *ibid.*; Captain H. L. Wells (1881), *ibid.*, pp. 144–53; H. B. Lynch (1889), *Proceedings of the R.G.S.* (new series), vol. xii.

AHWAZ TO BEHBEHAN.—Captain H. L. Wells (1881), *ibid.*

BEHBEHAN TO BUNDER MASHUR (*viâ* Deh Mullah).—J. S. Stocqueler (1831), *Fifteen Months' Pilgrimage*, vol. i. pp. 86–100.

BEHBEHAN TO SHIRAZ.—Baron C. De Bode (1840), *Travels*, vol. i. pp. 192–290; Captain H. L. Wells (1881), *ibid.*, pp. 156–63.

BEHBEHAN TO ISFAHAN (*viâ* Ardal).—Col. M. S. Bell (1884), *Blackwood's Magazine*, July 1889.

CHAPTER XXV

THE KARUN RIVER

From Atropatia and the neighbouring plains
Of Adiabene, Media, and the South
Of Susiana to Balsara's haven.
MILTON, *Paradise Regained.*

Fardah Inshallah—
Please God, to-morrow!
Persian Saying.

The Karun country

HAVING in the previous chapter supplied all the information in my power about the provinces of Arabistan and Luristan, about their peculiar and warring populations, and about the problems of local and foreign politics which they bring to light, I now turn to a description of my own journey up the waters of the Karun River, as far as the fanatical and crumbling city of Shushter. There is much in the country, in the river scenery, and in the character of the people upon its banks, that distinguishes this from other parts of Persia. Few Englishmen have visited, and fewer still have described this interesting corner of the Shah's dominions; and whilst those who have done so have recorded their experiences in compilations not devoid of romance and familiar to the student, though not perhaps to the public at large,[1] the local

[1] The writers who have dealt with the Karun river, Shushter, and the surrounding districts are as follows:—Dean Vincent, *The Commerce and Navigation of the Ancients*, 2 vols., 1807. Gen. W. Monteith, *Journal of the R.G.S.*, vol. xxvii. p. 108. J. M. Kinneir, *Geographical Memoir*, 1813. Capt. R. Mignan, *Travels in Chaldæa*, 1829. J. H. Stocqueler, *Fifteen Months' Pilgrimage*, 2 vols., 1832. (Sir) H. Rawlinson, *Journal of the R.G.S.*, vol. ix., 1839. Lieut. W. B. Selby, I.N., *Journal of the R.G.S.*, vol. xiv., 1844. (Sir) A. H. Layard, *Journal of the R.G.S.*, vol. xii., 1842, vol. xvi., 1846; *Early Adventures*, 2 vols., 1887. Baron C. A. De Bode, *Journal of the R.G.S.*, vol. xiii., 1843; *Travels in Luristan and Arabistan*, 2 vols., 1845. Col. F. R. Chesney, *Expeditions for the Survey of the Rivers Euphrates and Tigris in* 1835–7, 2 vols., 1850. W. F. Ainsworth, *Researches in Assyria, &c.*, 1838; *A Personal Narrative of the Euphrates Expedition*, 2 vols., 1888; *The River Karun*, 1890. W. K. Loftus, *Travels and Researches in Chaldæa and Susiana*, 1857; *Journal of the R. G.S.*, vol. xxvii. 1857. Capt. G. H. Hunt, *Persian Campaign* (1857). Gen. A. H. Schindler, 'Travels in S.-W. Persia in 1877–8,' *Zeit. d. Gesell. f. Erd. z.*

THE KARUN RIVER
AND BRANCHES
Scale of Miles
SHUSHTER
Bagh-i-Husainabad
Deh-i-Nao (Ruins)
Ab-i-Shaur
Ab-i-Diz
Shelailieh
Kaleh Bunder
Kaleh Kunahid
Neshan-es-Sebaza
Kut Said Mutlak
Kut Khairabad
Ab-i-Shuteit
Ab-i-Gerger
Kaleh Said
Dauletabad
Deh-i-Said Musa
Deh-i-Pir Mohammed
Kaleh-i-Falieh
Ghor el Ebaitan
Kut Kishmamieh
Bund-i-Kir
River Kerkhah
Kut Sowari
Kaleh Jemand
Kut Homus
Kut Abdullah
KARUN RIVER
Weiss
(Oweyes)
Karaduk
Kut el Khamisa
HAWIZEH (Ruins)
Kut Nahr Hashim
Kut Ailan
Ancient Bed of River Kerkhah
OLD
GHOR SAIAR
Rapids
Ahwaz
Bund-i-Nasiri
Karaishan
Abu Dobbi I.
Shikara
Um-et-temr
Kut-Abdullah
Maktueh
Kut Omeirah
Kut Maron
Beraikieh
Farsiat
Abdul Gaffar
(Ruins)
Seyid Karthom
Ismailieh
Subbah
Old Tomb
Idrisieh (Derrasieh)
Nussarah
Um Shahra
Ramanieh
Akarkieh
Um-el-Wawieh
Memleh
Salowieh
Khurma
Tomb Ali Ibn Husein
Kut el Howair
Jerahi R.
El Athera I.
Old Dorak (Jangari)
Tomb Rowah Ali
Huseinieh
FELLAHIEH
(DORAK)
Canal leading to
Fellahieh
Salmanieh I.
Dha I.
Sablah
Kaban or Gobban Canal
Gisbah
Karun el Amieh
SHAT EL ARAB
Salahieh I.
Felieh
Mohammerah
Dabbeh I.
Bahmeshir Chan.
48°
30'
49°
32°
31°
F. S. Weller.

conditions have very greatly changed since the majority of their narratives were written, and the drama of life is fast nearing the close of a chapter whose leaves will presently be turned back and sealed for ever. A riparian population of Arab tribes under native sheikhs, who sustain a fitful and expiring independence against the ever advancing encroachments of Persian governors and tax-collectors; an inland population of nomad tribes, of mixed origin and reluctant loyalty, who in their native hills still retain their old clan organisation and a vagrant liberty of life; townspeople, half Arab and half Persian, whose character is as composite as their origin; these ingredients alone suggest a tableau of dramatic outline and vivid contrast. How much more complex and absorbing is it bound to become when an outside competitor, in the person of Great Britain, steps upon the scene!

The Karun river

The Karun river is described in text-books of geography as the only navigable river in Persia. Rising in the knotted mountain range to the west of Isfahan, from which I have briefly traced its passage in the previous chapter, it pursues a westerly course through wild gorges and upland plains, until, emerging from the hills immediately to the north of Shushter, it turns sharply to the south and, after adorning that town with the waterworks that have rendered it famous in history and still leave it respectable in decay, pursues a sinuous course over the wide alluvial plain that stretches to the Shat-el-Arab and the Persian Gulf. On the way it receives, at Bund-i-Kir, its main affluent, the Ab-i-Diz, or river of Dizful; whilst lower down its channel is interrupted, and navigation is impeded, by the renowned rapids of Ahwaz. At the river-port of Mohammerah it flows into the estuary by which, forty miles lower down, at Fao, the combined waters of the Tigris and Euphrates enter the Persian Gulf.

Berlin, 1879, pp. 38–67 and 81–124; *Journal of the R.A.S.*, vol. xii., p. 312. *Proceedings of the R.G.S.*, March 1883, containing: Paper by Col. J. Bateman-Champain; Speech by Mr. G. S. Mackenzie; 'Surveying Tours in South Persia,' by Major H. L. Wells. Mme. Dieulafoy, *La Perse*,'1887; *A Suse*, 1888. Col. M. S. Bell, V.C., *Blackwood's Magazine*, April 1889. Gen. Sir R. Murdoch Smith, *Chamber of Commerce Journal*, March 5, 1889; *Journal of the Society of Arts*, May 10, 1889. W. Tomaschek, *Topogr. Erläuterung der Küstenfahrt Nearchs*, 1890. Mrs. Bishop, *Journeys in Persia*, 2 vols., 1891. Perhaps I may be permitted to add to this bibliography my own contributions on the same subject, which have been partly utilised for this chapter: Letter xi. of the series on Persia in the *Times*, February 4, 1890; 'Leaves from a Diary on the Karun River,' *Fortnightly Review*, April and May 1890; 'The Karun River,' *Proceedings of the R.G.S.*, September 1890.

With ancient history, and with the disputed questions of the Ulai or Eulæus, the Coprates, the Choaspes, the Pasitigris, and their identity with the modern river-beds in the Tigris and Euphrates delta, I shall not greatly trouble my readers. The channels, and even the entire course of the rivers of Susiana—where from time to time great masses of snow-fed water are suddenly propelled through a sandy and friable soil, and where vast artificial irrigation works have sometimes reversed the dispositions of nature—have shifted frequently and irrecognisably. Unless we adopt this explanation, which charity as well as nature recommends, we shall be forced to the conclusion that the ancient chroniclers and geographers who dealt with these rivers were a very muddle-headed set of people; an hypothesis to which I am only inclined by the discovery that the majority of their modern successors have been guilty of confusions at least as startling, but over which the impulse of common impartiality tempts me equally to draw a veil. I will merely say that I identify the Karun with the Pasitigris (i.e. Lesser Tigris),[1] up which Nearchus sailed with the Macedonian fleet to join Alexander. Other historical identifications will be reserved for the foot-notes as I proceed.

Ancient channels

Here we may take up the history of the Karun river at the moment when it first concerns ourselves, and when its commercial advantages began to be recognised, not by the British public, who are habitually ill-informed, but by the few pioneers whose invariable fate it is to be snubbed by their own generation and applauded by the next. It is just fifty years since the immense latent value of the Karun trade route, as an avenue of expeditious approach to the great cities and centres of grain cultivation in the west of Persia, and as an opening more especially for British and Anglo-Indian commerce, was first brought prominently before the attention of Englishmen by the united labours and writings of Sir H. Layard and Lieut. Selby. The former of these explorers, from his intimate relations, both with Mohammed Taki Khan, the great Bakhtiari chieftain, and with the merchants of Shushter, was enabled to guarantee Persian reciprocity in any such enterprise; and he penned at the same

Early negotiations

[1] *Pas* (vulgo *past*) and *pastar* are still used in modern Persian to signify inferiority. The same meaning—i.e. Lesser Tigris—was expressed in the name, given by others to the Karun river, of Dijleh Kudek, and in the Arab designation Dojeil.

time a report to the Home Government, and a letter to the Chamber of Commerce at Bombay, urging the prompt utilisation of so favourable an opportunity. Political convulsions in Persia frustrated the further prosecution of the design, and it was not till thirty years later that the opening of the Karun river to foreign commerce appears to have been made the subject of formal official communications between the Governments of Downing Street and Teheran. In 1878 Husein Kuli Khan, the second redoubtable Ilkhani whom the Bakhtiari clans have produced in this century, made offers of co-operation to Mr. G. Mackenzie, member of the large trading firm of Gray, Paul & Co. at Bushire, not less cordial than those which his famous predecessor had made to Layard; and the firm above mentioned volunteered to place steamers upon the river. The independent action, however, and conspicuous authority of these chieftains in each case excited the jealousy of the Central Government. The permission was refused; Layard's friend died in imprisonment at Teheran; Mackenzie's friend was put to death at Isfahan by the Zil-es-Sultan. At length, after seventeen years of diplomatic fencing, with feint and counterfeint, and all the diversified tricks of the Oriental school—in the course of which France at one time appeared as a combatant in the arena, and all but carried off an exclusive concession for the navigation of the river and the development of the surrounding lands [1]—the matter was, through the successful instrumentality of Sir H. Drummond Wolff, settled by a decree of the Shah, issued in October 1888, by which the Karun river as far as Ahwaz was, subject to certain somewhat vexatious conditions, opened to the mercantile marine of the world.

Enterprise of Messrs. Lynch

The leave, such as it was, having been obtained, Messrs. Lynch Brothers, of the Euphrates and Tigris Steam Navigation Company, who have for many years owned the English steamers navigating the Tigris, detached one of their boats for the Karun service, and have continued to run a boat at intervals of a fortnight from Mohammerah to Ahwaz ever since.

[1] This concession, twice granted and twice cancelled between 1876 and 1878, was obtained by the influence of Dr Tholozan, the French physician of the Shah, strongly supported by Russian influence at Teheran. It was proposed to rebuild the dam at Ahwaz, with locks (the French having the exclusive right of navigation), to irrigate the surrounding country, and even to work mines and forests. A French engineer was sent out to report upon the Ahwaz rapids, and, in connection with the projected enterprise, a line of French steamers was established between Marseilles and Busrah, and a French official was placed at Mohammerah.

The boat at first employed was the 'Blosse Lynch,' a fine paddle steamer employed in the Tigris navigation between Busrah and Baghdad. She was found, however, to be both too long for the abrupt bends and zigzags of the Karun, and of too deep a draught to pass over the shoals in low water. Accordingly, after running for some months, she was replaced by the 'Shushan,' a smaller stern-wheel boat, with three rudders to allow of her answering very quickly to the helm. The latter was one of seven or eight boats built by Yarrow, of Poplar, for the English Government at the time of the Nile expedition, but never apparently used for that purpose. Some of them were sold to Messrs. Cook for pleasure-boats on the Nile, while the 'Shushan' found its way to the Karun. She was supposed to be able to steam from ten to twelve knots an hour, but against a current running four miles could not certainly manage more than four. It was in the 'Shushan' that I ascended the river as far as Ahwaz. She was subsequently, in the spring of 1890, taken up the rapids in flood-time, and has since plied on one or other of the upper channels to Shushter. Advantage of the Karun concession was also originally taken by the Bombay and Persia Steam Navigation Company, who, for a short time, ran a small steamer named the 'Iran' up the river; but, finding that they obtained no return, gave up the experiment. Messrs. Lynch Brothers have, in spite of a steady loss, continued the service up to the present time, and in the face of the greatest difficulties have laid the foundations of what it is to be hoped may become an important and lucrative trade in the future.

Having thus disposed of the preliminaries necessary to a comprehension of what follows, I now proceed to a record of my own journey. One hundred and seventeen miles after leaving Bushire, the British India steamer which navigates the Persian Gulf, sailing from Bombay to Busrah, drops anchor for a while off the mouth of the Shat-el-Arab, until the rising tide shall admit of her passing over the bar. At high water there is a good eighteen feet upon the bar, but the tide rises and falls as much as from eight to ten feet, and vessels at all heavily laden have invariably to cut their way through a shifting bottom of mud, while they sometimes stick fast for days. No effort appears to be made to keep open a channel by dredging or other artificial means —an apt reminder that we are on the brink of Ottoman jurisdiction—and the present passage solved the difficulty by arbitrarily

The Shat-el-Arab

cutting its own course in the year 1880. The Shat-el-Arab, as is well known, is the estuary by which the mingled waters of the Euphrates and Tigris, uniting at Kurnah, the legendary Garden of Eden, fifty miles above Busrah, descend to the Persian Gulf. Its northern bank is Persian, to a point upon the river beyond Mohammerah; its southern bank is Turkish throughout. At its entrance from the sea it presents the appearance of a noble river, a mile in width, flowing between low banks which, especially on the Turkish side, are fringed with a dense and magnificent belt of date palms. The opposite shore is more sandy, and is marked by the occasional tomb of some departed saint.

The Turks in these parts are disposed to be very nasty towards the Persians, against whom they have cherished a particular grudge ever since the cession of the port of Mohammerah to the latter by the joint Anglo-Russian Commission more than forty years ago. They are jealous of the intrusion of any other power upon the Shat-el-Arab; and they are still more jealous of the rising fortunes of Mohammerah itself, which, in the event of any considerable development of the Karun trade route, will divert much of the traffic that now finds its way to Busrah and Baghdad, and, through their Custom-houses, to and from the Persian interior. Accordingly, they adopt every means in their power of hampering, irritating, and menacing their rivals' interests; the most conspicuous illustration of this attitude being the erection of a large fort upon a shelving sandspit at Fao, absolutely commanding the entrance to the Shat-el-Arab on the south. By a clause in the Treaty of Erzerum (1847) Turkey and Persia, the two contracting powers, bound themselves by a reciprocal engagement not to erect fortifications on either bank of the estuary, Great Britain and Russia being the two witnessing parties; and the action of the Turks appears consequently to be a violation of this agreement, which is not atoned for by their complacent invitation to the Persians to go and do likewise. In 1886 they commenced the construction of the fort, and in spite of frequent protests since, both from the English and Persian Governments, met by the traditional diplomatic disclaimer from Constantinople, they have now completed it to a point at which the guns only are wanting to render it a serious and intolerable menace both to their Persian neighbours and to the interests of the British trade and shipping engaged upon the Mesopotamian rivers. Some time ago an English telegraph-clerk

Turkish fort at Fao

from the neighbouring telegraph-station at Fao landed from a boat at the fort, meeting with no interruption, and succeeded in making drawings and plans of the fortifications. When this vagary was discovered the Turks were furious, and have since fanatically excluded every prying eye. But from the deck of each passing steamer enough can be seen to show the actual progress of affairs, and to reduce to their proper proportions the diplomatic denials from Stambul. When I add that early in 1890 the Turks also commenced to build two other forts in the immediate neighbourhood of Mohammerah higher up the river; that the soldiers at Fao fired without provocation upon the captain and boat's crew of a British man-of-war (an act for which an apology arrived just in time from Constantinople); and that daily and weekly they place every obstacle that a perverse ingenuity can suggest in the way of the (English) Euphrates and Tigris Steam Navigation Company, who own the right to ply with two vessels between Busrah and Baghdad, it will be seen that to represent their action as dictated by any other spirit than one of provocation both to Persia and this country is difficult.

Telegraph station

A little beyond the new fort is the joint British and Turkish Telegraph station at Fao, where the cable of the Gulf section of the Indo-European Telegraph Department comes up from the sea, and is prolonged by an overland wire to Constantinople. Two buildings or sheds accommodate the respective officials of the two nationalities, and recently provided a further illustration of the suspicious hostility of the Turks. For when the English superintendent began to build a low wall round his shed to keep off the encroachments of the river, the Sublime Porte, which is ready to detect a menace in any proceedings but its own, formally protested against the fortification on its territory of a hostile place of arms!

Haffar channel

About sixty miles above the bar outside the Shat-el-Arab, forty miles above the entrance to that estuary at Fao, and twenty miles below the Turkish port of Busrah, the present main exit of the Karun river flows into the Shat-el-Arab from the north-east by an artificial channel, whose etymology testifies to its origin, known as the Haffar Canal.[1] When this canal was cut no one knows, and I shall not attempt to conjecture.[2] The reason for

[1] Haffar signifies 'dug.'

[2] Mr. Watson, in his *History of Persia*, p. 445, says it was cut by Alexander the Great, in order to avoid the necessity of sailing down the Karun into the Persian Gulf. But I know of no ground for this hypothesis.

its construction was presumably to open a communication between the Karun, which then entered the Persian Gulf by an independent mouth, and the Shat-el-Arab, and thus to promote trade between Arabistan and the then existing predecessors of the Turkish ports of Busrah and Baghdad. Where it flows into the Shat-el-Arab, the Haffar Canal is about a quarter of a mile in width, with a depth of from twenty to thirty feet. The town of Mohammerah is situated upon its right or north bank, at a distance of a little more than a mile from the point of confluence; although the new buildings recently erected by the Persian Government in consequence of the opening of the river to foreign trade, and consisting of a governor's house and a warehouse, with a primitive quay made of palm trunks in front, have been placed on the shore in the angle between the two streams. The comfort of the future governor had not been forgotten, for a bathhouse, heated by a furnace, was appended to his mansion. In the interval before trade begins, the new quay, which is about fifty yards long, was being turned to practical use, having recently been ploughed and sown. On the opposite or southern side of the Haffar Canal are the ruins of an old Persian fort and castle, where the sheikh used to reside fifty years ago, and which, in co-operation with larger works on the northern bank, attempted to dispute the entrance of the river with the British in 1857, but was very speedily silenced and knocked to pieces by our guns. In the past year (1891) infantry and artillery barracks have been built upon this site by the Persian Government.

Here the British India steamer stopped her engines to put me down. At Fao the Turkish Custom-house officer had come on board, and it was thought likely that he might raise an objection to the vessel stopping at Mohammerah, to allow of my leaving her, although he could have no legal claim whatever to do so; Mohammerah being a Persian port, and the Turks having no right of control either over the boats of the British India Company or over the opposite side of the Shat-el-Arab. This forecast of the probable tactics of Turkish officialdom was not entirely mistaken, because, although the individual in question made no sign when I disembarked, he subsequently lodged a formal complaint upon arriving at Busrah, and swore that the captain had put me down in the face of his vehement protest. Upon this the Custom-house at Busrah fined the vessel 12*l.*, an act of impertinent

Ottoman amenities

malice to which, I am glad to say, the agents of the company absolutely declined to submit, and which was still the subject of heated controversy when I left the river a month later. I mention it only as an additional instance of the amenities of Ottoman officials in a region too remote from head-quarters to admit either of prompt intervention or becoming chastisement.

Disembarking in a *bellam*,[1] or native boat—a long, narrow craft, shaped rather like a racing punt, and either sailed with a big lateen on a single mast, or paddled, or poled—I was propelled in the last-named fashion round the corner of the Haffar Canal up to the town of Mohammerah. Against the opposite bank was moored the rusty and decaying hulk of an old steamer, owned many years ago by Haji Jabir Khan, the late Sheikh of the neighbouring Arabs, who had procured from the Government at Teheran a monopoly of the navigation of the Lower Karun as far as Ahwaz. The story ran that when laden with a cargo of petroleum the vessel had been destroyed by fire. Mohammerah, as I have said, is situated rather more than a mile up the Haffar Canal, the total length of which, from the Shat-el-Arab to the Karun proper is about three miles, with an average breadth of a quarter of a mile, and depth of from twenty to thirty feet. It is probable that in the passage of time it has been considerably enlarged, as the banks are liable to be chafed away in flood time, while the sea-tide flowing up the Bahmeshir, or original and natural mouth of the Karun river, piles up the waters of the latter and forces them into the Haffar channel.

Disembarkation

Those who, from the glowing accounts in the newspapers three years ago, formed a roseate conception of Mohammerah as a great trading emporium, will be disappointed to hear that it is a small and exceptionally filthy place with a ruined fort, a little over 2,000 inhabitants (of whom, however, 40 per cent. were said to have been swept off by the cholera in 1889), and as yet only an insignificant foreign trade. In the old days, six centuries ago, when Ahwaz, Shushter, and Dizful were large cities and the centres of popular districts and an extensive commerce, Mohammerah was a port of some renown.[2]

Mohammerah

[1] The word signifies originally 'cotton-pod,' and hence a cockleshell boat.

[2] On or near the site of the modern Mohammerah, Alexander the Great founded one of his numerous Alexandrias. This city having been destroyed by flood, it was rebuilt by Antiochus, and called Antiochia. Again washed away, it was again rebuilt, and called Charax; and having been captured by an Arab chief named

In 1820 Mohammerah was, for a short time, the head-quarters of the British Residency, which was moved hither from Busrah, in consequence of disturbances between the Turks and Arabs at the latter place, and the prevalence of piracy on the river above. Sir Henry Layard, in his 'Early Adventures'—one of the most romantic narratives of adventure ever penned, and so rich in incident that one is at a loss to understand why the author should have delayed its publication for forty years—describes the important part played by Mohammerah in the conflicts between Turkey and Persia in the first half of this century. Attacked and taken by a Turkish force, but subsequently abandoned by them, it was in November 1841 occupied by the Persian troops, who, under the infamous Motemed-ed-Dowleh, pilloried for ever by Layard's unsparing pen, had undertaken an expedition against the Ka'b Arabs of the Karun. When the fighting was over, the Turks claimed the territory on the ground that it was situated, not on the Karun proper, but on an artificial canal which appertained to the northern littoral of the Shat-el-Arab. On their side the Persians declined to withdraw, advancing the counter-claim that no one could certify the origin of the Haffar branch, which, for all practical purposes, was both a physical continuation and the natural mouth of the Karun river. Layard himself, who, from his intimate knowledge of the locality, was employed by Lord Aberdeen to report upon the matter, recommended its cession to Turkey; but the Russian Government, taking a strong line in favour of Persia, the English Government followed its lead; and when the Treaty of Erzerum was signed Mohammerah was left, and has ever since remained, in Persian hands. At a later date it cut a somewhat inglorious figure in the Anglo-Persian war of 1857, when it was hastily fortified by the Persians, and was incontinently shelled from the river by six British men-of-war. After the bombardment was over, and the British troops had landed to attack, the defending force vanished, without striking a blow, into the desert.[1] Now it is little more

Spasines, received his name—i.e. Spasini Charax. Ardeshir Babekan, when rebuilding the town about 235 A.D., changed its name from Kerkh Misan (Charax of Mesene) to Astrabad. *Vide* Sir H. Rawlinson, *Journal of the R.G.S.*, vol. xxvii. p. 185; and W. F. Ainsworth, *Personal Narrative*, vol. ii. pp. 168-9.

[1] There were four Persian batteries on the mainland and five on the opposite side of the river, with casemated batteries, exceedingly well placed. The Persian army consisted of 13,000 men, under Prince Khanlar. The British force was

than a local mart for the needs of the Arab tribes, and for a limited export of native produce, such as grain, opium, wool, and dates. Its customs were farmed a few years ago for 1,500*l.*; but as the duty was levied on the number of packages or bales, irrespective of bulk or value, no criterion was thereby afforded of the total volume of trade. Selby in 1842 laid stress upon the exceptional healthiness of the place, which he said was superior in this respect to any other part of the adjacent country, to which he attributed the continued immunity from bad fever of himself and ship's crew, and which he explained by the coolness of the snow-fed stream. This testimonial, if it be applicable to the river, which has been disputed by other witnesses,[1] can scarcely be transferred to the town, whose main street is also its *cloaca maxima*, and which riots in smells. Nothing, indeed, redeems the place from insignificance but its palm-groves, which are superb, and its physical situation, which in any other country and under any other government would long ago have been turned to enduring profit. In the river off the town were moored some twenty *mehalas*, the large native boat, ranging from five to fifty tons, and having a draught of from three to six feet, built with raking prow, lofty poop, and a single vast lateen sail, which is the immemorial cargo boat of the Karun.

Here I embarked on board the 'Shushan,' too late, however, to proceed till the next morning. The Persian Government maintained an agent at Mohammerah, one Mirza Kasim Khan, known as the Karguzar, to superintend mercantile operations, represent the Foreign Office, and watch Messrs. Lynch. The first of these functions was easily performed, because the

A Persian official

composed of 5,000 men, with twelve guns, four armed steamers, and two sloops of war. At daybreak on March 26, 1857, the British guns opened fire upon the Persian batteries, which were silenced in less than an hour. The troopships then advanced, passed the batteries amid musketry fire, landed under Sir H. Havelock, drove the Persians out of the batteries (these alone of the enemy showed fight), and advanced through the palm-groves towards the camp where the main Persian army was entrenched. The latter fled precipitately, leaving their tents, stores, ammunition, and sixteen guns. The officers were afterwards publicly disgraced by order of the Shah, being dragged along the ranks by rings through their noses, beaten, and cast into prison. The arch-coward, however, Khanlar Mirza, who ought to have been shot, having made a present of 8,000*l.* to the prime minister, received a sword and robe of honour.

[1] W. K. Loftus (*Travels in Chaldæa*, p. 278), W. F. Ainsworth (*Personal Narrative*, vol. ii. p. 175).

operations could not be said as yet to have begun; the second became an excuse for protracted delays, caused by a dutiful reference to official superiors; while the third offered a boundless field for meddlesome and nonsensical activity. It did not argue a high level of practical intelligence to insist that the import duty upon foreign merchandise should be levied on the price, whatever it might be, that the article would fetch at the moment in the local bazaar. But commercial law did not happen to be the *forte* of the Karguzar. On this occasion he was very much interested in myself and my future movements. He had already complained of the steamer being detained on my account; and had peremptorily ordered it, quite *ultra vires*, to quit. A series of messages now passed, the Karguzar requiring my passport, which had not once been asked for during three months of previous travel in Persia, and finally bidding me to call upon him at sunrise before starting next morning. This I felt myself quite unable to do; and leaving him to devise fresh toils for the bird that had flown, our steamer weighed anchor at 6 A.M. and started up the river.

Bahmeshir Channel

Some two miles above Mohammerah, and, therefore, three miles from the mouth of the Haffar, we come to the Bahmeshir (derivation disputed),[1] or alternative channel, by which a portion of the waters of the Karun still enter, and the whole, in all probability, once entered, the Persian Gulf. It runs in a line from north-west to south-east, parallel with the Shat-el-Arab, for a total length of over forty miles, and flows into the sea by a wide mouth at a distance of several miles from the embouchure of the estuary. Along its shores, as on those of the Shat-el-Arab near Busrah, are to be seen screens of reeds planted at low water level, in order to catch the fish which are left in great numbers on the muddy banks when the tide retires. In ancient times the Bahmeshir was the eastern mouth of the Tigris, and the Shat-el-Arab the western. The island enclosed between them, the Haffar, and the sea, is the Dilmun of the cuneiform inscriptions, and the Persian Mian-i-Rudan, i.e. Between the Rivers, or Mesopotamia.[2]

[1] Some spell it Bahr-el-Mashir (Sea of Mashir ?). But the name is probably a contraction of Bahman Ardeshir, to whom are attributed many works in these parts. The district on the lower Tigris was called Khorah Shad Bahman, the maritime border Bahman Ardeshir.

[2] It was also called Muharzi, from the port of Muharzeh at the north end of the island. Yakut described it as a triangle, with the Persian Gulf as base, and the two mouths of the Dijleh (Tigris) as sides.

Should the unfriendly attitude of the Turks lead at any time to positive collision, it may be of incalculable importance to Persia to have an alternative and independent way of entry into and exit from the Karun. Such a channel is provided by the Bahmeshir. With both its banks and its mouth exclusively Persian, and safely removed from risk either of Ottoman menace or violence, it may be that the Bahmeshir will once again be utilised for navigation. It was ascended by the steamship 'Euphrates' under Major Estcourt, in connection with the Euphrates expedition of 1836. In 1841 Lieutenant Selby steamed down it from Mohammerah to the sea and back, and found a channel of not less than nine feet at low water. Layard described it as having a good navigable channel to its junction with the sea of not less than four fathoms depth, and over half a mile in width, and said that its entrance at low water, during spring tides, was more than three fathoms deep, and therefore practicable for ships of large burden. Since then shoals appear to have formed outside its sea-mouth, pierced only by a tortuous and shifting channel. There is a rise and fall of tide of about nine feet, and the water throughout its course is rumoured to be growing shallower. It would be well if a careful survey were made of this channel; and it is possible that by dredging or other artificial means it might again become accessible throughout, and thus provide an exclusively Persian entry to the Karun. I doubt if the Persians themselves, who are commercially apathetic, except in the cause of obstruction, have at all realised the possible value of this stream. By us, however, it should not be overlooked.

Mohammerah itself is buried in palm-groves that would consecrate any landscape; but at Gisbah, about eight miles up the river, this edging of green suddenly ceases, and henceforward as far as Bund-i-Kir the banks are absolutely bare, or are covered only with low scrub and tamarisk bushes and willows,[1] here and there intersected by creeks or the desiccated beds of forgotten canals. In this lower part of its course the banks are everywhere low and flat, but farther on they increase in height till they attain an altitude above the water, sometimes of from twenty

Landscape

[1] This tree, half poplar and half willow, called *gharab* (or 'tear') by the Persians, is, without doubt, says General Schindler, the true *Salix Babylonica*, or willow of scripture (Levit. xxiii. 40; Job xl. 22; Psalm cxxxviii. 2; Isaiah xv. 7, xliv. 4). The tree which we know as *Salix Babylonica*, or weeping willow, is not found in Chaldæa or Susiana, but is the Persian *Bid-i-majnun*.

to thirty feet. Here, too, the Karun is in volume and dimensions a noble river, commonly from 300 yards to a quarter of a mile across, it not being till above Ahwaz that it is sometimes contracted in width to 200 yards. At this time the river was very full, a heavy fall of snow or rain in the mountains having just preceded; and mud held in turbid solution changed its waters to the colour of Turkish coffee, and its consistency to that of prison gruel.

At a distance of from ten to twelve miles above the Bahmeshir occurs a third, but now choked and disused channel of the Karun, by which also, in days probably anterior to the Bahmeshir, it once sought the sea. This dried-up bed, which is supposed to be that up which the fleet of Nearchus sailed to join Alexander the Great at Susa, is called the Karun-el-Amieh, or Blind Karun.[1] It was followed by the officers of the Euphrates Expedition in 1836 towards the sea, and was found by them to consist of a depression 200 yards in width, in the middle of which still existed a small channel that was filled by the flowing tide, but left with only one foot of brackish water at the ebb. The probability of this having been the original or earliest mouth of the Karun is enhanced by the fact that the Oriental geographers describe the Haffar Canal as being four parasangs, or about fifteen miles in length, figures which almost exactly correspond with the length of the present stream from the mouth of Karun-el-Amieh to Mohammerah; so that we should be justified in regarding the entire river-bed below the former point as an artificial creation. Support is given to this hypothesis by the fact that, in the time of the Elamites and Babylonians, we hear of a canal being cut from the lower Karun to the Bahmeshir, beginning at the present Sablah. It was in existence in Alexander's time. This canal, after being repaired by the Asad-ed-Dowleh, was called Nahr-el-jedid, or the New Canal, and Mukadessi, the Arab geographer, calls the top of the Bahmeshir, Fam-el-Asadi, i.e. mouth of the Asad.

Blind Karun

From the Karun-el-Amieh has been cut a canal conducting to the former Ka'b capital of Fellahieh, on the Jerrahi river, and variously known as Kaban or Gobban. In the last century a dam was thrown across the Karun at this point by Sheikh Salman, i.e. Suleiman, of the Ka'b tribe, with the

Kaban canal

[1] This name, if correct, is very curious; for to call a river 'blind' is not Arabic either in idea or expression. If the channel had been dry for a long time, the name might originally have been *Karun ila ma*, i.e. 'Karun without water.'

object of diverting its waters either into this canal or into the Karun-el-Amieh. In the Persian invasion of Kerim Khan this dam was destroyed, and the Blind Karun consequently achieved blindness. The canal is still navigable at seasons to Fellahieh. A long time before reaching it, the pyramidal tomb, in thirteen steps or stages, of Robein-ibn-Yakub, or, as it is sometimes called, Rewah Ali, on the right bank stands out the sole feature in the 'the level waste, the rounding grey,' appearing alternately on the right and left hand as the river twists and turns. Beyond, another small tomo, known as Imamzadeh Ali-ibn-Husein, shaded by a cluster of six palms, succeeds and is in turn caught up and left behind. Further on we pass Imam Sabah (i.e. Sâb'a, or the seventh) on the right bank, the half-way stage to Ahwaz. Beyond this, a post named Kajarieh has lately been established on the right bank, where is a Telegraph office and halting place of the steamers.

Arab camps

In the summer the banks of the river in this part are wholly destitute either of population or verdure. But at the time of my visit occasional Arab encampments were to be seen on the water's edge, consisting either of black tents or of a square enclosure composed of mat huts with a fence of thorns, the horses and cattle being folded at night in the interior to keep them from the attack of wild beasts. These nomads move upwards in the winter months from the date groves, loosely turn the soil with rude wooden ploughs drawn either by donkeys, horses, or cattle, scatter the seed, and await the harvest. Having gathered this in the early spring, and procured flour for bread and fodder for their horses during the remainder of the year, they

> Fold their tents
> And silently steal away.

In the neighbourhood only of these temporary encampments is cultivation to be seen, the rest of the country having the appearance of a desert. But the entire district is one of incredible natural fertility, and it is pitiable to see stores of potential wealth lying idle in a land that is always bewailing its poverty. At 8 P.M. the 'Shushan' dropped anchor for the night by the small village of Ismailieh, on the left bank. The tide from the Shat-el-Arab and Bahmeshir is felt as far as this place, and in the lower reaches of the river causes a rise and fall of from four to five feet.

Early in the following morning we passed Beraikieh, the first

TOMB OF ROBEIN-IBN-YAKUB

village of any size since leaving Mohammerah. It contains about three hundred inhabitants, Arabs, and their sheikh is subordinate to Sheikh Mizal Khan. Then follow a series of river loops and windings, so tortuous that we continually find ourselves steaming right away from the point at which we are due to arrive in another hour, while on the boat's deck we can never settle our relations with the sun. The next village, again on the left bank, is Kut Omeirah; while further on, at a distance of about thirty miles from Beraikieh, is Kut Abdullah, the main settlement of the Bawieh, who are also a sub-division of the Ka'b tribe. This is one of three places between Mohammerah and Shushter where the local sheikh formerly claimed the right of levying a custom duty or blackmail upon any goods passing up the river, either by boat or caravan. For convenience sake these tolls, which no one ventured to dispute, were subsequently amalgamated, and are still exacted from native merchandise at the two termini.

Riverain settlements

The scenery on the Karun in these parts cannot be styled otherwise than depressing. Fifty years ago travellers described the banks between Mohammerah and Ahwaz as being abundantly wooded with poplar, tamarisk, and small timber. A good deal of this has since disappeared, and a low scrub or brushwood in parts is all that breaks the flat monotony of the river's edge. On either side the plain, marshy, bare, and untilled, may be seen stretching away to the horizon. Where the banks are at all high the boat is quite concealed from view at the distance of a few yards; but over the level expanse its tall funnel can be seen for miles, projecting like a stick of black sealing-wax from the ground, and appearing to creep stealthily over the surface. For many hours before reaching Ahwaz we were in sight of the sandstone ridge with pointed summits that stretches across the country, and is responsible for the barrier there existing in the river bed. Throughout our journey we had seen a great variety of wild fowl on the river, duck, teal, snipe, pelican, and gulls. About two miles below Ahwaz some of us went ashore with guns and rifles to test the resources of the scrub on the right bank. Wild fowl rose in clamorous flocks from swamps and pools a little way inland; francolin [1] (called a partridge in these parts, but in

Wild game

[1] *Tetrao francolinus*; the male bird has a ring round its neck. This is the 'black partridge' of India. In Persia it is called *durraj*. *Vide* Layard's *Early Adventures*, vol. i. pp. 358, 476, and Yule's *Marco Polo*, vol. i. p. 101.

size and appearance more resembling a hen pheasant) jumped up at our feet and whirred away with a flight like that of a grouse; several hares scampered hither and thither. I shot a big wild cat which turned out to be a lynx, and was as large as an Indian cheetah, and some monster wild boar appeared within easy range. It would be difficult to ride them in this country, because of the swamps and deep nullahs or cracks in the surface; but some years ago pig-sticking expeditions were regularly organised from Baghdad. For anyone content with small game a richer preserve could not be found than the Karun valley; while, for the more ambitious, lions are also forthcoming, and further north, in the Bakhtiari Mountains, a number of antelope, ibex, and wild goat.

At 3 P.M. the 'Shushan' was anchored in mid-stream below the rapids of Ahwaz, having occupied twenty-three hours' steaming in the ascent.[1] The distance from Mohammerah by river is about 117 miles; the land march is much less, being calculated by different authorities as from seventy-four to eighty-two miles. Here I continued my walk up the right bank in order to inspect the ruins of the famous *bund* or dam, and the not less famous rapids. It should be added that the town of Ahwaz is 220 feet above the level of the Persian Gulf.

Ahwaz

Navigation is abruptly suspended at Ahwaz, and the crux of the Karun difficulty is created by the existence in the immediate neighbourhood of the river of a formidable outcrop of tertiary sandstone, which, after constituting the somewhat remarkable ridge already mentioned as rising with oblique stratification and zigzag outline, at a slight distance from the left bank, suddenly obtrudes itself in the shape of a number of ledges right across the river bed, and then vanishes under the surface of the plain, only to reappear in another and lower ridge some miles further to the west. It is the obstacle formed by these ledges, of which there are four, cutting the stream almost at right angles, and the abrupt fall of about eight to ten feet between the water level above and below, that constitute the rapids. There are

The rapids

[1] The descent subsequently occupied $11\frac{1}{2}$ hours, there being a great deal of water in the river. The average time occupied by the 'Blosse Lynch,' a much larger paddle-wheel vessel, with which Messrs. Lynch have resumed the navigation, was $16\frac{1}{2}$ hours in the ascent and $10\frac{1}{2}$ in the descent, in the high waters of the preceding spring. The velocity of a full current is from 4 to 5 miles in the hour; of a low current, from 1 to $1\frac{1}{2}$.

commonly said to be five of these; but three only present at all a serious impediment to navigation, the remaining two being very slight and, when the river is full, all but imperceptible. Below the lowest rapid, where the 'Shushan' anchored, the river contracts to a breadth of about 200 to 250 yards. It then begins to expand, and two large islands composed of silt occur in mid stream. Above this, at the point where are the middle and main rapid and the remains of the ancient bund, the right bank is deeply embayed by the impact of the current, and the distance from shore to shore is approximately half a mile. Higher up it narrows again, and resumes its normal width of about 400 yards.[1]

The great dam

Starting from the south and moving up stream, I found the first rapid, which is formed some distance below the point of the two large islands, invisible save for a slight swirl in the current, although the reef of rock which causes it was above the surface. The second rapids, two in number, formed by a ledge of rock at the head of the same islands, were also insignificant. Then came two more formidable barriers. The fall in the third set of rapids is very perceptible, and the rush of water was powerful, but not overwhelming. At the fourth rapid, above 150 yards higher up the stream, and in the full sweep of the bend, the water dashes with a roar through two gateways at the west extremity of a much more prominent rocky reef, stretching right across the river, and supporting the massive remains of the great dyke of Ahwaz. This famous structure, commonly attributed to the Sassanian monarchs, was designed to hold up the waters of the Karun, which were then diffused by means of ditches and canals through the surrounding country, at that time and for long after renowned for its rich plantations of the sugar-cane. The ruins of the dam, upon which it is likely that, as at Shushter, there may have been superimposed a bridge, survive in the shape of big masses of masonry, still held together by an indestructible cement, and built upon each of the rocky islets that here span the current. The abutment on the right bank is also visible, having withstood the floods of centuries. Though it is but little, yet enough remains to show the solid and imposing character of the ancient work, and to indicate the revolution that it must have effected in

[1] All figures of breadth, depth, or volume relating to the Karun vary considerably, according to the season of the year and the state of the water at the time of the writer's visit.

the physical condition of the neighbouring country. Both on the right and left banks passages and tunnels have been cut in the rock at the water level, in which water-wheels originally, and in the case of some on the left bank, still revolve. There are also to be seen in the neighbourhood of the town a large number of old circular mill-stones, which were used for the grinding of flour and the crushing of the sugar-cane. It is not known when or how the *bund* was destroyed, though the date may probably be assigned to the thirteenth century, when we read that the prosperity of the town and neighbourhood fell into utter decay. At the discussion before the Society of Arts General Schindler mentioned a local legend, which attributed the disaster to the wicked machinations of a mediæval sugar merchant, who cornered the market; but after a time, when the price had risen and he opened his bags, found them full, not of sugar, but of scorpions, whose tails were so sharp that they cut a thick felt carpet in two. Such myriads of these scorpions came out that the people fled, and have never returned.[1]

It is the twofold rapid racing through the gaps left by the destruction of the *bund* that has ever since constituted the main obstacle to the continuous navigation of the Karun. The main channel is the aperture between the right bank, which is steep and lofty, and the first rocky islet in the current, the passage varying from fifty to eighty yards in width according to the condition of the water, and there being an approximate fall of three feet in a distance of fifty yards. Between the islets and the main section of the sandstone ledge which dams the rest of the stream is a second and narrower rapid. Through both these gateways there was a swift and noisy rush of water—I can hardly call it a cataract, for it was not comparable to the headlong sweep of the Great Bab at the First Cataract of the Nile. It was by the larger or western channel that Selby took up the 'Assyria,' with Sir H. Layard on board, in March 1842. She was a paddle-wheel steamer, 100 feet long. They passed the lower rapids without difficulty, the river being full and the ledges completely concealed. Twice did Selby attempt to force the main rapid by steam alone, but the force of the current, running at the rate of 5 to 5¼ miles an hour, turned the 'Assyria' completely

Main rapid

[1] Two other versions of the tale are mentioned by De Bode (*Travels in Luristan*, vol. ii. p. 154).

round, and he was compelled to resort to more powerful means. Putting out a strong hawser or tow-line to the shore, and ordering the engines to be worked at full speed while the crew hauled upon the hawser, he again turned the ship's head towards the gap. For a few moments she stood trembling but motionless, and then slowly forged ahead, until presently, within less than half an hour from the first unsuccessful attempt, she was moored in the tranquil waters off the town. On her return journey, a short time afterwards, the 'Assyria' 'shot through the opening like an arrow.' It was through the same gate that the 'Susa,' the small launch in which I ascended the upper river, was towed up earlier in 1889, and here, too, the 'Shushan' passed without difficulty in 1890. I do not myself think that, in a favourable state of the water, there need be the slightest risk in taking up a steamer. The configuration of the river banks and rocks in mid-stream is convenient for the purpose. I even think that the conditions are not infrequent when engines of reasonable horse-power would suffice to take up a vessel alone.

Highest rapids

The fifth and final set of rapids are about half a mile higher up the stream, and a little above the village of Ahwaz. They are formed by a low double ridge of rock projecting like a hump across the river, and pierced by two channels in low water, but forming rapids when the river is full. Above them the Karun resumes its placid surface, and no further obstacle to navigation occurs till within a few miles of Shushter. The entire length throughout which the river is broken up by rocks and rapids is from $1\frac{1}{4}$ to $1\frac{1}{2}$ mile. Sharks of some size frequently come up to Ahwaz, and are seen swimming in the pools below the rapids. They even penetrate as far as Shushter. Just above the topmost rapid, the dry bed of an old canal leads in a southerly direction from the left or eastern bank of the river. It is supposed to have been dug for the purpose of diverting the main stream while the *bund* was being constructed, and is said to run far in the direction of Fellahieh.

Channel, canal, or tramway?

The difficulty of passing the main rapid, except under particular conditions of the water, is so great that, if continuous navigation is to be attempted, artificial means are a *sine quâ non*. Three projects have been suggested for the solution of the problem. The first of these is the cutting, blasting, or training of a channel through the rocks and in the bed of the river itself, which should be available for the passage of vessels. This scheme may be dismissed from consideration as being both costly in execution and problematical in issue, it being quite uncertain how the level of the two parts of the river would be affected by this sudden and violent readjustment of the fall. The second plan is the cutting of a canal with locks for a distance of about a mile and a half from the lower to the upper river, through the nearly level ground on the left bank. Though a perfectly feasible undertaking, and one that has the merit of obviating transhipment, it is not in the least likely to be commenced by the Persian Government, both because it would involve a considerable outlay, and because they would forfeit thereby their control of the upper river navigation. The third alternative, which I strongly recommended in writing to the 'Times,' was the construction of a light horse-tramway over the same piece of ground on the left bank, from the river below to the pool above the rapids. Traversing the distance on foot, I found it to consist of a slight slope with insignificant undulations, the distance, if the village of Ahwaz were skirted, being about a mile and three quarters. This work has since been undertaken by a native company, the Nasiri, of whom I shall have more to say later on. A tramway, however, only facilitates, without obviating, transhipment; and I incline to the opinion that should a railroad ever be laid upon this line it should be continued as far as Mohammerah, so as to prevent the double break of bulk in transhipment there and at Ahwaz; whilst the new road now being constructed from Teheran may even find it advisable to make Ahwaz rather than Shushter its terminus.

Ahwaz, or Aginis

The modern village of Ahwaz is situated on the left bank of the river, which rises to some height above the stream, at a point nearly parallel with the highest rapids. It is a wretched collection of mud-hovels, with a small rectangular fort in a state of ruin upon the brink, and an Arab population of about 700. Nothing redeems the place from abomination but the possession of a humble *imamzadeh*, or saint's tomb, whose white plastered cupola gleams agreeably from a cluster of dark green trees. This is all that survives in the room of the once famous Aginis,[1] the mediæval capital of a province, the residence of royalty,

[1] The yet earlier history of Ahwaz may be remitted to a footnote. Nearchus, ascending the Pasitigris (Karun), came to a lake, into the northern end of which the Tigris flowed, and on which was situated the Susian town or village Aginis,

the see of a Christian bishop, and a favoured resort of wealth and luxury. Gibbon has preserved in characteristic garb the tale of the 'gay Barbarian,' Harmozan, prince or satrap of Ahwaz and Susa, and his interview with the conquering Khalif, Omar.[1] It was in the time of his Abbaside successors at Baghdad that Ahwaz reached the height of its fame. Then the Arab historian Abulfeda described the banks of the river at this spot as 'adorned with gardens and pleasure-houses, and enriched by extensive plantations of the sugar-cane and other valuable products of the vegetable kingdom.' There is moderation as well, no doubt, as truth in this statement; but the most liberal exaggeration could hardly justify a native writer of the present century in describing the dimensions of the mediæval Ahwaz as forty parasangs (150 miles); or excuse the travelled Captain Mignan for confounding the sandstone ridge behind the town with the ruins of the ancient city, which he said extended for ten or twelve miles, and, in the opinion of the inhabitants, for a journey of two months.[2] The halcyon days of the

500 *stadia* from Susa. This lake, which has since disappeared, filled the depression west of the Karun as far as Hawizeh (i.e. Small Ahwaz). The Tigris left it somewhere near the present Suwaib, and then flowed into the Shat-el-Arab. The lake or swamp is called in Assyrian cuneiform inscriptions 'Agamme,' or 'Aghme,' and Nearchus' Ἄγινιν (accus.) probably stands for Ἄγμην. Nearchus did not enter the lake or go to Aginis, but ascended the Pasitigris to a bridge of boats on the road between Persis and Susa, 600 *stadia* from the latter. This bridge was probably near, or at, the present Ahwaz, which may also be the site of Ptolemy's Ταρείανα (an old Persian word meaning 'passage,' or 'ford'). Later on it was called Wajar Khuzistan, or market of Khuzistan. Its inhabitants were Elamites, named Huz or Huj; and the Arabs (*vide* Abulfeda) called the place Suk-el-Ahwaz, i.e. Market of the Huz (Ahwaz being plural of Huz). It was at the meeting-point of several roads—north to Asker Mukrem or Lashker, and Shushter; east to Persis (Fars); west, to Wasit on the Tigris; and south, to Busrah.

[1] *Decline and Fall of the Roman Empire*, cap. li.

[2] 'Memoir on the Ruins of Ahwaz,' contained in *Travels in Chaldæa*, p. 302. There cannot be a doubt that Captain Mignan, who visited Ahwaz in September 1826, did commit this extraordinary error, for he speaks of 'the immense mass of ruins that rears its rugged head behind the town' (p. 297), and argues that they must have been erected long after the days of Alexander the Great, otherwise they would have been noticed by 'that illustrious warrior' in his ascent of the Karun (p. 307). It is still more amazing that the usually intelligent Stocqueler, visiting Ahwaz five years later, in May 1831, compliments Captain Mignan on 'the accuracy and research of his sketch of Ahwaz,' and adds that he himself followed the same ruins for thirty miles and upwards without arriving at their termination, which, however, he subsequently encountered on the Persian Gulf at Bunder Mashur!' (*Fifteen Months' Pilgrimage*, vol. i. pp. 62, 84). Where was ancient Babylon, or Thebes the mother of cities, compared with this astounding Ahwaz?

old Aginis came to an end with the rebellion against the Khalifs of the African negroes who had been imported to labour in the sugar plantations. The revolt was suppressed; but the city and its surroundings never recovered, and fell into deeper and more forlorn decay, until the emigrant Ka'b Arabs turned their nomad steps in this direction, and reared their clay hovels amid the piles of débris that still mark the ancient site. Evidence of a yet earlier period and of a dead religion, as well as a vanished splendour, exists in the sandstone ridge above mentioned, where may be seen hollow excavations high up in the rock, hewn in the olden days of the fire-worshippers for the exposure of the dead, and in some of which bones were actually discovered by Lieutenant Selby's party. In the mountain cliffs near Shushter have been found similar rock Towers of Silence.

Ahwaz played a memorable but an even less distinguished part than Mohammerah in the incidents of 1857. After the occupation of the latter place, three small river-steamers, the 'Comet,' 'Planet,' and 'Assyria,' with 300 men, and three gun-boats in tow, were detached to pursue the retreating force up the river to Ahwaz. Captain Rennie was in command of the flotilla, Captain Hunt of the soldiers, Captain Selby commanded one of the vessels and acted as guide. At Ahwaz the Persian infantry, 7,000 strong, with a large force of cavalry, was found encamped a few hundred yards from the right bank; a garrison of 500 men held the town and fort upon the opposite shore. No sooner did the English prepare to land than the garrison decamped, while simultaneously the defending army melted into the desert. The dissolution was not less complete than when the mirage, so common on the neighbouring Chaldæan plains, wastes on approach into thin air. It is true, as I have said, that the Persian Commander-in-Chief, by paying the Grand Vizier a bribe of 8,000*l.*, or at the rate of about 1*l.* for every man who ran away, received a sword of honour from the Shah. But no historian will be disposed to speak harshly of so superlative a sample of Eastern equity.

War of 1857

Since the opening of the Karun to foreign commerce in October 1888, another small settlement, called Bunder-i-Nasiri, in compliment to the Shah (Nasr-ed-Din), had been established on a slight elevation overlooking the river at the point below the rapids where steamers come to anchor, and about one mile south of the native village. So far the reality hardly cor-

Bunder-i-Nasiri

responded to the grandiloquence of the title. The place consisted of four or five mat huts, in front of one of which floated the Persian flag, and a small gun was planted to fire salutes and to proclaim the majesty of government. Within resided the deputy of the Governor-General of Arabistan, an official named Mirza Akbar Ali, with whom I was now to make acquaintance, and in whom I found a model type of the genus Persian subordinate official, species first-class obstructionist. Another of the mat-huts was tenanted by the agent of Messrs. Lynch, who with great difficulty obtained permission to take up his residence here, and was obliged to pay a rent of 600 *tomans* (170*l.*) a year for quarters that would be exorbitant at 7*l.* This preposterous fine—for it was nothing else—was submitted to on the understanding that it was to be the rent of a substantial structure, which was forthwith to be erected by the Persian Government, with a suitable shed for stores. A year had elapsed, and the new residence was as much *in nubibus* as ever, although no mention had been made of any consequent abatement of rent.

Introduction to the Mirza

I was the bearer of letters of recommendation from the British Resident at Bushire to the Nizam-es-Sultaneh, Governor-General of Arabistan, requesting him to aid my journey by means of the Persian steam launch, the 'Susa,' lately placed upon the upper river. Being already three days behind time at Ahwaz, I heard with pleasure that the 'Susa' was lying at anchor above the rapids, waiting for the arrival of the 'Shushan' in order to proceed to Shushter. I therefore called upon the Mirza with my letter to the Governor, to request that the 'Susa' might be ordered to start upon its journey at daybreak on the following morning. It would have been possible for me, and far better, to have ordered horses on my own account and to have ridden to Shushter, the distance being only 56 miles by land. But I was informed that the route might be impassable from rain and mud, and—I did not yet know the Mirza.

His wily ways

The latter first attempted at the same time to put me off and to vindicate his own official importance by making the plea of illness an excuse for not receiving me. I replied that my business was urgent; and an interview was accordingly arranged, the imaginary illness not again figuring in the negotiations. I found the Persian seated *more Persico* on the ground in his mat-hut, with a carpet spread in front of him, on which candles were placed, while chairs were arranged opposite for myself and party. At first the Mirza was all compliance. After a slight show of hesitation he acceded to my request; the boat was to be ready to start at 7 on the following morning, and I was to be on shore at 6.30. He only required to see my passport, a demand with which I readily complied, the more so as I knew that he could not read a word of it, and only wished to make a show of official precision. He then rambled off into a lengthy disquisition upon the friendship of Persia and England, the common interest of the two countries, their common friends and foes (a sly dig at Russia), and his personal desire, to which Messrs. Lynch's agent could testify (here I am afraid that I exchanged winks with that gentleman, whose life had been rendered a burden to him for six months by the obstructive persecutions of the Mirza), to promote concord between these heaven-appointed allies. Having been for some months in Persia, I was now quite familiar with this formula, which I had many times heard, couched in almost identical terms, and, I imagine, learnt off by heart by every Persian official on his appointment. However, I reciprocated the compliments, and the interview closed.

Throughout this colloquy an interested audience had watched, without taking any part in the proceedings. On either side of the Mirza squatted two somewhat lugubrious-looking personages, who said nothing, but smoked the *kalian* as it was passed round. One of them was minus an eye, which gave him a rather ill-favoured appearance, but their mien was sufficiently distinguished to lead me to suppose that they were Persian gentlemen and friends of the Mirza. It transpired, however, that they were two malefactors belonging to the ruling family of the Bakhtiari tribe in the neighbouring mountains, who had recently killed their brother and nephew in cold blood, and had been captured while in the jurisdiction of the Mirza.[1] In the absence of any guard-house, they were now being kept in the Mirza's hut, where they shared his sleeping apartment, took their seats in the manner described at the durbar, and were on such general terms of familiarity that upon the Mirza accepting an invitation to dine in Messrs. Lynch's hut a few days later, he asked permission to bring his two guests with him. The harmony was enhanced by all

His distinguished guests

[1] They were Nasir Khan and Saif Allah Khan, who had murdered their brother, Mirza Agha Khan, chief of the Chehar Lang branch of the Bakhtiari Tribes. *Vide* the pedigree in cap. xxiv.

three getting drunk. Next the murderers sat two green-turbaned *seyids*, descendants of the Prophet, whose personal repute and illustrious descent lent a sort of balancing odour of sanctity to the proceedings.

Before 7 A.M. on the morrow I was on shore with my baggage, but the mules which had been ordered to convey the latter to the 'Susa' were not forthcoming; while the engineer was loafing about, waiting for instructions from the Mirza. Arousing this worthy, I requested permission to proceed at once in pursuance of his promise of the previous evening. I cannot relate in detail the incidents that ensued; but I may summarise them by saying that the next three hours were consumed in frivolous objections by the Persian, who had either repented of his premature amiability, or was frightened at the responsibility, or thought the occasion too good a one to be lost for demonstrating his own importance. He now protested that he had no authority to act without direct orders from the Nizam, that he could not look at my letters to the latter, because they were another man's property, and that he must have a formal guarantee testifying to my identity and absolving him from blame. A long time was spent in composing this ridiculous document, which had to be torn up after all, when I found that the Mirza had inserted in it an order to him from Messrs. Lynch to despatch the 'Susa'—an ingenious attempt to inveigle them into a false position—and a statement that the permission was only granted because I had official business to transact with the Governor, which I had not. It became necessary for me to adopt a more peremptory tone, and to insist either on compliance or refusal. This brought the Mirza to his senses; but another long interval ensued while the revised declaration was being drawn up, and a letter of explanation written to the Nizam; and it was not till eleven o'clock that I found myself on board the 'Susa,' and an hour later that she started under way. Exactly five hours had been consumed in the diplomatic caracoles of the Mirza, upon whom I was sufficiently human to vow vengeance if ever I arrived at Shushter.

The Mirza after a night's rest

At one stage of the morning's controversy the mat-hut presented an even more curious scene than on the previous evening. Not only were the same *dramatis personæ* present—the Mirza evolving interminable excuses, the pair of respectable but melancholy fratricides, the two holy men, and ourselves;

Dramatis personæ

but there was also a Persian gentleman who wanted to go up in the 'Susa' himself, and had intervened as peacemaker; the Arab sheikh of Ahwaz, a dignified old gentleman with grey beard; and finally, the sheikh's son, carrying a gun to protect his father, whose life was threatened by a blood feud, but himself attended by another man with a gun, being in reality a prisoner, like the Bakhtiari couple, and having been sentenced to the sticks for an act of robbery. In this mixed society of *seyids* and scoundrels, gaolers and prisoners, Persians, Arabs, and English—as diversified a *mejilis* on a small scale as was ever assembled—the momentous question was fought out as to whether I should travel sixty miles by river or by road.

Two more hours were wasted, and it was not till long after noon that we were under way, and had definitively entered upon the journey to Shushter. As the hours wore on, however, and against a current running less than 4 miles an hour the 'Susa' appeared unable to achieve a higher rate of progress than about $2\frac{1}{2}$ miles—a speed which enabled the villagers in the river-side camps to keep pace with us by slowly walking along the bank—I began to think that the victory over the Mirza and the loan of the 'Susa' had been somewhat dearly purchased. In 1889, after the Karun concession had been granted, this vessel, which is one of the two items composing the Persian Navy, had been taken by an English captain to Ahwaz, and towed by Persians up the rapids; since which time she had remained on the upper river, under the orders of the Nizam-es-Sultaneh, nominally for purposes of trade, but in reality serving no other purpose than to carry him up and down the river. Her draught of water was too great to allow of her being much used as a cargo boat, except when the water is high. She was piloted and steered by Arabs; but her engineer, a Turk from Baghdad, had never been on the upper river before, and vindicated his ignorance by a series of assurances that would have excited the jealous envy of the Mirza. I was to be landed without fail at Shushter at noon on the day after we had weighed anchor from Ahwaz.

The 'Susa'

Above Ahwaz the Karun is confined within lofty banks, varying from ten to twenty, and even thirty feet in height, with vertical profile of marl, and a bed of from 200 to 350 yards in width. Water for irrigation is drawn up from pools hollowed in the river bank, by means of leather skins and a pulley worked by oxen pacing up and down an inclined plane on

The Karun above Ahwaz

the top of the bank—the immemorial custom of Elam and Chaldæa. The Arab camps or villages, dependent for their existence on the water thus derived, are situated on the very brink, and the entire population, not working with the plough, would turn out to see us pass. Throughout the day we traversed a country devastated by locusts. They swarmed on the banks and hung in red festoons from the twigs of every bush and shrub; they dropped on the boat, scrambled into the cabin, and straddled all over the deck; and the drowned bodies of those that had not strength to cross the river floated in hundreds down the stream.

The first place of the smallest importance after leaving Ahwaz is the village of Weiss on the left shore, which, to a line of mud huts fringing the banks, adds the rare distinction of an *imamzadeh* and half a dozen palms.[1] This village marks the northern limit of Sheikh Mizal's jurisdiction, the territory beyond, though largely peopled by Arabs, being under the direct administration of the Governor of Arabistan. There is here a ferry across the river. Weiss is about thirty-five miles distant by water from Ahwaz, the river following a very serpentine course between; allowing for which circumstance it was still somewhat disquieting only to find myself abreast of the village at 1 P.M. on the day after leaving Ahwaz, or an hour later than the time at which I had been assured that I should reach Shushter, still nearly sixty miles distant by river.

Weiss or Oweiss

In the annals of earlier travellers Weiss has left a name for inhospitality quite uncommon among the Arab tribes. It was the furthest point reached, in his navigation of the Karun river in May 1831, by the adventurous Mr. Stocqueler, whose boat was stopped, plundered, and fired at by the sheikh and people of this place, and compelled to beat a precipitate retreat to Mohammerah.[2] Five years later, in November 1836, Major Estcourt's party, ascending the river in a native boat from Ahwaz, were refused provisions by the inhabitants, and were obliged forcibly to appropriate a sheep.[3] No more untoward demonstration took place on this occasion than the frantic shrieks of the juvenile population, who watched our passage from the

Shapur or Shaur river

[1] The *imamzadeh* is that of Oweiss ibn Karani, one of the companions of the Prophet, and the place is named from him.

[2] *Fifteen Months' Pilgrimage*, vol. i. pp. 63–7.

[3] W. F. Ainsworth's *Personal Narrative*, vol. ii. p. 222.

banks. Originally the Shapur, commonly pronounced Shaur river, which washes the western face of the great mound of Shush or Susa (Shushan the palace), flowed into the Karun from the north-west a little below Weiss. After deserting this bed it adopted a more southerly channel, joining the main river near Ahwaz. Later again it struck northwards, and at the time of Layard's and Selby's explorations in 1842, was found entering the Ab-i-Diz, or Dizful River, at a point twelve miles above Bund-i-Kir.[1] The comparatively recent and well-ascertained history of this river, whose various channels can be distinctly traced, is typical of that of all the rivers of Susiana, including the Karun itself, and accounts for the difficulty that has been felt by writers in identifying and reconciling the obsolete descriptions of the ancients.

For at least twelve miles above Weiss the Karun is followed in a perfectly straight line to Bund-i-Kir, where, for the first time since leaving Mohammerah, we find the river split up into several confluents; this being the point of junction of three streams, the Ab-i-Gerger, or artificial canal that runs from Shushter on the east; the Ab-i-Shuteit, or Karun proper, that runs also from Shushter in the centre; and the Ab-i-Diz, or river of Dizful, that runs from Dizful on the west. Comparing the singular straightness of the twelve-mile stretch of water below the angle of confluence with the accounts of old Arab geographers, who reported the artificial canal of the Ab-i-Gerger as being continued to Ahwaz, Selby thought that he saw therein a survival of the latter work; an hypothesis whose likelihood is only invalidated by the complete absence of any ancient bed, such as ought in that case to be forthcoming in the neighbourhood, of the main body of the Karun.

Point of confluence

Bund-i-Kir, called by Kinneir Bundekeel, and by Loftus Benderghil, signifies the *bund* or dyke of *kir* or bitumen, the stones of an artificial dam which, like those of Shushter and Ahwaz, once spanned the river at this point, and which tradition ascribes to Darius, having doubtless been cemented by that material. The members of the Euphrates Expedition found it in 1836 to be a small walled town, with a population of nearly 600; and General Chesney's book contains an illustration of the place as it then existed from the pencil of Major Estcourt

Bund-i-Kir

[1] *Journal of the R. G. S.*, vol. xvi. p. 57.

(vol. i., p. 198). In 1850 Loftus described it as a small Arab village of forty houses, entirely supported by the traffic of the ferry which is maintained across the various rivers at this spot;[1] and his account holds good of the present time. The hamlet is situated a little way inland on the projecting tongue of soil between the streams of the Shuteit and Ab-i-Gerger, and on the right bank of the latter. It is entirely surrounded, however, by the ruins of a large and important city, which were for the first time examined by Sir H. Layard in 1842, and found to belong to three periods, Kaianian, Sassanian, and Arab,[2] being identified by him with the remains of the early Persian city Rustam-Kowadh and the Arab Askeri-Mukrem.[3] At the time of my visit the old bricks were being utilised, by orders of the Nizam-es-Sultaneh, to construct a fort and telegraph station on the bank of the Shuteit, the Government having decided to establish telegraphic communication between Shushter and Mohammerah. These ruins, the physical surroundings of Bund-i-Kir, and the significance of its name, unite in eloquent testimony to a period, long dead and forgotten, when this wilderness blossomed like a rose, and when busy peoples, great public works, and a diligent cultivation beautified the now silent banks of the triple stream.

The three confluents

Layard represented the colour of the three rivers which here converge as being conspicuously different, that of the Ab-i-Diz being very dark, from the rich alluvial mould through which it flows, the Shuteit, or Karun proper, being of a dull reddish hue, and the Gerger canal a milky white. I did not observe this difference, which is probably more or less noticeable according to the state of the waters. At the point of confluence the first-named river appeared to me to be about 80 yards wide, the second 150 yards, and the third 60 yards, their united volumes occupying a bed about 300 yards in width.

The Ab-i-Diz

The Ab-i-Diz descends from distant sources in the mighty Zagros range. What is really its parent stream no two maps have hitherto agreed in indicating. Major Sawyer's explorations, however, in 1890, have proved that there are two main streams, one flowing from near Burujird and draining Silakhor, the other draining upper Feraidan and passing Baznoi. Hence he calls them the Ab-i-Burujird and Ab-i-Baznoi. Here,

[1] *Travels and Researches*, p. 290. [2] *Journal of the R. G. S.*, vol. xvi. p. 63.
[3] *Early Adventures*, vol. ii. p. 28.

however, I am only concerned with its lower course, when, after passing the town of Dizful, it meanders through a jungle-grown and untilled plain until its union with the Karun at Bund-i-Kir. This river has only once been ascended in a steamer, namely, by Selby and Layard in the 'Assyria' in the late spring of 1842, after their successful ascents of the Shuteit and the Gerger. Pursuing with some difficulty an exceedingly tortuous channel, they at length came to a spot called Kaleh Bunder, about twenty-five miles in a direct line, and a good deal more by water, from Bund-i-Kir. There they found the river divided into two branches by an island, and a natural *bund* or rocky reef stretching across both. Penetrating by an opening in the right barrier, they continued their ascent for a few miles further, and then, finding the stream very shallow and the current strong, turned round and steamed back to Bund-i-Kir. So far as I know, the Diz has never since been ascended or explored by an Englishman. The jungle on its banks is said to abound in lions, and I recommend it to any adventurous sportsman.

The Ab-i-Shuteit

The second river of the trio that unite at Bund-i-Kir, though locally known below Shushter as the Ab-i-Shuteit, is in reality the main channel of the Karun. It was the first of the channels navigated by Selby in the 'Assyria' in 1842. He ascended it to within six miles of Valerian's bridge at Shushter, where the boat ran aground, and was only got off by a lucky freshet of water descending from the hills. Both he and Layard described it as admirably adapted for steam communication, and as having a deep channel. It was reported to me as being broken up near Shushter into numerous shallow channels, separated by shoals or islets, and impassable to navigation; but it has since been adopted by the 'Shushan' as a preferable channel to the Gerger, although the steamer can get no nearer to Shushter than Shahrdinga, a distance of ten miles by land.

The Ab-i Gerger

My own course in the 'Susa' was to lie up the Gerger, or artificial canal, which, owing to its greater depth and less shifting bed, was at that time utilised as the river approach to the capital. How I ended by steaming down instead of up the Gerger, the circumstances which I shall now narrate will explain. It was 6.30 P.M. when we ran up alongside the bank at Bund-i-Kir; and the 'Susa' having already occupied more than eighteen hours' steaming, exclusive of twelve hours' stoppage at night, in reaching the half-way point between Ahwaz and Shushter, I began to be doubtful when, if ever, I should arrive at the latter place, the more so as the Ab-i-Gerger has a somewhat precarious channel, and it was not unlikely that the 'Susa' might ground on a shoal. The engineer, of course, assured me that if I remained on the boat he would deposit me at Shushter before noon on the following day. But my credulity had already been overstrained by his frequent promises that I should accomplish the whole journey in less time than had now been consumed upon half; while a simple mathematical calculation showed that no engineer in the world could take the 'Susa' up to Shushter in the specified time. I therefore decided to leave the boat and ride the remaining distance, instructing the 'Susa' to follow as best she could.

Night at Bund-i-Kir

Selby's report contains the amazing statement that the banks of the canal at Bund-i-Kir 'tower perpendicularly overhead to a height of 130 feet,'[1] an error which has been faithfully reproduced by Mr. Ainsworth.[2] It was up a bank of considerably less than 30 feet in height that I scrambled, and made my way to the nearest hovels. The villagers at first said that all their animals were out ploughing, and that they could let me have neither horses nor mules. But the magic name of the Nizam-es-Sultaneh, brought to bear upon the Sheikh—a benign old gentleman with well-dyed red beard—produced a startling revulsion of attitude, and I was promised the use of one horse and two mules for the morrow at the exorbitant rate of 12 *krans* each (7 shillings), the normal charge *per diem* being 3 or 4 *krans*. However, beggars cannot afford to be choosers; the bargain was concluded; the 'Susa' puffed off into the night, and I settled down as best I could in a mud hut, placed at my disposal by the Sheikh. A fire was lit on the floor in the middle of the room, which was sufficiently large to accommodate a good deal of smoke, as well as the Sheikh and his attendants, who, until requested to retire, seemed anxious to give me their company throughout the night.

Routes to Shushter

I was called at 4 A.M. the next day and started at 5. The sun did not rise for two hours, but there was a good moon, and happily the air was not cold. From Bund-i-Kir to Shushter there are three tracks by land, following respectively the left, the centre, and the right of the island formed

[1] *Journal of the R. G. S.*, vol. xiv. p. 241.

[2] *The River Karun*, p. 40.

by the two streams of the Shuteit and the Gerger, which separate at Shushter just as they reunite at Bund-i-Kir. I was conducted by the left or westernmost track, which is a full eight *farsakhs*, or thirty-two miles, in length, and is called Beni Hasan from the name of the Arab tribe encamped upon it. The middle road is called Beni Kaid Hasan for a similar reason, and is no doubt shorter, but appears to be impassable after rain. The easterly track, which was taken by Colonel Bell, strikes across to the right to Dowletabad, or Beni Daud, a distance of eleven miles, where it touches the right bank of the Gerger Canal, and follows the latter more or less closely to Shushter, twenty-one miles further on.

Sir H. Layard relates that in 1842, Selby and himself were confronted immediately outside Bund-i-Kir by a huge black-maned lion.[1] It was a curious coincidence that soon after starting we heard a lion roar a little way off. My guide, who was walking in front, informed me at the same moment that my horse was so much accustomed to go in advance, that he would himself facilitate my progress by dropping to the rear; an act of friendly consideration on his part for which I shall ever remember the Arab. The entire country between Bund-i-Kir and Shushter was crowded with game. Wild fowl of every description, mallard, teal, snipe, plover of two kinds, francolin, sand-grouse, pigeons, jackal—all these I saw within easy shot in the course of my ride; and a sportsman might without doubt make a large and varied bag. The fertility of the soil is beyond conception; and in the spring-time Layard has depicted the island as 'clothed with the most luxuriant vegetation, and enamelled with flowers of the most brilliant hues, the grass being so high that it reached to the belly of a horse.'[2] In winter there is no verdure, and the greater part of the ground is allowed to waste in jungle and swamp; no sign of cultivation being visible till I reached the Arab encampment of Beni Hasan, about twelve miles from Bund-i-Kir. There the entire population was abroad and astir, ploughing with horses, mules, buffaloes, bullocks, and even donkeys, and scattering the seed the moment the rude wooden share had scraped the

The island

[1] *Early Adventures*, vol. ii. p. 353. Lions are not uncommon in the jungle and brushwood bordering on the rivers, particularly the little-known and unexplored Ab-i-Diz. For some interesting remarks upon their haunts and peculiarities, *vide* the same work, vol. i. pp. 439–447; and De Bode, *Travels in Luristan*, vol. ii. p. 196.

[2] *Early Adventures*, vol. ii. p. 346.

surface. In industrious hands this island might become the granary of south-west Persia, producing not only wheat and barley, but cotton, rice, maize, tobacco, sesame, indigo, and opium in almost unlimited amount. Its fertility was well known to the ancients, and better utilised by them; and the omniscient Strabo described the soil as giving a return exceeding one hundred and even two hundredfold.

Sunrise

In the far east the sun topped the Bakhtiari mountains at 7.10 A.M., and threw a radiant gleam upon their snowy caps. A dense canopy of leaden clouds, hanging just above, with

> Ragged rims of thunder brooding low
> And shadow streaks of rain,

caused an atmospheric phenomenon which I imagine to be rare, and which I have nowhere previously seen. It appeared to have the effect, instead of absorbing the sun's rays as the disc arose, of resisting and throwing them across the heavens, so much so that in the opposite quarter of the horizon on the west was produced a very perfect reflection of the rising orb, in the shape of a circular nimbus of prismatic light. Too soon the vision faded and disappeared. At the Arab encampment, composed of parallel rows of reed huts, I struck the left bank of the Ab-i-Shuteit, here a fine river flowing between steep jungle-clothed banks with a width of about 250 yards. The track followed it for three or four miles, and then, at a point where a rocky bluff comes down to the right bank of the river, and there is a second Arab village on the left, struck across to the north-east in the direction of Shushter. I did not again see the Shuteit or Karun till above Valerian's bridge outside the city.

Outskirts of Shushter

As I neared Shushter, the ground showed abundant traces if not of present, at least of bygone cultivation. Dykes, water-courses, and the banks of dried canals intersected the country in every direction; while the recent rains had converted the track into a sea of mud. A village with palm-trees was passed on the left; a larger and thicker green fringe on the horizon gave suggestions of a better tilled and more populous site; a pyramidal spire crowning a ruined mosque appeared upon a hill-top; whitewashed cupolas shone amid the trees; and presently the panorama of a large town in a state of obvious decay unrolled itself upon the summit of a considerable elevation, evidently terminating on its right or eastern side in a steep gorge. Thick groves of *konar* trees[1] were scattered over what are now arable plots, but were once the famous gardens of Shushter; in the midst of which numerous brick towers of refuge—not unlike those that I have seen dotted in such numbers over the old hunting-grounds of the Turkoman freebooters in Transcaspia and Khorasan—showed that agriculture, even in the immediate vicinity of the town, can at one period have been far from safe, and paid an eloquent homage to the lawless proclivities of the Persian nomads in the past. I forded the shrunken stream of a canal, called the Minau, which formerly irrigated the suburbs to the south of Shushter, and of which I shall have occasion again to speak, passed the ruined *imamzadeh* of Abdullah on its isolated hill-top, the building being flanked on its northern front by two tottering minarets, and surmounted by a hideous plaster cone which looks, as Loftus said, exactly like the extinguisher of a candle; picked my way through heaps of débris that once marked a town wall, and emerged on to an open space round which, in open stalls, smiths and brass-workers were making a horrid din, and which was the wreck of a once extensive bazaar. Thus, almost before I was aware of it, I found myself in the interior of the capital of Khuzistan, and perhaps the most dilapidated city in Persia.

History

The derivation of the name Shushter is not positively certain, though it appears to be a comparative of the Pehlevi word Shus, signifying 'pleasant,' and consecrated to more than one site in this neighbourhood, particularly to the great mounds of Sus or Shush, commonly called Susa, and now definitely ascertained to be the ruins of 'Shushan the palace,' wherein Daniel relates that he saw the vision.[2] Whether or not the town was built by Shapur, the famous warrior king of the Sassanian dynasty (the probability being that it is of earlier date), that it has been the city of kings is certain, not merely from tradition but from the

[1] The *konar* (Greek, κόνναρος; Latin, *Zizyphus lotus vulgaris*) is a tree with dark green foliage and a long, yellowish berry, acid, but agreeable to the taste.

[2] Daniel, viii. 2. Sir R. Murdoch-Smith (*Journal of the Society of Arts*, May 10, 1889) suggested the derivation Shah Shatra, or City of the King. But the old Persian for these words would be Khshathra and Khshatya, out of which the modern Shushter, mediæval Tostar, and Sostrate, Sosirate, or Sostra of Pliny could never have been formed. Moreover, from Khshathra was derived the modern *Shehr* (e.g. Abu Shehr = Bushire), which originally meant a country, and has only in modern times stood for a city.

massive relics still surviving of a truly royal rule. Here, beyond doubt, the victorious monarch used occasionally to reside, and here he left perhaps the most striking and permanent among the many visible memorials of his zeal for public works and architectural splendour, that are still to be found scattered amid the mountains and valleys of South Persia. From this time forward, Shushter, elevated by the engineering works of Shapur into a strategical post of capital importance, continued to play a prominent part in history. At the time of the Arab invasion its inhabitants made a stout resistance, until betrayed by one of their own number. Profiting by this experience, when the next or Tartar wave of invasion beat against their gates, the Shushteris yielded to the power, and were the recipients of the clemency of Timur, who is even said to have repaired the dyke of Valerian. Half a century earlier, the Moorish pilgrim Ibn Batutah had thus described the city: 'On the first of the mountains there is a large and beautiful city, abounding with fruits and rivers, surrounded by a river known by the name of El Azrak, the Blue.' Later on, under the Sefavi dynasty, the town became a great centre of the Shiah propaganda, and a hotbed of religious fanaticism. It continued to be the capital of a province and the seat of government until the early part of the present century, when it was the residence of Mohammed Ali Mirza, son of Fath Ali Shah, and Governor-General of Kermanshah, Luristan, and Arabistan, at which time it is reported, though probably without truth, to have contained 45,000 souls. Depopulated, and all but destroyed by a severe plague in 1831–2, which carried off nearly 20,000 souls, and attacked by the cholera afterwards, it was superseded as the provincial capital by Dizful, and has never rallied since.

Population

The most conflicting estimates have been given of its numbers by different travellers. In 1836, Chesney reported it to contain 5,000 to 6,000 houses and 20,000 inhabitants. In the same year, Rawlinson returned the numbers as 15,000. In 1841, De Bode calculated the total as from 4,000 to 5,000, while in the following year Selby gave 8,000, and Layard 10,000 as the probable figure. At the present time, though it has again become the capital, the population is estimated as not more than 8,000, and these are spread over an extent of ground that would accommodate five times that number, but is little else than an indiscriminate pile of ruins. In a country remarkable for its dead and dying cities, for immense groups of human habitations, either wholly deserted or crumbling into irretrievable decay, Shushter earns a well-merited palm. Not even Isfahan, with all its majestic solemnity of ruins, can show, in proportion to its size, such heaps of débris, so many structures fallen, falling, or abandoned. What were once dwelling-houses are now formless mounds of brick, and many of the buildings still inhabited are in an intermediate stage between the two. A blight seems to overhang the spot, and Shushter might well stand for what a poet has dolefully styled the City of Dreadful Night. Among all writers there has been an absolute consensus of opinion that this fall of a once famous and inherently wealthy place has been due far less to visitations of nature than to the shameful iniquity and oppressions of the Persian Governors who have successively been deputed to this remote province, and have combined the rapacity of a Verres with the cruelty of an Alva.

Modern features

Such, however, as it is, Shushter possesses features uncommon in Persian towns. From the familiar clusters of low mud huts, it is with relief as well as surprise that we come to a place where the houses still standing are commonly of two storeys, the lower half of stone and the upper part of bricks embedded in clay, and that rise to a height most unusual in Persian habitations. The flat roofs of many of these edifices, which have a low parapet, and upon which the inhabitants sleep at nights, are over thirty feet from the ground. In the interior court there is commonly a large *aiwan*, or reception-chamber, one side of which opens, without either wall or doorway, into the court. The houses possess a further peculiarity, which redeems them from all risk of being forgotten. Shafts are pierced in the masonry of the walls from the roof to the ground, opening by an aperture or spout on to the street. They are the sole drain-pipe of each dwelling, down which the refuse is inexpensively discharged into the roadway, each vent being a nucleus of odours not less filthy than the filth which it exudes. A receptacle is provided below by a species of gutter which occupies the centre of the street, and which, in the absence of any scavengers, would be an impassable slough, were it not that, the town being situated on an elevation with a sandy soil, the rains sweep down much of the accumulations, and that these are found to have a marketable value in autumn as manure for the opium plantations outside the town.

Another remarkable feature of the place, not, however, visible from the exterior, is the almost universal construction of *shabedans*, or *shevedans*,[1] underground chambers hewn deep down in the rock upon which the city stands, ventilated by shafts conducting to the upper air. Almost every house is so provided; and one of these cellars that was shown to me, newly hollowed out beneath the Governor's palace, had been excavated to a depth of at least sixty feet below the surface, access to it being gained by a steep flight of steps, and light as well as air being admitted by a circular orifice in the vaulted rock-roof. In the months of July and August, when the heat is appalling, the inhabitants live almost entirely in these subterranean chambers, seldom stirring between 9 A.M. and sunset; and at such times the town becomes even more than ordinarily a necropolis in brick and stone.

Cellars

The trade of Shushter is equally inconsiderable with the agricultural development of its surrounding lands. Though possessed of a soil admirably adapted to the growth of opium, but little enterprise is shown in its cultivation, and only twenty or thirty cases are said to be exported annually to the Arabian coast and Muscat. Indigo is grown in some quantity outside the town, and is responsible for a predominant tone of blue in the costumes of both sexes. Selby, in 1842, though reporting the local trade as small, lamented that nearly all the cottons, woollens, chintzes, cutlery, hardware, and sugar were supplied by Russia, notwithstanding a long and tedious land-carriage from Isfahan.[2] Whatever may have been the case fifty years ago, I found that Russian ascendency had now completely ceased, there being few, if any, Russian articles in the town, and the European import trade consisting almost entirely of English or Indian goods, brought from Busrah either *viâ* Amarah on the Tigris and Dizful, or by Mohammerah and the Karun river. The sole local manufactures appear to be a species of bright-coloured carpet or matting, made of cotton and wool, and a felt of coarse pattern. The bazaar, which was once the largest in Khuzistan, consists only of two diminutive alleys crossing each other under a dome, of the stalls before alluded to, and of one or two open booths, with a roof

Trade and manufactures

[1] Elsewhere in Persia they are called *serdabs*, literally 'cold water.' Layard says they are known in Shushter as *shadrewan* (*Early Adventures*, vol. ii. p. 43); but this is a mistake.

[2] *Journal of the R.G.S.*, vol. xiv. pp. 234, 242.

resting on stone supports, that still survive in the centre of the miserable *agora*. There are no *khans*, or caravanserais, for merchants such as are usually found in Oriental cities.

Layard and Selby on the people

A very large proportion of the population are *seyids* (i.e. descendants of the Prophet), whose voluminous green turban, here even more than elsewhere, seems to be an excuse for insufferable airs, gross superstition, and an indolent life. Of their attitude towards strangers, however, the most conflicting accounts have been left by English visitors. Layard [1] and Selby [2] have spoken thereof in terms of the highest praise; and I cannot but attribute the favourable reception of Selby and his crew to the personal popularity and prestige of the great traveller under whose auspices they came.

Nor was the verdict of the quartermaster of the 'Assyria' much less complimentary, when in reply to a question from Sir H. Layard as to what he thought of Shushter, 'Well, sir,' he said, 'it ain't a bad place, but there bain't a public in it.' [3]

That Selby, however, felt a little nervous as to the justice of his tribute is evident from his next paragraph, where he says:—

> In writing thus highly of the Shushteris, I fear I may be considered as having drawn too highly-coloured and flattering a picture. Let future experience and knowledge of them decide the point, nor, until they are found unworthy of the character I have given them, let them be classed with their oppressive neighbours, the Persians.

Modern character

Unfortunately 'future experience and knowledge,' which we are now in a position to invoke, have decided the point both against Selby and his friends the Shushteris. Only eight years later, Mr. Loftus described 'the countenances of the inhabitants as not prepossessing, low cunning, deceit, and mistrust being universal among the lower classes;' [4] while the advent of Messrs. Lynch's agents and the opening of the Karun have supplied the present generation with the opportunity of giving the lie to the benignant assurances of their predecessors to Sir H. Layard. When Messrs. Lynch's representative first took up his abode there, in 1888, he found difficulty even in procuring drinking water and the commonest necessaries of life, so loth were the people to have any dealing with such 'an unclean thing;' and every obstacle was

[1] *Early Adventures*, vol. ii. p. 282; *cf.* pp. 44, 340, 357.

[2] *Journal of the R.G.S.*, vol. xiv. p. 230.

[3] *Early Adventures*, vol. ii. p. 357.

[4] *Travels and Researches*, p. 296.

still placed by the *mullahs* and *seyids* in the way of trade. The inhabitants had, in fact, been ordered not to purchase from the English, and the word for a general 'boycott' had been passed round. This unreasoning hostility might be expected in time to give place to a more sensible attitude; but it is illustrative of the difficulties with which Western influence is everywhere confronted in its first collision with Oriental prejudice, and which are often so little understood at home.

MERCHANTS OF SHUSHTER

Appearance and dress

The Shushteris, of whom I have said so much, are as peculiar in their origin, appearance, and dress as they are in their character and surroundings. Neither pure Arab nor pure Persian in descent, but a hybrid between the two, with a greater admixture of Arab blood, they seem to possess the less attractive features of either race. Their appearance is ill-favoured, and the reverse of healthy; a fact which may be due either to the drinking water, which is slightly brackish, or to the enervating heat in summer, or to their colossal neglect of the most elementary laws of hygiene, or to a combination of all three. Even in their apparel there is something distinctive, for along with the flowing cloak of the Arab they wear a dark or parti-coloured turban, one end of which is tucked up in front, while the other hangs down behind, not unlike the Afghan's head-dress. One who was well qualified to speak informed me that 'in character they are close, seldom spending money on anything but actual necessaries; that in bargaining they can hold their own with any Oriental people, and that to call them sharp in business matters is not saying much.' The town is divided into several wards or quarters, each with its own khan, and the population into corresponding factions; and where in England local conflicts are decided on November 5 by the peaceful arbitrament of the polling-booth, the Shushteri wire-pullers, who would probably confess a hearty contempt for representative institutions, adopt the more primitive method of fighting it out in the streets.[1] Finally, Layard may be quoted for the statement that 'the Shushteri ladies are renowned for their beauty, but not for their virtue;' with which concluding touch I may take literary leave of the good folks of Shushter.

Situation of town

In the situation of the town there is much that both harmonises with and accounts for the idiosyncrasies of its people. Unlike most Persian cities of any size, which are commonly built in plains at no great distance from the base of mountains whence they derive their water, Shushter is built upon a rock, and is at once sustained and fortified by the command of a noble river. Emerging from a pink sandstone ridge at a distance of about three miles to the north of the town, the Karun river, hitherto pent up in narrow gorges, and foaming over an obstructed bed, expands itself with all the luxury of new-found ease in the flat alluvial plains that stretch from here to the sea. By this mountain barrier, which is, so to speak, the advance-guard of the mighty Zagros range behind, Shushter is shut off from easy contact with the rest of Persia, and is brought into direct association both with the Iliats, or nomad tribes of the mountains, forming the various branches of the great family of Lurs, and with the Arabs of the plains. Its position at the outlet of the hills explains both its political and commercial importance; since it is at once the spot

[1] When the Nizam-es-Sultaneh was deprived of his post at No Ruz in 1891, and when news of the change of governors reached Shushter, that town and its people showed in their true colours. Everyone armed himself, and started out to wreak his private vengeance. Business was suspended; the shops were closed; the rival chiefs seized, and tortured, and mutilated each other; there was fighting in the streets; and patrols of armed men with difficulty kept the peace at night. The same phenomenon was repeated up and down Arabistan, and the governors of Hawizeh and Fellahieh were expelled by former tenants of their office.

from which these unruly tribesmen can be most effectively controlled, and the natural channel through which trade must pass to and fro between the rich inland districts of Burujird, Kermanshah, and Hamadan, and the Southern seas. To these advantages no inconsiderable strategical strength has been added by the happy natural juxtaposition of river and rock, as well as by artificial works which I shall now proceed to describe.

Water-works

It has already been indicated that the town is situated on an eminence at the northern extremity of an island formed by two branches of the Karun, the one the original river-bed, the other a canal partly cut by man, which reunite some twenty-five miles in a straight line further down at Bund-i-Kir. About 600 yards above the town, the Ab-i-Gerger canal diverges from the left bank of the main stream, and pursues a straight southerly course, intersected by two dams of which I shall speak, through a gorge artificially hewn for its reception in the rock upon which the city stands, thereby constituting an important military defence upon its eastern flank. Meanwhile the main body of the river, which from the point of bifurcation to that of reunion at Bund-i-Kir is popularly called the Ab-i-Shuteit, after parting with some of its waters in the manner described, makes a broad sweep to the west, laves the base of the rock upon which the *kaleh* or citadel, and behind it the city, stand, and then turns southwards, its channel being barred at this point by the celebrated *bund* and bridge of Valerian. While skirting the castle rock it sacrifices a further portion of its waters, which pass into a subterranean tunnel pierced beneath the citadel, and opening on to a further artificial canal on the western side of the town, manifestly designed in order to irrigate the suburbs, which are situated at too great an elevation above the Karun itself to get their requisite water supply therefrom. These three features, the Ab-i-Gerger, the Ab-i-Shuteit, and the Minau Canal, are the determining characteristics of the situation, and it is to their history, nature, and purpose, as well as to the elucidation of the problem in hydraulics which they present, and which Rawlinson described as 'one of the most intricate and contradictory objects of research upon which he was ever engaged,'[1] that I now turn. If my explanation or description does not exactly coincide with that of previous writers, it is not in either case given without careful study of all that has been written

[1] *Journal of the R.G.S.*, vol. ix. p. 75.

on the subject, nor without personal examination on the spot—a task which some of my predecessors appear to have discharged in the most perfunctory fashion.

1. The Ab-i-Gerger Canal. At the point of its divergence from the Karun, 600 yards above the town of Shushter, an artificial dyke is thrown across the opening of the canal. This dyke is constructed of large blocks of hewn stone, which in the low water of the summer months are left quite bare, with six sluices or passages for the water between. It appears to have been repaired, at the same time as Valerian's bridge, by Mohammed Ali Mirza, in the early part of this century, and to have then exchanged its previous name of Bund-i-Kaisar (a probable allusion to the legendary handiwork of Valerian in the reign of Shapur) for that of Bund-i-Shahzadeh, or Prince's Dyke. I did not, however, gather that either name is now in use.

1. The Ab-i-Gerger

At a little distance below this dam commences the artificial cutting in the sandstone rock through which the canal is conducted, and at half a mile from it occurs a second *bund* or dam, which now completely blocks the progress of the stream. The present structure cannot be of ancient date; for when Sir J. Kinneir visited Shushter in 1810, he describes this *bund* as 'a bridge of one arch, upwards of eighty feet high, from the summit of which the Persians frequently throw themselves into the water without sustaining the slightest injury;'[1] and Rawlinson, in 1836, still speaks of 'a bridge of a single arch,'[2] although, from his description of the lower part of the dam, I cannot help thinking that he was mistaken therein. Anyhow, by 1841, when Layard first visited Shushter, the arch had disappeared, and the present solid stone barrier had taken its place. This is in the form of a wall, about sixty yards long, and twenty-five feet high, built right across the artificial cleft in the rock, which is here nearly a hundred feet in depth; the masonry of the wall rising on the south side from a sloping dam, also made of big stones, with an approximate elevation of forty feet; so that the entire height of the *bund* from

Dams and mills

[1] *Geographical Memoir*, by J. M. Kinneir, p. 97. I shall have occasion more than once to allude to the extraordinary errors of previous writers in describing the waterworks of Shushter. But not one of them is comparable with that of Kinneir, who, both in his narrative and in his map, confounded the river and the canal, and reversed their geographical positions. After this it is not surprising to find him mistake the *bund* of Ahwaz for the continuation of an old palace wall across the river.

[2] *Journal of the R.G.S.*, vol. ix. p. 77.

the water to the parapet is about sixty-five feet.[1] A roadway, supplying the eastern entrance to Shushter, runs along the top; and from the fact of its having once led to the now deserted village or suburb of Boleiti on the farther side, caused the dam to be called Pul-i-Boleiti (i.e. bridge of Boleiti), a name which also appears to have passed into disuse. This *bund* has at no time borne any connection with irrigation, but was raised for a distinct and definite object. At a short distance above it four or five tunnels have been pierced in the rock on either side of the gorge below the canal level; and through these the water is diverted from the

DAM AND MILLS ON THE AB-I-GERGER

stream, emerging with a rush from several openings on the lower side of the *bund*, and turning in its passage a large number of wheels for the grinding of barley. The spectacle below the dam on the town side is indeed a very curious and interesting one; for there a number of pools are formed by the water as it gushes from the tunnels, and at different levels the mills have been placed so as

[1] Loftus (*Travels and Researches*), though correct in his description of the Pul-i-Boleiti in other respects, transferred these features—viz., the cutting through the rock and the solid masonry wall—to the upper dam, or Bund-i-Kaisar, of which neither of them is true.

to utilise the force, the grindstones revolving in small circular towers. The water passing on falls with a splash and a roar into the canal below, and the entire appearance of the place awakens positive though discordant recollections of the tunnels and cascades of the Horatian Tivoli. Of the further progress of the Ab-i-Gerger I shall speak when describing my return journey.

2. I now pass to the Karun proper, or Shuteit, and its co-ordinate system of dams, bridges, and canals. Immediately after the point at which it parts with the Gerger Canal, the main river takes a bend to the west, considerably widens its bed, and forms a broad sheet of water as it washes the base of the castle rock. This is the part of the river that was paved with stones by Shapur, and called, in consequence, Shadurwan, or 'flooring.'[1] Rounding the western angle of the citadel, the river then turns towards the south, and at a point about 500 yards lower down, where it is nearly a quarter of a mile in width, is spanned by the famous so-called *bund* and bridge of Valerian.

2. The Ab-i-Shuteit

Bund and Bridge of Valerian

These great works consist of a stone *bund* or dam, with sluices for the passage of water, constructed of massive blocks of granite, iron cramped, right across the stream, and of a stone bridge of forty-one arches, built upon the top of the dam. The *bund* was formerly called the Bund-i-Mizan, or Dyke of the Balance, for reasons which will presently be manifest; and the bridge, Pul-i-Kaisar, from the supposed authorship of the Emperor Valerian. The bridge has evidently been built and rebuilt scores of times, as may be seen from the differing character of the material and the different style and size of the arches.[2] The roadway upon it is cobble-paved, and is twenty-one feet wide, and the bridge, so far from being straight, winds about in the most picturesque and random fashion, its total length being 570 yards. It is approached from the town by a modern gateway adorned with gaudy tiles, while two pillars guard the further extremity. At the time of my visit a great gap, over seventy yards in width, yawned in the very middle of the bridge, both *bund* and bridge having been entirely swept away by a

[1] *Vide* El Istakhri's (misnamed by Ouseley Ibn Haukal) *Oriental Geography*, pp. 74–76.

[2] The oldest bridge was destroyed by Hejaj-ibn-Yusuf during the reign of Abdul Malek-ibn-Mervan (A.D. 684–705). The dam is said to have been repaired by Timur in A.D. 1393. *Vide* also M. Dieulafoy, *L'Art antique de la Perse*, part v. pp. 109–112.

SHAPUR'S BRIDGE AT SHUSHTER

powerful flood in the year 1885. This, however, is no uncommon experience. In 1810, Kinneir found the *bund* only just repaired, after a four years' restoration by Mohammed Ali Mirza (under the superintendence of General Monteith), at a cost, stated by De Bode as 60,000*l.* It was again destroyed by floods in 1832; and Rawlinson, in 1836, being in command of a detachment of Persian troops, had to take over his men and guns on rafts of inflated skins. It had been repaired before 1841, in which year De Bode crossed it on his way to Dizful. Selby mentions a further collapse in the spring of 1842, when the entire bridge was under water for two days; and Loftus, in 1850, found the passage obstructed by three of the centre arches, which had fallen in during the previous winter.

Broken section

After a long delay, steps had at length been taken in 1889 to reconstruct the fallen section. Two unsuccessful attempts were first made to rebuild the *bund*, and were each swept away. Finally, the Nizam-es-Sultaneh, unable directly to meet, had essayed to circumvent the difficulty by constructing a temporary dam of baskets filled with stones, a little way above the bridge, presumably with the object of diverting and breaking the full force of the current while the necessary repairs were carried out *in situ.* This dam, however, had been designed with very small engineering skill, for not only was it placed at the most unfavourable angle of the river, but, instead of being pushed out little by little from one bank, in order to drive the current towards the other, it had been commenced simultaneously from both banks, with the result that as the two arms approached, the whole volume of the river torrent swept through the narrow aperture between, and rendered the completion of the work impossible. It had, consequently, been suspended as a bad job, and through a gap of about fifteen yards the water was racing with foam and fury, while the two unfinished extremities were already beginning to subside and disappear. I am not surprised to hear that the restoration has since been altogether abandoned, and that the river bed in the gap has accordingly been scoured out to a depth of twenty feet below its former level.

3. The Minau Canal. This is the artificial canal that has been diverted from the main stream through a tunnel perforated in the face of the castle rock, in order to irrigate the high-lying lands to the south of the city, round which it winds in a deeply-

furrowed loop. Rawlinson and other travellers have designated it the Nahr-i-Darian,[1] or Ab-i-Miandab—the latter, which signifies 'river between two waters,' being a perfectly correct description of its situation, and being identical with the modern contraction Minau (i.e. Mian-i-ab)—while Colonel Bell calls it the Ab-i-Khurd. After leaving the cutting through the rock which is said by Rawlinson to be 300 yards long and 15 feet broad,[2] it passes into the sandy soil behind the town, and here its level was till lately regulated by artificial dams, of which the most curious is a *bund*, thrown right across the ravine cut by the canal and supporting a quaintly irregular bridge, the roadway of which is stone-paved, and runs sharply uphill on one side in order to reach the top of the bank, where is a ruined gateway and guard-house. This bridge is called the Pul-i-Lashker. When I inspected it no water was flowing through the arches of the *bund*, whilst I have already mentioned that on entering the town I was able to ford the shrunken continuation of the same canal at a point further to the east. The reason of its failure has been the rupture of Valerian's *bund* and bridge, by which the level of the river, at the point where it formerly fed the canal, has been seriously lowered, and its consequence is visible in the desiccation and sterility that have overtaken the small Mesopotamia which it was intended to irrigate.

3. The Minau Canal

I have so frequently used the terms Valerian's *bund* and bridge in speaking of the Bund-i-Mizan, that it will be well now to explain that I have only done so in deference to popular legend, and because they are always so called; but in no sense because I believe that the Emperor Valerian was personally engaged in their execution. It is well known that in 260 A.D. the Roman Emperor, in attempting to relieve Edessa, was taken prisoner by King Shapur, who for seven years kept him in captivity (it is said in the castle at Shushter), treating him, if we are to believe a somewhat questionable legend, with extreme cruelty and indignity, and perpetuating his insults even upon the monarch's corpse. In the Shah Nameh of the Persian epic poet, Firdusi, occurs an interesting passage, in which the conqueror is said to

Tradition of Valerian

[1] The name Darian (which is a contraction of Darabian) seems to suggest a connection with Darius, who may conceivably have anticipated the Sassanian kings in the waterworks of Shushter.

[2] *Journal of the R.G.S.*, vol. ix. p. 76.

have enlisted the engineering skill of a Roman prisoner, who was captured on the same occasion, to build, or perhaps to rebuild, the (broken) *bund* and bridge, the freedom of the captive being the reward of success. The Roman's name is given as Baranush, or Varanus, and with the spoil taken in the Emperor's camp the cost may very likely have been defrayed. I cannot, however, ascertain that there is any other historical basis than this very vicarious connection for the association of Valerian's own name with these works. There is no independent ground for believing that he was possessed of an aptitude for hydraulics; nor would a captive sovereign as a rule be of much service if converted into a civil engineer. Valerian's name is also attached to the first dam, or Bund-i-Kaisar, over the Gerger Canal; but upon no superior foundation.

Having described the character and features of the various masonry and waterworks at Shushter, let me now endeavour to explain the purpose which, severally or in combination, they were intended to serve. Of such explanations as have been furnished by earlier writers, and of which some are incorrect and others impossible, that of Rawlinson is based at once upon the most exhaustive knowledge and the most accurate information.[1] There are, however, I think, sufficient reasons why it cannot be implicitly accepted. It rests upon the assumption that Ardeshir, or his son Shapur, before any dam existed upon the Karun, or the latter had as yet been utilised for irrigation purposes, cut the artificial canal of the Gerger—a colossal work—for no reason whatever except possibly the strategical advantage that might thence be derived, and that the level of the main river being thus lowered, and the town deprived of water, the bed of the former was then paved, the big *bund* built, the Gerger dammed, and the tunnel pierced in order to supply the city and its suburbs. I venture to suggest a different order of events, more compatible both with probability and with the natural features.

Explanation of ancient hydraulics

Tradition, with probable justice, assigns either to Ardeshir or to Shapur the construction of the first great public works upon the Karun. We may believe that either the father or the son, recognising the results that might be expected from a proper fertilisation of the fields outside the town, ordered the erection of the great *bund* across the river in order to

Construction of the Gerger Canal

[1] *Journal of the R.G.S.*, vol. ix. pp. 73–6. I reject M. Dieulafoy's explanation, which is as unsatisfactory as his map is erroneous (*L'Art antique*, pp. 110–111).

hold up its waters, and the excavation of the tunnel and Minau Canal leading therefrom, in order to carry off a different portion of the waters so collected for irrigation purposes. Before long, however, the river, scouring a soft and friable bed, deepened its channel and ceased to fill the canal, a process which would be accelerated, if, as is probable, the *bund* had also broken down. It was at this critical juncture that we may assume the engineering ability of the Roman prisoner to have been invoked in order to redress the evil, and the series of waterworks which have made both the place and its founders famous, to have been initiated in their entirety. Realising the difficulty of repairing the *bund* and of adequately controlling the often swollen torrent of the Karun as long as there remained no other exit for its superfluous waters, the monarch or the engineer ordered the excavation of the Gerger Canal through the rock on the eastern side of the town. No sooner was the cutting finished than the entire volume of the Karun rushed through it, entirely deserting the old river bed, a fact which I regard as established by two considerations. At some distance below the Gerger *bund*, where are the existing water-mills, is another artificial *bund*, on which are the remains of numerous disused water-mills at such a height above the present level of the canal that it is obvious they must have been placed there when the canal occupied a much higher level. Further, throughout the entire course of the Gerger from Shushter to Bund-i-Kir, whilst the canal at present occupies a narrow bed of from 60 to 70 yards in width with steep banks, there are visible at distances varying from a few yards to half a mile from these inland, others and higher banks, now standing up like cliff walls from the plain, but unmistakably indicating a time when they formed the confines of a much larger and more powerful stream.

Building of the big *bund*

The Karun having thus been emptied into the Gerger Canal, the big *bund* was rebuilt, or, if no previous operations be attributed to Ardeshir, was now, along with the tunnel, constructed for the first time. Simultaneously the opportunity was seized for raising and paving the river-bed below the castle rock, in order to prevent any further detrition of the bottom. These undertakings being completed, and the system of irrigation which, according to my hypothesis, was their main, if not their sole *raison d'être*, being available for use, orders were now given partially to dam the Gerger Canal, so as to turn back the Karun into its original bed. At this stage, then, were constructed the various *bunds* that obstruct the course of the Gerger, whose diminished contents naturally receded from the broad channel which they had hitherto occupied, and in process of time cut for themselves their present narrow and sinuous track, which has only to be followed down to Bund-i-Kir to show that it cannot at any time have been artificially cut by man.

Such is the explanation which I offer of the hydraulic and engineering works of Shushter. They may be summed up in the following propositions:—Valerian's *bund* was built (the bridge being raised upon it so as to admit of communication with the opposite bank, and particularly with Dizful) in order to hold up the waters of the Karun for irrigation purposes.[1] The Minau Canal was cut in order to convey the waters thus dammed to the lands behind the towns, which were otherwise wholly without water-supply. The Gerger Canal was cut, not for independent purposes of irrigation, but simply in order to facilitate the above operations, and to carry off the surplus waters of the main river.[2] In fact, a utilitarian purpose was behind each of these great undertakings, which, at a distance of sixteen hundred years, survive to demonstrate the public spirit and the spacious conception of their illustrious founder.

Upon arriving at Shushter—which, thanks to my just appreciation both of the steam-power of the 'Susa' and of the mendacity of her engineer, I succeeded in doing about nine hours in advance of the passengers by the canal—I forwarded my credentials to the

[1] Consequently I reject the theory of Loftus, for which I do not see any foundation, that the Bund-i-Mizan was constructed, partly so as to provide a foundation for the bridge, partly to accumulate a sheet of water before the castle for the delectation of its occupant.

[2] The irrigation theory, and the recent date of the contraction of the Gerger, which have both been urged, are negatived by the fact mentioned by Layard, that 'the excavations at Shushter, and particularly the steps leading from the town to the bed of the canal, which are evidently very ancient, are carried *to the present level* of the Ab-i-Gerger (*Journal of the R.G.S.*, vol. xvi. p. 60). The origin of the name Gerger is doubtful. It may be onomatopœic (from the sound of the water gurgling through the tunnels of the dam). Compare the origin of the well Zemzem at Mecca. On the other hand, a native historian says it was so called from a colony, who came to Shushter from Gerger in Azerbaijan. In the time of Timur the Gerger was known as Do Dank, and the Shuteit (which is a modern appellation, diminutive of Shat, i.e. river), or Karun proper, as Chehar Dank, from the proportions of water—two-sixths and four-sixths—that flowed in the two channels. The name Mashrekan, strictly belonging to the Chehar Dank, was also commonly applied to both.

Governor, and intimated my desire to pay an early call. The customary civilities passed in the interim, consisting of presents of cakes, fruit, and sweetmeats from the Nizam, and tips of corresponding or superior value to his servants from myself. In the afternoon I rode to the citadel at the hour fixed for the interview. This building, to which are annexed barracks and an arsenal, is situated on the summit and at the extremity of the rock, where it rises with a precipitous face of over one hundred feet from the river-bed. Nature has designated this locality as the obvious site for a citadel, and from the days of Shapur downwards it has been occupied by a *kaleh*, or fort, which at the time of the Arab conquest was known by the name of Selasil.[1] The present edifice is a modern structure, containing no remains of the ancient castle, while it has been further altered and modernised by the reigning Governor, who has rebuilt the habitable portion in the shape of a lofty two-storeyed tower, from whose summit a magnificent panorama is enjoyed of the river scenery and town. The entire space occupied by the buildings is said to be three or four acres, and the walls of the barracks are loopholed towards the city, from which they are separated by an open plot—a very necessary precaution in a place of such unstable quietude as Shushter, where Governor and people have often been engaged in bloody conflict. The *kaleh* is entered by a gateway glittering with the showy tiles that represent the debauched taste of modern Persian art, and its interior contains some pretty garden-terraces and points of outlook. Nothing, indeed, could be fairer than the landscape from the large open window at which I sat with the Nizam. The river, emerging from the rugged mountain range, sunned itself placidly in the broad sweep below the cliff, while on its further bank stretched a park-like expanse of ground, dotted with venerable trees. One of the rooms in the castle contained a large tank of running water in the centre, above which was placed a wooden platform or lounge, for purposes of slumber or repose. It breathed a coolness beyond expression.

The citadel

The then Governor of Arabistan, whose official title was the Nizam-es-Sultaneh, had only within the last two years been appointed to that office, but during this time he seemed to have acquired a fair reputation for justice as well as energy of adminis-

[1] Identified by some with the Sele of Ptolemy and Ammianus Marcellinus, who mention it as one of the four great towns of Susiana.

tration. Though neither of good family nor distinguished antecedents, I found him to possess the inimitable manners of a Persian gentleman, which were also shared by his younger brother, the Saad-el-Mulk, then Governor of Bushire. His conversation contained the usual flattery and assurance of friendly sentiments towards the English people, pitched in a more than ordinarily persuasive key. Accepting his protestations, I asked him point-blank why he did not testify their sincerity by endeavouring to remove the obstacles that had been so gratuitously placed in the way of the English firm who, in response to an invitation from his sovereign, had commenced mercantile operations upon the river. He answered that he had done, and would continue to do, everything in his power—a statement that did not precisely tally with what I knew both of his previous attitude and of his personal interests, which were believed to be directly concerned in excluding the British from the upper Karun, some sort of concession for its navigation having been granted to his brother. Intimating courteously that it was open to him to give much more practical evidence of sympathy in the future, I next related the tale of his subordinate, the Mirza, upon whom he undertook to bestow a suitable rebuke.

The Nizam-es-Sultaneh

The Arsenal at Shushter which adjoins the Castle, and which I visited, was said to contain 3,000 Werndl rifles; though none of the garrison-troops whom I saw, and who are said to consist of six companies of infantry, as well as a detachment of artillery with two Uchatius mountain guns, were armed with that weapon. Included in the arsenal are also some old bronze guns, one of which dates from the Sefavi times, while the second was cast at Hawizeh by Nadir Shah, and the third was a present from Nicholas I. of Russia to Abbas Mirza at the close of the war in 1828. The Persians firmly believe that the latter was triumphantly carried off by them on the field of battle.

Arsenal

After I had left him, and during the remainder of my stay in Shushter, he continued to pay me every possible attention, placing the 'Susa' absolutely at my disposal for the return journey to Ahwaz, offering me a horse, which, as I proposed leaving by river, I could not accept, and subsequently a set of elegantly-chased silver coffee-cups, which also I declined, having no equivalent present to make in return. When I left the town, which was very late at night, in order that the boat might start at

Civilities

sunrise, he was most anxious that I should not ride out to the place of anchorage till the next morning, in order that he might send a large mounted escort with me.

The starting-point and terminus of navigation on the Ab-i-Gerger is at a spot called Shelailieh, between six and seven miles below the town, the course of the canal above that point being obstructed by more than one semi-natural, semi-artificial *bund*, although the 'Assyria' in 1842 succeeded in threading a passage to within two miles of the city. At Shelailieh, where is a miserable village on the right bank, boats are in the habit of lading or unlading their cargo, which must be conveyed to or from Shushter on donkeys or mules. I fancy that by a little blasting a channel could be opened to a point nearer the town, and that the nuisance of this rather lengthy land portage might accordingly be abridged. My descent of the Gerger Canal as far as Bund-i-Kir occupied 7½ hours, the same time being consumed between Bund-i-Kir and Ahwaz. The canal follows a very tortuous course, and has worn in time a bed deeply sunk between banks of clay, the old banks on the higher level looking strangely forlorn in the absence of the big stream which they once confined. There is far more and thicker jungle on the banks of the Gerger than on those of the Karun; and throughout our voyage winged game, starting up from the water's edge, whirred over our heads from one bank to the other. The average width of the canal is from 50 to 75 yards; and a boat of over 100 feet would find it almost impossible to make some of the turns.

Descent of the Gerger

As a special compliment the Nizam had sent two of his suite to accompany me as far as Ahwaz. They were also bearers of letters to the Mirza, whom, however, I had now so entirely forgotten in my satisfaction at having successfully accomplished the journey, and at having further caught the 'Shushan,' which was to wait for me up to a certain date at Ahwaz, that I went on board Messrs. Lynch's steamer without lending a thought to my obstructionist professor of a few days before. I was just turning in at 1 A.M., when a knock at my cabin-door revealed the figure of the Mirza, slightly the worse for liquor, and in a pitiable condition of mingled humiliation and fright. He explained that the Nizam had written him a severe reprimand, and had threatened to cancel a whole year's salary for his behaviour on my upward journey; and he submissively implored me to write a parting

The Mirza again

letter to his chief, saying that my vengeance was satisfied, and requesting that no further punishment should be imposed. I had no wish to inflict an injury upon the poor wretch, who had already suffered so serious a fright that he would be most unlikely to repeat the same tactics when the next English visitor should ascend the river; so I wrote the desired epistle, and we parted good friends. But whenever I hear mentioned the name of the Karun river, or of the rapids of Ahwaz, amid the din and whirl of the waters humming over the ledges there intrudes upon my memory the vision of that inimitable Mirza, seated in his mat-hut between the two melancholy fratricides, with the silent *seyids*, the imperilled sheikh, and the stalwart robber-son looking chilly and imperturbably on.

Opposition to British navigation

I will not here recapitulate the facts set forth at sufficient length in my communication to the 'Times,' and of which the attitude of the various Persian officials whom I encountered was only a casual illustration, that led me to believe that at that time a determined attempt was being made upon the spot to destroy, by means of a general 'boycott,' the value of the Karun Concession. The reasons for such a policy were not hard to seek. The Arab sheikhs, who with their tribes inhabit the banks of the river and have for long enjoyed a practical independence of the central authority, though exceedingly well-disposed to the English and hostile to the Persians, whom they detest, disliked the intrusion of an element that brought down upon them the attention, dictation, and exactions of the Government, and that located Persian officials at Ahwaz and Mohammerah. The local traders resented competition with the hallowed monopoly of their caravans. The Persian officials, alive to the great possibilities of the trade, were furious at seeing it slip through their fingers; and, though they had never hitherto lifted a little finger to develop the route themselves, were disgusted that the task should be undertaken by those from whom they could expect to make no *mudakhil* and to receive no bribes. Above all, some sort of concession for the navigation of the upper river appeared to have been given to the Governor of Bushire and to a wealthy merchant of the same place; and there was ground for believing that the Nizam's interests were preoccupied in the same direction, and that he was secretly aiming at retaining the monopoly of the upper river in Persian hands.

At the time I wrote that I did not think that these tactics would be likely in the long run to succeed; partly because every fresh introduction of foreign influence into Persia had met with, but by patience had ultimately vanquished, the same antagonism, partly because the intrinsic prospects of trade were so good that the Persians were unlikely for long to turn the cold shoulder upon a project by which money might stick to their own fingers, and because the Government, by the construction of public buildings and of a telegraphic wire, had already shown a personal, even if a selfish, interest in the development of the concern. After a lapse of one and a half year I will now narrate how far these anticipations have been realised, and what was the position of affairs in the summer of 1891.

Prospect in 1889

Of the steps that have since been taken for the furtherance of trade either by the Persian or the British authorities, three were recommended by me in 1889 as essential. The first of these was an arrangement for the navigation of the river above Ahwaz in correspondence with the steamers running below. The 'Susa' now navigates the Gerger to Shushter in connection with Persian vessels on the lower river, while the 'Shushan,' which was presented by Messrs. Lynch to the Persian Government, plies on the Shuteit in connection with the 'Blosse Lynch' below. There is thus a double steam service in existence from Mohammerah to Shushter. Secondly, a British Vice-Consul has most wisely been appointed at Mohammerah, and has already found time to pen an official report to his department.[1] And, thirdly, an attempt is now being made by the Imperial Bank, in co-operation with the Persian Government, to reopen the northern road from Khorremabad to Dizful, about which I have spoken as a future trade artery into the interior of Persia. The Persians are slowly building caravanserais upon this route, and in a still more leisurely fashion are taking steps to check the lawless vagaries of the Sagwand and Derikwand tribes of Lurs, who are usually out on the war-path, and who have up till now rendered this section of road quite unsafe for merchandise. A little firmness on the part of the Central Government would result in the suppression of these sporadic disorders, and would give the new commercial avenue that fair chance which has hitherto been denied to it. I think it unlikely that the through *fourgon*, or wagon-service, from

Subsequent progress

[1] Annual series of Diplomatic and Consular Reports, No. 826 (1891).

Shushter to Teheran, which has been talked about, will be organised for some time to come, owing to the expense that would be entailed in constructing the requisite roadway. But upon the rougher and more mountainous sections of the route mule transport may still be wisely employed, and with greater security improvements will gradually follow.

Among other measures that have been adopted by the Persian Government may be mentioned the reconstruction of a telegraphic wire formerly in existence between Khorremabad and Dizful (in connection with Teheran), and its extension to Shushter, Ahwaz, and Mohammerah. Like most such works, however, in Persia, this has been badly executed; and the wire is usually cut in the troubled belt of Lur country of which I have spoken. There are times, indeed, when in this region the authority of the Central Government is absolutely *nil*. If we turn our gaze to the Karun itself, a more gratifying advance may be recorded. My obstructive friends have disappeared from the scene, and have been replaced by officials, if not of perfect friendliness, at least of a superior stamp. Bunder-i-Nasiri, or the new settlement at Ahwaz, is now a flourishing place, containing a respectable cluster of government buildings, barracks for a detachment of artillery and two companies of infantry under a *sertip*, a large caravanserai and a bazaar at the landing-place below the rapids, and a similar caravanserai in course of erection on the opposite bank, in order to attract to the Karun the trade of Hawizeh, forty-five miles distant to the west. At Mohammerah the government buildings have been completed at the mouth of the Haffar, and the new settlement is called Bunder Sahib Kerani. Barracks have been raised on the other bank of the river. A weekly Persian post has been organised between Mohammerah and Shushter.

Public works

By far the most remarkable change, however, that has taken place is the active, though tardily aroused, interest of the Persians themselves in the river traffic. Instead of limiting their energies to thwarting the efforts of Messrs. Lynch, they have set about the task of cutting them out. The Nasiri Company, already mentioned, is responsible for this new development. Its leading spirit is the Muin-et-Tajar, a wealthy merchant of Bushire; Sheikh Mizal Khan, detecting a new loophole of salvation in co-operation with those whom he has hitherto distrusted and feared, has joined the undertaking; and there is

Native enterprise

not a doubt that behind both looms the powerful personality of the Grand Vizier, the Amin-es-Sultan. It is this company who have constructed the buildings already mentioned at new Ahwaz, and who have also laid a light horse tramway, with a three feet gauge, between the lower and the upper river. One of their steamers, the 'Nasiri,' plies on the lower river, in correspondence with the 'Susa' on the upper, towing after it two barges; it is shortly to be replaced by two larger vessels. Simultaneously with these evidences of activity, schemes have been heard of, also of Persian origin, for developing by irrigation the fertile plains on either side of the river, for establishing a pumping station at Kajarieh, and for extensive plantations of the sugar-cane, cereals, and the date palm. The value of land is rising at Mohammerah, and there is abundant reason for believing that the start thus made will be vigorously pursued.

British fortunes

It is only natural that this enterprise, which, while perfectly legitimate and even praiseworthy, has been conceived in a spirit of undeniable hostility to Messrs. Lynch, should to some extent have affected the fortunes of the English company. Native merchants are discouraged and even prohibited from shipping their goods by the English steamers, in spite of the lower freights offered by the latter. The old difficulty of dépôts, wharves, and warehouses remains unsolved, foreigners being forbidden to erect these necessary appurtenances of successful traffic themselves; and the Persian Government being slow to fulfil their part of the original concession. The long-promised regulation of the customs, though more than once authorised at Teheran, has never been carried out on the spot, and, in the utter insecurity of the country north of Dizful, facilities for caravan traffic into the interior may be said not as yet to exist. Messrs. Lynch have, with unabated energy, sustained their fortnightly service to Ahwaz, carrying, for the most part, their own goods, sugar, copper, and cotton fabrics, and, for return freights, buying wheat, sesame seed, and other local products. In the year 1890 they also conveyed 2,000 passengers. In the same year the figures of Mohammerah trade, both English and Persian, were returned as follows in the Vice-Consular report: Imports 146,140*l.*, exports 53,100*l.* Traffic is still, for the reasons that I have specified, chiefly local in character; but the interests of the Persians will lead them in time to insist upon those conditions by which a wider and proportionately more remunerative extension may be secured; and, as long as the rivalry is a fair one, and British commerce is not hampered by open *mala fides* or by a tacit conspiracy of obstruction, the development of Persian resources by Persian as well as by foreign means should meet, not with suspicion, but with encouragement. Personally, I hope that a day may arrive when the two agencies may be found engaged in sympathetic alliance. What I have said will show, that though affairs are moving slowly, they are yet moving, on the banks and waters of the Karun river. Anticipation, warned by the failure of those who blew so loud and foolish a trumpet over the opening of the river to foreign trade in 1888, should be careful not as yet to risk too jubilant a strain. But the omens are decidedly favourable, and another decade may be expected to mark a more positive advance.

CHAPTER XXVI

THE NAVY

The Spanish fleet thou can'st not see, because
It is not yet in sight.

R. B. SHERIDAN, *The Critic*, act. ii. sc. ii.

Persian dread of the sea

I MIGHT almost borrow a hint for the contents of this chapter from the famous chapter on Snakes in Iceland, which said merely 'There are no snakes in Iceland.' It is scarcely less difficult to discover the traces or existence of a Persian Navy. Brave and victorious as the Persians have shown themselves at different epochs on land, no one has ever ventured so far to belie the national character as to insinuate that they have betrayed the smallest proficiency at sea. It would be difficult, and perhaps impossible, in the history of the world to find a country possessing two considerable seaboards, and admirably situated for trade, which has so absolutely ignored its advantages in both respects, and which has never in modern times either produced a navigator, or manned a merchant fleet, or fought a naval battle. Cicero wrote in one of his letters to Atticus, '[Pompeii] omne consilium Themistocleum est; existimat enim, qui mare teneat, eum necesse esse rerum potiri.'[1] But no Persian monarch since the days of Xerxes[2] has shared the opinion of Themistocles or of Pompey, unless we except the Sassanian Shapur II. (310–379 A.D.), who is said to have gained the appellation Zhulaktaf or 'Lord of the Shoulders,' from having dislocated the shoulders of all his captives,[3] in a campaign against the Arab pirates of his maritime border, and

[1] *Ep. ad Attic.*, x. 8.

[2] The fleets of Mardonius and Xerxes were manned, not by Persians, but by sailors from the tributary provinces of the empire. In none of the Achæmenian sculptures is there any trace of naval affairs.

[3] This is the account of Masudi. Mirkhond says he strung his prisoners together by piercing a hole through their shoulders. Gibbon erroneously spells the title Dhulaknaf or Protector of the Nation.

to have traded with India. At times, indeed, in the pages of Persian history we come across ludicrous, because unconscious, examples of the terror of the marine element that is common to that people. In April 1442, one Abdur Rezak being sent on a mission from Shah Rukh, the grandson of Timur, to an Indian king, weighed anchor from Ormuz. The unwilling voyager has left the following delightful account of his sensations :—

As soon as I caught the smell of the vessel and all the terrors of the sea presented themselves before me, I fell into so deep a swoon that for three days respiration alone indicated that life remained within me. When I came a little to myself, the merchants cried with one voice that the time for navigation was passed, and that everyone who put to sea at this season was alone responsible for his death, since he voluntarily placed himself in peril. All with one accord having sacrificed the sum which they had paid for freight in the ships abandoned their project, and after some difficulties disembarked at the port of Muscat.[1]

The ambassador, however, dared not thus sacrifice his mission to his fears, and he succeeded in safely reaching his destination. Upon his return voyage from Mangalore ill fortune again condemned him to be caught in a storm; and again the anguish flowed in rich metaphor from his hyperbolical pen :—

With tears in my eyes I gave myself up for lost. Through the effects of the stupor and of the profound sadness to which I became a prey, I remained like the sea, with my lips dry and my eyes moist. The agitation of the waters caused my body to melt like salt which is dissolved ; the violence of the deluge annihilated and utterly dispersed the firmness which sustained me, and my mind, hitherto so strong, was like the ice which is suddenly exposed to the heat of the month Tamouz ; even now my heart is troubled and agitated as it were a fish taken out of fresh water.

In the previous century the poet Hafiz, having attained a great reputation in the East, had received an invitation from the Mussulman King of the Deccan to pay him a visit at his Court in India. The poet *venit, vidit, et victus est.* Having embarked at Ormuz, he fell so dreadfully sea-sick that he insisted on being put ashore again; and as soon as he regained his beloved Shiraz, composed an ode,[2] which was an unconscious imitation of the celebrated lines of his Roman prototype fourteen centuries before.

[1] *India in the Fifteenth Century* (Hakluyt Society), p. 7.

[2] *Vide* Brigg's *Ferishta*, vol. ii. pp. 348–9.

Illi robur et æs triplex
Circa pectus erat, qui fragilem truci
Commisit pelago ratem
Primus, nec timuit præcipitem Africum
Decertantem Aquilonibus,
Nec tristes Hyadas, nec rabiem Noti.[1]

Hafiz and Abdur Rezak were no unfair examples of their countrymen. In the Caspian Sea navigation by Persians was unknown. In the Persian Gulf it was entirely in the hands of the Arab tribes, who had crossed over from the Arabian mainland, and colonised the entire maritime border of Iran. They were as venturesome as the Persians were timid; from the eighth to the sixteenth century they retained the trade of the seas, and their merchant fleets penetrated to India, to Ceylon, to the Malay Peninsula, and to China; even to this very day the native navigation of the Gulf is in their hands. When that sea was thrown open to European vessels, by the discovery of Vasco da Gama, and the buccaneering expeditions of Alfonso d'Albuquerque, it was into European and not into Persian hands that the entire commerce fell; and the successive monopolies of Portugal, Holland, and Great Britain will be related in another chapter. So utterly deficient were the Persians in any naval capacities, that when Shah Abbas wanted to possess himself of the mercantile emporium of Ormuz, only a few miles from the mainland, then held by the Portuguese, he was compelled to invoke the aid of the British, to undertake the maritime part of the engagement.

Maritime ambitions of Nadir Shah. 1. The Caspian

It is no mean testimony to the genius of Nadir Shah, and to the wide range of his ambition, that, while for a brief moment he elevated Persia to the rank of the first military power in Asia, he also dreamed of creating naval resources, which should ensure her dominion over the shores of both the northern and the southern seas, i.e. over the Caspian and the Persian Gulf. On the former waters he was fortunate in securing the services of an able and adventurous Englishman, John Elton, whose career, as told by his fellow factor Jonas Hanway, is one of the most dramatic episodes of the time. Elton had gone out to Persia in 1739 in the employ of the British Moscovy, or Russian Trading Company, who had decided, mainly on his initiative, upon reopening the overland trade with Persia *viâ* Moscow

[1] Horace, *Carm.*, Lib. I. iii.

and Astrakhan. Jealousies, however, having arisen between the different factors, Elton, whose bold temper yearned for a more extensive field, entered the service of Nadir Shah, then at the height of his power, as naval constructor, and in January 1743 received a decree, confirming him in that position, and presenting him with the title of Gemal Beg. Nadir's designs, in contemplating a Caspian flotilla, were fourfold. He desired to check the piratical excursions of the Turkoman tribes on the eastern shore, to punish and subjugate the turbulent Lesghians on the western coast, to acquire a monopoly of the trade with Astrakhan, and to establish the Persian claim to sovereignty over as much as possible of this inland sea. The indefatigable Englishman warmly seconded these designs; and having, in the summer of 1743, conducted a survey of the east coast of the Caspian from Astrabad Bay to Cheleken Island and Balkan Bay, in the ship the 'Empress of Russia,' which he had himself built at Kazan on the Volga in the preceding year, upon his return, with no resources or trained assistance of any kind, he resolutely set about building a fleet on the shore of Gilan. The timber was hewn in the mountains and brought down to the coast; he fished for lost Russian anchors in order to supply his own needs; he manufactured sailcloths of cotton and cordage of flax; his only ship's carpenters were one Englishman, a few Indians, and some Russian 'renegadoes;' and of several vessels on the stocks he actually succeeded in launching one, intended to mount twenty three-pounders, which triumphantly flew the Persian royal flag.[1] These proceedings were equally distasteful to the Russian Government, who did not at all relish the idea of a Persian navy on the Caspian, and to the British merchants, who had engaged Elton to extend British trade, and not to humour the whims of a Persian despot. The former retaliated by a decree in November 1746 absolutely interdicting the British Caspian trade. The remaining British factors, having quarrelled with Elton, left the country. Elton himself, having procured a decree from Nadir Shah, commanding him to stay, remained on through the troublous times that succeeded the assassination of the tyrant, and was finally shot in a local rebellion in 1751. With him and with his employer perished the sole

[1] The relics of one of Elton's vessels were said to be visible near Lahijan as late as 1843, but were not seen by Holmes (*Sketches on the Caspian Shores*, p. 129).

attempt ever made by the Persians to institute a naval armament on the Caspian. The story is told at greater length in the fascinating pages of Hanway,[1] who adds, in confirmation of an opinion that I have previously expressed:—

> But there cannot be a stronger instance of the ignorance of the Persians in regard to maritime affairs than that of Myrza Mehtie (i.e. Mirza Mehdi) who was appointed Admiral of the Coast before he had ever seen a ship. This was the man who was afterwards nominated by Nadir to examine into the Christian religion.

The maritime ambitions of Nadir Shah were not limited to the northern Persian littoral. He possessed a fleet of between twenty and thirty ships in the Persian Gulf, built in Europe, Pegu, and Surat, and manned by Indians and Portuguese.[2] Not content with this, he designed the institution of a native dockyard on the southern sea, ordered timber to be hewn and transported from Mazanderan, and is said to have contemplated an interchange of inhabitants on his two maritime borders, a contingent of Arabs to be transported to the shores of the Caspian, to instruct the northern sailors in the science of navigation; and a batch of Mazanderanis to be moved to the southern coast as workmen in the shipyards. The only results of this project were the rude ribs of an unfinished vessel, which were visible on the beach at Bushire in the early part of the present century.

2. The Persian Gulf

Later in the same century, in 1775, Sadek Khan, the brother of Kerim Khan Zend, then ruling with the title Vekil, or Regent, at Shiraz, undertook an expedition against the Turkish port of Busrah: and marching himself by land was followed on the sea by a small fleet of thirty vessels from Bushire and Bunder Rig. But these were Arab-built, and Arab-manned; and I mention the incident only because, so far as I know, it is a unique instance of a Persian force, in modern times, operating on any other element than *terra firma*.

Kerim Khan Zend

[1] *Historical Account*, vols. i. and ii. Compare with this the *Voyages and Travels* of Dr. J. Cook, who was in Northern Persia in 1747, the year of Nadir Shah's assassination.

[2] C. Niebuhr (*Travels through Arabia*, vol. ii. p. 139) says that no Persian sailors being forthcoming, Nadir was obliged to engage Indians, who, being Sunnis, refused to fight against the Arab Sunnis, turned upon their Shiah officers, massacred them, and carried off the ships. In 1761, the remains of some of these vessels were seen by Niebuhr at Bushire.

Whatever dreams of naval ambition on the Caspian Persia may ever have indulged were rudely shattered in the early years of the present century by the treaty stipulations that concluded the two Perso-Russian wars. The Treaty of Gulistan in 1813 contained a clause, renewed and confirmed in the Treaty of Turkomanchai in 1828, by which it was declared that Russia alone should have the right of maintaining vessels of war on the Caspian, and that no other Power should fly a military flag on that sea.[1] So crushing a penalty has seldom been inflicted by the victor in any campaign upon the vanquished, and could only have been submitted to by a power as weak as Persia at the dictation of a power as strong as Russia. It has transformed the Caspian into a Russian lake, destroyed the last shred of Persian autonomy or authority on the northern sea, and left the Shah's dominions in a position of abject defencelessness on the north. It is true that Russia has herself elsewhere set an example, in which Persia might discover an apposite precedent here, by tearing up the Black Sea clauses of the Treaty of Paris. But modern Persia is not a power that can afford to infringe any treaty; nor are the modern Persians so untrue to the traditions of their nation as to be willing to run any risk for sake of the sea.

Treaties of Gulistan and Turkomanchai

The Russians have not been slow to profit by the advantage thus secured. Only ten years after the Treaty of Turkomanchai was signed, they made it an excuse for that occupation of the Island of Ashurada at the mouth of Astrabad Bay, the incidents of which I have narrated in an earlier chapter. The Persian Government, disabled from maintaining the police of the seas by a flotilla flying its own flag, had applied to Russia for the loan of two small vessels of war, in order to suppress the piratical excursions of the Turkomans. The Czar generously replied that he was willing to take the trouble upon his own shoulders; and as a consequence the island of Ashurada, which is as much Persian as the Isle of Thanet is Kentish, has ever since supported a Russian naval establishment. Hasan Kuli Bay, Chikishliar, Cheleken Island, and Balkan Bay—all of them points either nominally or actually in Persian territory upon the eastern shore of the Caspian—have since been similarly seized, and the impotence of Persia cannot be more forcibly demonstrated than by a coasting voyage along the 400 miles of maritime border which she owns

Occupation of Ashurada

[1] Treaty of Gulistan, Article V.; Treaty of Turkomanchai, Article VIII.

upon the north, in which entire distance not a single Persian craft will be encountered upon the waters.

It is true that on the Murdab, or Lagoon of Enzeli, the Shah possesses a small dilapidated paddle-wheel steamer bearing the proud title of 'Shahinshah Nasr-ed-Din,' which was specially constructed in order to convey his Majesty to the limits of Persian territory on his first journey to Europe. But not even is this royal plaything exempt from the stern law of the Muscovite taskmaster, for, upon one occasion, having proceeded as far as Baku, gaily flying the Persian flag, the vessel was greeted by a shot from the fort. The Persian commander, delighted at the graceful compliment, kept merrily on. Bang came another shot, rather closer than the first. Still he proceeded: a third brought him to his senses, and the Persian flag was hurriedly hauled down. Such is the majesty of the King of Kings on the Caspian.

The Shah's yacht

Thus cribbed and cabined on the north, the Persian Government has at times turned an aspiring eye upon the Persian Gulf, where no hostile Leviathan guards the waves, and dreams of naval supremacy whereon have occasionally floated before her eyes. About the year 1865, the Shah mooted the idea of a Persian naval flotilla in the Gulf, to consist of two or three steamers, manued by Indian or Arabian crews, and commanded by an English naval officer. The idea was discountenanced by the British Government, to whom it was known that the project really concealed aggressive designs upon the independence of the islands and pearl fisheries of Bahrein.

The Persian Gulf

Finally, in 1883, the scheme was revived in a more innocent shape, and there was then laid the foundation, and also the coping-stone of the modern Persian navy, which consists of the proud total of one vessel, designated the 'Persepolis.' In that year the son of the Mukhber-ed-Dowleh was despatched to Europe to order a man-of-war for the Shah. Having previously received a German education, he naturally went to Germany; and after protracted negotiations, and a still longer haggle when the bill was presented for payment, the 'Persepolis,' a screw steamship of 600 tons, of 450 horse-power, was turned out from the dockyard of Bremerhaven in January 1885, and despatched with German officers and a German crew to the Gulf. With her was sent out in sections, which were put together at Mohammerah, a

The 'Persepolis'

small river steamer of thirty horse-power, called the 'Susa.' The cost of the two vessels was 30,000*l.*; and their annual maintenance is said to have amounted to 3,500*l.* The 'Persepolis' is armed with four 7·5 centimètre Krupp guns; and was originally designed for the double purpose of bombarding refractory fishing villages, or intimidating local governors and sheikhs, and of conveying cargoes of dates and pilgrims. I am not aware that she has ever been used for the latter object; but in the intervals when she is in a navigable condition, she conveys the Governor of Bushire, and deputy of the Amin-es-Sultan on the Persian Gulf littoral, from one port to another, spends her powder, exercises her guns, and impresses the maritime population by firing salutes of seventeen guns, whenever that worthy arrives at a new port; and in general conveys to the Shah's subjects in these parts an idea of the overwhelming importance of their royal master. I saw and made a careful inspection of the 'Persepolis' at Lingah, whither she had come on one of these official errands. Her crew consisted of forty Persians and Arabs, officered by four Germans, who had picked up the English language in the Gulf. She possessed an Arab, though formerly she had had a German, engineer. In addition to the four Krupp guns, she carried two old brass muzzle-loading smooth bores in the forecastle for firing salutes; and an armoury of forty Mauser rifles and cutlasses. The ship was in spick-and-span interior condition, and below decks she was more like a comfortable passenger steamer than a man-of-war, having a large saloon, good cabin accommodation, and a fine apartment for the Governor in the poop, with a comfortable bedroom attached, which, however, was unoccupied by His Excellency, who, true to the national habits, preferred to court slumber on the floor. The 'Persepolis' had been laid up in the previous year in the dry dock at Bombay, in order to be cleaned from the shells and barnacles which had accumulated on her sides and bottom, reducing her speed from a nominal eight to ten knots an hour to five. Already, however, she had again become foul, and could not steam more than seven knots in the hour, and her commander, in order to avoid the expense of a second trip to Bombay, was searching for a suitable spot either on the shore of Kishm, or of the island opposite Laft, to beach her, and scrape and paint her again. The guns of the 'Persepolis' have never yet fired a shot in anger; but the general terror inspired by the four Krupps is so great, that immediately upon her appearance any disturbance as a rule ceases, and a threatened insurrection at Chahbar had incontinently collapsed in 1888.

The 'Susa'[1] is placed upon the upper Karun, and navigates the waters of that river between Ahwaz and Shushter. My own doleful experience of her powers of velocity has been related in the previous chapter.

The 'Susa'

In these few pages I have come to both the beginning and the end of all that there is to be said about the naval strength of Persia. *Ex nihilo nihil fit*; and I am even surprised at my own tale of bricks, with so modest an allowance of straw.

[1] The 'Susa' is a screw steamship (resembling what in England we should call a harbour-launch), with engines nominally of 30 horse-power, length about 80 feet, beam 16 feet, tonnage 36 tons, draught of water over three feet.

CHAPTER XXVII

THE PERSIAN GULF

'Tis true they are a lawless brood,
But rough in form, nor mild in mood,
And every creed and every race
With them hath found—may find—a place
But open speech and ready hand,
Obedience to their chief's command,
Have made them fitting instruments
Far more than ev'n my own intents.

BYRON, *The Bride of Abydos.*

Historical interest of the Gulf

AN account of the political condition of Persia and of the relations subsisting between her and Great Britain would not be complete that omitted all notice of the Persian Gulf,[1] and of the part played in its control by the representatives of this country. The majority of those at home probably regard the Persian Gulf as a sea whose northern shore is, perhaps always has been, Persian, whose southern shore belongs to they do

[1] This chapter has been compiled from three sources—(1) the results of my own observation or inquiries; (2) the works of previous writers, which have in each case been referred to by name; (3) Government records and official reports, many of which have not met the public eye. There are few, if any, authorities upon the Persian Gulf *per se*; but I shall devote a section of my bibliography to those writers who, either directly or indirectly, have dealt with it. In addition to the works there named, descriptions of parts of the Gulf will be found in the following authors: 1. among ancient writers—Istakhri, Mukadessi, Edrisi, Ibn Batutah, Abdur Rezak, Ludovico di Varthema; 2. among later writers—Purchas' *Pilgrims*, P. della Valle, Herbert, the Sherleys, Mandelslo, Tavernier, Chardin, Thévenot, Sanson, Le Brun; 3. among modern writers—Dupré, Kinneir, Morier, Ouseley, Buckingham, Fraser, Alexander, Binning, Goldsmid, Stack. Among official publications, the following are worthy of mention: *Selection from the Records of the Bombay Government* (new series), No. xxiv., 1856; C. U. Aitchison, *A Collection of Treaties, etc., relating to India and neighbouring Countries*, vol. vii. (1876); *Calendar of State Papers* (East Indies Series), vols. i.–iv. (1513–1629); and the annual *Administration Reports of the Persian Gulf and Muscat*, issued at Calcutta. The *Journal of the R.G.S.* contains some useful papers on the Persian Gulf, notably by Col. D. Wilson, vol. iii.; Lieut. Kempthorne, vol. v.; Sir L. Pelly, vol. xxxiv., and *Proceedings*, vol. viii. p. 18; and Lieut. Whitelock, *ibid.* p. 170.

not know whom, and where a British official can have little else to do but to protect British subjects and safeguard British commerce. Such a view would be at once narrow and erroneous. It is scarcely possible to imagine a quarter of the globe of similar physical configuration that has had so romantic and varying a past, that contains more diverse nationalities and clashing interests, or where graver responsibilities are imposed upon a foreign power than here devolve upon Great Britain. At intervals, from the earliest times, the Gulf has loomed large upon the stage of history. Along its shores, carefully noting in his log-book each island, and anchorage, and seaboard village, came Nearchus, the Admiral of Alexander, on his famous voyage in 326–5 A.D., from the mouth of the Indus to the Tigris delta. To this day we may identify the successive mooring-grounds of the Hellenic navigator. Down the Persian Gulf, from Busrah (Balsora) sailed the Arab Columbus, Sinbad, upon his seven adventurous voyages in the ninth century. From the same port sailed the argosies manned by Arab sailors, that throughout the middle ages interchanged in Turkish and Persian havens the products of the remote East and West. Upon this maritime field Portugal and Holland and England have fought out their battles for the supremacy of the seas; it is even now the theatre of the rival pretensions of discordant powers. Early in this century Arab corsairs desolated its shores and swept its waters with piratical flotillas; slave-hunting flourished; and security either of trade or dominion there was none. The hands by which this long-standing anarchy was subdued are also those by which present differences are composed, and a maritime peace assured that is one of the most successful achievements of practical statesmanship. The pacification of the Persian Gulf in the past and the maintenance of the *status quo* are the exclusive work of this country; and the British Resident at Bushire is to this hour the umpire to whom all parties appeal, and who has by treaties been intrusted with the duty of preserving the peace of the waters.

Synopsis. Northern coast line

A synopsis of the present situation will be best attained by pursuing in geographical order the circuit of the Gulf, and indicating the status, government, and interests of each port or district as it is encountered, finally drawing together the several threads, and weaving them, if possible, into a succinct and intelligible whole. From the Gulf of Oman and the Indian Ocean, the Persian Gulf is entered, at about 57° long. and

26° lat., through the Straits of Ormuz (properly Hormuz), so called from the celebrated island of that name, lying a few miles from the mainland on the northern coast line. Persian territory itself does not begin here, but at a point more than 300 miles to the eastward, where, at the tiny port of Gwetter, the frontier line between Persia and Beluchistan touches the sea. From Gwetter the coast line, running westwards, first to the Straits of Ormuz, next along the northern shore of the Persian Gulf, and finally to a point a little beyond Mohammerah on the Shat-el-Arab,[1] is exclusively under the control, directly exercised or delegated, of the Persian Government. The inhabitants of this maritime fringe are Persians, or Persian Arabs, i.e.—either Arabs under Persian rule or Arabs denationalised by long subjection and intermarriage. The latter are in the numerical ascendant in the coast villages and ports; but, as I shall show, have been powerless, from their own intestine feuds, to resist the encroachments of the Persian authority, which has been pushed in these regions with uncompromising vigour, not exempt from much injustice and cruelty.

Southern coast line

The southern coast line of the Persian Gulf, with which I shall here include the Kingdom of Muscat, or Oman, occupying the eastern shore line of the Arabian peninsula outside Cape Mussendom (Ras Musandim), extends in a north-westerly direction from that cape to where the estuary of the Shat-el-Arab mingles its waters with the sea. Broadly speaking, this extensive coast line is inhabited by tribes of Arab origin, either wholly independent, or admitting in different degrees the sovereignty of Turkey, now exercised from the *vilayet* of Busrah, which, in order to add to the prestige of Ottoman dominion, was severed a few years ago from that of Baghdad, and was constituted an independent Pashalik, with special reference to the claims of the Commander of the Faithful over Arabia.[2] The great trade that exists between the two shores of the Gulf, the occasional pretensions advanced by Persia to the right of interference on its southern littoral, the rival, and even hostile interests of Persia and Turkey on the Shat-el-Arab, and the position filled by England in

[1] The western, or Turkish, frontier of Persia was defined by the Treaty of Erzerum in 1847, and was demarcated by a mixed Anglo-Russian Commission during the following years. *Vide* cap. xvi.

[2] Busrah was first made a separate vilayet in 1875. In 1880 it was reincorporated with Baghdad. But in 1884 the experiment of independence was again tried, and is not now likely to be revoked.

relation to all parties, Persians, Turks, and Arab tribes alike, render a discussion of the southern shore and its concerns as necessary as that of the northern or Persian coast, even in a work professedly dealing with Persia alone. The order I shall follow will be that of my return journey down the Gulf from Mohammerah; at which point I will commence my survey of the Persian maritime border, and will describe such places as I personally visited as far as Gwadur, a little beyond Gwetter, in Beluchistan. Thence I shall cross over to Muscat, and with my face turned in the opposite direction shall proceed along the Arab coast, until, at Fao, I have completed the periplus of the Gulf.

Bunder Mashur and Hindian

I have, in an earlier chapter upon the South-West Provinces, described the present condition and waning fortunes of the once independent Ka'b Arab tribes, who are situated upon the banks of the Shat-el-Arab and Bahmeshir, eastwards of Mohammerah. Sheikh Mizal Khan still retains a nominal supremacy at the western extremity of the region which they inhabit, though every day falling more under the control of the Persian Governor-General of Arabistan. Further east, the country lying round the Jerahi river, and continuing along the coast nearly as far as Bunder Dilam, has been placed under the Persian deputy-governor of Behbehan, who is himself a subordinate of the Prince-Governor of Shiraz. This district includes the petty coast ports of Bunder Mashur and Hindian. The first of these, which has long ago seen its best days, is on a wide inlet that receives the waters of the Dorak or Jerahi River, descending from Dorak or Fellahieh, the easternmost settlement of the Ka'b tribe, and irrigating in its upper course the cultivated plain of Ram Hormuz. The second is a minor *entrepôt* of the inland trade with Behbehan. At both ports this local traffic is carried on by native craft, chiefly buggalows (probably from the Arabic root *baghl*, which means 'carrying a burden'), importing piece goods to clothe the people and dates to feed them, in return for an export of wheat, barley, wool, *ghi* (clarified butter) and rice.

Persian jurisdiction

At Bunder Dilam we come upon a strip of coast, inhabited partly by Persians, partly by Arabs, which in the political rearrangement of the Persian Gulf littoral that followed the fall of the Zil-es-Sultan in 1888, has been subjected to the Amin-es-Sultan, or Grand Vizier, as Governor of the Gulf ports, and has been committed by him to the local management of the governor of Bushire, an official named Mohammed Hasan Khan, and entitled the Saad-el-Mulk, brother to my amiable host at Shushter.[1] This functionary has been placed in direct supervision of the coast-line and islands from Dilam in a south-easterly direction to beyond Bushire, a strip which includes the ports of Dilam, Rig, and Bushire, and the islands of Kharg or Kharak and Khargu; and further eastwards, again, of a prolonged stretch of coast, with important ports and islands, which I shall presently mention. In the various maritime towns and villages, he leases the customs for a stipulated sum, as a rule, to some enterprising local merchant, frequently a Hindu Buniah; while, in the larger places, subordinate officers are planted to represent the central authority. The Saad-el-Mulk himself, with all the pride and circumstance suggested by a flotilla consisting of a single vessel, makes periodical tours of inspection in the 'Persepolis' to the various sea-ports within his jurisdiction; religiously exacts his salute of seventeen guns; and, amid salvoes of artillery from his flag-ship, feebly responded to by some old brass carronade on shore, no doubt fancies himself an heir to the august traditions of Albuquerque.

Bunder Dilam

Dilam was once a place of some size and importance. In the eighteenth century it was a trading-port of the Dutch, the remains of whose factory are still to be traced. Possessing one of the best roadsteads in the Gulf, it is the starting-point of the principal caravan-route to Behbehan and Ram Hormuz, though the town itself has dwindled to a petty village of a few hundred souls. From the interior are brought grain, cotton, wool, *ghi*, and dried fruits for transmission to the other Gulf ports; while sugar, tea, and cotton fabrics are imported in the main from Bushire, and dates from Busrah or Mohammerah. Its customs were farmed in 1889–90 for 7,200 *tomans*. Dilam, like Mohammerah, is one of those places from which an alternative route from the coast into the interior of Persia has been examined and reported upon by those who are anxious to expedite trade connection with Isfahan and Teheran. From Dilam the track proceeds to Behbehan, 48 miles, thence to Ardal, 265 miles, thence to Isfahan, 102 miles, total 415 miles. A shorter but more arduous diversion from Behbehan *via* Felat and Kumisheh would reduce this total to 345 miles. The time occupied by caravans over this journey is fifteen days, which is only about half of that now consumed on the

[1] The latter has since superseded him at Bushire.

Bushire-Shiraz line; while the distance from the sea to Isfahan is from 100 to 150 miles less. The insecurity, however, of the country, the absence of villages or caravanserais, where provisions for man and fodder for beasts can be procured *en route*, and the severity of the winter season, by which the passes are closed during four months of the year, have combined effectively to close this route against through communication; and it must be confessed that there is not the remotest likelihood of its being opened up.

Bunder Rig is a small port situated further to the south, on a creek by which one of the mouths of the Shapur or Rohillah River enters the sea. Here, in 1754, the English East India Company, whose Gulf trade had been seriously crippled by the troubles arising out of the Afghan invasion, endeavoured to found a factory, and sent out an agent. The attempt was a failure, owing to Dutch intrigues and opposition; but a few years later Bushire was selected as a substitute. Bunder Rig was one of the strongholds, a little later in the century, of a famous Gulf pirate, known as Mir Mohannah, whose fort was taken and razed by British troops.[1] Its local trade is of the same character as that previously described; and its customs are now farmed for 5,000 *tomans*.

Bunder Rig

We next come to Bushire, the principal landing-place (I cannot call it port) on the southern coast of Persia. I have already described the position and features of Bushire at the end of my Trans-Persian ride, and have there shown how slender are the qualifications that have secured for it the premier position. From the sea the town presents a more striking and compact appearance than any other port on the northern shore of the Gulf, completely occupying with its buildings the end of the peninsula upon which it is situated, and rising sharply with its two-storeyed houses and its somewhat pretentious sea-front from the water-level. Till about forty years ago, the town, whose indigenous population is Arab rather than Persian, was ruled by its own sheikh. But here, as at so many other points along the coast, the internecine feuds of the tribes supplied the central authority with the occasion which its own venturesomeness would never have won for it. Advantage was taken of one of these local conflicts; Persian soldiers appeared upon the scene; the weaker disputant was coerced, and Bushire received a Persian governor. It is re-

Bushire

[1] The history of this exceptional ruffian is related by Niebuhr (*Travels through Arabia*, vol. ii. p. 147).

gretted by many that the British did not retain possession of the place after their capture of it in 1857.[1] The harbour might then have been improved, or rather created; stone quays would have replaced the present mouldering sea-wall; the routes into the interior would have been definitely taken in hand; and in immediate contact with enterprise and initiative, backed by wealth, southern Persia might have found an earlier salvation.

Coast landscape

The mountain-wall, down which I climbed by the precipitous rock-ladders from Shiraz, and which fills the entire background at Bushire at a distance of thirty miles from the coast, rising on the north-east horizon to a lofty spike, 6,500 feet high (Kuh Khormuj, called in the charts Halilah Point), is continued along the coast almost without interruption from the Hindian River to Gwetter. From the ship's deck this unbroken rampart never leaves the eye. In places it approaches to the shore; but far more commonly it is withdrawn to a distance, varying from fifteen to thirty miles inland, admitting between its base and the sea a level expanse, the parts of which nearest the coast are often under water, and are little better than sticky mud flats when dry; while beyond are plains, sparsely cultivated, and dotted at rare intervals with small villages consisting of mud-huts dropped amid clusters of palms. These torrid plains, called by the natives Garmsir (hot region), extend to the foot of the hills, where a lower sandstone ridge frequently intervenes before the main range, or mountains proper, known as Sardsir (cold region), are reached. Upon these no speck of green, no token of life is visible. Pink they glow in the early morning under the rising sun; grey they glisten under the full noontide blaze, when their veteran scars can be traced or counted in the field-glass; lilac they linger longer on the landscape as the fugitive afternoon throws them into deepening shade; umber they merge and are swallowed up in the umber night. The last impression of the traveller, as he leaves Persia, is that wherewith he entered it. It is a land of mountains, and oh for a sight of green grass!

Thirty miles north-west of Bushire, and also under the jurisdiction of the Saad-el-Mulk, is the small island of Kharak, four and

[1] General John Jacob, a man possessed of remarkable political insight, was strongly of opinion, after the campaign, that England should retain Arabistan, Bushire, and Kharak Island (*vide* his *Views and Opinions*, edited by Captain Lewis Pelly).

a half miles broad by three miles long. Its inhabitants are a few miserable Arabs, who catch fish and supply pilots for the Shat-el-Arab. This tiny island once enjoyed a short-lived prosperity under the vigorous rule of the Dutch, who, retiring from Busrah because of a difference with the Turks in 1748, transferred their trading emporium to this spot, raised its population in a few years from a few hundreds to 12,000, and then as suddenly collapsed, being forcibly expelled by Arab pirates, under the famous Mir Mohannah, Sheikh of Bunder Rig, in 1765. The leading spirit of this enterprise had been one Baron Kniphausen, of whom an old chronicler said that, 'Beneath the character of a merchant he concealed the statesman and man of genius'; and the withdrawal of his inspiration preluded the national disaster.[1] Even in the time of its fame Kharak was always dependent upon the neighbouring islet of Kharaku (i.e. little Kharak) Khargu, or Corgo, and upon the mainland for its supplies; and it is related by one authority that the stratagem by which it fell was the employment by the invading corsairs of a ship containing poultry, whose cackling aroused no alarm in the garrison. In the fugitive appearances made by France upon the arena of Persian politics, Kharak has twice passed nominally into her hands. Kerim Khan Zend ceded it to the French by a treaty negotiated by M. Pyrault at Busrah, and signed at Paris; but the suppression of the French East India Company followed, and the treaty lapsed. It was again surrendered, or was about to be surrendered, to France during the short burst of Napoleonic ascendency in 1807–8,[2] but with the expulsion of the French Embassy from Persia in 1809, this second cession shared the fate of its predecessor. Sir John Malcolm was then instructed to occupy the island in defence of British interests in the Gulf;

Karak Island

[1] The story of the brief Dutch occupation of Kharak is told in E. Ives' *Voyage from England to India*, etc., pp. 207–226, the author having visited Kharak in 1758, while Kniphausen was still in command; by C. Niebuhr, *Voyage en Arabie*, vol. ii pp. 149–61, 164–6, and *Description de l'Arabie* (Heron's trans. vol. ii. cap. vii.), the writer having visited Kharak in 1765, the very year that it fell; and by J. Price, *Free Merchants' Letters*, p. 172. Ives draws a very flattering picture of the energy and activity of Kniphausen, who was a Prussian, not a Dutch, by birth. Niebuhr says that he presided over the Dutch factory for five years, and was succeeded by Messrs. Van der Hulst, Buschmann, and Van Houting. It was under the latter's rule that Mohannah, the pirate, being foolishly allowed to enter the fort with an armed retinue, seized the place and expelled the Hollanders.

[2] G. A. Olivier, *Voyage dans l'Empire Othoman*, etc., vol. v. p. 157.

but this design was not executed.[1] Later in the present century it has possessed a peculiar interest for Englishmen in having been, on two occasions, the scene of the first act in the drama of Anglo-Persian war. When the army of Mohammed Shah advanced against Herat in 1837, and the protests of the British Minister were contemptuously ignored, an Anglo-Indian force was despatched to the Persian Gulf; and Kharak was occupied in June 1838, the British Residency being at the same time moved here from Bushire. The Persians retired from Herat, after ignominious failure in the siege, in September 1838; but, owing to the shifty character of their subsequent diplomacy, the island was not evacuated till March 1842. The Herat fever of the Persian Government was again the signal, fourteen years later, for the reoccupation of the island. In defiance of the agreement of January 1853, a Persian army marched against Herat in March 1856. The city was forced by famine to surrender in October of the same year. War was declared between Great Britain and Persia in November. Troops were landed upon Kharak in December; and the military operations ensued, both at Borazjun and Mohammerah, to which I have elsewhere alluded. Upon the cessation of hostilities, after the publication of the Treaty of Paris (March 1857), Kharak was again evacuated, and has since remained in Persian hands. The Russians from time to time discover a mare's nest in the rumoured cession of the island to England; but a momentary spleen, which can only have been engendered in complete oblivion of the too faithful parallel of Ashurada on the Caspian, is soon discredited by the absurdity of the *canard*. At present Kharak contains, with the exception of a good supply of water, nothing more interesting than some curious underground aqueducts, which were found by the Dutch on their arrival, and are undoubtedly of ancient origin.

South-east of Bushire we come upon a strip of coast-line about 200 miles in total length, which is under the jurisdiction of the

Dashtistan and Kangun

Governor of Shiraz. The first section, containing the small port of Bunder Deyir, Dashti, and the district of Dashtistan (i.e. Land of the Plains), was, in 1888, placed by the Amin-es-Sultan under Prince Nowzer, but later on was given to the Governor of Shiraz, and administered by a *sertip* acting

[1] Malcolm, as his rival Sir H. Jones said (*Mission to Persia*, vol. i. p. 138), had a furious passion for the possession of an island in the Gulf. He wanted Lord Wellesley to purchase Kishm; and he twice tried to get hold of Kharak.

as his deputy. The second section, starting from Deyir, and containing the petty ports or, rather, maritime villages, of Kangun (Congoon), Tahiri, Shivu, Chiru, and Charak, and the islands of Sheikh Shuaib, Hindarabi, and Kenn or Keis, is administered on behalf of the Governor of Shiraz by his chief minister, the Kawam-el-Mulk. Of the above-mentioned places Kangun was once a trading port of renown, having been a Portuguese settlement, and still containing the ruins of the factory built by that people. In the first half of this century the Arab sheikh of Kangun was a chief of some authority, and ruled over a considerable tract; but the last occupant of the post, having quarrelled with the Persian government, was seized and strangled in 1880, and his district passed under the central control. Kangun justifies its ancient pre-eminence by the possession of an excellent roadstead, with good anchorage. Tahiri is interesting as being the site of the ruins of the once famous emporium of Siraf, which shared with Ormuz the mercantile supremacy of the Gulf. The island of Kenn or Keis was for a time, under Arab rule, after the destruction of Siraf, the centre of Gulf trade and shipping,[1] and the ruins of a large Arab city called Harira are still visible on its northern side. This, too, was one of the places where the English established a military station (afterwards abandoned) in their warfare with the pirates in the early part of the present century. Arab authority throughout this region has been successfully disintegrated by the Government, and has yielded to centralisation supported by guns.

Region of historic interest

Approaching the more important ports of the Gulf in its eastern portion, we now again touch the jurisdiction of the Saad-el-Mulk, which extends over towns and islands, from which is extracted a considerable annual revenue. The former include the ports of Lingah, Khamir, Bunder Abbas, Minau (Sif), and Jask; the latter the well-known names of Kishm and Ormuz, and the less known Larak, Henjam, and Sirri. Here we are brought into contact with a region that can boast historic memories, and has experienced many shocks of fortune. Situated

[1] It is the Kisi of Marco Polo and the Kis or Kish (not to be confused with Kishm) of Benjamin of Tudela (1160–1173 A.D.), who described it as the great emporium 'to which Indian merchants bring their commodities, and the traders of Mesopotamia, Yemen and Persia all sorts of silk and purple cloths, flax, cotton, hemp, mash, wheat, barley, millet, rye, and all sorts of comestibles and pulse, which articles form objects of exchange. Those from India export great quantities of spices.' *Vide* a note by Yule in his *Marco Polo*, vol. i. p. 66.

on the threshold of the Gulf, to which it commands the entry from the east, and opening up long-sanctified routes of communication into the interior of Asia as far as the yellow Oxus and the snowy Hindu Kush, its harbours have for centuries been battled for by European nations; have flown in turn the flags of Portugal, the Netherlands, Great Britain, Arabia, and Persia; have teemed with argosies of wealth, upon which historians love to linger; and now, in their last state, though shorn of all splendour, and protesting against their degradation with the mute appeal of ruined fortress and battered tower, still pour for the most part into foreign garners the wealth which their native peoples have never had the spirit or the capacity to retain for themselves. At Lingah and Bunder Abbas the chief traders are Hindu Buniahs from Shikarpur and the Sind province; the customs are commonly farmed by them; and the vessels that all but monopolise the carrying trade are those of the British India line. In this interesting quarter I am tempted to halt a little longer upon sites that have been celebrated by the travellers and historians of more than ten centuries, even though their glory be chiefly centered in the past.

Lingah is the first of these ports that is visited from the west, 309 miles distant by sea from Bushire. It is the prettiest and most attractive of the Gulf ports, if prettiness can, indeed, be predicated of any of these maritime towns. A long line of yellow houses, glittering in the recess of a wide bay; a fringe of tufted palms behind it; a stretch of desert; and then the mountains, rising first in strange, twisted contortions, in whose folds and hollows a violet mist seems perpetually to tremble, and further away, in a long rugged wall against the sky, a pale pink, and sometimes a silver grey in hue—this is the agreeable panorama that is visible from the sea. The mountain scarp behind rises in its highest points to 2,900 and 3,900 feet, one of these being marked on the nautical chart, presumably by some old sea-captain, as Grubb's Notch. The anchorage is in three fathoms of water, at a distance of about a mile from the land. Alone among the Gulf ports, Lingah possesses a small wet dock, defended by a wall from the sea, and filled or emptied by the tide. A couple of dozen vessels, ranging from buggalows down to small craft, were lying in it at the time of my visit. The sloping beach of sand is also utilised for shipbuilding purposes. Three or four of the largest buggalows, ranging up to 300 tons burden, are built here

Lingah

in the year; and I inspected one still on the stocks, which was to carry over 250 tons, and to cost, all complete, between 2,000*l.* and 3,000*l.* The workmen were employed in smearing shark's oil over the outer timbers, a local recipe for seaworthiness. The town possesses some forty boats of large size, engaged in the coasting trade both with the Persian and with the opposite Arabian shore; and at the time of the pearl fisheries about the same number of craft put out from its harbour to try their fortune on the banks.

Native craft

The smaller craft for shore use are simple dug-outs, and, there being no timber in the country, are imported from the African coast. I observed here a method of rowing the larger boats that I have not seen elsewhere. There are no seats in the boat; but four or five men sit facing each other upon the gunwale on either side in the fore part, and pull large oars respectively over their right and left shoulders. There is no rudder or coxswain, but the stern oar steers. I am generally disposed to think that each place has found out by experience the method of progression, the vehicle, or the craft, that is best adapted to the local conditions; though I confess to having been shaken in my hypothesis by the Russian tarantass and the catamaran of Ceylon; but I cannot help thinking that an elementary knowledge of dynamics would acquaint the simple boatman of Lingah with the fact that their method involves a quite unpardonable waste of force.

Trade

Lingah is the chief port for the Persian province of Laristan, and has long plied a thriving trade with Bahrein and the Arab coast. Its foreign trade is of more recent origin (the village of Kong, seven miles down the coast, having been the site of the Dutch establishment), but has had a very rapid growth. About 100,000*l.* worth of cotton goods is imported in the year; but on an average nearly one half of the total imports (in value) is in pearls, between 300,000*l.* and 400,000*l.* worth of which enter the port annually. That the bulk of these goods merely pass through Lingah in transit elsewhere is shown by the table of exports, in which the quantity and value of the same articles stand at almost the same figure. Persian tobacco is among the chief articles of export, and is destined for the Turkish market. On the other hand, a stronger quality is imported from Oman for local consumption. The manner in which the British Consular tables relating to this port have been compiled, the same items appearing in the columns both of export and import, render the total returns an imperfect basis of generalisation as to the true volume of trade. The customs, which in 1874 were valued at 6,500 *tomans*, were farmed in 1889–90 for 12,000 *tomans*; the revenues of the surrounding district were let in 1889–90 for 8,000 *tomans*.

Town and population

Lingah, like most Persian towns, contains a larger population than its external appearance suggests. The figures were given to me as 15,000, an estimate which I should be inclined to reduce to 10,000. The town is divided, so to speak, into two quarters, the fringe along the shore, in which there is a small covered bazaar of a single street, and a further cluster beyond the date groves a little way inland. The feature of which the inhabitants are most proud, is a number of *birkehs*, or tanks, outside the town, for the preservation of rain-water. It only rains here during a period of two or three weeks in the year, and, there being no wells or fresh-water springs in the place, it is entirely dependent for the remainder of the twelve months upon the storage of that brief interval. The rain-water is brought down in natural channels from the hills, four or five miles inland, and conducted into big circular reservoirs, twenty or thirty feet deep, which are covered over with a domed roof to prevent loss by evaporation or stagnation. There are thirty-six of these tanks in the town, and ten more at the village of Kong, before mentioned; and the united supply is said to be ample for a period of fourteen months. The population of the place is partly Arab, partly Persian, partly African, partly that nameless hybrid mixture that is found in every maritime town east of Port Said. The Arabs belong to the Kowasim (vulgarly pronounced Jowasmi) tribe, a branch of the larger stock who people the opposite Arabian coast at Ras-el-Kheimah. For generations the governorship of Lingah, and of the islands lying off the shore, has been an hereditary patrimony of the sheikh of this tribe, who resided at Lingah, and was always recognised by the Persians as deputy-governor of the town. The policy, however, of centralisation, which I have so frequently sketched, has been applied to the Jowasmi Arabs equally with the Kurds of Khorasan, the Beluchis of the Mekran coast, and the Ka'b Arabs of Mohammerah; and in the fate of Sheikh Kadthib, the last Arab governor of Lingah, Sheikh Mizal Khan may perhaps see a foretaste of his own. In 1887 a detachment of Persian troops landed here, occupied the town without resistance, seized the Sheikh, and deported him to Teheran, where, in 1889, he was still a prisoner. A barrack was then built at Lingah, and a detachment of 200 Persian regulars was quartered in the place. Simultaneously a Persian garrison was planted in the island of Sirri, which had been for generations an hereditary possession of the Jowasmi. Both proceedings excited a good deal of local antipathy at the time. But the inhabitants of these coast towns are very poor and have no means of organised resistance, besides being sad cowards into the bargain, and having a mortal fear of a soldier, even of a Persian soldier, at the butt-end of a muzzle-loading gun. Accordingly they soon settled down to the new order of things, and the Persian garrison of Lingah had now been reduced to twenty men. At the time of my visit the Saad-el-Mulk was staying here, and the 'Persepolis,' which had brought him, was lying at anchor in the roadstead. In an interview, I found him to be a man of pleasing appearance and courtly address; he professed the most friendly sentiments, and gave me a letter to his deputy at Bunder Abbas. He was reported to be fairly popular with the people, having quiet manners, and being perhaps less roguishly disposed than the majority of Persian officials.

Great Britain is represented at Lingah by a native agent, a jolly old Arab, who came rowing out in a boat flying the Union Jack, and whose sons, from frequent contact with English vessels and officers, could speak a little of our tongue.

Leaving Lingah, the boat skirts the southern shore of the large island of Kishm,[1] or Jazirat-el-Towilah (i.e. long island), which seems at one time to have formed part of the mainland, but is now separated therefrom by a channel sixty miles long, and from three to thirteen in width. The island is fifty-four miles in length, and varies from nine to thirty-two in breadth. In its centre is the village of Brukth or Urukth, the Oaracta of Nearchus and Arrian, who says that at the time of the Greek admiral's visit the island produced corn, vines, and fruit of all description. At the period of the greatness of Ormuz it supplied the latter with fruit, vegetables, and water; and the aid of water still renders a large portion of its soil amenable to the cultivation of grain, melons, grapes, etc., while large date groves are to be found in the interior. Fraser says that it once contained 360 villages, in the sixteenth century. A more moderate calculation fixes the number as seventy,

Island of Kishm

[1] The Quesomo of Thévenot and Kichmichs of Chardin.

with a total population of 10,000, before the pirates established their ascendency in the Gulf in the last century. It has greatly decayed since, and has suffered severely in recent years from earthquakes; but its customs are still farmed for 3,300 *tomans*, the bulk of which revenue is derived from its salt mines. Its population has been estimated in the past year at about 12,000 (Kishm 3,000–4,000, Laft 800–1,000, Deristan 800, Susa 400, Kauri 400, Ghuri 250, Basiduh 350). A coarse naphtha is also produced at some springs on the southern coast, near the village of Salakh, opposite the island of Henjam, and is used by the Arabs both for lighting purposes and as a remedy for rheumatic complaints. There is a good deal of game on the island, wild goats, partridges, and rock-pigeons in the hills; and abundance of small and beautiful antelopes or gazelles on the plains, which used to be hunted with greyhounds by the British officers at Basiduh.

British military settlements

To English readers, however, the chief interest of Kishm will lie in the fact that it has been, during the greater part of the present century, a British military or naval station. The principal town, called El Kishm, once held by the Portuguese, is at its north-eastern extremity. Two miles from this, and on the very site of the old Portuguese castle,[1] a cantonment of English and Indian troops, several hundred strong, was established in 1820, with the idea of overawing the Jowasmi pirates. This force, originally 1,200 strong, had been stationed first at the captured pirate stronghold of Ras-el-Kheimah, on the opposite shore of the Gulf, but had been compelled by the climate to evacuate that position. For their purpose the new station and the troops were equally useless; and the men suffered severely from the heat,[2] besides being almost wholly dependent upon

[1] The English flotilla, in conjunction with the land troops of Shah Abbas, besieged the Portuguese castle on Kishm from January 13 to 19, 1622 (on the latter day the garrison yielded), prior to their joint attack upon Ormuz. In the engagement only two Englishmen lost their lives, but one of these was the famous navigator, William Baffin, the discoverer of Baffin's Bay, who, having entered the service of the East India Company, sailed hither with the beleaguering squadron. As Mr. T. Wilson, the chyrurgion of the flotilla, quaintly wrote: 'Master Baffin went on shoare with his geometricall instruments for the taking the height and distance of the Castle wall, for the better levelling of his Peece to make his shot; but as he was about the same, he received a small shot from the Castle into his belly, wherewith he gave three leapes, by report, and died immediately' (Purchas' *Pilgrims*, vol. ii. lib. x. cap. 9).

[2] The appalling heat was the cause of a similar military retreat two centuries earlier; Tavernier being our authority for the episode, which is curious. After the

Bombay for food and supplies. Accordingly, the post at Kishm was abandoned. A move was then made to Deristan, on the southern coast of the island, opposite Henjam; but here, too, the insalubrity of the place compelled a retreat. Finally, the point of Basiduh, called by the English Bassadore, at the north-western extremity of the island, where also are the ruins of a once flourishing Portuguese settlement, became the headquarters of the Indian naval squadron, maintained for the same object in these waters; and here, until 1879, was stationed a company of sepoys belonging to the marine battalion at Bombay, their barracks being built upon a plot of land that is still the property of the British Government. The malarial feverishness of the spot, and the diminishing need for their services in the neighbourhood, led to their withdrawal in that year, and a coal depôt and agent are now all that is maintained by the Indian Government at Basiduh. Some eighty fugitive slaves from other parts of the island are living (1892) as fugitives on British territory.

An adventurer's career

I have also somewhere read a tale, which appeared to be authentic, of an English renegade, who, in the early part of the century, ended an extraordinary career of audacity and crime as Mussulman sheikh of Kishm. This remarkable man, whose real name was Thomas Horton, began life as a tailor's apprentice at Newcastle. In the course of his career he was successively a soldier in the Swedish army, the leader of a band of Tartar robbers in the Crimea, Russian inspector of the Caspian littoral, a Mussulman Haji, the principal merchant of Busrah, and agent at that port for the East India Company, and commander of the naval forces of the Arab sheikh of Kishm. During the passage of these years he was frequently guilty of murder (having once been sentenced to death by a Russian court), as well as of almost every crime known to the calendar. These atrocities he appropriately summed up by rebelling against his Arab patron, whom he deposed and strangled. Having married his widow he got himself elected sheikh of the island, and for a quarter of a century ruled with mingled severity and success, being

ambassadors of the Duke of Holstein to Shah Sefi I. had retired from Persia, the Dutch complained that they had drained the silk market, and had raised the price from 42 to 50 *tomans* a piece. They accordingly refused to pay more than 44 *tomans* themselves, and when the King declined to endorse this compromise, they besieged Kishm (in 1641-2), but were compelled to retire by the frightful heat.

respected alike for his mercy and his justice. He never spoke his native language, but affected the rigid Mussulman; though, when an English vessel was once wrecked upon the coast, he entertained his old countrymen right royally, and, hearing that the crew numbered 120 officers and men, graciously despatched an equal number of female slaves on board as a present.

Off the southern point of Kishm is a small island, about twelve miles in circumference, called Henjam (sometimes also Angam).

Henjam Island

It is now barren and supports but a scanty Arab population of about 450 males. Yet at one time it must have been densely peopled; for the remains of thousands of stone houses, as well as reservoirs faced with an indestructible cement, are scattered over the slopes, which also display the relics of terraced cultivation; and at the northern end stand the ruins of a considerable city with two mosques. The land-locked bay between Henjam and Kishm was recommended by Sir J. Malcolm to Lord Wellesley in 1800, as a naval station, having an easy entrance and excellent anchorage, even for the largest men-of-war; but it was never occupied. The geology and the mineralogy of Henjam are equally unique. The island contains a number of curious petrifactions, locally supposed to be the stems of date-trees, in the form of pillars of solidified mud embedded in some banks of calcareous soil; and some huge salt-caves, one of which is described by Mr. Floyer, who has written the most detailed account of the locality.[1] When the Indo-European Telegraph was shifted from Cape Musandim to Jask, a station was established for a while on Henjam, where it connected Jask with Bushire. It was abolished in 1881.

Rounding Henjam, and passing the further small island of Larak, on the north shore of which are the ruins of an old Dutch fort,

Ormuz and Bunder Abbas

the steamer now skirts the celebrated island of Ormuz, which it leaves on the right hand, and casts anchor, at a distance of 120 miles from Lingah, in the roadstead of Bunder Abbas. These two names are so richly fraught with historic memories, that I must here for the moment arrest my own footsteps, and supply a brief prologue to a modern description.

Ardeshir Babekan, the Sassanian king (211–241 A.D.), is said to have founded the original city of Ormuz on the mainland. This, too, was the site of the first Arab city bearing the name, whose

[1] *Unexplored Baluchistan*, pp. 123–126.

ruins have been discovered on the banks of the Minau creek (to the east of Bunder Abbas) some six miles south-west of the Minau fort. Towards the end of the thirteenth century Marco Polo twice (in 1272 and in 1293 A.D.) visited the city of Hormos, Hormes, or Curmosa, which was already the centre of a vast trade with every part of the East, receiving, especially from India, rich cargoes of spices, precious stones, pearls, ivory, silks, and cloth of gold. It was ruled by a line of independent Arab chiefs or kings,[1] the fifteenth in descent of whom, named Kutb-ed-Din, being pressed by a Mongolian invasion from the north, and finding that the exposed situation of his capital rendered it an easy prey to rapine, took the decisive step, in 1300 A.D., of abandoning the mainland, and founding a new Ormuz on a small island, distant at the nearest point about four miles from the coast, which has ever since borne the name. For 200 years the new city retained, in Arab hands, the fame and prosperity of its predecessor, and wielded a sovereignty that extended to Bahrein and Busrah. Ibn Batutah, the Moor, came hither in 1331 A.D., and reported the new Ormuz as being a large and beautiful city, containing the residence of the king.[2] A little later the reigning sovereign escaped the hostility, by becoming the tributary, of Timur. In 1442, Abdur Rezak, the reluctant seafarer and envoy from Shah Rukh, whom I have before quoted, starting for India from Ormuz, left on record that that place 'had not its equal on the surface of the globe,' that it contained 'merchants of seven climates and travellers from all countries,' and that 'the inhabitants united the flattering character of the people of Irak with the profound cunning of the Indians.'[3] Thirty years later the Russian merchant, Athanasius Nikitin, paid a similar tribute to the commercial glory of Ormuz.[4] Ludovico di Varthema, in 1504, three years before the Portuguese appeared upon the scene, described it as 'the noble city of Ormuz, which is extremely beautiful.'[5] The Latin tongue was even invoked by some scholarly eulogist, who thus rendered a couplet that had also an English version :—

History of Ormuz

[1] For a list of the Arab kings of Ormuz, *vide* Teixeira, *Relaciones del Origen, etc., de los Reyes de Persia y de Harmuz*, Coimbre, 1610; Traduction Française, 2 vols., Paris, 1681; also Purchas' *Pilgrims*, vol. ii. lib. x.; Herbert, *Some Yeares' Travels*, pp. 108–9; De Guignes' *Histoire des Huns*, vol. i. p. 345; and Yule's *Marco Polo*, vol. i. pp. 124–6.

[2] *Travels* (edit. 1829), p. 63.

[3] *India in the 15th Century* (Hakluyt Society), p. 7.

[4] *Ibid.*

[5] *Travels* (Hakluyt Society), p. 94.

Si terrarum orbis, quaqua patet, annulus esset,
Illius Ormusium gemma decusque foret.

It was at this period, namely, the opening of the sixteenth century, that the Portuguese, profiting by the recent discovery of the Cape of Good Hope route by Vasco da Gama, appeared in the eastern seas and, under the famous Albuquerque, laid the foundations of their short-lived but showy empire. In 1507, with a small armament, after sacking and destroying Muscat, he attacked Ormuz, and won a partial success, forcing the king to acknowledge himself a vassal of Portugal and to pay an annual tribute. Failing to receive the latter he reappeared upon the scene in 1514 with a much larger force, being now Governor-General of the Portuguese dominions in the East, captured the place, reduced the king (Seif-ed-Din) to complete subjection, and compelled him to admit a Portuguese garrison, but left him on the throne as a Portuguese *titulado*, or vassal, in receipt of an annual pension. Fresh treaties were made with his successors, regulating and raising the tribute exacted by the conquerors, which advanced from 15,000 to 100,000 seraphims, until, in the middle of the century, the Portuguese compulsorily appropriated the entire customs and became the *de facto* proprietors of Ormuz.

Portuguese ascendency

There was not anything in the locality itself, beyond its situation at the mouth of the Persian Gulf, and its possession of two good harbours, to recommend it as the site of a great city. The island, which is twelve miles in circuit, contains no natural products but salt, iron, and red ochre and sulphur. The hills are covered with a thick saline incrustation, under which they glisten white in the sun. There is not a well or water spring in the entire extent; and the rain of the short winter-falls was collected in artificial reservoirs or tanks, the ruins of which are still visible in the mountains. As Master Ralph Fitch, the English merchant, said, 'it is the dryest island in the world, for there is nothing growing in it but only salt.' All supplies, even the daily provisions of life, were imported from the outside; and anyone who visits the modern site, strewn though it be with ruins, will find it difficult to believe that it was once occupied by an urban population of 40,000 souls.[1]

Natural disadvantages

[1] The remains on the island of Ormuz now consist of parts of the Portuguese fort or castle, a lighthouse, a number of tanks in good repair, and the ruins of several hundreds. The modern town of Ormuz contains a population of 340. *Vide* a paper by Lieut. A. W. Stiffe in the *Geographical Magazine* of April 1874.

Nevertheless there is such an absolute consensus of testimony on the part of independent travellers of many nationalities that we are fain to believe that the city of Ormuz must have fully merited its world-wide renown. By the joint energy of Arabs and Portuguese this barren rock was converted into a rich and crowded mart, where the commerce of the two ends of the world changed hands, and in whose bazaars might be encountered all the hues of the Orient, from the tawny Arab of Oman to the darker native of Coromandel or Malacca, and the sable negro of Zanzibar. The Abbé Raynal, in his 'History of the East Indies' (translated by Justamond) delivers this glowing panegyric of Ormuz at the height of its fame:—

Splendour of city

At the time of the arrival of foreign merchants Ormuz afforded a more splendid and agreeable scene than any city in the East. Persons from all parts of the globe exchanged their commodities and transacted their business with an air of politeness and attention which are seldom seen in other places of trade. These manners were introduced by the merchants belonging to the ports, who induced foreigners to imitate their affability. Their address, the regularity of their police, and the variety of entertainments which their city afforded, joined to the interests of commerce, invited merchants to make it a place of resort. The pavement of the streets was covered with mats, and in some places with carpets; and the linen awnings which were suspended from the tops of the houses prevented any inconvenience from the heat of the sun. Indian cabinets, ornamented with gilded vases or china, filled with flowering shrubs or aromatic plants, adorned their apartments: camels, laden with water, were stationed in the public squares; Persian wines, perfumes, and all the delicacies of the table, were furnished in the greatest abundance; they had the music of the East in its highest perfection. In short, universal opulence and extensive commerce, a refined luxury, politeness in the men, and gallantry in the women, united all their attractions to make their city the seat of pleasure.

In 1583, four brave English merchants, John Newberry, Ralph Fitch, William Leedes, and James Story (the first named of whom had already in 1581 made the overland journey by Aleppo and Busrah to Ormuz and had stayed there six weeks),[1] their imaginations stirred by the great tales that were wafted westwards of the wealth and profits of the East, started for India on their own private venture. At Ormuz they were seized and thrown

English merchants

[1] Purchas' *Pilgrims*, vol. ii. lib. ix. cap. 3.

into prison by the Portuguese Governor, Don Mathias de Albuquerque, who did not at all relish the idea of British trade competition; and who sent them on as prisoners to the Viceroy at Goa, whence, after a further term of imprisonment, they finally escaped in 1585. Master Ralph Fitch wrote thus of Ormuz:—

The Portugals have a castle here, which standeth near unto the sea, wherein there is a captain for the King of Portugal, having under him a convenient number of soldiers, whereof some part remain in the castle and some in the town.[1] In this town are merchants of all nations, and many Moors and Gentiles. There is a very great trade of all sorts of spices, drugs, silk, cloth of silk, fine tapestry of Persia, great store of pearls, which come from the island of Bahrein, and are the best pearls of all others, and many horses of Persia, which serve all India.[2]

In 1627, five years after the expulsion of the Portuguese, Sir Thomas Herbert, landing at Ormuz, described in his own inimitable way the character of the city under their rule:—

Albeit the isle had little or nothing considered in itself, the city, nevertheless, being furnished from most parts of the Orient, abounded with all things requisite, and was capacitated to supply other parts with what was desirable either for the belly or eye. Such was the excellency of the situation for commerce, such the industry and commendable ingenuity of the Portugal. . . The laborious Portugal brought it to that perfection as it became the staple and glory of the Eastern world. The houses within were exceeding newly furnished with gilded leather and with Indian and China rarities; the Buzzar was rich and beautiful; the Churches splendid within; and both within and without the Castle so regularly built and so well fortified with deep trenches, counterscarp, and great ordnance commanding both city and Haven, that none exceeded it through all the Orient.[3]

1 When the town was taken by the English and Persians in 1622, T. Wilson, chyrurgion, wrote of it as follows: 'The citie of Ormuz was of great bignesse, the Houses all built of stone, and seemed a most famous thing to looke upon from the ships, with steeples and towres. They had fair and large Churches in it, strong and stately buildings; the castle of Ormuz was the fairest, largest, and strongest that ever I saw' (*ibid.* lib. x. cap. 9). On the topmost peak of the island, 650 feet, stood the chapel of Nostra Senhora de la Penha.

2 *Ibid.* lib. x. cap. 6.

3 *Some Yeares' Travels* (3rd edit.), p. 106. The worthy knight goes on to describe the disembarkation of Sir Robert Sherley, Sir Dodmore Cotton, and himself. 'Wrapped in smoak and flame, we landed safely, though Neptune made us first to dance upon his liquid billows, and with his salt breath seasoned the epicinia. The Cannons also from the Castle and Cittadel vomited out their choler, ten times roaring out their wrathful clamours, to our delight, but terrour of the Pagans, who, of all noise, most hate artificial thunder.'

Tavernier, a little later, recorded as a proof of the magnificence of the Portuguese that, 'the very barrs of their doors and windows were all guilt; the fortress was a noble thing; and they also had a stately church dedicated to the Virgin, where they were also wont to walk.'

Meanwhile the invaders had also possessed themselves of the port of Gombrun or Comron on the mainland, about twelve miles distant from Ormuz, having captured it in 1512 from the King of Lar, whose dominions had been severed from those of the first Sefavi sovereign. While the merchants and nobles lived at Ormuz, the bulk of the trade was conducted at Gombrun, particularly of that passing overland into or from Persia. Shah Abbas the Great, however, as he proceeded with the consolidation of his power and territories, looked with an increasingly jealous eye upon the usurpers in the south, who occupied posts on his mainland, picked the plums of his trade, and controlled his waters. 'The Sword of the Lord and of Gideon' had served the Portuguese very well as a motto for acquisition; but in the contemptuous neglect by them of the arts of peace, and in the absence of any genius for colonisation, it did not facilitate retention. The Portuguese were fanatical, oppressive, and destitute of the true commercial spirit. Instead of conciliating, they trampled upon Persian trade, compelling the Persians to purchase from Portuguese magazines, at prices fixed by themselves, and to ship their wares in Portuguese vessels. Shah Abbas accordingly looked around, and observing the rapidly growing power, both mercantile and naval, of the British, made an alliance with that people, by which, on certain conditions and in return for stipulated commercial advantages,[1] they were to assist him in turning out the Portuguese. In 1614 the Persian army under Daud Khan, brother of Imam Kuli Khan, the famous Governor of Fars, recovered Gombrun; and in 1622 the joint forces of the

Rupture between Portugal and Persia

[1] The articles of agreement were as follows: (1) the castle of Ormuz and all its ordnance and ammunition were to fall to the English; (2) the Persians might build another castle on the island if they pleased; (3) the spoil was to be equally divided between Persians and English; (4) Christian prisoners were to fall to the English, Mussulmans to the Persians; (5) Persia was to pay half the cost of victuals, wages, shot, powder, etc., expended during the operations; (6) the English were to receive half the customs of Gombrun in future, on condition of maintaining two ships of war in the Gulf to safeguard navigation; (7) the English were to be duty-free in Gombrun for ever.

British[1] and Persians, after capturing the Portuguese castle on Kishm, moved in conjunction against Ormuz. On February 9, the Persians attacked and gained possession of the city, the Portuguese retiring to the castle; a regular siege followed and breaching works were pushed forward until, on April 22, the garrison surrendered. The number of pieces of ordnance found in the castle was variously returned as from 200 to 600. The Portuguese, expelled from Ormuz, Kishm, and Gombrun, fell back upon Muscat, and in 1625 concluded a treaty with Shah Abbas by which they restored to him all his coast possessions, retaining only the pearl banks at Bahrein, and a moiety of the customs of Kong, of their factory at which place I have previously spoken.[2]

Persian *mala fides*

The alliance between Persia and the East India Company had no sooner succeeded in its object than the Persians began conveniently to forget the terms of their bargain, which were never carried out, and which were the cause of disputes that were protracted for many years.[3] The English did not get the castle; they only got half the ordnance; of the spoil their share did not amount to more than 20,000*l.*, of which 10,000*l.* went to the purse of James I., and 10,000*l.* to the Duke of Buckingham,[4] whilst their moiety of the customs of Gombrun was never fairly paid,[5] and dwindled in a few years from 40,000 to 1,000 *tomans*. As the factors plaintively remarked, 'Now we have

[1] The British force consisted of five vessels (the 'London,' 'Jonas,' 'Whale,' 'Dolphin,' and 'Lion') and four pinnaces (the 'Shilling,' 'Rose,' 'Robert,' and 'Richard'), under Captain Richard Blithe and Captain John Weddall. The Portuguese fleet consisted of 5 galleons and 15 or 20 frigates; their admiral, Don Ruy Frera d'Andrada, was taken prisoner at Kishm.

[2] The privileged position of the Portuguese at Kong only continued as long as they had a fleet in the Gulf strong enough to compel vessels to frequent that port. As their power declined, merchant vessels went elsewhere, and the Kong governor refused to pay the stipulated share of the customs. The Portuguese sent a fleet, and for a while the payment was compounded for 15,000 crowns a year. In 1711 it was stopped altogether.

[3] *State Papers*, vol. iii. Nos. 330, 388, 687. As early as August 1623 the factors presented a letter to Shah Abbas from James I., complaining of the *mala fides*.

[4] Assuming 100,000*l.* as the value of the various prizes taken by the forces of the Company in the Indian waters, the King and Buckingham, as Lord High Admiral, demanded one-tenth each (*State Papers*, East Indies, vol. iii. No. 303).

[5] Mandelslo, who was at Bunder Abbas in 1638, says: 'The English should by right receive one half of the customs, but they have hardly the tenth part allowed them, nay, they are obliged to take that little which they have in commodities' (*Travels into the Indies*, pp. 11–12).

broke the ice, the Dutch find good fishing.' Malcolm speaks of the *dénouement* in terms of unaccustomed warmth :—

The English had, it is true, revenged themselves on an enemy they hated, destroyed a flourishing settlement, and brought ruin and misery upon thousands, to gratify the avarice and ambition of a despot, on his promising to enrich them by a favour, which they should have known was not likely to protect them, even during his life, from the violence and injustice of his officers, much less during that of his successors. The history of the English factory at Gombroon, from this date until it was finally abandoned, is one series of disgraces, of losses, of dangers, as that of every such establishment in a country like Persia must be. Had that nation either taken Ormuz for itself, or made a settlement on a more eligible island in the Gulf, it would have carried on its commerce to much greater advantage; and its political influence, both in Persia and Arabia, would have remained unrivalled.[1]

Move to Bunder Abbas

The only immediate and practical result of the conquest, apart from the disappearance of the Portuguese, was that Gombrun received the name of Bunder Abbas, in honour of the victorious monarch, and that it became the headquarters, for a century from this date, of the foreign trade with the Persian Gulf. The English, French, and Dutch possessed factories there;[2] two forts protected the town on the east and west, and, about the year 1650, it was surrounded by a wall on the land side. Chardin says that in his day the place contained 1,400 or 1,500 houses, a mixed population of Persians, Jews (50), and Indians, and that it was fronted by a quay more than a mile long. The English and Dutch factories were in the centre of the town as it then existed, which was a good deal to the west of the modern site; but in 1698 the Dutch erected a new house on the eastern outskirts, which is the centre of the modern Bunder Abbas.

Nevertheless, small as had been the intrinsic recommendations of Ormuz as the site of a great city, and torrid as had been

[1] *History of Persia*, vol. i. cap. xii. Sir C. MacGregor (*Journey through Khorasan*, vol. i. p. 8) recommended a return from the mainland to Ormuz. But, seeing that the trade of Bunder Abbas is now a purely overland trade to the cities of central, southern, and north-eastern Persia, and that the mediæval trade route to Europe *viâ* Busrah, Baghdad, and Aleppo has ceased to exist, I can see no wisdom in a recommendation which would necessitate a double, instead of a single, shipment, and which would benefit nobody.

[2] The English alone possessed the privilege, in memory of their services against Ormuz, of flying their own flag on their agent's house.

its climate, the new port was far worse equipped in both particulars, and excited by its *désagréments* the irritated reproaches of travellers. Master Ralph Fitch, the worthy Elizabethan merchant before mentioned, thus expressed himself, in 1583, about its charms:—

Its climate

Nature seemed not to have designed it should be inhabited. It is situated at the foot of a ridge of mountains of excessive height; the air you breathe seems to be on fire; mortal vapours continually exhale from the bowels of the earth; the fields are black and dry as if they had been scorched with fire.

Chardin spoke of the 'foul and lethal air,' which compelled the people to retire for six months in spring and summer to the mountains. Herbert is, as usual, more comic than any other writer:—

The air is insufferable, so as some use to lie naked in troughs filled with water, which nevertheless so perboils their flesh as makes it both exceeding smooth and apt to take the least cold when any winterly weather succeeds the heat, which by that becomes little less offensive.[1]

Fifty years later the British tars who manned the vessel of Dr. Fryer expressed similar sentiments in a more professional vocabulary by declaring that 'there was but an inch-deal betwixt Gomberoon and Hell.'[2]

John Struys, the Dutchman, however, made the honest confession that the effect of the climate was 'enhanced by a liquor called Palepunsken, which is so bewitching that they cannot refrain from drinking it.'[3] So unanimous, however, was the general censure, that all writers combined in bewildered admiration of a famous banian-tree (*Ficus Indica*), which was situated about three miles from the ancient town, and was said to cover 400 men with its branches. Several of the seventeenth century travellers present illustrations of this curiosity.

In the anarchy that ensued upon the invasion of the Afghans in 1722 and the overthrow of the Sefavi dynasty, the English and Dutch merchants shut up their houses in Isfahan, and retired to

[1] *Some Yeares' Travels*, pp. 112–13.

[2] *Travels in Persia*, p. 228.

[3] *Voyages*, vol. iii. cap. 36. Can he mean 'pale punch'? The latter beverage (which Mandelslo calls *pauntz*) was said to have been invented by the Duke of Holstein's Mission to Persia, to which Mandelslo was attached, in 1637; and to have been so called from the five (*punj*, e.g. Punj-ab) ingredients used in its composition—viz. spirit, lime-juice, spice, sugar, and rosewater.

Bunder Abbas. But here, too, the prevailing insecurity was speedily felt, and commerce rapidly declined. In 1738 the English Company established an agency at Busrah, and a good deal of their Gulf business was shifted to that port. In 1750 Bartholomew Plaisted found nine out of ten houses at Bunder Abbas deserted. In 1758 Edward Ives still found there an English agent with five assistants, but said, 'The English and Dutch factory-houses are the only buildings remaining of any importance; the whole city besides is almost one entire scene of ruin.' In the succeeding year, the Comte d'Estaing, a Frenchman who had been released on *parole* from imprisonment at Madras, at the head of a fleet of four vessels flying the Dutch colours, entered the roadstead and attacked and captured the English factory; and from about this time, accordingly, may be dated the temporary cessation of the Company's establishment at Bunder Abbas. The latest records that have been preserved relating to this period bear the date 1763.

Collapse of the factory at Bunder Abbas

Almost simultaneously, however, with the retreat from Bunder Abbas occurred the foundation of a new English depôt at Bushire. The latter place had been selected by Nadir Shah as the site of a naval station, because of its proximity to Shiraz; and here, in confirmation of an agreement entered into with the local sheikh, the excellent Kerim Khan Zend (Vekil or Regent), by a document dated July 2, 1763,[1] granted permission to 'the Right Worshipful William Andrew Price, Governor of the English nation in the Gulf of Persia,' to build a factory, with exemption from all custom-duties, and a complete monopoly of the import of woollen cloths. Ever since that date Bushire has been the headquarters of British commerce in the Gulf.

Removal to Bushire

We next come to a curious episode in the history of these Gulf ports, in which another proprietor, the Arab Sultan or Imam of Muscat, appears upon the scene. It seems that Nadir Shah, conscious that his authority was somewhat precarious in these regions, and preferring a certain annual contribution to the revenue to an assertion of authority that might have provoked resistance, granted the district of Bunder Abbas and the islands of Kishm and Ormuz by a firman to the Arab sheikh of the Beni Maaini tribe. The subjects of one of his successors suffered so severely from misrule that in the last quarter of the

Claims of Muscat

[1] Quoted by C. R. Markham, *History of Persia*, Appendix A., pp. 530-1.

century they appealed for assistance to Sultan bin Ahmed, the powerful ruler of Muscat. Nothing loth, the Sultan appeared upon the scene, made himself master of the triple possession, and received a firman from the Persian Government, transferring to him in leasehold the port and dependencies of Bunder Abbas, i.e. a coast-strip nearly a hundred miles in length from Minau on the east to Khamir on the west. At the same time he remained in possession of Kishm and Ormuz,[1] which his successors always declared he had won by right of conquest from the Arabs, who had won them by a similar title from the Persians, whose suzerain claims accordingly were disputed by Muscat. The friendly terms which were consistently observed between the East India Company and the rulers of Oman enabled the former to negotiate a re-appearance at Bunder Abbas; and in 1798 a treaty was concluded between the two parties, Mahdi Ali Khan being the English signatory, which contained these words:—

> In the port of Abassy (Gombroon) whenever the English shall be disposed to establish a factory, I have no objection to their fortifying the same, and mounting guns thereon as many as they list, and to 40 or 50 English gentlemen residing there with 700 or 800 English sepoys; and for the rest the rate of duties on goods on buying and selling will be on the same footing as at Bussora and Abushahr.[2]

I presume that the two smooth-bore brass guns, stamped with the royal crown of England, and the initials G. R. (Georgius Rex) surrounded by the motto, 'Honi soit qui mal y pense,' which I saw lying upon the pier at Bunder Abbas, were either presents to this faithful ally of the British Crown or are reminiscences of the affirmative reply made by the Company to the above invitation.

From time to time the Persian Government, in moments of aggressiveness or elation, laid claim to the resumption of its possessions; but it was not till 1852 that, in the absence of Seyid Said of Muscat in his southern dominions at Zanzibar, they succeeded in ousting his deputy. The Sultan, returning in high dudgeon, despatched an expedition for the forcible recovery of the ports; but, meeting with little success, was obliged to conclude a new agreement upon much less favour-

Re-assertion of Persian authority

[1] In 1815 Morier found a garrison of 120 Nubian slaves and 80 Arabs, maintained by the Sultan of Muscat, at Ormuz, as a guard against the Jowasmi pirates.

[2] C. O. Aitchison, *Collection of Treaties, Engagements, and Sunnuds relating to India and neighbouring Countries*, vol. vii. No. xxxii.

able terms in 1855, his term of occupation being restricted to twenty years; the rent being raised from 6,000 to 16,000 *tomans* (7,600*l.*); and Persia plucking up courage to assert in the most emphatic terms her ownership of Kishm and Ormuz, as well as of the neighbouring land districts, 'that are all the very territories of the exalted government of Persia.'[1] The new arrangement continued in force until 1866, when, upon the assassination of Seyid Thoweyni of Muscat, the Persian Government seized the opportunity to instal as a Persian dependent the Arab governor under the late Sultan, who engaged to pay 20,000 *tomans* per annum. Presently, however, he declined to pay the increment; and the new Sultan, Seyid Selim, at the same time threatening to blockade Bunder Abbas unless the contract was at once rescinded, the Persians solicited the interference of the British Government, by whose offices the lease was renewed for another eight years from 1868, upon payment of 30,000 *tomans* a year, the progressive rise in rent indicating approximately the increasing prosperity of the revived Bunder Abbas. In the same year, however, the Sultan was expelled from Muscat by a successful revolt, and the Persian Government, taking advantage of a clause in the lease, allowing them to cancel the contract if a conqueror obtained possession of Muscat,[2] installed their own governor at Bunder Abbas, and have retained possession of the place ever since. In pursuance of the fussy policy which I have before described, Persian soldiers were stationed here in some numbers in 1888, where their presence was extremely distasteful to the Arab population. But the Government having recognised both its own mistake and the superfluity of the precaution, orders were issued in 1889 for their withdrawal.

The anchorage at Bunder Abbas is in four fathoms of water at a distance of at least two miles from the land.[3] There is a very

[1] Aitchison, vol. vii. Appendix III. Article ii. of this treaty contains an admission, quite engaging in its candour, of the sanctity of that method of procedure which I have previously described as so dear to the Persians. The distribution of the 16,000 *tomans* annual rent is there openly stated as follows: revenues, 12,500; *pishkesh* (i.e. present) for Prime Minister, 2,000; *pishkesh* for Governor-General of Fars, 1,000; present for Shuja-el-Mulk, 500.

[2] Aitchison, Appendix III., clause xii.

[3] Here, in full view of the shore—where, 'during two days' fight, Mr. Barker (the Factor) and the Sultan of Gombroon, sitting upon the houses, counted 16,000 shot, but in the greatest brunt the ordnance went off so fast that they could not tell them'—was fought a famous sea-fight on February 1, 3, and 14, 1624–5, between an English fleet of four vessels (the 'Royal James,' 'Jonas,' 'Star,' and 'Eagle'),

shelving sandy beach, with so small a slope that I had to be carried for some distance to the shore. The town, which is not to be compared with Lingah either in size or appearance, is situated upon the beach, the business of its motley bazaar and the life of its people being concentrated upon the narrow strip of yellow sand that glitters above the high-water line. Here are to be seen innumerable stalls covered with dates, almonds, raisins, and other fruits, themselves covered with myriads of flies; and strange forms, passing to and fro through the narrow passages, here the pious votary of Vishnu or Shiva, with the red or white sect mark daubed upon his forehead, there a swaggering pirate from an Arab port, here a cringing henna-bedyed Persian, there a six-feet black-locked Barabbas from Kabul. Bunder Abbas has a small stone pier projecting a short distance into the sea, and supporting a flagstaff, the two English guns before mentioned, and two old iron carronades as well. The horizontal lines of the town are broken by a large number of wind-towers, but are relieved by very few palms, which do not seem to flourish here as at Lingah. In the centre facing the sea is the customs-house and residence of the Deputy-Governor, once the Dutch factory, and afterwards the residence of the deputy of the Imam of Muscat. A little to the east are the ruins of two towers or bastions which were part of the fortified *enceinte* erected by Shah Abbas. The English and old Dutch factories, as I have said, were to the west of the modern town, and have disappeared. So also have the tombs of the Englishmen who died while residing at the factory here. Immediately behind the town is a low sandy ridge, and at a distance of fifteen miles a mighty mountain scarp, rising to a sheer height above the Gulf of 8,500 feet at its highest point. A little to the west the range dips to a gap, through which the caravan road strikes into the interior. The population of the town is peculiarly fluctuating, according to the arrival or departure of large caravans, and to the season of the year, the place being almost deserted in the heat of summer; but it was given to me by a merchant as 5,000 persons. The customs, however, are farmed for 53,000

Modern Bunder Abbas

commanded by Captain John Weddall, in alliance with four Dutch vessels, against a Portuguese fleet of eight galleons and sixteen frigates. The English lost 29 men; the Dutch nearly as many, including their commander; the Portuguese, 800, including their general and vice-admiral. The enemy were put to flight, and the allies were only prevented from continuing the chase by failure of ammunition (*State Papers*, East Indies, vol. iv., Nos. 121, 122).

tomans, as compared with the 12,000 of Lingah, a difference that illustrates the relative part played by the two places in the import and export trade with the interior. The revenues of the Bunder Abbas district are 30,000 *tomans*.

In the days of the Sefavi kings, when the northern avenues of access to Persia were barred by hostile nations or robber tribes, and before the Bushire-Shiraz line of communication had been opened, Bunder Abbas was the main, almost the sole port of Iran, and absorbed the bulk of its foreign trade. A well-worn caravan track led from thence, *viâ* Lar and Shiraz, to Isfahan, and has been described by Tavernier, Chardin, Le Brun, and other seventeenth or eighteenth century writers. With the opening of the Bushire route from the Gulf, of the Baghdad route to the western provinces, and of the Tabriz and Enzeli routes on the north, the importance of Bunder Abbas has naturally much diminished; and its trade is now restricted to the eastern portion of the Shah's dominions, and in some slight measure to the neighbouring districts of Central Asia and Afghanistan. Three main caravan tracks now strike into the interior from this port, single as far as Kerman, but trifurcating from there (1) to the important manufacturing centre of Yezd, and thence to Kashan, and finally Teheran—a total distance of 920 miles from the Gulf; (2) *viâ* Birjand and Turbat-i-Haideri to Meshed; (3) *viâ* Birjand and Yezdun to Herat and Kabul. Upon the first of these routes is conveyed the export and import trade of Kerman and Yezd, which I have elsewhere discussed; by the second are carried the tea and indigo which supply the bazaars of Meshed, and are re-exported to those of Bokhara; by the third had travelled the long-haired, loose-trousered desperadoes from Kabul, whom I encountered on the beach at Bunder Abbas. From Bunder Abbas in 1889 were exported 1,800 chests of opium for Hong Kong and China, with an estimated value of 70*l.* per chest, 1,300 tons of raw cotton valued at 33,000*l.*, 6,700 tons of dates valued at 20,000*l.*, 16,000 tons of salt valued at 2,700*l.*, and 1,000 tons of wool valued at 27,000*l.* The total value of exports, including specie, was 344,000*l.* There were imported into Bunder Abbas 9,000 bales of cotton goods, with a value of 156,000*l.*, thread and twist to the value of 24,000*l.*, 175 tons of indigo valued at 23,000*l.*, 1,400 tons of crushed sugar with a value of 25,000*l.*, 600 tons of tea valued at 69,000*l.* The total imports amounted to 360,000*l.* In an earlier chapter upon Khorasan I have urged the

Trade

adoption of measures for the greater security and convenience of this most important trade avenue into Persia.

Some fifty miles to the east of Bunder Abbas the river Minau (*lit.* muddy water) flows into the sea, past a town and fort of that name, containing some old Portuguese guns, situated on a hill about fifteen miles inland. Native craft run up and down a creek communicating with the sea, and do a trade in grain and dried fruits, the customs of the port, called Sif, being farmed for the comparatively large figure of 3,500 *tomans*. Minau, with its shady palm-groves, is the summer retreat of the parboiled citizens of Ormuz and Bunder Abbas, and has elicited by its picturesque and reposeful scenery the encomiums of such travellers as have passed over the fiery surrounding deserts. The river on which it stands is identified with the Anamis of Arrian, where Nearchus put in on the eighteenth day after leaving the Indus, and hauled up his ships on shore for repair, while he marched inland himself and visited the camp of Alexander. Here we take leave of the Persian Gulf, and passing through the straits of Ormuz, round the gloomy basaltic peaks of Cape Musandim, emerge into the Indian Ocean.

Minau

The next calling-point of the steamer is the promontory of Jask (Ras Jashak, sometimes written Jasques), 130 miles from Bunder Abbas. So far as I can ascertain, Jask is the site of the first mercantile settlement made by the East India Company on Persian soil. In 1616, in pursuit of the advice of Mr. Richard Steele, who in 1615 had journeyed through Persia, the directors sent a ship from Surat to Jask 'to make the first offer of a residence, and to get a kind of a possession.'[1] This vessel, the 'James,' commanded by Alexander Childe, took out Edward Connock, the first agent of the company in Persia, who, in his reports to the board of directors, spoke favourably of his reception by the local governor, living at Mogustan, and of the prospects of trade.[2] Childe wrote of Jask: 'It is the worthiest place for fish in all the Indies,'[3] a reputation, I may add, which it still retains. On December 17, 1620, occurred an indecisive

Jask

[1] *Vide* letter from Sir Thomas Roe, ambassador from James I. to Jehangir, the Great Mogul. Purchas' *Pilgrims*, lib. iv. cap. 17. Sir T. Roe himself earnestly dissuaded the venture (*Calendar of State Papers*, East Indies, vol. i., No. 1176).

[2] *State Papers*, vol. i., Nos. 1179, 1181, 1182, 1186, 1188.

[3] Purchas' *Pilgrims*, lib. v. Ap. II.

conflict between a Portuguese fleet, that was blockading Jask, and four English vessels[1] off Cape Jask, which on being renewed on December 28, resulted in the defeat of the Portuguese, but also in the death of the English commander, Andrew Shilling, who, being slain in the engagement, was buried at Jask. After the battle the English ships 'despatched their businesse at Jasques.'[2] The result of this successful engagement, and of the growing friendly relations between the English and Persian courts, was that in 1619 the East India Company founded their first Persian factory and erected a fort at Jask. I incline to the opinion that when, three years later, they obtained so much better a position at Bunder Abbas, they must have vacated this station.

Jask possesses a very different modern interest, as the point of convergence of the land and marine wires of the Indo-European Telegraph Department between India and the Gulf. Here the duplicate indiarubber and gutta-percha cable from Bushire, a distance of 499 miles, comes up from the sea; and its place is henceforward taken by a double overland wire to Kurrachi, a distance of 684 miles. A single submarine gutta-percha cable is, however, also continued to Kurrachi, and forms a section of the through cable line from Kurrachi to Fao. Originally the cable was laid from Gwadur to Cape Musandim, but in consequence of the abominable climate there encountered and of other reasons, it was shifted in 1869 to Jask and Henjam. The telegraph station and a few buildings surrounding it are situated at the extremity of a low spit of land or cape projecting into the sea; the native village and fort of Jask, now in ruins, being ten miles to the north, at a distance of one mile and a half from the shore.

Indo-European Telegraph

When the Indian naval station was withdrawn in 1879 from Basiduh (Bassadore) on Kishm Island, the company of sepoys, 100 strong, who had been posted there, was moved to Jask, and barracks were erected by the Indian Government for their accommodation. At that time the promontory of Jask was unoccupied, save by the English telegraph station, and its ownership was not strictly determined, the tribes along the coast and in the interior being Beluchis, who claimed independence, and the Persian authority being as yet precariously

Indian military station

[1] They were the 'London,' 'Hart,' 'Roebuck,' and 'Eagle.' W. Baffin, who was killed at Kishm a little more than a year later, sailed in this fleet, which left Gravesend in February 1619.

[2] *Ibid.*, lib. v. cap. 16.

established in those parts. When the telegraph station had been first opened at Jask in 1869, the cape was a barren piece of sand to which no claimant turned a thought. This tiny military settlement remained unnoticed and unobjected to until 1886, when the Persian Government, hearing that a small trade had sprung up since the arrival of the English, sent an agent to establish a custom-house. This individual detected an opportunity of personal distinction which was not to be missed. In a highly-coloured report, he represented the English as exercising sovereign rights upon Persian territory, and acquiring undue political influence over the Beluchi tribes (the village sheikh received a few rupees a year for the preservation of the wire running through the district); and himself as having by valiant measures restored seventeen townships to the Persian allegiance. He received his decoration, and subsided into satisfied obscurity. The two local sheikhs, however, who were quite innocent of anything in the nature of a conspiracy, were carried off in chains, and were only released after a long imprisonment. Meanwhile the Shah appealed to the Indian Government to withdraw the sepoys. Under similar conditions Russia would doubtless have replied, *J'y suis, j'y reste.* The Viceroy, however, respecting the susceptibilities of the Shah, and having no further need for the service of land-troops since the police of the Gulf is now so well assured, withdrew the detachment, and the quarters which they occupied at Jask are now empty.

Modern Jask

In their place has been built a square fort, which I found tenanted by a Persian deputy-governor, subordinate to the Saad-el-Mulk, with a guard of forty soldiers commanded by a corporal. He has no *raison d'être* except to assert Persian sovereignty over the strip of soil on which he is located, and to overawe the tribes in the interior by the display of his dingy body-guard. The Persian authority here, as elsewhere along this coast, is cordially detested by the local tribes, who have been accustomed to a life of independence, and who resent the appearance of the tax-collector and the *serbaz*, as the death-warrant of their old freedom. On shore, the British telegraph station and its surroundings, where there is a staff of six English officials, and in front of which the British ensign floats from a flagstaff, betray that neat and orderly appearance which may everywhere be associated with an English habitation, from Plymouth to Yokohama. Some trees have been planted, a fresh-water tank has been constructed, a little garden laid out, and a lawn-tennis court marked on the level clay. The British India Company's flag flies above the hut occupied by its agent; and a double row of huts accommodate the native *employés* of the various establishments. Such, and no more, is Jask: almost the only trade being in fish, of which an immense number—somewhat like whitebait—are caught at certain seasons of the year, and are shipped across to the Arab coast, where they are utilised sometimes as food, more commonly as manure for the date-palms. The customs are farmed for the modest sum of 500 *tomans*. At a distance of twenty miles inland, a remarkable conical hill, called by the natives Jebel Bahmedi, rises to a height of 3,100 feet above the sea.

Mekran coast

From Jask the steamer, as a rule, crosses to Muscat on the opposite coast of Oman, a distance of 133 miles. But before passing from Persia proper to a discussion of its *vis-à-vis* neighbours on the other side of the Gulf, let me complete my survey of the Persian littoral as far as the eastern frontier. From Jask, eastwards, the coast line is of a sullen mountainous character, and would seem to be wholly deserted by human habitation. We approach here the district commonly designated as the Mekran coast, though since Sir F. Goldsmid's able determination of the boundaries in 1871, it has been divided into the territories of Persian Beluchistan, terminating at Gwetter, and further east of Independent Beluchistan. In my chapter upon the South-eastern Provinces of Persia, I have described the state of affairs in Persian Beluchistan, and have shown how reluctantly there, as elsewhere, the indigenous population have submitted to Persian bayonets; although such are their weakness and destitution, that resistance becomes hopeless, and the mere appearance of the 'Persepolis' with its four Krupp guns off the coast throws its scanty inhabitants into paroxysms of dread.

Gwadur

Immediately beyond Gwetter is a strip of seaboard, about fifty miles in length, belonging to the Khan of Kelat, but separated from the remainder of the Beluch territory by a further and smaller strip, which has for 100 years been in the undisputed possession of the Sultan of Muscat. The latter consists merely of a few miles of coast, dependent upon the town of Gwadur,[1]

[1] The Beluchi Gwadur is the same name as Badara or Vadara, which occurs in the Ptolemaic Pinax, in Orthagoras, and in Arrian, and is either a Dravidian name, or of Aryan origin, in which case it might be derived from the Sanskrit *vadara* the cotton-plant, or *badara* the *Zizyphus* or jujube-tree.

the Muscat frontier being at the tiny village or fort of Pishkan, a few miles to the west of that port. Gwadur is also a station of the Indo-European Telegraph, and is sometimes spoken of as the possible maritime terminus of a railway line from Seistan, or British Beluchistan. The town is quaintly and even picturesquely situated on a long and low spit of sand, projecting into the sea, and narrowing to an apex, not more than half a mile in width, between two bays. Upon this low neck of land is built the port of Gwadur, with a population of about 4,000, and a trade in wool and cotton from the interior, and in fish from the coast. On the southern side, and immediately below the town, which is not at first visible from the sea, the narrow spit suddenly bulges into a rocky promontory, from 100 to 300 feet in height, the latitudinal section of which is perhaps six miles in length, and which, presenting its broad face to the sea, is exactly like the head of a hammer into which the haft is fitted at the point where is built the town. The anchorage is in 3½ fathoms of water, at about three miles from the shore, along which a nasty surf is heard booming. Gwadur was once one of the most popular stations of the Telegraph Line, and was regarded as the *sanitarium* of the Gulf ports, the temperature being very equable, and existence quite endurable even in the summer months. From some unknown cause, however, attributed by some to the sea-water, which is here so strongly impregnated with sulphuretted hydrogen that the fish are often killed in great numbers—a malarial fever has developed itself, which attacks every new-comer; and the place is now as much shunned as it was once sought. Till a few years ago, Gwadur was also the residence of a British political agent. But the increasing unhealthiness of the spot has led to the abandonment of the agent's bungalow as a permanent residence, and the political work along the Mekran coast is now discharged by an officer who pays an occasional visit in the course of a tour of inspection. It is highly probable that the climatic conditions may also lead to the abandonment of the telegraph station, which appears not to be essential to the efficient working of the line.

Upon the eastern side of the Gwadur Bay, where the spit joins the mainland, a stately cliff, called Jebel Mahdi, rises sheer

Coast scenery

from the sea to a height of 1,360 feet, its cloven summit being shaped at one point into two projections, that have procured for it from the compilers of the old charts the expressive title of the Asses' Ears. A neighbouring rock is known as the

Cathedral Rock, from its fantastic natural outline of pinnacles and spires; and the entire coast line is here so strangely fretted and moulded by nature, that we are reminded of Scott's description in the 'Lady of the Lake':—

> Their rocky summits split and rent
> Form'd turret, dome, and battlement,
> Or seem'd fantastically set
> With cupola or minaret,
> Wild crests as pagod ever deck'd,
> Or mosque of Eastern architect.

Traces either of Portuguese or of some foreign occupation are visible at Gwadur, in the ruins of a vast reservoir on the flank of the hill overlooking the town; while a rude archaic rampart dominates the same elevation. Nor is it altogether unknown in English history. For here it was that, in 1613, Sir Robert Sherley, returning from his embassy on behalf of the King of Persia to the Christian powers of Europe, in the good ship 'Expedition' (Captain Christopher Newport), and proposing to march overland to Isfahan, narrowly escaped a plot to murder both himself and the whole ship's crew, that had been formed by the 'Viceroy of Guader or Godel,' who is elsewhere described as 'a revolted duke from the Persians.'[1] The port and district are now governed by a Vali, or deputy of the Sultan of Muscat. The circumstances under which the latter potentate became possessed of the place occurred at the end of the last century, when a free gift of Gwadur and its surroundings, as well as of Chahbar, was made by Nasir Khan, the ruler of Kelat, to Seyid Sultan bin Ahmed, of Oman, who had retired from Muscat to the Beluch coast, after an unsuccessful attempt to oust his elder brother, Seyid Said. From that period the place was ruled by deputies of the reigning Sultan, until in 1871 Abdul Aziz, the younger brother of the late Sultan, with whom he was perpetually at war, on the occasion of one of his numerous exiles, installed himself at Gwadur and seized Chahbar, which had lately been occupied by local chieftains. The Persians, delighted at an opportunity of asserting their authority over Chahbar, expelled Abdul Aziz, who was also turned out of Gwadur by his brother; and the latter port has since remained in possession of the reigning

History

[1] Purchas' *Pilgrims*, lib. iv. cap. 10.

Sultan. From the small Gwadur district he derives an annual revenue of about 2,000*l*.

Survey

I have now completed the survey of the northern coast of the Persian Gulf, and have exhibited the Persian Government as exercising along its shores and over its islands a more extended and emphatic authority than at almost any previous epoch during the last 300 years. This authority is only enforced at the cost of a good deal of discontent, the result of corruption, misgovernment, and oppression; but it is not likely to be seriously disputed in the future, owing to the want of cohesion among the subject races, and to their inability to make any stand even against Persian regulars. The Oriental, moreover, is familiar from long experience with old orders yielding place to new, while his creed disposes him to a placid acceptance of the doctrine that God fulfils himself in many ways. He shrugs his shoulders and submits; it is only in cases of outrageous provocation that he actually rebels. Though it is upon the opposite coast of the Gulf that the responsibility of the British Government as guardian of the peace is chiefly called into action, yet disputes seldom occur, even on the northern side, in which the friendly offices of the British Resident at Bushire are not appealed to on one side or the other; and he is thereby enabled to exercise an influence which is both honourable to the nation that he represents and useful to the power to whom he is accredited.

History of Oman

In crossing to the Arab coast of Muscat, the mention of the internal politics and domestic broils of the reigning family of Oman, which the description of Gwadur has elicited, leads me to preface my account of that coast and its capital by a brief *résumé* of the recent history of this still independent Arab kingdom.[1] The Portuguese, in the eastward

[1] I have compiled the following brief bibliography of Oman: C. Dellon, *Voyage aux Indes Orientales*, 2 vols., 1685; E. C. Ross, 'Annals of Oman,' *Journ. of As. Soc. of Bengal*, vol. xliii.; C. Niebuhr, *Description de l'Arabie*, 1784; *Travels through Arabia*, 2 vols., 1792; Vicenzo, *History of Seyd Said of Muscat*, &c., translated by Sheikh Mansur, 1819; Major D. Price, *History of Arabia*, 1824; A. Crichton, *History of Arabia*, 2 vols., 1830; Lieutenant J. R. Wellsted, *Travels in Arabia*, 2 vols., 1838; A. Cole, *Journal of Bombay Geog. Soc.*, 1847; Rev. C. Forster, *Historical Geography of Arabia*, 2 vols., 1844; A. Caussin de Perceval, *Essai sur l'Histoire des Arabes*, 3 vols., 1847–8; *Selection from Records of Bombay Government*, No. 24, 1856; Salil ibn Razik, *History of the Imams and Seyids of Oman*, A.D. 661–1856, translated by Rev. G. P. Badger (Hakluyt Society), 1870; A.

outflow of their mercantile enterprise towards the Persian Gulf, did not confine their attention to its northern shore. On its way to Ormuz, in 1506, a naval squadron, under the redoubtable Albuquerque, appeared off the Arab shores of Oman, bombarded or demanded immediate submission from every port encountered, and presently anchored off the capital town Muscat, situated in a land-locked cove, at a distance of about 300 miles down the coast from Cape Musandim, and at less than half that distance from the opposite Persian shore.[1] The inhabitants of Muscat, who professed themselves subjects of the King of Ormuz, at first temporised, but, thinking that the quality of the great admiral's soldiers was probably not better than that of his guns, which were far from first rate, then ventured upon an ill-judged resistance. Albuquerque had no mercy. He landed his troops; the miserable defences were carried by storm; and the town, as a punishment for its contumacy, was given to the flames. From that time till 1650, the Portuguese remained in constant, though not undisputed possession of Muscat.[2] In the latter year the Arabs, recovering their strength, succeeded in ousting the intruder, whose prestige was now universally on the decline; after which they overran the shores of the Persian Gulf, scoured the seas with their buccaneering craft, established a foothold as far south as Zanzibar, and so terrified the King of Persia, that he made an offer to the English East India Company to give them the same privileges at Muscat as at Bunder Abbas, if they would co-operate with him in the reduction of the pirate stronghold. The Company, having at that time neither troops nor ships to spare for the operation, returned an indecisive answer. The Arabs now became very powerful; but in the second quarter of the eighteenth century were cowed into temporary submission by the iron hand of Nadir

Sprenger, *Die alte Geographie Arabiens*, 1875; Major Mockler and Colonel S. B. Miles, *Administration Report of Persian Gulf*, 1882, 1883.

[1] Prior to the appearance of the Portuguese, Oman had been governed for a period of nearly 900 years by a succession of independent rulers, entitled Imam, who owed their elevation to the popular choice, irrespective of family descent. This system continued down to the time of Nasir bin Murshid (1618–1644 A.D.), after whom the succession was vested in a single ruling family.

[2] In 1546 Muscat was bombarded by the Turks. In 1552 a powerful Turkish fleet under Piri Pasha anchored in the bay, and, after a protracted siege, took the town. In 1580 Muscat was taken and sacked by an Arab expedition from Aden under Mir Ali Beg. But after each of these vicissitudes the Portuguese either remained or returned.

Shah. In the distraction, however, that followed upon the dissolution of his kingdom, they saw their opportunity. One Ahmed bin Said, a man of humble origin, and a camel-driver by profession, aroused his countrymen, rose by his bravery to be Vali, or Governor of Sohar, a coast town 100 miles north-west of the capital, drove the Persians out of Muscat, and being elected Imam [1] by his grateful fellow-citizens, founded, in 1741, the Al-Bu-Said dynasty, which has occupied the throne of Oman ever since.

Ruling dynasty

Dying, after a reign of forty years, in 1783, he was succeeded by his second son, Seyid Said bin Ahmed, whose incompetence soon provided his younger brother with the chance of successful revolution. The deposed ruler was suffered to live in retirement, retaining, though destitute of all authority, the spiritual title of Imam, which has never since been worn by any ruler of Muscat. The victorious usurper, Seyid Sultan bin Ahmed, reigned both over Muscat and Zanzibar (which had been captured in 1784) till 1804, when he was killed in battle. His aggressive character and schemes for territorial and maritime aggrandisement continually involved in trouble both his own kingdom and the British Government, with whom he had established political and mercantile relations; but his fidelity to the English never wavered. In 1798 he concluded a treaty with the East India Company (previously quoted [2]), the main object of which was the exclusion of French agents and influence from Oman, upon which Napoleon had designs as a basis for naval attack upon India.[3] Two years later Major, afterwards Sir J. Malcolm, journeying to Persia on his famous first mission from Lord Wellesley, stopped at Muscat on his way, and negotiated a further treaty [4] with the Sultan, one clause of which provided for the residence at Muscat of 'an English gentleman of respectability on the part of the Honourable Company,' to act as an agent, 'in

[1] The title Imam implies spiritual headship, that of Sultan or Seyid (which here signifies 'lord,' not, as in Persia, 'a descendant of the Prophet'), the temporal sovereignty, in Oman.

[2] Aitchison, vol. vii., Appendix III.

[3] There was a brief resurrection of French influence in Oman in 1807, when the Sultan, impressed by the tidings of Napoleon's victories in Europe, despatched an envoy to Mauritius, and there concluded a treaty with General de Caen on June 1, 1807. But with the capitulation of the Ile de Bourbon and Mauritius in 1810, this Gallophile phase came to an end, and British influence was firmly and finally re-established.

[4] Aitchison, vol. vii. No. xxxiii.

order that no opportunity may be offered to designing men, who are ever eager to promote dissensions, and that the friendship of the two States may remain unshook to the end of time, and till the sun and moon have finished their revolving career.' The concluding paragraph was, perhaps, somewhat too rhetorical for modern tastes, and probably transcended the limited astronomical acquirements of the Sultan; but it expressed with becoming Oriental hyperbole the solidarity of an alliance which has lasted without interruption ever since, and under which the British Political Agent has always exercised a dominant influence at the Court of Muscat.

Seyid Sultan's successor was his second son, Seyid Said, who having, like his father before him, deposed his elder brother, Seyid Salim, ruled for the long period of fifty years. His reign was disturbed by constant warfare against the Wahabi Arab power in the interior, which had, at the beginning of the century, spread its ferocious influence along the entire southern shore of the Persian Gulf, enlisting on its side the piratical instincts of the maritime tribes, and continually threatening the territories of Oman. The Sultan was sometimes only saved from extinction at the hand of the Wahabis by the friendly intervention of the British Government, under whose arrangement he paid a yearly tribute to the Wahabi Amir. With England he joined in naval operations against the pirate tribes and slave-hunters, whom the Wahabi propaganda had let loose upon the seas, and in 1822, 1840, and 1845, concluded treaties with the East India Company, for the suppression of the slave trade, the seizure of slave-dhows, and the prohibition of traffic in slaves between the African and Asian coasts. In the latter part of his life the affairs of Muscat fell into great confusion owing to the prolonged absence of the Sultan at Zanzibar, which in 1840 he made the permanent seat of Government. Mr. Stocqueler had an interview with Seyid Said at Muscat in 1831, and described him as 'a mild gentlemanly-looking man of about forty years of age, a warrior and a trader, a just governor, and a chivalric lover,[1] just in his dealings and decisions, liberal of reward, anxious for improvement, and tolerant of the religions of other nations.'[2] He

Seyid Said, 1804–1856

[1] I do not know if Mr. Stocqueler here alludes to the fact that he left 34 children, with a fortune of 60,000 crowns to every son, and 29,000 to every daughter.

[2] *Fifteen Months' Pilgrimage*, vol. i. p. 3.

possessed a considerable fleet which, according to Fraser in 1821, consisted, in addition to native vessels, of five fine ships, including the 'Shah Alam,' a frigate of fifty guns, and the 'Caroline,' a frigate of forty guns; and, according to Stocqueler, ten years later, of twelve large vessels, including a seventy-four gun ship, and a frigate of forty-four guns, both of British build. His revenue was about 80,000*l.* a year, one-fourth of which was derived from the slave trade, before he abolished the latter by agreement with the English.

Seyid Said bequeathed the two portions of his dominions, Muscat and Zanzibar, to his eldest and fourth sons respectively; but the impossibility of governing the two territories without some more definite agreement, suggested to Lord Canning—to whom, on the old man's death in 1856, the inevitable dispute between the heirs was referred for arbitration—the wisdom of permanently separating the northern and southern states. His award, published in 1861 (the result of a commission consisting of General Coghlan and Rev. G. P. Badger), confirmed the arrangement of the late ruler, assigning Muscat to the elder and Zanzibar to the younger brother, the latter to pay compensation for the superior richness of his inheritance by an annual subsidy to Muscat of 40,000 crowns.[1] Seyid Thoweyni of Muscat reigned till 1866, when he was assassinated at Sohar. The gravest suspicions rested upon his son Seyid Salim, with whom the British Government for a while suspended relations.[2] A little later he was recognised; but the two years of his reign were marked by the rebellion of more than one pretender to the throne; and the wretched Salim fled the country, dying later on of small-pox at Kurrachi. After an interlude of usurpation by another member of the reigning family, Seyid Turki, a younger brother of Seyid Thoweyni, and one of the twenty-four sons of Seyid Said, returning from India, where he had been paid to live in exile, established himself in Muscat in 1871, and enjoyed a somewhat disturbed and inglorious reign till June 1888. Another brother, Seyid Abdul Aziz, was in continuous rebellion, and at one time pushed his success to the point of being admitted to a share in the government of Muscat; but being again

Muscat and Zanzibar

[1] Aitchison, vol. vii., No. xl.

[2] There were ten assassins engaged in the plot, nine of whom subsequently perished by a violent death. There is very little doubt but that Seyid Salim actually fired the pistol-shot that killed his father.

ejected, retired to the interior, whence sputterings of revolt were occasionally heard till Seyid Turki's death, and again broke into flame after his son's accession. Seyid Turki, though not a vigorous was a mild and liberal-minded ruler; he understood how to manage the Arab tribes under his control; and he remained consistently loyal to the British Government, by whom he was made a G.C.S.I. in 1886, and confirmed in his tenure of a throne which he had, on the whole, deserved, by an assurance of active support against unprovoked aggression. In 1873 Sir Bartle Frere concluded a treaty with him, consolidating the previous engagements for the suppression of the slave-trade, abolishing all public slave-markets in his dominions, and emancipating all slaves who entered his territories. At the same time his brother of Zanzibar having taken advantage of the disturbances in Oman to decline any longer to pay his annual tribute, the British Government, in return for the abolition of the free traffic in slaves between the African coast and the island of Zanzibar, charged itself with the payment of the annual subsidy to Muscat, and to this day hands over to the Sultan the sum of 7,200 rupees a month, or a little over 6,000*l.* a year. When Seyid Turki died in 1888, his second son, Seyid Feysul bin Turki, though the son of an African slave, and as black as a Nubian in colour, succeeded without opposition to the throne. Among Arab tribes there is no law or custom of primogeniture, and no prescription in favour of the eldest son. Within the limits of the reigning family might is right; the strongest hand seizes the sceptre and wields it. There being considerable doubt, however, as to the ability of Seyid Feysul to hold his own, he had not at the time of my visit been formally recognised by the British Government. In October 1888 he conducted an unsuccessful expedition against an old pretender to the throne, Ibrahim bin Kais, who still plays the game of rebellion from time to time; while his uncle, the veteran Abdul Aziz, after a long repose in the interior, suddenly resumed activity in 1889. The latter's rebellion was still undecided while I was at Muscat, but afterwards ended in the withdrawal of the pretender from the country. Seyid Feysul had the double advantage of youth and possession on his side. He is now (1892) only twenty-eight years of age; and if he exhibits sufficient tenacity to justify the support of the British Government, may possibly develop the ruling qualities in which some of his predecessors have excelled. The Wahabi power in the interior is a danger with which Oman is constantly threatened; but it may be that now, as heretofore, other and more pressing engagements will distract the attention of the Amir of Nejd.

City of Muscat

Muscat, the capital of Oman, is probably one of the most picturesque places in the world. From a distance immense granitic masses of rock, with jagged outline of cliff and crag, are seen ascending in gloomy abruptness from the sea. Far inland ridge rises upon ridge, splintered edge above and savage fissures between, the impression being that of a country upheaved from nature's primæval cauldron, and still scarred and blackened by those terrific fires. In this sea-wall of sheer rock a gap is suddenly disclosed, opening into a little cove, landlocked on three of its sides by these stupendous natural ramparts. In the furthermost recess of the bight, which is about one mile deep by half a mile in width, upon a narrow space of flat ground, left by some freak of nature between the mountains and the sea, is built the Arab capital, its plastered houses glittering against the sombre background like a seagull's wing against an angry sky. The town and bay face to the north. On the western side the rocks fall precipitously into the water, and not even a pathway can be carried round their base. Opposite, the eastern wall of the bay, no less lofty or steep, is actually an island, as its name El Jazirah shows, and, as is seen when we anchor off the town, a gap of 100 yards or more in width severing it from the mainland. To the English visitor this great metamorphic mass, whose slaty buttresses support not a grain of soil, much less a blade of vegetation,[1] appeals with a novel interest; for its rocks are seen to be freely bedecked at every elevation from the water's edge with the names of the British men-of-war who have, at different times, visited the station, painted in huge white characters upon any smooth surface that could be found. H.M.S. 'Osprey,' H.M.S. 'Kingfisher,' H.M.S. 'Woodlark,' H.M.S. 'Sphinx,' and many another goodly vessel, including even an American frigate, have thus left to later ages the proud record of their sojurn at Muscat These decorations, however, appear to be an evidence less of the æsthetic than of the too convivial instincts of the British mariner; for, upon inquiry, I learnt that the ship's crews of men-of-war are never allowed to land in the town of Muscat, for fear of the possible consequences of their hilarity; and

[1] Aucher Eloy, the botanist, said that, compared with the Muscat hills, those of Sinai itself are a garden.

that, accordingly, their only playground is this gloomy cone of rock, which admits of positively no other diversion than that supplied by the paint-pot.

Towards the inner hollow of the bay, which is here about a quarter of a mile in width, the town is commanded on either side by ancient Portuguese fortresses, perched on the summits of two craggy peaks.[1] These forts are not the only relics of the century and a half of Portuguese dominion at Muscat; a dilapidated building, now used as the Sultan's stables, being the remains of the old Catholic cathedral. The situation of the forts and town awakens sharp recollections of the entry to the harbour at Corfu. Indeed, Muscat might perhaps be brought before a reader's eye by describing it as a mixture of Corfu and Aden, combining the romantic outline of the one with the forbidding desolation of the other. I ascended to the eastern castle, and was shown over its defences by the commandant, a handsome bearded Beluchi. They consisted of a small detachment of Arab warriors, of venerable and tattered appearance, and of a battery of ancient iron guns, some lying on the ground, some on broken carriages half-tilted in the air. A few poked their rusty nozzles through embrasures in the wall, and were pointed at every conceivable angle to command the harbour and opposite rocks; but the majority were lying stranded on the ground; while one or two had tumbled down the cliff and were being playfully washed by the waves 200 feet below. One of the iron guns had stamped upon it the word Hollandia—eloquent witness to a vanished day—and a bronze gun bore the blazonry of the royal arms of Portugal.

Castles

From either of the forts a striking panorama can be obtained of the town. Occupying the small intervening space between the harbour and the mountains, it is defended on the sea front by the castles, and on the land side by a stone wall half a mile long with solid towers, and a fosse in fair repair

Panorama

[1] The westernmost of these, now called Merani (Fraser calls it Kumalli, Rev. G. Badger, in his map, Kaleh-el-Gharbieh), is a little the senior in origin. It was begun about 1550 by Dom Joao da Lisboa, and finished in 1588, when it received the title of Fort Capitan. The second, or eastern fort, originally called Sam Jao, but now known as Jelali (the 'Glorious'; Rev. G. Badger, Kaleh-es-Sharkieh) was completed about the same time—viz. in 1587, during the viceroyalty of Manuel de Souza Continho. How these big names and proud deeds of the old Portuguese conquerors contrast with the shrivelled possessions and the dissipated physique of their present descendants, the dingy domestic-servant population of Goa!

beyond. The mountains in the background are crowned on every peak and summit with small forts or sentinel towers; and the figures of the relief guard clambering up the rocky ledges to their posts could be seen silhouetted, as it were, in Indian ink, against the sky. Both town, walls, and forts, could be shelled with the greatest ease from the sea, or knocked to pieces by guns planted on any of the superior heights inland or round the harbour. For the purpose, however, of Bedouin warfare, pursued in the manner which I shall presently describe, the defences of Muscat are amply sufficient. Within the enclosed space is congregated a population of probably not more than 5,000 souls; but outside the walls are a large number of reed huts, which are occupied by Beluchi immigrants, but are hastily deserted whenever there is a prospect of an assault. Through them a road conducts to a spot about half a mile from the town, where are the wells from which it gains its fresh-water supply, and a pretty flower and vegetable garden belonging to the Sultan. Beyond, the road mounts by the sole accessible pass—and this of great ruggedness and difficulty—into the interior. Off the town are moored two steamboats belonging to the Sultan, one called the 'Sultanee,' of the size of a large steam yacht, the other more like a launch. They were presented to his Highness' father by his younger brother, the Sultan of Zanzibar, and, though armed with nothing better than pop-guns, are useful for a display of kingly force along the coast, or for bringing up levies from the more southerly ports for the defence of the capital. They are the only substitutes for the comparatively powerful fleet once owned by Seyid Said. In a small hollow at the foot of the western rock is a coaling depôt of the British Naval Squadron in the Indian seas, with storage accommodation for 1,700 tons of coal. Immediately facing the sea, which washes its walls, and in the centre of the outermost line of houses, is a plain substantial building, somewhat larger than its neighbours. A red flag flying from the roof indicates the residence of the Sultan. At the eastern extremity of the harbour front, a fine new house was being built for the British Political Agent, upon the site of the old Consulate, which had fallen to pieces. Now that it is finished it is the handsomest structure in the town; and, being situated close to a gap in the rocks where a side breeze comes in from the ocean, renders life less insupportable during the appalling heat of the summer months, when the sun's rays, refracted from the glowing rocks, seem literally to scorch, and the rocks themselves are like the walls of a brazen oven.

The climate of Muscat in summer is, indeed, an exceptional horror, and has tested alike the vocabulary and the imagination of the most fanciful writers. John Struys, the Dutchman, who was here in 1672, said that it was 'so incredible hot and scorching that strangers are as if they were in boiling cauldrons or in sweating-tubs.' But his description pales before the rhetorical flights of the worthy Abdur Rezak, before quoted, who in May 1442 had left on record that

Climate

> The heat was so intense that it burned the marrow in the bones; the sword in its scabbard melted like wax, and the gems which adorned the handle of the dagger were reduced to coal. In the plains the chase became a matter of perfect ease, for the desert was filled with roasted gazelles.[1]

Of more practical value as evidence will be the statement that in the heats between June and August, the ordinary thermometer bursts, and that those graded high enough have placed the solar radiation at 189° Fahr. The rainfall is only three and a half inches in the year, and the whole of this falls within a period of two or three weeks.

The town itself is one of no size or pretentiousness. The Sultan's house can scarcely be designated a palace. Inside the gateway a fine lion is kept in a cage on the one side. A miserable woman was immured in a similar den upon the other, and was said to have committed a murder. I asked whether this ominous juxtaposition portended the approaching doom of the culprit; but was relieved to hear that murder was by no means regarded in Oman as an offence deserving so bloody a retribution. The bazaar at Muscat is small and very narrow, there being barely room to pass in the alleys. Hindus monopolise the more respectable shops. Natives were busily engaged in cooking *hulwah*, a glutinous compound of clarified butter (*ghi*), flour, sugar, and water, flavoured with grated almonds or pistachios, which resembles half-melted butter-scotch, and is greedily consumed by the Arab stomach. Every man carried in his belt a small dagger with curving blade and scabbard richly ornamented with silver, and most were armed in addition with immensely long single-barrelled matchlock guns, also silver-plated, and with deer's hide bound round their stocks.

City and people

[1] *India in the Fifteenth Century* (Hakluyt Society), p. 9.

The women increase their natural hideousness by a kind of veil which consists of two strips of embroidery, with an aperture for the eyes between, a stiff band resting on the bridge of the nose, and connecting the two. Both men and women are extraordinarily black, the genuine Arab having been swamped here in the African type; and many of both sexes present the purely negro physiognomy. It was of the people of Muscat that the English ship's captain, being instructed, on visiting strange places, to make a report of the manners and customs of the inhabitants, penned the famous saying: 'As to manners they have none; and their customs are beastly.'[1]

Foreign representatives

America is the only other Power, besides Great Britain, that is represented at Muscat by a consul; an English merchant filling that post, and presumably having nothing to do but superintend the despatch of cargoes of dates, when the gathering season comes round. In addition to his political functions as adviser to the Sultan, the British Agent has extensive consular duties towards the Indian subjects of the Queen, some thousands of whom reside, for purposes of trade, in the town and neighbourhood, and who have gathered the import and export businesses almost exclusively into their own hands. From the demeanour of these men, and, in a no less degree, of the Arabs themselves, who commonly saluted or said Salaam, I inferred that British ascendency is a well-established and popular régime in Muscat. Oman may, indeed, be justifiably regarded as a British dependency. We subsidise its ruler; we dictate its policy; we should tolerate no alien interference. I have little doubt myself that the time will some day come when, as these petty native states crumble before the advance of a friendly civilisation, a more definite possession will be required, and the Union Jack will be seen flying from the castles of Muscat.

Trade

The chief local trade of Muscat, and indeed almost its sole neighbouring communication, is with the town and port of Muttrah, nine miles further to the west in another indentation of the same coast line. This is a larger and more populous place than Muscat, and the supplies of the latter come in the main to Muttrah from the interior, and are shipped in small buggalows round to the capital. Of the external trade of Muscat, the chief exports are, dates, fruits, fish, and limes. In spite of the

[1] Sir J. Malcolm's *Sketches of Persia*, cap. ii.

unpromising appearance of the coast, a profusion of excellent fruits is grown in gardens and orchards lying some miles inland. Grapes, mangoes, peaches, plantains, figs, pomegranates, melons, oranges, lemons, walnuts, as well as dates, and sour and sweet limes, are there produced ; and vegetables and flowers are grown with equal ease. For their fish the waters of Oman are famous; the harbour is sometimes alive with them ; and immense numbers are captured without difficulty, and utilised as food both for cattle and men. The chief imports are, Bengal rice, sugar, coffee, cotton fabrics (Manchester and Bombay), twist and yarn, silks, and oil, opium, pearls, wheat, and salt. The total value of exports for 1888–9 was returned as 210,000*l.*, of imports 280,000*l.* ; but, owing to the unscientific manner in which these statistics are calculated, the same item, if re-exported, appearing both in the import and export columns furnished by the Custom-house, they do not give an accurate idea of the total volume of trade. The customs, however, are farmed by a Bhatia merchant for 115,000 reals, or, approximately, 17,000*l.* ; a sum which indicates a total not far inferior to that above stated, a five per cent. *ad valorem* duty being charged upon all merchandise, imported or exported.

An old Pretender

As I have before mentioned, Seyid Feysul had for some time in 1889 been expecting a hostile movement on the part of his uncle Abdul Aziz. It was in October 1883 that the latter, who had now been in fitful rebellion against the reigning Sultan for a period of twenty years, but who never seemed to tire of the amusement, had made his last serious attempt upon the city. His followers, dressed in black so as to escape detection, assaulted the walls at midnight, but were repelled with a loss of 250 killed and wounded by the heavy fire and subsequent sally of the defenders. From that time forward Abdul Aziz had lain low in the interior; but since the death of Seyid Turki he was known to be meditating renewed mischief. A few weeks before my visit he finally began to advance, and a fortnight before had reached a position some twenty miles inland; whence it was reported that he was marching to the assault of the town. Sultan Feysul took immense precautions against the impending danger. The Bedouin clans were called upon to furnish contingents from far down the seaboard and from the interior. The Sheikhs, only too delighted to give their fighting men a holiday, gladly responded; and the men themselves, overjoyed at the prospect of free rations with nothing whatever to do—none of them having the slightest intention of fighting if it could possibly be avoided—obeyed the summons with equal alacrity. In this way a force of from 1,500 to 2,000 men was collected behind the walls of Muscat. Abdul Aziz was rumoured to be in the immediate vicinity, though with a small body of men, the tribes in general having declined to rally to his invitation, and another and more formidable insurgent named Ibrahim bin Kais, with whom the Sultan had lately been at war, having refused to throw in his lot with the Old Pretender. A detachment of Arabs was sent out from the city to effect a reconnaissance of the invading force, while the huts outside the wall were hastily evacuated by the humble population, who took refuge with their belongings inside. Night fell; when the cry was raised that the enemy was advancing, a movement being visible in the quarter of the deserted huts. In a moment the city walls and bastions, the forts, and mountain towers broke into a roaring line of fire. An Arab is seldom so happy as when letting off his gun, particularly if it be in the dark; and accordingly from every rock and parapet the bullets whistled into the night. The enemy, however, declined to advance; and, after three-quarters of an hour's vigorous firing, it was apparent that the assault had been triumphantly repelled. The next morning, when the field of action was searched for the slain, it transpired that the enemy had never moved from his encampment several miles away; but that the reconnoitring force, sent out from the town, preferring a certain spoil to a precarious brush with the foe, had turned back to the huts so recently abandoned by their own partisans, and had commenced to loot them of whatever contents had been left behind. The list of killed and wounded in this heroic defence of Muscat was said to have consisted of one old woman and a dog. After this I was scarcely surprised to read in an old volume of reports that there is a familiar Arab proverb, 'As big a coward as a Muscati.' The fact was that in this intestine warfare no one meant business. Either side was 'bluffing,' and wanted to see how far it could impose upon the other. Both parties belonged to the same people, many of them to the same tribe; an uncle was the principal on one side, a nephew on the other: and similar relationships were reproduced in their respective forces. No doubt, if the town were left unguarded, Abdul Aziz, or some other pretender, would be only too ready to slip in and dictate his own terms to the conquered. But as long as the Sultan kept a reasonable lookout, such a contingency was impossible; and the conflict was certain ultimately to resolve itself into a dispute as to the sum for which the invader should be bought off or persuaded to take himself out of the country.

Muscat was crowded with the doughty warriors who had taken part in this memorable conflict. They swarmed in the bazaar and

Arab warriors

crowded the streets, armed for the most part with long two-edged swords, like a claymore, and a small circular buckler or target on the left hand.[1] Everyone carried a venerable matchlock over his shoulder, and a powder-belt round his waist; while a few were equipped with double-barrelled percussion muskets. Having nothing better to do, they spent the time in executing a species of war-dance before an admiring crowd: making terrific slashes with their big swords, bounding like bucks off the ground, and discharging their crazy pieces either into the air or at the earth just in front of their own toes. All this took place to the accompaniment of a species of chant, and of two drums furiously beaten by a colossal negro. The firing went on the whole day; and, as everyone seemed much pleased, and in the best of humours, it was perhaps as innocent an expenditure of surplus energy and gunpowder as could be devised. On leaving Muscat, with its sable sultan, its lusty defenders, and its civil warfare, I could not suppress the reflection that 'C'est magnifique, mais ce n'est pas la guerre.'

Proceeding northwards from Muscat, we again enter the Persian Gulf, on our return voyage along its southern shore, by rounding

Cape Musandim

the stormy cliffs of Cape Musandim. At the end of a long and rugged promontory, whose black basaltic cliffs rise sheer from the water's edge, and are framed in a weird and solemn background of igneous heights, rising at their loftiest point to 6,750 feet, an isolated needle of rock is severed from the mainland by a gloomy channel only a few stones' throws in width,[2] winding between walls of basalt 800 feet high. This island is Ras or Cape Musandim, the 'Selama's sainted cape' of Moore, the

[1] These targets, which are as hard as wood, and appear to be of that material, are said to be made of hippopotamus hide, and to come from Zanzibar.

[2] Sir Ephraim Stannus, British Resident at Bushire in the early part of the century, once sailed through this channel in the East India Company's sloop of war 'Clive,' and it was thought a great performance.

Arabs, it is said, calling it by that name, or Mama Selemeh, in memory of a holy lady there interred. It has been written that

> The most advanced cliff is the 'Rock of Salvation' or of 'Welcome,' above which hover the protecting spirits of sea and air. When he launches on the boundless deep, the Arab navigator offers a sacrifice to this rock, and on his return presents it his thank-offering. The Hindu also strews the waves with flowers and cocoa-nuts in honour of the local deities, or else sends adrift a model of his vessel with its variegated sails and little cargo of rice. The omen is favourable if the tiny craft reaches the shore in safety; otherwise dangers of all kinds are imminent, and prudence enjoins a return to port.[1]

But, so far as I could ascertain, these pious superstitions, for an account of which I must refer my readers to the pages of Morier, have since succumbed to the iconoclastic influences of time. In the deep coves which ramify inland between the cliffs, projecting like the points of a stag's antlers, the waters boom against the rocks, and roar in hidden caves. On the peaks and crags of this mysterious promontory, fit denizens of so weird an abode, are found the fragments of an aboriginal race, driven forward till they have reached this final resting-place, where none can pursue them, above the sea. There are a few thousands of this people, known as Shihiyins, like the Arabs in feature, but darker; speaking a language unknown to the Arabs, but Arab also; and living on the capture of fish and preparation of sharks' fins, which are exported for soup to China. They dwell in caves on the cliff-side with a wattled thorn-fence in front, to save the inmates from falling into the sea, the children being usually tethered by the leg to this primitive domestic hearth.

Fifteen miles from the extreme point of Ras Musandim the promontory again narrows to an isthmus, named Maklab (place of turning), not more than half a mile in width, by which it is united to the mainland. On the eastern side of this isthmus a splendid bay, called by the natives Ghubbeh Ghazireh, but christened by the English Malcolm's Inlet, sweeps in from the sea. On the western side is an even finer natural harbour, more completely land-locked, and providing anchorage for the largest vessels, known as Elphinstone's Inlet. The station of Khasab, at the entrance to this wonderful cove, has before now

English occupation.

[1] Elisée Reclus, *Universal Geography*, vol. ix. p. 443.

been recommended for permanent occupation by the British, as a naval base in the Persian Gulf. Here the entire British fleet might safely ride at anchor. Curiously enough, this remarkable spot has once been occupied by the English under peculiar circumstances. When the telegraph cable was first being laid from Kurrachi to the Persian Gulf in 1864, it was taken by what was then thought the shortest and best line from Gwadur to Cape Musandim. Entering Malcolm's Inlet, the wires were stretched across the isthmus of Maklab, and re-entered the sea in Elphinstone's Inlet on the other side. But the drawbacks of the site, arising from the hot and horrid climate, the sterile neighbourhood, and the suspicions of the native tribes—all of which have been well described by Sir F. Goldsmid in his interesting 'Telegraph and Travel,'—compelled a retreat from a course which should never have been adopted; and in 1869, the cable was diverted to Cape Jask and Henjam. In the entrance to the Gulf, not far from Cape Musandim, lie five small rocky islands, which have been named the Quoins by English mariners, from their supposed resemblance to the quoin of a gun. Further in the Gulf, and about twenty-five miles from the western extremity of the island of Kishm, are two larger islands, known as the Great and Little Tomb,[1] the former of which abounds with antelopes, that were often coursed with greyhounds by the British officers from Basiduh.

Pirate tribes

Skirting the southern littoral of the Persian Gulf, we are now brought into contact with a number of Arab tribes of maritime residence and occupation, inhabiting a lengthy stretch of coast line from Ras-el-Kheimah on the east, to the promontory of El Katr on the west. These tribes have been addicted from time immemorial to piratical escapades, and to the simultaneous gratification and exhaustion of their energies in internecine warfare. Towards the latter end of the eighteenth century they were fused into an aggressive force of formidable character by the proselytising influence of the Wahabi movement, which, extending its activity from the interior of Arabia to the shores of the Gulf, invited the coast tribes, under the guise of piracy, to attain a secure salvation. So tempting a propaganda was sure of many converts; and within a few years' time the seas were scoured by hundreds of audacious buccaneers, who destroyed villages, carried off and sold their inhabitants, and faithfully plundered their way to heaven. These tribes

[1] Persian, *Gumbaz*; but Badger writes the names Tanb.

have ever since paid an intermittent tribute to the chief of Nejd; but, in the intervals of Wahabi aggressiveness, have enjoyed a practical independence. The events that first brought them under Wahabi domination also brought them into sharp collision with the British Government, which, in the interests of commerce and peace, and for the security of the large capital invested by British subjects in the Gulf trade, was compelled to charge itself with the repression of piracy in the Indian Seas. A period of hostility and conflict was followed by treaty engagements, and finally by a perpetual truce, under which the maritime security of the Gulf is now assured, and the signatory parties are entitled in diplomatic parlance the Trucial Chiefs of Oman.

The history of these relations, interesting alike in its stormy prologue and in its felicitous sequel, may be briefly summarised.[1]

[1] I will consign to a footnote the details that might be held unduly to encumber the text, and which I have culled from a variety of official and other sources:—

1805. The Jowasmi pirates captured two vessels, the 'Shannon' and 'Trimmer,' belonging to Mr. Manesty, British Resident at Busrah, and treated their commanders with great cruelty. A fleet of 40 sail also surrounded the 'Mornington' cruiser, and fired into her, but were compelled by her superior armament to sheer off. A British punitive expedition, in conjunction with the forces of Oman, was sent against the pirates.

1806, February. The first treaty was concluded with the Jowasmi pirates, binding them to respect the flag and property of the East India Company and its subjects.

1807. Piracy renewed. The Jowasmis seized Bahrein, and drove out the Oman garrison. They attacked H.M.S. 'Lion,' but were beaten off.

1808. Three pirate boats attacked H.M.S. 'Nereid.' Two were sunk, the third run down.

1809. H.M.S. 'Minerva' was attacked by a pirate fleet of 55 ships and 5,000 men, and, after two days' fighting, was boarded, and every man put to the sword. The chief of Ras-el-Kheimah demanded tribute of the British Government as the price of security for their vessels.

1809–10. Colonel (Sir L.) Smith, in command of a land force of 1,623 men, and the 'Chifonne' frigate (Captain Wainwright), assisted by a large body of Persian horse, were despatched against the pirates. They destroyed Ras-el-Kheimah, burnt 50 large ships, and, in conjunction with an Oman force, attacked and took the fort of Shinaz in the Indian Ocean.

1810–19. Piracies renewed.

1819, November. An expedition sailed from Bombay, consisting of a naval squadron under Captain Collier, and 3,547 men under Sir W. Keir Grant, which besieged and captured Ras-el-Kheimah (after a most gallant resistance) and the fort of Zyah, burnt 202 pirate vessels, released many Hindu prisoners, and returned, leaving a garrison of 1,200 sepoys at Ras-el-Kheimah.

1820. First general treaty with the pirate tribes. The British, in alliance with Oman, attacked the Beni-bu-Ali tribe near Ras-el-Hadd. Captain Thomson

It was in 1805 that the plunder of British vessels by the Jowasmi tribe provoked the first British naval expedition for their punishment. A treaty was concluded in 1806; but was so scantily observed that in 1809 a second expedition was necessitated, which took several ports and destroyed a large number of boats. Piracy, however, continued, not merely with unabated but with augmented virulence, the traffic in slaves being the main source of livelihood to these irrepressible buccaneers. Stronger measures were clearly required, and in 1819 a third expedition under Sir W. Keir Grant was fitted out, with instructions to crush the pirate power altogether. Ras-el-Kheimah was bombarded and taken; and in 1820 the first General Treaty was concluded between the British Government and the combined Arab chieftains of the coast.[1] Though a decisive check was placed upon kidnapping by this agreement, it did not prevent the traffic in slaves; and accordingly in 1838, 1839, 1847, and 1856, it required to be supplemented by further treaties, giving the right of search and confiscation to British vessels, and prohibiting the export of slaves from Arab ports. These engagements, however, which were mainly restricted to the slave-trade, were not found to have any effect in checking the combative instincts of the tribes among themselves, the loss of an outside field of activity encouraging them to turn their martial energies upon each other, in which occupation a little sly piracy was often possible under the guise of tribal warfare. In 1835 the British Government, visited with a happy inspiration, induced the combatant Sheikhs to sign a maritime truce by which they pledged themselves not to engage in hostilities by sea for six months, provided the British Government did not interfere with them by land. So successful was this engagement found to be by all parties that it was renewed in 1836, 1837, and annually till

Conflicts and treaties

led an expedition against Sur, but his entire force was annihilated, consisting of 7 officers and 303 men.

1821, January. A retaliatory expedition of 1,282 European and 1,718 Indian troops, under Sir L. Smith, sailed against Sur, and fought a battle with the Arabs, who, after a courageous resistance, surrendered.

1835, 1838, 1839, 1847, 1853, 1856. Further treaties.

In 1809, at the height of their power and depredations, the Jowasmi pirate fleet consisted of 63 large vessels (some with 40 to 50 guns and 300 men) and 810 smaller craft, manned by 19,000 bloodthirsty ruffians. For incidents of the anti-pirate campaigns, *vide* J. S. Buckingham, *Travels in Assyria*, vol. ii. caps. vi.–viii.; Captain Mignan, *Winter's Journey*, vol. ii. caps. vii.–x.

[1] Aitchison, vol. vii. No. xxi.

1843, when it was prolonged for another ten years. Its merits having been thus abundantly tested, it was, upon expiring in 1853, succeeded by a Treaty of Perpetual Peace, which provided that there should be a complete cessation of hostilities at sea between the subjects of the subscribing parties ; that in the event of aggressions on any one by sea the injured tribes should not retaliate, but should refer the matter to the British Resident in the Persian Gulf; and that the British Government should watch over the peace of the Gulf, and ensure at all times the observance of the Treaty.[1] This treaty is in operation at this hour; and its terms are explanatory at once of the happy results that have been produced, and of the commanding position filled by the British Resident at Bushire. The truce has not prevented, it was neither designed nor expected to prevent, warfare by land. These petty tribes exist for little else but internecine squabble, blood-feuds, puny forays, and isolated acts of outrage or revenge. With their internal relations Great Britain, who claims no suzerainty over Arabia, would have been foolish to interfere. All that she took upon herself to do was to secure the maritime peace of the Gulf; and in spite of occasional infringements of the treaty provisions, which are commonly punished by a fine, enforced by the timely appearance of a British gunboat, and never resisted by force of arms, she may reasonably congratulate herself that that object has been secured.[2] Trade is prosecuted in these waters with an immunity and security which, under any other *régime*, would have been impossible. One or more gunboats are at the disposal of the British Resident at Bushire, who has also a despatch boat for his own immediate use in the event of any emergency. Not a week passes but, by Persians and Arabs alike, disputes are referred to his arbitration ; and he may with a greater truth than the phrase sometimes conveys, be entitled the Uncrowned King of the Persian Gulf. It says much for the tact and ability with which Colonel Ross filled that office for the last twenty years that so little friction ever resulted, and (though this sounds a dubious compliment) that outside official circles so little was known of his extensive prerogative at home. The distinction of the post he

[1] Aitchison, vol. vii. No. xxvi.

[2] The slave traffic, in spite of every precaution, is not absolutely extinguished, but is still prosecuted, by all manner of surreptitious devices, between the old African slave ports and the Persian Gulf. The return from the Mecca pilgrimage is a favourite occasion for the clandestine importation of slaves. Several are still rescued and freed every year by the exertions of the British gunboats.

inherited as a legacy from his most capable predecessor, Sir Lewis Pelly.

The Trucial Chiefs

At the present time there are six of these Trucial Chiefs, whose tribes and territories occur in the following order, proceeding from the north:—

(1) *Ras-el-Kheimah.*—Present Sheikh, Hamid bin Abdullah, of the El Kowasim (Jowasmi) tribe.

(2) *Um-el-Kawain* (vulg. 'Gawain,' in earlier English records 'Amulgavine').—Present Sheikh, Ahmed bin Abdullah, of the Al-bu-Ali tribe.

(3) *Ajman.*—Present Sheikh, Rashid bin Hamid, of the Al-bu-Ali tribe.

(4) *Sharkah* (vulg. 'Shargah').—Present Sheikh, Sakar bin Khalid, of the Jowasmi tribe.

(5) *Debai.*—Present Sheikh, Rashid bin Makdum, of the Al-bu-Falasal tribe.

(6) *Abu Dhabi.*—Present Sheikh, Zaid bin Khalifah, chief of all the Beni Yas tribes.

Of the above places Debai is the most populous port on the pirate coast; and does a large export trade in dried fish, pearls, and dates. Of the Sheikhs by far the most important is the last-named, whose jurisdiction extends over the islands and along the coast as far west as Udaid (Odeyd) where it touches the semi-independent territories of El Katr, and the outskirts of Ottoman rule. A native agent is stationed at Sharkah by the British Government. He moves from place to place as is required, and reports to the Resident at Bushire.

El Katr

The unquestionable advantages of the Trucial Arrangement, and the disastrous consequences of a *laissez faire* policy, are manifest as soon as we quit the sphere within which that agreement actually prevails, and emerge upon a scene where an impotent controlling authority and turbulent subordinates plunge the seaboard into perpetual confusion. Adjoining the Trucial states upon the West is the rugged promontory of El Katr, projecting northwards into the sea, with a coast deeply indented by alternate capes and bays. The present Sheikh of this territory is one Jasim bin Mohammed bin Thani, a mischievous and disorderly character, who parades or denies his independence according as he is likely to profit by the one or the other assertion. By the British Government he is regarded and treated as one of the independent maritime chieftains, pledged to observe the maritime peace of the Gulf, and possessing a claim upon our support if he does so, or upon our retribution if he does not—a view of his status which rests upon a definite agreement not to commit any breach of the maritime peace, which was signed by his predecessor, independently of the six Trucial Chiefs, in 1868.[1] In 1871, however, thinking to escape this obligation, and to carry out with greater ease his projects for personal aggrandisement and conquest towards the south, Sheikh Jasim placed himself under Turkish protection and adopted the Turkish flag. The Ottoman Government, only too anxious, as I shall presently show, to extend its authority in these regions, gladly threw the ægis of its protection over the Sheikh, appointed him Kaimakam or Deputy-Governor of El Katr (to which district they have not the ghost of a claim), and placed a Turkish guard of 250 regulars, a coal-depôt, and a steam launch at El Bidaa, the principal port of the Katr coast. The claims of the Porte to sovereignty over the El Katr cape are not admitted by the British Government, and are the cause not merely of diplomatic controversy, but of positive anarchy in the districts concerned. For the Turkish officials are wholly indifferent to the suppression of piracy, or the observation of the maritime peace; and from the harbours and creeks of the coast alleged to be under their control, feluccas of desperate robbers, mostly of the Beni Hajir tribe, dart out upon the native craft plying to and from Bahrein; and after they have secured their spoil, retire again to the safe asylum of a Turkish anchorage.

Armati pelagum exercent, semperque recentes
Convectare juvat prædas et vivere rapto.

Sheikh Jasim himself is quite ready to coquet with any power that will forward his ambitious aims. He has for long been engaged in a savage blood-feud with the adjoining tribe of Abu Dhabi, and his son having been killed in one of the encounters in May 1888, he appealed for aid to the Turks, first at El Hasa, next at Busrah, and finally at Constantinople; and when he met with no response from his patrons, ended by invoking ths assistance of Ibn Rashid, the powerful chief of Nejd; an alliance for which, had it been granted, he would no doubt have had to pay the price of a

[1] Aitchison, vol. vii. No. xxix.

future tribute. The disturbances arising from these designs are not merely detrimental to the order of the Gulf; but they impose a special responsibility upon the British Government, inasmuch as the trade of the seaports is here, as elsewhere, mainly in the hands of Hindu merchants, who are British subjects, and whose lives and property are imperilled by the chronic outbreaks. Even Persia, whose aggressive mood is fired by the pettiest spoil, has been tempted to interfere by the prevailing disorder; and Persian agents have been heard of intriguing with the chieftains of El Katr and Bahrein with a view to their acceptance of Persian sovereignty.

Ottoman pretensions

Having been led to mention the pretensions of the Ottoman Government in this part of the Arabian peninsula, I will briefly indicate the steps by which the Turks have established themselves in this neighbourhood, and which will sufficiently demonstrate the justice or the reverse of their claims. In 1871, Abdullah bin Feysul, of the Wahabi reigning family, being engaged in a conflict for the throne of Nejd with his brother Saud, applied to Midhat Pasha, then Turkish Vali of Baghdad, to co-operate in his restoration to power. The latter was nothing loth. He cared little for Abdullah, and less for Saud; but the opportunity of extending Ottoman sway was too good to be missed. The Turks never went near to Nejd; but a Turkish army occupied the maritime district of El Katif, and the inland oasis of El Hasa,[1] which are the adjoining regions on the west to the promontory of El Katr. At the same time, in reply to the natural queries of the British Government, an explicit assurance was given that the Porte had no intention of seeking supremacy over Bahrein, Muscat, or the maritime tribes, or of undertaking naval operations. They have continued, however, ever since to keep possession of El Hasa and Katif (to which their ownership is not now contested), and are represented by an official, subordinate to the Vali of Busrah, who resides at Hufhuf in El Hasa, and bears the absurd title of Mutaserrif of Nejd, although a mountain range and the famous Nefud desert of shifting sand intervene between them and Nejd, to which the Turks have never attempted to penetrate. From the base of El Hasa the afore-mentioned claims to El Katr are put forward, in

[1] Hasa (pl. Ahsa) means literally soft or plain or sandy ground which retains rain-water below the surface.

defiance of the engagement above quoted. The Mutaserrif, who, like most subordinate officials in the East, thirsts for distinction at the expense of all decency, has even tried to assert the Turkish authority over Bahrein, on the ground that Bahrein, which has been independent for nearly 100 years, is a dependency of El Hasa.

Bahrein Islands

In the centre of the broad, V-shaped bay that separates independent but troublesome El Katr from Turkish El Katif, lies the object of much tender solicitude from all parties, viz., the Island of Bahrein,[1] famous throughout the world for its pearl fisheries, which rank with those of Ceylon. The island is thirty miles long, from six to nine broad, and contains two towns, Manameh or Bahrein, the port, and Raffar on a hill seven miles inland. Niebuhr says that it once possessed 360 towns and villages. Like most of the Gulf ports and trading settlements, it was taken, early in the sixteenth century, by the Portuguese, who established a station here and at El Katif, to ensure a monopoly of the pearl trade. Remains of the aqueduct and reservoirs built by them, as also of their fort, are still to be seen. The island further contains the remains of a ruined Arab city, with fragments of a palace and of a mosque with two minarets; and a number of sepulchral tumuli, of ancient but uncertain date, which were excavated, without much result, by Mr. Theodore Bent in 1889.[2]

Pearl-fishery

The pearl fishery lasts from June to October, and is pursued not only at Bahrein, but along the entire Arabian coast, which I have delineated in this chapter, and as far as Koweit. The Bahrein banks, stretching for a length of four or five leagues, are, however, the richest and most certain; and the boat-tax levied on every craft that comes to Bahrein to take part

[1] There are, in fact, several islands, of which one is large and the others small. The largest is commonly called El Bahrein, the second in size Moharrag. The name Bahrein signifies 'two seas,' and may be supposed to refer either to the bays on either side of it, or to the larger arms of the sea east and west of El Katr. It is identified by Oppert with the Tylos, or Tilvun, of the ancients, one of the sacred places where Chaldæan civilisation had its origin. From Tylos came that fish-god who, in the Babylonian myth, bore the Ark of the human race over the Deluge. In addition to accounts of Bahrein, in most descriptions of the Gulf, the following monographs may be mentioned: Whish, *Memoir on Bahrein*, 1859; F. Wustenfeld, *Bahrein und Jemamah*; De Goeje, *Mémoire sur les Carmathes de Bahrein*, 1863; Captain Durand and Sir H. Rawlinson, *Journal of the Royal Asiatic Society*, 1879; P. Frédé, *La Pêche aux Perles en Perse et à Ceylan*, 1887.

[2] *Proceedings of the R.G.S.* (new series), vol. xii. pp. 1–19 (1890).

in the fishing constitutes, along with the custom dues, the principal source of revenue of the Sheikh. At the season of the fisheries some 4,500 boats of every size and rig (of which it is calculated that 2,000 come from the pirate coast, 1,500 from Bahrein, and 1,000 from El Katr to Koweit) may be seen upon the banks, some with their sails bellied by the wind, others riding at anchor, all busily employed. They carry from five to fourteen men each, and the total number of hands engaged is said to be 30,000. The scene is one of the greatest picturesqueness and animation. The banks are open to all the maritime peoples of the Gulf; and there is scarcely a petty fishing village that does not send its contingent to the quest. The soundings vary considerably, from four to twenty fathoms; but the men as a rule decline to dive in deeper water than seven fathoms, although the best pearls are found at greater depths. The banks themselves are composed of corally rock and sand.

The method of working is primitive and does not materially differ from that employed on the banks of Ceylon. The diver descends weighted by a stone attached to his feet, his nostrils closed by a pincer of horn or bone,[1] and his ears plugged with beeswax. Round his waist is a net or basket into which he hurriedly gathers the oysters, and is then drawn up to the surface. Ibn Batutah in the fourteenth century declared that 'some remain under water an hour, others two hours, others less.' But either the worthy Moor was grossly misinformed, or the modern Arab is a very different creature from his ancestors, for the period spent under water is seldom more than fifty seconds, and often much less. Several men are killed every year by swordfish or sharks, though the latter are popularly said to be averse to coloured skins. When the diving is pursued in deep water, it is also apt to be fatal to life; and 250 men were reported to have died from this cause in 1885. It was these perils, I suppose, that inspired the affecting simile of Matthew Arnold:—

Methods employed

> And dear as the wet diver to the eyes
> Of his pale wife, who waits and weeps on shore,
> By sands of Bahrein in the Persian Gulf,
> Plunging all day in the blue waves, at night
> Having made up his tale of precious pearls
> Rejoins her in their hut upon the shore.

[1] This presumably is the 'tortoise-shell mask' mentioned by Ibn Batutah.

When the pearls have been picked out of the shells, they are handed to the master of the boat, who proceeds to sort them by the manipulation of a triple set of brass sieves, pierced with holes of differing diameter. The pearls that are unable to pass through the largest sieve are called *Ras*; the residue of the second sieve are *Batin*; while the resulting contents of the third sieve are known as *Dzel*. Made up into separate batches, according to their classification, the assorted pearls are then sold to the pearl merchant, upon an intricate scale of values, depending upon the shape, colour, specific gravity, and size. The merchant rearranges them in smaller packets, and despatches them to the Indian market, whence a great many come back again to Arabia and Persia.

Generally speaking the Bahrein pearls are not so white as Ceylon pearls, but are larger and more regular in shape; while they are said to retain their lustre for a longer period. The Ceylon banks require to be carefully watched, and fishing is only permitted by Government at intervals of years. On the other hand, the Gulf banks give no indication of failing supply. During recent years the harvest has been specially abundant; and as prices have risen within the same period, there has been a visible increase of prosperity in the Arab ports, and larger vessels have been built. Too often, however, it happens that the profits, which are supposed to be divided between the owners of the boats, the divers, and the crews, are absorbed by greedy money-lenders, to whom they have been previously mortgaged at usurious rates of interest. In each of the years 1888 and 1889, the total export of pearls from Bahrein and the Arabian cost of the Gulf amounted to about 430,000*l*., two thirds of this total passing through the custom-house of Bahrein. The chief imports of the island are, cotton goods, dates, grain, spices, tobacco, and coffee. The place is further remarkable for an almost unique phenomenon, viz. the presence of several fresh-water springs bubbling up in places at the bottom of the sea. These are found even at a depth of eighteen feet, and at a distance of some miles from the shore.

Produce

The history of Bahrein, since the expulsion of the Portuguese by Persia in 1622, has been one of constant vicissitudes, the result of the covetous appetites of the surrounding nations. In all the conflicts for the supremacy of the Gulf waged by Arabs, Persians, and Turks, each combatant has fixed his eye upon Bahrein, and the victor has invariably sought to make it his first

History

spoil. These selfish ambitions have only been controlled at the instance and by the interference of Great Britain, who, having entered into treaty engagements with Bahrein analogous to those concluded with the Trucial Chiefs, has always insisted upon their due observance, and has in return vindicated the independence of the island against the pretensions of whatever foreign power. After the expulsion of the Portuguese, the Persians enjoyed a lengthy though frequently interrupted domination over Bahrein, but were expelled in their turn by an invasion of the Utubi Arabs from the mainland in 1783. Muscat conquered the island and held it for a year in 1801, and the Wahabis established a foothold for nine years, till 1810; but from the latter date the Utubis have remained the paramount power, and have supplied the ruling dynasty; although their material and numerical weakness has rendered them a constant victim to more powerful neighbours, and has compelled them to pay tribute alternately to the rulers of Nejd and Oman. Their foreign allegiance has been still more diverse in its vagaries; and it is said that the British, Persian, and Turkish flags were on one occasion all flying at Bahrein at the same time. Since, however, Sheikh Suleiman bin Ahmed appended his signature to the General Treaty of 1820 for the pacification of the Gulf,[1] and his grandson, Mohammed bin Khalifah, to a further and independent treaty with the East India Company in 1847 for the suppression of the slave trade, Great Britain has steadfastly declined to tolerate the pretensions of other powers; although these have been freely put forward by Persia, by Turkey, even by Egypt. Sheikh Mohammed, above mentioned, was, nevertheless, an inveterate plotter; and a further 'Perpetual Treaty of Peace and Friendship' with Great Britain was considered necessary in 1861 to check his irrepressible intrigues. In this treaty he bound himself to abstain from war, piracy and slavery by sea, on condition of British protection against similar acts of aggression, and to permit all British subjects to trade with Bahrein on payment of an *ad valorem* duty of five per cent.[2] No form of words, however, or signature could bind the crafty old fox; and in 1867 he was found engaged in an outrageous act of piracy, which necessitated the bombardment of Manameh, and his expulsion from the island, and subsequent deportation to Aden. The British then set up his son Esau bin Ali, who, profiting by the

[1] Aitchison, vol. vii. No. xxi. [2] *Ibid.* No. xvii.

lesson of his father's life, has faithfully observed the terms of the original covenant, and has in consequence been protected against the ever-recurrent pretensions of foreign powers. Bahrein, in fact, supplies, in epitome, a vindication of the wisdom of the policy that has been pursued by Great Britain in the Gulf; and when its present condition is contrasted with that of El Katr, the true value of the *Pax Britannica* can with some accuracy be appraised.

The Wahabis

Mention has been so frequently made in the preceding pages of the Wahabi power of Nejd, that a few paragraphs are necessary to explain the introduction and significance of that strange phenomenon.[1] It was about 1740–50 that Sheikh Mohammed, son of Abdul Wahab of Busrah, disgusted with the laxity, the corruption, and the tyranny of Turkish Islam, first started the puritanical movement which has ever since borne his father's name. It would not be to the purpose of the present narrative to trace the steps by which the Wahabis established a temporal as well as spiritual authority throughout Arabia, carried their victorious propaganda far and wide, and in the early years of this century even captured the sacred citadel of the Mussulman faith. Here it is more relative to my subject to distinguish the moment at which they first came into contact with the British Government as the custodian of the peace of the Persian Gulf. From their stronghold in the Nejd, or Tableland, 250 miles inland from El Katr, and from their capitals Dereiyah and Riadh, situated on that mountainous plateau, they soon made their conquering influence felt along the maritime littoral, and have at different times in this century subjugated or extorted tribute from almost every Arab tribe from El Katif to Cape Musandim, and from Cape Musandim to Ras-el-Hadd. Proselytism in the guise of plunder was the bait which they held out to the natural pirates of the coast

[1] For accounts of the Wahabi Arabs, and for travels across this part of Arabia and to Nejd, *vide* L. A. Corançez, *Histoire des Wahabis* (ed. S. de Sacy), Paris, 1810; Captain G. F. Sadleir, *Diary of a Journey across Arabia in* 1819, Bombay, 1866; J. L. Burckhardt, *Notes on the Bedouins and Wahabys*, 1830; Sir H. Brydges, *History of the Wahauby*, 1834; C. Ritter, *Die Erdkunde von Asien—Arabien*, 2 vols. 1846–7; Dr. G. A. Wallin, *Notes of a Journey in N. Arabia in* 1848; W. G. Palgrave (1862–3), *Narrative of a Journey through Central and Eastern Arabia*, 2 vols.; C. Guarmani (1864), *Bulletin de la Soc. de Géog.*, Paris, Septembre 1865, *et seq.*; (Sir) L. Pelly, *Report of a Visit to Nejd*, 1866; Alb. Zehme, *Arabien und die Araber seit hundert Jahren*, Halle, 1875; C. M. Doughty (1876–7), *Travels in Arabia Deserta*, 2 vols.; Lady A. Blunt (1879), *A Pilgrimage to Nejd*, 2 vols.; Ch. Huber (1878–1882), *Bulletin de la Soc. de Géog.*, Paris, 1884–5.

ports. As has been well but cynically said, 'The leading tenets of Wahab's faith seem to have been those common to prophets, namely, to proclaim himself and the Unity of the Creator, and to kill or plunder his fellow creatures.' It was in 1787 that the first mention of the Wahabis is found in the Bombay Records; but the British Government, though taking strong measures against the piratical tribes whom their preaching had incited to plunder, was careful not to involve itself in hostile proceedings against the Wahabi Amir himself. Other nations, more intimately involved, undertook the task of crushing the schismatic upstart; and by 1818 Ibrahim Pasha, marching from Egypt, had captured the Wahabi capital and razed it to the ground, had sent the Wahabi Amir in chains to Constantinople, where he was decapitated, and had apparently stamped the heretical authority out of existence. Such, however, was the vitality either of the creed or of the dominion, that within a few years Turki, the son of the deceased Amir, had expelled the Egyptian governor, was proclaimed Sultan of Nejd, recovered all and more than his father's territories, and, by the judicious payment of a small tribute to the Egyptian Khedive, retained the throne till he was murdered in 1831. His son and successor, Feysul, upon succeeding to the throne, was at first rash enough to repudiate the Egyptian Suzerainty; whereupon Nejd was again invaded, El Hasa and Katif temporarily occupied by Egyptian troops, and himself banished to Egypt. In 1843 he managed again to return, and from then till his death in 1865 continued to rule in Nejd, and to push his sovereignty and claims to tribute far and wide among the surrounding tribes. Four times in this period the vigorous remonstrances of Great Britain, and the apparition of a naval armament off the threatened ports, whether of Bahrein or Muscat, were required to compel the retirement of the aggressive Sultan, not, however, without the extortion of a tribute in the case of Muscat, though not in that of Bahrein.

His son, Abdullah bin Feysul, who had long acted as Regent, succeeded him in 1865, and entered into an engagement with Great Britain not to molest the Arab tribes under British protection, particularly those of Muscat, but to rest content with the receipt of tribute from the latter. A prolonged fight ensued between Abdullah and his brother Saud, in which the latter was at first successful, but in which Abdullah, flying to Turkey, invoked that expedition from Baghdad which ended in the formal and permanent occupation of El Hasa by Turkey. The conflict being renewed upon Saud's death in 1874, Abdullah ultimately regained the throne, and held it till 1886, when events occurred that heralded the rise of another power in Nejd.

North-west of Nejd lies the mountainous district of Jebel Shammer, the residence of the Arab tribe of that name, forming part of the Wahabi dominion. It was in 1835 that one Abdullah ibn Rashid, with the aid of the Amir Feysul bin Turki, became Sheikh of that tribe, with his capital at the town of Hayil, and was appointed Muhafidh or frontier governor in dependence upon the central authority of Nejd. He died in 1846, but not before he had, by his great ability, laid the foundations of the power which has since swollen to such imposing dimensions in the hands of his even abler son. Tilal, the eldest of the family, at first succeeded his father as Sheikh of Jebel Shammer, and gradually, but surely, established his independence of the Riadh ruler. Tormented, however, by an internal malady, he shot himself in 1867. His younger brother, Mutaab ibn Abdullah, who succeeded him, enjoyed but a brief rule, being murdered by his nephews, the sons of Tilal, in the following year. One of these, Bander by name, then assumed the government. Meanwhile, the third and youngest son of the old Abdullah, namely, Mohammed ibn Rashid, who had been residing at Riadh as a fugitive, and had been kindly treated there by the Amir Abdullah ibn Feysul, was permitted to return to Hayil. His opportunity having come, the true character of the man was now revealed. Commencing by stabbing to death his nephew Bander with his own hand, he then killed the five remaining children of his brother Tilal, and became undisputed Amir and Muhafidh in Hayil in 1868. During the next eighteen years he consolidated his authority, acquiring more and more of the real power, and being engaged in intermittent acts of hostility against the Amir of Nejd, to whom, however, he never actually renounced his allegiance, until in 1886 the chance, for which he had waited so long and patiently, presented itself. In that year the Amir Abdullah bin Feysul was seized and imprisoned by two of his nephews, one of whom usurped the throne. Mohammed ibn Rashid, still wearing the mask of the loyal subject, marched from Hayil against Riadh, deposed the pretender, and reinstated

Mohammed ibn Rashid

Abdullah, although his next proceeding was to carry the Amir away with him to Hayil, leaving a younger brother as deputy governor of Nejd under the superintendence of an agent appointed by himself. The three rebellious nephews of Abdullah have since been put to death by the latter, and the fourth is detained at Hayil by Mohammed ibn Rashid, along with his uncle, the old Amir, to whom the successful pretender diplomatically concedes the spiritual title of Imam of Nejd.[1] He is, however, himself the *de facto* ruler, not merely of Nejd and Jebel Shammer, but of the whole of the Arabian desert from the confines of Syria to the Nefud, and wields an authority precisely analogous to that which was exercised so long in Japan by the dynasty of the Shoguns or Tycoons, who dispensed the temporal power at Yeddo in the name of an impotent spiritual *fainéant*, the Mikado, at Kioto. Though he has waded to his present position through the blood of his own kin, Mohammed ibn Rashid's government is understood to be both popular and just; while he has shown supreme diplomatic ability in the manner in which he has humoured the vanity of Turkey by professing himself the vassal of the Porte. By this purely nominal act of obeisance he secures an immunity from interference from El Hasa, and has practically no enemy to fear. Only fifty-six years of age, he is still in the full vigour of his manhood, and presents one of the most striking personalities in the East. During the past year a final, but futile, effort has been made by the old reigning family to shake off the yoke of Ibn Rashid and to recover their lost sway. A rebellion was organised by Abdur Rahman ibn Feysul and his son, and being vigorously supported by several powerful tribes, resulted in the expulsion of Ibn Rashid's agent from Riadh, and in temporary success. Ibn Rashid, however, marched against the hostile combination, inflicted upon it a severe defeat, and continues to rule in Nejd with an authority which will probably not again be disputed.

Koweit or Grane

Returning from the digression into which I have been led by the consideration of the Wahabi power, I resume the tale of the Persian Gulf littoral, at the point where I left it, viz. the Turkish position on the coast of El Katif, the southern limit of which may be fixed at the port of Ujair. Northwards from that place the Ottoman dominion is established without dispute as far as Fao, where we strike the estuary of the Shat-el-Arab

[1] Abdullah bin Feysul has since died.

and complete the circumnavigation of the Gulf. The sole place of any interest on the coast-line between El Katif and Fao is the excellent and flourishing harbour of Grane, or Koweit.[1] Here an Arab tribe, expelled from Busrah in the seventeenth century, came and settled, and by dint of sagacious policy and commercial aptitudes raised the population of the town to a total of 20,000 souls, and converted the harbour into one of the most prosperous and best managed ports of the Gulf. The stability of Koweit has also been greatly assisted by the phenomenal longevity of its chieftains, five only having ruled in the course of two and a half centuries. The best Arab horses are commonly brought down hither from the interior for shipment to India. In 1821–2 it was for a short time the headquarters of the British Resident at Busrah, who moved here in consequence of the insolent attitude of the Pasha of Baghdad. Koweit now nominally forms part of the vilayet of Busrah, to which it pays tribute; but it is not greatly interfered with by the central power, who have never attempted to place a garrison here. To English readers the name, in its alternative rendering of Grane, is more familiar as the suggested maritime terminus of the Euphrates Valley Railway, projected by General Chesney and advocated by Sir W. P. Andrew, the Duke of Sutherland, and others. If such a railway, as to the wisdom and chances of which I have spoken elsewhere, were to terminate in the Persian Gulf, Koweit would probably afford the best available harbour in the neighbourhood of the Tigris and Euphrates delta. On the other hand, were it to be continued by a line running, in whatever direction, through Persian territory, it would be absurd to locate the maritime terminus at a point so far to the west.

Fao

Fao is a quarantine and telegraph station of the Turkish Government, situated at the mouth of the Shat-el-Arab. The Indo-European Telegraph Department maintain a staff and occupy a building within the same precincts, Fao being the terminus of the submarine cable from Kurrachi *viâ* Jask and Bushire, and the point of junction with the overland wires from Baghdad. The place, which is otherwise insignificant, has lately developed a sudden, if somewhat spurious, importance from the steps that have been taken by the Turkish Government

[1] Grane is a corruption of the Arabic *ghern* or *kirn* = 'horn,' from the curving outline of the bay. Koweit, pronounced Quoit, is an Arab diminutive of *kot*, or *kut*, a fort.

to fortify the mouth of the river. I have described and commented upon these proceedings in an earlier chapter on the Karun river, and will not, therefore, repeat myself here.

Effects of British Protectorate

I have now completed the entire periplus of the Persian Gulf, and have shown the Persian Government along its northern shores exercising a more vigorous and undisputed sovereignty than at any period since the reign of Shah Abbas; upon its southern coast the Turks endeavouring to extend a precarious influence over Arabia; and small Arab states, retaining either wholly or only in part their original independence; while between all parties intervenes the sworded figure of Great Britain, with firm and just hand holding the scales. It is no exaggeration to say that the lives and properties of hundreds of thousands of human beings are secured by this British Protectorate of the Persian Gulf, and that were it either withdrawn or destroyed both sea and shores would relapse into the anarchical chaos from which they have so laboriously been reclaimed. That the Persian Government has been enabled to reassert its authority upon the north littoral; that the pirates of the opposite coast have been taught that rapine is not a safe religion, and, where they once swept the sea with laden slave-dhows, now dive harmlessly for pearls; that the Arab tribes, instead of being subjected to the curse of pashas, retain the liberty they so dearly prize, is due to the British Government alone. The very soundings of the channels and surveys of the shores, by which navigation has been rendered easy for the vessels of the world, were the work of the officers of the old Indian Navy, and have been transferred without acknowledgment to the charts of other countries navigating these seas. These considerations, to which I draw special attention from a belief that they are not generally recognised in England, are essential to an understanding of the attitude taken up by this country with regard to the future control of the Persian Gulf, and of her resistance to the possible intrusion of an enemy into the waters for whose security she has, both in treasure and in life-blood, spent so much

Every claim that can be advanced by Russia for the exclusive control of the Caspian Sea could be urged with tenfold greater force by Great Britain for a similar monopoly of the Persian Gulf. Hundreds of British lives and millions of British money have been spent in the pacification of these troublous waters. Where the Russians in the north have scared a few penniless buccaneers, the British in the south have effectively destroyed a pirate combination and fleet that recall the last century of the Roman Republic and the exploits of Pompey. A commerce has been fostered and multiplied that, if it is advantageous to Great Britain and India, is also the source of great wealth, and almost of livelihood, to Persia, to Arabia, and to Turkey. Thousands of British subjects peacefully ply their trade under the armed protection of the Union Jack. England, however, makes no such arrogant pretensions as Russia has insisted upon in the case of the Northern lake. She does not demand that the Persian Gulf should be a *mare clausum* against foreign trade. She does not impose treaties upon humiliated foes, wresting from them the right to fly their own flag in their own waters. The merchant navies of the world are free to plough these waves, and to fill their holds with incoming or outgoing treasures. But at least she must and does claim, in return for the sacrifices to which she has submitted, and the capital which she has sunk, and for the sake of the peace which she is here to guard, that no hostile political influence shall introduce its discordant features upon the scene. A Russian port in the Persian Gulf, that dear dream of so many a patriot from the Neva or the Volga, would, even in times of peace, import an element of unrest into the life of the Gulf that would shake the delicate equilibrium so laboriously established, would wreck a commerce that is valued at many millions sterling, and would let loose again the passions of jarring nationalities only too ready to fly at each others' throats. Let Great Britain and Russia fight their battles or compose their differences elsewhere, but let them not turn into a scene of sanguinary conflict the peaceful field of a hard-won trade. I should regard the concession of a port upon the Persian Gulf to Russia by any power as a deliberate insult to Great Britain, as a wanton rupture of the *status quo*, and as an intentional provocation to war; and I should impeach the British minister, who was guilty of acquiescing in such a surrender, as a traitor to his country.

Comparison with Russian claims

At Bushire, Bunder Abbas, Kishm, and elsewhere, I have spoken of the trying heats that have sometimes to be endured in the Persian Gulf. Though an agreeable place enough to the passing visitor in the winter months, in the summer-time this all but inland sea possesses a climate that to European constitutions is most trying; and political officers on the list of the Indian Foreign Office, or ships' officers in the service of the companies that navigate the Indian seas, hear with horror that they have been commissioned to what is spoken of, with a sort of grim personification, as 'the Gulf.' I have been told that under the awning on the deck of a Gulf steamer the thermometer has stood in the morning at 120° Fahrenheit, while on shore at Muscat a black-bulb solar thermometer has registered 187° in the sun. The intense heat is aggravated rather than relieved by the extreme humidity of the atmosphere and by the dust which the slightest wind raises in clouds from the Arabian desert, and blows in an opaque yellow pall across sea and land. The hot weather causes the skin irritation known as prickly heat, from which every one suffers; nor is the torment of the day redeemed, as it is further north at Baghdad, by the coolness of the night, although an abundant dew sometimes falls and renders sleeping in the open air a questionable relief. The prevailing wind is the *shamal*, or north-west, which blows down the Gulf from its western extremity, alternating in the winter months with the *sharki*, or south-east wind, which is cold and biting at sea, and is apt to bring short-lived storms of rain.

Climate of the Gulf

The mercantile navigation of the Gulf, as it now exists, is the creation of the last thirty years, and is largely to be attributed to the statesmanship of Sir Bartle Frere. In 1862 not a single mercantile steamer ploughed these waters. A six-weekly service was then started, followed by a monthly, a fortnightly, and, finally, by a weekly steamer. The opening of the Suez Canal gave an impetus to steam-borne traffic with the Persian Gulf which was further increased during the Russo-Turkish war in 1877, and has attained even more satisfactory proportions since. The principal trade, apart from the coasting traffic, which is in the hands of native buggalows, is now conducted by the steamers of the British India Steam Navigation Company, six of whose vessels, detached for this service, carry the mails, and leave Bombay and Busrah once a week, touching at the intermediate ports of Kurrachi, Gwadur, Muscat, Jask, Bunder Abbas, Lingah, Bahrein, Bushire, Fao, and Mohammerah; and occupying, with stoppages, a period of exactly a fortnight for a distance of about 1,970 miles. This is, of course, very slow progress; and except to those who are interested in the history, commerce, and politics

Mercantile navigation

of the Gulf, is apt to be extremely tedious. I may, perhaps console myself, if not others, by the reflection that it will at least provide time even for the reluctant reader to get through this chapter. At Busrah the up-steamers are in correspondence with the excellent boats of the Euphrates and Tigris Navigation Company, which ascend the Tigris in from three and a half to four days to Baghdad; an alternative, to which a European will never voluntarily resort, being supplied by the river boats of the Turkish Company, of which there are at present four in working order, running once or twice a week. At Bombay the down-steamers are in correspondence with the P. and O. mail boats to Europe. Steamers of the Bombay and Persia Steam Navigation Company, officered by Englishmen, but owned and controlled by native merchants, and working on a cheaper scale, also sail at irregular intervals between Bombay and the Gulf ports as far as Busrah. A French line of steamers for some time ran to the Gulf; but in spite of a heavy subsidy, was compelled to desist. There was a talk of the revival of a French line to Busrah, in correspondence with the Messageries Maritimes, who now run five boats monthly between Marseilles and Kurrachi. Messrs. Darby, Andrewes & Co. are the only English merchants now running steamers directly from England to Bushire and Busrah; though vessels are frequently chartered for single voyages by business firms.

In taking leave of the Persian Gulf, let me describe the last recollection that is imprinted upon the retina of the traveller's memory. The fore deck of a Gulf steamer presents one of the most curious spectacles that can be imagined. I have seen many quaint conglomerations of colour, race, language, and religion, but rarely any more diversified than this. Arabs in their soiled silk *kefiehs* and camel's-hair head-bands, frequently engaged in playing a sort of nursery whist with battered English cards, or sometimes reading aloud with guttural monotone from paper-bound books; a Persian dealer carrying horses to Bombay, and awaking bubbles from his eternal *kalian*; Mussulman pilgrims from the holy places of Sunni or Shiah, saying their prayers, kneeling, and touching the deck with their foreheads, while one chants the formula of devotion; orthodox Hindus conducting their ablutions in a corner, or cooking the food which no one else may defile by contact; a fat Turk sipping his gritty coffee; a Lascar having his head shaved clean save for a lanky topknot on the poll;

A Gulf steamer

Parsi merchants decked in Bombay-made clothes of doubtful English cut; Indian Buniahs in preternaturally tight white cotton pants, and with daintily-embroidered caps, stuck sideways on their heads; bearded Beluchis; an Afghan with unkempt black locks curling upon his shoulders, and a *poshtin* (sheepskin) waistcoat, which he would not relinquish on the Equator, and voluminous white pantaloons; Portuguese half-castes, with skins like boot-leather and features like monkeys; one or two negroes, with shining contrast of skin and teeth; men black, copper-coloured, slate-coloured, dust-coloured, and white; men with silver rings round their big toes and pearl buckles in their ears; men wholly dressed, half-dressed, and almost naked; men lying, sitting, squatting, singing, chattering, cooking, eating, sleeping; and all in the midst of a piled labyrinth of quilts, and carpets, and boxes, of sailcloths and ropes, of sheep, and birds in cages, and fowls in coops, of trays, and samovars, and cooking-pots, of greasy donkey-engines and clanking chains—surely a more curious study in polyglot or polychrome could not well be conceived.

CHAPTER XXVIII

REVENUE, RESOURCES, AND MANUFACTURES

Chaunting of order and right, and of foresight, warder of nations,
Chaunting of labour and craft, and of wealth in the port and the garner.

CHARLES KINGSLEY, *Andromeda.*

WITH some diffidence I approach in this and the succeeding chapter the question of the finances and trade of Persia, which, while giving scattered items of information throughout these volumes, I have not so far discussed with any completeness. My reluctance arises from the unscientific and not always reliable character of the data upon which I am compelled to rely. A system that is based upon covert exaction is not likely to favour the publication of details which would reveal its own clandestine workings; and, after Russia, where statistics exist but are systematically suppressed, I know of no country in which they are so difficult to procure as Persia, where they barely exist at all. British consular officers and merchants very willingly furnish information concerning the particular district, markets, or ports with which they are connected; but any wider calculations are largely of the nature of estimates; while no two estimates, even from the most competent of authorities, are found wholly to agree. Premising, therefore, that positive exactitude cannot be predicted of any statistics relating to Persia—the genius of whose people has never been trained to express itself in figures, other than in those of speech—I will proceed to give, from a collation of tables derived from a large number of sources, as near an approximation to the truth about Persian revenue and commerce as is obtainable.[1]

Persian figures

[1] Works relating to the Persian revenue are few. I may cite the following:—Sir J. Malcolm (1810), *History of Persia*, vol. ii. caps. xxi. xxii.; Sir J. Macdonald Kinneir (1810), *Geographical Memoir*; J. B. Fraser (1821), *Journey into Khorasan*, cap. x.; General J. F. Blaramberg (1839), 'Statistische Uebersicht von Persien,' vol. ii. of *Journal of Russian Imp. Geogr. Society*, 1841; (Sir) J. Sheil, note, p. 386, to Lady Sheil's *Glimpses of Life and Manners*; Cte. J. de Roche-

The revenue of Persia may be divided into two headings: the Maliat, or fixed revenue, and the Sursat, or irregular revenue.

Classification of revenue

The fixed revenue is derived from four sources: (1) regular taxation; (2) revenues of Crown lands; (3) customs; (4) rents and leases. The irregular revenue is derived from three sources: (1) *sadir* or public requisitions; (2) presents (*pishkesh*) on the festival of No Ruz (March 21, the Persian New Year's Day), and on the Prophet's birthday (Aid-i-Molud); (3) extraordinary *pishkesh*, arising from presents, fines, bribes, confiscations, &c. I will explain and deal with each of these in turn, foreshadowing that anything like precision, uniformity, or method cannot be expected of Persian finance, and that the theory is often widely divergent from the practice.

I. Maliat or fixed revenue. 1. Taxation

Regular taxation is nominally threefold in character, consisting of the land-tax, taxes on animals, flocks and herds, and taxes on shopkeepers, artisans, and trade. These various taxes are levied according to the differing nature of localities, peoples, and occupations.

Land-tax

The main and staple source of revenue in Persia is, and always has been, the land-tax. Postponing for a few moments the larger question of land-tenure throughout the country, I will merely here deal with the subject as regards its assessment by the Government tax-collector. Religious endowments, and lands held upon the basis of feudal service, are exempt from the land-tax; but it is levied on all other landed property throughout the kingdom, upon rice, cotton, corn, tobacco, and opium-growing fields, upon gardens, vineyards, and orchards, and upon date plantations in the south. In a land where all agricultural wealth is the result of irrigation, the assessment is commonly based upon the nature or amount of the water supply; and according to the character of the local produce, or to ancient custom, it is paid in cash or in kind. About one-fifth of the entire revenue is paid in the latter fashion, usually in wheat, barley, rice, or chopped straw. The principle upon which the land-tax rests is that one-fifth or twenty per cent. of the agricultural or horticultural produce is the right of the king. Formerly the Crown only claimed one-tenth; but this proportion was doubled by Fath Ali Shah.

chouart (1865), *Souvenirs*, caps. iii. xv. xix.; E. Stack (1881), *Six Months in Persia*, vol. ii. cap. xi. (on the Land Revenue). My own information is almost entirely first-hand.

In practice it is found that the assessment frequently amounts to thirty per cent., and twenty-five per cent. may perhaps be taken as a fair average. The system, however, varies absolutely in different parts of the country, and even in different parts of the same province; and in the course of a single journey, the inquiring traveller will perhaps encounter wholly divergent and inconsistent methods of application. Thus, in Azerbaijan, the chief agricultural province of Persia, the bulk of taxation is levied on the land and its produce, but in some cases it is levied on the number of oxen used in the plough, and in others on the land and oxen combined; while elsewhere, again, a poll-tax is imposed, *plus* a tax on horses, cows, asses, and sheep. In that province the revenue exacted is commonly as follows:—

If from the land alone, one-tenth of the produce.
If by a poll-tax, 3*s.* per adult male: 1*s.* 6*d.* from women and youths.
If upon oxen, 11*s.* 9*d.* per yoke of oxen.
If upon cattle, $8\frac{3}{4}d.$ per horse, ass, or cow; $1\frac{3}{4}d.$ per sheep.

A further anomaly arises from the fact that the taxes are levied sometimes from the proprietor, sometimes from the cultivator, local custom again being the determining cause.

Here, however, we are brought face to face with a truly Persian phenomenon. The system which I have sketched, though anomalous and intricate, yet rests upon a simple and intelligible principle, namely, a fixed contribution to the revenue, based upon the wealth-producing capacity of the soil, and levied upon those whose business it is to pay it. In practice, however, this system is wholly abandoned; it would not dovetail with the larger system of organised peculation upon which Persian government and society alike subsist, and would not provide those opportunities for extensive *mudakhil* which are so dear to the official mind. Accordingly, so far from the taxes being levied from the individual taxpayer by the revenue officers, we find that they are raised in lump sums from villages, towns, or districts, the taxes being, in fact, farmed out by the Government for a fixed money payment, and the allocation in subordinate areas being left to the arbitrary decision of local governors, chiefs, or headmen. Frequently the owner of a property farms his own taxes from the Government, so as to escape the visits of the official assessor; i.e. he compounds by an annual cash payment for the stricter obligation that would accrue from an official assessment if conducted.

Method of payment

Again, as regards the assessments themselves, these are not only neglected in parts, but are in the main wholly obsolete in date and character. Many of them were made in remote periods, beyond the memory of the oldest inhabitant, and have never been modified in spite of subsequent changes. Some villages continue to pay a purely nominal sum, though they have trebled or quadrupled in size, wealth, and population since the original assessment; others are mulcted for an exorbitant total, calculated upon the prosperity of a vanished day; these revolutions of fortune being both rapid and frequent in a country where all depends upon so capricious a factor as water. Some districts, therefore, are heavily over-taxed, others ludicrously under-taxed, the anomalies of an obsolete assessment being perpetuated by the consistent venality of the modern assessor, whose views of the situation are seldom proof against the persuasion of a bribe. Such a thing as a scientific or a periodical revision of assessment has never taken place, and would cause a thrill of horror to run through every class of Persian society above the peasant.

Herd-tax

The taxation on flocks, herds, and animals exists in two forms, either as a supplementary method of land-taxation, in the manner indicated above, or as the sole available method of contribution to the revenue by the Iliat or nomad tribes, who sometimes hold their lands on the condition of military service, or who do not practise agriculture except in a vagrant fashion, but whose wealth is expressed in large flocks, for the most part of sheep and goats. Mr. Stack mentions, as the common ratio of such taxation in its agricultural incidence, the sum of $\frac{1}{3}$–1 *kran* for a sheep or goat, $2\frac{1}{2}$–10 *krans* for a cow, 10 *krans* for an ass, and so on. From the nomad tribes the revenue is collected and paid over to the provincial governor in lump sums, the minor distribution of which is determined by the tribal Ilkhanis, or Khans, or *rish-sefids* (white-beards), or *tushmals* (elders). Thus, the Bakhtiaris pay partly to Arabistan or Burujird, partly to Isfahan, the Lurs to Luristan, the Pusht-i-Kuh Lurs to Kermanshah, the Kermanshah Kurds to Kermanshah, those in Persian Kurdistan to Sinna, those in Azerbaijan to Tabriz, the Kuhgelus, Mamasennis, Kashkais, Arabs of Fars, Bulverdis, etc., to Fars; the Shah Sevens in part to Azerbaijan and in part to Irak (Sultanabad), the Khalij partly to Saveh and partly to Irak, all the tribes in Khorasan to that province, the Afshars to Khamseh (Zinjan), the Karaguzlus to Hamadan. With a few tribes military service counts for revenue; but in the majority of cases the revenue is distinct, and the service is paid for separately.

Tribal blackmail

In Luristan there exist a number of peculiar methods of recruiting the revenue, which, both for intrinsic subtlety, and as illustrations of the resourcefulness of Persian finance, are worthy of mention. Each district and subsection is charged annually with a sum of 25–50 *krans* for a copy of the Shah's Diary of his First Journey to Europe. This tax dates from the period of that journey, viz. 1873, when it was imposed as a means of simultaneously acquainting the subjects with the majesty of their sovereign, and the sovereign with the pecuniary resources of his subjects. The tax has never been taken off, neither appetite being apparently as yet assuaged. Similarly, a favourite horse of the Shah having died, when he passed through Burujird many years ago, the district, which was obviously responsible for the misfortune, was fined in order to provide a substitute; which fine has been collected ever since by the local Governor. Another ingenious method is to issue a proclamation reserving certain pastures on the hill-sides for the Government mules and horses, and then to sell exemptions for the use of their own grounds to the real proprietors. Yet a further device is first to issue an analogous prohibition of shooting on the hills, then to prohibit pasturage on the ground of disturbance to game, and finally to exact a grazing-tax as the price of exemption.

Trade-tax

The tax on shopkeepers, artisans, and trade is one of the most capricious and unsystematic. Sometimes it takes the form of a capitation, or poll-tax; elsewhere I have heard it estimated as a 20 per cent. impost on the profits of trade. In older accounts of the Persian revenue system, I find that under this head are included the ground rents of houses, the rents of caravanserais, baths, shops, mills and factories; but, so far as I could ascertain, these taxes are rarely exacted, and a most legitimate and profitable source of income is thus allowed to escape.

On the other hand, in towns, the Governors have devised equivalent sources of profit which do credit to the Persian genius. The most successful of these, as elsewhere indicated, is the administration of justice. Nothing can be so welcome to a Persian Governor as a street-row, a blood-feud, a murder, or a quarrel, within his jurisdiction. Down come his officers on the delinquents, and from their pockets out comes the fine. If litigation ensues, so much the better for the provincial exchequer; since every wheel of the judicial machine will require constant greasing. Another device is the introduction of prostitutes into a district where they were previously absent. Using them as a decoy, the Governor suddenly pounces down upon some wealthy merchant, giving a convivial entertainment on the sly, and extorts a heavy blackmail as the price of silence. These and many other expedients are devised by the Governors, in order to meet the troublesome inquisition of the Ministry of Arrears, which has a beautiful way of producing all sorts of arrears, and deficits, and objections to provincial budgets. No final acquittances can be obtained without considerable 'palm-oil.

2. Revenue from Crown lands

Such are the component items of the revenue, as nominally raised by taxation upon land and labour. Scarcely distinguishable therefrom is the rent paid to the State by the cultivators of the Crown lands, which is fixed by immemorial custom as a certain proportion of the produce, determined by the relative contribution of the two parties to the expenses of cultivation. In some cases the Government provides the seed, and receives, in consequence, a larger fraction of the profits; but in the majority of instances the Crown is an absentee landlord, and no more. The terms upon which the contract between the State and its tenants is based appear to be reasonably favourable to the latter; and, subject to the payment of rent, they are rarely dispossessed. The revenue from the Crown lands is almost entirely ear-marked, to satisfy the annuitants, of whom I shall presently speak.

3. Customs

About one fifth of the *maliat* or fixed revenue is raised by Custom duties on the import and export of merchandise. In each province, district, or town, these are farmed out to the highest bidder, the sum paid by whom is matter of common notoriety, as well as the surplus, amounting as a rule to from 20 to 25 per cent., which he puts into his own pocket. Thus the customs of Bushire for 1889–90 were sold by the Governor for 91,000 *tomans*, plus a *pishkesh*, or bonus to himself of 5,000 *tomans*. The purchaser would then proceed to levy the 96,000 *tomans* thus required, plus the 20 per cent. profit demanded by his own interests. In other words, the sum actually raised would amount to about 115,000 *tomans*, although only 91,000 would enter the Government exchequer—a fair illustration of as corrupt and wasteful a system as could well be devised. Upon foreign merchandise, import and export, an *ad valorem* duty of 5 per cent. is charged once for all at the port or station of entry or departure, in accordance with the commercial treaties concluded with the majority of foreign powers. As I have shown, however, in my chapter upon Khorasan, foreign merchandise is sometimes compelled to pay more, in course of transit through the country, if it has passed into the hands of native traders. Thus British merchandise hailing from Trebizond which has paid 5 per cent. at Tabriz, will pay 2½ per cent. more upon entering Meshed, if introduced by a Persian house of business. From the Gulf the accumulation of dues is even more onerous; the 5 per cent. levied at Bunder Abbas upon Anglo-Indian goods being raised to 7½ per cent. as they enter Kerman, and to 9 per cent. if they pass through Yezd in addition. Native merchants pay a duty considerably less than Europeans at the port, commonly about 2 per cent.; but they are liable to road taxes and to town *octrois* en route, levied not upon the value, but on the number of loads, cases, or bales, the customary charge being 4 *krans* per load at each town. The sum total, however, of these contributions, except in the case of merchandise going far into the interior, when the accumulated tariffs are likely to exceed 5 per cent., and in a few individual cases, such as shawls, gold brocades, and so forth, is decidedly less than that paid by the European trader, and may probably be reckoned at an average of from 3 to 4 per cent.

It will excite no surprise that a system managed with such a complete lack of method, and resting in the last resort upon illegal extortion, should give rise to many abuses. One of these is noticed by Messrs. Stolze and Andreas. In order to make up the requisite surplus over and above the farm amount, it is to the interest of the farmers to attract as much trade as possible to their respective districts. With this object they endeavour to outbid the collectors in adjoining districts and in other ports. and, by agreeing to pass goods at much less than the official customs tariff, to induce merchants to desert other trade routes in favour of those passing their way. Thus, they sometimes find it prudent, even upon European merchandise, to exact no more than 2 per cent. This higgling, so to speak, of the customs market

Abuses

calls for corresponding calculation on the part of the merchants, and brings about frequent changes in the routes preferred.

A similar illicit sort of compact is entered into between the farmers and the merchants as the vernal equinox approaches. On that date (March 21, No Ruz) there is, as I have previously shown, a general shuffle of officials in Persia, from Governors of provinces down to petty collectors of customs. A Consular Report from Astrabad in 1882 thus stated what then occurs:—

> Incumbents are uncertain whether they are to continue in office or not, and are anxious to realise as much as they can. Consequently at this period the Customs officials are willing to reduce the dues leviable, and to take less than the legal tax. There takes place, therefore, at all ports where goods are exported, a regular bargain between the merchants and the Customs farmers. The former threaten, unless considerable reductions are made, not to export their goods until the new incumbent is nominated, and the latter endeavour to reduce the dues as little as possible. Importers also bargain with the farmers as to what abatement on the legal import duty the officials at the ports may be willing to make, before deciding where their imports shall be landed.

I append a table of the farm money, or sums received by the Government for the customs during the last decade, and of their equivalent, according to the prevalent rate of exchange, in pounds sterling. In each case it must be remembered that quite 20 per cent must be added, to make up the totals actually levied upon trade.

Year	Government receipts	Rate of exchange	Equivalent
	tomans	*krans* = £1	£
1879–1880	606,400	$27\frac{5}{8}$	236,400
1880–1881	708,629	$27\frac{1}{2}$	257,700
1881–1882	785,290	$27\frac{7}{8}$	281,600
1882–1883	807,770	$28\frac{5}{8}$	281,400
1883–1884	814,000	29	280,700
1884–1885	806,000	$30\frac{1}{2}$	264,262
1885–1886	838,000	$33\frac{1}{4}$	250,150
1886–1887	850,000	$33\frac{1}{2}$	253,730
1887–1888	820,000	34	241,176
1888–1889	800,000	34	235,294

Of the 800,000 *tomans* raised in the last named year by customs, 294,000 *tomans* were collected at Teheran, and the remainder at the Gulf and Caspian ports and in the frontier towns. The revenue from customs is allocated by the Shah to the payment of his Household expenses.

The next item will be more clearly explained by reference to the detailed table of the Persian revenue which I shall presently append. It is derived from the proceeds of various establishments, institutions, or concessions, owned and leased out by the Government. Such are the post, telegraphs, mint, mines, &c. In the year 1888–9 the sums thus raised amounted to a total of 107,000 *tomans*. I imagine that in the future this table will experience considerable augmentation, according as the Crown's share in the annual profits of the various concessions granted by the Shah to European companies (such as the Imperial Bank, and the Mining Corporation), is paid into the Exchequer. Should these institutions attain anything like the success that has commonly been predicted of them, the Royal treasury should profit to an annually increasing degree, quite apart from the large sum originally paid in hard cash by the concessionaire, which is, as a rule, quietly absorbed by the Shah.

4. Rents and leases

The irregular revenue, or *sursat*, i.e. the sums arbitrarily and suddenly levied to meet some temporary need, or forcibly elicited under the disguise of gifts, is still, to a considerable extent, and has been in times past to a much greater, a source of hardship and oppression to the people. For although it may appear at first sight that the sums thus extorted are wrung from rich grandees and corrupt officials, from whom no one would regret to see the literal pound of flesh exacted, yet in the last resort they are always ground out from the hapless peasant, upon whom, as the ultimate grade in the descending scale, the burden is certain ultimately to fall. Of these fortuitous exactions, the most arbitrary and tyrannical is that known as the *sadir*, a species of Persian ship-money, being a levy from a district or province, or even from the entire kingdom, in order to meet some special expenditure, such as the cost of warfare, an addition to the army, the construction of public works or royal palaces (the latter more often than the former), the reception of ambassadors, the official progress of governors, and other public officials. If the Shah, for instance, honours a portion of his dominions with his august presence, the cost of receiving and entertaining him and his enormous retinue must be thus defrayed by the loyal inhabitants. A fixed sum is usually demanded from the local or provincial

II. Irregular revenue. 1. Public requisitions

governor, who is free to manipulate the allocation as he will, there being no pretence to system or uniformity. In the form in which it reaches the taxpayer, it may be usually represented as a sort of graduated income-tax, levied according to the worldly circumstances of those from whom it is demanded. In the past year (1891) such a tax was levied on the district south of Tabriz in order to meet the expenses of the troops despatched to Suj Bulak against the Kurds. An interesting variety of this tax is levied in some districts when the Governor makes his tour of inspection. Supplies, in excess of all possible needs, are first exacted from the inhabitants; and the surplus is then resold to the villagers, who are compelled to buy back the very grain which, a few weeks before, they had been compelled to provide gratis.

2. Presents at No Ruz, &c.

The sums received by the Shah at the annual festival of No Ruz, which afford as graphic an illustration as the cynic could desire of the cynic's definition of gratitude as a sense of favours to come, were formerly one of the main sources of the royal income. Malcolm estimated their value in the time of Fath Ali Shah, who was notoriously avaricious, as 1,200,000*l.*; but his calculations, which in the case of the Persian revenue seem to have been uniformly pitched too high, are reduced to more probable proportions by the contemporary statements of Fraser, that they amounted to 1,000,000 to 1,200,000 *tomans*, or, at the then rate of exchange (1 *toman* = 12*s.*), 600,000*l.* to 720,000*l.*; and of Macdonald Kinneir, who named 943,000 *tomans* as the total of the whole annual *pishkesh* received by the Crown. These imposing totals have greatly dwindled in recent years, other and more ingenious means of levying a tax upon official wealth, or in other words upon official embezzlement, having been discovered; and the united values of the *pishkesh* received by the Shah on the two occasions of the No Ruz and of the Prophet's Birthday in the year 1888–9 amounted only, according to the figures presented to me, to 120,000 *tomans*, or, at the then rate of exchange, to 35,800*l.* I cannot be certain, however, that the correct amount would appear in these tables.

Malcolm estimated the value of the presents received in the shape of fines, bribes, confiscations, and gratuities, by the king as half of the regular Birthday *pishkesh*. There is no means whatever of ascertaining what is their modern amount, seeing that they are in the nature of private presents to the sovereign, and disappear, without more ado, into his voracious but silent exchequer. It may be added, however, that under the present administrative system, *pishkesh* of some sort is a necessity; for it is the only fund out of which the Shah can defray the cost of any extraordinary national outlay, e.g. upon military armaments or war. Hence it may be imagined that all public works being paid for neither out of a national surplus nor by means of a public loan, but out of the Shah's privy purse, every instinct, not merely of royal cupidity, but of caution, is arrayed against such proposals.

3. Extraordinary *pishkesh*

Before giving the figures and details of present revenue and expenditure, let me guard against a possible error in the comparison of recent totals. The revenue, calculated in *krans*, or in tens of *krans*—i.e. *tomans*—appears in all estimates to show a decided increase during the past fifteen years. This increase, however, owing to the rapid and till lately unchecked depreciation of the silver currency, was only ostensible. In 1875, when 25 *krans* were equivalent to 1*l*., a revenue estimated at 4,750,000 *tomans* equalled 1,900,000*l*. But when the *kran* fell to an equivalent of 35 *krans* to 1*l*., a revenue of 5,500,000 *tomans*, although showing a nominal increase of three-quarters of a million *tomans*, only equalled 1,570,000*l*.

Depreciation of currency

The following is the Budget account of Persia for the year 1888–9, as derived from official sources:—

I. Revenue derived from Taxes and Customs combined.

Name of Province or District	Payments in Cash	Payments in Kind						Prices at which Government compounds payments in grain for cash		Total revenue of the Province or District. Payments in kind calculated at Government rates
		Grain, wheat and barley	Straw	Rice	Gram	Grass	Silk	Wheat	Barley	
	krans	*kharvars* of 649 lbs.	*kharvars*	*kharvars*[1]	*kharvars*	*kharvars*	*man* of 13 lbs.	*kra*	*ns*[3]	*krans*
1. Teheran & dependencies	4,238,720	293	91	2,250	75	1,500	—	30	25	4,306,391
2. Azerbaijan . . .	7,861,420	54,873[2]	4,960	229	—	—	—	26⅔	16⅔	9,666,665
3. Khorasan . . .	5,082,686	60,123	11,699	725	—	—	—	30	20	6,586,932
4. Fars	6,420,402	7,700	—	—	—	—	—	40	30	6,689,902
5. Isfahan & dependencies	3,791,202	8,855	6,000	—	—	—	—	35	15	4,036,577
6. Kerman and Beluchistan	2,215,343	19,703	18,558	—	—	—	—	40	30	2,904,948
7. Arabistan . . .	1,427,359	1,600	800	—	—	—	—	30	15	1,466,538
8. Gilan	3,450,000	—	—	—	—	—	—	—	—	3,450,000
9. Mazanderan . . .	1,393,470	—	—	—	—	—	—	—	—	1,393,470
10. Kurdistan . . .	673,457	—	—	—	—	—	—	—	—	673,457
11. Luristan . . .	594,253	5,268	1,956	—	—	—	—	20	15	694,267
12. Irak, Kezzaz, Ferahan, Mahallat, Saveh .	727,357	17,405	2,228	—	—	—	—	30	20	1,200,079
13. Burujird. . . .	609,573	4,867	1,040	—	—	—	—	22	13	698,905
14. Yezd	1,794,920	—	—	—	—	—	—	50	40	1,728,023
15. Kermanshah . . .	936,935	10,170	3,800	—	—	—	—	20	10	1,104,685
16. Khamseh . . .	819,888	10,540	9,000	—	—	—	—	15	10	978,638
17. Kazvin	953,018	11,972	6,800	—	—	—		20	10	1,159,798
18. Astrabad . . .	171,899	—	—	8,984	—	—	1	—	—	351,779
19. Bostam and Shahrud .	93,366	3,542	3,827	—	—	—	—	25	20	188,369
20. Semnan and Damghan .	280,728	2,592	1,093	—	—	—	—	25	15	336,940
21. Kum	293,620	3,754	—	—	—	—	—	25	15	368,700
22. Kashan	712,006	1,052	921	—	—	—	—	25	15	736,730
23. Gulpaigan and Khonsar	225,811	1,767	216	—	—	—	—	30	20	269,986
24. Kamareh . . .	91,041	1,839	—	—	—	—	—	20	15	127,821
25. Gerrus	129,965	1,982	—	—	—	—	—	25	15	169,605
26. Hamadan . . .	673,635	9,306	-	—	—	—	—	30	20	906,285
27. Malayer and Tusirkan .	504,709	6,371	870	—	—	—	—	25	15	635,599
28. Nihavend . . .	280,303	7,317	4,941	—	—	—	—	25	15	446,407
29. Natanz	211,589	—	—	—	—	—	—	30	20	211,589
30. Asadabad . . .	23,435	2,572	—	—	—	—	—	30	20	87,735
31. Joshekan . . .	73,302	96	—	—	—	—	—	20	—	76,182
32. Khar	94,704	6,064	4,684	477	—	—	—	30	20	265,994
33. Kharakan . . .	51,102	1,467	—	—	—	—	—	30	—	95,112
34. Demavend . . .	22,910	1,447	—	—	—	—	—	30	20	59,085
35. Talikan	48,350	—	—	—	—	—	—	—	—	48,350
36. Kangavar . . .	17,671	527	159	—	—	—	—	20	10	24,942
37. Firuzkuh . . .	15,716	197	—	—	—	—	—	30	20	18,163
38. Chehardeh Kelateh .	10,892	48	—	—	—	—	—	25	—	12,092
Totals . .	44,076,757	265,309	83,643	12,665	75	1,500	1	—	—	54,177,740

[1] The Government price of rice in the husks, called *shaltuk*, is 20 *krans* per *kharvar* of 649 lbs.
[2] The Azerbaijan *kharvar* weighs 974 lbs.
[3] These prices are, as a rule, from 15 to 25 per cent. lower than the current prices obtainable in the market.

II. Revenue derived from Other Sources.

—	*krans*	—	*krans*
1. Mint establishment .	250,000	11. Zerger tribe	5,000
2. Telegraphs:		12. Brick kilns of Teheran .	120,000
(*a*) Persian telegraphs	100,000	13. Royal gardens . . .	65,000
(*b*) Indo-European Telegraph Co. . .	80,348	14. Meshed shrine . . .	10,000
3. Posts	12,000	15. Mines	147,500
4. Passports	130,200	16. Coal mine of Ustad Yusuf	1,500
5. Rent of quay at Bunder Abbas	3,000	17. Slaughter-houses of Teheran	80,000
6. Rent of coffee-shop at Doshan Tepe . . .	500	18. Rent of boxes at the Tazieh (theatre) . .	16,250
7. Press	5,000	19. Presents on the Prophet's birthday, Aid-i-Molud . . .	52,500
8. Kum-Road caravan-serais	6,000	20. Presents on New Year's Day, Aid-i-No Ruz .	66,000
9. Jask-Gwadur Telegr. .	30,000		
10. Nomad tribes near Teheran	10,978		
Total Revenue from other sources . . .			1,191,776[1]

Grand Total.

	krans	*krans*
I. Taxes paid in cash . .	36,076,757	
" " " kind . .	10,100,983	
Customs	8,000,000	
		54,177,740
II. Revenue from other sources . . .		1,191,776
Total Revenue of Persia . .		55,369,516
At the rate of exchange in 1888, $33\frac{1}{2}$ *krans* = £1 .		£1,652,820

Expenditure.

I. Local charges deducted from the revenue in provinces and districts.

(1) *Hak-el-hukumah*, governor's dues, charges for collection of revenue.

(2) *Takhfifat*, deductions from revenue on account of bad harvests, poverty of villages and districts, etc.

(3) *Sarf-i-tamir*, maintenance of Government buildings and repairs.

[1] Another authority says that the items for passports and slaughter-houses in the above column are much underrated; and that the following have been omitted: Taxes on coffee-shops, 400,000 *krans*; Rent of fisheries at Enzeli, 800,000 *krans*; Rent of boxwood, 170,000 *krans*; Teheran market, 10,000 *krans*, Grape-tax (?).

Name of Province or District	*Hak-el-hukumah*		*Taktfifat*			*Sarf-i-Tamir*			Total amount deducted from the revenue of province or district for local charges
	Cash	Grain	Cash	Grain	Straw	Cash	Grain	Straw	
	krans	*khavs.*	*krans*	*khar*	*vars*	*krans*	*khar*	*vars*	*krans*
1. Teheran and dependencies	32,133	—	33,970	700	1,740	2,000	—	—	} 174,510
" crown domains	—	—	11,387	478	1,750[1]	—	155	155	
2. Azerbaijan	143,600[2]	—	129,808	1,928	52	81,600	162	162	408,647
3. Khorasan	45,000	—	—	—	—	—	—	—	45,000
4. Fars	89,260	200	636,568	178	—	2,460	80	—	744,318
5. Isfahan	—	—	89,450	—	—	32,470	48	89	123,476
6. Kerman and Beluchistan	12,000	297	13,200	25	—	19,200	65	—	57,945
7. Arabistan	18,500	—	—	—	—	2,780	19	19	21,763
8. Gilan	30,000	—	204,000	—	—	10,290	—	—	244,290
9. Mazanderan	24,500	—	1,322	—	—	20,070	—	—	45,892
10. Kurdistan	29,650	—	—	—	—	7,650	—	—	37,300
11. Luristan	10,935	—	145,240	—	—	6,800	29	—	163,482
12. Irak, Kezzaz, Ferahan, Mahailat, Saveh	18,400	134	27,180	125	—	5,200	78	—	57,450
13. Burujird	10,400	—	47,540	380	—	400	14	—	65,235
14. Yezd	25,333	—	27,987	—	—	10,000	73	73	66,897
15. Kermanshah	9,870	—	32,083	67	400	8,104	73	73	54,049
16. Khamseh	8,060	—	9,430	256	293	5,400	—	—	27,262
17. Kazvin	—	—	12,820	87	—	4,700	16	16	19,129
18. Astrabad	—	—	12,606	1,512	—	1,644	16	—	44,810
19. Bostam and Shahrud	3,044	—	708	130	890	1,000	48	48	12,509
20. Semnan and Damghan	5,200	—	1,474	114	—	1,926	88	48	12,832
21. Kum	10,000	—	435	2	—	2,200	40	40	13,635
22. Kashan	6,000	—	24,650	113	207	1,610	25	25	35,948
23. Gulpaigan and Khonsar	4,600	—	17,880	533	—	1,000	—	—	24,812
24. Kamareh	3,200	—	240	6	—	—	—	—	3,560
25. Gerrus	2,670	—	3,840	17	—	400	10	10	7,490
26. Hamadan	7,960	—	17,730	154	—	1,090	58	—	31,080
27. Malayer and Tusirkan	7,730	—	2,150	14	—	1,400	14	14	11,896
28. Nihavend	6,400	—	37,040	438	—	2,000	—	—	54,200
29. Natanz	3,000	—	4,106	—	—	1,340	—	—	8,446
30. Asadabad	750	—	400	—	—	260	—	—	1,410
31. Joshekan	—	—	120	—	—	—	—	—	120
32. Khar	1,350	—	16,610	206	166	450	19	19	22,775
33. Kharakan	1,680	—	—	—	—	—	—	—	1,680
34. Demavend	800	—	2,760	83	—	200	8	—	6,035
35. Talikan	—	—	—	—	—	—	—	—	—
36. Kangavar	500	—	136	8	—	250	7	—	1,111
37. Firuzkuh	1,450	25	—	—	—	200	7	7	2,478
38. Chehardeh Kelateh	—	—	—	—	—	—	—	—	—
						Total Local Charges			2,633,472

[1] Also 2,111 *kharvars* of rice.

[2] The 143,600 *krans* for *Hak-el-hukumah* include 50,000 annual pay of the Vizier of Azerbaijan, and 20,000 *krans* subsidy for post-houses. The 81,600 *krans Sarf-i-tamir* include 20,000 *krans* for fire-works on festivals. The Crown Prince's allowance figures in the sum set apart for members of the Royal Family; it is 400,000 *krans* per annum.

II. Other Expenditure.

	krans
Army, including rations in kind and pensions to officers	18,000,000
Navy	100,000
Foreign Office: Ambassador at Constantinople, Ministers at London, Paris, Berlin, Vienna, St. Petersburg; consuls-general, consuls, and vice-consuls at various places, Foreign Office agents at various towns in Persia, Minister of Foreign Affairs, and a large staff at Teheran	1,000,000

OTHER EXPENDITURE—*continued.*

Revenue collectors, writers, accountants, secretaries in various administrations, priesthood, clergy	1,500,000
Colleges	400,000
Pensions of Government servants, ministers, &c.	8,000,000
Pensions to Afghans and Persian nobles	2,000,000
Subsidy to Kajar tribe	600,000
Allowances to princes of Royal house	3,000,000
Shah's establishment: pocket money, harem, guards, etc.	5,000,000
Total	39,600,000

GRAND TOTAL.

I. Expenditure for local charges	2,633,472
II. Other expenditure	39,600,000
Total expenditure	42,233,472
At the rate of exchange in 1888, 33½ *krans* = £1	£1,260,700

SUMMARY.

	krans		£
Total Revenue	55,369,516	=	1,652,820
Total Expenditure	42,233,472	=	1,260,700
Surplus	13,136,044	=	392,121

Surplus

This surplus is reduced by: 1. A deficit of over 8,000,000 *krans* per annum on the budget revenues; 2. Expenditure for building and repairing the Shah's palaces near Teheran, nearly 1,000,000 *krans* per annum; 3. Unforeseen expenses for purchase of arms, voyages of the Court, and other expenses caused by sending troops to the frontier, bringing unruly tribes to order, receiving foreign ministers,[1] &c.

It is increased by: 1. Presents made to the Shah by governors of provinces on appointment; 2. Voluntary presents made to the Shah; 3. Sums paid to the Shah for concessions granted by him to foreigners, and by royalties due to him on account of such concessions.

The reduction, in fact, is caused by such unforeseen expenses as, if not met by the aforenamed surplus, are reimbursed by the *sadir* or irregular requisition already described. The increase is due to the irregular *pishkesh*, whose amount I have previously declared my inability to estimate. After all payments have been made, the

[1] The reception of every new representative of a foreign power costs the Persian Government 1,000 *tomans* on an average.

ultimate surplus, whatever it be, goes into the private purse of the Shah, and assists to swell the great pile of hoarded, specie bullion, and treasure which is there amassed.[1] This surplus is said to be about 100,000*l.* annually; but, considering the impossibility of calculating the real amount received in *pishkesh*, I should hesitate too implicitly to accept this estimate, and should be inclined to rate the Shah's profit as somewhat higher. Common rumour in Persian official circles sets down the total annual receipts as 5,000,000 *tomans* (therein, as has been seen, not very greatly erring), and credits the Shah's privy purse with receiving a one-fifth share of this total, half of which fraction is supposed to be spent upon his *anderun*, or private household, and the remaining half to be stored in the Royal treasury.

Among the above-mentioned items of expenditure, the large sums spent upon pensions or annuities will have been noticed.

Annuities

This system is one of the worst but most cherished features of modern Persian finance. The number of pensioners is enormous, and is always being recruited. Every man's ambition is to obtain a *mustamari*, or annuity, upon any pretext, while the payments themselves tend to become more or less permanent, according to the status of the recipient. Upon the death of the latter, his surviving heirs do their best to purchase renewal, which can be effected by paying a cash percentage to the Shah in return for the favour, as well as a future annual rebate from the original grant. It is not safe, however, to be caught napping, for plenty of emulous pensioners are on the look-out; and keen is the competition for a *Dest khat*, or Royal Autograph assignment of the allowance, to be carried into effect as soon as a *mahal* or opportunity, by the death of the recent holder, occurs. Unless, therefore, the heirs have friends in high places, whose assistance they have conciliated by pecuniary means, they may find some rival candidate already standing in the dead man's shoes. These annuities carry with them no office, service, or obligation. The late Prime Minister, Mirza Yusuf, in virtue of his office of Mustofi-el-Mamalek or Chief Administrator of the Finances, had, before his death, accumulated

[1] The lowest, but perhaps the most reliable, estimate that I received of the contents of the Royal treasury fixed their value at 3,000,000*l.* On the other hand, a well-informed authority returned them twenty years ago as follows: specie, 1,500,000*l.*; gold furniture and plate, 500,000*l.*; Crown jewels, 2,000,000*l.*; total, 4,000,000*l.*

a great number of annuities in his own hands. By the judicious manipulation of pecuniary and other influences, his son, a mere lad, succeeded to the titular enjoyment of his father's office (though the actual duties were vested in another person) and consequently to the greater portion of these emoluments. People in the position of a *mustofi* have great opportunities of such illicit diversion, by which they freely benefit themselves or their relatives. One such individual was found to have secured a large number of annuities for his own son, by representing him as a number of different persons in different places with every possible combination of his real name, e.g. Mullah Ali, Mirza Ali, Ali Agha, and Ali Khan. These annuitants are mere drones and bloodsuckers, and are a curse to the State.

Abuses of present taxation

The system of taxation which I have described as prevailing in Persia is obviously faulty in the extreme. It is both inequitable in its incidence, and vicious in its operation. In the first place, almost the entire taxation of the kingdom falls upon the agricultural class, and among them with heaviest burden upon the humbler grades of the ryots, or peasants. Indeed, we may say that land and foreign commerce are practically the only commodities taxed. Towns and cities, urban property in general, and native wealth or trade, contribute scarcely any share to the revenue. There is no such thing as an income tax, or house tax, or property tax on the occupying householder. Even the large sums that are wrung in the shape of bribes or presents from the richer nobles and officials are in no sense a tax upon wealth, but are confessedly added to the totals which the tax-collector is required to levy from the people, the confusion of government offices in Persia (the governor being administrator, judge, and tax-gatherer in one) facilitating the operation. Under the abominable system of farming the unhappy cultivator pays a sum which has even been said to equal the legal assessment over again, the excess above the official scale merely going to fill the pockets of embezzling officials and spendthrift grandees. These latter maintain enormous establishments, and live in the lap of luxury, without contributing one penny directly to the revenue. If the sums at present raised in taxation were really paid into the exchequer, instead of providing a series of *mudakhils*, increasing in geometrical progression as the higher ranks are reached, an income would be forthcoming quite sufficient to pay for the public works which are now so deplorably neglected, as well as to provide the Shah with his annual surplus. If in addition a more equitable redistribution of the burden of taxation were adopted, the wealthiest classes in the community would no longer escape scot free, and the total revenue might probably be augmented without difficulty by half as much again.

Need for new assessment

In competent hands some approach to system might also be introduced into the haphazard method of land assessment at present in vogue. I do not say that a uniform assessment throughout the country would be either judicious or possible. The differing conditions and products of cultivation, as well as local custom or prejudice, would render such an attempt futile. But at least some sort of equalisation should be introduced, and agriculture in one province, even if pursued under a different system, should not be more heavily or less heavily burdened than in another. For a proper revision of the land tax, a cadastral survey of the entire country, conducted by trained European officials, is an almost indispensable preliminary. This should be followed by a new assessment for the whole kingdom, and would pave the way to periodical revisions, undertaken at stated intervals of time.

Public accounts

A more scientific or less slovenly method of keeping the public, provincial, and local accounts is another imperative reform. In the first place, every official should be called upon to present a budget estimate for his province or department at the beginning of the year. When the accounts are made up, there should be a clear division between the columns of revenue and expenditure, which are often now confused, owing to the deduction from the former of unspecified charges for cost of collection, etc. Further, the accounts made up should be officially audited and scrupulously preserved. At present the majority of officials tear up their accounts upon vacating office, in order to remove the evidence of their successful peculation. Some such reforms as these, in the methods as well as in the incidence of taxation, would result in a wonderful increase of the wealth of Persia, and would absolve her from the painful necessity of appealing for the smallest outlay of capital to foreign lands.

Fresh sources of revenue, in addition to the taxes on personal and on urban property already suggested, might easily be devised. Among those that I have heard suggested by competent authorities are the sale of Crown lands, which are constantly increasing in dimensions, with no corresponding gain to the State, the imposition of stamp duties upon all receipts, bonds, promissory notes, etc., a legacy duty regulated by the degrees of relationship, and excise duties upon the manufacture of wines and spirituous liquors. A clever financier would, no doubt, detect many other equally promising sources of wealth.

New taxation

Similarly with regard to the Customs, the present method of collecting which is equally unsystematic and venal, there is urgent necessity for reform. The farming system, as a fruitful parent of evil, should be destroyed root and branch. In its place, the collection of revenue should be conducted, as it is in every civilised country, by the salaried officials of a State department. Finally, much greater simplicity would be introduced, commerce would be both encouraged and expedited, the cost of collection would be lessened, and the openings for dishonesty would be curtailed, by an assimilation of the Custom dues imposed upon foreign and native merchandise, and by the abolition of the various internal road taxes and town *octrois* that are levied upon the latter. Native merchandise can scarcely be said to be protected against the foreigner by the present system. Indeed, I incline to the opinion that the European, paying his 5 per cent. *ad valorem* once for all, is in the better position.

Customs reform

I confess that, from what I have both heard and read of the present financial development of the Persian intellect, I see no immediate prospect of these or analogous reforms being carried out. In the 'Echo de Perse' for August 15, 1885, a Teheran newspaper which I have before mentioned, there appeared an article on Persian finance, which is so remarkable as to deserve a passing extract. 'There is nothing,' observed the philosophic writer, 'more curious than the financial condition of Persia. It is a virgin forest, where trees with strong branches grow close to trees not less strong, but rotting through age.' Intoxicated by this astonishing metaphor, the writer then went on to boast of a country without a national debt, a country whose expenditure was always less than its revenue, frequently by several millions, which forthwith passed into the Royal treasury. 'Here in Persia,' he sagaciously remarked, 'we undertake only such works as can be paid for out of the excess of receipts over expenditure. This is more modest, but it is also more sure. And if we have

Persian notions of finance

remained a little behind as regards public works, at least our minds are at ease, and debts do not haunt us.' And finally came this burst of patriotic exultation: 'What other country in the world finds itself in such an exceptional position? No national debt, no paper money, none of the nation's riches encroached upon, none of its revenues mortgaged for the future. The financial stability of Persia is still virgin and inviolate, in spite of the numerous temptations that have assailed it. May it never be prostituted in time to come!' I should scarcely have been tempted to quote this glowing eulogium of the Persian virgin, had I not observed, even in the pages of European writers, an unaccountable tendency to extol her charms. I have seen the absence of a national debt in Persia, the annual excess of revenue over expenditure, and her independence of foreign loans, paraded as evidences of a sound financial position and of administrative ability. The expenditure falls below the receipts, for the simple reason that the most necessary objects of outlay are scandalously neglected, stinted, or ignored, in order that the Treasury may receive its annual surplus. There is no national debt, because the country undertakes no expense, but is content with scrambling along as best it can from year to year. No foreign loans have been applied for, partly for the same reason, partly because the conditions under which alone they could have been granted would have involved that very mortgage of some of the country's resources to the immunity from which the Persian editor pointed with such innocent pride.

Persian land tenure

A discussion of the land tax and of land assessment leads me to say a few words upon the cognate subject of land tenure in Persia, with which it is inseparably connected. Owing to the wide expanses of sand, salt, and stones, that cover so much of the territorial superficies of Persia, the extent of soil under cultivation is said to be less than one fifth of the area of the whole kingdom. On the other hand, agriculture is believed to occupy the industry of nearly two-thirds of the entire population. Landed property in Persia is of four kinds: (1) Crown lands, known as *khalisah*, or *diwani*; (2) Lands held upon feudal tenure; (3) *Vakfs*, or religious endowments; (4) Private property, or *arbabi*.

The Crown lands of Persia are very extensive, but are chiefly, in their present ownership, the creation of the civil wars of the last century. Nadir Shah, and still more Agha Mohammed Khan

Kajar after him, found the old Persian families and estates broken up by the long continuing internal strife, much as the Tudor sovereigns found the English nobility after the Wars of the Roses. Like Henry VIII., Nadir Shah embarked upon a policy of ecclesiastical confiscation on a large scale, and the resumption of religious grants by the English monarch was more than equalled by the seizure of Church property in Iran by the Afshar usurper. These estates have ever since remained the property of the Crown. They have been further swollen, and are yearly increased, by the confiscation of private property, consequent upon the disgrace or delinquency of the owner, and by the semi-compulsory gifts which are so graciously accepted by the sovereign. I have already described the terms under which they are cultivated.

1. Crown lands

The feudal lands are those which have been granted in times past, on conditions of military service, chiefly to frontier tribes, such as the Kurds of the Turkoman and Turkish borders. Their tenure is dependent upon the provision of a cavalry contingent, and of frontier outposts and guards; and is sometimes accompanied by, sometimes free from, money contribution to the revenue.

2. Feudal lands

In spite of the sacrilegious cupidity of Nadir Shah, the mosques and *madressehs*, or religious colleges, have retained large endowments both in landed property and in the rents of caravanserais, shops, and bazaars. The mosque of Imam Reza, for instance, at Meshed (which was one of the few that were favoured by Nadir) possesses villages in all parts of the country, and derives from its possessions an annual income of 60,000 *tomans*, and 10,000 *kharvars* of grain. These estates are constantly augmented by the bequests of pious devotees, anxious to make their peace with heaven, and by secret agreements with public officials, who, in order to avoid sequestration of their property, bequeath it to the Church in return for a fixed life annuity. The *vakfs* are generally free from taxation; but a tax of 1,000 *tomans* a year is levied by the Government upon the endowments of the shrine at Meshed.

3. Religious endowments

Private property in Persia can be acquired by inheritance, by purchase, by gift from the Crown, or by right of reclamation from the desert. It is within the power of anyone to take up a portion of the *sahra* or dry land, to till, cultivate, and create for it a water supply, paying from any harvest or produce

4. Private property

that he may evoke the customary percentage to the State. As long as he fulfils the latter obligation, he is too useful a citizen to be dispossessed. The Persian landlord, however, as a rule does not farm his own property. It is let to tenants, who, without either owning or claiming proprietary rights, and blissfully ignorant of the Shibboleth of the Three F's, yet enjoy practical fixity of tenure so long as they pay the Persian equivalent to their rent. This is a portion of the produce regulatéd by the contribution of both parties to the working expenses, and varying in different parts of the country. In Azerbaijan I have seen it stated that the landlord only takes one-tenth, and, if he has provided the seed beforehand, an interest of 50 per cent. on his loan. In Mazanderan he is more exacting. The harvest there is divided into five parts, which are apportioned as follows, one part to each—land, water for irrigation, seed, labour, and bullocks. The landlord generally owns one or two, and receives accordingly one-fifth or two-fifths of the harvest. Sometimes he also supplies the seed, in which case he receives three-fifths, and the husbandman the remaining two-fifths. In other parts of the country other partitions prevail. Where population is so thin as in Persia, and where cultivation can only be achieved at the expense of steady industry and toil—not indeed in labour upon the land itself so much as in digging and maintaining *kanats*, and in regulating the measured supply—it is to the interest of the landowner to be on the best of terms with his tenant; and the Persian peasant, even if he can justly complain of Government exaction, has not found any one to teach him the gospel of landlord tyranny. He is poor, illiterate, and stolid; but in appearance he is robust, in strength he is like an ox, he usually has clothes to his back, and he is seldom a beggar. With the grossest ignorance he combines a rude skill in turning to account the scanty resources of nature, and though he neither expects nor aspires to prosper, he is patient and persevering. His times of misery occur when there is a break-down of the water supply, or when, after long drought, there is a famine in the land. Unfed and uncared for, the Persian peasantry then die off like flies. The conditions of agriculture might be enormously improved were the energy of Government to support that of individuals, and were certain sums annually set apart for the proper economy and storage of water. There are many places where invaluable supplies are allowed to tear a channel for themselves down the mountain gullies in flood time, and then to perish in swamps and pools in the desert. Reservoirs for such spates might be constructed in the mountains, like that formed by the well-known dam of Shah Abbas near Kuhrud; whilst any one who desires to see what can be done by a Government in the construction of tanks on a large scale for purposes of irrigation, has but to pay a visit to the island of Ceylon.

From the Persian Budget I pass to the material and industrial resources of the country—those possessions or advantages, in fact, which are capable of being utilised as means of wealth. First among a nation's resources must be counted its people; and I turn accordingly to the question of the Persian population. There can, I think, be no doubt that Persia was once much less sparsely populated than it is at present. Even if we reject the fifty millions ascribed by some writers to the time of Darius, and the forty millions mentioned by Chardin in the Sefavean days, as fantastic and absurd, I judge that the population must in former times have greatly exceeded its present total, less from the conjectural estimates of travellers and historians than from the evidence that everywhere meets the eye. Ruined cities, abandoned villages, and deserted bazaars, long lines of choked *kanats*, public works that once assisted to fertilise large districts now mouldering to decay, wide acres of cultivation since relapsed into sand and stones, —all these tell a tale whose significance cannot be mistaken; even although we remember that every abandoned site does not necessarily mean a corresponding extinction of life or industry, the Persians, in their corporate as well as in their individual capacity, having always exhibited a strange inclination to shift their place of abode, from the sovereign, who sought to immortalise himself by founding a new capital or building a new palace, to the peasant who vacated his predecessor's hovel. That the population of Persia, therefore, was once much larger than at present I think we may regard as certain; although I am unwilling to believe, in view of the physical conditions of the country, and of the constant warfare to which it has been a prey, that it was ever dense. Chardin himself supports my hypothesis, and supplies a corrective to his own exaggerated estimate when he elsewhere says:—

Population

The country is but thinly inhabited. I speak in general, the twelfth part is not inhabited nor cultivated; and after you have passed any great towns about two leagues you will meet never a mansion house nor people in twenty leagues more. As for the cause of the want of people it is very easy to comprehend. It proceeds on the one hand from the immeasurable extent of these monarchies, and on the other from the arbitrary government that is exercised there.[1]

Chardin further attributed the dearth of people to four subsidiary causes, namely, unnatural vice, immoderate luxury, early marriages, and constant migration to the Indies. Malcolm, in the early part of the present century, estimated the population as about 6,000,000, balancing against the checks upon its growth, which were identical with those named by Chardin,[2] the following advantages, viz., 'the salubrity of the climate, the cheapness of provisions, the rare occurrence of famine,[3] the bloodless character of their civil wars, their obligation to marry, and the comparatively small number of prostitutes.' Rawlinson in 1850 estimated the population as 10,000,000; but in 1873, after two desolating visitations of cholera and famine, as 6,000,000. The figures given by other writers during the last twenty years vary between 5,000,000 and 10,000,000. Nor, indeed, is any estimate based upon data that are either scientific or reliable. No census is taken in Persia, the machinery or means for doing so in at all an adequate fashion not being in existence, and the idea being repugnant to the religious orders. Neither the assessment for taxation which I have described, nor the military conscription list, affords a basis of calculation, which must therefore be in every case more or less a matter of guesswork. The two most recent estimates that I have seen differ as widely in

[1] *Voyages* (ed. Langlès), vol. iii. pp. 270–1.

[2] Dr. J. E. Polak, who was a physician, in his Report on Persia in 1873, gave the following as the main causes of the decline of population: (1) The unfavourable position of women, including the facility of divorce, early marriage and premature age, the length of the suckling period, and the thereby impaired fertility of the sex; (2) decay of sanitary police, and consequent greater ravages by typhus, dysentery, cholera, plague, and, more particularly, owing to the inadequacy of inoculation, by small-pox—the mortality of children in the second year of their age being very striking; (3) the exterminating wars of the Tartars, Mongols, and Afghans, the raids of the Turkomans in the eastern provinces, and sale of the inhabitants in the slave markets of Khiva and Bokhara, civil wars, and the mortality among soldiers enlisted for life, but swept away in masses before properly acclimatised to the different garrison stations; (4) emigration of non-Mussulman elements, such as Guebres, Christians, and Jews, to India, the Caucasus, and Turkey; (5) oft-recurring famine, caused by dearth of rain and snow, but intensified to the highest degree by want of means of communication, prejudice against the corn trade, bad condition of water channels, and misgovernment.

[3] This cannot, I think, be said with truth. In the second half of this century famines of greater or less severity have occurred at intervals of about ten years.

their totals as do any of their predecessors. One of these was drawn up by General Schindler—than whom no man is better qualified to pronounce, from his wide acquaintance with the whole country—in 1884. It was as follows :—

GENERAL SCHINDLER'S FIGURES.

Area of Persia about 628,000 square miles.[1]

	Families		Souls
99 towns containing	363,630	or	1,963,800
Villages and districts without towns			3,780,000
Nomads :—			
Arabs	52,020		
Turks	144,000		
Kurds and Leks	135,000		
Beluchis and gipsies	4,140		
Bakhtiaris and Lurs	46,800		
	381,960		1,909,800
Total population of Persia			7,653,600

This total he again subdivided, according to creeds :—

Shiahs	6,860,600
Sunnis and other Mohammedan sects	700,000
Parsis	8,000
Jews	19,000
Armenians	43,000
Nestorians and Chaldæans	23,000
Total	7,653,600

The above figures are clearly conjectural in many respects, my own experience having convinced me that the populations of several of the towns, in General Schindler's table,[2] are as much in excess of the real totals as some of the items in the second of the above tables, e.g. the figures of Jews, Nestorians, and Chaldæans, are below. If, however, we accept his grand total as the most available approximation to the truth, and add thereto a $\frac{3}{4}$ per cent. annual increase for each of the succeeding years, which have been free both from war and famine, we shall arrive at the following, as the total of population in 1891, viz., 8,055,500.

Russian estimate

On the other hand, M. Zolotaref published a much lower estimate in the Proceedings of the Russian Geographical Society in 1888.[3] He calculated the whole population as follows :—

[1] By others reported as 610,000, 636,000, and 660,000 square miles.

[2] Quoted in *Commercial Reports of the F.O.*, No. 7, 1885.

[3] No. ii. p. 120.

Persians	3,000,000	Arabs	300,000
Turks and Tartars .	1,000,000	Turkomans, Jamshidis, etc.	320,000
Lurs	780,000		
Kurds	600,000	Total . . .	6,000,000

These figures differ so widely from General Schindler's, both in total and in composition, as to give some idea of the precarious character of the data upon which any computation reposes. My own impression, which I hazard diffidently, not having visited some of the most populous quarters of the country, is that General Schindler's estimate errs modestly, and M. Zolotaref's ludicrously, on the side of depreciation. The recognised highways, which are traversed by the ordinary traveller, connect the principal cities, but they do not lead through the most fertile districts; and, owing to the terror inspired by the passage of armies, and even by the pacific progress of the monarch, or of provincial governors going to and from their posts, have repelled rather than attracted population.[1] In civilised countries the reverse is the case, and the main thoroughfares lead through the most populous districts. Herein we have one more witness to the backwardness of Persia. On the other hand, I have seen the reports and itineraries of many private travellers in out-of-the-way parts of the country, where strangers do not journey, where officials are rarely seen, and where the tax-collector seldom penetrates; and from the concurrent testimony which they afford to numbers of smiling villages, succeeding each other at the distance of a few miles over spaces marked by a blank in the maps, I am led to the opinion that estimates formed from journeys through the better-known parts of the country are likely to underrate rather than to exaggerate the totals. I should be disposed, therefore, myself to set down the present population of Persia as at least 9,000,000. When we remember that Persia is three times as large as France, while the above estimate leaves her nearly five times less populous, we can form some idea both of the gap that separates her in external appearance from a European country, as well as of the scope that exists for material and physical regeneration.[2]

From the population of Persia I turn to her indigenous products

[1] For an analogous condition of affairs, as the result of insecurity, compare Judges v. 6, 'In the days of Shamgar the son of Anath, in the days of Jael, the highways were unoccupied, and the travellers walked through byways.'

[2] Touching the ethnology of the Persians, I will refer my readers to Elisée Reclus, *Universal Geography*, vol. ix. pp. 107–8.

and manufactures.[1] She is a country rich in undeveloped resources. Possessing every variety of climate, from the extremes of tropical heat to the perpetual snow line, and every quality of soil, her vegetable productions are almost as numerous and diversified as are the mineral treasures that lie concealed beneath her surface. A scanty and diminishing rainfall, the desolation arising from frequent invasions in the past, ignorant agriculture, and gross maladministration, have impaired or reduced her capacities in the former respect just as effectively as the dearth of communications, the difficulty of transport, and the want of enterprise have impeded the development of the latter. In the one case, verdant plains have relapsed into stony wildernesses; in the other, no attempt has been made to profit by a natural endowment. Nevertheless, putting on one side her mineral resources, with which I shall deal separately, and at rather greater length, Persia at this hour can present a catalogue of products and manufactures remarkable, if not for its total bulk, at least for its ample variety of detail.

Products and manufactures

Grain, mainly wheat and barley (the latter of which, in the absence of oats, is commonly used as fodder for horses), is grown throughout the country, but in greatest plenty in the provinces or districts of Azerbaijan, Kermanshah, Luristan, Arabistan, Fars, Khorasan, Kerman, Yezd, and Isfahan. The Russians bought almost the whole of their grain for the Turkoman campaign of 1880–1 in Khorasan, the price rising so enormously in consequence, that there were very nearly bread riots in several of the towns; while the confidential reports of Russian military and diplomatic advisers invariably recommend the annexation of that province on the ground that, in the event of a movement upon India, its cereal wealth would be needed to supplement the scanty produce of Transcaspia. The implements of tillage are primitive in the extreme. A rude wooden plough-

Cereals

[1] For information on these points, I recommend: Sir J. Malcolm (1810), *History of Persia*, vol. ii. cap. xxii.; Dr. O. Blau (1858), *Commercielle Zustände Persiens*; Dr. H. Brugsch (1860–1), *Reise der K. Preuss. Gesandtschaft nach Persien*, 2 vols.; J. E. Polak (1865), *Persien, das Land und seine Bewohner*, 2 vols. (Leipzig); J. E. Polak (1873), *Persien* (Vienna); J. E. Polak (1883), *Notice sur la Perse au point de vue commercial*; F. Stolze and F. C. Andreas (1874–81), *Die Handelsverhältnisse Persiens* ('Petermann's Mittheilungen,' 1885); Sir R. Murdoch-Smith (1876), *Handbook on Persian Art*; S. G. W. Benjamin (1883–85), *Persia and the Persians*, cap. xiv.; A. Herbert (1886), *Commercial Report of the F.O.*, No. 18, 1886.

share, drawn by an ox or oxen, sometimes only by a donkey, has but to scratch the surface, on which the seed, lightly thrown, produces an abundant and unsolicited harvest. In spite of the thousands of acres of agricultural land lying idle, particularly in the western and south-western districts, the growth of wheat is already in excess of the needs of the home population, and grain is exported in some quantity to Turkey, the Caucasus, India (from Bunder Abbas) and even to England (from Bushire). Oats, as I have said, and rye are not grown; there is not much maize; but millet is produced in parts. Rice is largely cultivated in the low-lying and saturated strip of the Caspian littoral, whence it is exported to the Caucasus and to northern Russia, *viâ* Astrakhan.[1] A better quality is grown in a few places in the interior, where enough water can be spared for the necessary swamp, particularly in the neighbourhoods of Shiraz and Isfahan. The bulk, however, of Persian rice is locally consumed, the boiled grain constituting, next to wheat, the staple diet of the peasantry, and being a universal feature in every meal, whether of the high or low.

In olden times Persia was famous as a sugar-producing country, and the plantations of Ahwaz and the Karun basin enjoyed a wide renown. The sugar-cane is now sparsely cultivated in Gilan and Mazanderan, and also in the province of Yezd, where a coarse and ill-refined sugar is made for local consumption. The processes employed are very primitive and backward, and the area of cultivation appears to be diminishing rather than increasing. Beetroot, however, is very abundant, especially in Khorasan, and, in any other country than Persia, would long ago have been utilised to reduce the tremendous annual import of the French and Russian article. Formerly sugar used to be imported from India, Java, and Mauritius; but Marseilles and Astrakhan are now the chief ports of supply.

Sugar

Cotton grows with facility in Persia to an elevation of 5,000 feet above the sea. Over 100,000 bales leave the country annually, the greater part for the mills of Bombay,[2] some for those of

[1] The export of rice from Mazanderan and Gilan to Russia was given to me as 3,600,000 *pouds*, or 58,064 tons per annum; value from 1,000,000 to 1,100,000 *tomans*, or £285,700 to £314,000. For rice and sugar in Persia, *vide* a paper by A. H. Schindler in the *United States Consular Reports*, 1888.

[2] The Bombay Trade Returns show that the export to India began in the year 1884; the subsequent figures being 1884, 20,000 bales (3½ cwt. each); 1885, 23,000; 1886, 15,000; 1887, 15,000; 1888, 17,000; 1889, first six months, 17,000.

Moscow, the remainder being spun in the hand-looms of Yezd and Kerman. Persian cotton is, however, very short in the staple.

Cotton

Mazanderan, Khorasan, Semnan, Kum, Kashan, Isfahan, and the districts of Azerbaijan lying around Khoi and Urumiah, are the chief centres of cultivation; but I constantly came upon patches so planted in my rides through the country. The industry first received a forward impetus at the time of the American Civil War, when Persian cotton began to be seen in foreign markets; but it has never been properly developed, and is capable of much greater expansion. Jute is indigenous in Mazanderan, and is used for making sacks; but the amount raised is insufficient for the needs of the country, and there is a steady annual import by the Persian Gulf.

Silk

Of the silk industry, which first brought Persia within the ken of modern Europe, which was formerly so rich, but for long after the appearance of disease in 1864 remained on the downward incline, I have spoken at length in an earlier chapter on the Northern Provinces. Latterly, however, there has been a revival; and the figures for 1889, though furnishing a melancholy contrast to the brave totals before cited for bygone years, were given to me as follows:—

TOTAL PRODUCTION.

	Tabriz *mans*
Gilan and Resht	30,000
Mazanderan	15,000
Khorasan, Sebzewar, and Turbat	20,000
	65,000 *mans*, or 422,500 lbs.

In 1890 I hear that the value of exported silk waste alone exceeded 30,000*l*.

The bulk of the Khorasan crop is sent to Yezd, Kashan, and Isfahan—the Persian centres of the manufacturing trade—in whose looms about 15,000 *mans* are annually employed. Of the Mazanderan and Gilan crops, some 10,000 *mans* are either exported to Baghdad or are consumed at Kashan and Isfahan. The total remainder, i.e. 40,000 *mans*, are exported to Europe, the greater quantity to Marseilles, *viâ* Russia, a small quantity being shipped by Bombay.

The tobacco of Persia is known in every town and village in the western half of the Asiatic continent; and greatly to be commiserated is the European traveller or resident who, when either passing through or sojourning in that land, is guilty of indifference to the exquisite solace of the Persian water-pipe, or *kalian*.

Tobacco

Though I am no smoker, and derive little pleasure from the European modes of enjoying the weed, yet I never failed to succumb to the subtle influence of the Shiraz *tumbaku*, a few perfumed inhalations of which are sufficient to fill the remotest cells of the brain with an Olympian contentment. This superb tobacco, whose agreeable qualities are in part due to the quantity of nicotine which it contains, in part to the manner in which it is prepared, being soaked, squeezed dry, and then placed at the top of the pipe under lighted charcoal, whence its fumes are drawn through water to the smoker's lips, is grown chiefly in the districts of Shiraz, Kashan, and Tabbas, slightly inferior qualities being produced at Isfahan, Kum, Nihavend, Veramin, Semnan and Shahrud. On the ground it is purchased according to its quality at from 1–3 *krans* per *batman* (6½ lbs.), a price which, owing to the action of middlemen, is swollen by the time it reaches the city bazaars to 3–12 *krans*. The amount annually consumed in Persia alone has been estimated by M. Kitabji, Director-General of Persian Customs, as 18,000,000 *batmans*, or 52,230 tons.[1] Scarcely less popular is the Persian leaf in the neighbouring countries of the East, and an export, estimated at 1,500,000 *batmans*, or 4,350 tons, is conducted to Baghdad, Beirut, Cairo, Arabia, India, and Afghanistan. A second and different variety of tobacco, similar to that produced in Turkey, and used for smoking in pipes and cigarettes, is grown in Kurdistan, near Urumiah, and on the Caspian littoral, and, if developed, might prove a formidable rival to the Ottoman product. I have elsewhere mentioned that in the autumn of 1890 a concession was granted by the Shah for a tobacco régie in Persia, i.e. a complete monopoly of the purchase, sale, and manufacture of native-grown tobacco for a period of fifty years, and that a company entitled the Imperial Tobacco Corporation of Persia, with a capital of 650,000*l.*, was formed to work

[1] I cannot help regarding this as a most unscientific calculation; for it is simply based on the hypothesis that, given 10,000,000 as the total population of Persia (in my judgment an exaggerated estimate), one person in every five, without regard to sex or age, smokes 9 *batmans*, or 58½ lbs. per annum. The figures supplied to me represent the total production as only one half. For an account of the methods adopted in growth and preparation, *vide* a paper in the *Kew Bulletin*, April 1891.

this concession. In January 1892, however, the Shah revoked the entire concession, in consequence of popular outbreaks, arising from the hostility entertained by all classes in Persia to so inquisitorial an interference with the habits and practices of their daily life; an hostility which was skilfully inflamed by the *mullahs* to the verge of open rebellion. Statesmen will be as slow in future to touch the Tobacco Question in Persia, as they now are to touch the Temperance Question in England.

I now come to that which has for many years been a main, and will probably be an increasing, source of revenue to the Persian exchequer, namely, the growth and export of opium. From very remote times the poppy has been cultivated at Yezd for the native market, its use being recommended in the Persian pharmacopœia, and old people being in the habit of consuming its juice regularly. It was in 1853, however, that I find the first record of opium having been made an article of export from the district of Isfahan; though it was not till after the collapse of the silk trade in 1864–5 that the poppy was at all widely cultivated. At first the new industry was discouraged by the Government, whose financial acumen was not equal to detecting therein the possibilities of a large addition to the revenue, but who only saw that its development involved the diminution of the acreage under corn cultivation, and a consequent increase in the bazaar-price of grain and bread—a consummation usually attended by riots against the local governor, and general discontentment with the powers that be. Later on the trade was threatened by the short-sighted dishonesty of the native merchants, who adulterated the exported article to such an extent as seriously to jeopardise the fortunes of the nascent industry; and in 1882–3 a collapse was temporarily feared. Fortunately the Government exercised a resolute and wise interference; and under strict supervision the trade revived, and has now reached very large dimensions. Its growth may be judged from the following figures of the export from the two Gulf harbours of Bushire and Bunder Abbas, which are the main ports of exit—

Opium

1871–2 . . .	870 chests,	valued at	696,000 rupees		
1876–7 . . .	2,570	„	„	2,313,000	„
1880–1 . . .	7,700	„	„	8,470,000	„
1889–90 . . .	5,190	„	„	4,950,000	„

The chief areas of growth are Isfahan, Shiraz, Niriz, Khonsar,

Kerman, Yezd, Khorasan,[1] Kazerun, Shushter (the export from which, of very limited amount, goes, *viâ* Mohammerah, to Zanzibar), Burujird, Hamadan, and Kermanshah. The crops near Teheran and in Azerbaijan and Kurdistan are exported to Europe *viâ* Turkey. In the neighbourhood of Isfahan in particular, the poppy growth has now superseded all other industries: the yearly crop has been calculated as 250 tons,[2] and the export consists of 2,500 cases. A leading Isfahan merchant has estimated the total present export as 8,000 chests, with a value of 720,000*l.*—i.e. at the rate of 90*l.* a chest. In the returns, however, of the Gulf ports, I find the average value of a chest calculated at about 70*l.*; and this estimate corresponds with the figures of the total export from Persia for the year 1889, which I shall print later, and which were given to me as approximately 1,900,000 *tomans*, or 543,000*l.* In the infancy of the trade, the drug used to be sent to Java, whence it was reshipped to Hongkong and Singapore, next it went to Aden, and afterwards to Suez for transhipment. The purest quality is now despatched to London, for the extraction of morphine, and is in part re-exported to America. Three-fourths, however, of the total export, to some extent adulterated with sugar, starch, and grape-syrup, go to China *viâ* Hongkong. Persian opium has for some time driven the Turkish article out of the Chinese market, and is rapidly becoming a competitor with the Indian produce.

The process of cultivation, extraction, and despatch is as follows. The plant is sown in November, and sprouts early in the following spring, when it rears a stalk from three to four feet high, and blossoms. Later on the flower is succeeded by a poppy head; and now, at the beginning of June, the population turn out, tap the heads by a scratch or incision, collect the juice that exudes, and convey it in copper vessels to market. When it has dried it is made up into cakes weighing three-quarters to one and a half pound each, and wrapped in vine or fig leaves. These to the number of 192–196 are then packed into chests or cases for export, in order that, allowing for waste, evaporation, etc., the weight of each case on arrival in China may be one *picul* or 135 lbs. The opium of good quality, possessing 80 per cent. of

Processes employed

[1] The production of Khorasan in 1889 was valued at 180,000 *tomans*, or £51,430, of which over £37,000 was exported to China *viâ* India, and the rest to Constantinople.

[2] The tables which I give presently make it only 150 tons.

juice, will contain 9–10 per cent. of morphine. That exported to London or America contains up to 12 per cent.

Among the remaining vegetable products of Persia, attention must be drawn to the medicinal and colouring plants, of which there is a quite exceptional variety, the timber, and the flowers and fruits. Gum-tragacanth, the exudation of the *astragalus*, a low thorn bush, is collected in the hilly country from Kerman to Kermanshah, and is exported, the best qualities to London, the inferior to Russia. Gum-arabic is extracted from the *konar* tree in the south near Shiraz. Gum-ammoniac, galbanum, and sagapenum are produced in the neighbourhoods of Isfahan, Shiraz, Laristan, and Khorasan. Opoponax, sarcocolla, colocynth, and scammony are also known. The valuable, but odoriferous, gum known as asafœtida is extracted from a desert plant that grows near Birjand and Tabbas in Khorasan, and in many parts of Persian Beluchistan. The dried leaves and stem of this plant are also used in the form of a decoction for various ailments, and in solid shape as a medicinal condiment. Old men affect it as an aphrodisiac. The shrub is low and stunted, being seldom above 8 in. or 1 ft. high, with leaves like the Indian beetroot and a head like a cauliflower; but its root, from which the gum is extracted, is often as thick as a man's leg. The stem is sliced, sometimes as often as fourteen times in the year, and the juice is collected during the eight months from spring to autumn, until the root is exhausted, each plant being expected to yield 1 lb. weight. Anyone who has ever been near to asafœtida in the bazaars or on the wharves, is not likely to forget the overpowering sensation. The Persians themselves do not appear to understand or to take advantage of the medicinal properties of the gum, but it constitutes a remunerative export. Liquorice also grows wild everywhere.

Medicinal plants

The number of plants providing popular or serviceable dyes is also considerable. Indigo is grown in the south-west, near Shushter and Dizful, and in Laristan, and is used in the dyeing of cotton, and also (mixed with henna) in the colouring of beards. The latter plant, consisting of the pulverised leaf of the *Lawsonia inermis*, is cultivated near Yezd and Kerman, and is said to contain five or six times more dye stuff than any other specimen. A decoction therefrom is in wide use throughout the East for the beautifying of the beard, hair, and nails; and I entertain to this hour admiring recollections of the superb scarlet beard of Mirza

Colouring plants

Abbas Khan, formerly British Agent at Meshed. Nor has the memory of the Shah's red-tailed chargers, paraded during his first visit to England in 1873, yet faded from the public mind. Madder-roots, saffron from Yezd and Bujnurd, and gall nuts from the oak of Kurdistan, must be included among the valuable products, although the lamentable introduction of aniline dyes has diminished alike the growth of and the demand for native colouring materials.

In cataloguing the vegetable products of Iran, I must not omit the curious substance known as *gez*, and popularly identified with the manna of Holy Writ, which, although alleged to be the deposit of an insect, is yet found upon the branches and leaves of trees, particularly of the *gez* or tamarisk, flourishing chiefly in the neighbourhood of Isfahan. Chardin was evidently somewhat dubious as to the origin and character of this production, of which he spoke as follows:—

Gez, or Manna

> The leaves of this tree about Isfahan do in summer drop this liquid Manna, which they pretend is not Dew but the Sweat of the Tree congealed upon the Leaf. In the morning you may see the ground that lies under it perfectly flat and greasy with it.

As a matter of fact, *gez* is a white, glutinous substance, not unlike honey, and is said to be deposited in flakes on the leaves of the tamarisk bush by a small, pale-green insect.[1] It is gathered in the early morning by the natives, who go out with broad earthenware vessels or baskets, and shake the boughs over them. Carefully scraped off the leaves, it takes the form of a white paste. It is more commonly, however, made into a sweetmeat called *gezangebin*, with the addition of almonds and pistachios, being sometimes boiled along with the leaves, and allowed to harden into a species of greenish cake. I frequently tasted it, and, although clogging to the palate, found it decidedly agreeable, resembling a superior and less sticky form of *nougat*.

In the interior of the country the descriptions of my journeys will have acquainted my readers with the fact that, with the exception of an occasional straggling row of Lombardy poplars, and, in ancient towns or places of resort, of venerable *chenars* or planes, but little timber is to be seen. The patches

Timber

[1] This is denied by some authorities, who maintain that the substance is not an animal but a vegetable secretion, and that it exudes from the plant. *A priori* this is more probable. It is found not only on the tamarisk, but also in different places on the *bid* (willow), *khar* (thorn), and *belut* (oak).

or clumps of green that occasionally meet and entrance the eye, are almost without exception orchards. Konar trees in Arabistan, cypresses at Shiraz, groves of dwarf oak in the mountains of the south and west, corresponding with the juniper of the Khorasan ranges, walnut and mulberry trees, are almost the only other timber encountered in a journey of perhaps a thousand miles. On the other hand, in less frequented parts, which the traveller probably misses altogether, there is a growth as astonishing as the more ubiquitous dearth. The rich, humid valleys of the Caspian belt, and the lower slopes of the Elburz range rising therefrom, produce timbers of great variety and value, some of which are well adapted for ship-building. Here the ill-starred Englishman, John Elton, made his abortive attempt at a Persian navy in the service of Nadir Shah. Boxwood has existed in abundance in this region, and has been exported in some quantity to Astrakhan for Rostov on the Don, and even to Liverpool. But no system or science of forestry exists, and owing to the absence of regulation the supply has been well nigh extirpated. Among the other trees that are here met with are the oak, ash, beech, elm, alder, cherry, and thorn—all, or nearly all belonging to the deciduous class.

Flowers and gardens

A Persian garden bears no resemblance to its European namesake. There are no trim parterres, no close-shaven sward, no pattern or arrangement, no comely borders. The flower beds in the inner courts of the houses are promiscuously filled with blossoming plants, and the larger gardens are tangled wildernesses intersected with irrigation ditches. But for what they lack in method they atone in luxuriance, and their beauty in the flowering of the spring cannot be too greatly extolled. The perfumed blossoms of Iran have been sung in many an ode and stanza; and who has not read of the roses of Gulistan (literally, Rose-garden), and of the gardens and nightingales of Shiraz? Wild flowers are even more riotous in their abundance, and in springtime the drab and desolate plains of winter burst into a transient glory of colour and fragrance. From the far-famed Persian roses is extracted the rose-water that is celebrated throughout the East.

The fruits of Europe and of Asia meet and fraternise upon Persian soil. In the natural hot-bed of the Caspian belt, many of the former, as vines, plums, hops, raspberries, apples, and pears, grow wild, but are valueless in this state. The least cultivation will produce melons (reported to be the finest in the world, two of which are sometimes a load for a single beast of burden), nectarines, peaches, apricots (of which when dried there is a large export to the Caucasus and to Russia), oranges, pomegranates, cherries, tamarinds, mulberries, magnificent quinces, figs, pistachios, almonds. Dates are grown to a considerable extent upon the shores of the Persian Gulf, and are the source of an important trade both to the East and West, although the size and productiveness of the Persian date groves do not equal those of Busrah in the delta of the Tigris. In the neighbourhood of Rudbar, on the road between Resht and Teheran, and on the confines of the province of Gilan, there is an isolated, but plentiful cultivation of the olive. This industry supports the people of forty-three villages, owning from 80,000 to 100,000 trees, whose yield is on an average 6–9 lbs. of olives per tree per annum or, roughly, a gross annual produce of 750,000 lbs. Every olive tree is subject to a government tax of about 1½*d*. The process of extracting the oil is so clumsy and laborious that a great deal is wasted, and the residue has hitherto been used chiefly for the manufacture of a coarse soap. The olives are gathered in the late autumn, and are at once stored in a kind of large bin, where they are left to ferment till the early spring, when they are spread out to dry on the flat housetops. When perfectly dried, they are again packed till they ferment, and, after this second fermentation, they are trodden by men somewhat after the fashion in which grapes are trodden in the winepress. They are then boiled, and crushed in a sort of press between flat stones, beneath which is a receptacle for the oil. The ultimate refuse is used as manure. The value of the oil after a good harvest is 2 *krans* (1*s*. 2*d*.) per bottle of 2 lbs. at Resht or Teheran; after a bad harvest it rises sometimes to 5 *krans*, or 3*s*. In May 1889, a monopoly for the purchase and working of all the olives of northern Persia was granted by the Shah to two Russian merchants of Baku, and it is understood that they are about to introduce the best European methods of pressing and refining the oil.

Fruits

Next I come to the fruit of the vine, which in various forms, and usually the least innocuous, has played a large part in the life and trade of the Persians of all ages. As an article of present commerce, grapes are chiefly sold in a dry state, the Persian *kishmish* or raisins finding a large sale in Russia and

The vine

Turkey. In regard to this branch of export, there was an irreconcilable difference in the figures of my different returns. From one source I learnt that 200,000 cases go annually to Russia from the north, with an average value of over 140,000*l.*; on the other hand, I find the total stated in the exports of 1888–9 as equivalent to 45,000*l.*, a discrepancy which I cannot explain. From the south the fresh grapes of Shiraz are sometimes packed in cotton-wool and sent to India. Throughout the country this fruit is very abundant, and is met with in many varieties. In most native bazaars I found that good grapes could be purchased for prices varying from a fraction of a farthing to 1*d.* per lb.

Persian wine and wine-bibbers

It is, however, in its manufactured state that I desire more especially to speak of the fruit of the Persian vine, which from time immemorial has contributed to the merriment of a naturally hilarious people. Over 2,000 years ago we have the testimony of the excellent Herodotus that the Persians were much addicted to the consumption of wine,[1] fortified by the delicious story that they were accustomed to deliberate, first drunk and afterwards sober; whilst, if by accident the initial process was reversed, they made amends by reopening the discussion in the proper phase of intoxication. In modern times we can cite the witness of a number of credible authorities as to both the potency and the popularity of the native beverage. Thus spoke the incomparable Herbert:—

> Now concerning the Natives, the zone they live in makes them tawny; the wine cheerful; opium salacious. The Women paint; the Men love arms; all affect Poetry; what the Grape inflames, the Law allays, and example bridles. . . . At meals they are the merriest men alive. No people in the world have better stomachs, drink more freely, or more affect voracity; yet they are harmlessly merry, a mixture of meat and mirth excellently becoming them.

Tavernier wrote:—

> They say that the wine of Isfahan is cold upon the stomach, but that it fumes into the head. For its coldness upon the stomach I can say little; but I know it will warm the head if a man takes too much of it.

The history of the later Sefavi sovereigns, as related by Tavernier, Chardin, Olearius, Le Brun, and other contemporary travellers, is little else than the record of mingled debauchery and

[1] Lib. i., cap. 133: οἴνῳ δὲ κάρτα προσκέαται.

intoxication, the king being habitually drunk, and insisting on making his guests and courtiers share his orgies. Chardin, who reported that Persian wine was made in his day in Georgia, Armenia, Media, Hyrcania, Shiraz, and Yezd, remarked :—

Wine and intoxicating Liquors are forbidden the Mohammedans ; yet there is scarce any one that does not drink of some sort of strong liquor. The Courtiers, Gentlemen, and Rakes drink wine ; and as they all use it as a remedy against sorrow, and that one Part drink it to put them to sleep, and the other to warm and make them merry ; they generally drink the strongest and most heady, and if it does not make them presently drunk, they say : What wine is this ? It does not cause mirth.

The last-named idiosyncrasy remains a characteristic of the Persian to this day. He is not a tippler, but a toper ; not a drinker, but a drunkard. He sees no virtue in the mean, and no degradation in excess. That if a man drinks at all, he may as well get drunk, is his argument, the sole pleasure in drinking consisting in intoxication. There is an old Persian saying that There is as much sin in a glass as in a flagon ; and certainly such Persians as I met, who were content to be regarded as transgressors in this respect, profited by the agreeable latitude of this convivial canon.

Persia possesses at present several vintages of good, and one or two of very superior, repute. The three principal zones of the vine are : Azerbaijan in the north-west, Shiraz in the south, and Khorasan in the north-east ; and the chief centres of manufacture are : Shiraz, Isfahan, Kazvin, Hamadan, Kerman, and Yezd.[1] I also tasted local vintages at Kuchan, Meshed, Shahrud, and Teheran. The wine of Shiraz has by far the greatest foreign as well as native celebrity, being of the quality of an old sherry, and, particularly after being kept for a few years, constitutes an excellent beverage.[2] Its price is ridiculously cheap. In ordinary seasons it costs about 4*d.* a bottle, and is sold in the country at 8*d.* to 10*d.* a bottle within the year. The wine of Hamadan resembles a hock, and costs only 2*d.* a bottle to produce, although, owing to the expense of transport and middlemen, it is

Present manufacture

[1] Gmélin, in 1771 (*Histoire des Découvertes*, vol. ii., pp. 44–8), spoke of wine as being manufactured in Gilan and Mazanderan from the wild grape.

[2] For the method of manufacture, *vide* Wills, *In the Land of the Lion and the Sun*, cap. xxi. Tavernier, in 1666, gave the annual manufacture of Shiraz wine as 200,025 *mans*, or 4,125 tuns of 300 pints each.

sold for ten times that amount in Teheran. Isfahan manufactures two moderate varieties, a white wine with a Muscat flavour, and a strong red wine of the nature of port. The Yezd wine is said to be of very delicate flavour, the Kerman wine to be strong and rough. Teheran produces a nasty wine, somewhat resembling Burgundy; but the entire vintage is fortunately absorbed in local consumption. The Persians themselves are prohibited by the law from making either wine or spirits, although the right of private manufacture appears to be conceded to a few great families. The industry is almost entirely in the hands of Europeans, Armenians, Parsis, and Jews; but the appliances employed are of the rudest description, and adulteration is resorted to on a very large scale. The export of Persian wine is at present very trifling; but, looking to the facilities and cheapness of manufacture, as well as to the neighbourhood of suitable markets, the industry appears to be one that is both capable of extension and deserving of encouragement, even if we do not contemplate ever sitting down over a London table-cloth to the discussion of 'the yellow weeping of the Shiraz vine.' The Shah seems to be of the same opinion, though perhaps for more selfish reasons, having granted a concession to some Europeans for the sole manufacture of wines and alcohols throughout the Persian dominions in 1889, from which he was to receive an annual revenue of 7,000*l.*, and which has since been brought out by a company at Brussels entitled Société Générale du Commerce et Industrie de la Perse.

Spirituous liquors

Although the Persians are sternly interdicted by the Koran from the consumption of alcoholic liquors, yet in pursuit of their maxim that if drink is indulged in at all, it had better be hard drink, they consume large quantities of abominable spirits, which, indeed, they prefer in the 'neat' state to the choicest of wines. It is a mistake ever to hand to a Persian a brandy flask, at least if you expect to see any portion of its contents again. *Raki*, or arrack, a spirituous product of the grape with aromatic flavouring, is very popular; but the estimate of the annual consumption of wines and arrack in Persia as 8,000,000 gallons, and of the duties on wine and spirits brought into Teheran as 25,000*l.* per annum, which was given in the prospectus of the Concession, was purely chimerical. Another favourite intoxicant is *bang*, a preparation from hempseed, which is used both for smoking and drinking. Although I do not desire to advocate the extended production of these odious concoctions, yet I imagine that the manufacture of such spirituous liquors as are consumed in neighbouring countries, particularly Russia, and in the last resort of spirits of wine, might also become a profitable item of commerce.

In the animal world and in animal products, Persia can boast, if not of many, at least of exceptional, sources of wealth. The native breed of horses is widely known throughout the East. Three types are, indeed, obtainable in different parts of the country: the Turkoman, famed for its powers of endurance, although not perhaps for its symmetry, in the north; the Arab, originally imported and constantly recruited from the opposite coast of the Gulf, in the south; and the Persian, which is originally a cross between other strains. The Persian horse is thicker and sturdier than the Turkoman, and makes an excellent cavalry horse or rough hack. At certain seasons of the year few steamers sail from Busrah to Bombay without conveying large equine cargoes, which, having cost sums varying from 8*l.* to 20*l.* apiece in the country, realise a very considerable profit in the Indian market. In Persia itself the animal most frequently encountered is that denominated the *yabu*, a very serviceable beast, which can be procured for insignificant prices. The Persians, who, from the days of Herodotus downwards, have been born riders, take great pride in their horses, which they tend with the utmost care, and diligently swathe in felt wrappings at night.[1]

Animals: Horses

Better known even than the horses, are the mules of Persia. These excellent animals, although of no great size, being far inferior in this respect to the Spanish type, are possessed of extraordinary strength and endurance. Burdened with a load of from 250 to 350 lbs., or with an average of 3 cwt., they will march at the rate of three and a half to four miles an hour for distances of twenty-five to thirty miles in the day, for days, and almost for weeks at a time. The chief breeding zones are the districts of Isfahan, Shiraz, and Kazerun in the centre and south, the Bakhtiari country lying between Isfahan and Shushter, and the mountainous tract to the north of Shushter and Dizful. Scarcely a year passes in which officers of the Indian Army are not despatched to Persia with a commission to purchase several

Mules

[1] On the subject of Persian horses, *vide* C. J. Wills, *In the Land of the Lion and the Sun*, pp. 104–6; *Persia as it is*, cap. xxix.

hundred mules, the average price of which is from 12*l.* to 20*l.* in the native market, although, if it be true, as I have heard, that each animal so purchased costs the Indian Government 50*l.* by the time that it is delivered at Lahore, I can scarcely describe the process as an economical one, and cannot help wondering why rearing establishments are not instituted on a larger scale in India itself. In the Bakhtiari country the breeding of mules is an object of great care and solicitude. Donkey stallions and mares are kept for this exclusive purpose, the former being neither used as beasts of burden nor allowed to mix with their own species.

Camels

Of the powerful one-humped camel of Khorasan, I have spoken in my chapter on that province. He will not travel so quickly or so far as a horse or a mule, but he will carry double the burden, viz., 600 lbs., and proceed at the rate of twenty miles a day. The ordinary and inferior camel, which constitutes the bulk of most caravans, will carry 400 lbs. and march fifteen miles per diem.

Fisheries

The southern shores of the Caspian and the rivers there flowing into the sea are richly stocked with fish, principally sturgeon and sterlet, the export of which, both in dried state and in caviar, is in the hands of a Russian, who pays a very large annual price for the monopoly, and is said to make a handsome profit from his speculation. Polak, some years ago, estimated the annual production of caviar in the Caspian fisheries as 687 tons, at the rate of 1,000 fish to a ton.

Hides

Skins and hides are exported in large quantities to Baghdad and Russia from Khorasan, Isfahan, Shiraz, and Hamadan. At Shiraz is produced a native equivalent to the curled Bokharan lambskin of Kara Kul, near the Oxus, denominated in Europe Astrakhan. The quality is not so fine as the Central Asian skin, but it is very extensively used in the manufacture of the Persian *kolah*, or conical headdress. Hamadan is the scene of the principal tanneries and leather factories of Persia, and there the material known in Europe as Russian leather is said to have been originally prepared.

Wool

An increasing amount of sheeps' wool and of goats' hair is now being exported from Persia. The chief areas of production are Khorasan, Fars and Laristan, Azerbaijan, Kermanshah and Kurdistan. Of these the Khorasan flocks, especially those of Turbat-i-Haideri, and of the nomad tribes on the Perso-Afghan border, give the best wool. Sebzewar is the local centre of this trade, which is in the hands of Armenians, and which amounts to an annual export of 10,000 to 12,000 bales of 190 lbs. each.[1] A good deal of this wool now comes, *viâ* Russia, to England. It is very thick and long, but as exported is coarse and uncleaned. The best goats' hair is that produced by a species of Angora, in the neighbourhood of Birjand. It is used for the manufacture of shawls, and is also exported, *viâ* the Gulf and Bombay, to England. The total annual wool-crop of Persia was given to me as 1,750,000 Tabriz *mans* or *batmans*, i.e. 5,078 tons.

Mineral resources

In passing to the mineral resources of Persia, I am approaching a subject upon which has hitherto been expended a good deal both of loose statement and of vague conjecture, but an authoritative opinion as to which is only now for the first time coming within the range of possibility.[2] In the early years of the century Malcolm flew to one extreme when he wrote: 'Persia does not abound in valuable minerals; iron and lead however, are found in many parts'; a verdict the depreciatory character of which is falsified even by the pages of Chardin 150 years before. Half a century later, Polak, at the other extreme, writes: 'Scarcely any country of the earth can vie with Persia as to riches in metals, especially copper. Its unbounded wealth in coal, iron, and copper deposits only awaits exploration in order to set on foot a mighty industry.' It is between these two extremes that the historian of to-day will be disposed to seek, and will find, the truth.

History

Traces of mining operations have been discovered in many parts of Persia, that can only be referred to a period anterior to the Arab conquest, even if we hesitate to what preceding epoch to assign them. In post-mediæval times, it was to Shah Abbas the Great that Persia owed the first serious attempt to

[1] *Vide* Miscellaneous Series of F. O. Reports, No. 114, 1888; and Annual Series, No. 96, 1892.

[2] The bibliography of Persian mineralogy is as small as the subject itself is large. I can only mention: G. Melgunoff, *Das südliche Ufer des Kaspischen Meeres*, 1868; J. E. Polak (1865), *Persien, das Land und seine Bewohner*, vol. ii. pp. 174–8; A. Herbert, *Commercial Reports of the F. O.*, No. 18, 1886; Dr. E. Tietze, 'On the Soil and Geological Constitution of Persia,' *Mittheil. der k. und k. Geograph. Gesellschaft in Wien*, 1886, pp. 515–23, 561–75; Dr. E. Tietze, 'Mineralreichthümer Persiens,' *Year Book of Imp. Geological Institute*, Vienna, 1889; A. H. Schindler, 'Neue Angaben über d. Mineralreichthümer Persiens,' *Year Book*, Vienna, 1881; 'Aus d. Nordwestlichen Persien,' *ibid*, 1882; 'Die Gegend zwischen Sabzvar und Mesched,' *ibid*, 1886.

utilise her mineral wealth, his attention, according to Chardin, having been drawn to the presence of valuable metals beneath the soil by the abundant outflow of mineral waters. Chardin spoke of iron, steel, brass (i.e. copper), and lead, as the minerals most worked, and specified silver mines at Kervan in the Shah Kuh, four leagues from Isfahan, near Kerman, and in Mazanderan; iron mines in Hyrcania (i.e. Mazanderan), South Media (i.e. Kurdistan), Parthia and Bactria; copper mines at Sari, in Bactria, and near Kazvin; lead mines near Kerman and Yezd, the latter containing a large proportion of silver; naphtha springs in Mazanderan and Chaldæa (i.e. Arabistan); and turquoise mines near Nishapur and Firuzkuh. Of Persian steel he said that it was 'full of sulphur, very fine, with a mighty thin and delicate grain, very lasting, but brittle as glass.' But of the Persians as mining prospectors or engineers, he entertained a very poor opinion, for he declared: 'they are too slothful to make any discoveries.' [1]

About the same time or a little earlier (circ. 1650), Tavernier (who appears to have provided Chardin with some of his material, the same passages occurring almost *verbatim* in the two authors) wrote:—

Of late several copper mines have been found out of which the Natives make all sorts of Kitchen Household Stuff. Their lead comes from Kerman, their Iron and Steel from Korasan and Kasbin. Their steel is very fine with a smooth grain, and grown very hard in the water, but it is as Brittle as Glass. There are also some mines of Gold and Silver in Persia, wherein it appears that they have anciently wrought. Shah Abbas also try'd again, but found his expence to be more than his profit, whence it is become a Proverb in Persia, 'The silver mines of Kerven, where they spend ten to get nine,' which is the reason that all the gold and silver of Persia comes out of foreign countries.[2]

We hear little more of the mines of Persia till the days of Nadir Shah, when that adventurous monarch, in pursuit of his designs of universal conquest by land and sea, and particularly of naval ascendency on the Caspian, established an iron foundry near Amol in Mazanderan, where he cast cannon-balls and bomb-shells, forged horse-shoes, and contemplated the manufacture of anchors for his ships.[3] In the first quarter of the present century

[1] *Travels* (edit. Lloyd), vol. ii. cap. vii.

[2] *Travels*, bk. iv. cap. i. p. 143.

[3] J. Hanway, *Historical Account*, etc., vol. i. p. 288. Compare W. R. Holmes, *Sketches on the Caspian Shores*, p. 166.

Abbas Mirza, who with a somewhat flighty temper appears to have combined a genuine interest in his country's regeneration, at the same time that he introduced English uniforms, officers, drill and weapons at Tabriz, encouraged English mining experiments in Azerbaijan. About the year 1810, an Englishman named Williamson opened some extensive copper mines in the district of Sheikh der Aband near Turkomanchai, but was obliged to abandon them as a failure; owing, as one writer alleges, to the jealousy of Abbas Mirza.[1] In 1815, Captain Monteith was commissioned by the Prince to report on the best locality for iron works, and decided in favour of Dombre, south of the Aras (Araxes), and Masarud, saying, 'In no part of the world did we conceive it possible that a greater abundance of iron ore should exist than in the Karadagh range of mountains. For many *farsakhs* the soil appears to consist of no other stone.' Finally, in 1836, Sir H. Lindsay-Bethune brought out a steam engine and a number of skilled workmen from England, and sank a very large sum of money in the attempt to work both the copper and iron mines of Karadagh, apparently without any satisfactory results.[2] Brass cannon were, however, at this and earlier periods cast from Persian metal in the citadel at Tabriz.

Modern exploitation

In the present reign, as knowledge has become more widely diffused, and as European methods and appliances have slowly percolated to Persia, more numerous though deplorably imperfect attempts have been made to exploit the mineral wealth of the country, particularly in coal and copper; while the natural vanity of the Persians, inflamed by the inquiries or eulogiums of passing travellers, has disposed them to think that their native soil concealed an El Dorado of wealth whose spoils must ultimately fall into their lap. Most amusing stories are related of the mingled credulity and enthusiasm of these deluded Orientals. In 1877 it was reported to the Shah that an old man of Kavend, a village near Zinjan, had found some gold. Some Court officials were thereupon sent to Kavend to examine the man, who persisted

[1] Lieut. T. Lumsden, *Journey from India to London*.

[2] He had received the concession in the lifetime of the preceding Shah. Copies of the Firmans: 1. from Fath Ali to Abbas Mirza and Bethune; 2. from Abbas Mirza to Bethune; and 3. from Mohammed Mirza to Bethune, are printed in an Appendix to vol. ii. of G. Fowler's *Three Years in Persia*. W. R. Holmes (*Sketches*, p. 13) says that Bethune abandoned the works because of the difficulty of obtaining repayment from the Persians for the original outlay.

in his declarations that he had found the ore in a field while engaged in agricultural pursuits. In his excess of pleasure, the Shah, who already saw vistas of sturdy *hammals* staggering under sackfuls of gold into his subterranean vaults, despatched a superior officer with a large number of men, who, it being winter time, set about clearing away the snow and digging a large trench. Meanwhile a German prospector was engaged from Berlin, but, on his arrival, could find no gold. The original discoverer was then brought to Teheran, examined by the Prime Minister, and, it is said, by the Shah, and promised a large bonus as well as a pension if he could indicate the auriferous locality. The poor old fellow had told all he knew, and no pension in the world could elicit any more. Small pieces of gold or auriferous quartz were afterwards discovered, but the mountain, exhausted with this parturition, was left alone.[1]

An incident scarcely less droll happened in 1885, when a piece of ore from Azerbaijan was shown in the capital, and was found upon analysis to contain 70 per cent. of silver. Again the Shah had dreams of rivalling the Lydian monarch. Four generals and colonels were despatched to inspect the scene of production. Later it transpired that the specimen was a piece of scoriæ that had been stolen by one of the guards from the Royal Mint.

Persian Mining Corporation

Finally, in the spring of 1890 was formed a company, entitled 'The Persian Bank Mining Rights Corporation,' with a capital of 1,000,000*l.* to acquire and work the mining rights conceded to the newly established Imperial Bank of Persia by the Royal firman of the preceding year. These rights included the monopoly of all such iron, copper, lead, mercury, coal, petroleum, manganese, borax, and asbestos mines as belonged to the State and had not previously been ceded to other persons. Mines of the precious metals, and of precious stones (e.g. the turquoise mines of Nishapur, which I have described in Volume I., and to which I shall therefore not again refer in this chapter) were excluded. The term over which the concession extends is sixty years; it applies only to those mines the working of which is commenced within ten years of 1889; and sixteen per cent. of the net profits is the share exacted by the Shah. Immediately upon the formation of the company, a staff of competent engineers was

[1] This story is liberally embroidered and transmogrified by Madame C. Serena, *Hommes et Choses en Perse*, cap. xxviii. *Vide* A. H. Schindler, *Zeit. d. Gesell. f. Erd. z. Berlin*, vol. xviii.

sent out thoroughly to prospect the country; and although their movements have been to some extent retarded by sickness, by the trying extremes of climate, which render some parts of the country inaccessible in winter and others in summer, and by the dilatoriness of Persian officials, yet their reports enable us to form a clearer notion than has ever yet been possible of the extent and value of Persian minerals. It may be found that in a number of cases, principally at first, the operations of the company will take the form of a joint agreement and working of mines already known and leased with their present proprietors or lessees; the Persian Government having excluded from the monopoly all such mines as were of private property, or were rented from the State; and the majority of known mines naturally falling into this category. As time passes, and new mines are discovered by the prospecting engineers, independent working will become more and more frequent. Instead of recapitulating, encyclopædia-wise, the vague and unsatisfactory lists of places at which minerals have at different times been alleged to be found in Persia, I will divide the country into its several metalliferous zones, and will briefly report what is so far known for certain of each.

Mineral-producing zones

The mineral-producing zones of Persia are, roughly speaking, six in number: (1) The province of Azerbaijan in the north-west; (2) the northern and southern slopes of the main Elburz range between Rudbar near Resht, and Astrabad; (3) Khorasan; (4) Kerman; (5) the central districts between Kum and Shiraz, principally around Isfahan and Nain; (6) the Persian Gulf littoral and islands. I will devote a few lines to each of these in turn.

1. Azerbaijan

Owing to the severity of the winter and the deep snow, the province of Azerbaijan has not yet been investigated and reported upon by the company's engineers. About no district, however, is more information forthcoming in the scattered records of the past, and of no district is it known with greater certainty that its mineral possessions are both numerous and varied. Iron, lead, and copper ores exist in abundance, and have been frequently if unmethodically worked. The richest district is that of Karadagh in the north-east, where iron and copper mines have both been worked in this century, by Europeans as well as by natives.[1]

[1] I have seen a report on the mines of Karadagh, then being worked by Sir H. Lindsay-Bethune, which was sent by Dr. Riach to Sir J. McNeill in 1837. He

Lead has been continually extracted from the Khalkal region, 14 *farsakhs* from Tabriz, whence also copper and saltpetre have been derived. Coal is even now dug from a spot four miles to the north-east of Tabriz. Bordering on Azerbaijan on the south-east is the district of Khamseh, with its capital Zinjan, where are deposits of copper, lead, and coal, as also of mercury [1] (which was known in the middle ages) at Ak Derreh and Kiz Kapan to the west of Zinjan. Although it is as yet too early to predict anything with certainty of this zone, there is every reason to believe, from what is known of its unquestioned geological attributes, and from the presence in its centre of a great city as a purchasing market, that mining operations will successfully be commenced here in the near future. Of the marble pits of Dehkharegan, producing the petrifaction commonly called Maragha marble, I have elsewhere spoken.

2. Elburz range

It has been known, since Chardin's and Hanway's times, that the slopes of the Elburz were peculiarly rich in deposits of coal and iron; and from their greater proximity to the capital, as well as from this fact, it has arisen that these resources have been more freely exploited than any others in Persia. This zone may be divided into the northern and the southern slopes of the Elburz, facing respectively towards the Caspian Sea and the Teheran Valley. In the former sub-division the presence of several iron and lead mines is known; and certain of either class are worked, notably the iron mines of Naij, near Amol, about which Hanway wrote, and to export the produce of which (the ore contains fifty to sixty per cent. of iron) the Mahmudabad-Amol railway, which I have previously described, has in part been constructed. It is a noticeable and an encouraging fact that in this region the iron [2] and coal mines are generally found in close proximity to each other. More definite intelligence is in our possession regarding the southern, or coal-bearing slopes of the Elburz, where a certain

wrote of the entire district that 'it seems to be one enormous mass of the most valuable minerals, whole mountains being apparently composed of ores, perhaps the richest in the world—viz., iron, tin, and copper;' and of an unworked tin mine at Angert, he said that 'it is, perhaps, the most wonderful in the world.' Morier, speaking of the same region, quoted the words of Deut. viii. 9: 'A land whose stones are iron, and out of whose hills thou mayest dig brass.'

[1] Mercury is at present so rare in Persia that it costs 10*l.* per flask of 75 lbs., or 300*l.* a ton, in Teheran.

[2] The iron at present used in Teheran is almost exclusively Russian. In simple bars, it costs 3½ *krans* (about 2*s.* 6*d.*) per *man* (6½ lbs.). Russian pig iron costs 20*l.* per ton.

amount of ill-regulated activity has for some time prevailed, and whose coal pits supply the present demands of Teheran. Mineral deposits occur at many places along this range from beyond Kazvin on the west to Tash, between Shahrud and Astrabad, on the east; but the most productive areas lie to the north-west of Teheran, between the capital and Kazvin, and to the north-east in the direction of Demavend, and further east.

North-western district

The North-western District contains a number of coal mines, situated on the slopes about half-way between Teheran and Kazvin, at the distance of a few miles to the north of the postal road. Of these the best known are those of Abiek, Hiv, and Feshend, extending along a strip of country thirteen miles in length, and about 5,000 feet above the sea. All of these mines have been, or are being, tentatively and clumsily worked by native proprietors or by foreign lessees. The output of the Abiek mines in 1888 was 2,000 tons, of the Hiv mines 9,000 tons. The mine of Feshend has been leased by its native owners to a small syndicate of foreigners, entitled La Société de Charbonnage, of whom the moving spirit is that Jack-of-all-Trades of Teheran, M. Fabius Boital, and who have recently procured a concession for a small narrow-gauge railway to transport their produce from the pit's mouth to Teheran.[1] The work that has hitherto taken place in these mines has been abominably and wastefully conducted, the modern Persians not having the dimmest notion of mining science. They contain, however, useful seams of coal, easily accessible; and if properly worked with scientific implements and appliances, should yield a largely increased production.

North-eastern district

In the North-eastern District, the annual output of which has hitherto been 4,000 tons, the best-known coal pits are those of Lar, about forty miles from Teheran, where a number of shafts have been clumsily worked for some time, averaging six cwt. of coal per miner per day. It is understood that the mines of Hiv and of Shemsek, in the Lar district, have been acquired in part ownership by the Mining Corporation; and far better results, as well as a larger native consumption, which is

[1] The present annual consumption of coal in Teheran is about 15,000 tons. At the mouth of the pit it costs 4 to 7 *krans* a *kharvar* (649 lbs.), or 14 to 24 *krans* a ton. Thence it is conveyed on donkeys, mules, or camels to the city (the cost of transport being 30 to 32 *krans* a ton), where it pays 2 *krans* octroi at the town gate, and is sold in the bazaars at an average of 70 *krans*, or 2*l.*, a ton.

certain to follow upon reduction in price, may soon be anticipated.

The Governor-General of Khorasan boasted to me of the mineral wealth of his province; and the Khorasanis themselves say
3. Khorasan that it contains, in addition to the turquoise mines of Nishapur, twelve copper, seven lead, four coal, two salt, and even a gold mine, of which only three copper, one coal, and one salt mine have been worked, and that in a very perfunctory fashion. The well-known copper mines of Gurkhani, between Maomai and Abbasabad, on the high road between Shahrud and Meshed, which Fraser speaks of as having been worked up to Nadir Shah's day, but abandoned because of Turkoman depredations, are now full of water. A copper mine was seen, five miles from Meshed, by Colonel Val. Baker, who found the workings ancient and extensive, but not very rich. Good coal is said to be procured from Firizi and Ab-i-Kat, eight miles south of Chinaran. Some lead mines at Damghan and Sebzewar are leased to private individuals, and copper, coal, and iron are also found in the neighbourhood of the former place. Next to Gurkhani, the principal copper mines of Khorasan, many of them containing the remains of ancient working, but now under water, may be classified as follows: 1. Chund, Homai, and Nehru in the hills south of Sebzewar; 2. Batau and Dahaneh Siah further to the south, the latter being the most productive copper-mine in Persia; 3. several mines in the neighbourhood of Turshiz; 4. ditto in the Turbat-i-Haideri district; 5. Paghaleh, etc., in the Jagatai hills north of Sebzewar; 6. the Biarjumand district on the caravan route between Shahrud and Turshiz. One or other of these localities is likely to be taken in hand by the Mining Corporation. It must be remembered that though Polak declared that every district in Persia had its own copper mines, and that though there is not a village in the country where copper vessels and utensils are not a *sine quâ non* of domestic existence, even among the peasants, yet the local manufacture of the metal is insignificant in the extreme, the output of the Persian mines now worked hardly exceeding 3,000*l.* yearly in value, and almost the whole amount consumed in Persia being imported in sheets, principally by the Gulf from England.[1] Consequently there is a most favourable opening for an industry

[1] Copper sheets, rolled and finished, cost between 90*l.* and 100*l.* per ton, in the Persian market. Chili bars cost 60*l.* per ton.

that will find an eager market at the very threshold of production.

The next district, that of Kerman, is one of whose mineral wealth glowing accounts have always existed, although, owing to its great distance from the sea, and the enormous cost of transport, the export of its varied productions has never been, and probably never will be, profitably conducted, except in a few cases of especially valuable minerals. On the other hand, the market provided by the two great manufacturing cities of Kerman and Yezd must always create a considerable local demand. Chardin spoke of lead from Kerman as being used for many utensils; and it is still extracted in the districts of Kuhbenan, Jevarun, and Mahun.[1] At Kaleh Ziri, between Birjand and Neh, Khanikoff in 1859 inspected the extensive remains of ancient galleries, whence copper, lead, manganese, and turquoises had at one time been extracted, but which had apparently not been worked since the Arab conquest.[2] Stack, in 1881, was shown rich specimens of lead and copper ore from Tang-i-Mo-i-Aspan, four *farsakhs* from Pariz and two from God-i-Ahmer.[3] Coal exists at Bazergun thirteen miles north of Kerman city, at Deh Taki in the Hizumi Pass, to the north-east on the road to Rahwar, and throughout the Kuhberan district. Between Kerman and Shiraz at Parpa, near Niriz, are the iron mines of which Marco Polo, Tavernier, and Chardin spoke as steel mines, and which were extensively worked in ancient times. Very rich manganese ore is found at Heruzeh, sixty miles from Kerman on the road to Rahwar. Good borax comes from the Shehr-i-Babek district, to the north-west of Kerman on the northern edge of the Sirjan salt-desert. Asbestos was discovered only five years ago near the village of Gujar, in the Kuhbenan district, twenty *farsakhs* north of Kerman, where it is known as *sang-i-kakhur*, or 'wound stone,' being locally applied to stop bleeding. An excellent yellow, semi-transparent marble is quarried in the mountains near Yezd, the actual spot being Turun Pusht, forty miles from Taft, and fifty-six miles from Yezd. From it were made the superb marble throne, and the twisted marble pillars that now adorn the throne room, or Talar, in the Royal Palace at Teheran.

4. Kerman

[1] Almost the only use now made of lead in Persia is that of casting bullets and shot, and about 1,000 tons of the metal suffice for the needs of the whole country.

[2] *Mémoire*, etc., p. 169.

[3] *Six Months in Persia*, vol. i. p. 211.

Recent explorations have proved the entire strip of country between Kum and Isfahan to contain mineral ores of considerable richness and variety. A vein of iron ore, containing 60 per cent. of metal, and copper pyrites in addition, has been discovered at Kamsar, where it is reported that at least 100,000 tons of ore are lying on the slope of the hills. Lodes of good copper and iron ore have been exposed in the neighbourhood of Kuhrud. The fastidious folk of Kum are said to object to the use of coal in their sacred city, on the ground that it pollutes the air round the shrine of the holy Fatima; but it may be conjectured that future generations of worshippers will be less sensitive. A splendid iron ore, containing 59 per cent. of metal, is obtained in the Feridan district, north-west of Isfahan. Mercury exists in the Zardeh Kuh range, to the north-west of the city. Antimony and nickel and cobalt ores have been discovered within the last year near Anarek, in the district of Nain, between Isfahan and Yezd. The former, when powdered, produces the ingredient known to science as collyrium, to the Persians as *surmeh*, and to the Arabs as *kohl*, that is so widely used by the female sex in the East for beautifying the eyes. The nickel and cobalt ores have been found in old copper mines that have evidently been worked for centuries. Copper, lead, sulphur, asbestos, and manganese have also been discovered in large quantities in the Anarek district, which appears to be one of unusual richness.

5. Central districts

In the southern region we come upon a different mineral-bearing zone, and are confronted with a fresh variety of products. Rumours have for some time prevailed of the existence of good coal in the Dashti district, and in the Gisakun hills, to the north-east of Bushire; and it has been greatly hoped that these reports would prove to be true, owing to the near vicinity of so excellent a market as Bushire, where the steamers navigating the Gulf would be only too happy to buy fuel at a reasonable price.[1] The explorations so far conducted at Narestun, thirty-five miles south-east from Borazjun, in the region indicated, have not justified these anticipations, the alleged coal turning out to be only limestone strongly impregnated with bitumen. There is indeed a very marked bituminous vein running through these hills; and in probable connection therewith are the

6. Persian Gulf littoral

[1] Cardiff coal at present sells in Bushire for prices ranging from 33*s*. to 53*s*. a ton, the average price being about 2*l*.

naphtha wells of Daliki, which have long been cited among the unexplored Persian sources of mineral wealth. Two springs of greenish-coloured water here well up, with a temperature of 95° Fahr., strongly impregnated with sulphuretted hydrogen, which exudes a nasty smell, and flecked with drops of naphtha on the surface. A concession for the working of these wells was granted a few years ago to Messrs. Hotz, of Bushire, but after sinking an experimental shaft in an unsuitable spot, they desisted from further operations. The concession has since been transferred to the Mining Corporation, whose engineers have during the past year been engaged in sinking a bore to a considerable depth, and who are still at work. The naphtha-bearing zone apparently extends from here in a north-westerly direction, the next spot where the oil comes to the surface being in the district of Ram Hormuz, and in the vicinity of the River Karun. Here, according to the most recent surveys, there are three oil-bearing localities. The first is near the village of Shardin, about fourteen miles east of Ram Hormuz, where there are more than ten springs, yielding a dark and heavy oil, the three principal of which produce at present a daily average of only twenty-five gallons, but one of which gives pure oil. They are claimed by local *seyids*. The second site is about equidistant (twenty-four miles) from Weiss on the Karun, and Beni Daud, and is forty-five miles south-east of Shushter. Here there are six shallow pits in the bed of a brook, only one of which is at present productive, yielding thirty-four gallons of white oil per diem, which is used in lamps unrefined, being sold in the bazaars of Shushter,[1] Isfahan, and Teheran.[2] They are leased to a leading citizen of Shushter. The third group of wells is situated at Haft Sheid, eighteen *farsakhs* in a northerly direction from Shushter, beyond the Akili valley of the Karun. Owned by the Shushter *seyids*, these wells yield thirty gallons daily of a dark green oil, which is sold to the Arabs for rubbing on camels, and as a cure for itch. In each of these cases the conditions of locality are perhaps less favourable than at Daliki, the cost of transporting machinery being very large, and the tribes being superstitious and ignorant. Naphtha is also re-

[1] Ram Hormuz naphtha is sold at Shushter for 1 to $1\frac{1}{4}$ *krans* per *man*.

[2] In the bazaars of Teheran and Isfahan it fetches 50 per cent. more than Baku oil, and is used by painters and polishers. In the south it is employed to adulterate American oil.

ported to exist near Dizful, and near Kasr-i-Shirin and Kalhur, in the Kermanshah district of Persian Kurdistan. Outputs have further been observed at Ahmedi and Rudun, north of Bunder Abbas, and in the neighbourhood of Semnan. The only other place, however, where it is extracted for use, appears to be at Salakh, in the island of Kishm, where a coarse but promising oil is employed by the natives, both as an illuminant and for rheumatic complaints.

Mumiai

While speaking of naphtha I must not omit to mention a variety of bitumen known as *mumiai*, which is collected by exudation from rocks near Behbehan, and at Darab. It has long enjoyed a great celebrity in Persia, being credited with wonderful therapeutic properties, particularly when applied to broken limbs. Chardin,[1] Kaempfer,[2] Le Brun,[3] and the old travellers in general, give long descriptions of its character and efficacy, usually denoting it a precious drug or gum, and being apparently very much puzzled as to its origin. After being collected, it is made up into hard, cylindrical rolls, and is packed for transmission in gold or silver paper.

Rock salt and iron ochre

The islands of the Persian Gulf, though famous in past times as emporia of commerce, have now little claim to notice, except as the source from which is derived a large amount of rock salt. Ormuz and Kishm, whose harbours have sheltered the argosies of Portugal and Spain, now export in native sailing craft the salt and iron ochre which are their sole marketable commodities. The salt used to be collected from salt-pans by evaporation; but it is now quarried from the rock with crowbars or blasted with gunpowder, and is carried on camelback to the beach, where its price is 13 rupees a ton. The annual export of these islands is said to be 25,000 to 30,000 tons a year, the best salt coming from Nemekdan on Kishm, where there is a perpendicular cliff of pure rock salt, 200 to 300 feet high; and the markets to which it is despatched are Muscat, Zanzibar, Bombay, Mauritius, and Java. The salt is almost everywhere found in combination with iron ochre, locally known as *gilek* or *gilu*, the trade in which has lately been farmed for 650 *tomans* by a Persian. The annual export has hitherto amounted only to 1,500 tons; but it is probable that this could be largely increased. There are

[1] *Voyages* (edit. Langlès), vol. iii. pp. 311–12.

[2] *Amœnitates Exoticæ*, pp. 516–24.

[3] *Travels*, cap. xlv.; *vide* also Sir W. Ouseley, *Travels*, vol. ii. Appendix v.

many other parts of Persia where salt exists, and is quarried in great abundance, far exceeding the needs of the country itself. Among these may be mentioned Masreh, Aiwan-i-Kaif, Deh Nemek, Lasgird, Kafir Kaleh near Nishapur,[1] Kamarij, and two salt lakes between Kerman and Bunder Abbas.

Remaining minerals

Among the minerals which I have not yet mentioned, but which are found scattered through different parts of the country, are large supplies of gypsum, nitrates of soda and potash, alum (principally extracted from a number of mines near Kazvin, and also at Tash), sulphur, the chief mines of which at Khamir, on the mainland opposite the island of Kishm, used to be farmed by the Sultan of Muscat, but are now in Persian hands, saltpetre near Zinjan and Kum, zinc near Yezd, and tin (it is said) between Astrabad and Shahrud.

Future of mining in Persia

It is as yet too early in the day to venture upon any confident prediction as to the future of mining operations in Persia. The information which I have given, and which a later edition, if ever demanded, may enable me very greatly to amplify, will at least have shown that the arena of activity is various, well-stocked and large. I entertain no doubt that time will reveal other and equally remarkable sources of mineral wealth at present unknown or untested. The intrinsic value of the Persian minerals cannot be disputed. Their worth as articles of commerce is almost wholly dependent upon the locality in which they are situated, and upon the cost of mule or camel transport either to the coast or to the nearest town market. These difficulties, and others, arising from the severity of the Persian climate, the enormous cost of conveyance of machinery, and the humours of Persian officialdom, constitute an array of obstacles which only those who have practical experience can credit. If coal and copper can be produced in large quantities so as both to meet and to augment the native demand, and if the more valuable minerals of which mention has been made can be conveyed to a port at a cost which will render export either to Europe or to other Asiatic countries profitable, I believe that the future may be prosperous.

From the natural I pass to the manufactured products of Persia, which may be divided into two separate but not mutually exclusive

[1] The salt mines of Kafir Kaleh (i.e. Hill of the Infidel) produce 680 tons a year, and supply the needs of Khorasan and Meshed.

classes, viz., silk, woollen, or cotton tissues, and artistic fabrications. Broadly speaking, factories, as the term is understood and used in Europe, do not exist in Persia; and the multiplication and economy of labour-force, by the employment of steam-power, or even of water-power, is hardly known. The country has indeed been famous in times past for its industrial and artistic products, and, even in the decadence of native ingenuity, consequent upon the importation of cheap European substitutes, still retains traces of the ancient skill; but these manufactures were then, as they still remain, the output of private workshops, or the production of particular schools. In no country have I found trade more localised, not merely by the cheapness in a particular neighbourhood of the primary substance, but also by long tradition and local custom. Almost every town of any size can boast its own speciality, which it is impossible to procure elsewhere. Associations of workmen, or a species of elementary guild, exist in every manufacturing centre; and by these are regulated the habits and customs of the trade.

Manufactures

Of the textile fabrics, by far the most important and best known are the Persian carpets, which have attained so wide a celebrity that the upper-class householder in England or America is rare who does not think the acquisition of such an article, whether genuine or spurious, an indispensable testimony both to culture and to civilisation. Who that has once seen them can ever forget the imperishable colours, mellowed but uneffaced by time, the exquisite designs, and the predominant grace, of the genuine old Persian carpet? And who that has ever made such a study does not experience a pang at sight of the modern usurper that so frequently claims to bear the honoured name? The true Persian carpets have always been, and still are, entirely hand-made, being stretched on frames, either upright or horizontal, and, among the nomad tribes, being invariably worked by the women.[1] The varieties are considerable, and are marked by the strongest individual characteristics, so much so that it is impossible to mistake the products of different provinces or districts.

Carpets

[1] The men receive the orders, buy the wool, and get it dyed according to pattern; the women and girls do the work, three or four being employed upon a carpet of ordinary size. Every stitch is separately woven, a good carpet containing 10,000 stitches to the square foot, the very best 40,000. A single loom will give three or four carpets of ordinary size in the year; slow weavers will spend one or two years over one carpet.

Among the latter the principal are: (1) the districts of Kain and Birjand, in Khorasan, whose fabrics are very close in texture, of high quality, and command good prices; (2) Sarakhs, where the famous Turkoman carpets, of dull crimson and brick-coloured hues and velvety surface, can be procured; (3) Kerman, where an extraordinarily soft and well-wearing carpet is made, wholly of cotton; (4) the district of Karadagh, in Azerbaijan; (5) the district of Ferahan, whose capital Sultanabad is the centre of the carpet trade of Western Persia[1]; (6) Kurdistan, the fabrics of which are known throughout Europe; (7) Fars and Shiraz, among the best fabrics being those of Murghab; (8) the glossy, long-haired carpets made by the nomad Kashkais of the same province. Messrs. Ziegler and Co. and Messrs. Hotz keep European representatives at Sultanabad, to superintend the local production, which has in this locality been systematised and regulated, very much at the expense alike of originality and excellence. The introduction of aniline dyes, though strictly prohibited by the Government, has had a lamentable effect in causing the neglect, and in some cases even the loss, of native vegetable hues; while the necessity of rapid production, and of competition with the cheaper fabrics of European looms, has all but killed individuality of design, and has led to the monotonous reproduction of prescribed patterns. It is a sad reflection that, on purchasing a modern Persian carpet, the most elementary caution prescribes that one should rub with a wet cloth to see whether the colour be fast; and that one never feels safe unless the purchase be unmistakably old. In some places, particularly at Kerman, the manufacture is pursued under very unhealthy conditions, the artisans being obliged to work underground in order to escape the dryness of the outer air, while the elasticity of the threads is preserved by moisture from vessels filled with water. Most beautiful among the ancient Persian carpets of the Sefavean and even of later days were those manufactured of silk, than which I do not think that a more exquisite fabric has ever been woven by human hands. Silk carpets can still be procured to order, according to any pattern, size, or design; but the prices are so high as to be prohibitive to any but wealthy purchasers (ranging from forty to hundreds of pounds); and even here the application of a moistened

[1] In this district there are 150 villages, and some 5,000 looms, occupying, if all engaged, about 10,000 persons.

handkerchief is apt to be rewarded by the cruel but tell-tale daub. The lovely old prayer-carpets, formerly made in Kurdistan, Birjand, and elsewhere, are now very difficult to procure. I was informed by a leading merchant engaged in the trade, that the total annual export of Persian carpets amounts to from 90,000*l*. to 100,000*l*., mainly to Great Britain, France, and the United States. While speaking of carpets, mention must also be made of the wonderful *namads* or felts, manufactured of almost any size or shape, principally at Yezd, Kerman, and Isfahan, but rarely if ever seen out of Persia, by reason of their great bulk and weight. They are commonly made of camel's hair beaten into the requisite consistency, are left of the natural colour, i.e. a pale brown, and are extraordinarily soft and pliant, being sometimes as much as an inch and a half in thickness.

Shawls, prints, velvets, silks, embroideries

Among the remaining textile fabrics the most creditable are the woollen shawls of Kerman, made from the goat's hair of the nomads of Khorasan, and resembling to some extent in their pattern, while almost excelling in their delicate softness, the famous Kashmir fabric. At Meshed I saw a charming material made of camel's hair, and retaining the natural colour, called *berek*, not unlike the cloth that we call homespun in England. Cotton fabrics, chintzes, etc., are still manufactured in the country from native cotton, though not to the same extent as formerly. The *kalemkars*, or chintzes of Isfahan, in which flowery designs and patterns of flowers and beasts are printed by means of wooden hand-dies on a light ground, are the tastiest and best known; although the shirting on which the pattern is stamped is now for the most part imported into the country, while an imitation article is turned out by machinery in Manchester. The *kadeks*, or nankeen of Kashan, and *kerbas*, have also a good native sale. The richer tissues, such as silk, velvet, and brocade, which were made in Persia almost before they were known in Europe, have shrunk to narrow dimensions, although a few beautiful fabrics still emerge from the native looms. Kashan, Isfahan, Tabriz, and Resht are the centres of the native silk-weaving industry. Particoloured velvets are manufactured at Meshed, Kashan, and Isfahan, gold and silver brocades at Kashan and Yezd. The beautiful Persian embroideries which in times past stocked the bazaars of Stamboul have now almost disappeared, and it is difficult for any but a resident in the country, employing *dellals* to ransack the native houses, to procure good specimens. At Resht is manufactured a showy but somewhat vulgar embroidery, consisting of a species of coloured cloth patchwork, richly covered with broidered designs; and glittering arabesques of gold and silver, on backgrounds of black, green, and crimson velvet, are worked elsewhere. Nevertheless, to the traveller who, before starting from London, has made an inspection of the excellent and representative collection purchased for the South Kensington Museum by Sir R. Murdoch Smith, a visit to modern Persia will probably prove a great disappointment.

Artistic productions

By far the most famous of the artistic products of ancient and mediæval Persia were its earthenware and *faïence*, which still create such a splendour on museum walls with the imperishable lustre whose iridescence glints from the surface of tile and vase and plate and bowl. Truth compels the sad confession that the ceramic art of Persia is all but dead; although rude imitations of the ancient colours and designs are turned out at Isfahan and elsewhere, particularly in the form of showy tiles for the surface decoration of mosques, minarets, and city gates. But even a momentary comparison of the prototype with its pretentious successor is sufficient to dispel the illusion which distance alone can create, and affords a measure of the extent to which the artistic spirit in Iran has suffered eclipse. Metalwork was also one of the most renowned of Persian industries in bygone days. Perhaps the *mina* work, or enamelling in gold, silver, or copper, particularly for the bowls of *kalians*, upon which, in the midst of Oriental designs, are painted medallions of European beauties, is the best surviving relic, being still practised at Shiraz, Behbehan, and Isfahan. Kashan is a centre of copper and brass work, some of which is pretty and ingenious; but the pierced and chiselled brassware of Isfahan, though far superior to the coarse Indian analogue of Benares, is chiefly an imitation of ancient designs, intended for the European market. The damascened blades of Khorasan and Shiraz have once enjoyed a great renown, but the modern Persian prefers a gun to a sword. Almost the sole work in the precious metals worthy of mention is the filigree work of Zinjan. At Shiraz is executed a very ingenious and artistic mosaic work of bone, metal, and coloured woods, arranged in minute geometrical designs. The painting of mirror-backs, and *kalemdans* or pen-cases, is not what it was; but an order to the best native artists, and a sufficient amount of patience, will still procure a beautiful and valuable article. Persian ingenuity has ever excelled in carving; and on a small scale the pear-wood sherbet spoons of Abadeh and Gulpaigan, which are transparent, and yet carved in high relief on the surface, are a notable production.

Summary

I have now completed my survey of the chief indigenous products, manufactures, and exports of modern Persia, in which, if I have covered a wide field, I hope at the same time to have extracted therefrom both information and interest. From my narrative it will be seen that, in spite of her retrograde condition, which a study of history does more than anything else to accentuate, Persia, so far from being deficient, is richly endowed with those natural resources which it is a nation's own fault if it does not transmute into gold. Physical conditions, such as the scarcity of navigable rivers, the long distances to be traversed, and the interference of great mountain barriers between the interior and the sea, undoubtedly retard the development of many of these resources. But the apathy of the people and the neglect of the Government are greater obstacles still, and the notable disproportion of exports to imports in every table of statistics ever penned is a result for which the Persians themselves are entirely to blame. Improved means of transport, good cart roads, or even mule tracks, if railroads are not to be hoped for yet awhile, the circulation of a paper currency, and the facilitation instead of the wanton discouragement of foreign commerce on possible highways, such as the Karun, might work a revolution in a few years, and are measures which a sagacious sovereign and patriotic ministers might be expected, if not to initiate, at least to support. What has been done, is being done, or is capable of being done, for the exploitation of the nation's wealth, and for the promotion of trade, has in part been displayed in previous chapters, but will appear still more clearly in that which ensues.

CHAPTER XXIX

COMMERCE AND TRADE

PART I.—*History of Perso-European Trade*

PART II.—*The Modern Trade of Persia*

When Greek joined Greek, then was the tug of war.
NATHANIEL LEE, *Alexander the Great*, act iv., sc. ii.

The thread of history

IN pursuance of a claim which I have more than once made for this book—namely, that it aspires to fill up some of the unconsidered *lacunæ* of history, as well as to supply a picture of existing conditions—I propose to preface my account of the present commerce of Persia, and of the acute competition that there prevails in the field of trade between Great Britain and Russia, by a brief retrospect of the earlier stages of that competition, and of the events that, first bringing Persia into mercantile relations with European powers whose sun has long set, gradually opened her ports and markets to the all but exclusive control of two powers whose star had not then risen, and have ended by making them the regular and voluntary customers of Moscow, of Manchester, and of Bombay. I know of no work in which any consecutive attempt has been made to trace the history of the commercial relations that have now prevailed for three and a half centuries between this country and Persia, although for two and a half centuries of that time they superseded and filled the place of diplomatic communications, factors and agents acting the part of envoys and plenipotentiaries, and firmans and charters being substituted for treaties and alliances; and although the records of this period are full of episodes abounding in romance, and worthy of remembrance for the lustre which they shed upon the English name. In piecing together these scattered annals of the past, collected from many sources,[1] I hope, therefore, at the same time to fill a somewhat

[1] The chief of these, in addition to those mentioned in the text are Purchas' *Pilgrims*; Hakluyt's *Voyages*; *Early Russian Travellers* (Hakluyt Society);

neglected page of history, and to show of what long standing and of what high desert are the claims which I advance on behalf of this country to a predominant interest in the material regeneration of Iran.

Persia the connecting link

Situated midway between the far east and the west, and flanked by two navigable seas, Persia has from the earliest times played a prominent part in the mercantile intercourse between Asia and Europe. Immemorial caravans have furrowed their tracks across her deserts and plateaux, conveying to the Mediterranean the treasures of the Indies, of Tartary and even of China. The mariners of at least 4,000 years, from the Phœnicians down to the present day, have skirted her southern shores, and have established their most frequented marts upon her coasts or on her islands. The ruder conditions of northern life rendered the maritime route by the Caspian less open to use, but the history of its navigation by merchant vessels, though late in commencement, does not yield in dramatic episode to its southern competitor. It has even been said that 'ancient history is very much the history of the struggle for the transit trade of the East by the Persian Gulf and the Red Sea; just as the modern history of the Old World is almost altogether based on the opening up of the ocean way to India round the Cape of Good Hope.'[1]

The merchant nations

The number of peoples, and the diversity of powers, who have during this long period, coæval with the written history of the world, controlled or endeavoured to control the overland connection between Asia and Europe, and have thereby exercised a direct or indirect influence upon Persia, is extraordinary. Phœnicians, Assyrians, Babylonians, Greeks, Parthians, Romans, Arabs, Genoese, Florentines, Venetians, Turks, Armenians, Portuguese, English, Dutch, French, and Russians—the fingers of all have itched for the keys that should unlock the mysterious treasure-house of the East; merchants of each nationality have scoured every available track by land and sea,

Jonas Hanway, *An Historical Account of the British Trade over the Caspian Sea*; Abbé Raynal, *History of the Settlements and Trade of the East and West Indies*, (translated by J. Justamond), vol. i.; J. Bruce, *Annals of the East India Company*, 3 vols.; N. Sainsbury, *Calendar of State Papers relating to the East Indies*, 4 vols. (1513–1629); Sir G. Birdwood, *Report on the Miscellaneous Old Records of the India Office*; F. C. Danvers, 'The Persian Gulf Route and Commerce,' *Asiatic Quarterly Review*, April 1888.

[1] Sir G. Birdwood, *Report on the Records of the India Office*, p. 255.

many of them uniting the functions of the historian with the pursuits of the tradesman; the flag of each nation has flown in turn upon Persian waters, or its coinage has changed hands in Persian bazaars. In the dawn of recorded history and down to a time posterior to the Christian era, the great marts of interchange between the East and West were situated on the Chaldæan rivers, not far from the head of the Persian Gulf. Here were Babylon, 'a land of traffic, a city of merchants,' and Teredon. Here afterwards were founded Seleucia and Ctesiphon, Busrah and Baghdad. To the expedition of Alexander we owe the practical commencement of Indo-European trade, just as to the voyage of his admiral, Nearchus, we are indebted for our earliest minute acquaintance with the Persian Gulf. Under his Seleucid successors, and under their supplanters the Romans, the trade between Asia and Europe followed a triple line, either by caravans from the Oxus to the Caspian, or *viâ* the Persian Gulf and Syria, or by the Red Sea and Egyptian route to Alexandria. By one or other of these three routes came to Europe the precious stones and pearls, the spices and silks of the Orient. When the capital of the Empire was moved to Byzantium, the Egyptian route languished, and the overland route from India was preferred, leading through Afghanistan, Persia, and Asia Minor to the Bosphorus. Persia gradually acquired a monopoly of the silk trade, until in the reign of Justinian, two monks, travelling from China, brought with them the eggs of the silkworm in the hollow of a cane, and started a rival growth in Europe. A little later the conquests of the sectaries of Mohammed completed the mercantile ruin of Alexandria, and transferred to Arab hands the control of Eastern trade, and more especially of the Persian Gulf. Keis, or Kisi, and Ormuz successively became the emporia of Oriental commerce; and to Busrah were brought in Arab holds the commodities of far Cathay. Such was the situation when the commercial enterprise of the Italian Republics once again brought Europe as a competitor on to the scene, assisted by the re-awakened enthusiasm for the East that was the natural consequence of the wars between Cross and Crescent. Venice is said to have imported silk from the East as early as 555 A.D., and to date from 300 years later the commencement of her long mercantile reign. With Amalfi, and later with Florence, she reopened and engrossed the Egyptian route to India in the tenth century. Genoa, on the other hand, turned her attention to the northern avenues trading *viâ* the Black Sea and the Caucasus; and inaugurating at the dawn of the fourteenth century the overland route from Trebizond which is utilised to this day. In these hands for the most part remained the carrying trade between East and West, until in the last years of the fifteenth century an event occurred which has had a prodigious and almost unique effort in history, has revolutionised the balance of power, and has rewritten the map of the world. In November 1497, Vasco da Gama, the Portuguese navigator, doubled the Cape of Good Hope, opened a new waterway to India, and bequeathed to the Portuguese a brilliant century of riches and fame.

Portuguese ascendency

The new century was not two years old when the successful discoverer reappeared in command of a powerful fleet to appropriate what he had hitherto only explored, backed by a Papal Bull which conferred on King Emanuel of Portugal the proud title of 'Lord of the Navigation, Conquests, and Trade of Ethiopia, Arabia, Persia, and India.' Tristan da Cunha, Anthony de Saldanha, Francis, and above all Alfonso de Albuquerque, continued the work of forcibly planting the Portuguese flag upon every suitable point of vantage, and of giving to fire and the sword all who resisted the victorious soldiers of Christ. The proceedings of Albuquerque in the Persian Gulf have already been traced in the chapter dealing with that sea. By the time of his death in December, 1525, the Portuguese dominion had grown into an empire. In the middle of the century it was at the height of its renown. No vessel was suffered to navigate the Indian Ocean without a Portuguese permit. An absolute monopoly was rigidly enforced by the conquerors. From Japan to the Red Sea fluttered their unresisted flags; and while the cruelties of viceroys, the insolence and corruption of minor agents, and the fanaticism of those who thought to combine the quest of lucre with the championship of the Faith, were already undermining the fabric so arrogantly reared, rumours of their unbroken triumph rang through Europe, stirring keen chords of emulation in some hearts, but striking terror into the mass.

English initiative

Nowhere was the stimulus of competition more profoundly felt than in England, then trembling on the doorstep between the Middle Ages and the New World. Yet nowhere for a time was the common acceptance of Portuguese monopoly more humbly acquiesced in, or the idea of fighting her with her own weapons and on her own ground less seriously entertained. In their desire to get to India and to dip their hands in the fabled garners of the East, the explorers and merchants under the early Tudors could compass no better idea than to discover a new route for themselves which should escape Portuguese competition altogether, and provide a private maritime highway to the enchanted goal. The north-western and the north-eastern passages were each thought likely to supply this alternative channel, and were successively tried. In 1553 Sebastian Cabot obtained from Edward VI. a preliminary charter for the 'Company of the Merchants Adventurers for the Discovery of Regions. Dominions, Islands, and Places unknown, a nomenclature that sufficiently indicated the haphazard character of the undertaking, and testified to the admitted dearth of geographical knowledge. In the same year Sir Hugh Willoughby, starting with two ships on the north-eastern quest which was to end in the recovery of this new Golden Fleece, was frozen to death off the coast of Lapland. A third vessel, however, commanded by Stephen Burrough, and piloted by Richard Chancellor, sailed into the White Sea, and discovered Archangel. This accidental and unforeseen event was fraught with momentous consequences. Chancellor, travelling inland to the court of the Grand Duke of Moscovy, the famous Ivan Vassilievitch the Terrible, was favourably received by him, and laid the foundations of the British 'Russian or Moscovy Company' (whose chequered career I shall briefly relate), for the conduct of the overland trade through Russia with the lands lying to the east and south of the Caspian. In 1557, a formal charter of incorporation having been granted to the company by Philip and Mary in 1555, Master Anthony Jenkinson, in company with Richard and Robert Johnson, were despatched by the directors to explore and to open the projected trade routes with Central Asia. They journeyed *viâ* Moscow to Astrakhan; they flew for the first time the British flag (the red cross of St. George) upon the Caspian; they reached and returned safely from Bokhara, the first Englishmen, so far as my knowledge extends, that ever set foot in the Tartar capital; and they furnished the desired incentive for a more extended venture.

It was now contemplated by the company in include Persia within the sphere of its operations, for a twofold object. In the first place, the silk-producing provinces of that country, Shirwan, Gilan, and Mazanderan, lay in the north and in immediate proximity to the Caspian Sea, a fact which seemed to suggest an easy triumph over 'the Portugals,' who could only purchase and export this valuable commodity from the southern havens, at a distance of several hundred miles from the area of production. And secondly, through Persia it might be possible to tap the mysterious resources of Hindustan by overland caravan routes, which should divert to camelback and muleback the wealth that was now poured into Portuguese carracks and galleons. Accordingly the travelled Jenkinson was again sent out in company with one Edward Clarke to make the initial experiment, bearing with them 'cloth of golde, plate, pearles, saphyres and other jewels, as well as woollen cloths (karsies or kerseys),' and a letter from Queen Elizabeth to the 'Great Sophie, Emperour of the Persians, Medes, Parthians, Hyrcanes, Carmanarians, Margians, of the people on this side and beyond the river of Tygris, and of all men and nations betweene the Caspian Sea and the Gulph of Persia'—a compendium of his titles which could not fail to be gratifying to the Sefavi monarch, but which affords an amusing test of the knowledge of Persia possessed by the best informed English intellects of the Tudor time. The narratives of this and of the subsequent expeditions organised by the Moscovy Company, contained in a number of letters written by the principal actors, have been ably edited and republished, and constitute one of the most interesting volumes of travel ever penned.[1]

The Moscovy Company and Persia

During the twenty years from 1561 to 1581, six trading expeditions to Persia were despatched by the Moscovy Company, and assuredly commercial enterprise has rarely been prosecuted with greater gallantry or under more serious discouragement. Jenkinson himself received a rebuff at the start that would have deterred any less resolute pioneer. Having landed at Derbend, then a Persian town, in August 1562, and having proceeded to Kazvin, at that time the Persian capital, he was received in audience by Shah Tahmasp, to whom he presented the Queen of England's letter, but who returned to him this ungracious reply: '"Oh, thou unbeliever," sayd he, "we have no neede to have friendship with the unbelievers," and so willed mee to depart'; the reason of the Shah's reluctance to enter into commercial relations with Englishmen being that he had just composed his differences with Turkey, whose

Trading expeditions

[1] *Early Voyages in Russia and Persia* (Hakluyt Society), edited by E. D. Morgan and C. H. Coote. 2 vols. 1886.

merchants then monopolised the northern outlets of Persian trade to the Levant and Europe. Undismayed, Jenkinson spent the winter of 1562–3 at Moscow, organising a second expedition. Thomas Alcock and Richard Chenie were the factors who represented the company upon this venture, but their fortune was even more untoward. Abdullah Khan, the King of Shirwan (dependent upon Persia), who had favoured Jenkinson, was angry because a Mohammedan had been killed by a Russian. Deprived of the royal protection, Alcock was murdered on his way back to the coast, and Chenie only escaped with difficulty. The third expedition, which left Astrakhan in July 1565, in a boat of twenty-seven tons burden built for the company at Yaroslav, was as little exempt from personal misfortune, but found the commercial outlook more reassuring. Its history is related in a series of four letters by Arthur Edwards, one of the factors. Alexander Kitchin, one of his colleagues, and Richard Davis, one of the sailors, lost their lives from illness; but Edwards, arriving safely at Kazvin in May 1566, found the Shah in a much more amiable temper than heretofore. 'He was desirous of London clothes (i.e. cloths), three or foure of all sorts for example, being wel shorne and drest. The Persians talke much of London clothes, and they that knowe the wearing are desirous of them before the cloth of the women's making (i.e. native fabrics), for they finde it nothing durable, for when it cometh to weare on the threede, it renteth like paper.' Shah Tahmasp now gave a formal letter of privileges, or charter, to the Moscovy Company, guaranteeing them the following advantages: exemption from all tolls and customs, protection for their merchants 'from all evil persons,' and right of free way throughout the country, legal recovery of just debts, immunity from robbery, and assistance in unlading. Edwards sent home to his employers a list of the imports which might advantageously be sent into Persia from England, consisting of carseis or kersies,[1] tume, Brasil, redde cloth, and copper; and also of the exports which he proposed to ship from the Caspian, and which comprised 'rawe silke, peper, ginger, nutmegs, brimstone, allam (alum), rice, galles (gall-nuts), cloves, and yew for bowe-staves.' His letters also contain a curious allusion to the Russians, in which we may trace the first dawn

[1] These were woollen cloths, which received the name from the village of Kersey, in Suffolk, where the woollen trade had been established by a colony of Flemings.

of the mercantile jealousy that afterwards had such momentous results.

> The Russes are sorie that we doe trade into these parts. For wee are better beloved than they are; because they are given to be drunkards, they are much hated by the people. It is to be wished that none should serve your worships in theese parts that be given to that kinde of vice; and that your chiefe agent and factor should be able to rule and governe himselfe that no dishonestie should be imputed to him and us.

The fourth expedition consisted of Arthur Edwards, chief agent, John Sparke, Lawrence Chapman, Christopher Fawcet, and Richard Pringle. Arriving in Persia in August 1568, they found that a change had come over the spirit of the scene. They received no help in landing, in spite of the Shah's former decree; Chapman, journeying to Tabriz, found the market already overstocked by the competition of Turks, Armenians, and Venetians; in Kazvin no sale could be procured; the king, notwithstanding his former affability, on the strength of which 2,000 kersies had been ordered from England, declined to take any cloth; and the factors travelling in Gilan found Turkish agents everywhere. It was but a poor consolation that Chapman succeeded in extracting from Shah Tahmasp a further decree which granted the English free passage through Gilan and all parts of Persia, ordered native assistance in the event of shipwreck on the coast, and the safe custody and delivery of goods in the event of the agent's death, and conferred the right to camel hire at the ordinary rate, to the protection of roadguards, the supply of quarters and victuals, and the purchase or erection of houses.

The fifth voyage was fraught with even greater perils, and was more fatal to life than its predecessors. In the 'Thomas Bonaventure,' of seventy tons, there left Yaroslav, in July 1568, Thomas Bannister, Lawrence Chapman, Geoffrey Ducket, Captain Lionel Plumtree (the chronicler of the expedition), and others. On their way down the Volga they were attacked by the Nagay Tartars, who were only repulsed after a fierce fight, in which Bannister was twice wounded. When at length they reached Persia, Ducket made his way to Tabriz, where he stayed for two and a half years. Bannister went up to Kazvin, where, finding the Shah in a most benign mood, he succeeded in effecting a good sale and in securing most of his requests, though he was unsuccessful in the attempt to inaugurate a through trade with India, which project appears to have been broached upon this occasion for the first time. Disasters now fell fast and thick on the devoted band. Bannister died in Ganjeh in July 1571; Chapman died also. Five of the company died and two were robbed or murdered within the space of five weeks. The survivors, under Ducket, weighed anchor in May 1573, but the tale of their calamity was not yet complete. On the Caspian they were attacked by Cossack pirates, and after a valiant resistance, in which fourteen of the enemy were killed and every Englishman was wounded, were compelled to surrender the vessel in return for their lives. The corsairs turned them adrift in an open boat, in which they eventually reached Astrakhan. A further accident befell them on the return journey up the Volga, but in October 1574, Ducket, Plumtree, and Amos Riall again reached England, after as perilous a venture as ever befell English hearts of oak, even in those days of fearless enterprise and strenuous deed.

It was not till five years later, in June 1579, that the sixth and last expedition left Gravesend, the chief of the four factors deputed by the company being the same Arthur Edwards who had already shared and survived the perils of two of the previous undertakings. He was less fortunate on this occasion, for he died at Astrakhan in the following year. The same Nemesis that had dogged the footsteps of the preceding ventures now attended his companions. Shah Tahmasp had died in 1576, and his old enemies the Turks had seized the opportunity to invade the outlying portions of the Persian dominions. Sailing from Astrakhan in the spring of 1580, the English factors heard at Baku that Shirwan was in possession of Ottoman troops, and that Shemakha (Shumakhi) had been destroyed. Accordingly they landed and marched by the coast to Derbend, where they effected no great sale Their own vessel being leaky, they bought another, which was immediately driven ashore in a storm, and, when finally they succeeded in starting upon their return voyage, they were caught in the ice at the mouth of the Volga. After many hardships the survivors reached London in September 1581, and the company, whose speculation had been attended with as small pecuniary success as it had been pursued with dauntless courage, very wisely decided to abandon so hazardous a field of adventure.

In contrast with later experiences, it is with surprise that we read of a British mercantile undertaking, conducted by Russian invitation, with Russian countenance, and very largely on Russian rivers and soil. The reason of this strange phenomenon was the following: The Russians were at that time in far too backward a condition to embark upon any trading venture, or even upon any maritime expedition, themselves; and were content, therefore, to profit by the superior skill and industry of others. Moreover, Ivan the Terrible stood greatly in need of supplies, and particularly of warlike stores and ordnance, which could only be procured from the foreigner, and which the English merchants brought out to him from London in return for the exemptions granted to them in Russian territory. The failure of the British experiment was attributable to several reasons: imperfect acquaintance with the country, which had led the first voyagers to underrate the competition of the Turks, Armenians, and Venetians, whose long-established control of the Persian market was not easily to be shaken; bad management;[1] the risks arising partly from the navigation of the Caspian, partly from the Persian climate, and partly from the insecurity inseparable from barbarous manners and troubled times; but, above all, the exorbitant length and complexity of the sea, river, and land route employed, which rendered it impossible for merchandise so conveyed to compete with the more direct overland and maritime routes by which Persia was approached on the south and west. Nevertheless, history does not record a finer example of British daring; and the names of these forgotten factors are as worthy of remembrance as those of illustrious mariners who have bequeathed new titles to the shores and islands of the western main.

Causes of failure

For some time after this the northern route to Persia, *viâ* Russia and the Caspian. was abandoned by English merchants, the close of the century having witnessed the inauguration of a fresh undertaking, to which I shall presently turn. In 1600, however, Sir Anthony Sherley, an English gentleman and soldier of fortune, appeared in Persia, acting upon the suggestion of his friend the Earl of Essex, then Lord-Lieutenant of Ireland, with the double object of persuading the Shah to join in an alliance against the Turks, and of re-establishing commercial intercourse between Persia and England. At Venice he had

Grant to Sir Anthony Sherley

[1] A writer in Purchas' *Pilgrims* says that the 'evill success was owing to the forwardnesse of some few and evill doing of some unjust factors,' no doubt an allusion to Johnson.

encountered some Persian merchants, who had greatly flattered the last named desire. This self-accredited but gallant emissary was received with the utmost distinction by Shah Abbas, who formed for him a strong personal attachment, and who, besides sending him as his own plenipotentiary to the powers of Christendom, granted him a firman, 'which shall be of full effect and force for ever, without renuing, for me and my successors, not to be changed,' conferring freedom from all customs and tolls, legal recovery of debts, protection of person and property, religious liberty, and the right 'to repaire and trafique in and through our dominions without disturbances or molestations,' upon all Christian merchants.[1] It does not appear, however, that any immediate advantage was taken of this concession by English traders, although it doubtless encouraged them in their forthcoming essay in the south.

Early in the new century a fresh endeavour was made, by negotiation with the Czar of Russia, to reopen the overland route through his dominions, between England and the East. In 1646 Sir John Merrick arrived at Moscow on a mission with this object from James I. to the Czar Michael Feodorovitch, the first of the Romanoffs. The conservatism of the Boyars, however, would not admit of the concession; and, upon the plea that nothing could be done till the war with Poland was over, the request was refused.[2] In 1618 the Moscovy and East India Companies agreed to amalgamate their fortunes, and it was proposed to advance a loan of 100,000 marks to the Czar, in order to secure his support for the revival of the transit trade through his dominions.[3] Sir Dudley Digge was sent out as ambassador in the same year to negotiate a formal agreement; but again the mission failed.[4] Thirty years afterwards, when the English monarchy was overthrown and the Commonwealth established, the Czar revoked all privileges enjoyed by foreigners, and expelled all British traders from Muscovy, except from Archangel. It was not till a century later that, under a more liberal monarch, and in the hands of the Russia Company, the project again achieved a short-lived realisation.

Sir John Merrick

[1] For a copy of this grant, *vide Report of Sir Anthony Sherley's Journey*, 1600, quoted by Malcolm, *History of Persia*, vol. i. p. 353.

[2] *Calendar of State Papers* (East Indies Series), vol. ii. (1617–1621). Nos. 307, 308, 309, 310, 312, 313.

[3] *Ibid.* No. 306.

[4] *Ibid.* No. 467.

In 1619 we hear of one Giles Hobbs, an agent of the English East India Company, who was deputed by his employers to travel to Persia by the deserted route of Jenkinson from Moscow and Astrakhan, and who, after a hazardous journey of seventeen months, in which he suffered arrest and imprisonment, arrived at Isfahan, and suggested a reopening of this northern channel.[1] At that time the Portuguese enjoyed an absolute mercantile predominance in Persia, and the spleen of the worthy Englishman vented itself in the following paragraph:—

Giles Hobbs

Gentlemen, this your Persian trade, as it is in her infancy, hath many enemies: the Turks, Arabians, Armenians, and the proud Portugall, whose lying tongue ceaseth not to dishonour our kingdome and nation; but the Lord, I hope, will turne the dishonour upon his owne pate.[2]

Hanway says that, early in the seventeenth century, the French formed a design of opening trade with the Caspian and Persia, by way of Archangel and Moscow. This project, of which I have found no other confirmation, and which differs from the other French schemes to which allusion will presently be made, came to nothing.

French ambition

The next attempt to revive the northern trade route was made in a novel quarter. Early in the seventeenth century the silk manufactories of Holstein had attained some eminence in Europe; and it occurred to a Hamburg merchant, named Brucman, that a profitable speculation might accrue from the import of the raw material direct from Persia, and that the wealth which flowed into the coffers of the Portuguese and Dutch by their maritime advantages on the South, might be diverted into equally remunerative channels on the North. Not being strong enough, even in conjunction with his fellow merchants, to act alone, Brucman appealed to the Duke of Holstein, who at once entered into the spirit of the enterprise, and in 1637 deputed Brucman with others on a special embassy to the Court of Persia. On their way they made ruinous terms with the Grand Duke of Moscovy, for the right of free transit through Russia; and, upon arriving in Persia, soon found that customs and freight charges would leave no margin of profit. Brucman accordingly changed his tone and posed as a diplomatic envoy, courting an alliance against Turkey.

Holstein embassy

[1] *Calendar of State Papers* (East Indies), vol. ii. No. 753.

[2] Purchas' *Pilgrims*, lib. v. cap. xvi.

The record of the embassy, of its stormy fortunes and its abortive issue, has been vividly narrated by its secretary, Adam Olearius, who cherished a bitter dislike against Brucman.[1] The Shah, Sefi I., could not understand the confused and blundering accounts of the chief ambassador; and the latter was so universally admitted to have failed that, upon his return, he paid the penalty with his head.

Passing for the moment over the intervening and successful movements of British trade upon the south—a subject to which I shall presently revert—we arrive, after the lapse of a century, at an epoch when a second attempt, in no way less adventurous, and, alas! not less ill-starred, than its predecessor, was made by the British Russia Company, which had, in the meantime, shifted its headquarters to St. Petersburg, to reopen the Moscow-Astrakhan-Caspian route to northern Persia. In the interval since the last venture the Russians had begun to trade themselves, and had established their commercial base at Shemakha. There, however, they were seriously harassed by the inroads of the Lesghians, by one of which, in 1712, Yevreinoff, a Russian merchant, was despoiled of mercantile property worth 200,000 crowns. Peter the Great was now upon the throne, and among the far-sighted ambitions cherished by this remarkable man was the aim of attracting to Russia, by new as well as by recognised avenues, the transit trade of the East. In 1717 he sent the ill-fated Beckovitz to explore the old and new channels of the Oxus. In 1718 he issued a decree throwing open trade within his dominions to all foreigners. In 1722, taking advantage of the disorder in Persia consequent upon the Afghan invasion, and of the weakness of Shah Tahmasp, he made that armed descent upon the northern provinces of Persia which I have previously described. The silk trade of Gilan was one of the chief temptations that drew him thither, while, at the same time, he took steps to improve the Caspian navigation by engaging an Englishman, Captain P. H. Bruce, to make a survey of its shores.[2] Peter did not live long enough himself to witness the realisation of his schemes, but a few months before he died (January 1725) he made overtures through an English merchant named Richard Mainwaring to the merchants of London with a view to reinstituting the trans-Russian trade

Peter the Great and the Russia Company

[1] Adam Olearius, *Relation du Voyage*, Paris, 2 vols. 1639. Translated into English by John Davies. London, 1662.

[2] *Vide* Bruce's *Memoirs*.

between England and Persia which had been dropped 150 years before. His death put an end to the scheme; but in December 1734 the Empress Anne, in faithful execution of his ideas, signed a concession granting to British subjects the right of carrying merchandise through Russia to and from Persia on payment of a 3 per cent. *ad valorem* duty. A little later, in 1738, John Elton, an Englishman of rare, but impetuous, genius, and the real father of the revived scheme, having acquired some experience of Central Asia in the Russian service, and having formed the idea that the resources of the Khanates might be tapped by a new route proceeding from Astrabad to Bokhara, proposed to some of the factors of the British Russia Company in St. Petersburg to open this new artery of trade. With one Mungo Graham he left Moscow in 1739, sailed from Astrakhan, landed at Pir-i-Bazaar, and having addressed a formal petition to Reza Kuli Mirza, son of Nadir Shah, then ruling as regent at Meshed in the absence of his father in India, received a decree from the prince authorising him to land goods and trade everywhere in the Persian dominions from the Caspian to Attock on the Indus—an interesting corollary to Nadir's conquests six months before—to hire or to build houses at Resht or at any other place, and to pay custom dues only upon landing. Elated by this advantage, Elton appears to have formed an altogether exaggerated notion of the prospects of future trade. Returning to St. Petersburg, he wrote a magniloquent letter to the British minister, from which I have previously quoted, and so inflamed the imagination of the London merchants that, in spite of the strenuous opposition of the Turkey and Levánt Company, and of the East India Company, who were alarmed at competition from so novel a quarter, a powerful movement was organised by the Russia Company, the Government was won over, several members of the company were called to the bar of the House of Commons to give explanations, and finally an Act of Parliament was passed authorising and regulating the trade. The record of these and of the subsequent proceedings has been handed down to us by the graphic pen of Jonas Hanway, himself one of the leading spirits in the sequel, and a London citizen and philanthropist of high repute and intelligence.[1]

[1] *An Historical Account of the British Trade over the Caspian Sea, &c.* (4 vols. 1753; 2 vols. 1754, 1762). Jonas Hanway, though Dr. Johnson said of him that 'he acquired some reputation by travelling abroad, but lost it all by travelling at home,' was eminent both as merchant, voyager, public official, philanthropist, and

The British Government having received permission from the Russians to build two ships at Kazan on the Volga, these vessels were launched in June 1742. Elton, being placed in charge of the expedition, sailed in the 'Empress of Russia,' Captain Woodruffe. In the second vessel, the 'Elizabeth,' Captain Gilbert Blaire, sailed James Brown, Martin van Mierop, and Richard Wilder, the remaining factors. Jealousy soon broke out between the two parties, largely owing to the wayward and imperious temper of Elton, who, in January 1743, without any application to, or permission from, the Company, entered the service of Nadir Shah as naval constructor on the Caspian, under circumstances which I have narrated in an earlier chapter on the Persian Navy. Taking the 'Empress of Russia,' which had already prosecuted some trading voyages between Resht, Baku, and Derbend, he proceeded on a survey of the eastern coast of the Caspian as far north as Balkan Bay. Rumours of his action were transmitted to St. Petersburg, and excited the liveliest suspicions of the Russian Government. Jonas Hanway, at that time a partner in a mercantile house in the capital, was accordingly sent out by his employers to report on the situation. Upon his arrival in Persia at the close of 1743, he very speedily took stock of the situation. The amenities of courts were no guarantee for amity of commerce. He found Russian officials and traders everywhere jealous and hostile. Intent upon an independent venture, Hanway at once started off to carry out Elton's original project, and to open the route from Astrabad to Meshed. At Astrabad he came in for a local rebellion, his caravan, when about to start, was seized and the bulk of his property confiscated, and he himself narrowly escaped being handed over as a slave to the Turkomans. Having at length escaped, he returned through Mazanderan and Gilan to Kazvin, and proceeded from thence to Hamadan, where, finding Nadir Shah in camp, he procured from him an order for the restitution of his stolen goods.

John Elton and Jonas Hanway

author. Born in 1712, he became a partner in the house of Dingley, in St. Petersburg, in 1743, and in that interest travelled in Persia and Russia until 1750, when he returned to London. There he led a life of public activity, founding many excellent institutions, and particularly interesting himself in the welfare of the young. When he died, in 1786, a monument was erected to his memory in Westminster Abbey. *Vide* John Pugh, *Remarkable Occurrences in the Life of Jonas Hanway*, 1787, 1798. A contemporaneous account of the same Anglo-Persian venture is to be found in the *Voyages and Travels* by Dr. J. Cook, who accompanied Prince Galitzin, Russian Envoy to Nadir Shah in 1747. He disagrees in some respects with Hanway. *Vide* vol. ii. cap. xxxiii.

After a fracas with Elton, against whose shipwright's intrigue he had always protested, he left Persia with a cargo of raw silk in September 1744, and returned to St. Petersburg, where he resided for the next five years. His report upon the silk trade of Gilan I have already cited in my chapter on the Northern Provinces.

Abandonment of business

Of the factors of the Russia Company left in Persia, Von Mierop, went to Meshed and resided there for over two years, but met with no success. Graham was murdered at Semnan. Five out of the fifteen Europeans employed died at Kazvin between 1740 and 1744. Agues and distempers prostrated those who lived at Resht. The Russian Consul at the latter place, Bakunin by name, was particularly hostile. Nor did the action of Elton render the outlook more promising. The Russians were seriously irritated at the naval pretensions of Nadir Shah, and the Russian College of Commerce issued an order that 'no goods or merchandise consigned to Mr. Elton could be permitted to pass through the Russian Empire.' Thereupon the Russian Company in London, in much alarm, decided to recall Elton, allowing him a pension of 400*l.* a year, and to amalgamate their own business with that of Hanway. Elton, however, spoiled the arrangement by positively declining to come, and procured a decree from Nadir Shah (November 1745) ordering his detention in the country. Matters went from bad to worse. In consequence of the repeated protests and persecutions of the Russians the two British vessels were compulsorily parted with to Russian merchants at Astrakhan and were navigated henceforward under the Russian flag. In November 1746, the Empress of Russia issued a decree absolutely interdicting the British Caspian trade. The surviving English factors lingered on for a time in the vain hope of recuperation; but, after the murder of Nadir Shah in June 1747, they were plundered of 80,000*l.*, and in the subsequent disorder saw no opportunity of recovering either their property or their prestige. Accordingly they retired in 1748 and 1749, and the second and last determined effort of England to open the Caspian route to Persia perished as miserably as had done its predecessor. It was not out of harmony with the dismal issue of the venture that Elton, who was so largely responsible for the disaster, met with a violent death three years later.

During the six to seven years over which the enterprise extended, the business accomplished, if not considerable, had been remunerative. It consisted almost solely in the export of raw silk from Persia and in the import of English cloth and other European goods into that country. The attempt to trade with Meshed was, according to Hanway, a great mistake, and the factors would have done better to have stayed quietly at Resht and waited for, instead of running after, custom. The balance-sheet, as published by him, showed the following figures:—Imports into Persia 1743–6, 690,492 crowns, or 174,398*l.*; exports of raw silk from Persia 1743–9, value in Persia, 373,500 crowns, or 93,375*l.* Hanway mentions that the cost price of silk was about 10*s.* per lb., and that, deducting all expenses, it was commonly sold for 15*s.* 6*d.* —a profit of over 50 per cent.; and sometimes for 28*s.*—a profit of 180 per cent.; calculations which, in his opinion, justified the risks incurred, however great they might appear.

Balance-sheet

The reasons of failure were both commercial and political, but chiefly the latter. So brisk a competition prevailed between Russians, English, and Armenians, that the markets of Gilan were glutted with European wares, which could not be sold at a profit.[1] The British wasted their strength by dividing their business and by the jealousy that raged between the rival firms. Persia was in so miserable a plight at the time that the natives had not the wherewithal to buy. But beyond all other impediments must be counted the hostility of Russia, set in motion by the self-seeking though heroic obstinacy of Elton, and the appalling condition of Persia, of which, under the declining years of Nadir's reign, Hanway has drawn a picture of such terrible fidelity. In a society at once so degraded and so unruly there was small scope for the pacific operations of trade; and the moment for renewing the attempt was signally ill-chosen. The hostility of Russia was a sequel that might with equal certainty have been predicted, as soon as to a commerce which her people must have regarded with jealousy from the start, and which imperial policy was powerless to recommend to local agents, was joined an attempt to convert Persia into a naval power and to dispute the Russian mastery of the Caspian. The wonder is, that the Russians should have thought the revenue derived from transit-dues paid by the British a sufficient compensation for their admission to a field of whose spoils they themselves,

Reasons of failure

[1] The Armenians were even compelled to abandon the trade in 1745, four years before the British.

by their geographical situation, were in such easy command. This was the last occasion upon which the British flag has flown upon the Caspian, and it foreshadowed the events by which, in the present century, that sea was converted by formal diplomatic instrument into a Russian *mare clausum*.

Turkey and Levant Company

I now revert to the southern zone of commercial access to Persia, of which a short while ago we left the Portuguese, in the middle of the sixteenth century, in secure possession, their monopoly being an institution so well established that maritime rivalry with them by the Cape route was regarded as a dream. The first attempt to compete with their Gulf trade, made by Englishmen, was in the formation of the Turkey and Levant Company in 1581, whose scheme aimed at the export of Persian silk by Busrah, Baghdad, and Aleppo to the Mediterranean. Merchants proceeded by this route from England to Hindustan, and it was with an eye to the trade of the Indies that this project was really framed, Persia being regarded as an intervening station. The first Englishman to visit India by this route was Thomas Stephens in 1579. We hear of Master Thomas Hudson at Tabriz in 1580. In 1581 John Newberry made his first trip to Persia and Ormuz; and in 1583 was accompanied on a similar journey by Ralph Fitch and others, whose exciting adventures I have elsewhere related.

The East India Company

An event now occurred which not only had a prodigious effect upon the balance of power in Europe, but whose consequences penetrated to the remote Orient, and indirectly paved the way to the acquisition of the Indian Empire of the British Crown. In 1578 the Crowns of Portugal and Spain had become united in the person of Philip II., and Portugal was henceforth regarded as an appanage of the superior power; and in 1588 the majesty of the combined states, and their hitherto all-but-uncontested supremacy at sea, were rudely shattered by the destruction of the Invincible Armada in the English Channel. From this moment the expanding maritime ambitions of Great Britain demanded a wider range. A private trading venture to the East was organised by some London merchants in 1591, but resulted in failure.[1] In the following year a great Portuguese carrack, the 'Madre di Dios,' which had been captured by some

[1] This expedition was captained by James Lancaster and George Raymond, in command of the 'Penelope,' 'Merchant Royal,' and 'Edward Bonadventure.'

English privateers, was towed into Dartmouth, and in her, in addition to a great cargo of eastern merchandise, was found a register of the Portuguese trade and possessions in the East, upon which was based the memorial of the founders of the London East India Company to Elizabeth in 1599. In 1598 the ambitions of Englishmen were roused by the news that Cornelius van Houtman, a Dutch merchant, who, having been arrested for debt in Lisbon, had mastered while there all the particulars of Portuguese trade with the Indies, had broken the long monopoly of the latter by a successful voyage round the Cape of Good Hope. The time had arrived when England, although late upon the scene, must also follow suit. On December 31, 1600, the London East India Company, commonly called the London or Old Company, received its first Charter of Incorporation from Queen Elizabeth;[1] and in the succeeding year, the first expedition, consisting of four vessels under Sir James Lancaster, left Gravesend. Between 1600 and 1612 twelve of these expeditions were made, and were called the Separate Voyages from the fact that their cost was defrayed, not from the Joint Stock account, but by individual subscribers. The last of these expeditions, under Christopher Newport, was the first that visited Persian soil, taking out Sir Robert Sherley on his return from an embassy to England. From 1613 commenced the Joint Stock Voyages, in one of which sailed Sir Dodmore Cotton and Sir Thomas Herbert on their way to the Court of Shah Abbas in 1626.

The Company had not been long in existence before its agents, or those of the Turkey or Levant Company, which had received a charter from Queen Elizabeth in 1581, were found in Persia. In 1609, Joseph Salbancke and Robert Covert journeyed from India, *viâ* Kandahar, Seistan, Kerman, and Yezd, to Isfahan, and reported that—

First dealings with the Persian Gulf

At Hisfahan might be planted a profitable trade if our ships with safetie might lade in the Persian Gulfe; where fiftie in the hundred

[1] The principal events in the development of the Company may be summarised thus. Its first charter was from 1600 to 1615; but this was renewed in perpetuity by James I. in 1609. In 1635 Courten's Association of the Assada (Madagascar) Merchants was formed, but united with the London Company in 1650. A remnant of the former, called the Merchant Adventurers, remained independent, and obtained a charter from Cromwell in 1655, but amalgamated with the London Company in 1657, when a new charter was granted by the Protector. Further charters were dated 1661, 1677, 1683, 1693. In 1698 was incorporated a rival

may bee gained from Ormus to Hispaan, and that in eightie dayes travell ; whereof I was thoroughly informed by diverse prisoners and merchants of the Great Towne of Julpha.[1]

Chardin says that 'the English went for the first time into Persia (he is speaking of the trade from the south) about 1613.' The first record of a grant that I have been able to find is a firman granted on September 1, 1615, by Shah Abbas,[2] at the instance of Sir R. Sherley, to John Crowther and Richard Steele, who had also journeyed overland to Isfahan from India. Its terms provided 'that all governors of seaports in Persia shall kindly entertain the English shipping.' In 1617 we hear of British factors as permanently settled at Isfahan.[3] In the same year a further commercial treaty was concluded by Shah Abbas with Mr. Connock, the Company's agent.[4] In 1619 a factory was established at Jask,

association entitled 'The English Company trading to the East Indies,' but commonly called 'The English, or New Company' with a charter running to 1714. The greatest jealousy and friction prevailed between the rival corporations, until, in 1708–9, the two were finally amalgamated under the title 'The United Company of Merchants of England trading to the East Indies,' officially known as 'The Honourable East India Company,' whose charter was renewed in 1793, under whose administration was acquired the Indian Empire of Great Britain, and which finally expired in 1858.

[1] Purchas' *Pilgrims*, lib. iii.

[2] Quoted in *ibid.* lib. iv. cap. xi. xiii.

[3] An interesting account of the interior economy of the newly-established British factory in Isfahan in the years 1619–20 is to be found in an article by the late Sir H. Yule, 'Concerning some Little Known Travellers in the East' (on George Strachan) in the *Asiatic Quarterly Review*, April 1888. *Vide* also *Calendar of State Papers* (E. Indies), vols. i.–iv., *passim*.

[4] E. Connock, who, when he was sent out by the Directors to Persia as Chief Factor, was described by them as 'a man above any other factor in the kingdom,' appears to have offended them, and still more Sir T. Roe, by posing as Ambassador from James I., with a letter from whom he had been entrusted to Shah Abbas. His interview with the latter took place in April 1617. 'The King called for wine, and in a large bowl drank His Majesty's health upon his knee, saying that Connok was welcome, that the King of England should be his elder brother, that his friendship he did dearly esteem and tender, that he would grant us Jask or any other port we would require, and every freedom in every respect as his honour might grant.' The Shah then promised to deliver from 1,000 to 3,000 bales of silk annually, to be shipped at Jask, free of customs, at the price of 6*s.* to 6*s.* 6*d.* a pound. *State Papers* (E. Indies), vol. ii. No. 122. Cf. also Nos. 60, 155, 156, 339. Connock died at Isfahan in December 1617 (*ibid.* vol. i. No. 263). His successors, acting under instructions from Roe, proposed a new treaty to the Shah, which the latter refused to sign, although confirming the treaty made with Connock (*ibid.* No. 369). In 1619, however, he granted to the East India Company the monopoly of the silk trade by the Persian Gulf, and 'syned the same with his royal and imperial seal' (*ibid.* No. 753). The English were bound to pay the king one-third in money and two-thirds in commodities (*ibid.* No. 475).

from whence, before the port of Gombrun was opened to the English, the overland trade was conducted with the Persian capital. In the same year, Giles Hobbs, whom I have before quoted, reported that the annual consumption of Persian raw silk in Europe was 1,000,000 lbs. at 12*s*. the lb., or 600,000*l*., the cost price in Persia being 8*s*. the lb.[1] In 1622, the English, in alliance with the Persians, turned the Portuguese out of Ormuz, and acquired a position of commercial ascendency at Gombrun, now renamed Bunder Abbas, under circumstances which I have related in my chapter on the Persian Gulf.

The French

Here I must turn aside for a moment to notice the appearance of other European competitors on the scene. Almost simultaneously with the formation of the first English East India Company, a similar association was formed in France; 1604, 1611, and 1615 being the dates of the formation of successive French imitations of the English model. The first notice that I have discovered of proposed commercial relations with Persia was in 1626, when Richelieu deputed a certain Louis Deshayes on an embassy to Abbas the Great, to prevent Persia from allying with Spain against Turkey, and to procure facilities for French merchants by the Levant route. The envoy, however, never got beyond Constantinople, having quarrelled with the French ambassador there, and the mission fell to the ground.[2] Two years later, however, two Franciscan friars, Père Pacifique de Provins and Père Gabriel de Chinon, appeared upon the scene and were well received by the Shah, who allotted them a house in Isfahan.[3] In 1642 Richelieu formed a new East India Company. In 1664, Colbert, who was even more keenly interested in the Asiatic trade, and who had enlisted the assistance of the Dutch, initiated a further attempt. Three representatives of the French Company were sent to Persia, in conjunction with two gentlemen travellers, MM. de Lalain and Boulaye, who received a kind of roving commission as deputies of the French king. They were well received by Shah Abbas II., 'who had a peculiar love for the Europeans, and a mighty inclination to enter into the strictest

[1] Purchas' *Pilgrims*, lib. v. cap. xvii. In 1619, however, seventy-one bales of raw Persian silk were sold in London for 26*s*. 10*d*. a pound (*State Papers*, vol. i. p. 745).

[2] *Vide* 'An unpublished Instruction by Louis XIII. for a French Embassy to Persia,' by J. G. de Rialle, *Asiatic Quarterly Review*, January 1891.

[3] *Relation du Voyage de Perse*, par. P. de Provins, 1631. Cf. *State Papers*, vol. iv. No. 732.

leagues and bonds of friendship with our princes;' although the Persians appear presently to have become disgusted at receiving envoys of such small consideration from so great a monarch. The Shah, however, granted them a firman, conceding immunity from tolls and customs for the space of three years, and the same trading rights as other foreign nations, a formal treaty of commerce being promised as soon as sufficiently valuable presents were forthcoming from the French king or company. There were constant quarrels at Isfahan between the representatives of the two latter powers, and De Lalain died in 1666. The Board of the French East India Company decided in 1668 not to open trade with Persia; but a M. Gueston, a new director, having come out from India to renew the attempt and having died at Shiraz in 1673, the captain of the vessel that had brought him, one Berrier, and his clerk De Jonchères, decided that it would be very good fun to pose as ambassadors themselves. They procured a patent from the king giving them free right of trade throughout Persia, but do not appear to have secured any exceptional privileges, the Shah's minister inviting a fresh deputation from the Company before he made any further concessions. In 1708, M. Michel, sent out by Louis XIV., concluded a treaty with Shah Sultan Husein; and in 1715 Le Grand Monarque was humbugged into signing another at Versailles by a Persian adventurer, named Mohammed Reza Bey. The French establishment existed in Isfahan till the Afghan invasion in 1722, when they were compelled to retire; and they also possessed a factory at Bunder Abbas.

The Russians

About the same time, viz., in 1664, there appeared at Isfahan an embassy from the Grand Duke of Moscovy consisting of two envoys and 800 followers. They were received with great distinction, and were lodged in a royal palace, which they so defiled with their filthy habits that Shah Abbas II. called them the Uzbegs of the Franks, intimating, says Chardin, 'that as among the Mohammedans there is no nature so nasty, so meanly educated, nor so clownish as the Yusbecs, so among the Europeans there was not any that equalled the Muscovites in those foul qualities.' It was presently discovered that the object of the embassy was commerce, and that the guise of ambassadors had been assumed in order to evade the payment of duties on the merchandise which they had brought with them into the country. Indignant at this double-handed dealing, the Shah dismissed them with barely an answer. The Grand Duke's rejoinder was the Cossack invasion of Mazanderan to which I have alluded in the first volume.

A third and a much more formidable competitor had meanwhile entered the contest. In 1580 the Netherlands had declared their independence of Spain and Portugal, and had started upon a brilliant period of maritime and commercial fame.

The Dutch

They were greatly encouraged by the defeat of the Spanish Armada; and the successful voyage of one of their own countrymen, Houtman, which I have mentioned, and which resulted in the formation of a Dutch settlement at Java, roused such enthusiasm in Holland that several rival companies were formed to trade with the East. These were amalgamated by a decree of the States General in the Dutch East India Company in 1602, and in the course of the next twenty years the new comers had made themselves masters of the principal Portuguese trading possessions in Asia. They first appeared in Persia in 1623, and seem to have received permission to settle at Ormuz, whence they moved their factory to Bunder Abbas in the reign of Abbas II. They also possessed business houses at Isfahan and Busrah. Somewhat conflicting accounts have been handed down of their fortunes in Persia, their first agreement having pledged them to a direct commercial bargain with the Shah,[1] by which the latter appears to have been the gainer. In 1652 and 1666 Dutch ambassadors visited Isfahan in order to negotiate better terms, and there was a good deal of duplicity and cheating in the proceedings on both sides. Nevertheless, Chardin is to be believed when, in the middle of the century, he relates that no nation trading in Persia could be compared with the Dutch in cunning, and that they were the masters of Persian trade. The English suffered greatly from their competition, and in the seventeenth century occupied an admittedly inferior position in the Persian Gulf. Both suffered during the Afghan siege of Isfahan in 1722; but the Dutch, who had amassed a large profit by selling sugar at an exorbitant rate to the besieged, were forced by Mahmud to disgorge 400,000 crowns. In the eighteenth century, and par-

[1] In 1704, when Le Brun was at Isfahan, the contract was as follows:—The Shah was bound to deliver every year to the Dutch East India Company, 100 bales of silk of 40[illegible] Dutch lbs. each. The Company, on the other hand, were bound to deliver in Isfahan 1,200 cases of sugar, of 150 lbs. each. *Travels*, vol. i. cap. xliv.

ticularly towards its close, the tables were completely turned. The sordid and exclusive spirit which had led the Dutch to sacrifice everything to a monopoly of the spice trade proved their bane, and in the great wars Holland lost nearly all of her colonial possessions in the Eastern seas to her successful rival, Great Britain.

Meanwhile the fortunes of British trade in Persia may be briefly traced. Firmans were procured from each succeeding sovereign, confirming, extending, or modifying the terms of previous concessions.[1] The Sefavi monarchs appear to have been endowed with strong commercial instincts, and Shah Sefi I., in renewing the conditions granted by his predecessors, stipulated for an annual present of 1,500*l.*, and for the annual purchase from himself of 60,000*l.* worth of silk, one-third of which was to be paid in coin and two-thirds in goods. The English business does not seem to have been well managed at this epoch, and the jealousy of the rival English companies was even felt in Persian waters, from which dislike of the Dutch appears alone to have dissuaded the East India directors from retiring. The Persians had almost from the start violated the conditions of the Ormuz-Bunder Abbas compact, and in 1679 the Court of Directors again seriously considered the question of abandoning Persia altogether. A policy of protest and petition was, however, decided upon. Charles II. had already written a letter to Shah Suleiman, urging the reconsideration of an edict issued in 1670, by which the amount annually paid to the English at Bunder Abbas—according to the original agreement, one half of the customs revenue—was fixed at 45,000 livres or 15,000 crowns; but the Persian Government had declined to grant any redress, taking refuge behind the paltry plea that the customs were no longer its own to dispose of, having been farmed out to a third party, and that the English had failed to observe other portions of the original bargain. In 1683, accordingly, Sir Thomas Grantham was sent out from England with instructions to push the British claim;[2] but, finding the port of Gombrun blockaded,

British fortunes

[1] *State Papers*, vol. iii. No. 577, vol. iv. Nos. 852, 857; Bruce's *Annals, passim.*

[2] His commission and instructions are quoted in *The Diary of William Hedges*, agent of the East India Company in Bengal, edited by Sir H. Yule (Hakluyt Society), vol. ii. p. 163. The Company complained that, for many years, they had been deprived of their ancient privileges, viz., 'the Agent to sit in the King's divan or Councill, and an officer to sit in his Bundar or Custome House, to collect half the Customes of Gombroon,' and had only received 1,000 *tomans* yearly instead of 40,000 *tomans*, the stipulated moiety. They claimed arrears for five

and war proceeding between the Dutch and Persians, he returned *re infecta*. Soon after, however, the English agents in Persia were fortunate, in spite of Dutch opposition, in securing new and more favourable firmans, and in 1697 a payment of some portion of the Bunder Abbas arrears was made in silk. Throughout this period the chief British agent appears to have occupied a position of especial distinction at Isfahan, being regarded as an accredited representative of the Crown; and in 1699 the Shah conferred upon the English factory the peculiar honour of a visit, which compliment cost them the modest sum of 1,200*l*. The amalgamation of the old and new companies in 1708 put an end to an unfortunate interlude of bickering and rivalry, and was followed by the despatch of Mr. Prescott to Isfahan as chief agent of the United Company, with a letter from Queen Anne to Shah Sultan Husein. Then followed a period of general dislocation and anarchy, arising from the Afghan and Turkish invasions, and from the internal warfare that succeeded. The English were compelled to shut their establishment at Isfahan, and a little later at Bunder Abbas; and of their fortunes in this stormy period the Abbé Raynal writes:—

During this general confusion the English sales in Persia consisted of no more than a hundred bales of woollen manufactures, 2,000 cwt. of iron, and the same quantity of lead. These articles, taken together, brought them no more than from 1,200,000 to 1,300,000 livres paid in money (=554,687*l*. 10*s*.).[1]

In 1763 Bushire was selected as the headquarters of the Gulf trade of the company, and, although it was temporarily relinquished in 1770 in favour of Busrah, it was reoccupied three years later, and commercial residents were retained at both places under the Government of Bombay. At first only one vessel was annually despatched to Bushire, with a cargo of 60 to 100 bales of cotton fabrics, iron, sugar, and muslins.[2] But from 1790 the trade between the Gulf and India rapidly increased, and in 1809 had risen at

years, or 150,000 *tomans*, but offered to take 50,000 *tomans* in composition, and to be content with 10,000 *tomans* yearly in future. On the other hand, Dr. Fryer, who was in Persia a little earlier (1676–7) as doctor to the East India Company, says that the latter had failed in their part of the bargain by not keeping two men-of-war in the Gulf. (*Travels in Persia*, pp. 222, 353.)

[1] *History of the Settlements and Trade of the Europeans in the East and West Indies.* Translated by J. Justamond, vol. i. p. 362.

[2] From 1780–90 the establishment at Bushire was only maintained at a total annual loss of 1,800*l*. In no year did the aggregate of sales exceed 7,000*l*.; in one year it sank to 93*l*. (Milburn's *Oriental Commerce*, cap. x.)

Bushire to an annual importation of 600 bales of cotton goods alone. When Sir John Malcolm first appeared in 1800 at the Court of Fath Ali Shah, he negotiated with the ministers of that monarch a commercial as well as a political treaty, by which most of the privileges of the old factories were restored, and several additional ones granted. English and Indian traders were to be permitted to settle, free from taxes, in any Persian seaport, and to be protected in the exercise of their commerce. Englishmen were also to be at liberty to build and sell houses in any Persian port or city. English iron, lead, steel, and broadcloth were to be admitted into Persia free of duty, while existing duties on other goods were not to be increased. Unfortunately, this treaty was never ratified, and, along with its political contemporary, found its validity disputed. In 1828, however, Russia, by the treaty of Turkomanchai, which fixed an *ad valorem* duty of 5 per cent. upon all Russian exports and imports, set an example which has, in turn, been followed by every European nation trading with Persia. But it was not till 1841 that the treaty was negotiated by Sir John McNeill that placed Great Britain upon the most-favoured-nation footing, and provided for the establishment of commercial agencies in the two countries. Meanwhile, in 1810, the commercial residencies of Bushire and Muscat, and of Baghdad and Busrah, had respectively been amalgamated, and in 1812 the commercial residency at Bushire was abolished and a political agent left in its place. In 1822 a general revision took place of the various stations in the Persian Gulf. Factors and brokers were henceforward denominated residents and native agents, and the entire establishment was rendered a political charge. This change was an inevitable consequence of the events that had brought Persia within the range of European politics, and had transferred the relations between this country and her from the ledgers of merchants to the despatches of statesmen. Since Malcolm first landed on her shores the situation has been revolutionised, and whereas the Foreign Office at Whitehall scarcely knew at the beginning of the century where or what Persia might be, a regiment of clerks and secretaries now ticket and file the voluminous correspondence that flows in from Teheran. In 1872 the superintendence of the Persian Gulf littoral was transferred from the Bombay Government to the Government of India, and to this day the British Residents at Bushire and Baghdad and the political or consular agents at Muscat and Busrah are selected and paid from the Indian establishment. No longer the *employés* of a company, they safeguard the commerce of a nation; and the trade reports which they send home with unfailing regularity once a year, and which are published by the Foreign Office, afford the best possible indication of the value of their labours, and of the extent to which business has swollen under their fostering supervision. The development of particular branches or channels of trade in the present century will be noticed in the review of the modern commercial situation, to which I next turn. I shall consider the historical retrospect in which I have indulged more than justified if I have thereby persuaded any reader who has been patient enough to follow me that Great Britain, by her traditions and her services, has an inherited right to a commanding interest in Persian trade, and that the claim which I advance on her behalf to retain it is no offspring of national cupidity or desire for material aggrandisement, but is a legitimate testament from a past of which we have no reason to be anything but proud.

Part II [1]

In proceeding from a retrospect of the past to a survey of the present condition of Persian trade, we are confronted with an almost complete metamorphosis of physical conditions, and with a very different cast of actors upon the scene. With the exception of the single, or at the most the double, outlet

Change in the scene

[1] The chief sources of reference on the trade of Persia since the beginning of the present century are: A. Dupré (1808), *Voyage en Perse*, vol. ii. caps. lviii., lix.; J. B. Fraser (1822), *Travels on the Shores of the Caspian*, Appendix II.; (Sir) A. Burnes (1832), *Travels into Bokhara*, vol. iii. p. 356; J. H. Stocqueler (1832), *Fifteen Months' Pilgrimage*, vol. ii. cap. i.; General F. R. Chesney (1835–7), *Expedition to the Euphrates*, vol. ii. cap. xviii.; Dr. O. Blau (1858), *Commercielle Zustände Persiens*; Dr. H. Brugsch (1860–1), *Reise der k. Preuss. Gesandtschaft nach Persien*, 2 vols.; J. E. Polak (1865), *Persien, das Land und seine Bewohner*, 2 vols. (Leipzig); (1873), *Persien* (Vienna); (1883), *Notice sur la Perse au point de vue commercial*; Capt. M. A. Terentieff (1875), *Russia and England in the Markets of Central Asia* (Russian); F. Stolze and F. C. Andreas (1874–1881), 'Die Handelsverhältnisse Persiens' (Petermann's *Mittheilungen*, 1885); A. Kitabji (1889), *Etudes Persanes*; Dr. P. F. Traubenberg (1890), *Hauptverkehrswege Persiens*; and the Diplomatic and Consular Reports in the Commercial, Annual, and Miscellaneous Series, published by the English Foreign Office, relating to Persia in general and to the cities or ports of Trebizond, Tabriz, Resht, Astrabad, Meshed, Teheran, Bushire, Mohammerah, and Bussorah.

on the Persian Gulf, where the traffic was in alien hands, the trade of Persia in the former period was a land-borne trade. Occupying the neck between two seas, Persia was traversed by caravan routes that had been trodden from remote antiquity by the interchanging *kafilahs* of the East and West. But those lateral routes are now, for the most part, deserted; the age of caravans is fading from view; the advances in navigation and the invention of steam have driven commerce to the maritime highways; and the seas on the north and south, which were once the main protection of Iran, are now a means of aggression and a source of weakness. On the Caspian the Moscovite, in the Gulf the Briton, knocks at her gates, and the exports and imports, whose freight has allured or enriched half the nations of Europe, are conveyed in Russian or English holds. The pride of Portugal is dead; and her name is unknown in Persia, save for a few rust-eaten guns and crumbling towers. The Dutch, who formerly swept the Gulf and dictated terms to the Persian kings, support a vice-consul only at Bushire. Venice and Genoa have long ago disappeared from the category of independent states. Armenians still traffic and barter in Persian bazaars, and flourish by the profits of retail trade, as they will do till the crack of doom; but Armenia is not a nation, and her wealth is only that of households. The mastery of the seas has decided the long-drawn conflict. Pompey's aphorism has been proved true. The struggle has resolved itself into a duel between the maritime power of the north and the maritime power of the south. Germany, Austria, and France claim a portion of the import trade, but cannot be regarded as serious competitors. It is to a contemplation of the duel thus in progress, and to a balance of the position and prospects of the two combatants, that I now turn.

Russian ascendency in the North

Though the appearance of Russia as a formidable influence upon the scene was foreshadowed from the days of Peter the Great, and was facilitated by the collapse in the middle of the same century of the last attempted revival of the British Caspian trade, it was not till after the Russo-Persian wars in the first quarter of the present century, and more especially not till after the treaty of Turkomanchai in 1828, that Russian mercantile ascendency in the north could be said to have at all a stable foundation. By the earlier treaty of Gulistan in 1813, the Caspian had already become a Russian *mare clausum*; but in 1817 Yermoloff, the Russian ambassador, had pressed in vain for the appointment of a Russian commercial agent at Resht. Derbend, Baku, and Lenkoran had now, however, become Russian instead of Persian ports; and it was only a matter of time how soon the advantages of commanding position on the one side, and complete impotènce on the other, would be seized by the conqueror. In 1828 the political treaty of Turkomanchai, which sealed the strategical ascendency of Russia on the north-west, was accompanied by a commercial treaty, which did the same in the mercantile arena, and which, by fixing an *ad valorem* duty of five per cent. upon all imports and exports passing through Russian hands, set the model which has been followed in all similar engagements with foreign powers on the most-favoured-nation scale. It is only, however, within the last thirty years that Russia has awakened to the real value of the spoil, or has developed the means of adequately profiting by it. Within that period, the final subjugation of the Caucasus, the steps whereby first Poti, then Tiflis, and finally Batum, have been connected by rail with Baku, the simultaneous improvement of railway communications from Central Russia to the Volga and Astrakhan, the extended navigation of the Volga, and, above all, the creation of a large merchant marine upon the Caspian, have given an impetus to, at the same time that they have fortified the monopoly of, Russo-Persian trade on the north, that cannot possibly be exaggerated. The almost miraculous growth of Baku in particular, since the expansion of the petroleum industry, has created a large demand, and has provided a handy neighbouring market for Persian timber, skins, corn, rice, and dried fruits. More recently the construction of the Transcaspian railway, by opening a new gateway into Persia on the north-east, has extended the line of Russian superiority to Khorasan, and has handed to her the keys of the entire north of the Shah's dominions. Backed up throughout this period by a fiscal policy of rigid exclusiveness—a policy which led the Russians first to throw open the Caucasus to transit trade between Europe and Persia, in order to popularise and bring money to the route, and later on to close it altogether in order to keep a lucrative monopoly for themselves, and in pursuance of which the Russian Government habitually grants exemptions or rebates upon goods shipped for Persia and the East—the control of the northern markets has naturally gravitated towards Russian hands, and has only been successfully contested in cases where the manifest superiority of English goods has enabled them to survive the cost of the long caravan journeys from the Black Sea, from Baghdad, or from the Gulf. It should be noted further that the Russian approaches, both by land and sea upon the north, are far easier and more expeditious than are the corresponding avenues open to Great Britain upon the south and west. Though the Persian ports or landing-places on the Caspian can scarcely be distinguished, in point of execrable badness, from their rivals on the Gulf, they are yet situated within as many hundred miles of the Russian ports of embarkation or the reverse, as the Gulf ports are distant thousands from Bombay or from London. The Russian frontier is within eighty miles of Tabriz, the commercial capital of Persia. Russian steamers can unlade their goods within 160 miles of Teheran, the political capital and largest centre of population. No such stupendous passes intervene between the landing-stage and the market on the north as the tear-compelling *kotals* of the southern coast. Finally, contrast the distance that separates Teheran from Manchester with that between Teheran and Moscow!

Fortunately, this Russian predominance, which I shall presently analyse in detail, stands neither uncontested nor alone. It is balanced in the whole of Central and Southern Persia by a British ascendency, with which the distance of Russia from the Indian Ocean has never enabled her to compete, and which is now so firmly established as to defy assault. This superiority, though it was anticipated and founded by the meritorious part played by Great Britain in the pacification of the Persian Gulf from the beginning of the present century, is yet, in its later, and as yet unarrested, expansion, the work of a period even nearer to ourselves than that which has witnessed the corresponding growth of Russian trade on the north. It has been comprehended within the last twenty years, and may be said to date from the opening of the Suez Canal. In 1876 the tonnage of British shipping in the Persian Gulf was returned at only 1,200 tons. In 1889 115,000 tons of shipping, of which 113,000 were British, were cleared from the port of Bushire. In 1870 only a monthly steamer visited the Gulf from Bombay, and three or, at the most, four sailing ships a year from England. The weekly and fortnightly services that now ply with exemplary regularity have been named in my chapter on the Persian Gulf. This astonishing growth is to be attributed to four causes: to the

British ascendency in the south

immense reduction of distance by the Suez Canal route; to the greater security that prevails in Persia itself, and to the corresponding spread of knowledge as to its needs; to the exclusive policy of the Russian Government, which, by shutting the northern gates to every other power, has driven England to improve and develop her southern means of access; and, above all, to the vast improvement in steam service and the cheapening of maritime freights.[1] Where Manchester goods once entered Persia through Turkey, they now are shipped direct from England or are reshipped from Bombay. On the other hand, this traffic—the still improving condition of which is demonstrated by the prosperity of the Gulf ports, by the large profits made by mercantile houses, both Persian and European, and by the annually increasing yield from customs—is hampered by drawbacks greater than any that attend the northern avenues of commerce. The climate of the southern seaboard is fearfully and wonderfully made. The distances between port and market are enormous. The intervening passes are a byword and a horror. That Anglo-Indian trade should successfully vanquish these several obstacles, and should, in their despite, be steadily extending its borders, is no mean proof of industrial enterprise.

The middle ground

Such and so firmly rooted are the rival ascendencies on the north and the south, Russian predominance in the one quarter being met and balanced by British predominance in the other. Between the two exists a middle region over which both parties are emulously endeavouring to extend their sway, and the destiny of which, as yet undecided, will supply, in a manner, a touchstone of the respective capacities and probable future of the combatants. Into the controversy that is there being waged I shall enter with the comfortable advantage of being able to show that, thus far, the British have made more extensive inroads into the enemy's ground than the Russians have into ours.

Total of Persian exports

Before, however, I pass to this, which is, properly speaking, a sub-section of the larger subject of Persian Commerce as a whole, I would wish to summarise the present condition and to estimate, so far as possible, the total value of the latter, so as to give some idea of the nature of that prize for which British and Russians are contending. I have, in a previous

[1] In 1870, the freight on iron-bars from London to Bushire was 69*s*. 6*d*. a ton. In 1883, it had sunk to 30*s*., and is now less.

chapter on the Resources of Persia, furnished some accounts of the indigenous products and manufactures of the country, the surplus of which, after feeding, sustaining, or clothing its people, constitutes the bulk of his exports to foreign lands. I will not here recapitulate that information, but will content myself with presenting a tabulated summary of the value of the articles so exported, referring my readers for an explanation of the individual items to the chapter before mentioned. The following is an approximate statement of the value of Persian exports for the year ending September 30, 1889, my impression being that the figures, where they err, do so on the side of depreciation; and that the totals, both of bulk and value, may be reckoned at a rather higher figure:—

Exports from Persia for year ending September 30, 1889.

	Value in *tomans*		Value in *tomans*
Opium	1,900,000	Hides (cow and ox)	50,000
Cotton (raw)	500,000	Calico prints	10,000
Wool (unwashed)	64,000	Rice	1,000,000
Silk (raw)	1,300,000	Turquoises	20,000
Silk (cocoons, &c.)	50,000	Wine	1,000
Asafœtida	280,000	Horses	60,000
Gall nuts	100,000	Cattle	10,000
Gum tragacanth	100,000	Dates	25,000
Leeches	1,000	Drugs	30,000
Tobacco (*tumbak*)	300,000	Dyeing and colouring materials	90,000
Tobacco (for pipes and cigarettes)	50,000	Grain (wheat and barley)	200,000
Carpets	300,000	Provisions and stores	20,000
Shawls	35,000	Rose water	50,000
Raisins	160,000	Woollen goods	100,000
Dried fruits, pistachio nuts, &c.	250,000	Salt	10,000
Saffron	60,000	Spices	100,000
Skins (goat and sheep), untanned	20,000	Seeds	26,000
Skins (goat and sheep), tanned	10,000	Sundries	160,000
		Total	7,442,000

Calculated at the then rate of exchange (thirty-five *krans* to the pound) this total is equivalent to a sum of about 2,126,000*l.*

I now turn to the imports, the totals of which I shall merely enumerate here, postponing for the moment the question of British and Russian competition and the relative shares of the two nations. Richly endowed though Persia be with a wide diversity of natural products and manufactures, it will have been

Character of imports

noticed that she is singularly deficient in those materials which, in the eyes of the West, constitute the necessities and still more the comforts of civilised life. She makes little or no sugar, she grows neither coffee nor tea; and yet she consumes enormous quantities of the first and last, and a considerable quantity of the second. Her own oil-wells being untapped, her streets and houses are lit by Russian or American kerosine. Though believed to possess the precious metals in sufficient quantity to repay the working, she imports all her silver and gold. As long as her own copper and iron mines lie untested, the one must be purchased in sheets, the other in bars. It is a dismal reflection that, while every district in Persia is reported to possess its copper mine, barely a single cooking pot is made of the native metal. Hardware, cutlery, glassware, crockery, and porcelain—all these must be introduced into a country which can only work iron in the rudest fashion, which makes no glass, and which has all but lost the ceramic art. The assumption of European tastes carries with it the consumption of European wines, spirits, and liqueurs. The Persians are eminently a race of sportsmen, and, for all above the middle grades, arms and ammunition must be procured from the West. Jewellery, clocks, and watches are a further concomitant, if not a *sine qua non*, of civilisation. A Persian Minister or nobleman must possess his victoria or his brougham, and who ever heard of such a vehicle being built in the country? Finally, there is the illimitable department of dress, affecting both sexes and all classes, from the sovereign to the cultivator of the soil. Silks, satins, and broad cloth are the indispensable luxuries of the upper classes; prints, shirtings, and cotton fabrics are worn by all. The humblest peasant is clothed from Manchester or Moscow; the indigo that dyes the hood which his wife draws so closely round her ill-favoured physiognomy has been shipped from Bombay. Persia, in fact, from the highest to the lowest grade, is absolutely dependent upon the West; whence, perhaps, it arises that she struggles with such fanatical energy against an influence of which she wears the external signs, but which in her heart of hearts she abhors.

Foreign feeders

The main feeding grounds of Persian needs are Great Britain, Russia, France, Germany, Austria, and India. Roughly speaking, the imports from Great Britain may be said to consist of calicoes, chintzes, white and grey shirtings, Mexican or T-cloths, Turkey-red twills, broad cloth, copper, crockery, candles, arms, and ammunition; from Russia of cotton fabrics of every description, sugar, oil, candles, lamps, glassware, mirrors, crockery, hardware, carriages and harness, tea trays, samovars; from France of loaf sugar, glassware, china, and silk fabrics; from Germany and Austria of glass, woollen cloths, cutlery, sugar; from India of tea, indigo, tin and zinc, drugs, medicines, spices, muslin, gold and silver thread, and brocades.

Total value

The total of these imports for the year 1889, exclusive of bullion and specie, which constitute a large item,[1] but the figures of which I was unable to procure, was supplied to me as follows:—

IMPORTS INTO PERSIA FOR YEAR ENDING SEPTEMBER 30, 1889.

	Value in *tomans*		Value in *tomans*
Sugar (loaf)	1,000,000	Hardware (Austrian)	20,000
Sugar (candy and soft)	80,000	Hardware (Russian)	10,000
Tea	200,000	Glassware and crockery (Austrian)	120,000
Spices	1,000,000	Glassware and crockery (French)	80,000
Petroleum	180,000	Glassware and crockery (Russian)	100,000
Flour	1,000	Wine and spirits	10,000
Calicoes (English prints)	3,000,000	Jewellery, clocks, and watches	50,000
Calicoes (Russian prints)	500,000	Iron, in bars and plates	165,000
Calicoes (English white and grey shirtings)	3,000,000	Glass (window panes)	100,000
Silks, satins, woollens (English)	1,800,000	Coffee	50,000
Silks, satins, woollens (Austrian)	100,000	Drugs and chemicals	40,000
Silks, satins, woollens (French)	50,000	Indigo	150,000
Silks, satins, woollens (Russian)	50,000	Arms and ammunition	50,000
Cloth (Austrian)	1,000,000	Jute and canvas bags	20,000
Cloth (Russian)	500,000	Sundries[2]	200,000
Hardware (English)	70,000	Total	13,696,000

This total, at the same rate of exchange, is equivalent to 3,913,100*l.* The added values of exports and imports according to the above tables (the accuracy of which, though procured from official sources, I cannot positively guarantee) amount to 6,039,400*l.*, or, if we make a liberal estimate for the inclusion of specie in the imports, to 6,300,000*l.*, as the total value of Persian trade.

[1] The Consular Returns from the Persian Gulf show that in 1888 the value of specie imported into Bushire, Bunder Abbas, and Lingah was £216,740, and in 1889 £176,524. Whether these totals represent the whole value of specie imported, I cannot say.

[2] The import of copper appears to have been omitted from this table.

There is a further, though less strictly scientific, means of estimating the total value of Persian trade, viz., from the Custom-house returns. In the previous chapter I have explained the system on which the customs are collected, and have shown that, whilst on European traders the duty levied, both for imports and exports, is five per cent. *ad valorem*, on Persian traders it varies between three and eight per cent., or even more. I have also shown that, under the farming system which is universal in Persia, the farmer, besides paying in the stipulated sum to the governor or the Shah, makes a handsome profit for himself, which sum may be estimated as at least twenty per cent. in excess of the official return. Taking four per cent. *ad valorem*, therefore, as the mean of customs paid by all merchants, foreign and native, and adding twenty per cent. to the value of the farm-money actually paid, we arrive at the following rough estimate of the total value of Persian trade for the nine years from 1880 to 1889.

Estimate from custom-house returns

Year	Government Receipts		Rate of Exchange	Farm Money + 20 per cent.	Estimated value of Trade
	Tomans	£	*Krans*=£1	£	£
1880–81	708,629	257,700	27½	309,240	7,731,000
1881–82	785,290	281,600	27⅞	337,920	8,448,000
1882–83	807,770	281,400	28⅝	337,680	8,442,000
1883–84	814,000	280,700	29	336,840	8,421,000
1884–85	806,000	264,262	30½	317,114	7,928,000
1885–86	838,000	250,150	33½	300,180	7,504,000
1886–87	850,000	253,730	33½	304,476	7,612,000
1887–88	820,000	241,176	34	289,411	7,235,000
1888–89	800,000	235,294	34	282,352	7,057,000

It will be observed that the last-named total exceeds by no less than 700,000*l.*, that derived from the elaborate table before quoted, but which I have already stated that I regard as an under-estimate. My own impression, derived from a calculation of the volume of trade at the several ports or points of entry—a subject to which I shall next turn—is that the total commerce of Persia at the present time may be set down as from 7,000,000*l.* to 7,500,000*l.* —a rough estimate that was also given to me by two independent authorities—of which the imports constitute about two-thirds, and the exports the remainder.[1]

[1] Elisée Reclus gives the total volume of trade as £6,000,000. Whitaker's Almanack gives: exports, £2,260,000; imports, £3,850,000; total £6,110,000. The Almanac de Gotha gives: exports, £3,120,000; imports, £5,280,000; total £8,400,000. Mr. Herbert, Secretary of Legation at Teheran, in a F. O. Report of 1886 (Com-

Such being approximately the total value of Persian trade at the present time, I pass to an examination of its local distribution and of the shares in it that are claimed respectively by Russia and Great Britain. Already, in dealing with particular cities or provinces, such as Meshed, Tabriz, Isfahan, and Shiraz, I have supplied a more or less minute account of the existing mercantile situation; and in such cases will therefore merely summarise the results, referring my readers back for the details. In earlier chapters I have more than once found it convenient to make the tour of the Persian frontiers in order to explain with some system the various problems arising from their position or configuration. Let me once again repeat the journey, in order to elucidate the commercial *status quo*, pointing out at each stage of my advance the relative fortunes and opportunities of the two rivals. The number of principal trade arteries by which merchandise flows into or out of Persia is seventeen, which may be classified under the several zones of the north-west, the north, the north-east, the east, the south, and the west. I will deal with each in turn.

Persian trade arteries

In the north-west zone are included the two routes from Europe which converge at Tabriz, the largest distributing centre and city in Persia, and from there follow a common line to Kazvin and Teheran. Of these one may be described as the English line, the base of which is the Turkish port of Trebizond, on the Black Sea. The other is the Russian line, and starts from Tiflis, the capital of the Caucasus. The Trebizond trade route was first initiated about the year 1830 by Abbas Mirza, the son of Fath Ali Shah and Heir Apparent to the Persian throne,

N.W. zone 1. Trebizond-Tabriz line

mercial No. 18), calculating the totals on the basis of the Customs returns, gave the figures for 1884–5 as exports, £2,888,000; imports, £5,012,000; total, £7,900,000; which total he increased to £9,875,000, by adding a proportion of one-quarter for the trade of places from which no returns were forthcoming. In a later report (Annual Series, No. 113) he gave the following impossible figures for 1885: exports, £4,366,109; imports, £5,768,352; total, £10,134,461. This total, however, he somewhat reduced by adding 10 per cent. to the value of the exports, and deducting 10 per cent. from that of the imports, for these reasons: (1) because on exports the Custom-house officers are in the habit of accepting the merchant's declaration of value without examination; (2) because on the imports, the 5 per cent. *ad valorem* is levied on the merchant's price, which is largely in excess of what he has paid to the Indian or European manufacturer. He, therefore, represented the imports as roughly £5,250,000, and the exports as £4,000,000; or a total of £9,250,000. The items of his calculation can be shown, however, to have been exaggerated in every instance.

who despatched a vessel laden with English goods for Persia from Constantinople to that port. About the same time an English consul was first appointed by Lord Aberdeen at Trebizond.

2. Tiflis-Tabriz line

In 1830 only one English vessel entered the harbour of Trebizond out of a total of twenty-six European (other than Turkish) vessels; in 1832, two out of forty-two.[1] Mr. Stocqueler, travelling this way in the latter year, pointed out the future trade importance of Trebizond, suggested the institution of an English consul at Tabriz and of a commercial agent at Erzerum [we now have consuls at both], and said of the newly-founded trade:—

During the past two years a little has been carried on by two or three adventurous persons, who report that British manufactures are purchased with avidity. No less than 750,000*l.* worth of such goods have found their way through Erzerum to Persia.[2]

Encouraged by Abbas Mirza, a Mr. Burgess soon after opened trade *viâ* Trebizond with Tabriz and Teheran; and in 1836 Colonel Stuart reported that: 'Such is the rage for English goods that three princes went by night, not long ago, to make purchases at Mr. Burgess' warehouse [in the capital], though expressly forbidden by the King.'[3] The same writer observed:—

Of the exports, the Russians export nearly two-thirds more than the English. Our merchants, however, though unprotected by a treaty, daily acquire a superiority in the market. Their yearly exports from England by Trebizond, the greater part of which are destined for Persia, amount to 900,000*l.*, being about seven-eighths of the whole amount of goods brought into the county.[4]

The Trebizond-Tabriz route continued to flourish and to be patronised by British trade until the Russians opened the Trans-Caucasian railway from Poti, and, for prudential reasons, continued to maintain free trade in the Caucasus. In 1877, however, deciding that foreign competition was an impediment to their own

[1] British navigation with the Black Sea is still so scandalously ill-developed, in spite of the certain profits to be derived from direct connection with England, that in 1889 only twenty-six British steam vessels, with a tonnage of 26,425 tons, entered the port of Trebizond out of a total of 554, with a tonnage of 528,943 tons, the French in the same period being responsible for 110 steamers with a tonnage of 159,588 tons.

[2] *Fifteen Months' Pilgrimage*, vol. ii. p. 3.

[3] *Journal of a Residence*, p. 225.

[4] This is an interesting statement, as fixing the total amount of imports at the time, viz., about £1,030,000; and as showing how small was the proportion claimed by the Gulf trade.

industries, they first issued a prohibitory decree against the Caucasian transit trade. Merchandise was at once driven back to the Trebizond route, the cost of freight by the Russian railway under the plomb system [1] being so enormous as to be almost prohibitive.[2] The protective edict was subsequently modified, and for a time it was rumoured that a free trade policy was again to be pursued. But in 1883 all idea of the latter was finally abandoned, and the transit of foreign merchandise through the Caucasus may be said to have practically ceased.

For a few years after 1883 the Trebizond route did not appear to profit as it might have been expected to do by the closure of the competing channel, although it is uncertain how far the diminution of traffic was due to the diversion of merchandise to the southern or Gulf avenues of entry. Since 1887, however, the figures of Anglo-Persian import and export have exhibited a steady rise, and the total volume of trade between the two countries by this route in 1889 amounted to 610,140*l.* The route itself cannot be regarded as a very favourable one for the operations of British commerce, for, although no transit dues are levied by the Turkish Custom-house,[3] yet 500 miles of mountainous and, in winter, sometimes impassable road supervene between port and market; and if we contrast the distances by land or sea that require to be traversed by the merchandise of the rival nations, it is astonishing that a country handicapped so severely as is Great Britain can not only share, but, as I have shown in my chapter upon Azerbaijan, can almost control, the market-destination. The distance from Moscow to Tabriz by the shortest route—viz., *viâ* Astara, on the Caspian—is

[1] It is as follows: A sum, equivalent to the full value of the goods, has to be deposited in the Russian custom house at the port of entry, and the goods are then 'plombed.' On reaching the frontier the 'plomb' seals are examined, and of these be intact, and the goods bear no evidence of having been tampered with *en route*, certificates are granted by which the owner can get his guarantee-deposit refunded. But it is obvious that the merchant thus incurs a double loss of interest—on the capital sunk in his venture and also on the sum paid as security.

[2] The carriage of a piano from Marseilles to Teheran, *viâ* Poti, was £120 under this system, nearly the whole charge being incurred after entering Russian territory. A photographic apparatus cost thirteen francs in transit from Marseilles to Poti, 180 francs from Poti to Teheran.

[3] Lately the Turks have created a new difficulty, by insisting upon a second verification of the goods at a deserted spot named Kizildizeh, where there is no accommodation, and which is exposed to brigandage, in addition to the examination at Erzerum.

1,582 miles, of which 214 are by caravan. The distance from London to Tabriz, *viâ* Trebizond, is 5,176 miles, of which 520 are by caravan. If we compare the Tabriz figures with the Trebizond figures for 1889, as follows—

Tabriz.	£	Trebizond Transit Trade to and from Persia.	£
Total Imports	853,891	Imports from England . .	574,040
„ Exports	389,456	Exports to England . .	36,100
Total Trade .	£1,243,347	Total Trade . .	£610,140

we see that nearly 70 per cent. of the Tabriz imports, and 11 per cent. of the exports, or half of the entire trade, is in British hands, a result which appears even more satisfactory when it is seen, as demonstrated in the chapter before referred to, that, in the only fields where she seriously competes, Great Britain is practically master of the field.

In the same period the figures of the Russian trade with Tabriz, *viâ* Julfa, were returned as follows by the official 'Review of the External Trade of Russia on her European and Asiatic Frontiers,' published at St. Petersburg: imports from Russia, 22,220*l.*; exports to Russia, 120,035*l.*

Two subordinate trade routes also find their objective in Tabriz. One of these is the purely Russian line from the port of Astara, on the Caspian, which is hardly as much used as its physical advantages would lead us to infer that it might be. The Russian figures of trade by this route in 1889 were as follows: imports from Russia, 52,404*l.*; exports to Russia, 198,716*l.*

3. Astara-Tabriz line

The other is the Levant route, *viâ* Aleppo and Mosul, from Alexandretta on the Syrian coast, which is still followed by a few caravans. I have been unable to procure the figures relating to the latter route, and they are probably not in existence. They would not, however, be at all considerable. A small traffic also exists between Baghdad and Tabriz *viâ* Suleimanieh, but this line scarcely deserves to be included among Persian trade routes.

4. Alexandretta-Tabriz line

The second, or northern zone, has for its objective the capital Teheran and the supply of the provinces which are fed from that centre. Here the Russian monopoly of the Caspian and the prohibitory tariffs charged upon Russian railroads before reaching the

Caspian ports, have placed the bulk of trade in Russia's hands. She approaches and supplies the capital by two routes from the Caspian; the first, the principal caravan entry into Persia from the port of Resht; the second, from Meshed-i-Ser, a shorter but less organised, and on the whole costlier, journey. No one can compete with Russia upon either of these lines; and they give her a position in the Teheran market overwhelming in its physical advantage. From the Englishman's point of view, therefore, it is satisfactory to read in the Russian newspapers loud and reiterated complaints of the decline of her commercial influence in the north. For my own part, I think that these jeremiads are as uncalled for on the part of Russia as any exultation on the part of England would be premature and unwise. From careful questioning of those qualified to pronounce, I am led to believe that the following is the actual condition of affairs in the Teheran market. The import trade from the south, i.e. from the Gulf, which is almost wholly English, has very largely increased in the last ten years, and in certain goods enables our merchants to hold their own against Russia in spite of the enormous advantages possessed by the latter. Thus, in cotton goods the market is at present about evenly divided between the two rivals, England having, perhaps, a slight advantage. Austria claims the largest share of glassware and woollen goods. Russia has almost the exclusive supply of sugar, oil, and candles. The bulk of the trade is, of course, Russian, though much of it is in cheap articles, that aggregate no very imposing total. That Russia herself is dissatisfied with her present position is shown by the symptoms which I have already mentioned and by an exhibition of every variety of Russian goods that was opened while I was in Teheran by the well-known Moscow firm of Konshine, in order to attract local purchasers and to secure orders from Persian traders in general. I afterwards read in the Russian journals that the enterprise did not meet with the success to which its excellence, both in material and selection, seemed to me to entitle it; that the wares were too costly for the Persian taste; and that the most gratifying transaction recorded was the sale of a pair of decanters to the Shah. A feeling in Russia that her mercantile supremacy in north Persia is imperilled, may tempt her to undertake the construction of one of those northern railways of which I have spoken in an earlier chapter. My own impression is that, railway or no railway, in the bulk of imports she will retain

Northern zone. The Teheran market

the advantage, while in piece goods England will continue to compete with her on rather better than even terms.

It is difficult to analyse the items composing this northern trade, owing to the absence of any recent statistics. The latest figures

5. Resht-Teheran line

that I have seen relating to Resht are those of the year 1883, which return the trade passing through the Custom-house of Enzeli as: imports, 376,443*l.*; exports, 259,250*l.*; total volume, 635,693*l.* The figures for the same year relating to Meshed-i-Ser give the imports as 179,746*l.*; exports, 135,710*l.*;

6. Meshed-i-Ser-Teheran line

total, 315,456*l.* I cannot feel certain of the accuracy of either of these computations. In both cases the entire carrying trade by sea is in Russian hands, and the bulk of the imports will come from, just as the bulk of the exports will go to, Russia. Unfortunately, the Russian trade reports do not distinguish between the goods entering or leaving Persia at the several Caspian ports, but lump their figures together with those of the trade across the land frontiers.

Roughly speaking, the north-eastern zone consists of the extensive and wealthy province of Khorasan, upon whose trade I

N.E. zone

7. Gez-Astrabad line

have dwelt at length in my first volume. The lines of strategical entry into this region, previously indicated, correspond with the main avenues of commerce. These are two in number: the route for sea-borne goods from Gez, in the south-east angle of the Caspian, to Astrabad and Shahrud—again

8. Ashkabad-Meshed line

a Russian monopoly—and the new line in connection with the Transcaspian Railway at Ashkabad, of which the same control must be predicated. Prior to the opening of the latter during the last decade, the Gez-Astrabad route was the main avenue of entry for Russian merchandise into north-east Persia, which from that base was diffused throughout Khorasan, supplied Meshed, and penetrated to Herat. The returns for the year 1881, in which the Transcaspian Railway reached Ashkabad, and the last year, therefore, of the Gez trade route monopoly, were as follows:—imports, 287,640*l.*, of which 256,000*l.* were in piece goods (chiefly from Moscow, although some came from England *viâ* Constantinople); exports, 86,280*l.*, of which nearly half was silk; total, 373,920*l.*[1] These figures, which were compiled by Colonel Lovett, then British Consul at Astrabad, do not correspond with

[1] I have seen the figures for 1883 given as: imports, £209,448; exports, £274,515; but am at a loss to understand how the latter total could be explained.

the valiant totals published at St. Petersburg, but they are confirmed by local authority. Since the opening of the Transcaspian Railway, however, this route has lost much of its importance, eastern Khorasan, Meshed, and north-west Afghanistan being now almost entirely fed by the aid of General Annenkoff's line. Accordingly, the Gez returns show a marked decline, and the British native agent at Astrabad gave the figures of total native and Russian imports as 51,900*l.*, of which 19,090*l.* were Russian, and of total exports as 20,000*l.*, or a total trade of 71,900*l.* As regards the Meshed trade, I have shown in a previous chapter that the value of British goods imported into Meshed by the long overland route *viâ* Trebizond, Tabriz, and Teheran was in 1889 23,429*l.*; and of Anglo-Indian goods imported *viâ* Bunder Abbas, 60,871*l.*; while the value of Russian imports in the same period, mainly *viâ* Ashkabad and Kuchan, was 110,408*l.* I showed further that, in view of the marked advantages enjoyed by Russia over England in this quarter, her superiority may be expected to increase rapidly, the better quality and greater favour of English goods being unable to compete with a cheaper article imported from only a quarter of the distance.[1] The general commercial ascendency of Russia in Khorasan is, indeed, a fact which no one with a knowledge of the country and its markets can dispute, and which an inspection of the map at once explains. The utmost, as I have argued, that British commerce can there do is to concentrate its attention upon the southern or Anglo-Indian avenues of ingress, and to urge the improvement and greater security of the roads from the Gulf, at present in parts in an abominable condition, and the appointment of British Consular officers at Bunder Abbas, Kerman, and Yezd, so as to facilitate and extend the ingress of Bombay trade.

Transit route. 9. Meshed to Khiva and Bokhara

From Meshed a transit trade in Anglo-Indian wares, but more especially in tea, is conducted to Khiva and Bokhara. Out of 123,714*l.* worth of Chinese green tea imported into Meshed from Bunder Abbas in 1889, 122,857*l.* was in transit to the Khanates. It is scarcely credible, but it is true, that, owing to the exorbitant dues charged by the Amir of

[1] Before going to press I am afforded the opportunity (Jan. 1892) of confirming my own prediction by the figures of General Maclean's second Khorasan report (F. O. Annual Series, No. 976) for 1890–1. He shows that while Anglo-Indian imports into Khorasan have increased £71,500 in the year, Russian imports have increased £97,190; and that Russian piece goods are rapidly ousting British chintzes.

Afghanistan, this circuitous route to Bokhara is actually cheaper for Indian tea than the direct route from Peshawur *viâ* Kabul. A pound of tea costing 12 annas in India will cost 16 annas by the time it has reached Meshed, and 18 annas at Bokhara. If conveyed *viâ* Kabul it will cost 21 annas at its destination, the Amir of Afghanistan levying 80 rupees (5*l.* 13*s.* 4*d.*) on every camel-load of goods passing through Kabul to Bokhara, and the Amir of Bokhara levying 2½ per cent. *ad valorem* on the frontier.

A transit trade of no very great volume or importance prevails between Meshed and north-west Afghanistan. In 1889 the imports by this route into Khorasan were 17,272*l.*, consisting chiefly of *poshtins*, pistachio nuts, manna, and opium; the exports were 18,299*l.*, consisting of piece goods, sugar, iron, and steel.

10. Meshed to Afghanistan

In former days an alternative and a far more direct trade channel existed between India and North-east Persia by way of the Bolan Pass, Kandahar, Farrah, and Herat. The distance by this route from Chaman, the advanced point of the British railway in Beluchistan, to Meshed is only 680 miles, or less than 30 stages; but the Amir's paralysing exactions—amounting to no less than 2*l.* 2*s.* per cwt.—have caused its entire abandonment. In the winter of 1890–91, the late Sir R. Sandeman, the able British Commissioner in Beluchistan, surveyed and traversed the old *kafilah* route through Southern Beluchistan to Persia, *viâ* Las Bela and Pangjur, long deserted owing to the unsettled state of the country. As Beluchistan passes more directly under British influence, it is possible that this trade route may be reopened, and may supply an alternative line of entry from British India into Southern Persia. Meanwhile, it is gratifying to learn that another such route from the British outposts at Chaman in Pishin, through Seistan to Meshed itself has recently been opened and is now being tentatively pursued. Whereas the camel-caravans occupy seventy-five to ninety days between Bunder Abbas and Meshed, this route is only forty days in duration, and rests not upon a long sea-voyage but on a railway. We may hope and expect, therefore, to see it largely developed in the future.

11. Afghan transit route from India

I now pass from the northern zones, which fall naturally under the influence of Russia, in which that influence is, as might be expected, in the ascendent, but in which, in certain departments, it is being energetically contested by English or Indian competition, to the southern or maritime zone, where the balance swings almost exclusively and unassailably to the British side. The proximity of Bombay, the vast merchant fleet of Great Britain, and the consistent and intelligible policy that has for long been pursued in this quarter—almost the only sphere of Anglo-Persian relations for which this attribute can honestly be claimed—have given to this country the trading monopoly of the Persian Gulf and the unchallenged supply from that base of the towns and villages of Southern and, in a less degree, of Central Persia. Three ports along this coast —Bunder Abbas, Lingah, and Bushire—receive the main proportion of Anglo-Indian trade. In 1889, out of 114,396 tons of shipping that entered the harbour of Bunder Abbas, 104,496 were British; at Lingah the proportion was 82,780 out of 119,280 tons, and at Bushire 111,745 out of 118,570 tons. The published value of articles exported or imported to or from Great Britain and India is unreliable as a basis of calculation, because other European goods, such as French Marseilles sugar and Austrian glass, are imported, *viâ* Bombay, by English merchants in English boats, whilst at Lingah articles which are imported by sea and then re-exported by land, or *vice versâ*, are included by the custom-house officials in both tables.[1] Subject to these qualifications, the value of imports from Great Britain and India for the year 1889 to Bunder Abbas was 338,182*l.*, out of a total from all countries of 353,506*l.*; the exports to Great Britain and India, 185,258*l.*, out of a total to all countries of 336,129*l.* At Lingah the figures were: imports, 285,156*l.*, out of 589,939*l.*; exports, 379,988*l.*, out of 586,147*l.*– totals which, for the reason above mentioned, I regard as untrustworthy. At Bushire, imports, 744,018*l.*, out of 790,822*l.*; exports, 251,902*l.*, out of 535,076*l.* Of these ports, Bunder Abbas is the starting-point of the important caravan line running north to the large towns of Kerman and Yezd (a distance of about twenty-four stages from the coast), which are supplied, mainly from India, with piece goods, prints, and yarn, copper sheets, iron bars, lead, tin, sugar, tea, dyes, spices, glass, and china; exporting in return opium, wool, cotton, madder, almonds, pistachio nuts,

Southern zone.

12. Bunder Abbas-Kerman-Yezd-Meshed line

13. Lingah-Laristan line

14. Bushire-Shiraz-Isfahan line

[1] Thus, pearls appear in the import table of Lingah as £304,957, and in the export table as £306,667, the same article clearly doing duty twice. Similarly, specie appears among the imports as £157,812, among the exports as £146,325.

etc. Thence the caravans ultimately reach Khorasan.[1] Bushire is the starting-point of the principal caravan route in Persia, that upon which I travelled, leading from the Gulf, *viâ* Shiraz, Isfahan, Kashan, and Kum, to Teheran. Lingah is the port of the Persian province of Laristan.

I have already stated that this brisk and satisfactory condition of trade is the all but exclusive growth of the last twenty years, and is mainly to be attributed to the opening of the Suez Canal. I may here add, in closer particularisation, that the extent of this growth may be judged from the returns of the individual ports. In fifteen years, from 1873 to 1888, the value of the imports and exports of Bushire increased by about 5,000,000 rupees (one rupee = 1*s.* 5½*d.*). In a period of ten years, from 1878 to 1888, the trade of Bunder Abbas increased to a similar extent. In 1874 the customs of Bushire were farmed for 40,000 *tomans*, in 1889 for 99,000 *tomans*; in 1874 those of Bunder Abbas for 30,000 *tomans*, in 1889 for 53,000 *tomans*; in 1874 those of Lingah for 6,500 *tomans*, in 1889 for 12,000 *tomans*. I am glad to record my opinion that this growth is by no means exhausted; but that the total volume of Anglo-Indo-Persian trade by the Gulf may be expected to attain much larger dimensions in the future.

Rapid increase of trade

In the seaports and surrounding districts British predominance is of course unquestioned. Of greater interest is it to follow up the caravan line as it penetrates further into the interior, and to discover how far the difficulties and cost of carriage enable the superiority to be maintained, and where the dividing line is to be traced between the spheres of British and Russian control. Elisée Reclus says in his 'Universal Geography': 'Russian competition has already monopolised the trade of the northern provinces, leaving to the British dealer only a narrow zone round about Bushire.' I am happy to say that this is conspicuously untrue. The yearly spreading radius of Anglo-Indian trade extends from the Gulf ports even to the capital, a distance of 800 miles, and has for some time absorbed the intervening markets. Shiraz, at a distance of less than 200 miles from the coast, is so entirely within the dividing line on the

Trade of Shiraz and Isfahan

[1] The caravan route from Kerman to Meshed runs by Ab-i-bed, Rahwar, Naiband, and Tun. From Bunder Abbas the total distance is 940 miles, and occupies forty days for a mule, seventy-five days for a camel, exclusive of halts.

English side as to render any analysis of its trade superfluous. The value of its imports for 1889 was 327,657*l.*, of which nearly one-half was in cotton goods; of its exports 340,515*l.*, the excess of the latter being due to the large export of opium, amounting to more than one-half of the total value. It is when we come to Isfahan, next to Tabriz the largest distributing centre in Persia, that the question becomes one of lively interest. Situated at a point almost mathematically equidistant by road from the two seas, the Caspian and the Gulf—viz., 500 miles from either, Isfahan is, so to speak, a battle-ground where northern and southern influence might be expected to clash, and where much should hang upon the fate of the duel. It is gratifying, therefore, to be able to record that, from this crucial test, Great Britain emerges with easy laurels, four-fifths of the imports into the city being English or Indian, no Russian firms being established in the place (though native merchants trade in Russian goods), and Russia only making fitful efforts to compete from Teheran in certain styles of prints. From Bushire to Isfahan is a caravan journey for mules of from thirty to thirty-five days, and the freight of each mule load (two bales) is 41 krans, or 1*l.* 2*s.* 6*d.* From Resht to Isfahan is a caravan journey of about twenty-five days. I have seen it lamented in English writings, as an instance of the lack of enterprise among English merchants, that the European trade with Isfahan should be in the hands of a Dutch and a Swiss firm. The critic was in blissful ignorance of the fact that Messrs. Hotz and Ziegler, the firms in question, are English business houses, trading from England, almost wholly in English goods, with head offices at Manchester or London. A third English firm, trading under the name of the Persian Gulf Trading Company (formerly Messrs. Muir, Tweeddy, and Co.), have also opened a branch at Isfahan, and maintain representatives at Baghdad, Busrah, Bushire, Shiraz, and Teheran. Messrs. Ziegler have houses or agents at Isfahan, Yezd, Teheran, Tabriz, Sultanabad, Resht, Meshed, and Shahrud. Messrs. Hotz confine their energies to the central and southern zones, and have agents at Bushire, Shiraz, Isfahan, Burujird, Sultanabad, Yezd, and Baghdad and Busrah in Turkey. Messrs. Gray, Paul, and Co., large English merchants in Bushire and Busrah, also keep an agent in Isfahan. Messrs. D. Sassoon and Co. are represented by Europeans both at Bushire and Isfahan.

In my 19th chapter I gave a list of the main imports into and exports from the bazaars of Isfahan, with the countries from or to which they severally come and go. The upshot of the information there collected was that Isfahan may be regarded as the northern outpost of the zone of undoubted British influence, whence reconnaissances are being energetically pushed forward in the direction of Teheran and the populous cities of the west provinces. A few years ago it was quite anticipated that the trade of Isfahan would slip from English fingers, and dirges were chanted upon the impending doom. But a recrudescence of commercial activity in the south, attended by other circumstances which contributed to the same result, has led to a remarkable reassertion of British supremacy. Among the subsidiary causes must be counted the increasing luxury of the Persian upper and middle classes, and the unbusinesslike methods and long credits in which the Russian merchants, particularly at Tabriz, have indulged in their efforts to take the northern markets by storm. As a consequence, there has been a contraction of the total volume of trade in the north, and the corresponding expansion in the south which I have already sketched.

Western zone 15. Mohammerah-Shushter-Burujird line

Finally, I come to the western zone, which possesses one developed and one undeveloped avenue of commercial entry into Persia, the former at present absorbing a great deal of the trade which the latter will eventually attract. I allude to the Baghdad and the Mohammerah routes. To the latter, which can scarcely claim, as yet, to be included among the recognised channels of commerce, I have before made allusion in discussing the question of Persian roads and the navigation of the Karun River. From Shushter a caravan track, that has been explored and described by Mr. Mackenzie, Major Wells, General Schindler, and Mr. Lynch, leads by Mal Amir through the Bakhtiari country, a total distance of 260 miles, to Isfahan. But the rugged and perilous character of this route, and the absence of bridges or caravanserais, have prevented its adoption by the Isfahan merchants, and there appears to be no immediate chance, in spite of the Karun Concession, of its being at all widely utilised. The road scheme, of which I have spoken as now in course of execution, contemplates a branch road from Burujird to Isfahan, a distance of 210 miles; and I hear that the merchants of the latter place are looking forward with sanguine anticipations to its completion. As regards distance, it will not help them much for merchandise coming from the sea, as the distance from Ahwaz by road to Burujird and thence to Isfahan will be about the same as, if not a little more than, the present distance *viâ* Shiraz from Bushire, viz., 500 miles; but, being a wheeled track and equipped with a wagon service, it will provide both a speedier and a safer transit than do the horrible rock-ladders of the southern coast range. The great merit of the new route, when opened and organised, from a British point of view, will be that the cities and villages of Western and South-western Persia —Dizful, a more northern counterpart of Shushter, Khorremabad, Burujird, with 17,000 inhabitants and with a surrounding plain of great productiveness; Sultanabad, the centre of the carpet industry, and their dependent districts, which are among the richest corn-growing lands in Persia—will be brought within easy access of the Gulf, whilst their inhabitants will thereby be drawn into the mesh of the Lancashire cotton spinner and the Hindu artisan. Kermanshah with its 60,000 people, and Hamadan with 15,000, at present only served by the Turkish route from Baghdad, will also be brought within the southern zone of influence, and will swell the profits of Manchester and Bombay. A British Vice-Consul was appointed to Mohammerah in the autumn of 1890, and has since presented the first trade report ever issued from that town.[1] He estimates the total value of imports for the year 1890 (all but 1,500*l.* of which came from India) as 146,140*l.*, and of exports as 53,100*l.*, of which 49,540*l.* went to India. The imports, however, do not include those that are brought down stream in row-boats from Busrah. Nor must it be assumed that they are entirely destined for Persian consumption, there being a considerable traffic between Mohammerah, by way of the Bahmeshir, with Koweit on the opposite or Turkish side of the Persian Gulf, which imports its Indian merchandise in this fashion. The river steamers on the Karun are not as yet much utilised for traffic with the interior beyond Shushter, owing to the dilatoriness of the Persian Government in carrying out their promises for the simplification of customs.

Next comes the transit route from the Gulf to Western Persia by way of the Tigris and Baghdad. In this case, steamers of the British India Company and the Bombay and Persia Company trade from Bombay, carrying cargoes from India to the Turkish port of Busrah.

[1] Diplomatic and Consular Reports (Annual Series), No. 826, 1891.

Two business houses—Messrs. Darby, Andrewes, and Co., of Baghdad, and a native merchant of Busrah named Asfar, who charters vessels on a large scale—also run steamers direct from London to Busrah. There the goods are transhipped into the capacious river boats of the Euphrates and Tigris Steam Navigation Company (Messrs. Lynch Brothers) or into those of a Turkish Company, running on the Tigris between Busrah and Baghdad. There are at present two English and four Turkish boats engaged in this service. On these boats the goods are conveyed to Baghdad, where, after passing through the Custom-house, merchandise in transit for Persia proceeds by the caravan route which crosses the Turco-Persian frontier at Khanikin, and continues by way of Kermanshah and Hamadan to Teheran, a distance of 500 miles, and a caravan journey of twenty-eight days. Kermanshah and Hamadan are both the capitals of populous districts and the distributing centres of a wide area. For articles from Europe of uncommon bulk or value, such as carriages, pianos, and the like, whose destination is Teheran, this is the favourite road entry into Persia, owing to its shorter duration and to its immunity from the perilous *kotals* of the Bushire-Shiraz line. Merchandise travelling by this route has to pass two Custom-houses, Turkish and Persian, though the former is more to be feared for the artificial delays which it delights to enforce, than for the severity of its tariffs, 7 per cent. of the 8 per cent. *ad valorem* import duty exacted at Baghdad being returned when the frontier is crossed at Khanikin. The break of bulk at Busrah is one shortcoming from which this route suffers. But the Turkish quarantine regulations, which are skilfully devised so as to irritate and offend, are a worse. One day's quarantine is regularly imposed upon all vessels coming from Bombay, even when cholera is rampant in Turkey and extinct in India, the only motive that anyone has been able to suggest being the vulgar cupidity that is gratified by the extortion of quarantine fees. As I was descending the river from Baghdad an even more unwarrantable act of malice was perpetrated by the Turkish officials at Busrah. Five days' quarantine was imposed upon all vessels hailing from Persia, or that had touched at a Persian port, not because any epidemic could be alleged to prevail in Persia, but owing, it was said, to the British India boat by which I had come up from Bushire having stopped to put me down at Mohammerah—which it was entirely within its right of doing, the Turks having no control either over

16. Baghdad-Kermanshah line

vessels navigating the Shat-el-Arab, or over the Persian ports on its left bank—although I fancy that this was merely made the pretext for an act of incivility to the Persians and to Mohammerah in particular, of the rising fortunes of which the Turks at Busrah are intensely jealous, inasmuch as it must in the future divert a considerable part of the Persian trade that now passes through their voracious maw. In entering upon my travels, I narrated in my second chapter a fair sample of the amenities of Ottoman officialdom at Constantinople. In bringing them to a close I am compelled again to record that, for wanton obstructiveness and petty bureaucratic malevolence, no such people within my experience exists on the face of the globe.

Figures of transit trade

Figures are almost as hard to procure from Turks as from Persians, and no statistics have ever been published of the volume or value of the Persian transit trade passing through Baghdad. During my stay in that city, however, I procured from the best possible source the following estimate, which I was enabled to verify, and which, in respect of imports, I found to be substantially correct. From 20,000 to 25,000 laden mules annually enter and leave Baghdad upon this line. The goods imported by sea for Persian destinations which they carry, may be approximately classified as follows: Manufactures, chiefly Manchester piece goods, but also Continental woollen and cotton fabrics, 7,000 to 8,000 loads, valued at 150,000 Turkish *liras*;[1] Indian manufactures, 1,000 loads, valued at 20,000 *liras*; drugs, metals, &c.—comprising pepper, coffee, tea, sugar, indigo, cochineal, copper, and spelter—7,000 loads, valued at 100,000 *liras*; loaf-sugar, principally from Marseilles, 6,000 loads, valued at 30,000 *liras*. Total value, 300,000 Turkish *liras*, or 270,000*l*. Upon the assumption that every laden mule that left Baghdad for Persia had previously come into it from Persia, and that the imports and exports adjusted their values, my Baghdad informant fixed the value of Persian exports passing through that city for despatch by land or sea (chiefly wool, cotton, carpets, opium, gum, dried fruits), or, for local consumption (such as tobacco, *ghi*, dried and fresh fruits), at the same figure, viz., 300,000 Turkish *liras*, or 270,000*l*. Upon the same assumption, by which the total Persian transit trade would amount to 540,000*l*., he estimated it as constituting nearly a quarter of the entire trade of Baghdad, which is reckoned at

[1] The Turkish *lira* = 18*s*., or $13\frac{2}{3}$ rupees, or 34 *krans*.

2,475,000*l.*, giving a customs revenue of 115,000*l.* Subsequently, however, I was fortunate in procuring from two independent sources the figures of the Persian Custom-house at Kermanshah for the year 1889, which ought to be practically identical with the above, all traffic between Persia and Baghdad passing through that town, which is the first important place on the Persian side of the frontier. These figures were in substantial accordance with the Baghdad estimate as regards imports into Persia, the value of which they fixed, giving the details in each case, at 232,530*l.* But the value of exports from Persia was reduced by them from the hypothetical 270,000*l.* to the more modest total of 95,266*l.*, the entire volume of the transit trade *viâ* Baghdad being accordingly 327,796*l.*[1] Upon the Baghdad-Teheran line English trade is largely in the ascendant. The same reasons which keep Russia from the Gulf keep her from Baghdad; and in so far as she supplies Hamadan and Kermanshah, it will be *viâ* Tabriz from the north. Baghdad, in fine, falls under the category of the Gulf ports, and must be included in the zone of indisputable British supremacy.

A certain export and import trade also exists between Baghdad and Persian Kurdistan, particularly with Sinna, the capital of the
17 Baghdad-Persian Kurdistan line latter district; although, as it does not always cross a customs cordon, statistics of its volume are not easy to procure. There appeared, however, in the 'Journal de la Chambre de Commerce de Constantinople' of May 17, 1890, a copy of a report to the Turkish Minister of Foreign Affairs, in which the trade figures of Persian Kurdistan for 1889 were given as follows—Exports: carpets 4,000 Turkish *liras*, animals (principally sheep) 10,000, wool 2,000, dressed skins 2,000, butter 10,000, cereals, raisins, gall nuts, gum tragacanth, almonds, mastic, and tobacco 77,000; total 105,000 Turkish *liras*, or 94,500*l.*, of which 39,000 Turkish *liras*, or 35,100*l.*, were said to be exports passing into Turkey, and appertain, I conclude, to the route of which I am speaking. The imports from Turkey into Persian Kurdistan were given in the same report as: gall nuts 10,000 Turkish *liras*, undressed hides 5,000, stuffs 2,000; total, 17,000 Turkish *liras*, or 15,300*l.* The entire volume of Turco-Kurdish trade in this quarter

[1] The credibility of these figures is incidentally but strongly confirmed by those quoted by Mr. Herbert (F. O. Reports, Annual Series, No. 113) for the year 1885. The imports into Kermanshah from Baghdad were there valued at £218,700, the exports at £89,780.

was, therefore, only 50,400*l.*, and would appear to consist of local products or manufactures, and not, therefore, to fall within the sphere either of British or of Russian influence.

Summary

I have now again completed my tour of the Persian frontier and have discussed, point by point, the operations, actual or possible, of foreign commerce, just as I formerly did the chances of lines of rail. My survey may be summed up as follows: In the north-west, north, and north-east zones of influence a decided Russian superiority is met, and in parts disputed by vigorous British or Indian competition. In the south zone British ascendency is firmly established, and is yearly increasing. In the west zone it already exists, and is likely to be strongly fortified in the near future. In the middle ground, the British have gained a solid *pied à terre*, and are gradually but surely extending their borders. The total value of English trade with Persia is given in the latest Board of Trade Returns as: exports to Persia, 363,000*l.*, imports from Persia, 104,000*l.*; total, 467,000*l.*; but I am quite unable to reconcile these figures with those that I have before quoted or referred to in dealing with the several ports. The Consular returns from these show that, in 1889, the exports from Great Britain to Persia were as follows: Trebizond, 574,040*l.*, Bushire, 415,452*l.*, Lingah, 821*l.*, Bunder Abbas, 7,505*l.*, or a total of 997,818*l.*, nearly three times the Board of Trade figures. On the other hand, there is less discrepancy in the figures of imports into Great Britain from Persia, which appear in the same consular reports as follows: Trebizond, 36,100*l.*, Bushire, 83,990*l.*, Lingah, 9,915*l.*, Bunder Abbas, 137*l.*; total, 120,142*l.* In both cases it must be remembered that the totals which I have named and added up relate to four ports alone, although these are the chief of the many points of mercantile entry into Persia; and consequently that, if similar figures were forthcoming in the case, for instance, of Baghdad, the result would be even more imposing, and the Board of Trade Returns even more fallacious.

Volume of Anglo-Indo-Persian trade

For my own part I think that the fairest calculations are those which reckon the Persian trade with Great Britain and India combined, the manufactures of products of Hindustan being the result of the industry of British subjects, and being conveyed in British bottoms. Here we are assisted by the figures compiled in the Indian ports, and published in the annual statement of the Trade of British India.[1] For the year 1889 the returns were as follows:—

IMPORTS INTO PERSIA FROM INDIA.

	Rupees
(1) Indian Products and Manufactures	4,971,020 [2]
(2) British, Colonial, and foreign Manufactures . . .	12,256,030 [3]
Total	17,227,050

In the same period specie to the value of 1,048,890 rupees was imported from India into Persia.

EXPORTS FROM PERSIA TO INDIA.

	Rupees		Rupees
Merchandise . . .	8,039,160 [4]	Specie	1,309,580

Total of Indo-Persian trade, including merchandise only, 25,266,210 rupees, or 1,842,327*l.*; including specie also, 27,624,680 rupees, or 2,014,299*l.* Adding these to the figures of Anglo-Persian trade, *viâ* Trebizond, I am disposed to calculate the total annual value of Anglo-Indo-Persian trade as about 3,000,000*l.*, of which over 2,000,000*l.* will be in imports into Persia from Great Britain and India, and the remainder in exports in the inverse direction.[5]

No statistics of Russo-Persian trade, however loosely compiled, can show results even remotely comparable with these. From the Russian official publication before quoted, and issued by the Customs Department in St. Petersburg, I derive the following figures for the year 1889:—

Volume of Russo-Persian trade

IMPORTS INTO PERSIA FROM RUSSIA.

(1) Across the Caucasian frontier, and from Baku and Astara.

Food products	Raw and half-worked materials	Animals	Manufactured goods	Total
£496,241	58,760	5,189	144,718	704,908

(2) From Astrakhan.

Food products	Raw and half-worked materials	Animals	Manufactured goods	Total
£56,136	8,825	640	111,411	177,012
			Total	£881,920

[1] *Parliamentary Papers*, C. 6341, London, 1891.

[2] The principal items were: indigo 1,725,430 rupees, and tea 802,020 rupees.

[3] The principal items were: piece goods 7,322,830 rupees, sugar 1,135,490 rupees, tea 1,540,540 rupees, and copper, 516,120 rupees.

[4] The principal items were: raw cotton 2,441,780 rupees, wool 1,037,220 rupees, horses 179,260 rupees, fruits 1,261,080 rupees.

[5] Mr. Herbert, in his report, estimated the total value of this trade as £5,000,000 yearly, a calculation which was a mere rough shot, and, as I think, greatly exaggerated.

EXPORTS FROM PERSIA TO RUSSIA.

(1) Across the Caucasian frontier, and from Baku and Astara.

Food products	Raw and half-worked materials	Animals	Manufactured goods	Total
£510,811	131,692	39,229	117,627	799,359

(2) To Astrakhan.

Food products	Raw and half-worked materials	Animals	Manufactured goods	Total
£158,096	197,683	5	9,825	365,609
			Total	£1,164,968

In the same document the transit trade between Persia and Europe, *viâ* Russia, is returned as follows: imports into Persia, 2,568*l.*, exports from Persia, 112,076*l.*; total, 114,644*l.* The figures of imports show how completely the prohibitive policy pursued by Russia in the Caucasus has choked off foreign merchandise by that channel.

I cannot be positively certain, although I believe, that the above-quoted returns include the Russo-Persian trade with Khorasan by means of the Transcaspian Railway. Assuming that they do, the total annual value of Russo-Persian trade is a little over 2,000,000*l.*, or about 1,000,000*l.* less than the estimated total of Anglo-Indo-Persian trade. If we compare the respective situations and advantages of Russia and of Great Britain with her dependencies, including Hindustan, it cannot be denied that the balance is extremely creditable to the latter.

That this great volume of trade should have grown up between the Anglo-Indian peoples and Persia, is indeed a notable tribute to the continued existence of those qualities and instincts that have pushed this country to the front in the industrial competition of the world. For of Persia it certainly cannot be contended, in spite of commercial treaties and consular or ministerial protection, that the ways are made smooth for the foreign merchant. Of the physical drawbacks to trade, such as the absence of harbours, the character of the mule tracks, and, in parts, the absence of security, I have repeatedly spoken. The sudden and calamitous visitation of plagues, and the system of farming and collecting the customs, are each in their way impediments to the regular transaction of business. The corn trade is frequently disorganised and hampered by capricious embargoes on the export of grain, imposed in order to suit the whims or the speculation of some provincial governor, and promulgated or removed without the slightest regard to equity or to public con-

Obstacles to foreign merchants

venience. A further difficulty is that of remittances, arising, in the main, from the constantly fluctuating rate of exchange—a point in which the institution of banks in Persia may be expected to afford some relief. Another is the utter contempt for the most elementary principles of contract that is freely displayed by the Persian merchant. The Persian's conception of a contract is an agreement which is only to be adhered to if attended with certain profit to himself, but which may be hilariously repudiated if a fall in prices or some other oscillation in the market renders his own share in the bargain one of dubious issue. He will call upon the other party to the contract, and coolly inform him over several cups of coffee and amid repeated *kalians*, that he declines to take the articles agreed upon, which have very likely been ordered all the way from England, and are perhaps on the verge of arriving at their destination.[1] No scruples of morality, no stings of remorse, not even any fear of the consequences, affect the complacent egoism of the Persian trader; and in the absence either of any code of commercial honour or of any tribunals for enforcing legal obligations, the deluded merchant must grin and bear it. Sometimes no excuse whatever is forthcoming. I bought some articles myself of a dealer for the sum of 200 *krans*. Upon my sending the next day to inquire why they had not been delivered, the reply was returned that the owner had repented of the bargain and refused to part with them for less than 400 *krans*. Fraudulent bankruptcies, effected under the sanction of a *mujtahed* who has been bribed, are another favourite device of the Persian who is reluctant to pay. In fact, a commercial law, however rudimentary, is greatly needed to protect foreigners in their dealings with this amiable but hyper-ingenious people.

Such, so far as I have been able to appraise them, are the present aspect and partition of Persian commerce. If we turn to

The future

the future, the outlook, from an English point of view, may be regarded as eminently encouraging. The improvement of ports, if ever undertaken, the construction of roads

[1] That the Persians change not in this respect may be illustrated by a passage from the letter of Lawrence Chapman, one of the factors of the Russia Company in their fourth venture upon the revived British Caspian trade in 1568. He wrote: 'Such is the constancie of all men in this countrey, with whomsoever you shall bargen. If the ware be bought, and they doe mislike it afterwardes, they will bring it againe, and compell you to deliver the money for it againe, regarding the Shawgh's (Shah's) letter, which manifesteth the contrary, as a straw in the winde.'

already begun, the introduction of railways in the more distant future, will all of them swell the totals of Persian, and in particular of Anglo-Persian, trade. I have sometimes wondered whether more might not be done by individual enterprise to develop so promising a business. One of the most familiar Russian methods is an exhibition of Russian manufactures, skilfully collected and tastefully arranged, in some Oriental city still a comparative stranger to the implements and luxuries of the West. Why should not an exhibition of British and Indian products be held in Teheran? Delegates from Chambers of Commerce, commercial travellers, or trained middlemen, seem rarely, if ever, to include Persia within the sphere of their activity; and yet I know no country where a more watchful and instructed scrutiny is required to keep pace with the capricious movements of local fashion. The breadth of a strip, the structure of a pattern, the gradation of a colour, the width of a line, all these are of vital importance to so fastidious, and in a sense æsthetic, a people as the Persians. Moreover, taste and habit vary with the locality. What is stylish here is unacceptable there. What is popular to-day may be tabooed to-morrow. With a due regard for such local idiosyncrasies, and with a continuance of the larger enterprise that has already achieved such praiseworthy results, Great Britain may expect no mean consequences from the future of Persian trade.

Note on the Caravan-routes or Pack-roads of Persia.

To the analysis of the various avenues of trade entry into Persia, given in the above chapter, I subjoin a table of the stages or number of days into which the principal caravan tracks in the country are divided, and which I have taken from a pamphlet by Dr. Polak (1883). His figures, however, while fairly accurate with regard to the distance-divisions, require a slight addition, if regarded as a measurement of time, the muleteers insisting upon a halt of a few days whenever they come to a large town or city *en route*. Thus, the stages between Bushire-Shiraz, Shiraz-Isfahan, and Isfahan-Teheran, if added together, do not accurately represent the time occupied by a caravan in marching from the Gulf to the capital, a few days' repose being interpolated at Shiraz and Isfahan. The same applies to any route of tolerable length.

Route	No. of stages or days
1. Julfa-Tabriz	4
2. Tabriz-Teheran (*viâ* Mianeh, Zinjan, Kazvin)	14–16
3. Teheran-Isfahan (*viâ* Kum, Kashan)	10–12
4. Isfahan-Shiraz (*viâ* Kumisheh, Yezdikhast, Dehbid)	12
Isfahan-Shiraz (*viâ* the summer route from Yezdikhast)	10
5. Shiraz-Bushire (*viâ* Kazerun)	10
6. Teheran-Meshed (*viâ* Semnan, Shahrud, Nishapur) .	22
7. Teheran-Resht (*viâ* Kazvin)	9–10

Route	No. of stages or days	Route	No. of stages or days
8. Teheran-Baghdad (*viâ* Hamadan, Kermanshah, Khanikin)	24	15. Kerman-Bunder Abbas . .	20
9. Teheran-Meshed-i-Ser . .	6	16. Tabriz-Astara (*viâ* Ardebil) .	7
10. Teheran-Astrabad (*viâ* Sari) .	14	17. Tabriz-Resht (summer route *viâ* Masullah and Fumen) .	12
11. Isfahan-Yezd	10	18. Tabriz-Baghdad (*viâ* Suleimanieh)	20
12. Kashan-Kerman	25	19. Hamadan-Sinna	4
13. Yezd-Kerman	12	20. Hamadan-Shushter	15
14. Kerman-Bam	11	21. Resht-Astrabad	14

I may add that the contract mule-load is 350 lbs., but that the normal burden is 250–300 lbs. In 1889, the charge for mules on the principal pack-roads was as follows: Bushire-Shiraz, 30 *krans* per mule for 43 *farsakhs*; Shiraz-Isfahan, 40 *krans* for 70 *farsakhs*; Isfahan to Teheran, 45 *krans* for 81 *farsakhs*; Teheran to Baghdad, 81 *krans* for 143 *farsakhs*.

CHAPTER XXX.

BRITISH AND RUSSIAN POLICY IN PERSIA.

Why cut the thread of friendship with the shears of uncertainty?
ABDUR RAHMAN KHAN, *Letter to the Viceroy of India.*

Lest brute power be increased
Till that o'ergrown Barbarian in the East
Transgress his ample bound to some new crown.
TENNYSON, *Early Sonnets.*

IN previous chapters I have discussed at length the internal politics of modern Persia. This concluding chapter I devote to her foreign policy, a subject which practically resolves itself into her relations with the rival powers of Great Britain and Russia, her Government being only brought into contact with other European nations and with America in matters affecting missionaries and trade, that might almost be disposed of by consular officials, and seem to scarcely justify the expensive establishments maintained by France, Germany, Italy, and Austria at Teheran. Persia has, indeed, two Asiatic neighbours, with whom her frontiers are coterminous over a distance of many hundred miles on the east and west; but her relations with Afghanistan and Turkey do not here require more than a passing comment. With both powers she is on terms of ambiguous friendship, which the fears of either party alone prevent from assuming a less disguised expression. Both the Turks and the Afghans are Sunni Mohammedans; and a devout Shiah would almost leave off cutting a Christian's throat to shift his grip to that of a cursed Sunni. Both the Sultan and the Amir hold large tracts of territory that were once included within the Persian dominions. The possession of the sacred Shiah shrines of Kerbela and Nejef by Abdul Hamid is a sore point only excelled in bitterness by the spectacle of Abdur Rahman's flag floating over the ramparts of Herat. Persia, indeed, cannot forget that what is now Western Afghanistan has through the greater part of history been Eastern Khorasan, that Herat has been habitually ruled by

Foreign policy of Persia. Afghanistan

Persian sovereigns, viceroys, governors, or vassals, that it is inhabited by a people of Persian rather than Afghan traditions and sympathies, and that it is severed by no physical or ethnographical barrier from Meshed. Twice in this century has the cupidity of Persia for her old possession brought a Persian army to the walls of the Afghan fortress, entailing on each occasion diplomatic rupture, and on the second open war with Great Britain. Behind her weak barriers she now sits frightened and sullen, hating but powerless to prevent the reproach of an Afghan garrison in the ancient capital of Khorasan. It was to this sense of baffled cupidity that Lord Beaconsfield appealed when, in his contemplated partition of Afghanistan after the war of 1878, he committed the inexplicable error of proposing once again to hand over Herat to Persia, thereby giving the lie to one of the few uniform precepts that have been observed by Great Britain in her Central Asian policy of this century, and forgetting that, in surrendering Herat to the Shah, he was in reality vicariously abandoning the so-called 'Key of India' to the tender mercies of the Czar.[1]

The ill-feeling between Persian and Afghan was not mended by the result of the Seistan arbitration, which angered both parties, and particularly the Amir Shir Ali; nor was it improved after the last Anglo-Afghan war by the refuge, given under the form of a veiled incarceration, to Ayub Khan at Teheran. If it has since slumbered, it is only because Abdur Rahman Khan is too formidable a neighbour to admit of any tricks being played on the frontier, and because, weak and vacillating as the Asiatic policy of Great Britain has been in many respects, it has at least, with the single exception of Lord Beaconsfield's blunder, retained consistency in this—that it has always cried, and would still cry 'Hands off' to any attempt made by the Shah to regain an Afghan dominion that perished with Nadir Shah and can never be recovered. It may

[1] Lord Beaconsfield's plan of handing over Herat to Persia was explained by Sir H. Rawlinson in the *Nineteenth Century* of February 1880. General Grodekoff, in his Russian book, *The War in Turkomania*, vol. ii. p. 296, quotes the text of the proposed agreement (as to the accuracy or authenticity of which I am not able to speak). According to him, Herat was to be surrendered to Persia, an English resident was to be stationed there, English officers were to be admitted in order to fortify the city and drill the Persian garrison, no foreign agents were to be tolerated, and England was to have the right to introduce troops if any danger threatened the Persian domination. This was an attempt to shift the responsibility of holding Herat on to the shoulders of Persia, and could only have resulted in failure.

be added that the haughty and truculent soldiery of the Amir look with unconcealed contempt upon the Persian *serbaz*, and that the ranks of Eastern armies do not anywhere provide a more speaking contrast than the tattered Persian regular and the bearded braggart who wears the uniform of Abdur Rahman Khan.

Turkey

Touching the relations of Persia and Turkey, though the two countries have not been at war for over half a century, and though the immediate sources of provocation to either are less striking or numerous, yet the hereditary enmity of centuries still rankles, and it is with keen pleasure that Shah or Sultan witnesses a rebuff administered to Stambul or to Teheran. It was this jealousy rather than the reasons alleged to the public that accounted for the omission of Constantinople from the last European tour of Nasr-ed-Din. In times past the balance of advantage has been fairly equalised. If Persian forces have held Baghdad, Turkish armies have stormed and captured Tabriz. The Treaty of Erzerum, concluded in 1847, is the basis of the existing peace between the two countries; but the indeterminate state of the long Turco-Persian frontier from Mount Ararat to the Shat-el-Arab is both, as I have shown, the source of recurrent squabbles, and might at any time be magnified into a *casus belli*. The divided jurisdiction over the Kurds is a further element of trouble, which in the rebellion of Sheikh Obeidullah in 1884 nearly burst into a flame. In the south the rising fortunes of Mohammerah are as gall and wormwood to the Turks of Busrah and Baghdad, and how amiable the interchange of official civilities between the two powers can be my chapters on the Karun River and the Persian Gulf will have shown. Fortunately for peace, neither Persia nor Turkey in Asia is a country that can afford to fight; and the rivalry between the two powers seldom gets beyond petty territorial thieving and diplomatic recrimination.

Russia and Great Britain

In turning to the connection of Persia with the policies of Russia and Great Britain, and more especially of the latter—a subject which has rarely been absent from my mind's eye in the composition of this work—I cannot better emphasise the commanding claim which I conceive it to possess upon the attention of Englishmen than by quoting the language employed by Sir H. Rawlinson in the preface to his statesmanlike essays:—

The political affairs of a second-rate Oriental power like Persia cannot be expected to prove of engrossing interest to English readers; but it may be well to remember that the country is so placed geographically midway between Europe and India, that it can hardly fail to play an important part in the future history of the East; and that the condition of its people, therefore, and the temper of its Government, are entitled to the attention of thoughtful inquirers in a degree altogether disproportioned to the space which the dominions of the Shah occupy on the map of the world, or the rank which Persia holds in the scale of nations. The Persia of to-day is not, it is true, the Persia of Darius, nor even is it the Persia of Shah Abbas the Great; but it is a country which, for good or for ill, may powerfully affect the fortunes of Great Britain's Empire in the East, and which requires, therefore, to be studied by our statesmen with care, with patience, and, above all, with indulgent consideration.

This language is the utterance neither of apology nor of exaggeration. It is a faithful statement of the truth.

Preface to discussion of rival policies

In discussing the respective policies of the two Powers in Persia, I know that I am approaching an international question of some delicacy which, in the case of a writer belonging to either nationality, it is difficult to treat with complete freedom from bias. My previous writings, however, will, I hope, have absolved me from the charge of Russophobia; and in this case it will equally be my endeavour to handle the subject fairly and with justice to those whose interests in the East undoubtedly clash with our own. I shall put out of recollection the fact that Russia has to a considerable extent usurped the position, power, and prestige at the Persian Court which in the earlier years of this century were exclusively in British hands, because I conceive that the transformation, upon which our rivals are entitled to congratulate themselves, so far from being a ground for legitimate offence, is a condition of affairs for which our own policy, weak in its conception and calamitous in its results, has been mainly responsible; and that to cry over spilt milk is as futile an expedient in politics as it is in any other walk of life. It is sufficient to admit that the successive conquests of Russia, and her subsequent policy, pursued in Persia with much industry, if with no superabundant scruple, have placed her in a position where she exercises a powerful control over Persian affairs, and requires to be consulted in any readjustment of Persia's political relations. More to my immediate purpose will it be to discuss the extent to which that control actually or in prospect amounts, and the designs which it is beyond question that it is to be utilised to promote.

Firstly, then, as to Russia's claims and pretensions in Persia. I venture without fear of contradiction upon the statement that these are distinctly, and in parts avowedly, hostile. Surveying the history of the present century, we see that, piece by piece, partly by open war and partly by furtive nibbling, Russia has appropriated more and more of Persian soil.

Russian absorption of Persian soil

By the treaty of Gulistan, in 1813, she acquired from Persia the provinces of Georgia, Imeritia, Mingrelia, and Persian Daghestan, Shirvan, Ganjeh, Karabagh, parts of Talish, and the ports of Derbend and Baku, while Persia was prohibited from maintaining any armed vessels upon the Caspian. In 1828, by the treaty of Turkomanchai, besides confirming these conquests, she gained Erivan, Nakhchivan (including the Armenian religious centre, Echmiadzin), as well as a war idemnity of nearly 3,500,000*l.* Since then it is true that no open hostilities have occurred between the two countries; but the process of territorial absorption has continued under the cover of an amicable alliance, and is being stealthily pursued at this very hour. In the course of the Shah's recent visit to Europe I observed that some too flattering courtier congratulated His Majesty upon not having lost or ceded one inch of Persian soil during his long and, on the whole, meritorious reign. This compliment must have caused its recipient an inward twinge. Did he, perhaps, remember that in 1869, when the Russians occupied Krasnovodsk and Balkan Bay, he had protested against the act as a violation of Persian territory? And if this could be contended of those places, how much more would it hold good of Chikishliar and Ashurada? Even if it be admitted that the Persian sovereignty over Merv was but a shadowy claim (though it has been more than once acknowledged by the Tekkes themselves), yet it is beyond question that the Transcaspian conquests of Russia have transferred many Persian villages to Russian hands. The pastures of the Atek, lying below the Kopet Dagh, the villages of Kaahka, Mehna, Chacha, and Dushak, the position at Sarakhs —all these were once Persian property, but are so no more. In my chapters upon Khorasan I have shown that the erosive process is still going on; and the Persians have more than once complained of the too liberal interpretation of the Akhal Boundary Treaty of 1881, by which the Russians have included within their border the

Persian territories of Kulkulab, Germab, and Kelta Chenar, and are daily appropriating more and more of the head-waters of the mountain streams. These movements are typical of a policy which may temporarily content itself with such small pickings, but whose ambition ranges over a much wider ultimate horizon, and is supported by powerful guarantees of success.

Let us indeed pause to contrast the position enjoyed by Russia in relation to Persia now with that which she occupied at the close of her last war, over sixty years ago; remembering that any advantages subsequently acquired have been gained under shelter of peace, and without firing a shot, by the pressure of a diplomacy which, whatever its moral standard, has never committed the culpable error of forgetting or concealing its own strength. At the time when, by the treaties above mentioned, the Caspian Sea was first converted into a Russian lake, Russia possessed neither military nor mercantile marine upon those waters. Many hundred steamers now plough the Caspian waves and, in the absence of any other navy whatsoever, control its shores for purposes either of commerce or aggression. The great improvements in river navigation on the Volga have also brought the military resources of Kazan and Central Russia in general into close communication with her Asiatic dominions. Sixty years ago the Caucasus was unsubdued, and the countrymen of Schamyl were no slight thorn in the flesh. Tiflis is now the military capital of a territory whose army contains a peace strength of 101,500, and a mobilised capacity of 270,000 men. A line of railway connects the Black and Caspian Seas, and will shortly be brought into correspondence with the systems of European Russia. All possible opposition, every conceivable obstacle, has in fact disappeared upon the northern side, and has been replaced by conditions of overwhelming strategical superiority.

Ascendency on the N. and N.W.

If we shift our gaze to the east we observe a Russian vantage-ground which, if more tardily acquired, is not one whit less substantial. Prior to her Turkoman campaigns, and while the terror inspired by those greatly overrated robbers still rendered it doubtful whether a European power would ever venture upon the sands of the Kara Kum, Russia pursued her object in the eastern portion of the Shah's dominions under the more subtle guise of commercial benevolence. Consuls or Consular agents were gradually stationed at the various ports or towns, first

Position in the N.E.

at Resht, in the reign of Mohammed Shah, then at Astrabad, Gez, Meshed-i-Ser, Shahrud, and thence eastwards, culminating in the already chronicled appointment in 1889 of a Consul-General at Meshed. Where it was impossible or unwise to station an official representative, emissaries in mufti, usually Russian-born Armenians, and persons engaged in trade, were employed to conduct the same process; and thus gradually was spread a network of intrigue throughout Khorasan disseminating far and wide a sense of the tremendous power of the Northern Colossus, and a skilfully exaggerated notion of the benefits to be derived from Russian rule. The impression so created was fortified by the *éclat* arising from the fall of Samarkand, the capture of Khiva, and the subjugation of Bokhara, names that were typical to the Eastern mind of the power and traditions of the hitherto unhumbled Orient. Each of these triumphs was further regarded as a blow to the prestige of Great Britain, whose name had not stood high in Central Asia ever since the Kabul disaster and Jugdulluk massacre of 1842; the rivalry between the two Powers being a subject of daily discussion in the bazaars and coffee-shops of the East, where a sounder grasp of the situation is, on the whole, more likely to be met with than on the benches of the House of Commons. Next in order came the Russo-Turkish war of 1877–8, the result of which was again a triumph for Russia, all the more notable in its effect upon Asiatic peoples that the vanquished combatant was Turkey, the traditional enemy of Persia, and the greatest Mohammedan power in Asia.

Finally, upon the top of these successes came the Turkoman campaign of 1880–1, in which Skobeleff, in order to magnify his victory, contrived a massacre of those dreaded, but not really formidable, Borderers, that echoed like a thunder clap through the surrounding nations. In addition to the prestige acquired by this conquest, troops of released Persian prisoners, returning to their homes, confirmed the sentimental *kudos* already accruing from the captives of Khiva and Bokhara; and, while they showed the gall marks of Tekke chains, extolled the clemency of the conqueror to whom they owed their freedom. The practical advantages resulting from the annexation of Turkomania have since been both consolidated and infinitely multiplied by the construction of the Transcaspian Railway, to the effect of which upon Persia and the Persian Question I must devote a passing paragraph.

Conquest of Turkomania

The commercial influence of General Annenkoff's line upon Khorasan has already been traced. I have shown that by its means Russia is acquiring a hold upon the trade of that northern province which, unless counterbalanced by some corresponding British advance from the south, cannot possibly be contested. I have also shown that in the panorama of Russian advance the pedlar precedes the *tchinovnik*, and that the process, whose first stage is the advent of bales bearing a Moscow label on the backs of camels or mules, is apt to find its last in the introduction of a permanent garrison. Politically the neighbourhood of the Transcaspian Railway and of a great Russian administrative centre at Ashkabad, whence perpetual communications and a steady flow of presents can be maintained across the border, is gradually converting into Russian vassals or agents the khans and chieftains of the contiguous Persian districts; the fond hope of Russia being that, either upon the death of the Shah, or when some other opportunity of disorder presents itself, a movement in this quarter may justify their advance, or an appeal for protection from the conspiring chieftains may suggest a suzerainty that shall afterwards take a more substantial form. But it is in their strategical aspect that her new position and railway communication with the Caspian have done most to strengthen the control of Russia over Khorasan. The old Gez-Astrabad-Shahrud route of invasion, hampered by the terrific obstacle of the Kuzluk Pass; the Atrek valley route from Chikishliar, which was adopted by Lomakin and Tergukasoff in their first Turkoman campaign, but abandoned by Skobeleff in 1880; the Teheran-Meshed postal route —all these methods of entering Khorasan, which alone were accessible to a Russian army up to 1881, may now be set on one side. Their place has been taken by the new military *chaussée* from Ashkabad to Kuchan and Meshed, by which a column could march from the Russian to the Persian capital city in less than ten days; by the Dushak-Meshed route; and by the Sarakhs-Meshed route, both of which are sometimes spoken of as lines of future railway advance. The Transcaspian Railway can bring to the point of detrainment the forces alike of Transcaspia and of Turkestan; the battalions of Samarkand can unite with those of Merv, Kizil Arvat, and Ashkabad; and admitting a caution that would in reality be superfluous, I can see no reason why a Russian army of 10,000 men should not be in bloodless occupation

Effect of the Transcaspian Railway

of Meshed within three weeks of the commencement of hostilities.

It cannot be denied, therefore, that the military position of Russia along the entire northern frontier of Persia from the Aras to the Tejend is one of overwhelming superiority; she overlaps 1,000 miles of border, at every point of which she is in a condition to threaten and to sustain her threats by armed force. From her military stations at Tiflis and Erivan she can easily overrun Azerbaijan. Her command of the Caspian enables her to dictate to the capital. Her new railway in Transcaspia, which, to a weaker power than herself would be a source of danger from a stronger power than Persia, enables her to do exactly what she pleases with Khorasan. The only Persian troops of any value in the capital are the so-called Cossack regiments, under Russian officers; and in the event of political convulsion it is doubtful whether they would not prefer the country of their uniform to the country of their birth. Whenever Russia desires to enforce with peculiar emphasis some diplomatic demand at Teheran, a mere enumeration of the Russian garrisons within a few hundred miles of the Persian capital is enough to set the Council of Ministers quaking, and to make the sovereign himself think twice. When the Shah came to Europe in 1889 a similar policy was pursued. I asked a Persian Minister what had struck him most in England, and what most in Europe. 'The number of the industrial population in the great towns of the interior,' was his reply to the first question; and 'the number of soldiers in Russia,' to the second. Soldiers were displayed everywhere—along the railway, at the stations, and in the streets—and the Persians came away with the idea that along with the country of Medea the Czar has inherited her secret of the dragon's teeth, and can sow inexhaustible crops of armed men.

Synopsis of Russian position

What, then, are the designs which this commanding position, and the power of bullying that it confers, are being utilised to promote? There is no concealment either as to their character or their scope. Russia regards Persia as a power that may temporarily be tolerated, that may even require sometimes to be humoured or caressed, but that in the long run is irretrievably doomed. She regards the future partition of Persia as a prospect scarcely less certain of fulfilment than the achieved partition of Poland; and she has already clearly made up her own

Aggressive designs

mind as to the share which she will require in the division of the spoils. It would be safe to assert that no Russian statesman or officer of the General Staff would pen a report upon Russian policy towards Persia and the future of that country that did not involve as a major premise the Russian annexation of the provinces of Azerbaijan, Gilan, Mazanderan, and Khorasan—in other words, of the whole of North Persia, from west to east. I do not doubt that the steps to be taken, in the event of war, disorder, or some equally favourable chance, for the realisation of these ambitions have been authoritatively discussed and approved. Russia covets the splendid province of Azerbaijan for its 40,000 square miles of rich and varied country, its stalwart Turkish peasantry, the military aptitudes of its population, and its great commercial capital of Tabriz. Contiguous over a long stretch of frontier with her Transcaucasian dominions and within easy reach of her military capital, Tiflis, it could be invaded with ease and annexed without difficulty. Next adjoining is the maritime province of Gilan, with its capital, Resht, the main port of Teheran, and its unexplored wealth in timber, in rice, sugar, cotton, and silk. Somewhat similar in character, but richer in natural resources, both vegetable and mineral, is the adjoining province of Mazanderan, which is said to contain the most industrious population in Persia, and to be a mine of unprobed riches. For reasons that I have previously given, and which result from the physical peculiarities of these provinces, their malarial climate, their impregnability if properly defended against attack, and the difficulty of holding them, even if acquired, I have elsewhere argued that the Russians would probably be guilty of an error in judgment did they contemplate, at least as an early step in their forward movement, an occupation in force of the South Caspian seaboard. But whether my judgment be sound or false, there is no question that the absorption of these provinces figures largely in the programmes that emanate from the *bureaux* on the Neva. Their seizure would bring Russia to Astrabad, and would dovetail agreeably with the probably already effected annexation of Khorasan; so that, were this scheme to be realised in its entirety as I have sketched it, the entire north of Persia would thereby pass from Persian into Russian hands.[1]

[1] Such a scheme was contemplated by Russia as long as sixty years ago. Captain Mignan, travelling in 1830, said (*Winter's Journey*, vol. i. p. 161): 'At a *levée* in Tiflis, Count Paskievitch declared in my hearing that he only awaited

It may, however, be thought that I am doing the Russians an injustice by attributing to them designs which they would repudiate themselves, and which may be only the figments of a disordered imagination. Lest I should be suspected of such an offence against honesty and truth, let me give a definition of Russia's attitude towards Khorasan as enunciated by her own spokesmen. On December 1, 1888, the following passage appeared in the 'Novoe Vremya':—

Evidence of the 'Novoe Vremya'

> Our attention has been the more concentrated upon the necessity of subordinating Khorasan—which is closely connected with Transcaspia, and should be economically and industrially dependent upon it—to the exclusive influence of Russia, as through Khorasan lies a convenient road in the direction of Herat, and in the event of military operations against India, Khorasan will form the victualling base for our operations further on. It is also of great importance, because within its limits rise the streams that irrigate the cultivated belts of the Akhal and Atek territories, the control of the distribution of whose waters is accordingly a necessary condition to the prosperity and success of our new Transcaspian province.[1]

When the cat is to be let out of the bag, commend me to a Russian newspaper for the uncompromising manner in which the operation is performed! Here we have definitely recommended (1) a suzerainty, or exclusive political control over Khorasan; (2) the actual appropriation of its soil; and (3) its ultimate utilisation as a base of military operations against the Indian Empire of Great Britain. The 'Novoe Vremya' might have added, what every soldier knows, that one of the reasons for which Russia looks with such feverish anxiety upon the future of Khorasan, is because the Transcaspian Railway, invaluable as a military weapon though it be, is threatened along a flank 300 miles in length by the mountain

the commands of the Emperor to annihilate the kingdom of Persia, and to render her a province of the Russian Empire.'

[1] The only prominent Russian spokesman who, so far as I know, has ever directly denied the covetous intentions of Russia with regard to Khorasan was General Skobeleff, who said, in an interview with the late Mr. Marvin: 'Why should we occupy Khorasan? We should only get provisions from the province, and we could get them as it is. We derive a revenue from Khorasan now by its trade with Nijni Novgorod; but we should lose this if we occupied it. I do not believe Russia will ever occupy Khorasan. I think the new frontier will be permanent.' This was only a piece of *blague* on the part of Skobeleff. We remember that he was equally confident that the Transcaspian Railway would not go beyond Ashkabad, and that Merv would never be annexed by Russia!

border of this Persian province, and because she knows that it could be wrecked at a score of places by a hostile power in possession of those heights. That Russia should have laid her railway over a line thus exposed is in itself an evidence of the security of her supremacy and of the contempt with which she quite justifiably regards any hostile movement on the part of Persia. To the latter her designs are presumably as well known as to herself, and have, indeed, been officially condoned in advance. For is it not one of the open secrets of diplomacy that in 1883 or thereabouts, in one of the chronic intervals of Russian menace and Persian humiliation, a secret treaty (never yet revealed) was concluded between Russia and Persia, by which, under certain conditions, Russian forces are allowed to occupy Khorasan?[1] He who thinks, be he Shah or private individual, that the Cossacks, when once they have marched down the Khiaban of Meshed, are likely ever again to evacuate it, must be but a blind student of the way in which Russia makes history in Central Asia. It will matter little that her Government may have given the most solemn assurances of the integrity of the Persian dominions to England, or to any other power. When Khiva was taken and Merv annexed, what became of the paper guarantees of their freedom?

Russian services to Persia

Let me, in justice to Russia, explain that not without reason she boasts of having rendered genuine service to Persia in the direction more particularly of Khorasan—service for which she may not unreasonably look for some return. She liberated, as I have mentioned, several thousand Persian captives at Khiva, at Geok Tepe, and at Merv, and returned them, without demanding ransom, to their homes. By her subjugation of the Turkoman tribes she has relieved the whole of northern Khorasan from the scourge of perpetual devastation, has rendered life secure and agriculture possible. By her annexation and firm administration of the Transcaspian province she has

[1] Mr. Benjamin, who was Minister in Teheran at the time, says in his book (*Persia and the Persians*, p. 481): 'It was also stated at the time (1883) that Russia goaded the Shah into secretly signing an offensive and defensive treaty with Russia, in which he agreed to side with that power and against England in the event of war. When this transaction came to light, England at once declared that it was impossible for such a treaty to be in existence; and Russia dissembled, as the time had not yet come for full revelation of her purposes. But I have every reason to believe that a treaty of such nature was drawn up; whether it was signed is more doubtful.' Mr. Benjamin need not have doubted. The signatures were there.

diminished the prestige and weakened the power of the border chieftains of Khorasan, and enabled the Central Government at Teheran to establish an authority over them which before was habitually disputed and never assured. These services are undoubted, even if less unselfish than a Russian might be disposed to contend. Whether they entitle her to a recompense that shall take the form of a forcible seizure of the best provinces of Persia, every individual is competent to judge for himself. Were such the ethics of international relationship, well might the Shah re-echo the plaintive protestation of the Trojan, 'Timeo Danaos et dona ferentes.'

Such, then, are the designs of Russia upon Azerbaijan, Gilan, Mazanderan, and Khorasan. But here again let me guard myself by saying that I do not rest these statements upon newspaper avowals, or upon covert references or admissions alone. With full knowledge of what I am writing, I make them as statements of fact. If any Russian disputes my thesis, let me suggest that he should procure a glimpse of the famous secret scheme for the invasion of India, drawn up by General Kuropatkin in 1885, and understood to be the officially accepted outline of the next Russian advance in Central Asia. I shall be surprised if he does not there find the incorporation of Azerbaijan, Gilan, Mazanderan, and Khorasan regarded as a primary object of Russian policy; Khorasan, in particular, being regarded as an indispensable preliminary acquisition to a movement upon Herat. It might be interesting also to inquire of the Shah how many times he has actually been threatened by Russian diplomats at Teheran with the forcible seizure of one or other of those provinces unless he proved himself more immediately amenable to Russian desires.

Official corroboration

But Russia's appetite for territorial aggrandisement does not stop here. Not content with a spoil that would rob Persia at one sweep of the entire northern half of her dominions, she turns a longing eye southwards, and yearns for an outlet upon the Persian Gulf and in the Indian Ocean. The movements that I have previously sketched along the south and east borders of Khorasan, the activity of her agents in regions far beyond the legitimate radius of an influence restricted to North Persia, her tentative experiments in the direction of Seistan—are susceptible of no other interpretation than a design to shake the influence of Great Britain in South Persia, to dispute the control of the Indian

An eye on the Gulf

Seas, and to secure the long-sought base for naval operations in the east. This can only be accomplished in either of two directions —by a war with Turkey and the capture of Baghdad, or by a semi-peaceful advance through Persia to the Gulf. Of these processes the second is the more hopeful and the less risky, and there is a fascination about its beckoning finger that draws the Russians irresistibly on. Here, again, lest it should be thought that I am wronging Russia by an insinuation of designs so incompatible with her general assurances, let me invite any injured partisan of that country to make inquiries in the Foreign Office at St. Petersburg as to whether, at the time that the Kuropatkin memorandum was penned, a secret agreement was not either concluded or sought to be concluded with the Shah, by which the advance of a Russian column into Khorasan was to be followed by the cession to Russia of the Gulf port of Bunder Abbas; and whether the most recent railroad concession pressed for by Russian agents at Teheran did not postulate a maritime outlet at Chahbar, on the coast of Persian Beluchistan.

Russian tactics

The solid advantages possessed by Russia in Persia, and the easy execution of her ambitious, but (if probabilities be fairly weighed) not altogether extravagant schemes, appear to be quite needlessly discounted in that country by tactics that exhibit a marked contrast to her general *bonhomie* and affability in dealing with Oriental peoples. Perhaps the theory is that amiability ought only to follow upon acquisition, and severity to go before. Her representatives and agents in Persia assume so dictatorial a tone, that, while it may impress, it cannot conciliate. It is notorious that the late Russian Minister at Teheran on several occasions gave great offence by his curt demeanour. I have elsewhere recalled the fact that rather more than two years ago a diplomatic squall was raised about the institution of a Russian Consul-General at Meshed. Upon that occasion the officer in question was actually nominated and his appointment gazetted in the St. Petersburg newspapers before the Shah was informed or applied to for an *exsequatur*. Upon his declining for a while to grant the latter—a very natural and dignified step—the real feeling of the Russians towards Persia glimmered out in an incautious note of fury from the 'Novoe Vremya':—'This refusal is almost without a parallel in the history of Russian diplomacy, and is the more insulting as coming from Persia, a country with a barefoot army, a population half composed of beggars, and crumbling political institutions.' Shortly before my arrival in Meshed a *seyid* had been banished from the city by the Prince-Governor, in obedience to the imperious requisition of the Russian Consul, but no sooner had the letter of the demand been complied with and the exile left the walls, than the *mujtaheds* persuaded the Governor to issue private orders for his recall. Nor can I think that Russian interests are materially forwarded by the intrigues in which Russian emissaries are constantly engaged, and not infrequently caught—e.g. the employment of Russian agents to stir up the Yomut Turkomans against Persian rule—a curious service to render to an ally—and the secret transactions with Ayub Khan in 1885, when the latter was a so-called prisoner at Teheran, and was urged by the Russians to escape, and was provided with funds for that purpose, so as to embroil England and Persia. Again, the Russians may have their own opinion about the venality of the Persians, and they may or may not be right therein, but their convictions in this respect are somewhat incautiously revealed when, with a reckless manipulation of numerals which only a Russian journal can successfully accomplish, the 'Novoe Vremya' exclaimed:—'The Queen of England lately raised the budget of her representative in Persia to 250,000*l.*' (it is really 5,000*l.*). 'If with 100,000*l.* Sir D. Wolff acquired the Karun, what will not his victories be when millions are at his command?'

Former Persian opinion

It is amusing to contrast the present position of Russia in Persia, and the political vantage-ground that enables her to pursue these tactics with impunity, with the estimation in which she was held when first she 'broke ground' in Persia more than 200 years ago. I have already narrated the story of the Muscovite ambassadors in the reign of Shah Abbas II., and of the unfavourable impression produced by their coarse and unmannerly habits upon the scrupulous and critical Persians. Chardin, in his description of the coronation of Shah Suleiman, in 1677, says:—

> The Persians looked upon the Moscovites as the most paltry, narrow-souled, and infamous among all the Christians, and in derision call 'em the Yusbeks of Europe, thereby expressing the small esteem they have of 'em, for the Yusbeks are the most abject people of all the East.

The Uzbegs now own as lords and masters these very Muscovites, with whom they were then compared; but for abjectness I am not sure that the modern Persians, though still independent, are not more deserving of the charge than the Uzbegs, who at least fought for their freedom sooner than be unmurmuringly absorbed.

Russian attitude towards internal reform

For my own part, while I hesitate to pronounce a decided opinion upon a foreign policy which may perhaps find recommendations or excuses that I have overlooked, and while I admit that Russia is free to play her own game in the manner that she thinks best, I yet hold that her attitude with reference to the internal politics of Persia can be seriously arraigned, and that she can in nowise escape condemnation for the resistance that she consistently offers to any proposal that has for its object the genuine requirements of a distressed and backward country. It may safely be averred, not merely that the opening of Persia to Western influence, the extension of roads and railroads, and the breaking-down of the barriers of obsolete tradition, might have been hastened by years had Russia chosen to lend her powerful influence to the effort; but—and this is a much graver charge—that no scheme for the strengthening of Persia and the unselfish expansion of her resources can be proposed that is not certain to meet with the most strenuous opposition that Russia can exert. It is notorious that the first Reuter Concession in 1872 was revoked because of the menacing tone adopted by the Russian Government when the Shah visited St. Petersburg in the following year. When a batch of Austrian officials came out to organise a postal service in Persia, in 1874, Russia threw every conceivable obstacle in their way; and when, in spite of her efforts, the present system of internal post had been established, she did all in her power to prevent Persia from being admitted into the International Postal Union. The navigation of the Karun river, having been all but conceded by the Shah on more than one occasion, was again and again postponed owing to the obstructive tactics of Russian Ministers. As soon as it was finally granted, an indignant shriek was raised in Russia, the favourite French doctrine of compensation was invoked, and the outcry was not allayed till counter-concessions on a large scale had been made to gratify her wounded pride,[1] the real interests or benefit of Persia never entering for one

[1] The terms of this secret convention, concluded in the spring of 1889, have never been revealed, but they are said to have included the following concessions

moment into her egotistical calculations. The institution of the Imperial Bank of Persia in 1889 received no aid from Russian sources, but on the contrary has been consistently thwarted by that Power; and the number of railway schemes which successive Russian Ministers have received instructions to oppose would fill a respectable obituary column in the 'Times.' I have previously noticed the twofold check more recently imposed by Russian influence upon the experiment of railway development in Persia, in the shape of the prohibitory agreement exacted, first for five, and afterwards for ten years, by the Russian Minister at Teheran, whereby no line can be laid anywhere in the country during that period without the Czar's consent; a document upon which I have placed the frank interpretation that it is obstructive, and nothing else. I will go further and state again, with knowledge of what I am saying, that no single scheme for the material or industrial amelioration of Persia has been proposed in the last twenty years that has not provoked, and too often been crushed by, Russian antagonism. Over 150 years ago the apocryphal will of Peter the Great, which, though of spurious origin, yet enshrines with admirable fidelity the leading principles that have guided the Asiatic policy of his countrymen ever since, contained these words: 'Hasten the decadence of Persia, penetrate to the Persian Gulf, re-establish the ancient commerce of the Levant, and advance to the Indies, which are the treasure-house of the world.' As regards Persia, a truer definition of Russian policy could not be given. Her desire truly is, not that Persia should be emancipated, but that the chains of servitude should be riveted closer upon her neck; not that she should become a useful ally, but that she should fall an easy victim; not that her political vitality should be resuscitated, but that it should rot and decay. If I cast an unfair aspersion upon the integrity of Russia's designs, it is entirely within her own power, by a more generous policy in the future, to falsify the accusation.

Neither can I feel any sympathy with Russia in her lust for territorial aggrandisement, at the expense of Persia, in the north.

to the outraged dignity of Russia: (1) the free navigation of the Enzeli Lagoon and of the rivers flowing into the Caspian (only one of which, the Sefid Rud, is navigable); (2) the construction of wharves and depôts; (3) the construction of a proper road from Pir-i-Bazaar to Teheran; (4) the construction of the Ashkabad-Kuchan road; (5) the Five Years' Railway refusal. The two last-named, anyhow, are *faits accomplis*.

Herein I am actuated by no narrow prejudice or national jealousy, inasmuch as I am profoundly convinced that England neither wants to possess, nor ought to possess, nor ever will possess, those territories herself. Nor am I a tainted witness as regards Russia in the East; for in my previous work I have admitted, and I here repeat the admission, that in her career of Central Asian conquest she has, though by devious and often dishonourable means, achieved a successful and salutary end; and that she deserves the praise due to those who substitute order for anarchy, and are the pioneers even of a crude civilisation. I have wished her well in Transcaspia and Turkestan, and I would be a party to no movement for disturbing her rule. But I do not say the same of Persia. On the contrary, the very pleas which have extenuated and justified Russian advance elsewhere in Central Asia, and which she is always quoting in self-defence, are wanting here. No one can contend that the Persians of Khorasan are a gang of lawless freebooters like the Turkomans; that they are a peril to their neighbours and a scourge to society. No insecurity of life or property in Khorasan or Azerbaijan demands the installation of a military despotism for the coercion of unruly elements. No sluggish pools of superstition or prejudice require to be stirred by the wand of a European magician. On the contrary, the Persians are far too timid a people to constitute a danger to anybody else, and are in many respects quite as advanced in civilisation as the Russians themselves. Regarding them as a distinct nationality, resident in the territories which they have occupied from time immemorial, under a sovereign and with a language, religion, customs, and individuality of their own, I can see no reason for suppressing their independent existence and subjecting them to an alien sway. The Government of Persia is in many respects bad enough, but that of Russia is not likely to be so immeasurably superior as to outweigh the claims to respect which an ancient and illustrious history and the main conditions of national existence (even in the absence of a national spirit) combine to create. A superiority of influence in North Persia, and in the districts coterminous with her own borders, is an advantage to which Russia from her position is entitled, and which no fair man will be disposed to grudge her. But influence is a different thing from ownership, and where the one is legitimate the other may be both mischievous and unpardonable.

No justification for territorial aggression

Still more strongly do these observations apply to her designs upon South Persia and the Persian Gulf. Here not only would any Englishman protest in the interests of Persia, but any English Government would be bound to protest in the interests of Great Britain. No plea that the most sophistical of logicians could devise can be advanced to justify any such proceeding. The safety of India, which is the first duty of Great Britain, the *pax Britannica* that now reigns in the Southern Seas in consequence of her temperate control, the sacrifices that have been made by her in the pursuance of that end, the utter absence of any Russian interests for thousands of miles, the perfect ability of Persia in these parts to look after herself, are incontrovertible arguments against any such aggression. It can only be prosecuted in the teeth of international morality, in defiance of civilised opinion, and with the ultimate certainty of a war with this country that would ring from pole to pole.

Or for designs on the Gulf

The criticism which I here pass upon Russian policy is no monopoly of English opinion, but is shared, and would be endorsed, by the majority of Persians themselves. Political acumen is one of the gifts with which the Persian character is most richly endowed, and it is no rare experience to find a very fair *aperçu* of the political situation formulated by men in a comparatively humble station of life. The Persians, from the Shah downwards, are tolerably well acquainted both with the designs and with the methods of Russia. They see in her, not the unselfish champion of distressed nationalities, but the future enemy of their political liberties, and their secret sympathies would be almost unanimously enlisted in the opposite scale. But they are at once deplorably weak and fatally conscious of their own weakness. And where amid a people of finer moral fibre such a consciousness might lead to a resurrection of national spirit and a manly effort for self-redemption, with the Persians it has the contrary effect of leaving them despondent and cowed, helplessly awaiting the catastrophe which they have made up their minds that they cannot avert. They are afraid of Russia, and they tell you so. The limit of their self-sufficiency is that which is permitted by their fears, and the crisis has never yet occurred in history where such a spirit has nerved a sturdy blow for freedom.

Persian weakness

If it be evident, as I have contended, that Russian policy in

Persia has a hostile object and aggressive intent, it is, I shall now hope to show, not less evident that British policy neither has, nor is again likely to have, any but the most opposite characteristics. It is only thirty-five years since this country was at war with the reigning Shah—an episode already so buried in oblivion that nine Englishmen out of ten are probably unaware that it ever occurred, while the tenth will not be able to say what it was about. The reception twice given to the Persian monarch in England, the large space that is now occupied in the public press by Persia, the vigilant interest with which our diplomacy in that country is watched at home, the increasing movement of Englishmen and English capital towards its shores, are evidences of a new-born, or at least re-aroused, concern in its welfare, and of a consciousness that its existence is in a measure bound up with our own. No more convincing illustration could be afforded of the impossibility of regarding British interests from an insular standpoint—that scatter-brained fallacy of a moribund school—than the contemplation of this distant country and its interesting people.

English interest in Persia

I trust that, from the information and reasoning that have been supplied in these volumes, the importance of Persia to England will have been made sufficiently manifest. The figures and calculations which I have given relating to trade, and more particularly Anglo-Persian trade, the analysis of the indigenous resources of Persia, the character and chances of the still undeveloped schemes for internal amelioration, the field thus opened for the judicious employment of capital, are all of them appeals to the practical and business-like instincts of Englishmen. In the furious commercial competition that now rages like a hurricane through the world, the loss of a market is a retrograde step that cannot be recovered; the gain of a market is a positive addition to the national strength. Indifference to Persia might mean the sacrifice of a trade that already feeds hundreds of thousands of our citizens in this country and in India. A friendly attention to Persia will mean so much more employment for British ships, for British labour, and for British spindles.

Mercantile

But I should be sorry to rest a demonstration of the importance of Persia upon mercenary grounds alone. If the physical position of that country, coterminous with Afghanistan along a border of many hundred miles, and almost contiguous to the western limits of our Indian Empire, be not sufficient to establish its overwhelming political significance to Englishmen, at least the description which has been given of Russian policy, and Russian tactics in Persia, will. That Russia covets Meshed because it will assist her to Herat; that she covets Seistan because it will open to her Beluchistan; that she covets the whole of Northern Persia because it will supply her with resources in which her own Central Asian possessions are woefully deficient, and which will render her military and offensive strength far more formidable than it is at present; that she has an eye upon the Persian Gulf because it may give her a dockyard and ships in the Indian Seas,—all these are points which to my mind no man in his senses can doubt. Neither can I think that she is ill-judged in her aspirations, ample and even exorbitant though they may appear to be. The history of her Central Asian advance has taught her that to get much she must lay claim to much; that to be successful she must be encroaching; and that she can with impunity ignore the most elementary axioms of international ethics. But in England we are not called upon to regard the question from a Russian, but from an English point of view. Unless, therefore, we are prepared to see Persia fall into the plight of Bokhara and Khiva, and to concede to a Power whose interests in Central Asia may in the future, if they do not now, clash with our own, an incalculable accretion of strength, Englishmen must be up and stirring, and the preservation, so far as is still possible, of the integrity of Persia must be registered as a cardinal precept of our Imperial creed.

Imperial

The recognition of this principle by British Governments has prevailed at intervals of greater or less frequency, and with greater or less earnestness—too often the latter—throughout the present century. Since Sir John Malcolm first landed at Bushire in 1800 down to the present day, Persia has alternately advanced and receded in the estimation of British statesmen, occupying now a position of extravagant prominence, anon one of unmerited obscurity. At one time she has been the occasion or the recipient of a lavish and almost wanton prodigality; at another, she has been treated with penurious meanness. Public opinion in this country and in India with regard to Persian politics has been either at a white heat, or has subsided into an inert stupor. We have made treaties with Persia, imposing upon our-

History of Anglo-Persian relations

selves the most solemn offensive and defensive obligations. When the occasion arose for redeeming them, we have shirked the responsibility and have subsequently bought our release from the self-inflicted tie. We have courted and waged war against the same Persian sovereigns; we have both trained and routed the Persian army; we have at once pampered and neglected the Persian people. Our Persian policy in each successive stage, whether of interest or apathy, has ever been characterised by the note of exaggeration. At the dawn of the century, when Lord Wellesley first opened negotiations with the Persian Court, we entertained exaggerated notions of the danger to India arising from a possible Afghan invasion. We next regarded with an equally exaggerated apprehension the installation and designs of the French at Teheran. When the Afghan cloud had blown over, and the French bubble had burst, we thought that Persia could be propped up against any other enemy by the double buttress of the drill sergeant and the rupee. It was an exaggerated hope. In 1833, in 1837, and again in 1856, we entertained a probably exaggerated opinion of the danger likely to arise from a Persian movement against Herat. We embarked upon the first Afghan war, with its attendant train of horrors, from an exaggerated alarm at these aspirations. A phase of equally exaggerated languor succeeded, and the subsequent epoch has not been free from analogous spasms of solicitude and torpor. It has been well said of British policy with regard to Persia throughout this century that *Nil fuit unquam sic impar sibi.* The political record of the first three quarters of this period down to 1875 has been compiled by the masterly hand of Sir H. Rawlinson, and to his pages may be referred any reader who desires to trace the balancing vicissitudes of lethargy and zeal. The ensuing decade was not less fruitful than its predecessors in illustration of the same phenomenon; for whereas in the hands of the brothers Sir Taylor and Sir Ronald Thomson, both of whom had lived so long in Persia as to yield somewhat to the pressure of their environment, and to lack the initiative that comes from change of atmosphere and scene, British influence sank to a very low ebb in the councils of the Shah,[1] Russia in the same

[1] Justice compels me to state that this decline was quickened by events for which neither of the Ministers named shared the smallest responsibility, viz. the calamitous policy pursued by the British Government of 1880–5 in various parts of the empire. The retreat from South Africa, the evacuation of Kandahar, the ever-

period making a corresponding advance; yet, first under Sir A. Nicolson, who from 1885 to 1888 acted as *chargé d'affaires*, and still more under his accomplished and capable successors, Sir Henry Drummond Wolff and Sir Frank Lascelles, there has during the past six years been a striking recrudescence of British activity and power, which has placed this country in a position of greater authority at Teheran than its representatives have exercised at any time since the death of Fath Ali Shah. Of the consequences of this recovered influence I shall presently speak.

The history of Anglo-Persian relations in this century falls, so to speak, into four parallel columns, according as it is concerned with the departments of diplomacy, military administration, commerce, and the electric telegraph. I have summarised the contents of the first-named category above, and will not presume to repeat at greater length what has been said with the fullest knowledge and authority by Rawlinson. The history of British connection with the Persian army has been related in the chapter upon the latter institution. The history of Anglo-Persian trade has similarly been treated in my discussion of Persian commerce. There remains for me only, in order to complete the picture, to say something of the steps by which the electric telegraph was introduced by Englishmen into Persia, and of the effect which that agency has had both upon the country itself and upon international relations. The main interest of such an inquiry will be found to be, not scientific, but political; nor, had the consequences that have ensued partaken only or principally of the former character, should I have judged them worthy of extended notice in this place.

Fourfold division

It was from no special desire to bring Persia into telegraphic connection with Europe, nor with any direct intention of conferring upon her the enormous benefits that have resulted from the introduction of that system into the country, that sprang the first proposals for so startling an innovation as a through wire from the western frontier of the Shah's dominions to the Persian Gulf. It was her geographical position that made Persia the fortunate recipient of this not wholly disinterested boon. Had her territories not lain upon the high

Indo-European Telegraphic schemes. 1. Turkish line

lasting disgrace of Khartum, the 'bolt' from the Murghab—all these incidents rang like a trumpet blast through the whispering-galleries of the East, and were interpreted as presages of an impending ruin.

road between Great Britain and India, she might have waited long for the outside pressure necessary to effect so bewildering a revolution. During the Indian Mutiny the need of direct telegraphic communication with Hindustan was seriously and increasingly felt in England; a period of nearly three months elapsing at that time between the despatch of a message and the receipt of a reply. In 1859 the British Government made the first attempt at direct through connection with India by laying a cable in the Red Sea, in correspondence with the wires of a private company that stretched from Marseilles to Alexandria in the Mediterranean. In the then primitive condition of the science of marine telegraphy, the attempt proved an utter failure, the line being only open for three weeks.[1] In the same year, however, a proposal was received from the Ottoman Government for continuing a Turkish telegraphic line that had been constructed under British supervision, after the Crimean war, from Scutari to Baghdad, in the direction of India; and a very able officer, Colonel Patrick Stewart, whose early death in 1865 was deplored by all Englishmen in the East, was deputed by the Indian Government to examine the Persian Gulf with the view of laying a cable from India that should connect upon Turkish territory at Fao, on the right bank of the Shat-el-Arab, with an overland wire, *viâ* Busrah from Baghdad. It was not proposed, however, to lay the cable for the entire distance from Kurrachi; a land line was projected along the Mekran coast, from Sind as far as Gwadur; and the surveys of this coast strip, which were entrusted to Sir F. Goldsmid, furnished that officer with the valuable information that subsequently stood both himself and the British Government in such good stead in the political demarcation of the regions concerned. In October 1863 the Protocol confirming these arrangements, and in September 1864 the complete Convention with the Porte, were signed; and by the end of the latter year the combined lines were open for the transmission of messages.[2]

[1] In consequence of a Government guarantee of 5 per cent., which was shared by Great Britain and India, both Governments have been saddled ever since with an annual payment of 18,000*l.*, which has not yet expired.

[2] The direction followed by this line is as follows: From London to Constantinople, either *viâ* Paris, Strasburg, Munich, and Vienna, or *viâ* Lowestoft, Zandvoorf, Cologne, and Vienna; from Constantinople to Fao *viâ* Scutari, Sivas, Diarbekr, Baghdad, and Busrah; from Fao to Kurrachi *viâ* Bushire and Jask. The distances are as follows: London to Newhaven, 56 miles, Dieppe 64, Paris 124, French frontier 211, German frontier 292, Turco-Austrian frontier 578, Constantinople 752, Fao 1,845 miles, Kurrachi 1,208 nautical miles.

It seems, however, to have been felt, while these negotiations were proceeding, and even when they were satisfactorily concluded, that the line thus opened would prove inadequate for its purpose, and might suddenly break down. Between London and Baghdad the gauntlet of quite a host of nationalities with different languages required to be run; and between Baghdad and Fao the climate of Mesopotamia was reported to be very unhealthy, while from the Arab tribes camping on the banks of the two rivers was expected a troublesome and permanent hostility. The two latter apprehensions proved, as time went on, to have been as much exaggerated as the first was reasonable; but the three in conjunction were sufficient to induce the Home Government, simultaneonsly with its negotiations at Stambul, to approach the Court of Teheran with the view of establishing an alternative line to the Persian Gulf, running through Persian territory from the Turkish frontier at Khanikin (whither the Anglo-Turkish Convention, already concluded, had stipulated for an extension from Baghdad) *viâ* Teheran to Bushire. British influence was not at that time at a very high-water mark in the councils of the Shah, and the proposal met not only with the strenuous resistance of the reactionary party in Persia, who detested all innovations, but with the jealous suspicions of the Shah's advisers, who suspected that some sinister purpose lurked behind. Colonel Stewart surveyed the line, and then retired *re infecta*. Early in the following year, however, the news came that the Persian Government had relented in its hostility, and the first Telegraphic Convention with the Shah was concluded in February 1863. Its terms differed very widely from those that afterwards obtained, and that still regulate the existence and business of the department in Persia, but they indicated the nervous apprehension with which the Persian Ministers originally regarded the new thing. The line was to be laid by Persians under British supervision, but it was to belong to Persia and to be worked by a Persian staff, the English being allowed to transmit messages thereupon at a fixed tariff. It was really the prospective income derivable from the latter source that overcame the Shah's suspicions; and its punctual payment ever since has smoothed the way for more practicable arrangements. By the end of 1864, the new line, consisting at that time of only a single wire on wooden posts, was completed from Khanikin *viâ* Kermanshah and Hamadan to Teheran, and from Teheran *viâ* Isfahan and Shiraz to Bushire,

2. Persian line

where it joined the marine cable to Kurrachi. It was not laid without much difficulty, and many exasperating impediments, arising from the obstinacy of local governors, and the depredations of nomad tribes. These and all other obstacles were, however, overcome by the unwearying patience of the officers employed, and so rapidly did the opposition of the Persians subside, that an agreement having been concluded in 1864, which allowed for management of the line by British officers for five months, at the end of which period they were to leave the country, a second Convention was signed in November 1865, which provided for a second wire to be used exclusively for European messages, and extended the period of residence for the English *employés*, whose maximum number was fixed at fifty, to five years. These consecutive modifications of the original terms were so many tributes to the tactful behaviour of the foreigners, and to the impossibility of working the line without their assistance. As a matter of fact, the Persians were not less the gainers by this second Convention than the English; for they secured thereby a free wire for local use, a maximum royalty of 30,000 *tomans*, or 12,000*l.*, for the right of transit enjoyed by the foreigners, and the ultimate reversion of the entire property. The Shah's advisers would have been ill-advised themselves had they thwarted so excellent a bargain.

The next step in chronological order was the opening of a third Perso-European line in 1866, by the junction of the Russian and Persian wires on the Caucasian frontier. By none of these three systems, however, viz. the Anglo-Turkish, the Anglo-Persian, or the Russo-Persian, were good results obtained. The staff in no case was competent, transmission was very slow, there was hopeless confusion of dates arising from the different calendars recognised, and the mutilation of messages consequent upon the frequent translations and retranslations by ignorant clerks into English, French, Dutch, German, Italian, Greek, Bulgarian, Wallachian, Servian, Russian, Turkish and Armenian, reduced the patrons of the various lines to a state bordering upon frenzy.

3. Russian line

A way out of the difficulty was suggested by a private firm. Messrs. Siemens Brothers, in 1867, conceived the idea of a special double line from London to Teheran, to be constructed by a European company and to be used exclusively for Indian messages. Their peculiar and influential relations with the various Governments concerned enabled them in the course of the same year to secure the requisite concessions from Germany, Russia, and Persia, the unique advantage of the projected line being that between Lowestoft and Kurrachi the wires only passed through the territories of those three powers; the concession was then disposed of to the Indo-European Telegraph Company; and finally, on January 31, 1870, the new line was opened between London and Teheran, where it joined the already existing wires to Bushire and Kurrachi.[1]

4. New Indo-European line

Almost simultaneously the confusion existing upon the land lines had caused the revival in another quarter of the abandoned scheme for a submarine cable between England and India; and in the same year, 1867, the Eastern Company was formed for the construction of such a line by the Mediterranean and Red Seas to Bombay. Two cables were laid from Falmouth, *viâ* Gibraltar, Malta, Suez, and Aden, and in 1870 the marine route was opened at about the same time as its overland rival. The Indian Government has entered into a joint-purse agreement with both companies, and the division of the traffic between the three existing lines from England to India is now as follows: The Eastern Company gets 64 per cent., the Indo-European Company 34½ per cent., and the Turkish Government 1½ per cent. Meanwhile the tariff between England and India, which in 1865–8 stood at 5*l.* for a message of 20 words, has, owing to the healthy competition thus engendered, and to the subsequent improvements in telegraphy, fallen by successive stages, until by either of the companies' wires it now stands at 5 francs a word, and by the Turkish lines, which are much slower, at 4½ francs a word. Simultaneously there has been a proportionate improvement in the speed of transmission. In 1867 a message was considered fortunate if it reached India within three days of being despatched from London. When the companies opened their lines in 1870, this was reduced successively to one day, eight hours, and six hours, and at the present time there is an average interval of only one and a half hour between despatch and delivery.

5. Submarine cable

[1] The line followed by the wires of the combined management, Indo-European Company and Indian Government, is as follows: London to Lowestoft 117 miles, Emden 274 knots, Thorn (i.e. through Germany) 720 miles, Julfa (i.e. through Russia *viâ* Warsaw, Odessa, Kertch, and Tiflis) 2,600 miles, Teheran 456 miles, Bushire 810 miles (i.e. through Persia 1,266 miles), Kurrachi 1,065 knots.

Indo-Persian section

Confining our attention to the Indo-Persian section of this great international scheme, we find that the present state of communications is as follows:—

1. Kurrachi to Jask, (*a*) Mekran coast line,[1] 2 wires .	683½	miles
,, ,, (*b*) submarine gutta-percha cable .	540	knots
2. Jask to Bushire, 1 gutta-percha and 1 indiarubber cable	519	,,
3. Bushire to Teheran, 3 wires (2 international, 1 Persian)	810	miles
4. Teheran to Julfa ,, ,, ,, ,, ,, .	456	,,
5. Bushire to Fao,[2] submarine gutta-percha cable .	152	knots

As regards the diplomatic agreements upon which the working of this section depends, the second Convention of 1865 was succeeded by a third in December 1872, which provided for three wires, one for local and two for international traffic, and which reduced the annual royalty paid to the Persian Government to 12,000 *tomans*, or 5,000*l*. This convention extended to 1895, a term that has since been protracted to 1905; at which period, unless new arrangements are made to the contrary, the entire plant will fall in to the Persian Government.[3] The utter inability of the latter to work a system of such magnitude by itself, and the immense advantages which Persia derives from the present system, constitute a sufficient guarantee for its continuance; and the future may be anticipated without alarm.

Staff and business

The management of the Persian section was originally committed to a separate department, the successive Directors-in-Chief of which were, Sir F. Goldsmid 1865 to 1870, Sir J. B Champain 1870 to 1887, Sir R. M. Smith 1887 to 1888. In the latter year the Persian Telegraphs were transferred to the Indian Government, and placed under the Director-General of Telegraphs in Calcutta, the command in Persia being given to an officiating Director, Colonel H. L. Wells, R.E., who in 1891 has

[1] The intervening stations on this line are Ormara, Gwadur, and Chahbar. Sonmeani and Pusni were also used at first, but were abandoned in 1871. The line from Kurrachi to Bushire was first laid by the Musandim Promontory in 1864, but was diverted to Jask in 1869.

[2] To superintend the marine section of the lines from Kurrachi to Fao, a cable-steamer is maintained by the Indian Government. The first ship so employed was the 'Amberwitch' from 1861 to 1879. She was replaced by the 'Patrick Stewart,' a screw steamer of 500 tons, making seven knots when clean.

[3] The Indo-European Telegraph Company have, in 1891, procured an extension from 1905 to 1925, in consideration of an advance to the Shah of the royalty for ten years. Their example has since been followed by the Indian Government.

been appointed Director-in-Chief, the importance of the Persian department thoroughly justifying this step. When a British staff first came to Persia, nearly thirty years ago, to construct and to work the line, non-commissioned officers of the Royal Engineers were chiefly selected, owing to their peculiar qualifications for the task. A few only of these now remain, and the line, though under military direction, is almost entirely civilian in its *personnel.* The present staff, comprising directors, superintendents, medical officers, line inspectors, and signallers of four grades, consisted in 1890 of forty-four persons; and it is among the most agreeable incidents of Persian travel to come, at intervals of sixty or more miles along the principal routes, upon a telegraph station occupied by an English official, who dispenses a generous hospitality, and as a rule is excellently informed about the country in which he has lived and worked so long. I entertain the most friendly recollections of evenings, lightened by the intercourse and rendered comfortable by the attentions of these gentlemen, upon whose amiability travellers, it is to be feared, have sometimes been disposed to presume. The extent of the business passing through their hands may be estimated from the fact that an average of 320 messages a day to and from India are transmitted along the wires; a total which, during a temporary derangement of the Red Sea Cable line in 1888, was swollen to 1,200. The following figures are interesting:—

1887–8	Govt. messages, 3,615	Paid messages, 71,894	Paid words, 1,184,799
1888–9	„ „ 5,722	„ „ 102,707	„ „ 1,565,481

And yet, in spite of this great concentration of business, most of which is embodied in code or in cypher, in an average of only one word in 200 is there the most trivial error in transmission. When the line was first made in Persia, wooden poles were employed, but it was found that these were constantly upset by the camels, who could not resist the opportunity of a good rub, or shattered by mischievous natives who regarded them as a capital mark for rifle practice. Accordingly iron poles were universally substituted; and, while cases of wilful violence are much less frequent than they used to be (the local governors being held responsible for any such damage), there remain, as causes of occasional interruption, atmospheric phenomena, gales, snow, and the humours of camels and birds. As soon as interruption occurs, the signallers from both stations between which the break-down is chronicled ride out along the line, whatever the weather, until they meet at the point of dislocation, which is immediately repaired. These duties, in addition to the obligation of being present at the instrument for the purpose of testing at fixed hours between sunrise and sunset, render the lot of the English telegraphist in Persia, even though personal danger need not now be feared, by no means a bed of roses. His service is for thirty years, at the end of which time he retires upon a pension equivalent to half-pay.

Influence upon Persia

From these details, which, though to some extent technical, are not deficient in interest,[1] I turn to an examination of the effect that has been produced upon, and in, Persia itself by the telegraphic system and establishment that I have described. This effect has been fourfold, and from whichever point of view we regard its operation, the influence of the telegraph has been enormous. I am disposed to attribute to it, more than to any other cause or agency, the change that has passed over Persia during the last thirty years, and the results of which I have chronicled in these volumes. To begin with, the telegraph for the first time brought Persia into contact with Europe, with the result of making her a member of the comity of nations. Europe learned to be interested in the distant country of which hitherto she knew little beyond the fact that it was the degenerate heir of the glories of Cyrus and Darius. Persia, on the other hand, became acquainted with European constitutions, customs, and standards, and whilst retaining an unshaken belief in her own ineffable superiority, discerned both the charm of novelty and the force of example in her new discovery, whose superficial characteristics she proceeded with imitative facility to absorb. But for the electric telegraph she would have lingered drowsily on, plunged in the self-satisfied stupor from which how many an Oriental kingdom and khanate has only been aroused to find itself upon the brink of doom, and would have rotted slowly away until the Muscovite trumpet rang its final summons in her ear, and Europe was invited as a spectator to the funeral feast. Whatever of civilisation, or reform, or regeneration has been introduced into Persia

[1] For the history of the introduction of the telegraph into Persia, *vide* Sir F. Goldsmid, *Telegraph and Travel*, 1874; *Report of Parliamentary Committee on East India Communications*, 1866; and papers by J. R. Preece in *Journal of the Society of Tel. Engineers*, 1879; and Sir R. M. Smith in *Scottish Geographical Mag.*, January 1889.

in the last quarter of a century, and has been traced in these pages, may indirectly be attributed to the influence of the telegraph. I doubt if otherwise the Shah would ever have journeyed to Europe, or have heard himself toasted by kings and emperors, and cheered by the *gamins* of Paris and London. From 1864, in fact, may be dated the appearance of Persia as a recognised figure upon the international stage.

Secondly—and this consequence has been scarcely less momentous or considerable than the first—to the introduction of the electric telegraph into Persia, followed as it has been by the spread of subsidiary lines throughout the country, must be attributed, even more than to the personal character of the sovereign or the altered spirit of the times, that consolidation of the royal authority which has made Nasr-ed-Din Shah the most powerful monarch of Persia since Nadir Shah. With a few rare exceptions, the licensed independence of the great border chieftains is at an end. Their capitals are connected by telegraph with Teheran, and the Shah has a predilection for placing himself at the other end of the wire. Such a phenomenon, for instance, as occurred upon the accession of Mohammed Shah in 1834, when at least three candidates for the throne were in the field at the same time, though ignorant of each other's movements, is no longer possible. News of the smallest outbreak in any outlying province is now sped along the wires to the capital; and long before sedition or mutiny has attained a head, troops are in motion, and the mere rumour of artillery has probably shattered the designs of the would-be rebel. The telegraph has also very much impaired the administrative independence of provincial governors, for, whilst it renders them liable to constant supervision from Teheran, it also enables them to refer any critical question for decision to the Central Government, a resort of which local functionaries freely avail themselves when pursuing the customary Persian tactics of procrastination or obstruction. Not the least, therefore, among the indirect services rendered by England to the reigning Shah has been that gift by which he has been enabled to collect his annual revenue with a precision very welcome to his economical instincts, to suppress local disorder or frontier turbulence, and, within the contracted limits of the modern Persian kingdom, to find himself everywhere acknowledged supreme.

Consolidation of royal authority

Thirdly must be ranked the friendly relations that have been developed by the social and official contact of nearly thirty years between Persians and Englishmen. Scattered throughout the country, where they are brought into frequent connection with all classes of the people, from a governor passing along the highway to his official post to the peasants of the neighbouring villages; constantly riding to and fro along the lines; possessed sometimes of a little medical knowledge, and willing to dispense a modest charity; above all, absolutely superior to bribes, the English telegraph officers in Persia may be considered mainly responsible for the high estimate in which English character and honour are held in that country. They are often made the unofficial arbiters of local disputes; the victims of injury or oppression fly to the telegraph office as a sort of *bast*, or sanctuary, where they are free from pursuit; and in the great towns the officers of higher rank are the friends, and sometimes the advisers, of governors and princes. If we contrast this state of affairs with the conditions under which the first engineers and sappers entered the country, in the face of daily obstruction, insult, and danger, we can arrive at some appreciation of the good work that has been done. Jealousy has been succeeded by confidence, and enmity has given way to friendly intercourse. Lastly, among the benefits that have accrued to Persia from the presence of the British telegraph staff upon its soil, has been the local knowledge acquired by English officers in this service, and subsequently utilised by the Persian Government in the settlement of disputes affecting the region concerned. It was, for instance, the knowledge of Mekran gained by General Goldsmid while laying the land wire from Kurrachi to Jask, that enabled him to act as arbiter in 1871 in the boundary dispute between Persia and Beluchistan, and to suggest and demarcate a new frontier for those countries.

Friendly relations

Nevertheless, prodigious though the effects of the Indo-European Telegraph have been in Persia, and honourable as is the reputation which its officers have acquired, I am myself astonished that a more ample use has not been made by the British Government of the local influence and knowledge of these men. Had they been Russians each one of them would have been an unaccredited but industrious agent for the country of his birth. I am not suggesting that any such spirit of irresponsible activity should be encouraged or even allowed; but, looking back upon the policy that has hitherto been

Suggested employment of telegraph officials

adopted, I cannot but regard it as unfortunate that over a period covering more than a quarter of a century so little advantage has been taken of the fortuitous presence on the spot of so splendid a band of pioneers. No effort, or but the scantiest effort, has been made by the British Government to utilise their knowledge, their services, or their possible influence. In one or two cases conspicuous local authority has caused a telegraph official to be entrusted with political duties; but these cases can be counted upon the fingers of one hand. This was mainly attributable in the past to a long-standing jealousy between the British Legation at Teheran and the Telegraph Department, who worked in haughty independence of each other and resented anything like common action. The Department was, indeed, a sort of *imperium in imperio*, and conducted negotiations with local governors, &c., on its own account, neither receiving nor soliciting diplomatic assistance. But now that these foolish jealousies have ceased to exist, it is worth while considering whether such of these officials as are competent might not be encouraged to extend their knowledge of the country by travel and surveys—an object for which engineers and sappers were presumably originally selected for the service—and whether their superior officers, who are frequently the first authorities upon the districts with which they are familiar, might not be put *en rapport* with the Government, and permitted to use their influence, which is often considerable, in the facilitation of the work of progress in Persia which England is now seriously taking in hand. How great the weight of personal influence with such a people may be was recognised by none more clearly than Sir J. Malcolm in the opening years of this century. The wise words with which he admonished his suite, then for the first time entering Persia, may still be borne in mind: 'In the absence of books the Persians will peruse us, and from what they see and hear, form their opinion of our country. Let us take care, therefore, that nothing is found in the page but what is found in England, and believe me that with such a people more depends upon personal impressions than upon treaties.' I am not unaware that there is another side to the case. The maxim *Ne sutor ultra crepidam* will be quoted, and it may be said that telegraph officials, if the recipients of even a tacit commission, will give themselves great airs, will neglect their duties, and will report mere gossip to Teheran; that if attached to the Legation they will involve the

British Government in disagreeable responsibilities, and that if not attached they will decline to obey the Minister's orders. There is much force in these objections, particularly if applied to anything like a wholesale or indiscriminate scheme of employment. But in cases of approved merit, I conceive that they do not hold good; nor should they discourage that exploration to which I believe that many a telegraphist would gladly devote his holidays were there any chance of receiving either the encouragement or the thanks of Government.[1] Within a few miles of some of the telegraph lines the country is still unexplored and almost unknown, although colonies of the most adventurous race in the globe have been planted for a quarter of a century in the neighbourhood.

Such, then, has been the history of British relations with Persia in this century, as conducted respectively by the statesman, the soldier, the merchant, and the civil engineer. The second and the fourth of these have, for the time being, finished their work. The future is in the hands of the first and the third. The statesman must at the same time avoid the shameful folly of indifference, and yet, according to my judgment, must hold aloof from the rupee policy of Malcolm and his immediate successors, who, where they thought to attach, did but degrade. His policy in the future is the guidance of Persia along the pathway of material expansion and internal reform. Backed by him, and profiting by the openings which it is the object of his diplomacy to secure, the function of the merchant is to supply Persia with that which she needs, and by commercial channels to win her to sympathy with Europe and with civilisation. In the matter of moral regeneration, it is difficult, if not impossible, for foreigners, save by the force of example, to interfere; and if Persia prefers to remain buried in moral and intellectual torpor, there exist no means of directly combating her resolution. But in the enterprise of mercantile and industrial development is to be found a vast and, as yet, almost

Work for the statesman and the merchant

[1] The only instances known to me of such performance in the past are the journey of J. R. Preece from Shiraz to Jask, published in the *Supplementary Proceedings of the R.G.S.*, 1886, and E. A. Floyer's exploration of Beluchistan, the tale of which is told in *Unexplored Beluchistan*. At the present time the Telegraph signallers and clerks are barely able to leave their offices at all, inasmuch as they are required to test five times a day, at the hours of 6, 10, 2, 5, and 9, in order to see that through communication is unbroken.

untilled field, whose features give promise of abundant return, and in which successful experiments have already been made. If moral progress is not yet to be expected from the people themselves, material progress, instituted by others, may facilitate its advent, and Persia may eventually be compelled to take an interest in herself by observing the interest which others take in her.

If, then, I were asked what is the policy of Great Britain towards Persia, I should answer in the following terms. It is not now, nor at any time in this century has it been, one of territorial cupidity. England does not covet one square foot of Persian soil. The eighth and tenth Commandments stand in no danger of being violated by us. In the war of 1856–7 British forces captured, and, for a short time, held both Bushire and Kharak Island, in the Gulf, and Mohammerah and Ahwaz on the Karun. It would have been easy to establish a permanent foot-hold in the Gulf, and to have settled the Karun question for all time by retaining these positions. In the absence of any reason rendering such a step compulsory, we gave them up. The Persians themselves, who had fully expected at least to lose Bushire, were bewildered at our clemency, and have come in time to believe that they ousted us by superior force. But the action remains an indisputable evidence of pacific purpose, and may appositely be contrasted with the Russian tactics at Ashurada in the North. Of the true character of British policy towards Persia a better description cannot be supplied than that which was given by Lord Salisbury in his speech at the Guildhall banquet to the Shah in July 1889:—

Policy of Great Britain

> We watch with intense interest and sympathy the policy which His Majesty has inaugurated in Persia. We wish for it the greatest possible development. We wish the highest possible stage of prosperity for himself and his people. We hope that those communications with the outer world which are the condition of prosperity in this age will increase and multiply in his country ; and we desire above all things that Persia shall not only be prosperous, but be strong—strong in her resources, strong in her preparations, strong in her alliances—in order that she may pursue the peaceful path on which she has entered in security and tranquillity. And we entreat our illustrious guest to believe that in seeking this commercial as well as political friendship we are asking for no exclusive privileges for ourselves. . . . We are urging upon him no friendship with us that shall end in any of the exploits or desires of aggression or of war. All that we desire are those

acquisitions which are achieved by industry and by enterprise, and which carry a common reward, not to one nation, but to all nations of the world.

In other words, the development of the industrial and material resources of Persia, the extension of her commerce, the maintenance of her integrity, the rehabilitation of her strength—these, under the pressure and by the aid of a friendly alliance, are the objects of British policy. The time for an offensive and defensive alliance has passed. Early in this century England might, with less risk and with possible advantage, have taken such a step. But the opportunity vanished with the events that led up to Turkomanchai, and with the drying of the ink that installed Russia in a position of permanent superiority on the north. Any such engagement now might implicate us in warfare at a tremendous distance from our base, with every disadvantage of position and resource, and against an enemy long and firmly entrenched. The last time that such a contingency might have been discussed was during the Crimean war, when Persia was quite willing to throw in her lot with Great Britain on condition of the restitution and guarantee of her lost provinces.[1] But *le jeu ne valait pas la chandelle* then, and still less can it do so now. We can undertake no responsibility for provinces which Persia has been so weak as to lose, and which she is no longer strong enough to keep; for the bargain would be a one-sided one, and the reciprocal advantage to ourselves would be small. But by dint of a friendly alliance, by the exercise of prudent advice, by encouragement of the flow of capital eastwards, and by its application to purposes of ascertained stability, having for their object the re-invigoration of the country, we can help to place her in a position which may render the hostile schemes of her neighbours, if not impossible, at least precarious.

Above all we may make it certain that, whatever destiny befall her in the north, in regions beyond the sphere of our possible interference, Persia shall retain inviolate the centre and south, and be able to say to an invader, 'Thus far and no further.' British ascendency, commercial and political, in the southern zone, which I

[1] In the absence of any sign from England, it is said that Persia was bribed by Russia during the Crimean War to place an army-corps on the Turkish frontier. In 1877, again at the request of Russia, Persian troops were concentrated at Khoi, Zohab, and Mohammerah.

have more than once described, is the only means by which this aim can be secured. A line can be drawn across Persia from Seistan on the east, *viâ* Kerman and Yezd, to Isfahan, and prolonged westward to Burujird, Hamadan, and Kermanshah, south of which no hostile political influence should be tolerated. Within those limits England asks for no exclusive privileges, exercises no dictation, and employs no threats. She will not require to move a soldier; she need never fire a gun. Geok Tepes and Panjdehs have never been to our taste; and any future triumphs that we may gain in Persia will be won, not by powder and shot, not by bluster or bullying, not even, as the 'Novoe Vremya' seems to think, by bribes; but by the amicable stress of common interests, working in the direction of industrial development and domestic reform.

British ascendency in the centre and south

If it be asked whether the omens are propitious for such a policy, an affirmative answer can, I think, unhesitatingly be returned. Natural inclinations might be expected to impel the Persians towards a British alliance; but, remembering the extent to which they are a prey to their fears, and the manner in which those apprehensions are habitually played upon by adversaries in a superior position, I own I have been surprised to find British influence so powerful at Teheran as I take it to be. But a short time ago this claim could not have been made with any scrupulous regard for truth. For more than thirty years Great Britain has pursued a policy towards Persia which, under the familiar disguise of masterly non-interference, has assumed the dimensions of unpardonable neglect. As the Grand Vizier said to me, 'A little more, and British influence would have been dead in Persia.' That this fatality did not occur, and that so notable a revival has taken place, is to be attributed in part to the tactical blunders of our rivals, in part to a juster estimate of British policy by the Persians themselves, but in a higher degree to the remarkable energy and wholesome influence of the late British Minister in Persia, Sir H. Drummond Wolff. The value of his services and the effect produced by his inexhaustible activity could, perhaps, be judged better from the frantic outcry of the Russian press than from the interested encomiums of a countryman, and I will, therefore, do no more than recall to my readers the weekly delirium of the scribes of St. Petersburg and Moscow. Personally, I believe the impression

British influence at Teheran

to be gaining ground in Persia that British counsels are framed, not with a purely selfish object, but with an honest desire for the country's gain. The Shah has given practical evidence of his sympathies in the concessions with regard to the Karun river, and the Imperial Bank. His recognition of the commercial aspect of English influence was shown by the interest with which he scrutinised the operations and productions of our manufacturing industries when on his tour in the summer of 1889 through the smoky capitals of the Midlands and the North. With the bulk of his subjects I believe that the English are personally popular, except when they adopt the brow-beating tone, a line of conduct which is in the last degree abhorrent to a people who pride themselves on civility of deportment, and possess a natural dignity. To the question propounded by myself in my opening chapter as to the impression produced in Persia by the great reception given to the Shah in England, the reply may be made that in the absence of newspapers or means of transmitting foreign intelligence, the majority of his people are probably ignorant of it altogether; that the minor officials, who in Persia are among the most conceited and intolerable of the human race, would be disposed to regard it as a symptom of British weakness and of the transcendant importance of their own sovereign; but that the higher ranks of society, the Ministers and men of influence, whose opinion alone is worth considering, were much and favourably impressed both by the tokens of friendly feeling and by the evidences of national strength. The greater the intercourse between the two peoples becomes and the wider the interchange of mutual amenities, whether of commerce or society, of good-fellowship or business, the speedier will be the recognition of common interests, and the arrival of the moment when Persia shall look upon Great Britain as her most natural ally, and Great Britain upon Persia as her willing friend.

Russian influence

Whilst to my surprise and satisfaction I discovered the existence of so powerful a British influence in Persia, I found the control exercised by Russia, in spite of her tremendous physical superiority, to be by no means so great as I had been led to believe. I found that Persian ministers declined to be browbeaten by Russian ministers; that Russian diplomacy was by no means uniformly successful; and that the Shah, if properly backed up, could even return a decided No to his very good friend the Czar. I am quite unable, therefore, to agree either with the estimate of the Frenchman, M. Orsolle, when he said that

> The Shah is only the viceroy of a Russian Province. The real sovereign is not he who lives in the Ark, but the diplomatist in the mean palace in the corner of the Ark near the bazaar (i.e. the Russian Minister).[1]

Or with the remark of my own countryman, Dr. Wills, that

> Our influence in Persia, thanks to ourselves, is next to nothing. There are few resident British subjects who are really Englishmen. England to the Persian is a mere phrase, Russia a power—a power to bow down to and to fear. Russian subjects are protected. English ones take their chance as a rule. . . . The Russian drill-sergeant and Russian influence are paramount; while England, her influence gone and her trade a shadow, has fallen into contempt.[2]

I do not know at what precise epoch these words were penned; but I cannot conceive a more misleading description of the present situation.

British hold over Southern Persia

Apart from the actual estimation in which England and Englishmen are held in Persia, and which dates from the days of Fath Ali Shah, and has been fortified by many friendly acts, as, for instance, the large British contribution towards the Persian famine fund in 1871–2, the position occupied by Great Britain in the south is such as to enable her to pursue the above indicated policy of ascendency in the centre and southern regions of Persia with every hope of permanent success. Her naval power in the Mediterranean, her hold of a possible base in Cyprus, her practical command of the Suez Canal, her possession of Bombay and Kurrachi, and her undisputed supremacy in the Persian Gulf, are conditions of preliminary advantage. Her control of the markets of the entire Persian littoral from Gwetter to Mohammerah, and of the inland towns and cities as far north as Isfahan, is a second and not less valuable guarantee. But more potent than either is the feeling that prevails throughout Southern Persia, from the Persian Beluchis on the east to the Bakhtiari Lurs on the west, that the power to which they must look alike for the vindication of their manhood and the maintenance of their freedom is Great Britain. I could give many instances of this phenomenon that have come under my own notice. While Persia

[1] *Le Caucase et la Perse*, p. 333.

[2] *In the Land of the Lion and the Sun*, pp. 175, 182.

has been extending a forcible and unwelcome sway over the Beluchi tribesmen on her eastern border, many are the petitions for protection that have poured in upon the British Resident at Bushire. There is not a traveller in the intervening regions of Kerman, Laristan, and Fars who has not recorded similar and unsolicited appeals; whilst in the west there is no prospect to which Bakhtiari chieftains, bullied and maltreated by the Persian Government, and Arab sheikhs, who have never professed more than a lip loyalty to the Shah, look forward more keenly than that of at once retaining and vindicating their independent nationality under the ægis of Great Britain. If Russian advance has sometimes been solicited by the craven populations of Khorasan, a not less genuine and a more creditable 'Come over and help us' has sounded in the ears of England from the warlike tribes of Southern Iran. And yet, well assured as is the British position in Southern Persia, and essential though it be that it should never be disputed, I have positively encountered the argument that Russia should be suffered to come down to the Gulf, in order to provide ourselves with a point of attack. Never previously had I heard of the generalship which could admit the enemy to a secure lodgment on the glacis of a fort, in order to have the luxury of marching out to attack him.

There is one condition intimately connected with the maintenance of British prestige in Persia, about which a marked difference of opinion prevails even among those who know, viz. the *personnel* and affiliation of the British Legation at Teheran. There are some who support the present system, under which, although a large part of the expenses of the establishment are borne by India, both the Minister and his staff are appointed by, and are subordinate to, the Foreign Office in London. There are others who contend that Persia, falling within the category of Oriental nations, and her politics standing in a particular relationship to those of India, the entire charge should be cast upon the Indian Exchequer, with the corollary of making the *personnel* and establishment entirely or mainly Indian in composition and qualification. History affords illustrations of either status from the time when, at the beginning of this century, the East India Company and the Home Government quarrelled so seriously about Persia, that their rival ambassadors, Sir. J. Malcolm and Sir Harford Jones, were both on Persian soil at the same

Question of the Legation establishment

moment, down to 1860, when Sir H. Rawlinson resigned his post as Minister at Teheran upon the final restoration of that office to the department at Whitehall. Throughout the century, indeed, English statesmanship has been quite unable to make up its mind as to which was the better solution, and has chopped and changed about in this respect quite as irrationally as in almost every other branch of Persian politics. The East India Company, as I have said, were first in the field; but they were soon ousted by the Crown. In 1823, however, Anglo-Persian relations were restored to the Indian Government, and an envoy of the Governor-General took the place of a Plenipotentiary of the Sovereign. In 1834, the process was again reversed. The see-saw continued until 1859, when, upon the government of the East India Company being transferred to the Crown, the Teheran establishment was placed under the Secretary of State for India, although the post of minister remained a Crown appointment. In the following year the Teheran Legation was restored to the Foreign Office, under whose charge it has remained ever since. The question of a change has been frequently mooted; and the House of Commons Committee, appointed to inquire into the constitution of the Diplomatic and Consular Services in 1870, reported as follows:—

That, while they have received conflicting evidence of the highest authority, on either side of the question, your Committee on the whole incline to the opinion that the Persian Mission should be placed under the authority of the Secretary of State for India ; but that if the responsible advisers of the Crown decide that such a change is not for the public interest, your Committee recommend that the members of the Persian Mission generally should be selected by the Secretary of State for Foreign Affairs from Her Majesty's Indian Service, and that the present charge of 12,000*l.* a year on the Indian Revenues for the expense of such Mission should be diminished, so as to throw a larger proportion of the expense upon Imperial revenues.[1]

Nevertheless this recommendation has never been acted upon. The Teheran Legation retains its English, or rather European, complexion and the 12,000*l.* are still drawn from the Indian Exchequer. There is undoubtedly a good deal to be said on either side of the question. It seems fair that India, paying so large a contribution, should be allowed a somewhat larger control, the more so as the remaining Anglo-Persian establishments at Bushire

[1] *Vide* Sir H. Rawlinson, *England and Russia in the East*, pp. 98, 289.

and Meshed and the adjoining Residency at Baghdad are Indian, both in appointment and pay; [1] as the Telegraph Department in Persia is subordinate to the Indian, and not to the Home Government; and as, in the event of British troops being required for the defence of Persia, Bombay, and not Portsmouth, would be the port of embarkation. It is also true that the conditions of service and life in Persia are more analogous to those of Hindustan than to the customs of European courts or cities, that the Persian language is more likely to be known by members of the Indian Civil or Military Services than by Foreign Office *attachés*, and that the latter are sometimes disposed to regard Teheran as a penal settlement, to be tolerated only with sullen mortification. It is, I think, less true than may formerly have been the case, that Indian interests in Persia are shelved or postponed in deference to the needs of European diplomacy. On the other hand, while the above considerations suggest a larger infusion of the Indian element than at present prevails, I am strongly of opinion that the broad question of control must be decided in favour of Downing Street rather than of Calcutta. The introduction into Persia of the electric telegraph, the visits of the Shah to Europe, and above all the menacing attitude of Russia on the north, have brought Persia distinctly within the purview of European politics, and render it impossible for British diplomacy in that country to be regulated upon strictly Indian lines. The Persian Question has become a branch of the great Eastern Question, that simultaneously agitates the cabinets of London, St. Petersburg, and Constantinople. The British Minister at Teheran must be in constant correspondence with the British Ambassadors at the two latter capitals. The presence of accredited representatives of the principal European Powers at the court of the Shah is a further evidence of the extent to which Persia has been lifted out of a purely Asiatic environment and is now regarded as a piece upon the international chess-board. I do not doubt that the Shah himself would regard it as an affront to his dignity were any proposal now made to restore the Teheran

[1] The appointments at Bushire, Meshed, and Baghdad are the result of a curious sort of compromise between the contending parties. The nominations are made by the Indian Government, but the appointments hail from the Foreign Office. To exemplify the twofold arrangement the occupants of all three posts are designated Residents or Political Agents in their relations with India, but Consuls-General in their relations with Whitehall. This peculiar system works well.

Legation to India, and I may add that the new work upon which I have described the British Government as having entered in Persia, viz., the resurrection of that country by the aid of British capital and brains, is one that takes its origin and receives its direction from English, and not from Indian sources. I have, therefore, no hesitation in saying that the Teheran Mission should, in my opinion, retain its present character as a European appointment, although some of the very pertinent objections, before quoted, to the composition of the staff might be obviated, according to the suggestion of the Parliamentary Committee, by a combination of Indian with Foreign Office nominees. Some slight approximation to such an issue has recently been attained in the appointment of an Indian officer of great experience, General T. E. Gordon, as British Military attaché at Teheran.

Impediments to reform

In conclusion I turn from the rival policies of Russia and Great Britain in Persia to Persia herself, and I proceed to the interesting question of her future in so far as it can be judged from the signs of the times, from the lessons of the past, or from the character of her people. In what I have written I have not deluded my readers as to the true condition of that country. He is but a doubtful friend either to Persia or to England who represents her as in a robust or satisfactory state of health. Expectations can only be aroused and projects encouraged by a false diagnosis that will recoil with disaster upon both parties. Persia is neither powerful, nor spontaneously progressive, nor patriotic. Her agriculture is bad, her resources unexplored, her trade ill-developed, her government corrupt, her army a cypher. The impediments that exist to a policy of reform, or even to material recuperation, are neither few nor insignificant. There can be no doubt that in the passage of time the natural conditions of the country have changed. The thoughtless destruction of timber and the waste of the existing water-supply have very much diminished the general average of fertility. There is less rain-fall than was formerly the case, and the long foot-slopes at the base of the hills represent a detritus which the present volume of water is powerless to sweep down and distribute over the plains. The outward evidences of decay are numerous and pathetic, and the casual traveller who sees everywhere spread around him deserted towns and cities, abandoned bazaars, crumbling walls and fallen towers, gardens relapsed into wildernesses, caravanserais in ruins, and bridges broken down, is apt to think that all virtue has gone out both of the people and of the country, and that the finger of doom has already traced its fatal *Mene*, *Mene*, *Tekel*, *Upharsin*, upon the wall. Proud as the Persians are of their heritage, and convinced that Iran is the first of nations, they are woefully deficient in patriotism in any but the most passive sense of the term. They are ready enough to swagger about the glory and the beauty of their country,[1] but there is not one in a hundred who would pull his sword from the scabbard to vindicate its independence. In every manifestation of national spirit or activity they appear to have succumbed to a creeping paralysis which is slowly making its way upward from the extremities to the head. By the least display of statesmanship, combined with a sufficient demonstration of force, they might have pacified the Turkomans of Transcaspia, instead of leaving them a prey to the tender mercies of Russia. Any government less careless or corrupt would have made of the Kurds on the north-west and north-east, and of the Lur tribes on the south-west, the most magnificent frontier garrisons in the world. As it is, they abhor the Central Government, and would be useless in the hour of danger. There is a total lack of initiative in public no less than in private life. Just as a Persian cottager would sooner absorb disease from a filthy pool at his threshold than walk 200 yards to a fresh spring,[2] so does the State require to be prodded and goaded into any act of administrative energy or vigour. Just as a Persian gentleman will build a mansion of mud when there is a marble quarry almost at his door, so will the Persian Government, if left to itself, prefer the outworn furniture of Oriental existence to the novel paraphernalia of European commerce and culture. Peculation is dear to the heart of every official in the country, from the most powerful governor to the meanest clerk, and he asks nothing better than that the blessed word *mudakhil* shall sum up the vocabulary of possible happiness in his time. Persia knows well enough that she is weak, but at the bottom of her heart she would prefer to be left alone in her weakness. She is certainly not thirsting, like Japan, for a new life, and when she

[1] There is great continuity in national character; 2,300 years ago Herodotus said of the Persians of his time *νομίζοντες ἑωυτοὺς εἶναι ἀνθρώπων μακρῷ τὰ πάντα ἀρίστους* (lib. i. 134).

[2] When Colonel Val. Baker was at Kelat-i-Nadiri in 1873, he found the people decimated by typhus from drinking bad water, though there was an excellent spring at a little distance (*Clouds in the East*, p. 202).

puts on the strait-jacket of civilisation, it is with as wry a face as the victim of the Spanish Inquisition when first confronted by the thumbscrew or the rack. I can also well believe that her redemption will not be accomplished without some outbreak of fanaticism; it may even be retarded by the recoil consequent upon a too precipitate advance. Just as in modern Japan there exists a party, recruited, not from the older, but among the younger spirits, who resent the Europeanisation of their country, and whose baffled patriotism finds vent in occasional outbursts of violence or despair, so I can conceive that in Persia, at any time of public disorder, a strong reaction might be set on foot by the retrograde and priestly party, and that the life and property of Europeans might be in temporary peril. Already there is a widespread feeling of discontent at the policy of concessions to foreigners upon which the Shah has latterly been persuaded to embark, and the recent successful outbreak against the Tobacco Corporation has stimulated a movement which a stronger Government might easily have repressed. *Mullahs* have publicly preached against the Europeans, and cursed them in the streets; anonymous letters have been sent broadcast throughout the country inciting to rebellion; it is said that the Shah's life has been threatened, and that the palace guards have been doubled. These rumours may in some cases have been exaggerated, or, if true, may have been partly the handiwork of personal intrigue. Still, it is not surprising that in a country still so fast bound in the manacles of Mohammedan prejudice and superstition there should be some recrudescence of bigotry at the admission of the foreign element upon so large a scale. The native usurers see their illicit percentage reduced almost to vanishing-point by the Imperial Bank; merchants and landowners detested the inquisitorial control of the Tobacco Régie; and governors and grandees find their chartered license of prerogative seriously curtailed by the remonstrance of ambassadors and the operation of treaties. I do not say that these hostile ebullitions, even if they assume a more serious form, will permanently jeopardise the good work that is being taken in hand, but they should render the outside public not unprepared for a serious phase of reaction.

Such are the impediments that exist to the progress of reform. On the other hand are features of more than balancing encouragement and advantage, an examination of which may lead us to be still of good cheer. In the first place, barren and naked as much of the country is to the outward eye, the soil remains the same, and is in its intrinsic capacities one of the finest in the world. It was by water that its former fertility was produced; and by water this can again be conjured into existence. No physical or climatic change has passed over Persia sufficient to replace productiveness and verdure by a permanent sterility; and in fifty years, by a proper economy of water supply, and with less primitive methods of tillage, the cultivable area might be doubled. Again, defenceless as the frontiers of Persia now are, in the absence of any army capable of utilising their enormous advantages for defence, she yet possesses in her mountains and ravines the most magnificent natural ramparts, which Providence would seem to have conferred upon her for her own protection. Similarly, stagnant though public spirit in Persia may be, and happy in its stagnation, nerveless and craven though the manhood of the people may have become, under a system of government which has allowed no scope for enterprise or independence, there is yet in the Iranian character that unconquerable and lighthearted vitality which has caused her people to be dubbed the Frenchmen of the East, which has kept them a nation in the face of repeated invasion and disaster for over 2,000 years, which has enabled them to conquer and to absorb their conquerors, instead of being obliterated by them, and which gives them, even in their decay, a certain strange homogeneity that no nation in the world, so externally weak, can claim in an equal degree. Even in his misery the Persian peasant is not a pauper; even in its decay the national manhood is not extinct. Feeble as an ally and impotent as a foe though Persia has become, she is not despicable; nor, though her administration is rotten, is it incapable of reform; nor, because the army is at present valueless, is it to be ignored or despised under a purer *régime*. Above all we must remember that the ways of Orientals are not our ways, nor their thoughts our thoughts. Often when we think them backward and stupid, they think us meddlesome and absurd. The loom of time moves slowly with them, and they care not for high pressure and the roaring of the wheels. Our system may be good for us; but it is neither equally, nor altogether good for them. Satan found it better to reign in hell than to serve in heaven; and the normal Asiatic would sooner be misgoverned by Asiatics than well governed by Euro-

Omens of good cheer

peans. The Persians are a suspicious people, strangely deficient in patriotism themselves, and inclined therefore to mistake interest for self-interest in others, and to see a cloven hoof beneath the skirts of every robe. Rome was not built in a day, and Persia will not be reformed in a decade; but if the physician will be long-suffering, the patient will in time become amenable, provided always that a rival practitioner from a Northern establishment does not insist upon tearing up his prescription.

Progress already made

I derive similar omens from an inspection of what has already been accomplished. In previous chapters I have quoted passages showing what was the state of affairs when the present Shah came to the throne, and how dismal the forebodings framed by competent authorities as to the future. My pages have demonstrated the falsity of many of those predictions; and if, during the past half-century, the bulk of which period must be classified under the old *régime*, so marked and visible a progress has been made, both in public security, in consolidation of the royal power, and in the somewhat tentative introduction of reform, we may, now that the country is on the threshold of a new era, look for swifter advance and for more durable results. Already the electric telegraph, regular posts, European banks, the small beginnings of a railway system, and the employment on a large scale of foreign capital for the exploitation of the national resources, have been introduced. The Persians are sufficiently clever to know that they cannot for ever stop here. Among their rulers are many enlightened men who deplore the condition and who recognise the needs of their country. In the course of my travels I enjoyed interviews with some dozen of the leading statesmen of Persia, and found in many of them a sincere desire for improvement, handicapped by a sense of powerlessness against the abuses which have fastened their coils around the nation, and which it requires stronger men than some of them are to shake off. The sovereign, however, has done much for reform—more certainly than any Persian monarch since Kerim Khan—and, if he dared, would probably do more. It is among the misfortunes, incidental to an Oriental system, that we are still almost entirely in the dark as to the reception which his policy—on the whole a creditable and praiseworthy policy—will meet with from his successor.

Nevertheless, whatever be our doubts or fears in this respect, nothing I am sure is to be gained by an attitude that is likely to encourage political unrest or to facilitate intrigue. Most writers appear to take it for granted that upon the death of the Shah a general convulsion will ensue, and in all probability a contest for the vacant throne. It is even discussed which candidate is to receive the suffrages of this or that party, which to be the Russian and which the British nominee. Any disposition to encourage false pretensions or to depart from the recognised canons of inheritance is very much to be deprecated, as likely to plunge the country into disorder and to give opportunities for aggression to those who are so minded. If it were known that England and Russia, the two strongest external powers, were resolutely united in their support of the legitimate heir to the throne, though the Shah were to die to-morrow, the security both of the Crown and of the country would, I believe, be absolutely assured.

The succession

If I turn from the public to the private character of the people, and proceed to draw any inference from their manners or behaviour as evinced in their every-day existence, I arrive at a conclusion which, after a balance of contradictory items, still leaves us just on the right side. The Persian character presents many complex features, elsewhere rarely united in the same individual. They are an amiable and a polished race, and have the manners of gentlemen. They are vivacious in temperament, intelligent in conversation, and acute in conduct. If their hearts are soft, which is, I believe, undeniable, there is no corresponding weakness of the head. On the other hand, they are consummate hypocrites, very corrupt, and lamentably deficient in stability or courage. They stand in the sharpest contrast to the peoples who surround them, the truculent Kurd, the haughty Afghan, the sullen Turk, the listless Hindu. With none of these do they share many common characteristics. The physical conditions of their country, and the possession of a separate faith, have accentuated a racial difference that must always have been extremely marked. Whilst, as individuals, they present many attractive features, as a community they are wholly wanting in elements of real nobility or grandeur. With one gift only can they be credited on a truly heroic scale; and this, though it may endear them to the student of human nature as a fine art, will excite the stern repugnance of the moralist. I allude to their faculty for what a Puritan might call mendacious, but what I prefer to style imaginative, utterance. This is inconceivable and enormous. After being in Persia, one is

Persian character

tempted to think that Epimenides must have mistaken the subjects of his famous aphorism. Notwithstanding long experience this accomplishment never fails to startle, and sometimes even to bewilder; and it divests nine-tenths of a Persian's assurances of the smallest value. I am convinced that a true son of Iran would sooner lie than tell the truth; and that he feels twinges of desperate remorse when, upon occasions, he has thoughtlessly strayed into veracity. Yet they are an agreeable people—agreeable to encounter, agreeable to associate with, perhaps not least agreeable to leave behind. From this composite presentment it is perhaps difficult to extract any really reliable basis of sanguine prognostication. Nevertheless there remain three attributes of the Persian character which lead me to think that that people are not yet, as has been asserted, wholly 'played out'; that they are neither sunk in the sombre atrophy of the Turk, nor threatened with the ignoble doom of the Tartar; but that there are chances of a possible redemption. These are their irrepressible vitality; an imitativeness long notorious in the East,[1] and capable of honourable utilisation; and, in spite of occasional testimony to the contrary, a healthy freedom from deep-seated prejudice or bigotry. History suggests that the Persians will insist upon surviving themselves; present indications that they will gradually absorb the accomplishments of others.

Festina lente

I feel compelled, however, to end with a word of caution. Colossal schemes for the swift regeneration of Persia are not in my judgment—though herein I differ from some other authorities—to be thought of, and will only end in fiasco. Magnificent projects for overlaying the country with a network of railways from north to south, and from east to west, and for equipping it with a panoply of factories and workships and mills, can only end in financial disaster, and bring discredit upon their promoters. Hot-headed concessions for making or exporting or importing every article under the sun, from telephones to tobacco, and from rose-water to roulette-tables, contain no element of durable advantage, and are seldom devised with any other object than to put money into the pocket of the originators of the scheme. Money will flow more smoothly, and industry will be more rapidly developed, by following the recognised channels.[2] The same may be

[1] Again let me quote Herodotus (lib. i. 135): ξεινικὰ δὲ νόμαια Πέρσαι προσίενται ἀνδρῶν μάλιστα· καὶ εὐπαθείας τε παντοδαπὰς πυνθανόμενοι ἐπιτηδεύουσι.

[2] How true were the above words, which appeared in one of my original letters in the 'Times,' has already been proved by the collapse of the Tobacco Régie.

said of internal communications. Mule tracks will in many cases require to precede roads, and roads to precede railroads. Hundreds of pounds had better be devoted to a certain benefit here than thousands staked upon a venture there. Persian capital must be interested in the exploitation of Persian resources, for a monopoly of the finance by foreigners excites jealousy, and suggests the idea of usurpation. Nor must it be forgotten, while agitating for this or that practical benefit, that the foundations of the system, which shall render the comprehension of its advantages simple and their appreciation universal, have in many cases yet to be laid. I have said that the people are shamefully ill-educated. I have shown that they live in an atmosphere of corruption. Civilisation will not be popular until it is taught in the schools. Respect for law, regard for contract, or faith in honesty will not be generated until the institutions by which they can be safeguarded have been called into being. This will be a work of time; but in due time it will come. Remote and backward and infirm Persia at present is; but, for all its remoteness and backwardness and present debility, I hope I have shown it to be a country that should excite the liveliest sympathies of Englishmen; with whose Government our own Government should be upon terms of intimate alliance; and in the shaping for which of a future that shall be not unworthy of its splendid past the British nation have it in their power to take a highly honourable lead.

INDEX